Criminal

P.J.Goddard

First published in the United Kingdom in 2005
by Hilltop Publishing Limited

ISBN 0 9536850 5 5

Printed and bound in Great Britain by Biddles Ltd, Kings Lynn.

Typeset in Bembo by Avocet Typeset, Chilton, Bucks.

Hilltop Publishing Limited
Brill
Buckinghamshire
U.K.
www.hilltoppublishing.co.uk

For R.F.
Semper fidelis

Author's note

My thanks and appreciation to …

Messrs Ferris & Papathanassiou for the music; the divine Ms A for the words; Mark Auty for his counsel both literary and legal; Jah for his enlightenment as to the iconography of the royal coat of arms; Deary and Tonge for the 'orrible Tudor slang; Kingston Crown Court for letting me in (and out) of their cells; Hilltop for continuing to bear the faith and, finally, Mari, Julius and all my family and friends for their kindness and support.

PJG
Spring 2005

Heaven help me for the way I am
Save me from these evil deeds before I get them
　　done
I know tomorrow brings the consequence at hand
But I keep living this day like the next will never
　　come

Help me but don't tell me to deny it
I've got to cleanse myself of all these lies until I'm
　　good enough for him
I've got a lot to lose, so I'm betting high and I'm
　　begging you
Before it ends just tell me where to begin

What I need is a good defence
Because I'm feeling like a criminal
And I need to be redeemed to the one I sinned
　　against
Because it's all I ever knew of love

Fiona Apple
'Criminal'

Part One

The Way I Am

Chapter 1

It was an old, narrow street – one of the few that still remained of the original Tudor town. Pausing before stepping on to its gnarled cobblestones, Miles Coverdale looked around to see if there was a sign showing that it led to the Courts of Justice. The courthouse was definitely down in that direction – he could see its distinctive, crenellated roof above the tops of the buildings just a few hundred yards away – but he didn't want to walk the length of the street only to discover that it was a dead-end or that he couldn't get through. Moving over to the left hand pavement, he attempted to get a better view, but, at the far end of the street, a large flame-red bush, its leaves blazing brightly in the clear spring sunshine, obscured what looked like an underpass leading to the front entrance of the courthouse. Looking around again, Miles caught sight of the words 'St. John's Road' picked out in faded orange-red tiles between the ground and first floor of the building opposite. It was peculiar that he had never noticed this street before: he must have driven past it dozens of times over the years on his way around the Kingston one-way system. Checking his watch, and seeing that it was only twenty past nine, he decided to give it a try. According to the information pack that he had received, jurors weren't required to register until nine forty-five, so, even if it was a dead-end and he had to turn around and come back again, he would still be in plenty of time. Besides, there appeared to be a couple of oldy-worldy shops up ahead and maybe he could pick up something interesting for his son's birthday.

St. John's Road did indeed lead to the courthouse, although the shops proved to be rather disappointing. The quaint, oak-beamed building half way down that had caught his eye turned out to be a women's boutique and from that point onwards the street seemed to degenerate into a succession of anaemic building societies and cruddy kebab houses; he would have to try and find something for Jake later. Stopping in front of the last shop in the street – a ramshackle newsagent – he stared at the surly Asian woman behind the counter and thought about going in and buying a copy of *The Mail*. A week ago, it had published a deeply incriminating photograph that Miles had taken of the MP, Angus Lamb, and he was still warmly basking in the heat of the scandal it had generated. In the end, he decided not to bother. The News Office had promised to keep copies of everything for him whilst he was on jury service and besides, he had listened to the radio over breakfast and there appeared to have been no new developments in the story overnight.

Walking up the slope of the underpass towards the courthouse, Miles found himself in the grip of a pleasant but unexpected sense of anticipation. At his request *The Mail* had managed to get him excused from jury service twice in the past four years, and would have done so a third time if the jury officer had not put his foot down. However, now that he was actually arriving for his first day, he was surprised to find that he was quite looking forward to the experience: after three gruelling weeks of keeping Lamb under virtual twenty-four hour surveillance, this was just the sort of break he needed. Walking up the wind-swept steps of the courthouse, Miles caught sight of the huge coat of arms above the entrance. Standing well to one side so as not to obstruct the other people arriving for court that morning, he gazed appreciatively at the large, wrought iron construction: it was unusual to see workmanship of this quality nowadays – even on the front of such a prestigious public building. The structure was at least six feet tall and decorated with quite the most intricate combination of gilding and enamel-work that he had ever seen; someone must have spent months making it. As he looked admiringly upwards, Miles recalled a lesson on the symbolism of the royal coat of arms to which he and his classmates had once been subjected by a particularly patriotic housemaster. The emblem was in fact a pledge – a sacred vow that consciously harked back to the covenant between God and the twelve tribes of Israel. The unicorn represented the people and the unsecured chain around its neck democracy – the system that guaranteed them the right to make the laws by which they were governed. The lion rampant in turn symbolized the Monarchy, positioned opposite and equal to the unicorn and thereby solemnly pledging its assent to those laws. Turning and walking towards the entrance, Miles smiled to himself, pleasantly surprised that he could still remember his housemaster's lecture twenty years after the event.

Passing through the revolving doors, Miles looked around the broad, high-ceilinged entrance hall – the inside of the court building was just as imposing as the outside. Although he had never been obliged to attend Kingston Crown Court in his professional capacity as a photographer, Miles was aware of its reputation as one of the most modern and well-equipped in the country. Two years ago it had hosted a huge child pornography trial – the largest ever in the UK – involving police services from over a dozen different countries. Some of the evidence, he recalled, had even been presented to the jury on-line over the internet. Although the probability of his ending up on a comparably high profile trial was no doubt quite small, he was nevertheless intrigued to think that he might be summoned as a juror to any one of the wide variety of different cases held at a major Crown Court like Kingston.

As he strolled across the marble floor, Miles warily fixed his eyes on the two uniformed security officers up ahead. It was an automatic reaction: having lied or bluffed his way past countless such individuals in his career, he had only to glimpse a row of brass buttons or a thickly-stitched epaulette instantly to embark upon an assessment of the likely sharpness, or gullibility, of the individual they adorned. The first of them was a tall, portly man in his mid fifties with an enormous handle-bar moustache. Miles dismissed him with a single glance – he knew his type all too well. The woman who stood beside him, however, was an altogether different proposition. Attractive, late twenties, with a stern but intelligent face, Miles could see even at a distance that she possessed that particular combination of objectivity and vigilance essential to the professional security officer.

'Good morning, I've, er, come for jury service,' he said, waving his information pack cheerily and fixing her with his most charming smile.

She turned to look at him; there was not a trace of warmth or humour in her face.

'If you'd like to remove any keys or metal objects from your pockets, sir, and go through the gate over there …'

You are good, thought Miles, still smiling as he walked through the scanner. As she returned his car keys to him from the plastic tray, he looked down at her skirt. It was long and tightly contoured. Standard issue uniforms never fitted like that. She had obviously had it altered.

'Thanks, er, where do I go now?'

'Over there and to your left, sir. Take the lift to the third floor.'

'Oh, right, cheers,' replied Miles with a grin, thanking his good fortune to have crossed paths with such a formidable security officer on one of the few days of the year that he wasn't actually working.

The jurors' waiting lounge seemed so large that at first Miles thought he had ended up in the wrong room. Half an hour later, though, when the induction video started, it had begun to appear, if anything, a little too small. Giving up his seat to a latecomer, an elderly woman carrying a shopping bag filled with knitting, Miles leant against one of the radiators and gazed at the tightly packed ranks before him. Twelve jurors per court for each of the seventeen courtrooms meant over two hundred jurors in all; handling that number of people along with all the associated defendants, witnesses and legal staff had to be a considerable logistical challenge. Slipping off his sports jacket, Miles turned his attention to the video which ran in turn through the procedures that jurors had to follow, the various rules and regulations to which they were subject and finally the catering and other arrangements laid on for their comfort. As soon as the video finished, the jurors began to make their way towards the canteen at the far end of the waiting lounge. Watching the queue beginning to form, Miles decided to explore the other rooms on the third floor, resolving to return to the canteen later once the crowd had died down.

The usher announced his name over the tannoy just after one-fifteen. Replacing his plate and coffee cup on the canteen counter and nodding in gratitude to the staff behind, Miles turned and walked across the lounge to the front desk where the other jurors who had been selected for court number eight had gathered. Their smart suits and air of nervous apprehension put him in mind of a group of eleven year olds on their first day at secondary school.

'Mr Coverdale?' enquired the usher.

'That's right,' he replied with a smile.

'Good, we're all here. Now, ladies and gentlemen, if you'd like to follow me, I'll take you down to the courtroom.'

The jurors marched one behind another along several corridors before travelling down two floors in a lift and then filing along a further series of corridors until they reached the waiting area outside court eight. Again, Miles was struck by the sheer scale of the operation – the court complex really was very large indeed. When the last juror had arrived, the usher addressed them in a friendly but authoritative voice.

'All right everyone, in a few moments you'll be going on through to be sworn in. Now, it's very important that you let me know immediately if you recognize anyone in the courtroom – not just the defendant, anyone at all. I'll be standing by the door – just come straight over and tell me. OK?'

Turning on her heel, the usher went through the heavy steel-panelled doors into the court. Now that the jurors had been left to their own devices, Miles expected them to descend into self-conscious silence, but no sooner had the usher disappeared than a conversation sprang up.

'Does anyone know what this case is?' asked a middle-aged man in a check suit.

'It's a burglary.'

All eyes turned to a young man in a leather jacket leaning against one of the concrete pillars. Miles noticed he was the only man apart from himself not wearing a shirt and tie.

'Really?' replied the man in the suit.

'Yeah.'

'How d'you know?'

'I saw it on her paperwork,' answered the young man, nodding towards the doors through which the usher had just departed and then adding as an afterthought, 'They do a lot of burglaries and thefts here.'

'Have you done this before, then?'

'Yeah. Eighteen months ago.'

A silence then descended on the group in deference to the unexpected presence of a veteran within their ranks. A few moments later, the usher reappeared.

'Could you please come on through now and line up next to the wall on your left. '

The first thing Miles noticed about the courtroom was how cold it was; he wondered whether the court authorities deliberately kept the temperature low to ensure that everyone stayed awake and alert. As the line of jurors came to a halt, he looked around the large, empty room. The walls and ceiling, which were of bright, highly varnished beech wood, seemed to add to the frosty atmosphere, and, although in no way overawed by the process in which he was involved, Miles shivered involuntarily as the judge turned to address the jurors.

Having firstly wished them good day, the judge then repeated the usher's instruction to inform a court official should they recognise anyone – especially the defendant. At this point, along with the rest of the jury, Miles turned to look at the slight West Indian youth in the dock who was dressed in a white sweatshirt and jeans. Surprisingly, the man showed not the slightest inclination to return the jury's gaze, but merely stayed slouched in his seat, staring indifferently into space. Miles wondered whether this was because he had been charged with something relatively trivial or because he simply didn't care whether he was found guilty or not; somehow, he rather suspected the latter. In front of the defendant stood his barrister, a slim, pale-complexioned man of indeterminate age who was poring intently over a file of papers. After the second juror had taken the oath, the barrister finally raised his eyes and, standing upright, surveyed the jury with a probing, incisive stare. Immediately Miles found himself wanting to reach for his camera and almost groaned out loud when he remembered that he did not have it with him. The visual contrast between defendant and defender was really quite remarkable: the white barrister in his black, formal gown, his brow furled in concentration; the black defendant in his white sweatshirt, his head slumped in nonchalant indifference. No sooner had Miles appreciated this striking counterpoise, than the barrister leant forward to look at his notes again and the juxtaposition between the two men disappeared. However, as Miles took the bible from the juror on his left and began to read aloud the oath on the card, he smiled to himself in satisfaction. For, just over a week ago, on a crisp spring evening, he had seen Angus Lamb and his mistress aligned in a similarly magical photographic moment, but, on that occasion, he had been able to capture the scene forever.

'Could you please state your name?'

The first witness had taken the stand.

'Albert Gregory Marks.'

'And where do you live, Mr Marks?' asked the prosecuting counsel, his rich, clear voice filling the spacious courtroom.

'Flat seventeen Lindley Gardens, Putney, London SW15.'

'And your home is on the first floor of an apartment block, is that correct?'

'That's right.'

The witness was in his late fifties, stout, with a blue checked jacket and a thick mane of silvery grey hair. He wore large framed glasses of a type that had gone out of fashion well over a decade ago, but which nevertheless perfectly suited his rugged, characterful face. Miles thought he looked the very picture of honesty.

'The, er, living room of your apartment, Mr Marks, could you explain to the jury what you see when you look out of the window?'

'Yes, my living room overlooks the roof of the flat below.'

'How far down is the roof exactly?'

'About four or five feet.'

'Thank you. Now, I'd like to ask you to cast your mind back to the afternoon of the twenty-fifth of August last year. Could you tell the jury what happened that day?'

'It was just after twelve-thirty. I was fixing myself some lunch in the kitchen when I heard a noise out on the roof, so I went across the living room to take a look. I've got net curtains on the window, and when I pulled them back I saw a man there. I looked straight into his face. He was standing on the roof, trying to look inside my flat.'

'Were you able to see his face clearly?'

'Oh, absolutely. He was only two feet away from me.'

'Can you describe this man?'

'Yeah, he was a coloured fella. About twenty-five to thirty, short cropped hair, T shirt …'

'What did you do then, Mr Marks?'

'Well, the window was on the latch – it was a hot day, you see – so I grabbed the handle and closed it quick. Then I went straight over and phoned the police.'

'What did you tell them?'

'That I'd just seen a bloke trying to break into my flat.'

'What made you think that was what he was trying to do?'

'Well, it was obvious,' replied the man, assuredly. 'If he'd been up there for any other reason he wouldn't have been peeping through my window like that.'

'So what did you do then?'

'I went back to the window to check, but he'd gone by that time – scarpered.'

'And what happened next?'

'Well, the police turned up about half an hour later. They interviewed me and that was it really.'

'Thank you, Mr Marks.'

As soon as the prosecuting barrister sat down the defence barrister straightaway stood up, although he paused deliberately before speaking, and, when he did so, looked not at the witness but directly at the jury.

'Mr Marks, just one question, if I may. The man you saw at the window, is he in the courtroom today?'

'No.'

'He is not the gentleman in the dock, then?'

'No, definitely not.'

'Are you sure of that?

'Oh yeah, a hundred percent. I got a good view of the bloke and that's not him.'

'Thank you, Mr Marks,' replied the defence barrister and then abruptly sat back down again.

As the witness made his way out of the stand, Miles looked around at his fellow jurors wondering what they had made of this negative identification. If the defendant hadn't been the man up on the roof, then why had the police arrested him and charged him with burglary?

'Your honour,' announced the prosecution barrister, standing back up again. 'I'd like to call Police Constable Warren Moore.'

The judge nodded, and a few seconds later a young, uniformed police officer took the stand. He was quite short for a policeman, but appeared muscular and very strong. Miles imagined he would make a first rate scrum-half.

'Could you state your name and rank, please?'

'Police Constable W-147 Warren Gerald Moore. Richmond Road police station.'

'PC Moore, could you tell the jury about the events of August the twenty-fifth? Do feel free to consult your notebook if you wish.'

'Yes, certainly,' replied the policeman, taking his notebook from his top pocket. His voice was clear and loud, and, unlike the previous witness whose gaze had strayed back and forth between the judge and the defence barrister, he addressed the jury directly.

'At twelve forty-eight that afternoon I received a call from Richmond Road station informing me of the attempted burglary at seventeen Lindley Gardens as reported by Mr Marks. I drove straight there arriving at about a quarter-past one. Having made contact with Mr Marks and radioed in my whereabouts, I then proceeded to investigate the area around and about the apartment block. Finding no sign of a suspect, or any visible evidence of a break-in, I interviewed Mr Marks, taking from him a full statement.'

'Were you alone at this point, or were you accompanied by your colleagues?'

'I was by myself at the actual scene, but I was in radio contact with two of my fellow officers from Richmond Road who were in a mobile unit carrying out a reconnaissance of the streets surrounding Lindley Gardens.'

'A mobile unit – you mean a police car.'

'Yes.'

'Please continue.'

'Just before a quarter to two, I decided to leave Lindley Gardens to return to the station. As I got into my car, I noticed an open window on one of the ground floor flats – I later discovered it was in fact flat number eleven. I went over to investigate and immediately found signs of forced entry – the window frame had been jemmied open with a screwdriver or a similar implement. I then radioed in requesting forensic assistance and waited inside for it to arrive, having discovered that the back door to the property was also open. The forensic team reached the scene at two thirty-five ...'

As the policeman paused, looking for the next relevant page in his notebook, Miles detected a slight movement on the other side of the courtroom where two people were noiselessly taking their seats in the large, otherwise empty public gallery. Not wanting to miss any of the police officer's continuing evidence, Miles at first merely cast a quick look in their general direction, but, as soon as he saw them, found himself completely unable to look away. The man was a powerfully-built West Indian, wearing a spotless white double-breasted jacket and a heavy gold chain around his neck. The woman was white, in her early twenties and unambiguously dressed like a gangster's moll. Shaking his head in disbelief, Miles looked across at the defence barrister. It seemed incredible that neither he nor the defendant's solicitor had warned their client about the risks of guilt by association. However strong his alibi, it couldn't fail to suffer in the eyes of the predominantly white middle class jurors by the arrival of acquaintances such as these.

'Jesus!' whispered a voice on Miles's left. 'Get a load of those two.'

Miles turned to look at the juror sitting next to him who obviously had also just caught sight of the two people in the public gallery. It was the young man in the leather jacket who had earlier identified that the case was a burglary. Catching his eye, Miles grinned in response. To his surprise, the man then leant slightly towards him and extended his hand for him to shake, holding it low under the parapet so that neither the judge nor the court officials could see.

'John. How d'you do?' he whispered.

'Miles,' he replied, grasping the man's hand and warming both to his sociability and the fact that, unlike the other jurors, he seemed not in the least bit phased by the formality of occasion.

In the witness box, the police officer cleared his throat, having finally found the right page in his notebook.

'After the forensic team had left, I ascertained that flat eleven was owned by a Mr Roger Wilson, a financial planning officer employed by Citibank Corporation based in Moorgate. Accordingly, I radioed through his details to Richmond Road asking that they make contact with him. At two forty-five I then proceeded to join my colleagues in the mobile unit in their search of the surrounding area, rendezvousing with PC Wilkes and PC Blake just after three o'clock on the main Putney Road.'

'And what did you discover while you were there?'

'While investigating Holly Park Avenue – one of the side roads off Putney Road – I came across a person whom I later learned to be the defendant, Mr Lewis. He was emerging from an alleyway that leads to the gardens at the back of the houses.'

'What time was this?'

'About three-fifteen.'

'Carry on.'

'I called out to Mr Lewis to stop – I wanted him to identify himself and explain what he was doing there – but he turned and ran back down the alleyway. I again called upon him to stop, and, when he did not do so, I ran after him in pursuit. I then radioed to my colleagues that I was now chasing a suspect, urging them to make their way quickly along Holly Park Avenue as it was likely that the alleyway would even-tually lead back on to it. This in fact proved to be the case, and after chasing Mr Lewis for about a minute, all the time repeatedly calling

18

upon him to stop, I saw him emerge from the other end of the alley into Holly Park Avenue where PC Blake and I then apprehended him.'

'Did Mr Lewis put up a struggle?'

'No. As soon as he saw PC Blake ahead of him, he stopped.'

'And what was his reaction?'

'You mean his reaction to being caught?'

'Yes. Did he look disappointed, scared …?'

'Disappointed definitely. He waved his arms downwards, like this, as though angry with himself that we'd headed him off.'

'What did you do then?'

'I proceeded to question Mr Lewis, asking him what he had been doing in the alleyway.'

'And what was his reply?'

'He said he'd stopped there to urinate. I asked him why he had run. He replied that it was because I had undoubtedly assumed that he had been up to no good.'

'Did you ask the defendant where he had been going?'

'Yes, he said it was a nice day, so he'd gone out for a walk. I then asked him where he lived. In reply, he gave me an address in New Malden, Surrey.'

'How far is that from the street in which you apprehended him in Putney?'

'Five or six miles at least.'

'Five or six miles? Quite a walk.'

'Yes, that's what I thought.'

'What happened next?'

'At three twenty-six I arrested Mr Lewis on suspicion of burglary. He was then held in the mobile unit whilst PC Blake and I made an investigation of the area.'

'And did you find anything?'

'Yes. Half way down the alleyway we found a silver Rolex watch in a clump of grass next to a garage – it appeared to have been thrown aside there.'

'Were there any identifying marks on the watch?'

'Yes, the watch carried an engraved inscription reading 'To Roger, with all my love Alexandra'. Its rightful owner was Mr Roger Wilson of flat eleven Lindley Gardens. He later identified the watch as being his property.'

'When you found the watch, did you realise it belonged to Mr Wilson?'

'I wasn't sure, but I thought the probability was very high.'

'Because you had stood guard over flat eleven Lindley Gardens whilst waiting for the forensic team to arrive, and because it was you who had discovered by means of a search of the flat that it was in fact the residence of Mr Roger Wilson?'

'Correct.'

'If you would, er, complete the record of that afternoon's events for the jury, Constable Moore ...?'

'Yes,' said the policeman, once more raising his notebook and reading from it. 'Having bagged the watch as evidence, I then took Mr Lewis to Richmond Road Station where he was placed in custody at four-fifteen for subsequent questioning by my CID colleagues.'

'Thank you, Constable Moore.'

As the prosecuting barrister sat down, Miles turned around to look at John who grimaced in response. Things were looking pretty bad for the defendant. Although he hadn't been identified as the person up on the roof, he must have been involved in the subsequent burglary in one way or another, having ditched the watch whilst being pursued by PC Moore. As the defence barrister stood up to begin his cross-examination, however, he looked anything but downhearted by the apparent weight of evidence against his client.

'PC Moore ...' he announced, letting the phrase hang ominously in the air for several seconds. 'Where shall I begin? The twenty-fifth of August was a hot day, wasn't it?'

'Yes, I think so.'

'How hot, can you remember?'

'... er, fairly hot.'

'Let me tell you how hot it was. Thirty-three degrees centigrade, according to the meteorological records for London for that day; absolutely sweltering in fact.'

'Yes, I recall it was very hot.'

'In your evidence, you told the jury that you arrived at Lindley Gardens, made contact with Mr Marks at flat number seventeen and then carried out a search of the other apartments. This search, however, revealed no evidence of a break in.'

'That's correct.'

'Then you went off to join your colleagues, got into your car and saw the window that had been broken into at flat number eleven – a ground floor apartment.'

'That's right.'

At this point the defence counsel paused, shaking his head wearily like a kindergarten teacher confronted with a child's hopelessly knotted shoe laces that he was somehow going to have to undo.

'Why didn't you see it first time around – when you had first made a check of the other apartments?'

'I must have missed it.'

'Didn't you walk right past it?'

'I believe I may have done …'

'When you finally did see it, you were in your car, is that correct?'

'Just getting into my car, yes.'

'And how far was your car parked from flat eleven?'

'Oh, er, hard to say. Perhaps about … twenty-five yards.'

'So the break-in was obvious at twenty-five yards, but not at two or three feet – is that what you're asking us to believe?'

'I guess I, er, just didn't see it.'

'Were you paying attention?'

'I believe I was.'

'Come now, PC Moore,' urged the defence barrister, 'it was a boiling hot day. Mr Marks had just told you that the burglar had run off over forty-five minutes ago. You were taking things easy, weren't you?'

'No, I believe I was paying attention, sir,' answered the policeman a little too quickly: the barrister had clearly touched a nerve.

'But you certainly took it easy after you got into the burgled flat, didn't you?'

'Er, no …'

'Well, you said in your evidence you did,' he continued, theatrically raising his notes up off the desk and reading aloud, 'Just before a quarter to two I decided to leave Lindley Gardens … the forensic team reached the scene at two thirty-five.' In the intervening fifty minutes you just hung around inside Mr Roger Wilson's flat, didn't you?'

'I did wait inside Mr Wilson's flat, yes.'

'Nice and cool in there, was it?'

'Yes, it was cooler than outside,' replied the police officer, who was looking more and more uncomfortable by the moment.

'You didn't really break into much of a sweat after that either, did you? Once again according to your evidence you joined your colleagues PC Wilkes and PC Blake at Holly Park Avenue just after three o'clock. Now, this is one and a half hours after they had begun their search of the surrounding area and over two and half hours since Mr Marks had first seen a man up on the roof. Didn't it occur to you that the burglar would have been long gone by then?'

'I thought that might be possible, yes.'

'Might be possible ... not highly likely?'

'Yes, there was a strong possibility that he'd gone, but he could also have moved on to look for opportunities to burgle other nearby properties.'

The defence barrister didn't respond straightaway, but simply curled his lip in barely disguised contempt.

'That's what burglars do, is it, in your experience?' he said, finally. 'After they've been identified by a member of the public and the area's crawling with police. Hang around for a couple of hours more in the hope of spotting an open bathroom window?'

'They may remain in the vicinity, sir,' replied the policeman stiffly.

Suddenly, the barrister dropped the irony from his voice and adopted a dry and objective tone. Miles had the feeling, however, that he was merely doing so in preparation for coming down on the police officer all the harder.

'PC Moore, when you saw Mr Lewis, how far down the alleyway was he?'

'About ten or fifteen yards.'

'And he was walking towards you, yes – back on to Holly Park Avenue?'

'Yes.'

'In a manner consistent with a man who had just stopped in an alleyway to urinate.'

'Possibly so, yes.'

'Did he see you first, or did you see him?'

'I believe I saw him first.'

'How many seconds away was he from emerging out of the alleyway and walking on to the road?'

'I don't know.'

'Roughly.'

'Five or ten seconds perhaps.'

'So, why did you call out to him?'

'I beg your pardon?'

'Why did you call to him?'

'I, er, wanted to attract his attention.'

'Well, yes, PC Moore, obviously, but from what you have said you needed only to have stood still and waited a few seconds and he would have walked right up to you. Wouldn't that have been better? As it was, you panicked him and that's why he ran off, wasn't it?'

'People who don't have anything to hide don't run off,' countered the policeman.

'Oh, no? What were the exact words you used when you called out to him?'

'I can't remember exactly … something like, "You there."'

'Wasn't it 'Oi! You!' That's what the defendant claims.'

'Yes, it could well have been …'

'Earlier you stated, "I wanted him to identify himself and explain what he was doing there," so why didn't you call out something to that effect, rather than "Oi! You!"?'

'Well, it just came out that way.'

'Oh, no, PC Moore. It wasn't an arbitrary exclamation. You used those words for a very good reason – because you were of a mind to arrest the first likely looking suspect that you found that afternoon.'

'That's not true. It was just my intention to question him.'

'In that case, then surely you would have said something like 'Excuse me, sir,' wouldn't you?'

'Not necessarily.'

'PC Moore, your words and actions that afternoon were consistent with one intention and one intention alone: to make an arrest. Mr Lewis, though completely innocent, sensed that intention and that's why he turned and ran.'

'I don't believe that's true.'

'And arrest him you did, didn't you? Without any evidence whatsoever. You said yourself you didn't find the watch until after you had arrested Mr Lewis, handcuffed him and trussed him up in the back of your 'mobile unit'.'

'I arrested him because I believed there was sufficient evidence to warrant such an arrest.'

'Evidence? What evidence? Being black and walking down a street a mile away from where a crime had been committed nearly three hours previously? The weather might have been hot that afternoon, PC Moore, but I put it to you that your police work was anything but!'

Standing in the wooden witness box with his hands clasped behind his back and his eyes staring upwards, PC Moore looked less like a policeman giving evidence than a martyr about to be burned at the stake. Looking at the pensive expressions on the faces of his fellow jurors, Miles was genuinely impressed by the defence barrister. He recalled having once read that advocates often receive details of a given brief only a few hours before it is due to be heard. He did not know whether that had been the case with this barrister, but, in any event, by his skilled, incisive questioning he appeared to have swung the pendulum back in favour of the defendant.

'Your honour,' said the prosecution barrister, tetchily, 'my learned friend is directing statements towards the witness, not questions.'

'Do you have any more questions for the witness?' asked the Judge quietly.

'Just one, your honour. PC Moore, after you had removed Mr Lewis to Richmond Road Station did you take his fingerprints?'

'His fingerprints were taken, but by the duty officer, not by me.'

'And the watch that you had found, was it dusted down for fingerprints, too?'

'Yes.'

'And were Mr Lewis's fingerprints found on the watch?'

'No, they were not.'

'I have no more questions, your honour.'

The judge called a halt to the afternoon's proceedings at half-past three. As Miles began walking through Kingston's central shopping precinct, he looked at the line of shop windows ahead and resolved not to return to his car until he had got something for Jake: there were only three days left until his son's birthday and he wasn't going to get a better opportunity to buy his present than this. Spotting a pair of roller blades in the window of a sports shop, he stopped and stared at them thoughtfully. Keeping up with the rapidly changing tastes of a fifteen year old was no doubt difficult at the best of times, but Miles and his wife were separated and because of the crazy hours that he had to work as a photographer and the fact that

Jake lived with his mother, they were often unable to see each other for weeks on end. Moreover, during the last eighteen months or so, Jake had become increasingly quieter and more withdrawn and, although it was doubtless only an adolescent phase, communication between them was nevertheless at something of an all time low. Frowning, Miles recalled his own teenage years. He had been fanatical about sport and if his father had presented him with a pair of blades such as these he would have been over the moon. However, children's interests were more sophisticated nowadays and understanding what was in or out of fashion at any one given point in time was no simple matter. In the end, Miles put his best foot forward and decided to buy them. Jake had been very keen on skating when he had been younger and only a few days previously Miles had seen a boy his son's age performing wonderful acrobatic feats on the ramps at the skateboard park a few hundred yards away from his flat.

Making his way back to the multi-storey car park, Miles began to feel a little more confident about the gift that he had just purchased: even if the skates weren't exactly what Jake wanted at least he would know that his father had made an effort. Placing the gift-wrapped parcel in the boot, he decided to take it around straightaway. He had told Elizabeth that he would call at her flat on Thursday, but not knowing what might happen with his jury service, it would be safer to go there now. There was a queue to get out of the car park and another to get around the Kingston ring road and it was nearly seven before Miles arrived at the apartment complex where Elizabeth and Jake lived. As he positioned his car in one of the visitors' parking spaces, he looked up at the cluster of modern, three storey blocks and suddenly had a flashback to the courtroom that afternoon, wondering how often these apartments got broken into – maybe he would ask Elizabeth about it when Jake was out of the way. Pressing the illuminated button on the entryphone, he stood back and waited for Elizabeth's voice.

'Hallo?'

'Hi, Liz, it's me. I've brought Jake's present round.'

A pause. Miles frowned. He really should have phoned to say that he would be coming a couple of days early.

'He's not here,' she replied. 'I thought you said you were going to bring it on Thursday …'

'Oh, er, sorry, I'm not sure what's going to be happening later in the week, so I thought I'd drop it off now.'

25

'You'd better come on up, then.'

'If it's inconvenient, I can come back …'

The buzzing of the automated lock cut Miles off mid sentence and, springing quickly forwards, he leant his shoulder against the door to ensure that he got through before Elizabeth took her finger off the button. Crossing the lobby, he summoned the lift, but it seemed to take an age to arrive and, as he stared at its polished stainless steel doors, blank and unmoving, he felt his spirits begin to drop. Here he was once again on Elizabeth's doorstep – having turned up out of the blue – an empty, guilty feeling in the pit of his stomach. How many times since their separation had he found himself in this exact same position? How many times had he stood on this very spot waiting to play out his part in the same forlorn, recurring scene that he knew would inevitably follow?

'Hi.'

She had had her hair highlighted. It made her look younger.

'Hi. Come on in.'

'Are you sure it's all right?' he replied, hesitating before entering the flat.

'Yeah, I wasn't doing anything, don't worry.'

'I like your hair.'

'What?'

'Your hair.'

'Oh, that. I had it done ages ago. I've got used to it by now. Come on through. D'you want a cup of tea or something?'

She always offered, just as he always refused – it was all part of the litany.

'No, no, I won't stop.'

'You sure?'

'No, no. I've got to get on. So, Jake's not about, then?' enquired Miles, looking around the spacious, brightly-lit living room, as tidy and as ordered as ever.

'No, it's half term. He's stopping over at his friend Gary's tonight and tomorrow.'

'Oh, right.'

'He's just had exams, so I thought the break would do him good.'

'How'd he get on?'

'Oh, fine. Sailed through.'

'Great.'

'Most of his friends feel overwhelmed by the amount of homework they get. He just seems to thrive on it. I have to drag him away from his schoolwork half the time.'

'Yeah?'

'Yeah. Especially English.'

'Good. Nice to hear.'

'I'm really pleased. He's doing so well. It's his GCSE's next year and all the teachers says he's going to fly through …'

Suddenly she stopped and pursed her lips. It always happened like this: she always cut their conversations short. Conversations made them close – especially about Jake. Close. Like they had been before. On the night that she had asked for a separation, he had begged her to give their marriage another try, certain that the bonds of affection between them were fundamentally strong. In response, she had replied that it was simply too late; that her love for him had drained away after fifteen long years of taking second place to his career; that he would never change and that she no longer even wanted him to. But then, as now, he could not help but see in her mannerisms tell-tale signs of feelings that her heart had not yet relinquished, no matter how much her mind might wish them gone. Perhaps he was deluding himself that these gestures denoted anything meaningful. Perhaps they were merely phantoms. But in the intervening six years she had not remarried and although he knew he had no right whatsoever periodically to make these impromptu visits to her home, in all the times he had turned up on her doorstep she had never once sent him away.

Finally, she broke the silence.

'So, is that it, then?'

'What?'

'The present.'

'Oh, yeah, yeah,' he replied, clumsily lifting up the polythene bag containing the skates.

'D'you want to leave it, or bring it around later in the week when he's back?'

'Er, yes, I think I will come back after all – if that's all right. Is Thursday still OK?'

'Fine. Yes, Thursday'd be fine. So, er, how's work, then?'

'Good,' he replied, and then added enthusiastically, 'no, actually, more than good. Brilliant. Couldn't be better.'

'Yeah?'

'Yeah. D'you know a bloke called Lamb – the junior Minister for Overseas Development?'

'The one that's been in the news for the last few days?'

'That's him. It was my photo.'

'What, in the hotel room with his secretary?'

'Yep.'

'Well, that must have been quite a coup.'

'Best picture I've taken in ages.'

'Oh, congratulations.'

'Thanks.'

Again the pursed lips. Again the awkward silence.

'Well, I'll be off then. Thursday evening – is that all right?'

'That's fine. I'll make sure he's here,' said Elizabeth, turning and making her way towards the front door.

'Oh, one other thing …' said Miles, pausing on the threshold.

'Yes?'

'These apartments. Do they ever get burgled?'

'Burgled?' she replied, in surprise. 'I don't think so. Almost never. I mean each block has its own caretaker. Why d'you ask?'

'Oh, no reason, really. It's just, well, nothing. See you on Thursday.'

'Oh, right. Bye,' replied Elizabeth, closing the front door, as always, with a tolerant, reserved smile.

Returning to his flat an hour later, Miles hung his jacket on one of the coat hooks in the hallway, slipped off his shoes and then went into the lounge and poured himself a large glass of scotch. He felt tired and washed-out – he hadn't eaten anything since the sandwich in the court canteen at lunch-time. Slumping down on to the sofa, he looked across the lounge towards the kitchen. After he had finished his drink he would fix himself some food and then turn in for the night. No sooner had he taken his first sip of whisky, however, than the door bell rang. Sitting up with a start, Miles put the glass down on the table and hurried to the front door, checking his watch as he went; he rarely had visitors at his flat, let alone at this hour of the night.

'Hello, old boy. I've got the right place, then.'

'Tom!' exclaimed Miles, astonished to see his boss standing on the doorstep. 'Come on in; come on in.'

'Thanks,' he replied, stepping through the doorway and wiping his feet on the mat energetically. 'Hope you don't mind me just turning up at your place like this.'

'No, not at all.'

'It's just I've got a bit of good news,' continued Tom, with a conspiratorial wink. 'I thought I'd come around and tell you in person.'

'Oh, great, well, come on through and take a seat. Fancy a drink?'

'Ah! Excellent idea!' chuckled Tom, rubbing his hands together in glee as he followed Miles down the hallway.

Knowing that Tom preferred his whisky on the rocks, Miles went through to the kitchen to get some ice out of the freezer. Levering several of the cubes into a glass, he wondered what on earth could have prompted his boss to come around to his flat. He had worked for Tom Cranmer for almost four years, and, although they were good friends, by tacit but mutual consent they kept their personal lives very much to themselves and had never once visited each other's homes; whatever this news was, it had to be important. As he made his way back into the lounge, Miles could see that Tom had not in fact taken a seat, but was standing staring at the small gallery of photographs that hung in the alcove between the bay windows.

'So this is where you hang your scalps, then?' exclaimed Tom, shaking his head slowly in admiration. 'What a collection! I've never seen your work altogether like this before. Most of these made the front pages, didn't they? Yet not a single one of them would look out of place in a west-end photo gallery.'

'I have to keep them somewhere,' replied Miles modestly, passing Tom his drink. These were a dozen or so of the best photographs that he had ever taken: the pictures that had done most to make his reputation.

'This chap here,' asked Tom, curiously, pointing to the picture in the top left hand corner. 'I don't remember him. Who was he?'

It was a black and white photograph, taken at night, of a man in his early fifties warily emerging from a doorway and stepping out into the frosty darkness. The street was misty and the man had just exhaled – his steamy breath forming a cloud that almost completely obscured his face.

'Oh, it's quite an old one, this,' said Miles, stretching up and taking the photograph off the wall so that Tom could look it at more closely. 'I took it before either of us worked at *The Mail* – ten, eleven years ago, maybe.

His name was Dr Gregory Llewellyn. He was a back street abortionist.'

'What, in England?'

'Yeah – London. This street's just off the Peckham High Road.'

'I thought all that sort of thing disappeared in the fifties.'

'Oh, no – it still goes on even today. Llewellyn's speciality was girls from the Irish republic. They'd come over on a cheap flight for the weekend, check into a B&B and he'd do the operation in the room for them. After he'd been arrested, he claimed his motives were philanthropic – said the girls were better off with a qualified physician like him than some cack-handed butcher.'

'Really?'

'Yeah. Still charged 'em fifty quid a time, mind you.'

'What happened to him in the end?'

'He got struck off,' replied Miles with a shrug, hanging the photograph back on the wall once more. 'So, anyway, what's this good news you've got for me?'

'He's going,' replied Tom abruptly, turning and grinning at Miles. 'Tomorrow – first thing.'

'Who?'

'Lamb.'

'What, he's resigning?'

'Yep. He'll be gone by lunch time.'

'Wow, that is big news.'

'Isn't it just?' said Tom, moving over to the armchair and settling down into it comfortably. 'He's hugely popular with the public, of course, but the government's had enough of the embarrassment – what with a general election next year and everything. And besides, he's pissed an awful lot of important people off since he got the job – asked too many difficult questions. So, that's it. He's out on his arse. He's been told he no longer has the party's confidence, apparently. He'll keep his parliamentary seat, I gather, but as a minister, he's finished – his reputation's shot to pieces.'

'Are you sure about this?'

'Absolutely,' replied Tom, tapping the side of his nose confidentially. 'I've had it on the very best authority. So, how does it feel having occasioned the biggest political resignation of the year?'

'Pretty good, I suppose,' replied Miles.

'Cromwell called me earlier. He's pleased, too.'

'So, he should be,' huffed Miles, resentfully. 'It's the only decent exclusive he's managed to get his hands on all year.'

'Come on,' coaxed Tom, 'he's not doing such a bad job. Although it's certainly one in the eye for his full-timers only policy. Rather vindicates both our positions, wouldn't you say?'

'Yeah, that's true.'

'So, here's to infidelity everywhere, then,' beamed Tom, lifting his glass in a toast. 'Long may it flourish. Cheers.'

'Cheers.'

Taking a sip of his whisky, Miles had to agree with his boss's assessment. When he had joined *The Mail* seven years previously it had been as a member of a small group of thirty or so photographers that the paper retained on semi-permanent contracts – salaried freelancers who were allowed to pursue whatever material they wished in return for rights of first refusal on their work – an arrangement that Miles had quickly found suited him perfectly. A couple of years ago, however, after two consecutive quarters in the red, the paper's long-standing editor had been fired and Cromwell had been brought in. A tireless and ruthlessly efficient administrator, Cromwell had immediately set about dismantling *The Mail*'s numerous outdated systems and practices and within a year had brought the paper back into profit. Unfortunately – and in both Tom and Miles's view, wrongly – Cromwell regarded all employees on semi-permanent contracts as spongers and had either sacked or harassed most of them out. Today, Miles was one of less than half a dozen photographers still retained in this way, all of whom reported to Tom, the news features editor. But Lamb's resignation was set to become the biggest news story that *The Mail* had broken all year, and the fact that it had come from a photographer on a semi-permanent contract would inevitably cast doubt on Cromwell's entire policy.

'So, how was jury service, then?' asked Tom, cradling his whisky glass between his hands. 'Have you been twiddling your thumbs all day?'

'No, I got called up on a case straightaway.'

'Oh, really – I'd heard it was all sitting around for days on end.'

'Well, maybe for some people, but not for me – they got me right in there doing my civic duty from day one.'

'So, what was it, then?'

'What, the case?'

'Yeah.'

'Some bloke accused of stealing a watch.'

'Hold the front page.'

'Well, exactly, but I am enjoying the break.'

'Good, you deserve it. And, er, how's your son? Are you seeing much of him lately?'

'Sorry?'

'Your son – Jake, isn't it? Are you seeing much of him lately?'

Miles paused before answering – more than a little surprised by the question. Not only had Tom taken the unusual step of coming to his flat that night, but was now proceeding to enquire about his family life.

'He's fine, yes, fine,' answered Miles, guardedly.

'I didn't mean to pry,' continued Tom with a frown, clearly conscious that he had strayed into unfamiliar territory. 'It's just that I may have a job for you – one that by its very nature would mean your not being able to see him for possibly, well, several months on end. I wanted to ask you whether you'd be interested, given those conditions.'

'What sort of a job?'

'I can't exactly say at this point, old boy. It's very hush hush. I mean, I can say that I think you're absolutely ideal for it. More than that, in fact, you're the only person I know who could pull it off. But it will mean your being out of commission, as it were, for quite long periods of time.'

'Well, I can't say. Not without more information …'

'But you wouldn't be against it in principle?' asked Tom, swiftly.

'Er … No, I suppose not.'

'Good, good,' he continued, once again gently rotating his tumbler of whisky and staring down at the ice as it swirled around inside. 'It might be dangerous, too. I have to tell you that.'

'Dangerous?'

'Almost definitely.'

'It's not some conflict or other somewhere, is it? War photography. I mean, you know that's not my bag.'

'No, no, nothing like that,' replied Tom, with a shake of the head. 'What are you doing on Friday? In the evening?'

'Nothing I can't cancel.'

'I can tell you more about it, then, if you really are interested.'

'OK,' said Miles, starting to feel a little intrigued.

'Come to the Tower – about seven. It'll be me, you and number one. This whole thing was his idea originally.'

'Oh, Tom, for God sake!' exhaled Miles, despairingly. 'Not another one of Cromwell's half-arsed schemes. Please! I mean I know he's the boss and all that and you've got to keep in with him, but I choose my own material – my own stories – I always have done. You know that better than anyone.'

'I'm not talking about Cromwell,' replied Tom, quietly.

'What d'you mean?'

'I said I'm not talking about Cromwell.'

'No?'

'No.'

'Who then?'

'King.'

'King!'

'Yes, King.'

'Really?'

'Yes. Shall we, er, say eight thirty?'

'OK. I'll be there.'

'Good,' said Tom with a smile, standing up and making his way back towards the door. 'I thought you might be interested.'

Looking through the window and watching his boss drive away, Miles frowned thoughtfully. Tom was right: he was interested – very interested. Because Henry King was much more than the number one man on *The Mail* – more, even, than the number one man of the media empire of which *The Mail* was a part.

He owned it.

Chapter 2

The moment Mary Lamb opened her eyes she was completely awake. Turning her head slowly, she looked around at the bedside clock. Five twenty-three. It had been just after one when she had last checked the time, squinting restlessly at the alarm clock's luminous green dial. Although she had only managed to get four hours sleep, it had been deep and dreamless – the first proper sleep she had had in over a week – and she was grateful for it. Wrapping her dressing gown about her, she went into the kitchen and put a match to the crumpled up newspaper underneath the pile of coals in the grate. For several minutes she stood watching the flames flicker into life, waiting until she was sure that the fire was burning safely before going back across the kitchen to make a pot of tea. Her son Angus was very concerned about her old, Victorian open fire, worrying that it was both inefficient and dangerous, but she always turned down his kind offers to replace it with a modern gas appliance and instead made sure to keep a wary eye on it at all times. She had grown up in front of this hearth and, if it had been good enough for the first seventy years of her life, it would be good enough until the day that God in his wisdom decided to call that life to an end. Pouring herself a cup of tea, she sat down in one of the two chairs in front of the fire, wrapped a blanket around her legs and waited in the silence for the dawn to break; the dawn that would herald the day every mother dreaded.

She got changed at a quarter past six. The kitchen had warmed up considerably and the central heating had also come on in the rest of the house. Walking down the corridor that connected her ground floor annex with the main part of the house, Mary slipped silently into the large downstairs kitchen and put the kettle on to make tea for Angus and Madeleine. She had been listening for the last half hour and there had been no sounds of movement from the first floor. They were still sleeping. That was good. They needed all the rest they could get.

As the kettle was taking time to boil, Mary wandered restively along the hall and into the front room. Sitting on the arm of the sofa, she stared at the heavy velvet drapes that covered the window facing the street outside. The first of them would already be out there waiting on the pavement, thirsty for blood – Angus's blood. With a shudder, she turned and retreated back into the relative security of the kitchen. Opening up the cupboard, her fingers reached for the tea cups but alighted instead on one of the brightly painted mugs that they had bought in Sicily the previous summer. It had been a wonderful holiday – probably the best they had ever had together. With melancholic reverence, Mary took one of the mugs down and placed it on the worktop. On the first day they had split up, keen to investigate the maze of shops in Taormina's old town: Angus had gone off in one direction and she and Madeleine had gone off in the other. An hour later they had met up in the main square, each of them clutching an identical bright orange ceramic mug, each of them having been told the same story by a different shopkeeper of a brother-in-law who carefully crafted the pieces by hand in his mountainside pottery. Certain that their new purchases had actually been manufactured in China, the three of them had then walked off together arm in arm, laughing as they had made their way to eat their packed lunch in the magnificent amphitheatre overlooking the bay.

As she began putting the tea things on the tray, Mary suddenly stopped in panic. At the end of the hallway, she could see light coming through a gap in the dining room door: they must have left the curtains open overnight. What if one of those awful people had climbed over the back fence and was waiting in the garden to snatch a photograph? Abandoning her preparations, she hurried down the hall, across the dining room and hastily pulled the curtains together. What a state of affairs – prisoners in their home. Sitting down to catch her breath for a moment at the long, twelve-seater table, Mary looked across at the photo of Angus and Madeleine on the fire place. Madeleine had not believed the lies about her husband for a moment, but she, of course, also had a career, and however strong her own conviction it would not prevent the tongues wagging behind her back or the knowing looks as she walked down the corridor. Frowning, but with a growing feeling of resignation, Mary made her way back across the darkened dining room towards the kitchen. Things would be easier after today. It was going to be a difficult day for Angus and Madeleine certainly – perhaps the most difficult of all – but once they had got through it, the spotlight would soon turn upon some other poor unfortunate and they would be forgotten. No, she shouldn't feel sorry for her family or herself. In the long run, it would not be they who would suffer by Angus's enforced departure, but rather the tragic host of nameless, faceless victims that he had spent his entire life striving to defend.

'Couldn't you sleep?'

He was standing at the bottom of the stairs in his pyjamas. The bags under his eyes were visible even in the darkened hallway

'No, no, I slept well – don't worry about me. Go on back upstairs, I'm making you some tea.'

With a sad, grateful smile, he turned and went to make his way back up the stairs, but then stopped and looked at her again.

'If I'd have known, when I first went into politics, that it was ever, ever going to hurt Madeleine or you in any way … I would never have done it.'

'Then I'm glad you didn't know,' she replied, quietly.

With a shake of his head, Angus Lamb stared in admiration at the diminutive figure of his mother. How was it that those slight, aged shoulders were so able to bear the anguish and pain of others?

'After all this is over, we'll go away again. The three of us. OK?'

Walking slowly down the hall towards her son, Mary smiled and placed her hand on his arm.

'Come on. Get back upstairs and spend some time with Madeleine. She's going to have to be very brave today; you both are.'

Walking back down the hallway with the tea tray a minute later, Mary heard a snatch of laughter from the street outside and, looking through one of the clear panes of glass at the side of the front door, saw two men on the far pavement setting up a camera tripod. Later, in their studio, they would splice and edit their photographs of Angus, seamlessly pasting together the parts that they needed for their evening editions or their special weekend pullout supplements.

But the man himself, she knew, could not be put back together so easily.

Despite the prosecution barrister's strenuous efforts the following morning, the jury eventually returned a verdict of not guilty, just as Miles had suspected they would. As soon as they had settled in the jury room, a vote had been taken, and, although it had been eight to four in favour of guilty, the subsequent discussion had revealed that the three women and one man had been so influenced by the defence barrister's demolition of PC Moore that they had no intention of changing their minds. As the most experienced juror, John, in particular, had found their obduracy exasperating in the extreme, pointing out that there had been no reference to the defendant being 'of good character' – which automatically meant that he already had a criminal record – and that his refusal to take the stand had undoubtedly been rooted in the fact that he had no innocent explanation as to why he had been caught hanging around in an alleyway that was over five miles from his home. In spite of this, the four jurors had continued to stand firm, insisting that the defendant deserved the benefit of the doubt. After an hour's increasingly heated debate, Alec, the retired accountant who had been elected foreman, had announced that their discussions had effectively become deadlocked and that they therefore had no alternative but to inform the judge that their final vote was eight to four in favour of guilty. John had scoffed at this suggestion, however, declaring that the judge would simply send them straight back to the jury room to continue their deliberations; a subsequent vote of ten to two might then possibly persuade him to accept a guilty verdict, but, if it remained at eight to four, he would simply dismiss the case. Fifteen minutes later they had gone back to court and returned a verdict of not guilty. When Alec had actually stood up and announced it, the defendant had smiled and shaken his head several times – a gesture which Miles and John had later agreed was less indicative of his gratitude towards the jury than his disbelief that they could have been so naïve as to have let him off.

So it was that at half-past eleven on Tuesday morning, Miles and the other eleven members of the court eight jury went back into the pool of available jurors and it was then that the waiting to which Tom had referred began in earnest. Miles and John spent the rest of that day exchanging life stories – Miles listening with interest to John's account of his twelve years in the Royal Engineers and his subsequent decision on returning to civilian life to embark upon a completely new career as an estate agent. On Wednesday morning, a rumour went around the waiting lounge that three new trials were about to begin, but one leisurely conversation passed into another without a single juror's name being announced over the tannoy all day. By Thursday morning, Miles and John had more or less run out of things to say to each other and instead simply lay sprawled in adjacent seats swapping newspapers and taking turns to buy the coffee. After lunch the much heralded three new trials all suddenly began at once, but the two men were not summoned to them and instead remained a part of the ever-smaller band of stand-bys until mid afternoon. At three-thirty, the usher then gathered together the forty or so people who were left in the waiting room and explained to them that although preparations for two further trials had been completed that afternoon, it was now too late in the day to initi-ate the actual proceedings and they were therefore free to go. It was thus with a considerable feeling of release that Miles emerged from the courthouse at a quarter to four and drove off to deliver his son's birth-day present.

'Oh, you're early,' announced Elizabeth's voice from the entry phone.

'Yeah, sorry,' said Miles, sheepishly. 'It's not inconvenient, is it?'

'No, no, come on up,' she continued, brightly. 'Charlotte's here, actu-ally.'

'Great,' he exclaimed, although as he entered the apartment block he was grimacing painfully: much as he was fed up with the jurors' waiting lounge he would have gladly hung around there for another hour if it meant that he could have avoided meeting Charlotte Burgess – Elizabeth's oldest and closest friend. Twenty years previously, when Liz had first introduced them to each other, Charlotte had seemed to take to him straightaway and a mutual fondness had quickly sprung up. But as Miles and Elizabeth's romance had started to become more serious, Charlotte's affections towards him had correspondingly cooled. When Elizabeth had finally informed her that they had decided to get married, she had received the news calmly, although by then Miles had been certain that she regarded him as simply not good enough for her best friend. All the way through their married life and on the few occasions that he and Charlotte had met since their separation she had treated him with politeness, but, beneath the veneer of civility Miles was in no doubt that her antipathy towards him remained as strong as ever, and, as he came out of the lift and approached the front door of Elizabeth's apartment, he mentally prepared himself for the tacit hostility that awaited him on the other side.

'Hello,' said Elizabeth, opening the door.

'Hi,' replied Miles, stepping into the hallway. 'So, is, er, Jake back from school yet, then?' In response, Elizabeth nodded in the direction of Jake's bedroom. Inside, Miles could see his son sprawled out on the bed, his eyes closed, listening to music through a pair of headphones.

'He'll be in in a minute. Come on through.'

Walking down the corridor, Miles followed Elizabeth into the living room. Charlotte was seated in one of the room's two armchairs, dressed in a stylish, and typically champagne socialist, full-length camel coat. On the table between the two armchairs were a couple of half-drunk cups of coffee: his arrival had obviously disturbed a cosy little tête-à-tête.

'Hello, Miles,' she said, pleasantly, 'how are you?'

'I'm fine, thanks, you?' he answered, guardedly, moving over to sit at the dining table.

'Yeah, very well, thank you,' replied Charlotte, nodding at the plastic bag that he was carrying. 'Have you come to bring Jake his birthday present as well?'

'Yes.'

'Oh, right,' she smiled. 'Me, too.'

'Good, good,' replied Miles, forcing his face into a smile to match hers.

'Do you want a coffee?' asked Elizabeth.

'No, no, thanks, I'm OK – I've been drinking it all day,' said Miles, continuing to smile but feeling his eyes drifting towards the living room door: the sooner Jake finished listening to his music the better.

'So,' ventured Charlotte, 'how's work then, Miles?'

'Yeah, fine. Fine.'

'Come on now, Miles, better than fine,' urged Elizabeth, who, as always, seemed largely insensitive to Miles and Charlotte's mutual antipathy.

'Oh, yes?' asked Charlotte with interest.

'Well, all right, pretty good, then,' conceded Miles.

'Some nice photos of the royals, maybe?' enquired Charlotte, arching an eyebrow.

'No, actually,' answered Miles, feeling the hair rise on the back of his neck – how typical of Charlotte to characterize him as a low-grade paparazzi drone. 'A bit weightier than that.'

'Miles took that picture of Angus Lamb,' continued Elizabeth. 'You know – the Minister: the one who resigned earlier this week.'

'A thousand yards, at dusk, with a telescopic lens,' said Miles. 'It was quite a shot, though I say so myself.'

'Don't tell me you took that photo?' gasped Charlotte, her jaw dropping and a look of horror rapidly spreading across her face.

'Yes.'

Miles and Elizabeth stared on in surprise as Charlotte's complexion all of a sudden completely drained of colour. Pursing her lips, she then sat stiffly up in the armchair.

'Well, I hope you're proud of yourself …'

'What do you mean, I hope I'm proud of myself?' asked Miles.

'What's up, Charlie?' said Elizabeth.

'He was one of the best Ministers for Overseas Development this country's ever had. And you've gone and got him sacked … and for no good reason, at all.'

'He was having an affair with his secretary,' exclaimed Miles in astonishment.

'She wasn't his secretary. He's had the same secretary for the last twenty years – she's in hospital now, having an operation. That woman was a temp. A three month temp.'

'Oh, so that makes it all right then, does it? It's OK to screw your secretary as long as she's a temp?'

Looking around, Miles could see that Elizabeth was almost as amazed as he at Charlotte's response. Suddenly, though, Charlotte sat forward in her chair and began to speak quickly.

'I don't suppose you know anything about this, Elizabeth, but I heard all about it from a friend of mine at the Charity Commission. The temp that Lamb had employed had just been through a divorce. She was distressed and emotional. He tried to help her out, but she completely misread his interest.'

'Really?'

'Yes. She was the one who booked the hotel room. It was all a big mistake – an awful misunderstanding. The moment he found out what she'd been thinking he put her right. That photo of him with his arms around her? She'd just burst into tears – he was comforting her.'

'Oh, yeah, like hell …' responded Miles.

'It's true!' snapped Charlotte. 'My friend talks to Lamb's department all the time. She was absolutely devastated when she found out he might have to go. She told me the whole story.'

'And you believed her, did you?'

'Of course, I believed her!'

'Well, more fool you, then,' scoffed Miles, dismissively. 'The guy's a fake – a charlatan.'

Charlotte looked as though she were about to explode with rage at this comment, but before she had time to reply, Elizabeth spoke first.

'So why did he resign if he was innocent?'

'Because he knew nobody would believe his story,' exclaimed Charlotte. 'And, because the knives have been out for him for ages – in Whitehall and in the cabinet – he's put too many noses out of joint.'

'Did you know about this?' said Elizabeth, rounding on Miles.

'No, I didn't,' retorted Miles, irritated that Elizabeth seemed so ready to credit Charlotte's version of events, 'and I don't believe it for a moment, either. I'll bet Lamb just put that story around to try and save face.'

'How could you possibly know that?' retorted Charlotte.

'Because I followed those two around for nearly three weeks. It was obvious that there was something going on between them. I mean, they never left each other's side from dawn till dusk.'

'That's because he works his guts out!' countered Charlotte, hotly. 'Everybody knows that. That's how he's managed to get so much good done over the years.'

Out of the corner of his eye, Miles could see Elizabeth looking at him uncertainly. It was true that as soon as he had taken the photograph he had rushed straight back to his flat to get it developed – wanting to confirm that the couple he had glimpsed in the hotel room through his telescopic lens for the few short moments before the lights had gone out had indeed been Angus Lamb and his secretary. It was therefore just conceivable – albeit highly improbable – that they had not actually remained in the room overnight but had turned around and walked straight back out again.

'Oh, get real, Charlotte! Any politician with half an ounce of sense is never going to allow himself to wind up in a compromising situation like that!'

'Sense! Sense!' raged Charlotte. 'It's got nothing to do with sense! He's a genuine, kind man. He felt sorry for the poor woman. He shouldn't have to be scared of that. He shouldn't have to feel guilty about demonstrating a bit of compassion. Although, God knows I wish he had, with gutter journalists like you hanging around to frame him!'

Miles felt a surge of anger rush through him, accompanied at the same time by an exhilarating sense of release. At last, Charlotte had come out into the open and declared her hostility and, at last, he would therefore be justified in declaring his.

'Listen,' he hissed through gritted teeth. 'I know you don't like what I do. But there's a big difference between me and the sort of gutter journalists you're describing – and that is they make things up and I don't. When they can't find a story, they invent one. I've never done that, not once. It doesn't make things easy, though, being all hung up on the truth. It means I have to work twice as hard, three times as hard, as all the others. But that's just the way I am. Angus Lamb was in that hotel room with his secretary and he had his arms wrapped around her. I didn't do anything to bring that situation about. I didn't fake anything, I didn't lie, I didn't bribe anyone, I just waited and waited and then I photographed what I saw. That picture was the result. What's the significance of it? I don't know. It's not for me to judge. People have to make up their own minds about it.'

'You can't just wash your hands of responsibility like that!' cried Charlotte. 'Pictures have context. What on earth are people going to think if they see a photograph like that in *The Mail* with all the other salacious shit it prints?'

'People have to make up their own minds about all that stuff, too! As grown adults, interpreting what they see on the basis of their own experience – of what they know of the world and its ways. And besides, I work for the paper, I don't own it. I've got no control over what's in the next fucking column let alone what's on the next page!'

Miles and Charlotte sat glaring at each other, but, on detecting a sudden, flinching movement from Elizabeth, both turned and looked sharply around.

'Oh, hi, darling,' said Elizabeth. 'Your father and Aunt Charlotte are here. They've brought you your birthday presents.'

It was Jake, standing pale and motionless at the half-open lounge door.

'Hello, Jake,' said Charlotte quickly, 'how are you?'

'Hello, sport,' echoed Miles.

The young man didn't speak, but merely stood staring at the three adults, uncertain as to how he should react to the situation into which he had stumbled.

'Happy birthday,' said Charlotte, giving him her most reassuring look and holding out a neatly wrapped package. 'I hope you like it.'

Finally, Jake smiled, walked slowly towards Charlotte and took his present.

'Thanks.'

'You're welcome. I won't ask for a kiss now you're fifteen and all grown up. It's the book you asked for. Read it and let me know what you think. It's one of my favourites, too.' So saying, Charlotte leant forward, squeezed Jake's hand and then in one graceful movement lifted herself out of the chair. 'Right, well, I'd better be going. I'll leave you with your Mum and Dad. Thanks, Elizabeth.'

'Thanks, Charlotte — and thanks for the present,' said Elizabeth. 'Come on, I'll see you out.'

Turning swiftly on her heel, and without acknowledging or even looking at Miles, Charlotte followed Elizabeth through the door.

'Sorry about that, old man,' said Miles, after they had gone. 'You know Charlotte and me don't exactly see eye to eye on everything.'

'That's OK,' replied Jake.

'Come on; let's go to your room. I've got a present for you myself.'

As they went out into the hallway, Elizabeth was coming back from the front door. Catching Miles's eye, she frowned and then strode purposefully into the kitchen. Seeing the look that his parents had exchanged, Jake averted his eyes and carried on walking down the hall towards his room. As Miles followed, he cursed Charlotte for setting Elizabeth and him against each other like this. It was bad enough that they happened to be separated, but even during the darkest days of their break-up they had never once argued in front of Jake. Could there be anything more painful to a child than an open display of disharmony between its parents? Miles's own mother had died when he was six, and although many years later he had learned from his uncle that there had been more than a little acrimony between her and his father, his childhood memories were completely unsullied by even the remotest recollection of parental strife and were all the more precious for it.

'So, here you are, this is it,' said Miles, sitting down on the bed and handing his present over to Jake. 'Go on. Open it.'

'Oh, thanks,' said Jake, joining him on the bed and then clicking apart the plastic fasteners on the heavy, polythene bag. 'Oh, great – roller blades. They look really good.'

'The guy in the shop said they're just about the best pair you can get. Hope they fit you, but if they don't just let me know and I'll get them changed.'

'Yeah, right, thanks,' replied Jake.

'So …' continued Miles, uneasily, 'how's school?'

'OK.'

'Your mum says you're doing really well.'

'Yeah, all right, I suppose.'

'Aren't you going to open Aunt Charlotte's present?' asked Miles, hoping that his interest in Charlotte's gift might imply that their mutual dislike was not as intense as it had doubtless seemed.

'It's all right; I know what it is already. It's a book. I asked for it.'

'Oh, right …'

'What were you arguing about?'

'Oh, er, difficult to explain, really,' replied Miles, taken off-guard by the question, 'I suppose whether I can take photographs of anyone I like except people Aunt Charlotte approves of.'

'Oh, right. I see.'

Looking at the shy, slimly built young man sitting on the bed next him, Miles felt overcome by an uncomfortable feeling of concern tinged with estrangement. His own teenage years at boarding school had been a wonderfully satisfying period of his life. Academically he had easily matched his peers, and in sport – especially rugby and athletics – he had even more easily excelled them. For Jake, however, adolescence was clearly an altogether more complex experience that was driving him inwards upon himself, not outwards into the company of others.

'Did it upset you – our argument?'

'No, why should it?'

'Well, no one likes to walk in on other people having a row.'

'Don't worry about it,' replied Jake. 'I didn't mind'

'Good man,' said Miles with relief. Stretching out his hand, he went to tousle Jake's hair but then stopped mid gesture and instead punched him lightly on the shoulder with his fist. Much as he disliked Charlotte, he had been impressed by the way that she had resisted the impulse to kiss Jake. Even if he didn't quite know how to deal with his son's passage into adulthood, he too had to come to terms with the fact that it was happening and that he should no longer treat him like a child. 'Listen, I've got to go now. Do you want to get together in a few weeks time? Yeah? Go and see a match maybe?'

'Yeah, all right.'

'OK, I'll give you a call,' said Miles turning and walking towards the door. 'Don't fall off your skates, now.'

'Don't worry – no chance of that,' replied Jake.

Walking thoughtfully down the hallway towards the kitchen, Miles tapped lightly on the door and then entered. Elizabeth was standing by the window, cutting up vegetables on a chopping board.

'I'll be off now,' he said, quietly. 'Thanks for letting me come round.'

'I'm sorry about all that with Charlotte,' replied Elizabeth, putting down the kitchen knife and turning to face him. 'I hope it didn't spoil your giving Jake his present.'

'No, it's all right. He was OK about it, and besides, Charlotte's got every right to say what she thinks'.

'Yes,' conceded Elizabeth, 'and when she wants to she does precisely that …'

Miles paused before continuing, wanting to ask Elizabeth about Jake but knowing how easily she might retreat into one of her silences if he overstepped the mark. Finally, he closed the door carefully and took a few paces across the kitchen towards her.

'I do worry about him, you know. He seems so withdrawn nowadays. He is all right, isn't he?'

'He's fine,' replied Elizabeth, smiling sympathetically. 'Honestly. It's his age – he just needs a bit of space, that's all. I mean, even I've backed off a little bit lately. But he's doing OK. He's happy. He really is.'

'Well, that's good to hear,' said Miles, with relief. 'You always know what he's thinking better than anyone. OK, well, I'd better get going. I'll let myself out.'

'You sure?' said Elizabeth, turning as though about to accompany him to the door.

'No, no, it's OK, you get on with the dinner,' he replied, pointing to the vegetables that Elizabeth was preparing.

'Oh, yes, OK. See you, then.'

'Bye.'

As the front door closed with a muffled click, Jake slipped the CD insert that he had been idly reading back inside its case and put it on the window ledge with the others in his collection. Sitting down on the edge of the bed, he picked up one of the roller blades and indifferently spun its rear wheel around once with his forefinger. With a shake of the head, he then packed both skates away and, with a quick look down the hallway to check that his father had indeed gone, picked up the heavy box and slid it deep beneath his bed. Looking at the clock and noting that dinner was still about a half an hour away, he took the book that Charlotte had given him out of its wrapping paper, lay down on the bed, and with concentration and interest, began to read.

Hearing his name announced over the tannoy, Miles took his jacket off the spare seat next to him and walked out of the canteen back into the jurors' waiting lounge. It was two forty-five and because he had been summoned to a new jury he would not now be able to sit out the next forty-five minutes until the usher let the stand-by jurors go home at half past three. That evening he was due to meet one of the most influential media figures in Britain and, although he would not now have the opportunity to return home first and get cleaned up, he was quite happy to go straight to the meeting from the courthouse: it would be good to have something else to occupy his mind for the next couple of hours, rather than speculating about the intriguing but apparently dangerous job that it appeared he was going to be offered that night. As he made his way across the lounge, he watched the other jurors gathering around the usher's desk, noting with interest that three of the people from the court eight trial had also been summoned. Hearing John's name announced also, Miles went over to the usher to tell her that he had gone down to the ground floor smoking room five minutes previously and would be back in a few moments.

On first sight, court three appeared to be identical to court eight in every respect save that it was about half the size. As with the previous trial, the clerk of court began proceedings by reading out each prospective juror's name in turn and then pausing to give the defence barrister the opportunity to object. When the first of the jurors started reading the oath, Miles looked across at the man in the dock. Once again he was in his late twenties, but thereafter all similarities with the court eight defendant completely ceased: whereas the black youth had appeared indifferent to the point of arrogance, this sallow-complexioned young man was plainly overawed by the situation in which he found himself; whereas the former defendant had exuded a stylish street cool, this man had come to court in a suit which, although quite smart, was fractionally too small and had the unfortunate effect of making him look rather seedy, albeit in a somewhat pitiful fashion. As he watched the defendant shift nervously backwards and forwards in the dock, Miles began to suspect that what would be revealed over the next couple of hours would be a tale not of human greed, but of human weakness. At that point, his own name was read out and, taking the bible from the juror next to him, he held it aloft and read the oath aloud.

'Could you state your name and occupation, please?'

The first witness was a middle aged man in a coal grey suit. He wore expensive cufflinks and had a neat but rather artificial hair style that reminded Miles of the black and white photographs of highly coiffeured male models that used to be hung in barber shops when he was a boy.

'Thomas Arthur Myland. I am the South East regional sales director for Jaycon Electricals.'

'Thank you, Mr Myland. Now, could you please tell the jury about the events that took place in February of last year?'

'Certainly. Towards the end of that month I was informed by our haulage contractor that one of their delivery vans had been broken into overnight and that six packing cases of Vortex Fours had been stolen.'

'The Vortex Four is a vacuum cleaner imported by your company, is that correct?'

'Yes, that's right.'

'And six packing cases amount to how many machines in total?'

'Er, twenty-four; there are four per case.'

'So, what did you do on being presented with this information?'

'We put together all the necessary documentation and then submitted an insurance claim.'

'And after having submitted that claim, what did you do then?'

'Well, nothing, really. We lose a certain proportion of goods each year in pilferage. This wasn't a major haul by any stretch of the imagination, so we just forgot about them really.'

'And what happened to revive your interest in that particular consignment?'

'Three months later, at the beginning of May, we received one of the guarantee cards back filled in with the name and address of the owner. We keep a database of everything we sell, and when the customer service assistant went to input the details, she found that the piece of equipment with that serial number had been red-flagged as having been part of the consignment that had been stolen.'

'So, what did she do?'

'Well, she informed me and I informed the police – the same day.'

'The vacuum cleaner in question – the, er, Vortex Four – could you identify it as being of the type that is being brought into court now? If the clerk of court would kindly, please … thank you …'

Along with the rest of the jury, Miles turned to look at the blue plastic vacuum that the usher had just brought into court.

'Yes, that's a Vortex Four,' confirmed the sales director.

'Thank you Mr Myland. Just one final question; what was the name and address on the guarantee form?'

'Mrs Jeanette Clarke, forty-three Omega Mansions, Kingston.'

'Mrs Jeanette Clarke, ladies and gentlemen,' said the prosecuting barrister, inclining his face towards the jury for a moment, 'is the defendant's wife. Thank you, Mr Myland.'

The prosecuting barrister then turned to the defence barrister at this point, but, in response, he merely shook his hand to indicate that he did not wish to question the witness. As the sales director left the stand, the prosecuting barrister spoke again.

'Your honour, I would like to call Detective Constable John Reid.'

A minute later a tall, powerfully built man took the stand and began to read the oath. He was in his mid fifties with a gruff but intelligent voice. Judging by his age and appearance, Miles guessed that he was a far more experienced police officer than PC Moore.

'Could you state your name, rank and serial number, please?'

'Detective Constable John Reid, KI202, Kingston Road CID.'

'DC Reid, I would like to refer you to the enquiries that you undertook in April of last year in connection with a quantity of stolen and counterfeit goods being stored at a lock-up garage on the Oxford estate, Kingston. Could you tell the court about these, please?'

'Yes. Following a series of surveillances, on April the twenty-seventh,

48

myself and two colleagues carried out a raid on the home of a Mr Mark Smith, the owner of a garage on the Oxford Estate. Amongst the stolen goods that we recovered were six Vortex Four vacuum cleaners with serial numbers matching those of the stolen consignment referred to by the previous witness. Mr Smith was subsequently arrested and prosecuted for the possession of a variety of stolen goods recovered both from his garage and from his home.'

'For which he received a sentence of two years imprisonment last month at this very court,' added the prosecution barrister.

'That's correct,' replied DC Reid, looking up momentarily.

'If you would continue, please ...'

'Yes. Shortly after Mr Smith's arrest, on the seventeenth of May, acting on information received from the CID in Havant, I called at the defendant's house and interviewed his wife Mrs Jeanette Clarke, concerning the Vortex Four vacuum cleaner for which Jaycon Electricals had received a guarantee card.'

'And what did she tell you?'

'She informed me that she had received the vacuum cleaner as a present from her husband several weeks previously. I asked her if she knew where he had obtained the vacuum cleaner, but she replied that she didn't. I then asked her to ask him to make contact with me as soon as possible as we had reason to believe that the article had been stolen.'

'Did the defendant Mr Clarke make contact with you?'

'He did. He made an appointment to see me two days later.'

'And what did he say about the manner in which he had acquired the vacuum cleaner?'

'He said he had been given it as a gift.'

'By whom?'

'By a customer. Mr Clarke explained that he was a mini-cab driver and that several weeks previously he had helped out a customer – an elderly gentleman in a light brown suit – and that as a token of his thanks he had given him the vacuum cleaner.'

'What was your reaction to this?'

'I said I thought a two hundred pound vacuum cleaner was a rather generous gift.'

'And what did he say?'

'He said he thought so, too.'

'Did you ask him for the name and address of this benefactor?'

'I did. He said he didn't know the man's name but that he knew the street where he lived – Seymour Road – and that he could find the house again if necessary.'

'So, were you able to trace the gentlemen in question there?'

'No, we weren't. On the twenty sixth of May, the defendant accompanied by myself and another police officer, went to number two Seymour Road, but there was no one in. I returned to the property three days later and having spoken to the next door neighbours was led to believe that it was in fact unoccupied – its previous owner having recently died. Further enquiries revealed the owner to have been a Miss Elaine Ballard who had passed away at the end of March – a fact confirmed by the firm of solicitors administering her estate, Fraser, Black and Owen of Clerkenwell, East London from whom I took a statement on the second of June. They informed me that they were unaware of any surviving relatives and that her will made no reference to such – only instructions for her house to be auctioned after her death and the proceeds given to a variety of charities and good causes. I then interviewed two neighbours in the street, obtaining from them statements confirming that to their knowledge she had lived alone there for well over ten years.'

'What was Mr Clarke's reaction to this information?'

'I interviewed Mr Clarke again at Kingston Road station on June the fourteenth in the presence of his solicitor, but he was unable to account for this situation.'

'Really?'

'Yes, he continued to maintain his story concerning the elderly gentleman in the light brown suit.'

Thank you, DC Reid. Just two final questions. How far is the defendant's flat from that of Mr Mark Smith who was convicted of selling these stolen vacuum cleaners?'

'Mr Smith lives in the same tower block as Mr Clarke – in flat number sixteen. Mr Clarke occupies flat number forty-three which is two floors above.'

'And how far away from Mr Clarke's flat is Seymour Road?'

'Several miles away – four, perhaps five.'

'Thank you.'

As the defence barrister stood up to begin his cross examination, John turned and grimaced at Miles in a manner that left little doubt as to his thoughts: all the evidence appeared to be indicate the defendant's guilt and his alibi sounded like a complete spur of the moment invention. Despite this, Miles couldn't help thinking that the case was far from over. At this same point in the first trial things had looked just as gloomy for the defendant, yet his barrister had still managed to turn the case around.

'I have just one question, DC Reid. Did you check if Mr Smith had sold one of the stolen vacuum cleaners to Mr Clarke?'

'We did. According to the original examination that had led to his conviction, he was not able to remember any of the people that he'd sold them to'.

'Thank you. That's all, DC Reid.'

With a nod towards the judge the policeman left the stand. The defence barrister remained on his feet until he had left and then turned to the judge who raised his pen at him as a sign to speak.

'Your honour, I'd like to call the defendant, Mr William Clarke.'

The judge nodded in response and within two minutes the defendant had taken the stand and been sworn in.

'Mr Clarke, do you have a criminal record?'

'No, I don't,' replied the defendant in a choked, tense voice which, after the studied clarity of his barrister's elocution, sounded virtually inaudible.

'May I ask you to speak up from now on, Mr Clarke? The jury needs to be able to hear what you are saying. For those members of the jury who were unable perhaps to hear what you did say, let me restate it: Mr Clarke has no criminal convictions of any nature whatsoever. He is therefore regarded in the eyes of the law as a person of good character.'

As the defence barrister paused for breath, Miles remembered what John had said in the previous trial about the importance of good character. With an active, premeditated crime like burglary it no doubt constituted a powerful argument in favour of the defence, but in the case of a more passive misdemeanour such as receiving stolen goods, he couldn't help feeling that it counted for a lot less.

'Now, Mr Clarke, could you tell the jury a little more about the kindness that you claim you showed this old gentleman – this man in the light brown suit – that encouraged him to give you this gift?'

The defendant stumbled over his words at first, but slowly managed to get into his stride.

'I picked him up at terminal three late one Thursday night. He'd, er, just come in on an international flight – the middle east, he said. He looked very tired. It was a cold night, and he'd only got on this, like, light brown suit, so I turned up the heating in the car. He didn't look well, so I said when you get home you can have a nice cup of tea, but he said there wouldn't be anything in the house so I said, why don't we stop on the way and buy you some. So we stopped at this twenty-four seven place. And then I took him home.'

'Did you help him with his luggage?'

'Yeah, I carried it into the hallway for him. He looked knackered.'

'And what happened then?'

'Well he thanked me and paid me and then said would I like to take him to the airport again three or four days later. I said all right and he asked me to write my phone number down for him because he had an open ticket and wasn't exactly sure when he was going back.'

'And did he phone you?'

'Yes, he did.'

'And did you go and pick him up three days later?'

'Yeah, I did.'

'And what happened when you called for him?'

'Well, I knocked on the door and he had his cases ready so I put them in the boot. When I got back he was still standing in the hall. That was when I saw the vacuum cleaner – it was all boxed up. He asked me straightaway if I wanted it. He said it was brand new and had only been used twice. I said no at first, but he said I'd been really kind to him and that he wasn't going to use it again so I could have it if I wanted to. So, I took it.'

'Did he explain why he'd only used it twice?'

'No. I asked him when we were driving along a few minutes later, but he'd gone, like, all quiet by then, so I just sort of shut up and left him alone.'

'Mr Clarke, have you any idea of how this story probably sounds to the jury?'

'Yes.'

'It's not very believable, is it?'

'No.'

'Fantastic, almost.'

'Yeah.'

'The police arrested the man downstairs didn't they – Mark Smith? The jury are going to think you bought the vacuum cleaner off him, aren't they?'

'Yeah.'

'Did you know Mr Smith?'

'Not really, I knew him to look at. I mean, I knew who he was after the police told me they'd arrested him.'

'Did you buy that vacuum cleaner off Mr Smith?'

'No, I didn't. I got it free from the man in the brown suit. I remember it like it was yesterday. I can still see his face now.'

'My lord …'

So saying, the defence barrister sat down. As the prosecuting barrister stood up to begin his cross examination, the defendant gave a sudden, nervous twitch as though he had just received an electric shock. Looking around at his fellow jurors, Miles had the distinct feeling that despite his highly improbable story the defendant had managed to gain their sympathy. He wondered whether the prosecuting barrister had sensed this and would ease off the defendant as a result: to humiliate such a pathetic figure might well leave them pitying him all the more.

'Mr Clarke. You say you picked up the old man at the airport on the Thursday night. Did he book a taxi through the mini-cab firm for which you worked?'

'No,' replied the defendant, uncomfortably.

'So, how did you pick him up, then?'

'I, er, went up to him and asked him if he wanted a cab. He looked a bit lost, you see.'

'Isn't that illegal – to solicit for business like that at an airport – even for a licensed taxi driver, which you are not?'

'Well, yeah, I suppose so …'

'You suppose so,' echoed the barrister dryly. 'Mr Clarke, not only were you illegally soliciting for business, but you were moonlighting as well, weren't you? Which is to say you were not paying a percentage of the fare to the mini-cab firm for which you worked.'

'Yeah, that's right.'

'You were cutting them out – lying to them – so you could make some extra money for yourself on the side.'

'Yes, I was, but I'd already worked for them five nights solid that week and I needed the money. Things were a bit tight at home, we'd just had a baby and my wife's birthday was coming up and I wanted to get her something nice.'

'Oh, yes, your wife, I'm glad you mentioned her,' said the barrister with heavy irony. 'When you gave her the vacuum cleaner, did you give her the impression that you'd bought it?'

'Yeah, sort of. I mean it was a present, wasn't it?'

'So you lied to her, too, didn't you?'

'Well, yeah, but ...'

'That's why she filled in the guarantee card, wasn't it? Because she thought you'd bought it legitimately. You lied to her, like you lied to your mini-cab company, like you lied to the police and like you are lying to us.'

'No!'

'Oh, Mr Clarke, please, please – spare us any more of this embarrassing charade,' said the barrister with a pained look on his face. In the jury box, Miles smiled to himself in admiration. The barrister had indeed recognized the sympathy that the defendant might garner and was shrewdly countering it with an air of tired exasperation.

'That old man gave me the vacuum cleaner. I didn't buy it off Smith.'

'Mr Clarke, are you really asking the jury to believe that you did not acquire this stolen vacuum cleaner from someone living directly below you who had a garage full of them to sell, but instead from a man whom you did not know, who did not live at the address you say and of whom no trace could be found six weeks later?'

'Maybe he was her husband, I don't know.'

'Who's husband?'

'That Ballard woman – the one who died. Maybe he was her husband, the man in the brown ...'

As the defendant's voice trailed away, the prosecuting barrister avoided administering the coup de grace by pointing out that the court had already been told that Miss Ballard had not been married, and instead turned to look at the judge.

'I have no more questions, your honour.'

'Ladies and gentleman of the jury,' announced the judge. 'We shall now adjourn until half-past nine on Monday morning at which time you will hear summaries from both the prosecution and the defence. Thank you for your cooperation this afternoon.'

Having watched the dock officer leading the defendant away – his head bowed despondently – Miles suddenly noticed the court clock out of the corner of his eye, and, seeing that it was approaching five o'clock made his way quickly from the courtroom.

Illuminated against the late evening skyline of docklands London, the Tower looked truly magnificent. King Media had moved its entire operations to the imposing ten storey building just over a year ago but, because Miles was on a semi-permanent contract and was not required regularly to attend *The Mail*'s fourth floor offices, he had only ever seen it during the day and had not appreciated its full majesty until now. Walking across the foyer to the reception desk, he gave his name to the receptionist who asked him to wait whilst she called through to Tom Cranmer. Sitting on one of the enormous black leather sofas, Miles watched the lifts open every thirty to forty seconds and a succession of office workers pile out and make their way homewards through the giant revolving doors. Henry King's organization was truly enormous and had diversified into every known form of media; from traditional, broad-based film and television production companies, through specialist technical and academic publications, right up to the latest in virtual ezines and cyberjournals. Yet, somehow, from amongst its myriad employees, Henry King had hit upon a venture for which Miles Coverdale alone appeared to be qualified. For the first time since Tom had spoken to him, Miles felt a flutter of nerves. Thankfully, before he had time to dwell on his apprehension, his boss appeared from one of the lifts and walked over to him, smiling.

'Miles, old boy. Good to see you,' he said, grasping Miles's hand cordially.

'Good to be here.'

'Come on, this way – Henry's dying to meet you. He's been talking about nothing else all week.'

Tom led Miles back towards the lifts, but instead of taking one of them up to King's office on the eighth floor, walked past them and then proceeded to go through a small, anonymous service door that Miles had not noticed before. A concrete staircase on the right hand side led sharply downwards towards the basement car park, but, before reaching it, his boss turned left and went through a second unmarked door that led into a narrow, plushly-carpeted corridor.

'Secret passages!' whispered Tom, over his shoulder.

At the end of the corridor was a windowless, hardwood door above the handle of which was an electronic security access lock of a type that Miles had not seen elsewhere in the building. Swiping a small green card through it – that once again Miles did not recognize – Tom opened the door which led into a second reception area, similar to the one in the lobby but very much smaller.

'Mr Cranmer,' acknowledged the single security guard, respectfully. Behind the man's shoulder, Miles could see a bank of closed circuit televisions displaying various parts of the Tower.

With a nod at the security guard, Tom turned to his left and pressed a button on the wall to summon what was obviously a small, private lift. He then winked playfully at Miles as the doors opened and they got in.

'Going up,' announced Tom, pressing one of only three buttons on the console.

'Where does this go to?' asked Miles, curiously.

'Henry has a penthouse at the top of the building.'

'Really?'

'Yes.'

'I didn't know that.'

'It's quite a closely kept secret, actually.'

'Well, you learn something every day,' replied Miles, attempting to appear at ease but feeling the nervous flutter in his stomach return once more.

Seconds later the lift came to a halt and Tom stepped out. Following after him, Miles was expecting to see another reception area and was thus completely unprepared for the sight that greeted him as he walked through the doors. They had emerged into a vast, cavernous room, empty of all furniture save for a long oak table. In the centre of the room, was a rugged, brick-built fireplace in which a number of logs were burning heartily, casting a rich, flickering light around the otherwise unilluminated room. Suspended above the fire was a black metallic hood, the flue of which stretched upwards into the gloom. Following its course towards the roof, Miles at first thought that the ceiling was painted black, but, spotting a number of small pin pricks of light quickly realized that it was made entirely of glass and that the darkness above them was in fact the night sky.

'Mr Coverdale. Welcome.'

He had emerged from the shadows and was standing facing Miles with his back to the roaring fire. With his feet planted firmly apart and his arms hanging loosely by his side, he had the air of a prize-fighter waiting for a bout to start. Miles remembered reading that as a young man Henry King had boxed semi-professionally and even now, in his late fifties, his imposing, powerful frame still retained an unmistakably pugnacious air.

'Mr King,' answered Miles, walking over to shake his hand.

'From now on, I'd like you to call me Henry,' replied King, grabbing Miles's hand and shaking it vigorously three times as though pumping a shotgun. His complexion was remarkably pale and, Miles imagined, would probably appear almost entirely colourless were it not for his tightly cropped ginger beard.

'OK … Henry.'

'You must have been wondering why Tom and I summoned you here,' said King with a nod in Tom's direction.

'Yes, I have,' replied Miles, shortly.

'Well, I don't want to beat about the bush, but there's one thing I must say before I tell you and that is I want you to keep everything we discuss here a secret. You'll have understood from what Tom's said that we've got a job in mind for you. If you don't take it − and the final decision in that respect is absolutely one hundred per cent yours − we'll more than likely abandon the project entirely: the chances of our finding someone else with your character and qualifications are small, but there's just a possibility that we may do and I wouldn't want that person compromised in any way. At the moment, there are only two people in the world who know about this, and that's Tom and I. I'd like to keep it that way.'

'You can rely on me,' said Miles.

'I believe we can, I believe we can,' replied King, fixing his pale blue eyes on Miles's face. Returning his gaze, Miles once again found himself observing King's extraordinary facial features − the small, pursed mouth and the slender, aquiline nose. Gesturing him to follow, King walked over to the oak table, on top of which was a single, slim, buff-coloured folder.

'Ten days ago, this file arrived by post at the offices of *The Mail*. It was addressed for my private and personal attention. Please. Open it.'

Leaning forward, Miles flipped back the front leaf of the folder and thumbed through the sheaf of papers inside. There appeared to be about twenty sheets of A4 in all, each of which had a black and white photo-graph of a different man or woman in the top left hand corner; judging by the image quality, Miles guessed that many of them had been taken with a telescopic lens. Beneath each photograph were a name and an address.

'These thirteen men and four women,' continued King, 'are a gang of housing benefit fraudsters based in Feltham, West London. Earlier this year, the Department of Social Security attempted to bring them to justice, but the case was rejected by the Crown Prosecution Service because they found that the evidence had been compromised. Shortly afterwards the investigation was closed down and the fraudsters got off scot-free, having successfully cheated the British tax payer out of over two million pounds; from what we understand, they're still at large now and still active.'

'Who sent you this?' asked Miles.

'I don't know,' answered King, 'and whoever it was made sure that they could never be traced. The package was posted in central London and there is nothing that we have been able to detect in the documents to indicate their origin. We're almost certain, however, that the infor-mation came from somewhere inside the DSS and was collated into this summary format specifically for the purposes of leaking it to us.'

'Our guess,' said Tom 'is that this file was drawn up by a disillusioned Social Security investigator or some other employee connected with the case. The note that came with it is at the back of the file.'

Opening the file again, Miles took out the anonymous, typewritten letter clipped to the back describing the aborted prosecution and read through it carefully twice.

'Is this true? I mean, did you check it out?'

'We couldn't,' replied King. 'There's no way of substantiating a claim like this if the case never makes it to trial – the information just ends up being buried in the DSS archives. We think that the sender knew the case was never going to see the light of day again, and that's why he or she made up this file and sent it to us. What we did do, though, was have the first five names checked out for previous convictions; Tom's got a friend at Scotland Yard.'

'And?'

'Three of the five had criminal records,' responded Tom. 'All juvenile stuff, but significant all the same.'

58

'So you think the file's genuine, then?'

'We can't be a hundred per cent sure, but …' Tom left the sentence unfinished.

Miles flicked through the sheaf of papers again. The photographs had an unmistakable life-like quality and he knew from his experience that they were genuine surveillance pictures; the addresses were complete even down to the postcodes. Closing the file, he replaced it on the table top and then turned to look at King again.

'How did they do it, d'you know? Defraud Housing Benefits of all that money. What system did they use?'

'We don't know and we don't think the authorities know either. Tell Miles what you found out, Tom.'

'The DSS publishes very little specific information about how social security fraudsters operate, so I had nothing official to go on. So, what I did was scour around for articles from our own archives, other newspapers, what have you …'

'And what did you find?'

'The picture that emerges is one of barely resourced investigators chasing increasingly sophisticated and well organized fraudsters. As soon as the DSS cracks down on one system, the fraudsters come up with another – they're constantly developing new techniques. The net result of all this is that each year somewhere between eight to ten billion pounds disappears in benefit fraud.'

'Eight to ten billion pounds!' proclaimed King, walking off with arms outstretched towards one of the penthouse's huge plate glass windows. Miles's eyes had now become accustomed to the light and he could make out the silhouettes of several more pieces of furniture and what looked like a partition at the far end of the room; he doubted that King actually lived here – it was probably just where he did his thinking. 'Eight to ten billion pounds disappearing every year in bogus claims for properties that don't exist, for injuries that never occurred and for dependants who've never been born. And where does that money come from, Miles? Hm? From me, from you and from the ordinary tax-payer, of course. From the Joe in the street who pays his dues every day of his life and would never dream of cheating anybody out of anything.'

'From the average Mail reader, in fact,' added Tom.

'Exactly!' exclaimed King, leaning against the window rail and staring out over the London skyline. 'Not that social security fraud is new, of course – it's been going on for years – and we're by no means the first people to find it absolutely scandalous. But there's something special about these people, Miles, about this particular gang of seventeen. D'you know what it is? I'll forgive you if you don't recognize it straightaway. I mean, it took me a week of staring at those pages before I finally worked it out – a whole week …'

'I don't know, tell me,' replied Miles, without picking up the file again.

'They've got faces, Miles, they've got faces!' Pausing before continuing, he stared out over the city for several seconds more and then turned around to look at Miles and Tom. 'Think about it. Think about every other type of criminal in this country's history. Murderers; who wouldn't recognize a photograph of Myra Hyndley or Thomas Shipman? Gangsters: the Kray twins are virtually national icons. Bent politicians and cabinet ministers: every single one of them since Profumo has had their faces plastered all over the daily papers. But the fraudsters – no one knows what they look like. I can't recall ever having seen a photograph of a single benefit cheat, not even through the window of the meat wagon as they're driven away from court. Up until now they've remained absolutely anonymous. And because the public have never seen them before … that makes them news.'

Walking back across the room to the table, King picked up the file and handed it to Miles. Opening it up once more, he stared at the photograph of the first of the fraudsters. Richard Michael Thompson – 14 St. Helena's Road, Feltham. King was right. There was something sinister, yet at the same time deeply intriguing about the man's face. Closing the file, he turned to face King and Tom.

'So, what do you want me to do, then? Photograph these people?'

For a moment the two men exchanged an unmistakably nervous look, clearly uncertain as to which of them should answer the question. Finally, placing the flats of his hands down on the surface of the table, King leant forward and stared unblinkingly into Miles's eyes.

'No, Miles. We want you to join them.'

'Join them?'

'Yes, join them,' replied King, steadily. 'Our idea is this. One day, one ordinary day, in three or four weeks' time, you come into the office and have a row with Tom here – your boss. It gets more and more heated and you end up getting fired. I don't know the reason for the disagree-

60

ment: you're dissatisfied with your salary, your terms and conditions, Cromwell's interference in your work – whatever – in any event, you act like a complete prima donna and he's forced to fire you. A few weeks later, you sell your flat and put your furniture into storage. There aren't many people close to you, but the few that are – your ex-wife, one or two friends – get a call from you to say that you've been offered a two year contract working overseas. And then … you disappear. A few days later the word gets around *The Mail* – source Mr T. Cranmer here – that you've been sighted on the continent. You're doing really well, apparently – enjoying yourself. At about the same time, in Feltham, West London, a man in his late thirties rents a flat. Nobody knows him. He's not from the capital – he's from Yorkshire, just like you originally were. Except he doesn't look like you. Not a bit like you. He's a labourer. He has a shaved head – he wears an earring. He's looking for work. In time he falls into the company of the gang you saw in that file. They're suspicious of him at first. Seriously suspicious. But he's not in a hurry. He's ice-cool. And he's useful, too. And, after a while, they accept him and let him hang around.'

'We thought long and hard about this, Miles,' said Tom. 'You have every quality that we can think of required to pull this off. It's not simply that you know cameras inside out and can film these people, but it's that you have a uniquely photographic eye – an eye perfectly attuned to the visual image.'

'You're a loner,' continued King. 'You're level-headed, you're patient, you're resourceful – but more than anything you're immensely dogged. All your professional life you've done things in your own, inimitable way and no one's ever been able to argue with your results. It's not just Tom here who's told me about your modus operandi, it's every other editor, too: you're famous for it. You leave the office one morning in pursuit of your story – in pursuit of your prey. You disappear for weeks, sometimes months on end – nobody hears from you – and then one day you just walk back through the door with that picture. That definitive picture.'

'Like you did with Lamb,' added Tom.

'Exactly,' confirmed King, 'that photograph of Lamb – it sealed it for us, absolutely sealed it. We want you for this job, Miles; you're our first and only choice.'

'If you agree to do it,' said Tom, 'if you do go under cover, we'll give you the absolute right to pull out at a moment's notice. If things start to look even remotely dangerous, you can just turn around and walk away – no questions from us, no recriminations.'

'But our hope is that you will succeed,' said King, 'that you will break into this gang and over five or six months using a concealed camera amass sufficient film footage of them. Then, one day, at a time of your choosing, you disappear from Feltham. You take a holiday – grow your hair a bit. A couple of weeks later you're Miles Coverdale again, back from the continent to see his family and friends. Then, after a month or two, when you're ready, you go under cover again.'

'What, back to these guys in Feltham?' asked Miles.

'No. A different undercover operation. If you're still able to face it, that is.'

'What do you mean, a different undercover operation?'

'I mean I want you to make a television documentary series for King Media, Miles. Tom and I have settled on the title already – *Criminal Britain*. The series will expose the faceless criminals. The ones who suck the lifeblood out of our country, out of our communities, who get away with it year after year – unknown, unrecognized, unpunished.'

'For the second program in the series,' continued Tom, 'Henry's idea is that you examine drug pushers. Think of our readers on *The Mail*. They see drug dealers on the television – in soaps and crime dramas – but who are the criminals that really ruin their kids' lives? Who are the dealers that destroy their children, even before they've made it into adulthood? What do they really look like?'

'Faces, again, Miles,' exhorted King. 'We want you to show us their faces!'

'You said second program,' responded Miles. 'How many are you thinking of altogether?'

'Four,' replied King, slowly lighting up a cigar, 'a maximum of four. That probably sounds like a tall order, so it's important you understand this. *Criminal Britain* is to be a documentary series, not a police investigation. You are under no constraint to amass legally binding evidence against these people, let alone a water-tight case.'

'Of course,' added Tom, quickly, 'we want you to do your best to find out how they work, how they operate, but what we're really after is for you to characterize them. For you to show the public how they behave, where they live, what they think and say.'

'Who would I be working for?' asked Miles, cautiously.

'Me,' replied Tom, quickly.

'As you know,' said King, 'Tom had ten years in television news before joining *The Mail* – that makes him more than qualified to handle this. Also, you know him and he knows you: if he's going to be your controller then it's important there's a strong bond of trust between you. The only other person involved – the only other person who'll know about it at all, in fact – is me. It's absolutely essential if you're working under cover that we limit the chances of anyone ever making a connection between Miles Coverdale the photojournalist as was and the person that you will have become. We know almost nothing about these criminals beyond what's in the file, but we have to assume that they're both highly organized and very dangerous. They must surely be on their guard all the time for investigators and if they find out that you're really a reporter, it could be very bad for you.'

Opening up the file once more, Miles slowly examined each of the pages in turn, but without really seeing the photographs or the addresses printed beneath them. Instead his mind was whirling as it struggled to comprehend what he had just heard. For the entire length of his professional career, he had resisted every attempt to influence his work. In the early days, before he had made his name as a freelance, this had resulted in some very lean periods indeed and he had slipped into debt on a number of occasions. For the last few years, his semi-permanent contract with *The Mail* had stabilized his income, but when this had recently come under threat from Cromwell's program of rationalization, he had made it very clear that he would resign rather than give up the right to choose his own material. Closing the file, he lifted his head slowly and looked first at King and then at Tom. There was anticipation in their eyes, but respect also – it was absolutely unmistakable. Hitherto he had been a maverick on the fringes of King Media – his free-spirit originality tolerated only as long as it continued to produce the occasional exclusive photograph. But, now, suddenly he had been catapulted right into the very heart of the organization – now, suddenly, he was a unique asset. Once the idea had occurred to King, it was easy to imagine he and Tom running one by one through the staff-photographers and reporters on *The Mail*, only to dismiss each of them in turn as lacking the character and self-belief required to succeed in such an undertaking. Placing the file back on the table, Miles allowed himself an ironic smile: this was where a lifetime's stubborn independence had led him; he would never have foreseen it. *Criminal Britain* was without doubt the journalistic opportunity of a lifetime, but one crucial question still remained: was the price that he would have to pay for it, the very independence that had qualified him for the venture in the first place?

'So,' he said finally, 'five or six months on the first investigation, then a break, five or six months on the second – is that your idea?'

'Something like that,' answered Tom.

'What about the third and fourth documentaries? Do I get any input as regards the subject matter?'

'Absolutely,' exclaimed King, emphatically pointing his cigar at Miles. 'Once you get on the trail of these fraudsters, our guess is that you'll see criminal activity going on all around you – all sorts of things that Tom and I here can only even dream of. We want to hear about them. We want your every idea, your every suggestion. *Criminal Britain* will be your series, Miles, make absolutely no doubt about that, and if you succeed with it, just think of what we'll have! Footage of Britain's unseen criminals that we could promote through all seven divisions of King Media – not just in the UK, but worldwide. Television, print, internet. It would be one of the greatest pieces of investigative reporting ever, and it would make you one the most famous undercover journalists on earth. Come. Come with me, here ...'

Leading Miles across to the window, King pointed a fat, muscly finger out over the shimmering London skyline.

'I won't even attempt to hide the dangers from you, and you must take your time to decide – we don't want to hurry you. But they're out there, Miles, the criminals we talked of, they're out there. Find them for me. Film them ... and then let's show the world their faces.'

Chapter 3

Following the other eleven jurors into the jury room, Miles realized that he had sat through the entire court proceedings that morning without really having taken in a word that had been said. Over the weekend, too, in his flat, he had found himself staring at a number of domestic chores that he had completed without actually remembering having performed the individual tasks concerned. Exactly a week ago, he had arrived at Kingston Crown Court utterly content with the niche that he had carved out for himself in the world of photojournalism, and with his life proceeding along wholly predictable lines. But the discussion with Henry King had shattered those certainties and Miles had left the Tower that evening promising to give Tom an answer within the next three days to a proposal that would effectively turn his entire existence on its head: at the time the file had been leaked to *The Mail*, the fraudsters had still been active, but they could easily cease operations at any moment and he would therefore have to go in search of them as soon as was practicably possible.

As the jury set about the task of electing a foreman, Miles poured himself a glass of water from the carafe in the centre of the table and sipped at it thoughtfully. He did not for a moment doubt his ability to work under cover – to adopt a series of new identities and carry them off convincingly. Furthermore, King had been wrong to think that his proposal would necessarily disrupt Miles's personal life – ironically, it was much more likely to help straighten it out. Elizabeth had said that what Jake needed more than anything at the moment was space to breathe, but the same was true of her. Miles had been turning up like a lap-dog on her doorstep for far too long – it was time he broke the cycle for good; she would only respect him for it. The real problem with King's proposal, of course, was that there would be no life to return to afterwards, personal or otherwise, if someone were to put a bullet in the back of his head. Similarly, even if his life did not actually come under threat, all of the investigations would be accompanied by dangers of one sort or another, but as he had no way of knowing their eventual outcome how could he judge whether they would be worth the risk? The fact of the matter was that he simply lacked sufficient information to make a rational risk-benefit analysis. Nevertheless, by tonight, he had to decide whether he was going to take the gamble.

'Oh, OK, then if nobody thinks I'm trying to hog all the limelight …'

Snapping out of his thoughts, Miles realized that Alec, the retired accountant, had somehow managed to end up being elected foreman once again. Turning to his left, he looked at John who raised his eyes heavenwards in exasperation: in the last trial, Alec's woolly bonhomie had annoyed him intensely.

'Just as well it's an open and shut case,' he whispered under his breath.

'So, er, shall we start off by taking a vote, then?' said Alec, turning and beaming benevolently around the table. 'Would all those people who think the defendant is guilty as charged please raise their hand?'

At first it appeared as though all twelve arms had been raised, but the jurors soon realized that one of their number had in fact demurred.

'Oh, Jesus, not again,' winced John, placing the flats of his hands over his eyes and then dragging them slowly down his face.

The woman's name was Jo. In the previous case she had been the staunchest proponent of the young black youth's innocence – or, more accurately, the staunchest critic of the lack of definitive evidence of his guilt. Although Miles had indeed paid little attention during the morning's proceedings, one of the things that he did recall hearing had been the judge's direction that the jury should reach a unanimous verdict. Clearly, John could see the combination of Jo's pedantic liberalism and Alec's less than dynamic leadership resulting in hours of fruitless debate followed by the eventual acquittal of a second patently guilty man.

'I, er, take it that you do not concur?' ventured Alec, politely.

'No, I don't,' she replied, quietly.

She wore no make-up and had long, straight brown hair that was tied back in a single knot, making her appear at one and the same time both formidable and trustworthy – like a female doctor or a teacher. Around the table the other jurors fidgeted uncomfortably. It was clear she was not in the least bit intimidated by finding herself utterly alone in her opinion and, moreover, felt no need immediately to justify it.

'But his story was obviously completely made-up,' exclaimed one of the other jurors somewhat despairingly.

As Jo leant forward to reply, John shook his head wearily in anticipation of her repeating the identical arguments that she had used last time: there had been no witnesses to the actual crime; the defendant was innocent until proven guilty and it was therefore up to those jurors who thought he was guilty to convince those who thought he wasn't – not the other way around. When Jo did answer in her calm, measured voice, however, her reasoning was altogether different.

'I realize the defendant's story sounded preposterous, but what made me disposed to believe it was the detail. It wasn't just a house somewhere; it was a particular road and a particular number. It wasn't just an old man; it was a sad, distracted old man in a light brown suit. Now, the defendant didn't look too bright to me, and, if he was lying, I don't think he'd embellish his story with quite that level of detail.'

'You've obviously never met many liars before, then,' grunted John, dismissively.

In response to this slight, she merely raised an eyebrow. One of the things about Jo that had infuriated the guilty camp in the previous trial, but which Miles had rather admired, had been her ability to remain completely calm in the face of all remarks that challenged her opinions – even those that were deliberately confrontational in intent. As if in recognition of this, one of the other jurors, an attractive woman in her mid forties, leant forward and addressed her in a far more reasoned manner.

'I know what you mean – I noticed that, too. But don't you think it's much more likely that the man in the brown suit really did exist, but that he didn't give the defendant the vacuum cleaner? What I mean is, the defendant might have actually had the old man as a customer on another occasion, and the old guy might have, I don't know, given him a big tip or something, and then, when the defendant found he'd been caught receiving stolen goods, he peopled his alibi with the most realistic sounding character he could think of.'

'Or, then again, he could've just made the whole bloody thing up,' repeated John, sullenly.

'What amazes me is this case came to court in the first place,' observed a middle-aged man in a sports jacket who was seated next to Alec. 'I heard it costs twenty thousand pounds a day to run a trial here. Twenty thousand pounds for a two hundred quid vacuum cleaner! It's ridiculous.'

Suddenly, three jurors who were sitting at the other end of the table all sat forward at once. Miles had the feeling that they knew each other from having previously been on a jury together.

'That's nothing,' said one of them, a bright-looking youth in a red fleece. 'You should have been on the case we had last week.'

'What was that, then?' replied the man in the sports jacket.

'We had a woman up for stealing two cans of lager.'

'What!'

'They weren't even worth two quid, let alone two hundred.'

'Jesus!' exhaled the man.

'There are loads of cases like this apparently,' continued the youth. 'They should really be sorted out at the magistrate's court, but people think they've got a better chance of acquittal at a jury trial. The whole system's clogged up with them.'

'And all the while the real criminals are getting away with it, aren't they, eh?' responded the man in the sports jacket, shaking his head bitterly. 'The muggers and the rapists. A two hundred quid vacuum cleaner. I mean even if the bloke did buy it, it's not exactly grand theft, is it? There's somethin' wrong with the system if they've got us all in here talkin' about this sort of thing when the real criminals can go unpunished.'

As the other jurors murmured and shook their heads in assent, Miles was struck by how the man's words totally validated the concept underlying *Criminal Britain*. Henry King had really hit on something – there was no denying it. These ordinary, decent people did indeed yearn for the faceless criminals to be brought to justice and were acutely resentful of the anonymity behind which they hid. When he had set off for the court that morning, Miles had regarded the coming day's jury service as an unfortunate annoyance – an unwanted diversion that would swallow up the bulk of a day on which he was due to make one of the most important decisions of his life. In fact, it had provided him with a vital spark of insight: there could surely be no stronger confirmation of what he stood to achieve by accepting King's offer than the discussion to which he had just been party. Originally, he had planned to get away from court as quickly as he could and spend the remaining part of the afternoon and evening alone in his flat thinking through his final decision. But his fellow jurors had made up his mind for him. He would do it. He would make *Criminal Britain*.

'What are you lookin' so happy about?' whispered John, with a nod in the direction of Jo, who was protesting that even though the offence was relatively trivial, they still had a responsibility not to burden the defendant with a criminal record unless they were certain of his guilt. 'We're gonna be stuck in here for ages yet.'

In response, Miles simply smiled, deciding not to wait until the evening to call Tom but do so as soon as the trial finished.

Three hours later, after the judge had finally accepted the jury's verdict of eleven to one in favour of guilty, Miles returned to the jurors' waiting lounge and called Tom from one of the public phones. For the rest of the afternoon his mind buzzed with excitement, but, on arriving back at his flat that evening, he began to get second thoughts about the enormity of the decision that he had taken. Having poured himself a glass of malt, he stood in the living room doorway and stared at the familiar objects all around him: the tall, Kenyan mahogany sideboard his father had bequeathed him; the illuminated display cabinet containing his collection of pre-war, Leica cameras; his old, comfortable, four-seater leather sofa. Within a few weeks all these would disappear – packed off into storage. Shortly afterwards, someone else would start renting the flat and all trace of Miles Coverdale would be gone. Moving across to the telephone he slowly dialed Elizabeth's number. King's idea had been that he should tell her about his fictitious job on the continent after he had been fired from *The Mail*. Worrying after all about the effect his protracted absence might have on Jake, he decided to sound out her opinion on the matter.

'Hello?'

'Hello, er, it's Miles,' he said, 'sorry to call you up like this, but have you got a moment ...?'

For a second there was silence and he could almost see the frown forming on Elizabeth's brow: after his two visits to her flat the previous week she was no doubt beginning to think that he was making even more of a nuisance of himself than usual.

'Yes, I'm OK, for a minute. What do you want?'

'It's just that, er, this job's come up – or rather a chance of a job, I don't know whether it's definite yet or anything – and I wanted to sort of run it past you.'

'Miles,' she replied, with a short, quizzical laugh. 'It's not up to me to decide which jobs you take.'

'Well, it's just that it's overseas, you see – on the continent – and if I take it, which is to say if I get offered it in the first place, it may mean that I'll be gone for quite long periods of time and won't be able to get back to see Jake when I'm away.'

'Right,' she continued, plainly more puzzled than annoyed, 'but, what's that got to do with me?'

'Well, I'm asking your advice – about whether it might have a bad effect on him. I mean, the other week he seemed a bit, well, you know, withdrawn and I was wondering whether with me being away and everything it might make things worse.'

'I shouldn't think so,' she replied. 'I mean how long will you be gone?'

'Well, it might be four or five months at a time. I'm not sure exactly, although I do know at the end of each stretch away I'll definitely be getting six or seven weeks off, so I'll be able to catch up on lost time then.'

'Well, if you're happy with that sort of an arrangement, then I imagine he will be, too.'

It was as simple as that. Again, Miles felt the excitement beginning to well up inside him. Elizabeth and Jake were extremely close and if she thought that it would do him no harm, then there was nothing to stop Miles going ahead.

'Do you really think so?'

'Well, I don't know, it's for you to decide how you should handle your relationship with him, not me. But certainly he is going to be pretty busy over the next twelve months with his GCSE's and every-thing, so maybe it's not a bad time for you take this job; you'll have to decide for yourself, though.'

'Oh, right, thanks, thanks.'

'When are you going to know for definite?'

'Oh,' replied Miles, hesitantly, 'a few weeks yet. Like I say, it's not exactly certain I'll get it or anything. I mean, even if I do get offered it, I haven't made up my mind yet whether I'll take it or not.'

'Well, let me know either way, won't you? OK?' she replied, sympathetically, but with an undertone to her voice which clearly indicated that she wanted their conversation to come to an end.

'Yeah, yeah, I will, of course, thanks.'

'OK, bye now, then.'

'Bye. And give my love to Jake.'

'Yep. Bye.'

Putting down the receiver, Miles was filled with a great sense of calm. He had made the right decision after all. Jake was going to be fully occupied with his exams for at least the next twelve months and it was well past time that he backed off and let Elizabeth get on with her own life. Looking at the alcove in which he kept the small gallery of his best work, he sipped his whisky thoughtfully. Each picture had its respective merits and each in its own way had served to advance his career. But now, with Tom and King's help, he had the chance to do something truly unique. Turning and looking around the room once more, he tipped his glass towards it in a toast: the flat had served him well, but nothing in the world was going to hold him back now. As soon as his jury service finished, he would serve his landlord with notice of his intention not to renew his tenancy from the next rental period, and then make arrangements to have his furniture put into storage.

The Mail's fourth floor offices were open-plan and, as he came out of the lift, Miles stared with a mixture of distaste and despair at the ranks of desks and filing cabinets stretching into the distance before him. Cromwell was a fervent advocate of the partition-less environment as a means of stimulating the cross-fertilization of ideas, but each time Miles went to the fourth floor, its oddly muted, dispassionate atmosphere seemed to depress him a little more. Just after his twelfth birthday, he had accompanied his father to visit one of his old friends who worked for a national daily in Fleet Street, shortly before computerization and trade union intransigence had fatefully combined to sweep away the centuries of newspaper tradition to which that single road had proudly laid claim. The experience had made a deep impression on Miles, laying the foundations of his later decision to take up a career in photography: the runners and messenger boys, scarcely older than he, darting in out of the journalists' offices; the smell of coffee and tobacco smoke mixing with the tangy aroma of acetone rising up from the printing presses that hummed in the basement; the sense of being at the epicentre of events

– the feeling that news was taking place all around you. That was how the offices of a national daily were meant to be – not the insipid, uninspiring environment in which he now found himself: the place felt more like an investment bank than a newspaper.

Making his way down the corridor that ran around the perimeter of the fourth floor, Miles nodded at the various colleagues that he met on the way to Tom's office. As News Features Editor, his boss was one of only a dozen or so executives fortunate enough to be granted the sanctuary of his own, private room, but as it came into view, Miles was disappointed to see Tom standing outside the door talking to Cromwell.

'Well,' exclaimed Cromwell, raising his eyebrows sarcastically. 'Aren't we the privileged ones, then? To what do we owe this honour?'

Staring at the editor's fat, snub-nosed face, Miles wondered how he had managed to last a full two years without telling this ruthless, yet deeply unimaginative man what he really thought of him.

'Miles has come in for his annual salary review,' said Tom, smoothly. It wasn't actually due for three months, but they had agreed it would provide credible grounds for their argument.

'I'd better make myself scarce, then,' sneered Cromwell, turning to walk down the corridor. 'I wouldn't dream of holding up such an important event.'

When Cromwell had goaded Miles like this in the past, he had been careful not to let himself be provoked into responding. However, as he and Tom were going to stage a fake but very public dismissal in just a few minutes time and answering Cromwell back would lend credence to his intended display of prima donna pique, Miles decided that on this occasion he would grasp the offered bait.

'I'm thinking of asking Tom to put me on to performance related pay, actually,' he called out to Cromwell's retreating back. 'Linking it to circulation, perhaps.'

Cromwell stopped dead in his tracks. Since he had taken over the editorship of the paper two years previously circulation had dropped and, although it was an industry-wide trend affecting all of *The Mail*'s competitors in equal measure, he was nevertheless known to be extremely sensitive about the issue.

'What did you say?'

Cromwell was physically quite a well-built man and, moreover, exuded a formidable air of disdainful superiority. Miles, however, had never really respected him, believing that he totally lacked any semblance of editorial flare, and, as he stared flippantly back into Cromwell's infuriated face, did not feel in the least bit intimidated.

'Circulation,' he repeated, cheerfully. 'You know – the number of newspapers we sell. I heard it shot right up on the day of the Angus Lamb photograph. What was the figure, Tom? I can't quite remember.'

'Er, eight hundred thousand,' replied Tom. His voice sounded reluctant and embarrassed, but from the look in his eye Miles could tell that he had astutely realized why Miles was being so deliberately provocative. He and Tom had always been on the same wavelength and it was deeply reassuring to think that once he went under cover he could rely on that long-standing rapport.

'What's the matter?' cried Miles, continuing to stare at Cromwell insolently; it was amusing to see that for once the big man had lost his tongue. 'Don't you think it's a good idea? I mean, I can try and take photographs that reduce circulation if you like, but I've always been led to believe that's not a terribly good thing ...'

For three or four seconds, Cromwell hovered backwards and forwards on the balls of his feet, clearly unable to decide whether to engage in what could quickly become a very public slanging match. Behind him, Miles could hear that Tom's secretary had stopped typing and, on the other side of the corridor, he noticed that several office workers were looking across in their direction.

'Can I have a word later, Tom,' said Cromwell, finally, through gritted teeth, 'when you've finished?'

'About half an hour, OK?' replied Tom.

'Thank you,' answered Cromwell, stiffly, turning on his heel and walking off back down the corridor.

Closing the door of the office behind him, Miles sat down in the chair on the other side of the desk from Tom. In the three weeks since he had decided to take up King's offer, it had never crossed his mind that he would have the opportunity to get his own back on Cromwell and the encounter in the corridor had thus been a pleasant and unexpected bonus.

'You enjoyed that, didn't you?' said Tom, wryly.

'I have to say I did, yes,' replied Miles with a grin.

'He probably asked to see me afterwards to tell me to fire you.'

'Well, he should be delighted when he finds out that you already have.'

'Yes, I suppose he will,' said Tom, reaching into his drawer and taking out a bottle of whisky and two glasses. 'Although if I was him, I wouldn't go around gloating too much over your dismissal, or anyone else's for that matter …'

'What d'you mean?' said Miles, taking the glass from Tom. At first his boss didn't answer, but simply stared thoughtfully at Miles over the top of his gold-framed glasses. Finally, leaning forward in his chair he raised the index finger of his left hand and drew it slowly across his throat.

'What – he's not for the chop, is he?' gasped Miles in astonishment.

Again Tom didn't reply, but merely narrowed his eyes enigmatically.

'You mean King's going to fire him?' probed Miles again. Although he had little respect for Cromwell as an editor, it was impossible to doubt his managerial skills; the way that he had succeeded in bringing *The Mail* back into profit within a year had been nothing short of miraculous.

'I think so,' said Tom, at last.

'Did King tell you that?'

'No, he didn't. I mean, I'm not even sure he realizes it himself yet.'

'So, how d'you know, then?'

'Henry and I go back a long way,' answered Tom, quietly, 'a very long way. He hasn't said anything, but I can sort of hear it in his voice when he talks about Cromwell – see it behind his eyes …'

'Why? The paper's back in profit now – has been for over a year.'

'You put your finger on it yourself actually; circulation.'

'That's not his fault, though, is it? I mean you know I've never liked the guy but even I'd have to admit he's holding his own given the current climate.'

'I agree,' replied Tom. 'And I'd go further than that. I'd say in time he probably could get the numbers back up – if he was allowed to get on with it.'

'So, why get rid of him, then?'

'Because deep down there's one thing Henry King can't abide,' said Tom, his eyes narrowing once more. 'And that's coming second. There are no excuses for it in his book. None.'

'Well, what d'you know?' said Miles, ruefully, leaning back in his chair and folding his arms contentedly: the day was simply getting better and better.

'Maybe, I'm wrong. Time will tell.'

'I'm sure it will.'

74

'So,' continued Tom, his face brightening once more, 'have you got your lines all prepared for our little row?'

'Pretty much. You?

'Yep.'

'I noticed as I was coming in there's a spare computer keyboard on the desk outside. I've decided I'm going to throw it at you, so be warned.'

'Isn't that going a bit far?' laughed Tom.

'Well, not actually throw it right at you. I thought I might sort of just pick it up and sling it in your general direction. I'll be careful, of course, but if you are going to fire me on the spot, I have to give you proper grounds, don't I?'

'So, you've obviously not had second thoughts, then?' said Tom.

'No, none.'

'Are you absolutely sure of that? Nobody could blame you for getting cold feet, old chap, and if you are thinking of pulling out, this would be the perfect time to say so.'

'No. No going back.'

'Well, here's to the success of our little venture, then,' said Tom, lifting his glass. Cheers.'

'Cheers.'

'Right,' continued Tom, taking a large, padlocked wooden box out of a drawer on the left hand side of his desk. 'A fair bit's happened since we last spoke. Let's start at the top. Number one – I've found us a safe house.'

'Excellent! Where?'

'Clapham,' said Tom, unlocking the box and passing an envelope across the table to Miles. 'The address and the keys are in here. It's a quiet back street. Lots of rented flats – the faces change all the time: should be ideal.'

'Great.'

'Meet me there on July the twenty-third. That's two weeks on Friday. Eleven a.m., OK?'

'Fine.'

'Bring two passport photos with you. My friend in the Met's given me the name of someone who deals in fake papers; it cost me a crate of scotch to prize it out of him, mind you, but a passport's essential to a credible cover.'

'So, what is my cover, then?' asked Miles. 'Did you and Henry decide?'

Leaning back in his chair, Tom looked at Miles with his shrewd, grey eyes. When they had last spoken over the telephone the previous week, Tom had said that he and King had given hours of thought to expanding the personality profile that they had tentatively suggested to him in the penthouse.

'Your name,' began Tom, 'is Michael Angel. You're thirty-seven years old. You were born in a small village in Yorkshire. You left when you were in your early twenties and have moved around a lot since, so you've lost your accent. You're a builder by trade — unskilled, although you've never been scared of a bit of graft. You've got a wife and two children — a boy and girl — but she ran out on you at the end of last year and took them with her. It was the gambling that did it: you liked the horses too much. They were good to you for a time, the nags, but then you had a bad spell and got into debt; she couldn't stand it any more. After she left, you sold the house, but you didn't get much for it and by the time you'd paid back everything you owed, you'd only got a couple of grand left and your car, of course. You love your car, you see. A red BMW 3 series. A bit old, now, but beautifully maintained. You used to spend hours in the garage with it. It drove her mad. She reckoned you cared more about that car than you did about her and the kids.'

'Have you got me a car like that?'

'Yes. West Yorkshire number plates. I bought it last week. It'll be ready for you when we meet at the safe house.'

'Driving licence?'

'No, not yet. But once you've found somewhere to live, let me know the address and I'll get the same chap who's going to do your passport to knock one up for you.'

'And I've come to London looking for work, yes?'

'That's right — and sooner rather than later that's exactly what you have to do. If the fraudsters decide to check up on you afterwards, it's important they find a consistent cover story stretching back some time. Also, you've got to be patient when you first get to Feltham: you can't go straight after them from day one — it's going to be very difficult, but you've got to force yourself.'

'OK. I'll give myself some time to settle in. So, have you found out anything more about their system?'

'Not as such,' replied Tom, extracting a second envelope from the box, 'but what I did do was get this report produced for us by a social sciences researcher at London University which details all the known social security scams. It's a real eye-opener – the chap's an authority on the subject.'

'Great,' said Miles, taking the thick buff envelope from Tom, 'I'll read it.'

'Do – I'm sure I don't have to preach to you about the value of research. His name and address are at the front there, so call him whenever you need to.'

'OK, I will. Did you ask him what he thought the fraudsters' system might be?'

'No, I didn't want to tell him anything about the documentary: I just said we were doing general background research into social security fraud as a whole – at this stage, I think we've got to keep things very close to our chest like Henry said. What I did do, though, was check to see if any of the systems he describes in the report correspond with the information in the file that was leaked to us.'

'And do they?'

'No, not as such.'

'Oh.'

'But there's plenty of food for thought in there, all the same.'

'Yeah?'

'Yes. I mean, this is all just speculation at this point and I'll be interested to hear what you think, but a number of things struck me. Firstly, just how big the gang is – seventeen people, that's a lot. There are all sorts of different systems in the report, but almost all of them are perpetrated by individuals fraudulently submitting claims on their own behalf or perhaps for one or two members of their family. So, if our gang's got seventeen members, it must be for a good reason. If it were possible to carry out the same fraud with just two or three people then they surely would: fewer gang members would mean tighter security and of course a bigger share of the loot.'

'So, you don't think it's a computer-based scam they're operating, then? I mean, you wouldn't need seventeen people for that.'

'It doesn't look that way, although we can't rule it out; just as we absolutely can't rule out the possibility that they could be highly computer literate and could use those skills to try and investigate your background as and when you get close to them. I can't stress that point enough, Miles; we have got to be so careful about electronic data. If they manage to access your phone records and find a connection to *The Mail*, or a financial transaction between us, then your cover will be completely blown.'

'Understood.'

'Good. Right, motivation was the next thing that occurred to me.'

'How d'you mean?'

'Two million quid is a lot of money. All the swindles in the report appear to net their perpetrators thousands of pounds, so how come our gang's up in the millions? And once they'd got into the millions, why didn't they cut and run? How come they're still at it?'

'What, d'you think they could be political? Fundraising for a terror-ist group or something like that?'

'It's a definite possibility — and if they are politically motivated, defrauding the state would no doubt be an exquisitely satisfying means of raising funds for their activities. A more likely scenario, though, is that they're career criminals — organized crime, in other words. As you'll see in the report, when fraudsters are apprehended they generally tend to give themselves up. Sentences are surprisingly light and almost all of them plead guilty when they go to trial.'

'But these guys have kept on going even though they might have known they were being investigated.'

'Exactly. My guess is that they're so savvy they're confident of not yet having made a single mistake; it wouldn't surprise me if that was what prompted one of the investigators to overstep the mark and that's why the investigation got kicked into touch when it came to light that it wouldn't stand up in court. Maybe there was an element of entrapment, or they did a search without a proper warrant or something. And that in turn would explain why the person who put the file together decided to leak it to us.'

'Because he thinks the fraudsters are so smart they're never going to get caught.'

'Quite.'

'Anything else?'

'Yes, just one final point — something that I only discovered today in fact.'

'What's that?'

'This,' replied Tom, taking the leaked file out of the box and opening it up on the desk in front of Miles. 'I brought it in this morning for you. Just before you arrived, I took one final look at it and I noticed something.'

So saying, Tom flicked through the pages pointing to the name of each fraudster in turn.

'What?' asked Miles.

'Can't you see?'

'No.'

'They're in alphabetical order.'

'Are they?'

'Yes. With one exception.'

'Which one?'

'The first one.'

Taking the sheaf of papers from Tom, Miles looked again at the photograph of the fraudster on the front page; Richard Thompson, the man whose face had so intrigued him that first night in the penthouse.

'What d'you think the significance of that is?'

'I don't know.'

'D'you think he could be the leader?'

'Yes, that's my instinctive feeling. The only other reason I could think of for placing Thompson at the front was that the person who sent us the file didn't get his photograph until last. All along we've assumed that the information about the fraudsters was readily available to him. But what if he had to gather it together from a number of different sources over a number of weeks? Imagine how he would have felt compiling the file. The expectation. The anxiety. It wouldn't be at all surprising that by the time he got hold of the last photograph he was a nervous wreck and just stapled it on top so that he could get the file off his hands straightaway. I mean, he must have gone through hell worrying about being caught doing all this.'

'Especially if he'd been involved in the original investigation.'

'Quite.'

Closing the file, Tom passed it across the table to Miles who put it inside his briefcase with the other documents.

'Is that it, then?' asked Miles.

'Yes, that's all for now. I'll call you tonight about eight and let you know the fallout from our little dismissal drama: I'm sure it's going to be the talk of the office all day. Now, do you want to bang the table first or shall I?'

'Well, if I'm supposed to be throwing the fit of pique, I guess it should really be me.'

'OK, then,' replied Tom with a grin, 'after you, old chap.'

The junction at the intersection of Brixton Road and Mall Lane is one of the busiest in the capital, with a complex set of traffic signals controlling the flow of vehicles and pedestrians between the two major trunk roads and a half dozen equally busy side streets. All day and for most of the night, motorists hurtle back and forth across the junction's scarred tarmac, accelerating to get through the traffic lights before they switch to red, whilst on the pavement the four cavernous exits of the tube station disgorge a never-ending stream of commuters and travellers. If you cross over Brixton Road, though, and follow the paved pedestrian walkway northwards around the perimeter of the common, it is remarkable how quickly the traffic noise dies away, blocked out by a thick blanket of bushes and the rows of sycamore trees that encircle the grassy expanse. The architecture, too, quickly becomes more pleasing – the tacky, plastic shop fronts of the Brixton Road giving way to the stately stucco facades of the Edwardian homes that overlook the common. As the paved walkway narrows into a lane, St. Alexius Primary School becomes visible through the trees on the right hand side and, in term time, if you listen carefully, the sound of children's voices can often be heard from the playground at the rear. A few yards further along the lane, it is quite possible to believe that you are not in a city at all, as the verdant slopes of the common relax the eye and there is little to disturb the ear beyond the singing of birds and the sound of the wind blowing through the trees.

As Miles strolled along this lane, he thought back over the previous few weeks. Although he had taken the decision to proceed with *Criminal Britain* whilst on jury service, he had only really come to experience the full thrill of the adventure upon which he was about to embark when he had been dismissed from *The Mail*. Despite the fact that he would not have entertained the idea of going under cover at all if Tom had not promised to stand by him every inch of the way, he had been able to hurl at his boss a stream of vitriolic abuse that had shocked the entire fourth floor into silence. During his career, he had pretended to be all manner of different people for the purposes of talking his way in or out of a particular situation, but, on each occasion, his conscious mind had been in control of his words and actions throughout. However, as he had strutted back and forth in front of Tom's office, alternately mouthing insults and egotistical hyperbole, he had felt his whole personality undergo a transformation: it had not been an act – for those explosive five or six minutes he had become a completely different person. When he had got back to his flat his mind had still been humming with exhilaration at the intensity of the experience, and, when Tom had called him that night, there had been an awed respect in his voice: Miles's performance had exceeded even Tom's own high expectations and if he managed to be only half as convincing when he went under cover, the series was bound to be a success.

Two days later he had phoned Elizabeth. Having been forewarned of the possibility of his going overseas, she had been relaxed – off-hand, almost. The next twelve months were going to be an extremely stable period for her and Jake. Every evening and most weekends he would be studying for his exams, and her duties as a deputy headmistress would similarly ensure that she would be fully occupied. Miles should go. If he was fed up with his job on *The Mail* and an excellent opportunity on the continent had presented itself, he should take it. As long as he phoned first and Jake was available, he could fly back and see his son more or less whenever he wanted.

The following weekend the removal men had come to put his furniture into storage and for the final three nights he had slept in a sleeping bag on the bare floor boards in the living room. Lying awake in the darkness each night until the small hours of the morning, Miles had let his mind meander through the life of Michael Angel – the fictitious unskilled labourer whose personality he was to adopt – imagining the faces and conversations that had accompanied his descent into debt, divorce and his eventual decision to move to London. Hearing an occasional car drive past the flat and listening to the sound of its engine recede into the night, Miles could feel himself drawn into his despair – sense his inescapable need to turn his back on everything he had ever known and seek refuge in a place where no-one knew his name.

Arriving at the end of the lane that boarded the Common, Miles came to an ornamental iron gate that led back on to the street; according to the map that Tom had given him, the safe house was to be found half way down the third road on his left. As he closed the gate behind him and crossed on to the pavement, he thought back over his last morning as Miles Coverdale. Having cooked breakfast and then thrown away the little food that was left in the fridge, he had locked the front door for the last time, and, without even once looking back at the flat in which he had lived for the previous six years, had walked the three quarters of a mile to the estate agents and given them the keys. He had then gone to a charity shop and traded in his sports jacket and sleeping bag for a black leather jacket he had found crammed into one of the tightly packed racks of second-hand clothes. It was old and a little cracked in places, but sturdy and comfortable and, most of important of all, it was exactly what Michael Angel would wear; he had known as much in a single glance. Five minutes later, he had walked into the first hairdressers he had come across and asked them to shave his head; they had pierced his ear for an extra five pounds.

The safe house was a three-bedroomed semi-detached and was quite as nondescript as Tom had suggested. Walking down the short pathway to the front door, Miles deliberately avoided looking left or right at the adjacent properties: although he and Tom might occasionally meet here for discussions, the house's principal purpose was a bolt-hole where he might hide out if he was forced to lie low for a while and it was there-fore essential he avoided attracting attention to himself. Turning the key in the lock, Miles peered into the frosted glass of the front door: he could make out almost nothing of the hallway, and if Tom had already arrived, he certainly couldn't see him. Closing the door quietly behind him, he walked down the carpet-less hall to what he imagined was the living room at the rear. The house smelt old and slightly damp. He guessed no one had lived there for several of months.

'My God!' gasped Tom. 'I don't believe it.'

He was sitting on a packing case in the corner of the empty living room. Behind him were a set of French doors looking out over an over-grown back garden.

'Good or bad?' asked Miles, walking slowly around the room so that Tom could get a full view of his front, back and profile.

'Scary,' replied Tom. 'I mean it. I would never have recognized you ...'

'I'll take that as a compliment,' answered Miles, who had been sur-prised but reassured by the guarded, respectful looks that his hard-man image had elicited from a number of passers-by that he had met after emerging from the hairdressers.

'When did you get it done?'

'This morning after I'd dropped off the keys to the flat. I thought about having it cut yesterday but didn't want any of my old neighbours to see me. I thought it best that they should only remember me with my hair long.'

'Good thinking, although to be honest I doubt they would've recognized you. Where did you get the jacket?'

'Cancer research shop.'

'It's spot on, old chap.'

'Thanks.'

'Anyway, listen, sorry about the lack of furniture – I'd planned to get it organized for yesterday afternoon but something came up.'

'No problem,' replied Miles.

'There's a table and a couple of chairs in the kitchen, though. Let's go on through.'

'OK.'

Following Tom back into the hallway and through the door on his left, Miles looked around the kitchen – it was a little old-fashioned, but very solidly built.

'So, are you nervous, then?' asked Tom, sitting down at the table.

'No, not really.'

'Good man. You certainly look the part, anyway.'

'Thanks.'

'Right, well, let's get started, then,' said Tom, opening up his briefcase and placing a thick brown envelope on the surface of the table. 'First of all, money. In here are three thousand pounds in cash and the key to a safe deposit box at Barclays Bank, Moorgate in which you'll find a further twenty-five thousand. Keep the two sets of funds separate. Open up a bank account in Feltham when you get there, put the three grand in and use it for your Michael Angel expenses – for your day to day living. When you need to buy cameras or any other equipment, go to Moorgate and take the money straight from the safe deposit. If you get into that routine, then there's no way anybody will ever be able subsequently to discover from your financial transactions that you have a second source of funds inconsistent with your cover.'

'OK. I've got you.'

'Insurance next,' continued Tom, fixing Miles with his most forthright stare. 'Henry and I talked it over last night and we'd like to propose a sum of five hundred thousand pounds – payable to your next of kin in the event of your death. Is that acceptable?'

'Yes. That's fine,' answered Miles, an image of Elizabeth and Jake flashing before his eyes.

'Is your will up to date?'

'It is. I called my solicitors last week.'

'Good. Well, I'm sure it won't get to that, but we want to set your mind at rest that everything's in place.'

'I appreciate that, Tom. Thanks.'

'It's the least we could do,' replied Tom, with a nod. 'Now, have you brought your photos?'

'Here,' said Miles, taking his wallet from his inside pocket and extracting the strip of passport photographs that he had taken at the tube station.

'Good show. As soon as you find yourself a place to live in Feltham, get a spare set of keys cut and send them to me here along with the address. I'll get the passport made up and send it back to you a week or two later.'

'OK.'

'In which regard,' said Tom, taking another envelope from his briefcase, 'in here is a list of Bed and Breakfasts in Feltham and the names and phone numbers of a few local estate agents. They might come in useful.'

'Great. Thanks,' replied Miles, taking the envelope.

'As regards communication between us after you get to Feltham, we have got to try and keep all links completely secure until we know exactly who we're dealing with. So, at first, I suggest you don't get a mobile phone and, whenever you want to call me, do so from a public call box. If the accommodation you find has a phone, don't use it – it'll be too easy to check the records afterwards.'

'Agreed.'

'You can phone me at the office or at home if you have to, although, as you know, I don't usually get back there until late. Probably the best thing to do therefore is contact me here – there's an answering machine which I'll check regularly. In an emergency, however – that is, if you need me to come and pull you out immediately – call me on this mobile.' So saying, Tom took a mobile phone from the top pocket of his suit. 'I'm going to keep it with me twenty-four hours a day. Tell me the time and place where you want to meet me and I'll go straight there. Don't use it except in the very last resort. If you call, I'm just going to drive straight to where you tell me on the assumption that the game's up and you don't care about your cover any more.'

'I understand,' replied Miles.

'The number's in the envelope I just gave you along with the phone number for the safehouse here. I suggest you commit them to memory and if you do eventually get your own mobile don't programme them in.'

'Got you.'

'For my part, I won't call you under any circumstances unless you specifically tell me to, in which case, once again, we should try and speak over a public phone. If I do need to talk to you, we should meet here, and with that in mind I've had an idea for a messaging system. It goes by overnight mail so it's a bit slow, but it's a hundred per cent secure and that's the main thing.'

'What are you thinking of, then?'

Opening up his briefcase, Tom took out two postcards.

'This amber coloured postcard means come to the safehouse when you can – preferably within a couple of days of receipt; call me at the office when you arrive and I'll come and join you here. This red coloured postcard means make immediate contact. Now, I'm not sure of the circumstances in which I might need to use either of these cards – and we might later develop a better system – but we'll run with them for the moment if that's all right with you.'

'Yeah. Sounds fine.'

'Next – your car. When you send me your address, I'll get you a driving licence made up in the name of Michael Angel as soon as I can. Here are two sets of keys. The car's parked about twenty yards down on the other side of the street. It's a red BMW 320 – you can't miss it. I've left you a London Street Index on the back seat as well.'

'Great, wouldn't want to get lost.'

'Quite,' smiled Tom. 'So, that's all from me. Any questions from your side?'

'Nope.'

'Well, in that case, all I have to say is good luck, and ask you to remember that I'll have this phone with me twenty four hours a day. Whatever scrape you're in, if you need me – call. I'll come and get you. You have my solemn promise on that.'

Looking across the table, Miles was struck by the expression of absolute sincerity on Tom's face; it was clear that he meant every word he had said. Standing up, Miles extended his hand for him to shake. His boss clasped it warmly and held it firmly for almost half a minute.

'OK, then, old chap,' he said, finally, his expression breaking into a smile, 'I guess this is it – time to cast off. I suppose we ought to leave separately.'

'Yes, perhaps we should.'

'I'll go first – give me ten minutes before you leave yourself. You can have a look around the house in the meantime, if you like. There are a couple of bedrooms upstairs; I'll get a bed and some linen when I order the furniture.'

'OK.'

'Bye then.'

'Bye.'

With a frank and reassuring smile, Tom turned to go, but, just as he put his hand out to open the kitchen door, he stopped and turned around to face Miles again.

'Oh, one other thing – I almost forgot.'

'Yes?'

'This.'

So saying, Tom reached inside his jacket pocket, took out a small envelope and passed it to Miles. Unlike the other two envelopes he had given him that morning which were standard office stationery, this was plainly the very highest quality vellum and, moreover, had been sealed with a small and perfectly circular droplet of blood-red wax.

'What is it?'

'Psychological stuff.'

'What d'you mean?'

'It's from a spy: a chap who went under cover in the early sixties during the cold war. He lived behind the iron curtain under an assumed identity for over three years, apparently. I know you're mentally very tough, Miles, and you can meet me here to talk whenever you feel the need, but all the same you're going to be living a double life for long periods of time. You can't expect to do that without encountering a certain amount of mental stress.'

'So, what's in the letter, then?'

'I don't know, I haven't read it – as you can see, it's sealed. The chap's a security consultant now. I rang him without telling him my name, explained very roughly what we were doing and asked if he'd be prepared to give you some advice about surviving under cover for protracted periods of time. He said he would, but only on condition that I passed it to you unopened.'

'Hm, peculiar,' remarked Miles.

'Maybe not. I've never met the chap – he was recommended to me by an old friend of mine – but apparently he's something rather special, so I think he wouldn't have done it without good reason and whatever he's got to say is probably worth reading. If not, well, just dispose of the letter as you see fit.'

Taking the envelope, Miles shook Tom's hand once again, and then watched as his friend walked down the hallway and out of the house.

The BMW was adorned with a number of rather garish accessories, but had nevertheless clearly been very well maintained. Gingerly turning the ignition key, Miles listened appreciatively to the sound of the healthy, powerful engine. Slipping off his jacket, he put it on the back seat and picked up the street index that Tom had left for him. The journey would take him about an hour and a half; he should get to Feltham just after one o'clock. Drawing the seat belt across his chest, he frowned thoughtfully as his hand brushed against the letter from the East European spy in his shirt pocket. After Tom had gone, he had opened the envelope straightaway, but had not known what to make of the two carefully handwritten pages within. From what Tom had said, he had been expecting to find advice as to how he should maintain his equanimity whilst under cover. Instead, the letter had spoken of one thing and one thing alone: betrayal. From the moment that Miles adopted his counterfeit identity, the spy had warned, the spectre of betrayal would begin to stalk him and would remain his dread companion for the rest of his days: half a century ago, the spy had insinuated himself into the lives of people whom he had regarded as enemies of his country, but yet still today suffered pangs of guilt at having betrayed their trust. It was an aspect of the operation Miles had not considered before and whose significance he knew he was not yet able properly to absorb. When he got to Feltham, he would put the letter in a safe place and go back to it at some time in the future.

Putting the engine into gear, Miles paused before driving off, savouring the final few moments prior to departure – once he pulled away from the curb, his undercover life would begin in earnest. Sitting with his hands resting on the leather-covered sports steering wheel, he suddenly thought of Charlotte, Elizabeth's best friend. When they had last met, she had avidly seized upon Angus Lamb's improbable alibi as a means of criticizing him and his work. If it had been true and he had indeed ruined a decent man's reputation – which he still did not believe for a moment – and if the photograph in question had been the only one that he had ever had published, her opinion of him might well have been justified. But the shot of Lamb and his mistress was merely one in a long line of such photographs, stretching right back through his career, that had exposed hypocrisy and deceit which otherwise would have remained hidden. And that, ultimately, was the reason why he had wanted to make *Criminal Britain*. King had been right – he was by nature a loner. But that did not mean he felt removed from his fellow countrymen. On the contrary, deep down he nursed a real desire to make the land that they shared a better place in which to live. It was a private and intensely personal conviction, which he had never once confided to anyone, but which nevertheless underpinned every photograph that he had ever taken of any value. Charlotte Burgess was entitled to her opinions – to her view of the truth – which no doubt sounded eminently reasonable at the cultured dinner parties and in the chic, brightly-lit cafés that she frequented. He, meanwhile, would continue to go in search of the truth in the places that he had always looked – behind closed doors and down darkened night-time streets – and, when the right moment came, point his camera so that others might also see what he had beheld with his own eyes.

With a wry shake of the head, he gently released the clutch: he could forget about Charlotte now, it was time to go. Arriving at the junction at the end of the road, he wound down the window to let in some air and, as he did so, was greeted by the smell of freshly mown grass wafting in from the common. Summer had been on the verge of breaking through for weeks, but now, at last, it was here. And, as the wonderfully fresh aroma filled his nostrils, Miles Coverdale smiled to himself. It was a good omen. A good omen for a man whose former life had come to an end that morning.

A good omen for a man about to be reborn.

Part Two
These Evil Deeds

Chapter 4

For residents and visitors alike, a given location in Feltham is usually understood with reference to its position on the 'Uxbridge', a two and a half mile trunk road that runs in a straight line from one end of the suburb to the other. Beginning in East Feltham amongst the warehouses and storage yards ranged around the perimeter of Heathrow airport, the Uxbridge Road passes on through a succession of brick-built residential estates, past the old town and then finally comes to an end at Apex Corner, the busy six-exited motorway junction that marks Feltham's most westerly point. It was via this motorway that, for two reasons, Michael had decided to make his approach. Firstly, he could tell from the street index that all three Bed and Breakfasts were located in West Feltham and, secondly, the essence of maintaining an undercover identity was routinely to act in concert with it: this was exactly the route that someone travelling down from Yorkshire would have taken.

Turning off on to the long, two-lane slip road, Michael gradually cut his speed as he approached the roundabout beneath the elevated section of motorway. This was it. He had arrived. Turning left, he came to a halt at a pedestrian crossing. Up ahead of him the Uxbridge Road stretched out straight ahead into the distance. What was Michael Angel thinking as he stared at this unknown town? How was his self-esteem coping with having arrived here with little more than a road map and the clothes on his back? What resolutions had he dared to make about his future, with three hundred miles between him and the failures of his past? The pedestrian who was crossing the road came into his field of vision. He was a middle-aged man wearing a full-length overcoat that would have made him look quite respectable but for the filthy training-shoes on his feet. Michael grunted to himself. They gave everything away, those shoes: the man was a tramp and had more than likely stolen the coat. Michael Angel might have slipped in the world, but he would never slip that low.

The first of the Bed and Breakfasts turned out to be less than a quarter of a mile away. It was on a side street next to a large Victorian house which, judging by the brightly coloured paintings on the windows, had been converted into a children's nursery. The rooms were thirty pounds a night – payable in advance. As the landlady led him up the well-swept, carpeted stairs, she surveyed him warily out of the corner of her eye: she obviously didn't like the look of him – his haircut and earring, probably. He didn't like the look of her much either, but she wanted his money and he needed the room, so that was that. Depositing his overnight bag at the bottom of the bed, he went straight out to find something to eat. It had been a long drive down from the north and he hadn't stopped once on the way.

The café on the corner of Uxbridge Road did all-day breakfasts at a fiver a time. It looked OK. Sitting in the corner by the door Michael waited for his food to arrive. In his inside pocket, pressed against his chest, he could feel the bulky envelope containing the three thousand pounds that Tom had given him. As soon as possible he had to get it into a bank – if it got stolen, he would be completely penniless. The next thing was to find some work. As he ate he thought about what he would do. Although he wasn't a skilled craftsman, he was strong and fit and there was money in London – everyone knew that. After he'd sorted himself out a place to live, he'd go looking for some general building work. He was bound to be able to pick up something.

He came out of the café just after four. Feeling a lot better for the food and not wanting to go back to the B&B until the evening, he decided to take a walk to try and get a feel for the district. To his right were Apex Corner and the Motorway. There wouldn't be much down that way. He'd go left along the Uxbridge Road towards Feltham old town.

The shops soon gave way to rows of semi-detached houses that seemed to increase in size but drop in quality the nearer he got towards the old town. The B&B was obviously in the posh end of Feltham which would explain why his landlady had been so stuck-up. Crossing over the next junction by the public library, Michael was surprised to see that several of the houses on his left had military vehicles parked in their long, narrow driveways. There were two jeeps, a troop carrier covered with a tarpaulin and a huge amphibious landing vehicle sporting a US military star on the side. How bizarre that a group of enthusiasts had somehow all ended up living next to each other on this same street! Pausing for a moment, Michael stared back down the road along which he had just come. On the opposite side of the junction to the library was a grey concrete office block, on the roof of which – for some unknown reason – there were literally dozens of antennae of various shapes and sizes. Suddenly, he found himself wanting to laugh out loud. It would only take the smoke from a householder's Sunday morning garden fire to make this entire place look like a war-zone. It was more like a suburb of Beirut than of London. Perhaps he would come back early one morning and photograph this extraordinary combination of urban features. Or then again, maybe he wouldn't. Because Michael Angel knew nothing of the visual arts: for him, photographs were representational and cameras were what you used for taking snaps of the wife and kids – if she hadn't left you and taken them with her.

He walked for nearly an hour and a half before at last stopping on the outskirts of the airport and then turning around to come back again. A number of black cabs passed him on the three-mile journey back to the B&B, but he'd only rarely used taxis in Yorkshire and he'd heard they were ridiculously expensive in London. On the way he passed half a dozen pubs, but despite the thirst he had built up wasn't tempted to go into any of them. There would be time enough for that once he was working again. As he approached the old town he thought about taking a diversion to check it out, but decided in the end not to bother. It was nearly seven o'clock now and there was something comforting about the familiarity of staying on the same stretch of road that he had walked along earlier.

Finally, half a mile from the B&B, he stopped at a newsagent and bought a packet of cigarettes. On the other side of the road was a small park that he hadn't noticed on his journey down and, even though it was getting dark, he crossed over and went in. In the distance he could see a woman walking her dog, but apart from that the place was completely deserted. Sitting on a bench, he looked at the building on his left which he thought at first might be a park keeper's lodge but in fact turned out to be a small training centre for the St. John's Ambulance Brigade. The sound of voices was coming from inside the building, but he couldn't really catch what they were saying; he guessed they ran evening classes there or something like that. At the front of the building was a large wooden sign. The paint was cracking around the edges and someone had daubed graffiti over the Brigade's logo, the black and white cross of St. John. He had been in Feltham for less than five hours and had spoken little more than a dozen words since he had arrived, yet somehow he felt he had established himself here. Turning around, he looked out over the park at the line of houses around the perimeter. Behind those doors and windows, couples were asking each other how their days had been, children were doing their homework, families were sitting down to dinner together. He doubted that they felt much in common with each other beyond the fact that they all lived in Feltham. To Michael Angel, however, sitting on a park bench on that quiet evening in July, they had a special unity all of their own. For he had come to discover the truth about the criminals who lived in their midst.

With a camera that he wasn't wearing.

And a life that wasn't his.

'Mr. Angel?'

'Yeah.'

'I'm awfully sorry to be late. Have you been waiting long?'

She looked more anxious than apologetic. He wasn't sure whether that was because of him, the district or both.

'No, not long.'

'I really do apologize. I'll just find the keys and we can go on in.' Locking her car door, the estate agent cast a nervous glance down the dusty, litter-strewn street and then fumbled in her handbag for the keys to the flat. 'The traffic was absolutely awful and I must confess I got a little lost. To be honest I'm not terribly familiar with our properties on this side of the motorway.'

'No problem. Don't worry about it.'

'You're most kind. Here we are. Let's go on up, shall we?'

Actually, he was glad that she had been late. It had given him the opportunity to check out whether the property was just as good at the back as it was at the front and sides. As a first-floor, end-of-terrace flat its aspect was ideal: anyone approaching or watching the building was visible from fifty yards away. Having looked over the garden wall and discovered that there were no alleyways at the rear, Michael had begun to think that he may have found his fortress: the only way into 144 Balam Road was via a frontal assault up the concrete staircase that led to the front door.

'OK. Now, let's see. Through here is the bathroom, over there the, er, kitchen, and this is the living room and the bedroom. Do please take your time and look around.'

Her invitation for him to view the flat at his leisure was delivered with a smile, but he could see that she wanted nothing more in the world than to get straight out of this dreary, council-built hovel back to her well-heeled clients in the town houses and maisonettes on the other side of Apex Corner. He decided to ignore her: a wrong decision now could spell disaster for him later. The kitchen and bathroom were small but adequate. Going through into the living room he looked around at the faded white paintwork and the scruffy, unimaginative furniture; just what you'd expect in a working man's one-bedroom flat. Walking over to the window, he pulled back the net curtains and peered through the smog-smeared pane. Beyond the slip road in front was a grass verge and, beyond that, a two-lane section of the Uxbridge Road along which the late afternoon traffic was speeding noisily. The view was every bit as all-encompassing as he had hoped. Both of the flats he'd seen in the morning had been on residential estates and had been completely surrounded by places from which he could be observed.

'Are you renting at the moment?' She spoke with her hand holding back the curtain of the hallway window so that she could keep an eye on her car. Michael hadn't spotted any kids playing around outside but noted well her demonstration of unease; the BMW was a very passable getaway car but would be totally useless with its tyres slashed. As regards the exterior of the flat, the side and rear windows were safe – no one could get up there without a ladder – but he'd have to put a mortice lock and some heavy duty bolts on the front door: there was no point risking his life with an undercover camera just to have some twelve-year-old housebreaker fence it for his next tube of glue.

'No, I'm in digs up the road. I just moved down here from Yorkshire a couple of days ago.'

'Oh, I see,' she replied, her brow furling slightly. 'Are you in employment?'

'Not yet.'

'Oh, right. Well, you do realize that in that case the landlord will require a six month deposit, don't you?'

'That's not what they said when they gave me the details,' he replied.

'Ah, yes, I'm sorry about that,' she gushed, regretfully. 'They really should have brought it to your attention.'

'They said three months.'

'Yes, well, you see, er, that's in the case of a tenant who is in employment. And, er, also we can only let out the property on a six-month renewable contract, too, I'm afraid.'

Listening to her invent new terms and conditions as she went along, Michael guessed what was going on. The other two flats had been advertised in the local paper, but he had got this one from one of the estate agents that Tom had recommended. Visualizing a map of Feltham, Michael realized that the train station connecting to central London was only about a half a mile away: the landlord and estate agent were obviously hoping to rent the place out to a young, salaried commuter who would only come back there to sleep. Six months rent was almost three thousand pounds – it would wipe him out completely. Moreover, if the fraudsters ever found out that as an unemployed labourer he'd handed over such a large amount of money without a second thought, it might well confirm their suspicions. He looked at the estate agent's voluminous bosom and flabby double chin. They'd only have to click their knuckles and she'd tell them everything.

'Could I have another look in the kitchen?' he asked: the longer he kept her here, the more uncomfortable she'd feel and the more chance he'd have of negotiating better terms.

'Er, yes, all right, if you wish …'

Walking through into the hallway, he looked down at the floor boards which were bare in every room; they hadn't been revarnished for years and whoever had done the job last time obviously hadn't taken much care. Looking around the kitchen he recalled his visit to the safe house four days previously: the difference between the two empty properties was striking. Whereas the kitchen in the safe house was old, it had clearly been properly constructed in the first place and just needed a good clean to make it presentable once again. This kitchen, however, exuded a sorry drabness: the fridge and cooker were almost decrepit and above the stainless steel sink unit was a line of stained kitchen tiles, many of which looked ready to drop off the wall at any moment. Looking out of the kitchen window, Michael frowned thoughtfully: the apartment block behind was over a hundred yards away. As a one-bedroom flat 144 Balam Road was horrendously over-priced; as a secure and inconspicuous operational base for an undercover reporter it was absolutely ideal.

'Who lives down below, do you know?' asked Michael.

'Oh, er, an elderly lady, I believe ...' replied the estate agent, with a vague wave of her plump, stubby hand.

Couldn't be better, thought Michael, extending his arm to suggest that they return to the hallway.

'OK, I'll take it.'

'That's wonderful. Could you ...'

'But not on six months deposit. I want three – like I was told. And no six-month contract, either. Annual – with three months notice on either side.'

'I'm sorry, Mr, er, Angel, but ...'

'I haven't finished yet,' interrupted Michael. 'I can understand you're worried because I haven't got a job yet – you've gotta look after the landlord's interests, I know. So, you can have three months rent in cash now and a further two months in four weeks time. Also, I'll paint the place. The floors need resanding, so I'll do them too, and I'll grout those tiles in the kitchen while I'm there.'

'No, I'm sorry, Mr Angel, but it's company policy. We have to abide by our rules, you know.'

'All right. Well, thanks for your time and good luck with the next tenants you'll be showing around. After you.'

With a sober and uncompromising stare, Michael took a step backwards to let the estate agent make her way out of the front door first. As he stood watching her, the left side of her mouth twitched involuntarily. Casting another glance out of the hallway window she looked at her car in the slip road. A piece of newspaper whipped up by the wind had draped itself around her wing mirror. It was obvious that she didn't want to come back here again unless she absolutely had to.

'Well, Mr. Angel, as we may have misinformed you when you first picked up the details, perhaps I could have a word with the landlord and see what we can do.'

'I'll call you tomorrow then, all right?'

'Please do,' she replied, making her way out of the door and then adding with a smile, 'you drive quite a hard bargain, you know.'

Remembering that might one day save my neck, thought Michael, smiling back in response.

Three days later, he went to the DIY superstore next to Apex Corner to pick up the materials for the flat. The paint, grouting and varnish were cheap enough, but when he saw the cost of the solvent stripper needed for preparing the floor boards, he decided to buy petrol instead: it was a tenth of the price and would do the job just as well. Having ascertained from one of the assistants the location of the nearest plant hire shop, Michael then set off to rent a sanding machine. On the way, he stopped at a service station and bought two ten litre plastic canisters which he filled with petrol: he would keep the second of them in the boot of the car for emergencies. The sanding machine cost thirty pounds a day to hire, but the man behind the counter told him that if he took it out last thing on Thursday night, he could bring it back on Monday lunch time and they'd only charge him for two days. Having thanked the man and asked him to reserve a machine for him on the following Thursday, he made his way back to the B&B. Sanding all four floors over the space of a single weekend would no doubt be a back-breaking job, but Micky Angel had never been scared of a bit of hard work and besides, once it was done he could forget about it altogether.

He moved into Balam Road two days later. Having unpacked the few items of clothing that he had brought with him, he sat in the quiet of the living room and began to think through the question of surveillance equipment. A top of the range lap-top with a high-density hard-drive would be ideal for storing and transmitting the large number of images that he intended to generate, but despite these obvious attractions he decided against it. Even if he encrypted his files, the very presence of a computer would be a complete give-away: what would an unskilled labourer be doing with a three grand lap-top? A VCR, on the other hand, would not be in the least bit out of character. He would have to find somewhere to hide the tapes, but it was clearly the best alternative. As for the cameras, he was going to need some very well camouflaged and extremely high-tech equipment; even with twenty-five thousand pounds to spend, he wondered whether it would be technically possible to meet the specifications he had in mind. Smiling, he got out of the armchair and picked up the keys to the flat from the living-room table.

The cameras could wait for the time being. For now, he had a some-what less technologically challenging task to carry out. Just down the road from the B&B, he had spotted a shoe-repairer that also cut keys. Picking up his jacket, he made his way out of the flat, imagining Tom's face as he opened the envelope and let the keys drop into his hand. It would be the first sign that their documentary series was underway.

Six days later, he set off to check out the first of the fraudster's addresses. The work on the flat had been just as hard as he had imagined, but the place looked better now and the dirt on his hands and the smells of the various materials had helped him mentally adjust to his new profession. Having stored the paint brushes and the half-empty canister of petrol in the cupboard outside the front door, Michael made his way down the stairs towards his car. For the first few days he had parked it on the slip road in front of the flat, but, having discovered a small area of waste ground at the rear that was visible from his kitchen window, had decided to leave it there in future.

The first address was less than a mile away in a particularly rundown area close to the old town. Although there were several empty parking spaces on the opposite side of the road to the small terraced house, he resisted the temptation to stop and simply drove past the front door. Parking a third of a mile away, he locked the car and walked back to the end of the road. Stopping on the corner he lit a cigarette, but instead of walking down the road past the house, carried on straight ahead, looping back to the car through a series of left turns: there had been no signs of life – he hadn't anticipated there would be. According to the report that Tom had commissioned, multiple addresses and multiple identities were the stock in trade of housing benefit fraudsters and, whatever the system they were using, he should expect them routinely to be on the move between different locations.

Returning to the car, he opened up the street index and checked the route to the next house. He had been careful not to mark the pages in any way but instead had memorized the three addresses he intended to check out that day. What he was looking for in this first round of sur-veillance was an address that lent itself to being observed from a posi-tion of relative security. Most of Feltham was flat – as was West London in general – but if he could find a slight hill, or a park, or some other feature that allowed him to get a complete view of the property from a reasonable distance, he'd stake it out until he spotted signs of life. Without the photographs in the leaked file, exact identification of the fraudsters would no doubt be extremely difficult, but because he knew their faces, Michael was fairly certain that he need only maintain a patient round of surveillance and eventually he would spot one of them going in or out. Thereafter, he could track them to a favourite haunt – a pub or club – and then try and make contact.

Winding down the window to let in some air, he drove to St. Helena's Road. This was the address at which Richard Thompson lived – the fraudster whom the unknown informant had placed on page one of the file and whom Tom had speculated might be the gang's ringleader. The previous evening, Michael had gone over every centimetre of the file with a magnifying glass and had discovered that the grain of the photograph of Thompson was of particularly poor quality. Without knowing the exact telescopic lens that had been used he could not be absolutely certain, but he wouldn't be surprised if the photo had been taken at a range of well over a quarter of a mile. Had Tom's hunch been right? Was Thompson the criminal mastermind who sent his operatives into the field whilst he himself hid in the shadows? Michael didn't know, but for the moment it felt like a good working proposition.

As he approached St. Helena's Road, Michael felt a thrill of anticipation. As soon as he turned into it, however, he knew immediately that the house was not going to be an easy a target for observation. The road was one-way, with single yellow lines on both sides and there was thus nowhere to park except on the driveways in front of the actual houses themselves. Driving past number fourteen he only managed to glance at the house fleetingly and so decided to circle around again. The second pass afforded a better view and he was able to catch a brief glimpse of something hanging from the ceiling of the upstairs bedroom. Going to the end of St. Helena's Road, he turned left, drove for another five hundred yards and then, frowning, brought the car to an abrupt halt. It had been a baby's mobile. It was only an instinctive feeling, but something of the innocence of that gently swaying object had created the powerful impression that fourteen St. Helena's Road was just an ordinary suburban home. Had Thompson sold up and left? According to the informant's note, after the Crown Prosecution Service had rejected the DSS's investigation the fraudsters had simply carried on regardless. But that had been over two months ago. A lot could have happened since then. If Thompson was cunning enough to have masterminded the system in the first place, he was cunning enough to get out the moment that he smelt the authorities were getting too close. Slowly sliding back into his seat, Michael tried to think his way into the fraudsters' modus operandi. So far he had only considered the notion that they were permanently based in Feltham. But what if they actually anticipated detection and only worked a given district for a number of months before moving on – like a plague of locusts sweeping across the land? Wiping the sweat from his brow with his shirt sleeve, Michael lit up a cigarette. If that was the case it would be even more difficult to pick up their trail without their becoming alerted to his presence. And, if their system really did involve keeping on the move, would they ever be in one place long enough for him to be able to infiltrate them successfully? Putting the car in to gear, Michael drove off to find the third of the addresses. There was no point in speculating until he had carried out a more thorough investigation. For the moment he would just have to continue checking out each of the properties in turn on the assumption that eventually he would catch sight of one of the fraudsters.

Four days later, he did precisely that.

'Well, I can't help you there, mate, but I know a man that can. If you'd like to follow me …'

'Oh, OK, thanks,' replied Michael, waiting for the assistant to manoeuvre his way out from behind the sales counter and then following him across the shop to a narrow, low-ceilinged workshop at the rear.

'Jim, this gentleman'd like a word with you,' said the assistant. Looking up from the printed circuit board on which he had been working, Jim switched off his micro soldering iron and unhurriedly removed the magnifying glass from his right eye. 'He's got some rather special requirements. I'll, er, leave you two to talk.'

The assistant left, closing the door behind him. Looking around at the densely packed racks of electronic components and reels of cable covering the walls of the workshop, Michael sat down on a plastic stool on the other side of the bench from Jim. He was a young man – he scarcely looked older than Jake – but exuded that irrefutable air of authority peculiar to technicians with an absolute knowledge of the field in which they work. He sat and stared at Michael, his face completely expressionless. This tiny room, less than eight feet square, was his domain and here he clearly reigned supreme.

'I'm looking for a concealed camera system,' began Michael, 'body worn; colour; wide angle lens with a light sensitivity of point nought five lux. I need high-resolution – three-eighty lines minimum. I can compromise on running times: it doesn't have to go for twelve hours or anything – two or three's OK as long as there's an on-off switch – but it can't have a bulky power pack or anything recognisable as a conventional twelve-volt battery.'

'How many gig d'you wanna transmit at?'

'I don't want the camera to transmit signals to a remote receiver because of the risk of going out of range; it has to record on to a portable unit – once again body worn.'

'But nothing recognisable, yeah?'

'Exactly.'

'D'you need audio?'

'Yes – with a recording range of about, say, ten to twelve feet.'

Narrowing his eyes, Jim sat back in his chair and thought for a few moments. Michael knew that what he was asking for was probably technically impossible and was impressed to see that Jim hadn't simply refused outright to consider his requests.

'What you gonna be wearing?'

'Sorry?'

'Your clothes. Suit and tie; a variety of different types; what?'

'No, no tie. Informal – always informal; like this.'

'Casual.'

'Yeah, casual.'

Again Jim went deep into thought for several moments, rubbing his hand over his smooth, unstubbled chin. Michael had steered well clear of the camera shops he had known before moving to Feltham – he had found this one amongst the dozen or so stores that advertised custom surveillance devices in the security equipment section of Exchange and Mart and had chosen it because of its central London location.

'It's impossible to incorporate all that into a single unit, you do realize that, don't you?'

'Yeah, I guessed as much.'

'You could do it with several smaller units, but they'd all have to be connected up and as a rule you wanna keep the number of wires down to an absolute minimum – it's too fiddly otherwise; I reckon we might be able to do it with two, though. Can you carry a mobile phone?'

'Yeah, no problem,' replied Michael; Tom had suggested that he avoid using a mobile for the time being, but that didn't prevent him from carrying one.

'Good.' Opening one of the drawers, Jim took out a mobile phone and placed it on the work bench. 'Concealed inside here is a miniaturized video camera with a running time of just under three hours. The phone itself is fully functioning: the manufacturer's original circuitry is completely intact and even an expert would be hard pressed to spot the modifications; ditto the SIM card and phone number – they're both exactly as originally supplied by the retailer. The clever bit's here, in the battery pack. We've taken out one of the two power cells and replaced it with components from a stripped down DAT. Because the phone's already got a set of speech and video chips built in, we didn't need to incorporate the support IC's – amplifiers, A to D converters, that sort of thing – which meant that all we had to fit inside the battery pack were the two tape reels and a motor.'

'Does the phone have to be switched on before the camera works?'

'No. The ring volume control on the side here doubles up as an on-off switch – up for on, down for off.'

'How d'you take the tape out?' asked Michael, running his fingers over the battery pack's apparently flawless exterior.

'You can't – unless you use a hammer. The tape mechanism's moulded into the casing. It's completely invisible – the only way to spot it would be an X-ray machine or something like that.'

'So how does it work then?'

'The tape's on a permanent loop – there's no fast forward or rewind. When you switch on, it starts recording until the tape reaches the end, at which point it switches itself off. When you turn it back on again, it automatically starts up in playback mode. You can either look at what you've recorded on the LCD display, or you can download it via the external digital interface socket.'

'Impressive.'

Ignoring the compliment Jim pointed his slim, bony forefinger at a small aperture above the phone's display, 'The microphone is here – at the top. You've got to keep it close to the lip of your pocket or you won't pick up any sound – or if you do it'll be muffled.'

'What about the lens?'

'There's an internal lens here next to the LCD display – which it defaults to when it's not attached to an external lens – but it's not wide angle and the resolution's quite low. It's OK if you want to talk into the camera yourself, but for good quality covert recording you really need an external lens. Can you stick to wearing that jacket or at least one like it?'

'I can do, if necessary.'

'Then do. Leathers are brilliant for pinhole lenses because they're stiff and padded out with loads of lining and stuff. You said you wanted colour images, right?'

'Yes,' answered Michael, watching fascinated as Jim took a small anti-static box off the shelf behind him and opened it up. Inside was a single, finely-etched printed circuit board about half the size of a man's thumb-nail. Taking it out with great reverence, like a learned monk showing a visiting pilgrim the monastery's most sacred relic, Jim placed it on a coated polythene sheet and slid it across the table for Michael to inspect.

'This is what you want. It's not made of glass, it's silicon – it's what they call a charge coupled array. It's a bit thicker than most of the pin-holes we do 'cos it's high-res, but it should fit in behind the top button of your jacket just fine. Now, to power it up you're gonna need a button battery. Did Bill tell you about those?'

'Who's Bill?'

'The guy out front – the one who brought you in here.'

'No, no, he didn't.'

'I haven't got one in the workshop to show you, but basically it's a lithium battery – you know, like you get in a wristwatch – only made into the shape of a button. We do dummies as well because you'll have to replace all the buttons on your jacket otherwise the power button'll look out of place.'

'How long does the battery last?'

'Oh, ages. The lens doesn't draw much current.'

'So, how's the lens connected to the camera?'

'Ribbon cable,' answered Jim, 'connected to a micro-connector sewn into the bottom of whichever pocket you're gonna keep the mobile in and then looped back up through the lining of your jacket to the top button.'

'Clever,' replied Michael.

'Just a bit,' replied Jim, seeming to accept the compliment this time. 'Now, there's one more feature you should know about as well. The phone functions both as a body worn and as a remote recording device. If you want to leave it somewhere to film an event at which you're not actually gonna be present yourself, turn it on, press 1-2-3 and then switch it straight back off – it'll immediately start recording using the internal lens. You'll have to experiment a bit to get used to positioning it right, but you'll get the hang of it soon enough, don't worry.'

'OK. I've got you.'

'Any questions?'

'Yes. Could you get the sewing done for me? I wouldn't trust myself to get the lens and the ribbon cable absolutely right.'

'Sure, we know a good seamstress. If you leave your jacket with me, I'll have it ready in a few days; you'll have to pay extra, mind you.'

'Money's the least of my problems.'

'That's what all my customers say,' observed Jim casually, picking up the circuit board and replacing it carefully in its box.

The fraudster's name was Geoffrey Harper and Michael had spotted him at the eleventh of the seventeen addresses in the leaked file. When he had returned to his flat afterwards, Michael had felt his heart thumping in his chest as he had sprinted up the front stairs to check that the face in the photograph had indeed been that of the tall, hook-nosed thirty year old he had seen walking into the three-storey house in East Feltham. The moment he had opened up the file he had realized that he had got his man: Harper had thick dark hair, shaved two inches above his ears and feathered at the front and back so that it protruded straight upwards like a small, black crown resting on the middle of his head – there probably wasn't another person within a twenty-mile radius with that exact same hairstyle. The following day, Michael had found Jim's camera shop in Exchange and Mart and had gone off to order the equipment he would need. Whilst it was being customized and his jacket was being fitted with the necessary wiring, he had stayed away from Harper's house, resisting the temptation to carry out any further surveillance. The waiting had nearly driven him mad, but, as he had paced around the flat smoking and drinking innumerable cups of coffee, he had forced himself to curb his eagerness; it was pointless going in until he was fully kitted out. Finally, five days later, at six o'clock in the morning, he once again parked his car at the end of the slip road on the industrial estate from which he had first caught sight of Harper. It was a perfect spot to carry out a surveillance – the row of ornamental trees decorating the edge of the estate providing ideal cover behind which he could watch the house from his car.

Leaning back in his seat and lighting up a cigarette, he found himself thinking about Jake. The last time that they had met he had promised to call him and arrange to go to a rugby match together. That had been over eight weeks ago and Michael realized with regret that in the flurry of preparations he hadn't actually spoken to him in person to tell him that he wouldn't be able to make it – or at least not for a few months. Tom had warned him about feelings like this. Apparently, for undercover operatives, the need to reach out to their families was always most acute just before going into action. Staring across at the façade of the shabby Edwardian building Michael wondered how long it would be before Harper appeared – or, indeed, whether he would appear at all that day. The temptation to get in touch with Jake and Elizabeth was going to get stronger as time went by and he would therefore simply have to learn to take solace in the thought that one day, recognizing the dangers he had faced and being proud of what he had done, they would under-stand why he had had to stay out of contact for such long periods of time.

For the first half hour there was little to disturb Michael's patient sur-veillance. Between six-thirty and eight, however, it became increasingly difficult for him to keep his eyes facing forwards through the wind-screen. In his rear view mirrors he could see that in the slip road behind, groups of men were gathering in two and threes. Every now and then a transit van or a truck would drive by, speak to one of the groups and pick them up and drive them away. Over the years Michael had main-tained numerous early morning stake-outs but had never quite seen anything like this before. Most of the vans were unmarked, but just before seven one of them did a three point turn and he noticed the words 'JT Construction' written on the side. The slip road was obviously a pick-up point for casual labour. By eight o'clock, the last of the strag-glers had gone and Michael was able to return his full attention to the house. Nevertheless he was glad that he had seen the activity behind him. Some time soon he was going to have to start picking up a couple of days building work each week to help maintain his cover and, by good fortune, he had obviously stumbled across the best place in Feltham to find it.

Harper came out at ten past ten. Hastily screwing the top back on to the bottle of water from which he had been drinking, Michael reached inside his jacket pocket for the tiny pair of micro-binoculars that he had purchased at the camera shop when he had picked up his jacket and the camera the previous day. Harper was wearing a baggy, faded green T-shirt, the arms of which had been ripped off to give it a purposefully ragged appearance. His complexion was pale as though he had only had a few hours sleep and he clearly hadn't shaved for two or three days. Leaning forwards in his seat, Michael watched Harper walk out of sight behind the electrical store on the corner of the street only to reappear a few moments later with a paper and a bottle of milk. Unable to get the binoculars to focus sharply enough, Michael could not identify the newspaper exactly, but got the clear impression it was not a tabloid. It was his first clue about the fraudsters: this one, at least was bright enough to want to read an intellectually demanding newspaper. Putting down the binoculars as Harper disappeared back into the house, Michael scratched his cheek thoughtfully, wondering whether the fraudsters' system involved computers and, if so, what the implications would be of having to seek some specialist help.

The rest of the morning was quiet, but then, at twelve thirty-five, Michael found himself facing a crunch decision. Seeing Harper leaving the house again – this time carrying a jacket and some sort of small package – Michael had to decide whether to stay where he was or leave the car and follow him on foot. Sensing by his purposeful stride that Harper had a clear destination in mind, he got out of the car, locked the door and, jumping quickly over the small brick wall at the end of the slip road, followed him in the direction of the Uxbridge Road. When he had caught up to within about thirty yards, he reached in his top pocket and pushed the ring volume control button on the mobile phone upwards.

'The man up ahead is Geoffrey Harper,' said Michael in a steady voice – conscious that his personal observations would be a vital feature of the documentary series. 'I'm following him from his home – or what I understand to be his home – in East Feltham. Hang on. He's turning off the road up ahead here. I don't know where he's going but I certainly don't want to get too close. Or at least not yet.'

Reaching the corner of the road, he was just in time to see Harper disappearing into a large, scruffy looking pub called The White Horse. Noticing a Newsagents shop on the other side of the road, he slipped through the busy Uxbridge Road traffic to buy a newspaper: no one looks at a man sitting on his own in a pub reading a paper. Leaning forwards to pick up one of the tabloids, he stopped mid-movement and instead chose a copy of *The Racing Post* which he purchased along with a fifty pence biro. The horses. They'd been kind to him once – before the debts had got serious – perhaps they would be again.

'A pint of lager, please.'

The barman nodded and took a glass off the shelf. Out of the corner of his eye, Michael could see Harper at a pool table at the far end of the bar, holding a cue in one hand and a hand-rolled cigarette in the other. Resting his elbows on the counter, Michael turned and casually glanced in the direction of the pool table. There were three men with him; two of average build and the third youngish, but very tall – taller even than Michael. As they were concentrating on the game and were not looking in his direction, he continued to stare at them whilst the barman poured his drink. None of the other three men appeared in the file – he was certain of that – he had been staring at the photographs for weeks and knew every one of their faces by now. The two smaller men were standing side by side and had what looked like paint stains on their clothes. Michael wasn't sure, but he guessed they were a couple of workmen on their lunch break who had somehow got into a game of pool with Harper and his friend.

'Two pound thirty.'

'Thanks,' replied Michael, turning around and handing the barman a five pound note. Sitting down at a table at the other end of the bar he took off his jacket and placed it on the seat next to him with the top button facing back across the room. The pool table was at least fifteen yards away and the light inside the dingy pub was poor – he wondered how the camera would cope.

It was ten minutes before he looked up again from his scribbled calculations in the margins of *The Racing Post*. The workmen had gone. Harper and his friend were playing a game together, the latter in particular seeming to concentrate intently on his shots – the two men evidently took their pool seriously. Taking a swig from his glass, Michael allowed himself his first proper, uninterrupted stare at Harper. Standing straight-backed with his cue by his side and with his distinctive plumed haircut, he seemed to possess a rigid, almost soldierly stature. Placing his glass back on the table, Michael recalled a pub in South London called 'The English Bowman' that he and Elizabeth had frequented in the early days of their courtship. On the brightly painted sign outside there had been an illustration of an archer depicted in a similarly erect pose holding a longbow by his side. But whereas that man had valiantly fought for King and country, this one cynically defrauded them both. Harper's friend potted a shot, stood upright and then held out his hand with a smile. Reaching into his back pocket Harper took out a ten pound note and passed it across to him grudgingly.

'Time to make myself scarce,' whispered Michael, leaning over the microphone. 'I don't want to make myself too conspicuous, and besides, I've had my fill of watching these two gambling away taxpayer's money.'

Without a second look at Harper or his friend, Michael replaced his glass on the bar and left the pub.

He got back to the flat about twenty minutes later. Checking his watch, he could see that the phone still had over half an hour to run before he could download its contents. Removing it from his top pocket, Michael decided to film himself getting to grips with a task that had been nagging away at him ever since he had arrived in the flat – that of finding a safe repository for the video tapes that he would amass of Harper and the other fraudsters. At first he had thought about mailing them to Tom at the safe house, but had quickly dismissed the idea because he would not be able to refer to them at short notice if he so needed: the tapes wouldn't just contain the eventual documentary footage, they would also be a valuable audio-visual library of everything he learned about the fraudsters. The problem was that the flat had no storage place whatsoever beyond a cupboard in the hall and another in the bedroom and if he stacked the cassettes up on a shelf in the living room they could be discovered too easily.

'What I need is a hiding place,' said Michael, holding up the phone to his face; he had to get used to recording his thoughts aloud whenever the camera was running. Walking through into the kitchen he ran his hands over the chimney breast – the only one in the flat that had not been removed. Whereas he had felt quite able to paint it, he doubted he would be skilled enough to take out its bricks and convert it into a workable yet fully concealed storage cabinet. Back in the hallway he looked at the cupboard. It probably wouldn't be too difficult to rig up some sort of false bottom, but it was made of such cheap MDF board that one hefty kick and the whole thing would fall apart. Suddenly, Michael caught sight of a piece of threadbare carpet in the passageway leading to the front door. Kneeling down, he removed the wicker entrance mat and examined the faded turquoise carpet underneath. It must have been laid down a very long time ago because the tacks – which were loose along the edges of the wall – were of the old-fashioned, dangerously sharp type that had long since been replaced by underfloor grips. Pulling the carpet and underlay away, he looked at the dusty floor boards beneath and then balanced the mobile phone against the wall so that he could record what he was going to do next.

'This is where I'm going keep the tapes,' he said, hoping that the light in the gloomy passageway was strong enough for the camera to pick out the cavity below the two floor boards he had just pulled up. 'I'll have to wrap them in polythene to keep out the dust – it's filthy down here – but it's pretty dry and there should be enough room for a couple of dozen cassettes.'

For the next twenty minutes he experimented with re-laying the carpet such that if anyone ever did get into the flat looking for evidence of his activities there would be nothing to indicate the hiding place beneath. The narrowness of the passageway was a major advantage. There was so little room to manoeuvre inside it that, having got through the front door, one immediately felt impelled to walk straight into the hallway ahead. When one looked back towards the passageway from the hall, its sole purpose appeared to be that of providing a space in which the front door could swing on its hinges. As long as he made sure each time to push the tacks back firmly into place, Michael was certain that no one but the most determined investigator would ever find his hiding place.

Sitting down on the sofa, Michael placed the mobile phone on the cushion next to him. Keeping his hand on the battery pack, he waited for the tape to reach the end. Five minutes later, just as Jim had described, the ring volume button slipped silently back into the off position without any perceptible vibration; it was good to know that the phone switched itself off without making a noise. Moving across the room to the VCR that he had purchased the previous week, Michael slipped in a cassette and, having placed one end of the digital download cable into the phone and the other into the socket on the back of the video recorder, switched on the television.

The sound was perfect; the images razor sharp. Shaking his head in admiration, Michael took a bottle of whisky out of the sideboard and poured himself a celebratory glass. What an incredible device. Tom would be amazed when he saw the quality of the footage. And it wasn't just the standard of reproduction, either. As the download proceeded, Michael found he was able to watch the whole game of pool between Harper, the tall man and the two painters that he had been unable observe in the pub through fear of being caught staring. When Jim had told him that the phone cost three thousand six hundred pounds he had thought it probably a little overpriced, but he now realized he had got more than his money's worth. The game ended with Harper and his friend winning comfortably. Again he saw ten pounds disappearing into the tall man's back pocket. Pouring himself another whisky he sat back in the chair thoughtfully. Harper and his friend obviously liked to gamble.

And so, of course, did Micky Angel.

'Where you from, then?'

'Yorkshire.'

'Yeah? Where?'

'Small town. You wouldn't know it.'

Playing a safety shot, Michael took a few steps backwards and, picking his packet of cigarettes up off the window sill, unhurriedly lit one up. The tall man, whose name was Jez, cast a suspicious look at Harper who stared back at him impassively: when they had arrived at The White Horse together at ten past twelve they had found Michael practising at the table by himself. Having ordered a pint for himself and Harper, Jez had then immediately come over and suggested a match for a ten pound bet. The game had gone slowly at first as Jez had tried to determine whether Michael was any good or not, but the tempo was now beginning to pick up.

'Twelve. Top left,' announced Jez, leaning over the table. Michael had noticed on the tape that it was habit to proclaim in advance of taking a shot which ball he intended to pot and into which pocket, despite the fact the rules didn't call for it. As the purple twelve clunked into the top pocket, Michael took a swig of his drink. Psychological tactics were one thing. Skill was another.

'What d'you think of it down south, then?' asked Jez, dropping to his knees to get a better view of his next shot. 'Nine, bottom right.'

'Ahh, it's all right, I suppose,' replied Michael, disinterestedly – his flattened Yorkshire vowels seeming to imply that he had not yet deigned to give the matter much thought.

'Been here long?'

'A couple of weeks.'

'New kid on the block, huh?' replied Jez, slamming the nine into the bottom right pocket with an elaborate flourish. From his menacing expression when he had asked for the game, Michael could tell that Jez had felt territorially threatened at having found someone already ensconced on his favourite table. 'You played a lot of pool up north, did you? Sixteen, top right.'

'A bit,' replied Michael, recalling the three hours he had spent at Feltham municipal leisure centre the previous afternoon practising in turn on each of their four tables. At the end of the session he had come to the conclusion that unless both pool table and balls were properly maintained it was impossible to rely on the same shot always producing the same result. As if to prove him right, the sixteen ball bounced frantically back and forth between the lips of the top pocket and then suddenly stopped, seeming to lose all momentum just at the point at which it was about to drop in: the baize in front of the pocket must have a minute ruffle. Michael looked around the table. The spotted balls that he had to pot were bunched together quite nicely and only the purple seemed to require a difficult shot to lever it off the cushion.

'Yours,' announced Jez, taking a step backwards. Although he had an unnecessarily ostentatious style, Michael judged him nevertheless to be a reasonably proficient player who probably won more games than he lost. At the far end of the table, seemingly indifferent to the match, Harper was taking tobacco out of a large metal tin and rolling himself a cigarette. One by one, Michael patiently set about potting the spotted balls. Having sunk four of them in succession, he attempted a screw shot on the yellow but missed it. All the same, he still had only three balls left to pot; the yellow, the problematic purple and the last ball – the black. Jez, on the other hand, had four, all of which, as a direct result of his hard-hitting style, were widely spread around the table and would thus require a series of long pots. Returning to the table with a swagger, Jez resumed his bravura self-commentary.

112

'Ten bottom left. No problem. Fifteen top right. Thank you. Eleven top right. And, last of all thirteen. Top right again.'

He missed.

Walking to the far end of the table, Jez stood ostentatiously shoulder to shoulder with Harper, who was now absent-mindedly smoking his roll-up. The threat that Jez was attempting to imply – lose, or risk being beaten up – was very clear, although Michael got the distinct feeling that Harper would not necessarily back his friend up. Brushing the blue chalk across the tip of his cue, Michael returned to the table. The worst thing he could do would be deliberately to flunk his shots – if at any future point he ever came under suspicion Harper would remember that on the very first day that they had met Michael had purposely shied away from beating and thus offending Jez. But, conversely, if a fight did break out it might ruin any chance of his ever getting close to Harper at all.

The yellow went in easily. Standing back from the table to take a swig of his beer, Michael looked around the pub. The barman, who had obviously sensed the increasingly tense atmosphere around the pool table, had stopped polishing glasses and was staring nervously across at the game. Michael looked at Jez. He guessed his age at not much more than twenty-five. Despite his size, Michael doubted he could fight, although instinctively he would know how to brawl. Turning his gaze back towards the table, Michael weighed up his options. The simplest shot would be to direct the purple to the same top left pocket into which Jez had failed to sink the eight. He would have to strike it just that fractionally bit harder.

'What's your name, mate?' asked Jez, suddenly.

'Mick,' replied Michael, moving forwards to the table.

The purple hit the left hand jaw and disappeared into the pocket. Only the black was left with a medium distance pot to the middle pocket – an easier shot than the one he had just made. He looked across at Jez and saw his eyes narrow. Bending over the table, he remembered his argument with Tom in the office on the day that he had been fired. Character. If you wanted to be convincing, you either acted in character or not at all. Across the bar he could see his copy of *The Racing Post* protruding from the pocket of his jacket. Michael Angel was a gambling man. He bet to win, not to lose.

The black went straight in.

'Ten quid, yeah?' he said, walking over to Jez who stared back at him unspeaking. Michael doubted that Jez had concluded he was a pool ace who scoured the bars looking for unsuspecting amateurs to fleece – his play had been too careful and ponderous for that – but nevertheless some deep feral instinct inside the young man's brain was clearly telling him that he had been beaten in a way and for a reason that he did not fully understand.

'I don't think so,' he answered finally.

'Don't pay your debts down south, then?'

Scowling, Jez took a step forward as though preparing to punch Michael, but the instant he moved forward Harper called out from behind.

'Pay the man, Jez.'

'But …'

Harper shook his head once. Despite his friend's comment, Jez turned back towards Michael again, his lip curled in a sneer, seemingly wanting to start a fight after all, but just at that moment there was a loud commotion at the door and the two painters whom Michael had seen on his first day in The White Horse came noisily in. Immediately sensing the atmosphere of tension they joined everyone else in the pub in staring at Michael and Jez.

'Ten pounds,' repeated Michael, holding out his hand. After a further moment's indecision, Jez's shoulders finally dropped and he reached into his back pocket and handed the money over.

'You wanna be careful, Mick,' he said, his eyes narrowing once more, 'careful you don't go round pissing off the wrong sort of people.'

Ignoring the comment, Michael picked up his drink and cigarettes and went back into the bar area to get his jacket. Finishing off his pint, he turned to leave the pub and, as he did so, saw Harper watching him move towards the door. For a second their eyes met and Michael could see a brief, humourless smile pass across his face. Letting the double doors slam behind him, Michael walked casually off across the car park. It was hard to judge the significance of that look – like all of Harper's mannerisms that he had so far observed, it had been brief and inexpressive – but whereas it hadn't gone as far as to denote approval, neither had it seemed to indicate any hint of suspicion.

Making his way back to the flat in the bright afternoon sunshine Michael found his plans for the next month falling clearly into place.

Three or four times a week, at different hours during the day, he would go back to The White Horse and immerse himself in that day's copy of *The Racing Post*. He had made his presence known and now he had to play the patience game. If he saw Harper or Jez he would pay them no attention – just as he had done on the first day that he had gone to the pub: to place himself so directly in their path once more after such a tense first meeting would be to risk alerting their suspicions. Only after a few weeks, once they had got used to seeing him around, would he be able to make his second approach. As for the other fraudsters, whom he had not yet tracked down, he would have to ignore them for the time being. There could be no more surveillance whilst he was pursuing Harper: if he was spotted anywhere near the houses of the other gang members, he would be finished. Reaching inside his top pocket he ran his hand over the mobile phone. Despite the fact that Jez now resented him, he didn't regret the way he had played the game. Maintaining the integrity of his cover was an absolute priority: as long as it remained intact, so would he. Next week he would go in search of the building work that was essential to his persona as the solitary, casual labourer. He was looking forward to it. Not just because it would allow him to enter right into the character of Michael Angel, but also because his brief was to show the world Britain's faceless villains and he had a very strong suspicion that attempting to authenticate his story for this first group of anonymous criminals was going to propel him straight into the midst of a second.

Chapter 5

Michael went to the slip road on foot, arriving there just before five to seven. Taking up a position about fifty yards short of the spot from which he had observed Harper's house, he stood waiting for the first of the vans to arrive, rubbing his hands together against the early morning cold. He had left his jacket and phone at home on purpose: although it was chilly now, it would be sweltering by eleven o'clock and not knowing where he might end up that day he didn't dare risk having them stolen. Apart from Michael and a group of three men standing behind him the slip road was deserted. It had been a Monday when he had carried out the surveillance of Harper's house, but today was a Wednesday. He guessed that a lot of jobs ran on a weekly basis and that on the first day of the week contractors would try and secure all the labour they needed for the following five days. Nevertheless the presence of the three men seemed to suggest that work could be found mid-week and so he lit up a cigarette and waited patiently for a prospective employer to show up. He had no idea what the going rate was for a day's casual labour. For today, at least, he would just have to take whatever he was offered.

At seven fifteen a large white transit van pulled up in front of the three men. After a short conversation the driver got out and then opened up the back of the van to let them get in. Slamming the doors, he stared undecidedly across at Michael for a moment, but then climbed in himself and drove away. Gazing at the now empty road, Michael frowned and looked at his watch. If he had had no joy by nine thirty, he'd go back to the flat: maybe Wednesday was too late in the week after all. Moments later, however, a 4 X 4 Landcruiser came speeding around the corner and pulled up directly in front of him.

'Lookin' for work, mate?'

'Yeah.'

'I got some drillin' if you're interested – a bit of hoddin', too.'

'How much you payin'?'

'Fifty quid a day – take it or leave it.'

'OK.'

'Hop in then, quick. I'm late.'

Not bothering with a three point turn, the man bumped the Landcruiser over the opposite pavement and sped off back down the slip road again.

'What's your name?'

'Michael.'

'You've done drillin' before, ain't you?' It was more of a statement than a question.

'A bit,' lied Michael.

'I'm Roger,' said the man, extending his hand for Michael to shake but without taking his eyes off the road. 'I'm glad I found you – I've got a real rush job on. Groundworks. I gotta get 'em finished by Friday or I'm in dead shit.'

'Yeah?'

'Yeah. I've got a whole stack of concrete that needs breaking up. I had a bloke lined up to do it for the rest of the week but he fuckin' pulled out on me. A Croat he was – they're lazy bastards, they are. You ain't a Croat, are you?'

'No.'

'Thank God for that.'

With a resentful grunt that seemed to indicate their conversation was now at an end, Roger stretched over to the dashboard and switched on the radio. Leaning back in his seat, Michael rubbed his hand over his jaw thoughtfully. This was an excellent start. It had been the awkwardly tailored clothes and swarthy complexions of the labourers he had seen in his rear view mirror the previous week that had made him suspect that the majority of them were illegal foreign workers – presumably of Southern and Eastern European origin. Looking around the 4 X 4's plush interior, Michael guessed that Roger made a very handsome living out of paying them below the minimum wage and skimming off their tax and national insurance contributions to boot. Having arranged to meet Tom at the safe house on Friday to show him the footage of Harper and Jez, he had decided to suggest that whilst tracking the fraud-ring he could explore the murky world of illegal immigrant labour as a possible subject for the third documentary. It would be easy for him to research the issue as obtaining casual labouring work was essential for his Michael Angel cover. Moreover, the two topics complemented each other perfectly: Roger was just as guilty of defrauding the British tax-payer by not contributing to the exchequer as Harper was by stealing from it.

Twenty minutes later, in a street on the outskirts of East Feltham, the Landcruiser came to a halt outside the remains of what appeared once to have been a brick-built warehouse. Stepping out of the car, Michael looked at the rusting metal screen in front of him that was supposed to cordon the site off from the pavement. It was just as well the houses opposite were derelict and uninhabited – shaking in the early morning breeze, the rickety safety panel looked ready to collapse at any moment.

'I've got to go and get some derv for the scoop,' shouted Roger through the passenger window, pointing to a small bulldozer parked next to the building's one remaining wall. 'Go and see Naz, he'll sort you out …'

As the 4 X 4 roared off down the street, Michael turned to look at the site. There were five other workmen, all of whom were foreign – judging by their dark skin colour possibly from North Africa or the Middle East. Walking up to the first of them, a broad-shouldered man in a baseball cap who was brewing a kettle over a portable stove, Michael asked where he could find Naz. The man didn't reply but merely smiled – a set of brilliant white teeth appearing in the middle of his thick, dark beard – and pointed towards a second man who was standing on a flat patch of concrete about twenty-five yards away. Picking his way through the bricks and rubble strewn across the site, Michael approached him – although only in his late twenties, he was obviously the site foreman.

'Are you Naz?'

'Yes, yes, I am Naz,' replied the man with a smile, extending his hand for Michael to shake. 'How do you do?' He had a deep baritone voice that rumbled up richly from the base of his chest.

'Er, fine, yeah. I'm Mick. Roger told me to come and see you. You've got some drillin' you need doin', right?'

'Oh, yes, yes, good,' he answered, stamping his foot on the concrete platform on which they were standing. 'Is this. We have to break this.'

'Yeah?'

'Yes. Is big job for one man, I think. But I help you later when my friends have knocked down wall, OK?'

'Yeah, yeah, OK.'

He was several inches smaller than Michael and thinner too, but beneath his open neck cheese-cloth shirt his muscles were sinewy and taut: Michael guessed that he was physically very strong indeed. Unlike the first man, he did not have a beard, so the full extent of his intelligent, although somewhat forlorn face, was revealed.

'Where's the drill, then?'

'This way, come, I show you,' replied Naz, walking across to the other end of the platform.

'Are we supposed to get this all broken up today?' said Michael, following after him.

'Roger he say yes, but I think no. Is two days work, maybe three.'

'So we're not gonna finish by Friday, then?'

'With more men, maybe, but we are only five – six with you now. Is not enough. These are drills. You pick one you like. I take other later.'

Michael looked at the two battered, grimy machines. There was almost nothing to distinguish them from the various other pieces of scrap metal lying abandoned around the site: if they hadn't been leaning up against the portable generator he would probably have failed to notice them altogether.

'This one'll do. Shall I get started?'

'Is good idea. Later it will be hot. You make start now, you take more rest later. You want cuppa?'

'Er, yeah, yeah. Thanks. No sugar.'

'OK, I bring over you ten minutes. You start concrete this end first, OK?'

Smiling again at Michael, Naz switched on the portable generator and moved briskly off across the site. Gingerly picking up the pneumatic drill, Michael walked over to the edge of the concrete and took up position. The functions of the two buttons on the front – red and green respectively – were self-evident, but he wasn't sure about the metal bar underneath the left of the grip handles. It was probably a throttle – he would just have to try it out and see. Looking up to make sure that neither Naz nor any of the other workmen were close enough to observe his efforts, he hit the green button and then squeezed.

The noise was ear-splitting and Michael had to fight back an instinctive urge to let go of the throttle immediately. At first the drill seemed to bite into the concrete but then suddenly skidded off at a tangent. Releasing the throttle to stop the machine from shooting out of his hands, Michael looked around the site. Thankfully none of the other men were paying him any attention. Pressing the throttle again, he activated the drill once more and this time it punctured the surface of the concrete and he was able to make a small incision of about six inches in length. He guessed the right way to proceed would be to fit the drill bit into the hole he had just created and then work his way forwards across the stretch of concrete.

By the time Naz reappeared with a mug of tea Michael had made what he thought was quite good progress, but when he hit the red button to switch the drill off he realized that not only were his ears and the sides of his head in pain, but that his fingers were already starting to blister.

'You got any gloves or anythin'?' he asked Naz.

'You no bring own gloves?'

'No.'

'Oh.'

'Won't Roger have some?'

'No,' replied Naz, his brow furling in a mixture of sympathy with Michael's predicament and surprise at his question. 'Roger no give gloves or hats or things. He say safety gear your problem, not mine. But there is shop on main road down street, I think. You can go buy later maybe …?'

'Oh, yeah, I'll do that. Thanks for the tea.'

'Is new work for you, yes?'

'Er, yeah, sort of,' replied Michael: although he hadn't noticed Naz watching him, his amateurism must have been all too apparent even from fifty yards away.

'Here, you drink tea. I show you.'

Gripping the machine tightly to the lower part of his body, Naz raised himself up over the drill and, keeping his arms absolutely straight, leant his full weight down on top of it.

'Stand in this way. Make short drilling. One, two, three … off! One, two, three … off! Like this, see?'

120

Slamming the green button on the front, Naz made several slow forward movements with the drill. It seemed to cut through the concrete like butter.

'Oh, right. I got you.'

'See. Is easy.'

'Thanks, thanks.'

'And these. You take these. Is extra pair.'

Putting his hand into his shirt pocket, Naz pulled out two small plastic bungs and handed them over to Michael.

'Great. Thanks.'

'You no go deaf now.'

With a wink and a smile, Naz turned on his heel and made his way across to the front of the site where the Landcruiser had just pulled up and Roger was already noisily shouting instructions. Taking a sip of his tea, Michael looked at his watch. 08:20. It was going to be a long day.

Naz and the four other men turned out to be renting a house together in East Feltham. Just after five o'clock, when Roger had chained up the bulldozer for the night, he came over to Michael and offered to give him a lift back with them. Although Balam Road was situated at the other end of Feltham, a good three miles away, he decided to accept – if he could, he wanted to get some time with Naz on his own.

'You done good today, Mick. Are you all right for the next couple of days?' asked Roger, peeling off fifty pounds from the enormous wodge of notes that he kept in the inside pocket of his jacket.

'Tomorrow, yeah, but not Friday, though,' answered Michael, thinking both of his meeting with Tom and his aching shoulders and back; after several more weeks he would no doubt toughen up, but for now, two consecutive days of this hard, physical labour was probably his limit.

'What's the matter, got a better offer?' replied Roger, sourly, slapping the notes into Michael's swollen hand.

'Somethin' like that,' answered Michael.

'What about Saturday – if we run over?'

Even though the six of them had worked like Trojans that day, it was fairly plain even to Michael that there was still a good three days work left before the site would be ready for the construction team who were due to arrive the following week.

'Yeah, I suppose so.'

'I'll talk to you tomorrow night, then, before you go for your day off,' replied Roger unpleasantly, walking off towards the Landcruiser.

Pushing the notes into his inside pocket, Michael looked around at the other five men who were collecting up their gear for the night. He hadn't seen Roger handing money over to any of them, so presumably they were paid weekly. He wondered how much they were getting; whatever it was, it wasn't enough. Seeing Naz unscrewing the generator power cables, Michael jumped over a pile of bricks and walked across to catch him while he was by himself.

'Hey, Naz, you fancy a drink tonight?'

'Oh, er, no, I'm sorry I cannot.'

'I'm payin' mate. I owe you for today, like. You helped me out right well.'

'No, is OK, Mick, thank you.'

'No, I'm serious. I really appreciated it. And anyway, listen, I was lucky on the horses earlier this week. You gotta let me buy you a pint. I'll have to drink on me own otherwise.'

'Oh, OK, I think about it ...' replied Naz, walking away with a slightly troubled smile. Michael guessed that it wasn't just lack of money, but that he thought it would be disloyal to go off and leave his friends. Although he was the youngest of the group, Michael could easily see why he had come to act as their foreman and spokesperson; tireless and resourceful, he possessed that particular combination of concern and competence common to the best team leaders everywhere.

'Come on, come on!' shouted Roger. 'You might not have wives to go home to but mine's got dinner on the table!'

Running from all corners of the site like school children streaming across the playground at home-time, the six men converged on the Landcruiser, crammed together into it and were soon on their way. Ten minutes later they arrived at the junction of two narrow residential streets and one by one got out on to the pavement. Michael looked to his left and right trying to recall if he had passed down any of these roads during his two weeks of searching for Thompson, Harper and the other fraudsters, but none of them seemed familiar.

'Six-thirty here tomorrow, boys – on the dot, all right?' called Roger. 'What about you, Mick. Can you make it here by then?'

'No, it's all right, I'll make my own way to the site.'

'Don't get lost, now, will you? I had enough hassle with that Croat wanker. I don't wanna have to go looking for somebody new two days runnin'.'

Ignoring the comment, Michael turned his back and walked over to speak to Naz. He had only been working for Roger for a day, but had already found that he only needed to glimpse his new boss's face to be gripped by an overwhelming desire to punch it in.

'So, what about it, Naz? Got time for a pint?'

Naz seemed just about to refuse again when Mustafa, the tall man in the baseball cap, called out something in what Michael now believed to be Turkish and waved his hand towards the end of the road. With a shrug, Naz turned to face Michael and smiled: his friends obviously didn't begrudge him a few minutes well-earned relaxation.

'OK, a drink with you, my friend. Thank you. We go pub over there, maybe. Is OK?'

'Yeah, sure, sure.'

As they crossed over the road and made their way towards a large, old-fashioned pub at the end of the street, Michael looked back at the narrow, terraced house that the five men occupied. It was even less pre-possessing than his flat – two of the upstairs windows being boarded up with heavy fibreboard.

'What happened to your windows?'

'Is kids from Abaddon estate over there,' replied Naz, pointing towards three high-rise blocks on the horizon. 'They drive past – eighty, ninety miles an hour. They throw rocks and things. Is crazy.'

'Are they picking on you 'cos you're, like, foreign?'

'No, no, is not only us. All the houses, you see?'

Looking along the street, Michael could see that several other houses also had smashed or boarded windows.

'Wow, I can see what you mean.'

'For first three months we come here is not so bad – maybe only Friday, Saturday night. But two weeks ago, man down street, he fed up, he bring out gun and shoot at kids one night. Boom. Boom. Since then, oh, is crazy.'

'What, you mean it's got worse?' asked Michael, incredulously.

'Now, is every night,' replied Naz with a doleful shake of the head. 'For the kids it is a – how you say – big dare. Now they throw rocks to see if they can escape crazy man with gun.'

'What about the police?'

'Kids throw rocks them too,' replied Naz with a shrug, opening up the door of the pub and letting Michael go through.

'What d'you want. Lager? Bitter?' asked Michael, walking over to the barman who was standing half-in half-out of the service hatch smoking a cigarette.

'Pint lager, please. I like English bitter but is so hot today, yeah?'

'Yeah, you're right,' replied Michael, indicating Naz to sit down and ordering two pints. As he watched the barman pour the beer, Michael thought about asking Naz how he had got in the UK but then decided against it. Just as with Harper, he needed to be patient – needed to take time to work his way into the Turk's confidence.

'So, here's to you and, er, thanks for today,' said Michael, as he passed the glass across to Naz and sat down opposite him.

'Thank you, Mick. Cheers.'

Putting down his glass, Michael wiped the back of his hand across his mouth. He couldn't recall the last time that beer had tasted this good.

'So, is Naz your full name, then?'

'No, no, is Nasruddin.'

'I thought so: I heard one of the others call you that.'

'Nasruddin is Turkish hero. Seven hundred years ago. Very famous. My parents call me after him. Funny man – write funny stories – you should read one day.'

'Yeah, I'd like to. So, is that where you're all from then, Turkey?'

'Hm,' replied Naz with a nod.

'Which bit?'

'Pardon?'

'Where in Turkey, which town?'

'Oh, I am from very small village. You don't know, I think.'

'Me too, I'm from a small village as well. Nobody's heard of it in London, either.'

'Yes?'

'Yeah.'

'Is nice place?'

'Oh yeah, beautiful.'

'So why you leave – come London? Huh? Work on buildings?' asked Naz with a frown.

'I had some problems. My marriage split up. I lost my job, my house – you know ...'

124

'Sorry. I should not ask.'

'That's all right, forget it. So, what about you? How long have you been in London?'

'One years before. I stay one more year. I send money home to family. We all do same. Me, my friends.'

'Why did you choose England?'

'Is easy get job here. Easiest in Europe, I think. Before England I go Germany. Three months. I have cousin there, but is bad – very bad. You have no ID card, police they chase you all time, you know? But here, police no care. Too busy chase hooligan with rocks. Ha!'

With a doleful smile, Naz took another sip of his beer. Although he was obviously starting to relax, Michael decided not to quiz him any further about his homeland: it would be better to let him volunteer the information in his own time, or return to the subject again in a subsequent conversation. Meanwhile, tomorrow or possibly on Saturday, after he had filmed the dangers of the building site, he would try and get some footage of Naz's house. If the inside was as depressing as the outside it would make powerful viewing.

'When did you start workin' for Roger then?'

'Is second week. We finish this Saturday, then no more – he not live London like us.'

'No?'

'No. Some town north of London. I don't know.'

'Is this what you mostly do, then, groundworks? That sort of thing?'

'We find work, we take it. Buildings, car wash, kitchen – anything.'

'What did you do back in Turkey?'

'In Turkey I train electronic engineer.'

'An engineer? What you doin' in England, then?'

'No work. I could go Istanbul – big city – look for electronic job, maybe, but not easy to find. My wife, my son, my parents – they need money now. They cannot wait.'

For the second time in just over a week, Michael felt a pang of loneliness for Elizabeth and Jake. If he called for a taxi he could be at their flat within an hour, although just like the family of the weary, mournful man seated opposite, they may as well have been a thousand miles away.

'Have you got a picture of them?'

'A picture?'

'Yeah, you know, a photograph of your wife and son.'

'Yes, I have picture. But not here. Back in house.'

'Will you show me?'

'Yes, I show you, my friend,' replied Naz, gently. 'You come our house one night. I happy show you.'

'I'd like that very much,' said Michael, meaning every word of it.

For the first couple of seconds after the video of the pool game had finished, Tom said nothing, but merely sat on the edge of the sofa, slowly shaking his head from side to side. Since Michael's initial visit to the safe house six weeks previously, Tom had acquired some quite decent items of furniture for it, although, for some reason that he could not quite fathom, he rather preferred the place as it had been before, empty and characterless.

'Spot on, old boy,' said Tom, finally. 'Absolutely spot on.'

'You like it, then?'

'It's exactly what Henry's got in mind. Exactly.'

'Glad to hear it.'

'How many times have you seen Harper since this was taken?'

'Twice.'

'In The White Horse?'

'Yeah, both times.'

'But you didn't talk to him or make contact in any way?'

'No. I just sort of spotted him out of the corner of my eye. You know, I was aware he was there, but I didn't take things any further.'

'And did he see you?'

'Yeah, I'm almost certain he did.'

'How long are you going to leave it before you approach him again?'

'I dunno – a week, ten days maybe.'

'What are you going to say to him?'

'I'm not sure. I haven't decided yet.'

'What about the other one. The one you nearly had the fight with?'

'Jez?'

'Yeah, him.'

'He seems to have disappeared,' replied Michael, walking across to the table and pouring himself a cup of coffee; Tom had also procured a coffee-maker for the flat along with a microwave and a fridge-freezer. 'I mean I was there for nearly three hours at lunch time the other day and he never showed up the whole time.'

'Maybe you scared him off.'

'I don't think so, somehow,' answered Michael, doubtfully.

'What about this system of theirs – have you had any more ideas?'

'Not as such,' replied Michael, 'but one thing I have discovered is that Thompson seems to have flown the roost.'

'Really?'

'Yes. I went around to the house – it was the second address I visited. I mean, I can't be sure but I got the distinct impression he's not there any more.'

'Do you think he might have moved to another patch – another district altogether?'

'I thought so at first – in fact, I was quite worried to be honest. If the gang is mobile I don't want to be chasing them up and down the country. But given that Harper's still there and the other addresses I visited all seem to be inhabited, my guess is that it's just Thompson who's particularly careful not to stay in one place for too long.'

'Hm. So, what next?'

'More trips to The White Horse – three, four times a week. Meanwhile, I've found something else to work on ...'

'Oh, yes?'

'Yeah. This.'

Taking a video tape out of the inside pocket of his jacket, Michael passed it over to Tom.

'What is it?'

'It's footage of the building site I'm working on at the moment. I took it yesterday. Apart from me it's entirely manned by illegal immigrant labour.'

'Really?' said Tom, holding up the cassette tape with interest.

'Really. There are six of us and the contractor – a bloke called Roger. Two weeks work and not a single penny's gone to the exchequer. No income tax, no national insurance, nothing. It's a total black economy venture.'

'Interesting.'

'The site's a health and safety disaster, too. No protective clothing, no hard hats, no medical facilities if anything should go wrong – or not as far as I could see. There aren't even any toilets: we have to go to the public ones three hundred yards away on the main road.'

'So, what are you thinking?'

'King wants me to find him the faceless criminals – the parasites that feed off the rest of society, right? Take a look at Roger if you want to see a prime parasite in action and then tell me what you think. I'm going to try and follow him back to his home tomorrow evening – after the job's finished. I doubt he personally brings illegal immigrants into the country himself, but he certainly lives off them. The whole subculture's absolutely fascinating in a depressing sort of way. I mean these immigrant labourers work their guts out for an absolute pittance. It's modern-day slavery.'

'Are you thinking of researching the subject at the same time as filming Harper and the others?' asked Tom.

'I can't not research it. It's right before my very eyes every day. All I've got to do is turn on the camera and there it is in front of me.'

'OK, I'll take it away and watch it back at the office – if it looks right I'll show it to Henry, too and see what he thinks. Now, what about your family, how have you been coping?'

'Well enough, I suppose.'

'You haven't called ...'

'No, no,' interrupted Michael quickly. 'I felt like it, but I remembered what you said so I wrote this letter to Jake instead. It tells him that I'm getting on fine and the new job's great and everything.'

'Did you use the PO box address in Geneva I gave you?'

'Yes, I did.'

'Great,' said Tom, taking the envelope. 'I'll send it off to have it forwarded to him from there tomorrow – he should get it in about a week. I've already put the rumour around the Tower that you've moved to Geneva, by the way.'

'Great, thanks, Tom.'

'My pleasure. So! What about a drink, old boy? Celebrate your successes so far. It's not too early in the day is it?'

'It's never too early.'

'Right!'

Going over to the newly installed sideboard, Tom opened up the left hand cabinet. Inside were six unopened litre bottles of whisky.

'Jesus,' gasped Michael. 'That's not all for me, is it?'

'No, to tell you the truth, it isn't,' replied Tom, taking out one of the bottles and unscrewing the cap. 'I stop off here most evenings to check the answering machine and if we're going through a heavy spell at the office I sometimes stay overnight: a quick night-cap, head down and then the next morning fifteen minutes in a cab and I'm in the Tower. Wonderful! It certainly beats trudging all the way back to Kent on the last train. You don't disapprove do you?'

'No, no, not at all.'

'Good chap!'

As Tom poured out two generous doubles, grinning all the while like a schoolboy sharing his secret store of tuck, Michael looked on with a smile that slowly changed from mirth to admiration. At the Tower, Tom was widely regarded as something of a happy-go-lucky character – an enthusiastic amateur who had wandered into the clubhouse one Saturday morning and somehow ended up playing for the first team. Nobody doubted his thoroughness, his tact and his capacity for hard work, but such was his overwhelmingly convivial personality, that even the sharpest minds at The Tower were prone to attribute his achievements to a combination of charm and good fortune. The one exception was Henry King – and if his choice of Michael as the ideal operative for *Criminal Britain* had been exactly right, then his choice of Tom as his controller had been positively inspired. For who better to run an under-cover documentary series demanding the utmost secrecy than a man with the unique talent always to appear to be running along happily with the pack when he was in fact always one step ahead of it?

Michael arrived at the site just before eight o'clock on Saturday morning. Intending to follow Roger home that evening, he parked his car two streets away and then went the rest of the way on foot. For all his bluff vulgarity, Roger was a sharp operator – as long as he didn't know that Michael owned a car, there was no risk of him spotting it in the Landcruiser's sizeable rear-view mirror. As usual, Mustafa was brewing up the tea and, seeing Michael arrive, gave him a thumbs-up sign to indicate that a mug would be ready for him in a few minutes.

'Cheers, Muzzie!' shouted Michael, waving a hand in thanks and then walking over to Naz who was bending over unlocking the padlocks on the mini-bulldozer.

'OK, Naz?'

'Oh, Mick. Welcome back,' said Naz standing upright and shaking Michael's hand warmly. Looking into the Turk's delighted, beaming face, Michael felt less like a labourer coming back to work after a day off than a long departed son returning to the bosom of his family.

'Thanks. You got a lot done yesterday, didn't you?' replied Michael, looking around the now nearly completed groundworks. It was amazing to think that four days ago the site had been covered by the remains of an entire building.

'We work late last night. Extra money. Is good, you know?'

'Great. But you haven't left anything for me to do!'

'Oh, is plenty, Mick. You no worry, is plenty,' replied Naz with a grin.

'So, where's Roger then?'

'He come late today. Nine. He go pick up roller from hire people: we make surface nice smooth, you know?'

'Oh, OK,' replied Michael, stretching upwards and placing his jacket inside the cab of the bulldozer behind the seat.

Despite the fact that the site looked a lot neater, Naz proved to be correct in his assertion that there was a still a good deal of work left to do and Michael and the five Turks worked continuously until lunch time to remove the remaining rubble. By two o'clock they had at last begun to feel that the job was nearly complete, but then Roger suddenly announced that they needed to dig a long, shallow trench at the far end of the site. It was as he started to explain this in detail that Michael first began to suspect that something was wrong. There was only one set of plans relating to the site and Roger kept them with him all the time. When he showed them the location of the trench, Michael noticed that instead of spreading the plans flat out on the bonnet of his Landcruiser, he held them up in the air awkwardly in such a way that only the drawings were visible. There was clearly something around the margin of the plan – probably in the bottom right hand corner – that he didn't want them to see. Was it the name and address of the principal contractor for whom he was working? Was it his name and address? Michael wasn't sure, but mentally noted the fact for subsequent reference: perhaps when he followed him in the evening he would learn more. An hour later Roger told the men to remove all their belongings from the mini-bulldozer as the plant hire company closed early on Saturdays and he had to return it promptly along with the roller. After he had driven off, the men finished the trench and, having brewed up a final cup of tea, stood and surveyed the results of two weeks of toil. It was while Michael was looking around the completed site that it suddenly dawned on him what had happened.

'Naz, can I have word, mate?'

'Yes, Mick.'

'Erm, over here, like, in private?'

'Yes, my friend,' replied Naz, walking away from the other four men who were standing patiently with their gear packed waiting for Roger to return and take them back to their house.

'Can I ask you something?'

'Surely.'

'It's a bit personal, so, sorry and all that, but, er, did Roger pay you for that extra work yesterday?'

'No, he will pay tonight.'

'He's paying you weekly, is he?'

'Yes, yes, he pay last Friday for last week, today for this week. I have record here.'

So saying Naz reached into the back pocket of his jeans and extracted a small piece of paper on which he had carefully noted in pencil the hours that each man had worked over the previous eight days. Looking down at the pathetic little scroll that the Turk clutched in his dirt-stained hand, Michael shook his head in dismay. Ever since the morning at court when he had decided to accept King's offer he had expected that the experience of uncovering his first crime would be exquisitely sweet, but now all he felt was a sickening, sour taste in his stomach. Whilst the six of them had been working on the trench, Roger had stowed every last item of his equipment into the back of the Landcruiser.

'Do you have a phone number for Roger? A mobile or a home number or anything?' said Michael, knowing the answer to the question already.

'No,' replied Naz, his honest, handsome face still not betraying the remotest suspicion of what had befallen him.

'Oh, shit.'

'Something is wrong?'

'I'll get my car. You'd better tell the others.'

'Tell others what, Mick?'

'He's not coming back, Naz,' exhaled Michael, with weary sympathy. 'Not coming to take you home. Just because he paid you last week doesn't mean he's going to pay you this.'

'What! I no ...'

'He's a con man, mate. A thief. He's cheated us – cheated you. This was a cash in hand job – his hand. Because you don't know where he lives you can't go around to his house and get your money out of him. And because you're not working legally you can't report him to the police and get him taken to court.'

Finally, Naz understood. His facial muscles dropped, his mouth opened slightly and his sad grey eyes misted over with an air of stunned disbelief.

'We work hard. Why he …?'

Sensing that if he displayed even a fraction of the anger that he was feeling, it would upset Naz still further, Michael controlled himself and instead placed his hand on Naz's shoulder and squeezed it in sympathy.

'I'll get the car. It's going to be tight, but we should all fit in …'

Once around the corner, Michael let out a stream of curses not at Roger's deceit, but at his own wretched impotence. Although there was a shot of the Landcruiser's number plate on the tape he had made two days previously and given to Tom, he dare not risk jeopardizing his investigations by using it to hunt down Roger on behalf of his new-found friends: there could be no knowing where such a course of action might eventually lead. Grim-faced, he opened up the car and gunned the engine into life. Despite the warmth that they had showed him, he couldn't interfere, couldn't dissipate his efforts, couldn't do anything, in fact, that might compromise his cover: they had to fight their battles and he had to fight his. As he approached the five men standing crest-fallen on the pavement in front of the site, he recalled the two pages of hand-written notes from the former East European spy that Tom had procured for him to help him cope with living undercover. At first he had been surprised to discover that the spy had written about betrayal to the exclusion of all other subjects, but, little more than a month into his new identity, he was already beginning to understand what he had meant. So far he had only considered the guilt he might feel at betraying evil people whose trust he had gained. Pulling up by the side of the curb, he wondered if it could be any worse than the guilt he was feeling at having to turn his back on such generous men as these who had treated him as one of their own and whom he knew it was well within his power to help.

They did all fit in. Mustafa was so large, however, that he needed the front seat to himself meaning that the other four men were crushed on top of each other in the back. In other circumstances, they would have no doubt found the situation quite hilarious: six mates crammed into a motor on a Saturday night. But Naz and his friends weren't going out on the town, or even simply returning home to their families. As they drove across East Feltham in silence towards the house, Michael calculated what they had probably earned over the last two weeks based on the figures that he had seen on Naz's note. A hundred and seventy-five pounds for around a hundred and twenty hours back-breaking, physical labour. That equated to less than one pound fifty an hour. Paper boys probably got double that.

When they reached the house and got out of the car on to the pavement, things took a still further turn for the worse: the downstairs front window of their house had been smashed. During the day some of the youths from the Abaddon estate must have driven past and thrown a brick through it. Looking at his watch, Naz groaned in dismay. It was quarter past six. Michael then heard him mumble a sentence in Turkish to the other men that contained the word DIY. He guessed he was saying that the local hardware shops would already be closed and it was thus too late to buy some board to cover up the window. Hearing this, Mustafa's anger snapped and he ran over to the metal dustbin in front of the house and began kicking it violently, streams of enraged curses pouring from his mouth.

'Look, I'm really sorry, mate,' said Michael to Naz, conscious that his words could provide no consolation.

'Is OK, Mick, is OK. We work again next week.'

'If there's anything I can do, like ...'

'No, no, it's OK – you very kind. Thank you for ride.'

'Let's keep in touch, all right?'

'Yes, Mick, we do that.'

'I'll come around one night like you said. You can show me that photo of your wife and kid.'

The reference to his family was probably ill-judged and Naz could only manage a listless wave of the hand to bid Michael good bye. Turning towards the house Naz called out something to Mustafa who gave the bin one final despairing kick and then disappeared through the front door. Getting back into the car, Michael set off for Balam Road, but then changed his mind, deciding to head for The White Horse instead: he hadn't been there since Wednesday night and he really needed a drink to help block out what had happened that day. Twenty minutes later, though, as he turned off the Uxbridge Road towards the pub, Michael's blood once again hit boiling point. For there, occupying two whole spaces in the middle of the car park was Roger's Landcruiser.

Jamming on the brakes, Michael thought about leaving his car exactly where it was – blocking the exit to the car park so that Roger could not get out. But after a couple of seconds' thought, he positioned it in one of the unoccupied spaces. The White Horse was three and a half miles from the building site and Roger was probably not in too much of a hurry to get away: certain that the Turks didn't possess a car, and not knowing that Michael did, he must have returned the mini-bulldozer and the roller to the plant hire company and then stopped off for a drink before driving back up the motorway. Getting slowly out of his car, Michael looked down the Uxbridge Road across towards the elevated section of the M3 in the distance. It all made sense – The White Horse was the last pub before Apex Corner. Looking across at the Landcruiser again, Michael thought about going over and letting down one of the tyres but then changed his mind. There was only one exit from the pub – if he went straight in, Roger would be cornered.

'Mine's a pint of lager,' snarled Michael, coming to a halt behind Roger who was leaning casually up against the bar.

Roger was scowling as he turned around, but the instant he saw Michael every muscle in his face dropped.

'Mick …'

'A pint of lager,' repeated Michael, his voice as hard as granite.

'Yeah, yeah, sure,' said Roger, hurriedly, nodding at the barman and handing over a five pound note. 'So, where was you, then? I got back to the site and you'd all fucked off!'

Smiling grimly at Roger's rapidly returning bravura, Michael took out his cigarettes, lit one and leaned on the bar.

'How much did you make, Roger? Eh? On the whole deal.'

'Well, come on, that's my business, innit?' replied Roger, with fake cheeriness.

The Barman put the glass of lager on the bar in front of Michael, who stared at it for a moment and then turned to face Roger again.

'How much?' he repeated.

'Look,' said Roger, leaning forwards with a congenial smirk as though he and Michael were the oldest of friends. 'OK, I was taking the piss a bit. I'm sorry about that. I'll make it up to you. But those fuckin' Turks.

I couldn't give a shit about them. They don't even live here, do they? Arseholes. So, why don't we just …'

Roger never finished the sentence. Slamming his fist down on the counter Michael roared out.

'Every penny! You give me every fucking penny you owe us!!'

Standing back from the counter, Roger squared up to Michael. The only two people in their area of the bar rapidly moved out of their seats, and the far end of the pub, where the majority of customers were congregated, went completely quiet. To his left Michael could sense rather than see the Barman inching towards the telephone.

'Now, I'm still prepared to be reasonable about this,' said Roger, 'so like I said, why don't we just …'

Without finishing what he was about to say, Roger threw a punch at Michael, but Michael had been ready for it from the moment that he had walked into the pub: for three years whilst he had been at College he had studied judo and of the many lessons he had learnt, the first – and ever since the most consistently useful – was to feint to the left when an inexperienced opponent leads with their right.

Rolling with the blow, Michael balanced himself on the heel of his left foot and then kicked out at Roger's leg with his right. Despite the anger that was raging through his mind, he then began to calculate precisely the punch that he would throw next. Side stepping away from the bar to ensure that he could properly follow through and thus inflict maximum damage, he slammed his fist straight into Roger's right eye. Propelled across the room, Roger knocked over a table and landed in a heap next to the fireplace. Rubbing his grazed knuckles backwards and forwards over his lips, Michael then went slowly over and, leaning down, slipped his other hand into Roger's inside pocket. The roll of notes was enormous: he had probably got paid for the job that very evening. Splitting the notes down the middle he stuffed half back in Roger's pocket and then went over to the bar.

'Sorry about that,' he said to the Barman. 'D'you do off sales?'

'Yeah,' replied the Barman, nodding cautiously towards the rear of the counter.

'Twenty cans of lager and a bottle of whisky. Keep the change for all the trouble.'

Depositing three fifty pound notes on the bar, Michael then turned and walked back over to Roger who was now slowly getting to his feet.

Grabbing hold of him by the lapels, he dragged him over to the double doors.

'Now, listen to me you greedy cunt. If I ever see your face again – here or anywhere else – you're fuckin' dead.'

Lifting Roger up, Michael hurled him towards the double doors through which he catapulted out into the car park with a resounding crash. Turning around, Michael then went back to the bar, took a swig from the pint that Roger had bought him, and, lighting up another cigarette, waited patiently for the Barman to bring the drinks. Around him the pub slowly returned to life, although he could sense that several of the customers were still staring guardedly in his direction. But he didn't care. In fact, he wanted them to look at him – wanted them to remember what they had seen.

Because no one fucks with Micky Angel.

No one.

The Barman returned a few minutes later with a bottle of Bells and twenty-four cans of lager shrink-wrapped together on a cardboard tray. With a nod of thanks, Michael tucked the beer under his left arm and, gripping the bottle of whisky by its neck in his right hand, made his way towards the exit: he doubted that Roger was waiting for him on the other side, but he had to be prepared all the same. In fact, as he went through the doors he could hear the Landcruiser coming back across the car park. Just as it drove past, Michael impulsively leapt forwards and lashed out with his boot, planting a large dent in the offside rear door. In the front seat, Roger flinched in alarm, but carried on driving. Walking over to his own car, Michael smiled darkly to himself. A good panel-beater could probably fix the door in a couple of hours, but there wasn't a physician on the planet who could do anything about the black eye that Roger would wake up with the following morning – he'd still have the bruising in a month.

He got back to Naz's house just after seven. Still buzzing with pent-up energy he knocked the front door a little too hard and, no doubt anticipating some form of harassment, it was opened a minute later by the two biggest of the Turks, Mustafa and Seremi. For a moment they stared at Michael open mouthed, but when he placed the beer and whisky on the floor and then pulled the wodge of notes out of his inside pocket, they both immediately sprang to life, Mustafa hastily ushering him into the hallway and Seremi racing off into the back room to find Naz.

136

'Mick, Mick what is it?'

'It's Christmas, mate. Christmas come early. You have Christmas in your country, don't you?'

Seeing the bunch of notes, Naz's eyes opened wide in astonishment and, speechless with surprise, he stepped back to let Michael walk into the living room where the other men were assembled. Sitting down at the dining table, Michael fanned the notes out on the surface. They stared at the cash in complete consternation: it was obviously more money than any of them had ever seen in their lives.

'I found Roger,' exclaimed Michael. 'I found him in a pub and got the money off him. Oh, yeah, and a nice fat bonus, too.'

Before Naz had time to question Michael, the others all began gabbling at him at once, begging him to translate.

'I don't know how much there is yet,' said Michael, unable to stop himself laughing at their excitement. 'Open up the drinks and I'll count it.'

The Turks partied even more efficiently than they worked. Within seconds a radio-cassette player had been plugged into the wall and a tape of Turkish dance music inserted. A minute later, the first of several trays of food appeared and, in no time at all, the table was groaning with kebabs, pitta bread, olives and yoghurt. Soon everyone was dancing, drinking and laughing, until Naz suddenly stepped forward and turned off the tape. A reverential calm then descended on the room: Michael had finished counting the money. There was a little over three thousand three hundred pounds in all – almost seven hundred pounds each. When Naz translated this, the other four men stared at the cash in total incredulity. Walking across the room to the sideboard, Naz took out six glass tumblers and poured a shot of brandy into each for a toast to Michael. The drinks were downed, a huge cheer went up, and seconds later the music began and everyone was dancing once more. For the next two hours the same pattern of dancing and cheering continued until there was only enough brandy left for a final toast. Standing up on a chair, Mustafa made what appeared at first to be a highly solemn speech in Turkish – until he reached the end at which point all five men burst into howls of laughter and downed the final drink.

'What was that last toast for, then?' Michael asked Naz as he put down his glass.

'That was for Roger's mother.'

'Oh, yeah?'

'Roger's mother and her, how you say, sexual needs.'

'Oh, right,' laughed Michael. 'I can imagine …'

'I don't think so,' replied Naz, with a shake of the head.

'No?'

'No. You no have donkey in England.'

Laughing once more, Michael looked around the room. Seremi was sprawled out in the arm chair with his eyes half-closed seemingly on the verge of sleep, whilst the other three men were sitting on the thread-bare sofa engaged in what Michael guessed was some sort of political discussion. It seemed like the right moment to leave – it had been a long day.

'Can, er, I have a word outside?' he asked.

'Surely,' replied Naz.

Walking out into the front garden, Michael buttoned up his jacket and drank in the cool night air. In his top pocket he could feel the mobile phone pressed against his chest. Although he hadn't been able to follow Roger, and get the pictures he had been hoping for that evening, he wasn't disappointed: there would no doubt be plenty more similar opportunities in the future and, in any event, the impromptu party had cheered him up enormously.

'Listen, I'm gonna make my way home now.'

'Oh, OK! I get others …' said Naz, turning to call his friends.

'No, no, leave it, mate,' interrupted Michael, 'let 'em relax and enjoy themselves – it's all right. I'll, er, just – you know – get off and leave them to it.'

'OK,' replied Naz, with a smile, clearly sensing that Michael wished to slip away quietly. 'But Mick, is fantastic day for us. We are so grateful you.'

'That's all right. It was my pleasure.'

'You know that money is more than I earn in month. I send my family now next week. They very happy. Very happy because of you, Mick.'

'They deserve it, I'm sure.'

'You need anything from me,' said Naz, extending his hand for Michael to shake. 'Any time. Any time. You ask. I do for you if I can.'

'Thanks,' replied Michael, grasping Naz's hand and then nodding his head to bid him goodnight. As he began to walk back towards his car, however, Naz spoke again.

'I mean what I say, Mick. If you need some help to find this thing you are looking for, please ask me.'

Pausing at the front gate, Michael slowly turned and looked around. 'Sorry?' he enquired.

'You are not workman, Mick,' said Naz, discreetly closing the front door behind him. 'I know first day. And tonight, too.'

Taking a few paces back down the path, Michael stared into Naz's astute, intelligent face. There was no denying the significance of what he had just heard: he was little more than one month into his first investigation and someone had already seen through his cover.

'I can tell you no work building site before,' continued Naz, deliberately lowering his voice. 'And then this evening you share money from Roger five ways – not six. You take nothing yourself, not even ten quid. Micky Angel is not workman – this I can see. So, why he take hard job on buildings – shitty job? Only one reason, I think. Because he looks for something.'

Mentally, Michael scolded himself for his carelessness. He hadn't for a moment thought to take a share of the money – a reaction that could not have been more out of character with the penurious, down-on-his-luck labourer that he was seeking to portray. For the future, it was essential that he took care to act in character all the time – not just when he was directly on the trail of a criminal. On the other hand, even though he had slipped up, he had to be adaptable, wherever possible turning his errors to his advantage. Naz was shrewd, discreet and – more to the point – considered himself in Michael's debt. Without a moment's further thought, he decided to take him up on his offer.

'It's not something I'm looking for – it's someone.'

'Who?'

'Someone in your world – someone who exploits illegal immigrants.'

'You immigration man?' asked Naz, with a frown.

'No, no – I'm not from immigration. Trust me. I know you and your friends are working here illegally, but you've got nothing to fear from me in that regard. '

'So who are you, then, Michael Angel?'

Sitting down on the garden wall, Michael smiled as he once again scrutinized Naz's face. He would definitely make a useful ally, but, for his own safety, it was probably not a good idea to let him know too much.

'I can't tell you who I am exactly. Let's just say I'm an investigator, looking for someone making money out of people like you. I think you have a hard life, Nasruddin, and you meet some hard people. So maybe you will know the person I am looking for when you see him.'

'Maybe,' he replied.

'You don't have to help me if you don't want to. I know you're only here to support your family and you don't want any trouble, so …'

'I said I help you, Mick,' interrupted Naz, 'so I help you.'

'Then find me someone,' replied Michael, his voice dropping to a whisper. 'Someone in your world – like Roger. Someone who lies and cheats and steals, but always get away with it. Find me a criminal, Naz. Find me a criminal.'

The following morning, Michael made his way to the sports centre where he had practised pool prior to the game with Harper and Jez. Walking over to the cluster of payphones at the far end of the foyer, he dialled the number of the researcher at the University of London who had compiled the report on social security fraud for Tom. From several references therein to organized crime, Michael guessed that he had a certain amount of knowledge of the trade in illegal immigrants – if he didn't, he could always ask him to refer him to one of his colleagues.

'Hello?'

'Hello, could I speak to Lloyd Hall, please?'

'Speaking.'

'Hello, there. My name's, er, Andy Byatt, I work for Tom Cranmer on *The Mail*.'

'Oh, right,' replied the researcher, cheerfully.

'Yes, it's about the report you produced for him a couple of months back on social security fraud – I've got a couple of questions on a sort of related topic and I wondered if you could help me out.'

'Certainly – I'll do my best.'

'Is it convenient for you to talk now?'

'Absolutely!' replied Hall enthusiastically. 'Please, please, Mr Byatt – fire away!'

Listening to the researcher's polite, obliging voice, Michael's imagination conjured up a picture of a lanky, frizzy-haired academic sitting in an office crammed to the ceiling with books and research papers. He hoped his knowledge was as comprehensive as this mental image suggested.

'OK, well, I'm doing a piece on immigrants working here illegally, and what I wanted to know first of all was how they generally get into the country.'

'I take it you're not talking about asylum seekers, are you – you're just referring to economic migrants?'

'Yes, yes. I'm interested in the criminals who bring them in and the various ways they're exploited once they arrive.'

'Right, well, the short answer is it depends on how long the individuals concerned intend to stay. Attempting to live permanently in the UK calls for a completely different set of measures from just coming here to work for a year or two to send money back home. In the former case, documentation is essential – passports, birth certificates etcetera – and that's where organized crime often gets involved. In the latter case, well, it varies. Some temporary economic migrants will turn to criminal gangs to transport them into the country, especially if they're travelling from a long way away, but a very large proportion of them simply just walk straight in.'

'Sorry?'

'They just walk in – arrive at an airport on a tourist visa, give an address where they're supposed to be staying and then just wander off and get a job.'

'Really?' replied Michael with surprise – he had automatically assumed that some far more complex form of subterfuge would be necessary.

'Yes.'

'What about paperwork? I mean National Insurance numbers and everything.'

'Well, most of the places they'll be working won't ask for them and those that do will just give them temporary numbers.'

'Can they do that?'

'Oh, absolutely,' replied the researcher with a chuckle. 'I can give you one now if you like.'

'Are you serious?'

'Oh, yes! What was your date of birth, Mr Byatt?'

'Er, November twenty fifth, nineteen sixty-six.'

'Right, well, you're male and we need TN for temporary number so that makes you … TN 25 11 66 M. When can you start work?'

'Is that really a valid NI number?' responded Michael with a laugh.

'Oh, yes, perfectly. I mean you couldn't use it for any length of time, of course – you'd get found out. But if you're only staying in a job for a couple of weeks – you know, in general catering or some other unskilled situation – it's more than adequate.'

'So, how many workers are there like that in the UK?'

'No one knows exactly. The last government estimate I heard was about three hundred thousand but you can treble that at least.'

'What!'

'Yes, around about a million, I'd say – maybe less but probably more.'

'My God, where do they all work?'

'Oh, on building sites, in car washes, clearing tables in motorway service stations – all over the place. I mean if you really want to see them, take an early morning tube journey across London. Not seven o'clock when the first of the city commuters start appearing, but really early, you know, half past five or something like that. There's a whole separate sub-culture down there. It's quite amazing.'

'What's the government doing about it?'

'Well, there are inspectors and periodic raids and what have you, but no real political will to confront the situation in any meaningful way.'

'No?'

'Oh, no. The circumstances of the casual labourer have never been a priority in Great Britain, Mr Byatt. We were the first European country to industrialize but one of the very last to introduce a minimum wage. If it took us three hundred years to get around to basic measures like that for our own nationals, it's hardly surprising that illegal foreign workers don't attract much attention. Besides there's a lot of money to be made in keeping the cost base down – low wages equate to high profits, don't they?'

'They certainly do,' replied Michael, remembering the thick wodge of notes in Roger's pocket.

'In the best case, of course, these people are able to make more money than they can at home. In the worst, they're very much at the mercy of the sort of criminals you describe. Young women are particularly vulnerable. There's a huge amount of prostitution – much of it enforced – to which east European women in particular fall prey.'

'Well, er, thank you, that's very useful information, Mr Hall,' said Michael. 'Can I call you again if I've got any more questions?'

'Oh, yes, of course, please do. And give my regards to Mr Cranmer as well, won't you?'

'I will. Bye for now.'

'Goodbye.'

Replacing the receiver, Michael turned and walked thoughtfully back out of the sports centre. The moment that he had seen the group of men on the slip road in his rear-view mirror, his journalistic sixth sense had become alerted, and now that he understood a little more about the plight of such people he was even more certain that he was on to a good story. Making his way back towards Balam Road, he felt a surge of excitement pass through him. Even if he never heard from Naz again, it should be possible to track down criminals involved in trafficking or exploitation by himself, given the staggering number of illegal foreign workers that the country appeared to be harbouring.

After the fight with Roger, he decided to wait a while before returning to The White Horse, finally going back there five days later at half past seven in the evening. In the area around the fireplace there was no evidence of their tussle. The barman was different and gave him a drink without any sign of having been told not to serve the shaven-headed northerner in the black leather jacket who had caused such a commotion the previous Saturday night. Taking a seat, he took out his copy of *The Racing Post* and began to study the next day's form. The television was on, however, and was showing an international soccer match, which, after a few minutes, he found himself watching.

'Good game, is it?' enquired a voice behind him.

It was Harper, standing holding a pint of beer in his hand and smiling down at him sardonically. Michael felt his heart begin to race, but before he could think of anything to say, Harper pointed at the vacant seat opposite to indicate that he would like to sit down. Nodding in response, Michael picked his packet of cigarettes up off the table, ostensibly to give Harper room to put down his drink but in fact so that he could slip them into his top pocket, switching on the mobile in the process. Harper sat down three feet away, directly in its line of sight.

'It's Mick, right?'

'Yeah, that's right.'

'Geoff,' replied Harper, sizing Michael up and down with his misty, grey-blue eyes. Staring back at him, Michael had to fight both his own nervousness and his natural inclination to carry the conversation forward: Harper had approached him – not the other way around – and it was therefore up to Harper to say what was on his mind.

'People don't seem to like paying you very much, do they, Mick?' said Harper with an ironic smile.

'How d'you mean?'

'I was in here on Saturday. I saw you kick shit out of that bloke,' continued Harper. Just above his collar bone, Michael noticed that he had a small tattoo of an anarchy symbol – he hoped that the light was good enough for it to be visible on camera.

'Tried to do me and my mates out of our wages.'

'Yeah, I heard. The whole pub heard.'

'I suppose they did,' observed Michael, dispassionately. 'So, where's your friend?'

'Who?'

'The bloke you play pool with.'

'Jez? Hah! He's not my friend – it's much worse than that, I'm afraid.'

'Yeah?'

'Yeah, he's my nephew. Aggressive bastard. I try to keep an eye on him but he can't stay out of trouble for five minutes.'

'Better keep him away from me, then.'

'Oh, don't worry, he won't be showin' his face again in a hurry.'

'No?'

'No, he's inside. He went down ten days ago. Twelve months at her Majesty's pleasure.'

'Might come out a better pool player.'

'Might not come out at all if he's not careful,' grunted Harper. 'D'you want another pint?'

'Yeah, lager, thanks.'

'Heineken?'

'Yeah, ta.'

As Harper stood up and slouched lazily over to the bar, Michael swallowed heavily and tried to keep calm. Leaning forward, he whispered quickly into the microphone.

'Geoffrey Harper's come over to talk to me. I haven't got a clue why, but this could be the break I've been waiting for …'

Harper returned two minutes later and put the drink down in front of Michael.

144

'Oh, cheers, d'you want a cigarette?' said Michael taking the packet out of his top pocket: the sound would be even clearer now.

'No thanks – got my own,' replied Harper. 'So, what d'you think of sunny Feltham, then?'

'It's all right, I suppose. I've been in worse places.'

'Not very friendly, though, is it?'

'Ah, it's OK.'

'You got a room or a flat or something?'

'Yeah, a flat,' replied Michael, 'about a half a mile up the Uxbridge Road.'

'Nice?'

'Yeah, it's all right.'

'You workin' much?'

'A bit – when I can.'

'You claiming?'

'What, benefit?'

'Yeah.'

'No.'

'No?' exclaimed Harper. 'Why not?'

'I dunno. Never done it before. Wouldn't know how.'

With a disbelieving shake of the head, Harper sat back in his seat and took out his tin of tobacco. Just as he was about to speak again, however, both he and Michael became conscious of someone walking towards them. Turning around, Michael looked up and saw a gaunt, thin-faced woman approaching their table. He guessed she was in her mid thirties, but her hard, uncompromising features made her appear much older. Beneath her unbuttoned blue cotton jacket she was wearing a sweatshirt emblazoned with the design of a Chinese dragon – its bulging, blood-shot eyes seeming to fix Michael in their frenzied gaze.

'Hi, Ange,' said Harper.

Without replying, the woman sat down next to him and then looked suspiciously across the table at Michael. Putting his hand on her knee, Harper spoke softly to her – so softly that Michael worried that the microphone in his top pocket would not pick up his voice.

'This is Mick. He doesn't know how to claim his benefit. We can help him out, though, can't we? For a small cut, of course ...'

Chapter 6

Harper and Angela came round three days later. Having observed at first hand that Harper customarily rose late in the morning, Michael wondered whether he would keep his promise to arrive at Balam Road at ten o'clock, but, true to his word, he and Angela got there exactly on time. Coming out of the living room to answer the front door, Michael took one final, careful look around the flat. Despite an attack of last-minute nerves, he felt reasonably safe. The only two things that could incriminate him were concealed respectively about his person and underneath the floorboards. Slipping his hand into his top pocket, he switched on the phone and then opened the door.

'Hi, Geoff, Ange – you all right?'

'Yeah, fine,' replied Harper, in a clipped, workmanlike tone quite different from his bonhomie of three days previously. Angela didn't answer at all, but merely nodded her head moodily. She had scarcely spoken the night that they had met in the pub and appeared even more taciturn this morning. As Michael stood back to let her go into the living room, he noticed that she had deep bags under her eyes. He wondered what she had been up to the previous night.

'D'you want a cup of tea?' asked Michael, conscious that the question somehow sounded terribly genteel. These people had come around to his house to plan a crime, not make arrangements for the village fete.

'Eh, yeah, thanks,' replied Harper.

'Me, 'n' all,' added Angela. 'And have you got any paracetamol?'

'Yeah, yeah, I've got some in the kitchen somewhere. I'll bring 'em in,' replied Michael, trying not to sound too desperate to please. Instinctively, he could sense that Angela had some sort of a hold over Harper. It might just be because they were a couple – he wasn't sure – but, for whatever reason, Harper definitely appeared in thrall to this scrawny, morose woman and Michael knew in his bones that he would do well not to get on her wrong side. As the kettle boiled, he thought about putting the milk and sugar out separately on a tray, but then changed his mind: once again he didn't want to risk appearing too refined. Pouring a splash of milk into each mug, he took the sugar bag out of the cupboard, stuffed a teaspoon inside and then carried it into the living room.

'Cheers,' said Harper, as Michael passed him the mug. He had chosen to sit at the dining table whilst Angela lay sprawled out on the sofa, her head leant right back and her hand over her brow. She looked so washed-out that, despite not wanting to appear obsequious, Michael felt it would seem strange not to ask after her health.

'You all right, Ange?'

'Yeah, I'm OK,' replied Angela, leaning wearily forwards and taking the tea and paracetamol from him.

'The sugar's on the table.'

Ignoring the offer and without saying thank you, Angela leant forward and quickly opened up the bottle of tablets. Michael sat down at the table opposite Harper, who, having taken a sip of tea, then took off the small satchel that he had strapped across his chest and began removing documents from it.

'Right. This is your NHB1.'

'What's that?'

'It's a Housing Benefits claim form,' replied Harper, folding over the first page and beginning to fill it in with a black biro. 'OK. *Surname.* You are Brian Morgan. Your wife – Angela here – is Wendy Morgan. *Address.* 144 Balam Road, right?'

'Right.'

'*Phone number?*'

'It's not connected at the moment.'

'OK, we'll leave that blank. *National insurance Number.* I've filled that in already along with your date of birth. I've made a note of both here on this piece of paper so you can keep a record. Don't lose it. *Do you pay rent for the place in which you live?* We tick yes. *How much?*'

'Are those real?' interrupted Michael, remembering his conversation with the researcher Lloyd Hall the previous week.

'What?'

'Those National Insurance numbers – for the Morgans.'

'Yeah.'

'Won't they check up on them, then – the authorities?'

'Wouldn't matter if they did. Neither of these people are already claiming housing benefit.'

'How d'you know?'

''Cos they're dead.'

'Oh, right.'

'*How much is your rent?* Seven hundred and fifty pounds a month.'

'Will I get all that back?'

'No. They'll assess it. I reckon you'll probably get six hundred a month tops. Here's your rent book. Have you got one already?'

'No. I pay the estate agent each month on one of those direct debits.'

'Good. Wouldn't look good to produce the wrong one. *What is your landlord's name?* Mr Michael Fry. *What is his address?* 43 Temple Place, Feltham, TW13 7QY.'

'Who's he?' asked Michael, already knowing the answer.

'Me,' replied Harper abruptly. 'I'll back up your story if they decide to check up. Right,' he continued, '*From which date do you wish to claim benefit?* We put down three months ago which would be the twenty-sixth of June.'

'Why three months ago?'

'Back rent. You can claim up to twelve weeks. *Are you receiving a disability allowance?* No. *Blind?* No. *Are you claiming income support?* Definitely no.'

'What's that – social security?'

'Yes – and don't either.'

'Don't what?'

'Don't claim social under this name or any other – that could really fuck us up. *Are you claiming child benefit?* No ...'

As Harper continued to read through the questions, Michael pondered the issue of why he had told him not to claim income support. One of the key observations in Lloyd Hall's report had been that fraudsters commonly claimed multiple benefits from multiple agencies and would be much easier to apprehend if only these agencies could improve communications between each other. Harper's housing benefit system, however, could clearly be put in jeopardy by claiming the dole.

148

'OK, *Declaration* – sign here and date it. Also, you need to sign this additional form – a CTB – to claim back your Council Tax. I'll send 'em off together.' Taking the second form out of his satchel, Harper passed them both across to Michael to sign.

'How should I sign them?'

'What d'you mean?'

'My own handwriting or what?'

Out of the corner of his eye Michael could see Angela looking across at Harper with a frown. She obviously had a bad headache and Michael's stream of questions was clearly not making it any better. Sensing that he was dangerously close to trying their patience, he decided not to quiz Harper any further.

'Your own handwriting,' replied Harper, delving into the satchel once more. 'That way, when you next have to sign anything it'll look the same. Now, marriage certificate. You've lost the original. This is what's called a certified copy. Don't worry, though, they'll accept it – it's a legal document. Now, that, your rent book and your NI number are the three things you absolutely must have and must be able to produce – don't lose 'em.'

'What happens next?'

'Right, I'll send these forms off today. In a couple of days you'll get an acknowledgement. About ten days to two weeks after that, you should get confirmation that your claim's been accepted. The money'll follow about two weeks later. Call me when it arrives and then pay me my cut each subsequent week after that. OK?'

'OK.'

'Now, this is the important bit, in about three weeks time – just before they start payin' you – you'll get a visit from the housing benefit inspectors. It'll be at very short notice and you'll need to be ready for them. What's your mobile number?'

'0767 394561,' answered Michael, having decided that the time had come to take the plunge and actually start using the mobile as a phone.

'Are you sure that's right?' asked Harper, staring at the line of digits that he had just written down.

'Yeah.'

'Can't be,' replied Harper.

'Why not?' asked Michael, nervously.

'It's only got ten digits.'

'Oh, yeah, right,' said Michael, suddenly realizing what he meant. 'It's an old number. It came with the phone when I bought it.'

'How old is it?'

'What?'

'Your mobile phone. How old is it?' repeated Harper.

'Oh, er …' murmured Michael, attempting to look casual but feeling his stomach beginning to twist into a knot. 'I've had it four or five years, I suppose.'

'Let's have a look at it.'

'What?'

'Fuckin' hell, Mick, do I have to repeat everything twice? Show us your phone.'

Taking hold of the handset, Michael removed it from his top pocket and, holding his breath, passed it across the table to Harper. Jim had insisted that its modifications were invisible – even to the trained eye. If he was wrong, then Michael's cover was about to be blown into a thousand pieces.

'Christ, it's ancient!' exclaimed Harper, contemptuously. 'It hasn't even got text, has it? What you walkin' around with this old thing for?'

'I, er, just, you know, never had the money to, like, upgrade …' mumbled Michael, desperately hoping that his persona as a hard-up and slightly feckless labourer appeared convincing.

'Well, if you can't afford a new one, then at least get yourself a booster chip to screw into the aerial,' replied Harper, curtly, passing the phone back to Michael. 'They only cost a fiver, but they ramp the reception up two or three bars – even on an old handset like this. We can't have you drifting in and out of range when we need to talk to you.'

'Oh, right, yeah, I'll do that,' replied Michael, relieved that Harper was moving off the subject, but mentally wincing at the fact that his attention had been drawn to it in the first place.

'Anyway, just before the inspection, we'll call you on that number and, if you're not already in the flat, get yourself back here as fast as you can. Ange and I'll be waiting for you.'

'Right.'

'Now, the inspectors are clever bastards, so you gotta be prepared. They'll check the flat and your documents to make sure everything's the same as on your declaration – they'll be all chummy and everything – and then they'll hit you with a question.'

'Like what?'

'Like … What did you do for your wedding anniversary, it was last week, wasn't it?', when it's not for five months. Or, 'How does it feel been married for fifteen years?', when you've actually only been married for six. So, learn your dates – all of 'em. If you're confident about the question, answer it straight. If not, don't answer at all. Now, we're gonna agree three or four basics. Remember these. Where did you two first meet?'

'At a disco in Leeds,' announced Angela from the sofa.

'Is your wife working?'

'Two days a week waitressing,' intoned Angela again.

'What do you earn?'

'Er, nothin', I'm still looking for a job,' volunteered Michael.

'Have you done any casual labouring work since you got to London?'

'No. I've got a bad back and can't lift things easily.'

'Nice one, you're learnin'. Right that's it,' said Harper, closing the satchel and putting it over his shoulders again. 'Thanks for the tea. Come on, Ange, we'll get you home.'

'Oh, right, thanks …' said Michael, watching Harper go over and help Angela to her feet.

'We'll let ourselves out,' said Harper, as he and Angela moved towards the door.

'Yeah, all right, see you.'

As the front door slammed, Michael looked at Harper's half-drunk cup of tea and then across the living room at the clock on the wall.

They had been in the flat just nine minutes.

Three days later Michael went to see Jim. The news was not good. A booster chip for the aerial of his current mobile was simple enough, but installing a full set of surveillance electronics into a more modern, up-to-date handset was an altogether different proposition. Recent mobile phones were so small that it would be extremely difficult to fit a tape mechanism into one of the new-style, slim-line battery packs; Jim would be delighted to try, but in all probability it would result in a lower spec-ification device. Having thanked him for the advice, Michael left the shop and made his way back to Feltham on the train, pondering the quandary with which he was now confronted. On the one hand, he wanted to stick with the original handset, but Harper had already expressed his reservations about it and he didn't want it to continue to attract his attention. On the other hand, if he bought a brand new mobile phone solely for the purposes of communicating with Harper, it might look suspicious if at some point in the future Harper were to see him still carrying his old one in his top pocket. In the end, Michael decided to hang on to the original phone but try and find a brightly-coloured cover for it: a snazzy facia might just be enough to make it look a little less old-fashioned and thereby help avert any further awkward questions.

Going straight from the station to the nearby municipal leisure centre, Michael made his way to the payphones in the foyer and dialled through to the Tower. Although he had no intention of keeping Tom apprised of every minor development, the progress with Harper had been so significant that he had decided to call him directly; today was a Thursday – the one day in the week that he could be certain that his boss would be at his desk, preparing for the weekly management meeting that afternoon.

'Hello, could I speak to Mr Cranmer, please?'

'Who's calling?'

'Mr Angel.'

'Mr Angel, you say?'

'Yes. Mr Angel,' insisted Michael.

'Please wait a moment; I'll see if Mr Cranmer is available.'

Michael grimaced as he listened to the tinny Beethoven sonata that was being played whilst he was on hold. He had always disliked Eva Osbourne, Tom's disdainful, sarcastic secretary, and was glad to think of him now walking across his office and shutting the door on her so that they could have their conversation in private.

'What's your number?' hissed Tom. 'I'll call you straight back.'

Reading the number off the dial, Michael put down the receiver. Ten seconds later the phone rang.

'What's up?' asked Tom, quickly.

'It's like buying house insurance,' he replied, with a laugh, 'or a personal pension or something like that.'

'Sorry?'

'It's like buying insurance – except the sales people aren't so smarmy. I've been trying to think how to describe it to you all morning; it just occurred to me a few minutes ago on the train.'

'What's happened? Have you made contact?'

'Yes. Harper came around to the flat on Monday with his girlfriend – a woman called Angela.'

'Hang on, you're losing me. What exactly did they come round for?'

'To fiddle my housing benefit for me, of course. I get a nice handsome cheque each week, they get a commission – everybody's happy; and all from the comfort of my own living room.'

'Great!' cried Tom, excitedly. 'Tell me all about it. What did they do?'

'Well, she didn't do anything, just sat in the chair with her hand over her face. She looked half dead – God knows what she'd been up to the previous night. And he just, like, delved into this ancient school satchel thing and then pulled out a whole load of forms. Sign here, sign there, and then bingo – the first cheque'll be with you in a month.'

'Did you get all this on film?'

'Every last second – in glorious technicolour. The tape's already packed away safe and sound under the floor boards. I'll bring it with me to the safe house next time.'

'Fantastic, old boy! So, how does this system of theirs work?'

'I'm still not sure, but I'll tell you one thing, they are very, very well organized. They're using the National Insurance numbers of deceased people; perhaps they hacked into some sort of government database to get them or something, I don't know. They've got fake marriage certificates that are extremely good quality – I mean I've checked the one they gave me and it's not a colour photocopy or anything, it's properly printed on original vellum. They've got all the relevant Housing Benefit forms; NHB1's and CTB2's – you name it – they just produce them like that.'

'Fascinating! Although, I suppose the big worry is that Harper might start to keep his distance from now on.'

'How d'you mean?'

'I mean once your claim's been processed, what's to stop him ignoring you and just taking his cut? You compared it to buying insurance, but it sounds to me more like a sort of pyramid selling organization. Harper and the others could have recruited numerous people like you and just be taking a slice of everything they earn. '

'You could be right,' said Michael, recalling the speed and efficiency of the previous day's encounter, 'I just don't know, but the next stage in the process is a visit from the Housing Benefits inspectors so I'm going to be meeting him one more time at least.'

'That'll be at the flat, yes?'

'Yes. Harper's going to call me just before the inspectors turn up. Angela's pretending to be my wife to bump up my claim, so she'll have to be there for it, too.'

'Right, well, let me know how it goes, won't you? And well done. This is fantastic news. Have you processed the pictures yet?'

'Yes, and they're fine,' laughed Michael. 'I told you that already.'

'Excellent!'

'So, anyway, what about King? Did you show him the illegal immigrants tape?'

'No, I didn't. He's been out of the country since last week and only got back yesterday afternoon.'

'But you did manage to get a look at it yourself, though?'

'Yes, I did – I looked at it very carefully.'

'And what did you think?'

'I don't think it's right for us.'

'Pardon?'

'I said I don't think it's right for us.'

'What! Why not?' gasped Michael, astonished by the tone of finality in Tom's voice.

'Simple, old boy. Illegal immigrants might read newspapers and watch documentaries but they don't read our newspapers and watch our documentaries, do they?'

'What d'you mean?'

'Well, I know it's just raw footage at the moment, but it's pretty obvious that the really gripping part of the story – the human interest bit, if you like – is the exploitation of those Turkish chaps, isn't it? They're the victims. But they're not the victims we want. They're not our victims – they're somebody else's. Our victims are first and foremost the British public.'

'But what about the arsehole Roger – he's not paying a penny in tax or anything!'

'Possibly so, but it isn't he that leaps out at the viewer from your tape. I mean, don't get me wrong, I think that the world you've uncovered through these illegal immigrants chaps is absolutely spot-on. It's got all the right elements for the series; crime, squalor and a wonderful air of seedy dishonesty, but the problem is that the story just generates the wrong emotional response.'

'Meaning what exactly?'

'Meaning *Criminal Britain* is founded on anger, not sympathy. Take that first tape you did in the pub. Why was it so good? Because just like you the average viewer is going to see Harper handing over ten pounds after that game of pool and immediately say to himself, 'That's my money he's gambling with!' Or take King's other suggestion about drug dealers. The same viewer is going to see some pusher selling drugs to a sixteen year old girl and say to himself, 'She could be my daughter!' That's the reaction we're after. Anger. Outrage. That's the emotional undercurrent we need to have running through all four documentaries. And at the end of the day, of course, that's why it'll be such a powerful series.'

'OK, OK, I see what you mean,' replied Michael, suddenly beginning to feel a little naïve.

'I mean I can see exactly why you suggested the idea. You had to work on that dreadful building site, so it's no wonder that you identified with those Turkish chaps, and I'm sure somebody ought to tell their story one day, but not this time around – it's not what King's after at all. He won't buy it for a moment – take my word for it.'

'OK. I get you.'

'You're not too disappointed are you?' asked Tom, solicitously.

'No, no. I get what you mean. I guess I just hadn't thought things through properly, that's all.'

'Good man!' declared Tom, appreciatively. 'But listen, whatever you do keep the ideas coming. Maybe this one wasn't exactly right, but, like Henry said, this is your series and we absolutely want to hear every suggestion you've got.'

'OK. Will do,' replied Michael, grateful for Tom's efforts to keep him encouraged.

'Excellent! Now, before I forget, I sent the letter to Jake like you asked. He should have received it in the last couple of days.'

'Thanks.'

'My pleasure. Now, you hang in there, old chap, won't you? And chin up, OK?'

'OK.'

'And once more, great news about Harper. It's really made my day.'

'Thanks, Tom. Cheers.'

'Bye.'

Replacing the receiver, Michael left the sports centre and began slowly making his way back to the flat. Walking towards the Uxbridge Road past a row of neat, red-bricked terraced houses, he stared at them blankly, thoroughly taken aback by the conversation that he had just had. Over the many years that he had worked for Tom, he had provided him with a wide variety of different material, none of which he had ever rejected outright and much of which he had personally sanctioned for publicity. How could he himself have been so wide of the mark on this occasion? It was blindingly obvious that he had got the editorial emphasis completely wrong. Of course he had identified with Naz and his friends, but that shouldn't have overridden his objectivity. What was happening to him? It was just as well that Tom hadn't actually shown King the tape. If Henry thought that he was incapable of realizing the concept underlying *Criminal Britain*, he wouldn't hesitate to call an end to the entire venture immediately.

Reaching the Uxbridge Road, he paused at a battered pedestrian railing and, gripping its cracked paintwork in both hands, stared uneasily at the speeding traffic beyond. He had always had faith in his own abilities and now was the one time in his life that he absolutely could not afford to lose it. He had made a mistake – he hadn't thought things through – but it had no direct bearing on his investigation into the fraudsters and he couldn't let it undermine his self-confidence. With a shake of the head, he resolved to put the entire experience behind him and concentrate on the tasks at hand. Harper had expressed qualms about his mobile phone. Allaying those suspicions was thus a top priority – he had to start looking for a cover that would disguise its age without further delay. After that, the next priority was to find some casual work. Micky Angel's funds were running dangerously low – he needed money and he needed it quickly.

He found a cover for his mobile phone three days later in a bargain bin at Woolworth's. Returning to the flat just after four o'clock in the afternoon, he began to unwrap it as he walked up the concrete steps to the front door. Half way up the stairs, he noticed the net curtain in the flat below tremble slightly. During the two months that he had spent at Balam Road this was the first time that he had spotted any sign of the old woman whom the estate agent had told him occupied the flat below. Pausing, he thought about going back down the steps, knocking the front door and introducing himself: knowing everything he could about those around him and any suspicions that they might harbour – however remote – was essential to maintaining his peace of mind about his undercover identity. It was for precisely that reason that he had spent so much time looking for the facia for his mobile phone. In the end, he carried on walking up the stairs and went into the flat. For now, the reclusive old woman would have to wait. However, as he sat down and began attaching the metallic-blue cover on to the front of his phone, he couldn't help feeling a measure of concern at not knowing whether this was the first time that she had observed him from her window or whether she had been doing so every day.

He arrived at The White Horse just after eight o'clock that evening. As soon as he got through the door, he spotted the unmistakable figure of Harper leaning over the pool table. Not recognizing the three men with whom he was playing, Michael decided to ignore him, and, having bought a drink, sat down by himself to read *The Racing Post*. Looking up ten minutes later, he could see that the game was still in progress. With a shrug he returned to studying the next day's form. He had to stick to his plan of playing the patience game. It didn't matter if he didn't speak to Harper at all that evening: his Housing Benefit interview would come around soon enough and, merely by virtue of his presence in the pub, his persona as the dour and solitary northerner was gaining further credibility.

'D'you ever win?'

It was Harper, holding two pints of lager and looking down at Michael's newspaper. Out of the corner of his eye, he could see that the men with whom he had been playing pool had left the pub. Harper was smiling, but Michael was nevertheless right on his guard: had the fraudster come over to speak to him to be sociable or for some other reason?

'Sometimes,' he ventured, cautiously.

'You know you never actually told me where you're from,' observed Harper, putting the drinks down on the table and moving around to sit opposite – in the second that he turned his back, Michael slipped his right hand into his top pocket and switched on the phone.

'Boltby,' he replied, nodding in acknowledgement at receiving the pint. 'A small village in Yorkshire called Boltby.' Tom had sent him a map of the village so that he could memorize the major street names.

'Oh, ah?'

'Small place. You know, everybody knows everybody else's business ...'

'Not like in the smoke, then?'

'No. Which is one good thing about London I suppose,' conceded Michael. 'So, what was the matter with Ange the other day?' he continued: if Harper was trying to probe him about his background, perhaps the best riposte would be to ask some searching questions of his own.

'Oh, family shit,' he replied, shaking his head in disgust. 'You wouldn't wanna know.'

'You don't have much luck with your relatives, do you?' said Michael 'What with Jez 'n' all ...'

'No, you're right, I don't.'

'Welcome to the club.'

Looking at Harper's rueful smile, Michael fought down a sudden burst of excitement. His partner's family was dysfunctional; he mentored a nephew he patently disliked; he played games of pool with complete strangers. Geoffrey Harper might well have come over to talk to him because he was suspicious, or he might have done so because he was lonely.

'So what about you?' continued Michael, lighting up a cigarette. 'You lived in Feltham all your life?'

'Pretty much. Except when I was at college.'

'College?'

'University actually.'

'Yeah?'

'Yeah, Newcastle. Not far from your neck of the woods, I s'pose.'

'What did you study?' asked Michael, once again trying to control his excitement. A University educated social security fraudster? Tom was going to love this.

'Economics.'

'Oh, yeah?' said Michael, recalling the newspaper he had seen Harper carrying on the first day of his surveillance. 'So you must know a fair bit about the subject, I suppose.'

'Enough.'

'What d'you reckon to this country's economy, then? In your expert opinion.'

'Superficially sound, fundamentally flawed. That's economist speak for all fucked up.'

'Was that before or after you started defrauding it?'

158

For a fraction of a second Michael felt a rush of horror at this spontaneous Freudian observation, but rather than provoking an antagonistic response from Harper it merely seemed to amuse him.

'I'm not defrauding it,' he replied, leaning back in his seat with a wry grin. 'I'm just contributing to its inevitable downfall in exactly the way it expects me to. And so are you now.'

'Yeah?'

'Yeah.'

'And how are we doin' that, then?'

'By taking our share of the protection money.'

It was a curious comment and Michael stared at Harper for a couple of moments, unable to fathom exactly what he had meant. Suddenly, he recalled Tom's speculation that the size and scope of the fraudsters' activities might be indicative of a political rather than a criminal motivation. Inside Harper's shirt collar, he could see his anarchist tattoo at the base of his neck. Despite the beer that he had just drunk, Michael's throat all of a sudden felt very dry. If Harper and the others were members of an extremist group, what would they do to him if they were to discover that he had been trying to infiltrate them? Fighting to stop his mind clouding over with his worst imaginings, Michael strove to make his reply sound as dispassionate as possible.

'I don't get it.'

'Of course you don't,' replied Harper enigmatically, stroking his chin between his thumb and forefinger. 'There are a lot of powerful people out there who don't want you to get it – politicians and the like. Although I can shed a bit of light on the situation for you, if you want ...' he added amiably.

'All right, then,' replied Michael, cautiously.

'What percentage of the national budget actually goes on welfare, d'you know?'

'No idea.'

'Thirty-five percent – it's the Treasury's biggest single expenditure by a mile; the second is the health service at about seventeen percent or somethin' like that. Just think about that for a moment. A third of the nation's entire wealth taken up in social security. Doesn't it seem a bit much?'

'I suppose so, now you come to mention it.'

'So what'd happen if they cut it? Eh? Stopped payin' out. Go and have a walk around the Abaddon estate if you need any help on that one. You know the place I'm talkin' about, don't you – over the other side of Feltham?'

'Yeah, I know where you mean,' answered Michael, recalling the three forbidding tower blocks that he had seen from the end of Naz's street.

'They are not a nice bunch of people over there – take my word for it. Ninety per cent of 'em are on social of one type or another. What d'you think they'd do if the dole suddenly dried up one day?'

'Go ape shit, I suppose.'

'Dead right they would. The city of London's twenty-five minutes away on the train. They'd be down the square mile, dragging every executive they could find out of his office and smashing his brains out on the pavement before you could say 'single parent family'. It's Danegeld, Mick – social security. You know what Danegeld is, don't you?'

'No,' replied Michael, staring back into Harper's shrewd, sardonic face. Once again his throat felt dry and he swallowed deeply. Did Harper suspect him after all? Was this just pub politics or a clever cat and mouse game – a subterfuge to tempt Michael to break his cover as a poorly educated builder by drawing him into an intellectual discussion?

'It was gold the English Kings used to give the Vikings every year to stop 'em from comin' over and wreckin' the place,' said Harper, taking a swig of his lager and then wiping the froth from his lips. 'Although buyin' off the superfluous masses is only a part of it, of course. To understand what's really goin' on you need to take a step back and have a look at the big picture – at the really big numbers. That's when it all starts to make sense. Look at North Sea oil for example.'

'What about it?'

'Well, it's all gone, hasn't it? Been pissed away. None of it got spent on anything permanent – on any sort of infrastructure – like the railways or what have you; they're less efficient than they were two hundred years ago. North Sea oil – the country's most important natural resource ever – pissed down the drain in forty short years of tax cuts and buyin' off the unemployed. It's the biggest financial scandal in this country's history – irresponsible asset management on a colossal scale. But have you ever seen anythin' about it in the press? Have you, fuck. Because the newspapers don't want you to know what's going on either. Journalists aren't paid to tell the truth, are they?'

Michael could feel his heart pumping wildly in his chest. It seemed

160

like a direct challenge – as though Harper had specifically brought the conversation around to the subjects of journalism so that he could mockingly demonstrate to Michael that his fake identity was now known to him. As he struggled to think of how he might reply, an image of the flickering lace-curtain in the ground-floor flat suddenly came to mind, blocking out his thoughts completely. *Criminal Britain* was a failure. He had fooled no-one in Feltham – everybody had been able to see right through him. Reaching into his pocket for his cigarettes, he lit one up and then tried to attempt a casual-looking shrug: somehow he had to keep Harper talking – even if it was only to learn that he had indeed been unmasked.

'So, what is really going on, then, Geoff? Perhaps you'd better tell me.'

For several seconds, Harper didn't reply, but merely continued to stare silently at Michael across the table. Again Michael's imagination went into free fall, as he pictured the other sixteen fraudsters suddenly marching through the door of the pub and encircling him like pagan priests around a human sacrifice. But Harper's partners in crime did not appear. Instead, he merely leant forward in his seat, narrowed his blue-grey eyes and began to speak in a soft yet steely voice.

'The country's cannibalizing itself – gorging itself to death on its own intestines – in a vast asset-stripping bonanza that's laughingly passed off as prosperity. London's got one of the biggest stock markets in the world, but the place is just a massive casino – ninety-nine percent of the transactions it handles are speculative. The country's not investing in its future, not in anything concrete – in bricks and mortar – even less in its people. Look at the education system. Schools churning out kids who can't think with arm-full's of qualifications that don't mean anything. I'd give the UK twenty years at most. We grow less than forty per cent of our food, produce less than twenty per cent of our manufactured goods. Even before the oil runs out the international bankers are gonna get twitchy and start callin' in the national debt. Next thing the pound'll dive, the property market'll collapse and the bastards who've been runnin' the show for the last fifty years'll all fuck off to their villas in socialist France so fast you won't be able to see their trails for dust. That's why the establishment doesn't give a toss about handin' out welfare to the likes of you and me, legitimate or otherwise – they've already ripped off far more than we could ever dream of.'

'So we might as well get our share while we can then, yeah?' said

Michael, enthralled by Harper's morbid fanaticism, yet at the same time thankful that he appeared to be moving away from the subject of journalists. His relief, however, was short-lived, as, without for a moment relaxing his piercing gaze, the fraudster responded chillingly.

'Exactly, mate. But don't get me wrong. Economic collapse and anarchy isn't a bad thing – in fact, it's just what the country needs. And, when the chance comes along to hurry the process up, those of us in the know have to make sure we take it …'

Michael awoke the next morning hung over and in the grip of a deep and brooding sense of insecurity. The drinking session with Harper had gone on for over three hours, until the portly, bearded publican at The White Horse had finally locked the doors behind them just after half-past eleven. From the moment that King had suggested infiltrating the fraud-ring, Michael had imagined that the process would be essentially linear in nature – breaking down the fraudsters' suspicions bit by bit until they at last accepted him as one of their own. But the previous night's discussions had been bewilderingly ambiguous, with just as much evidence to suggest that Michael was the deceived as the deceiver. After his tantalizing reference to contributing to the destruction of the British state, Harper had not returned to the subject of politics, leaving Michael maddeningly unsure as to whether the fraudsters really were politically motivated and, if so, why Harper had chosen deliberately to hint at such. Instead, Harper had gone on to quiz Michael at great length about his family and life in Boltby. Ostensibly, his expressions of sympathy at Michael's divorce and the break-up of his family had sounded utterly genuine. But even as he had told his story, embellishing it with the wealth of small details that he had worked out over so many sleepless nights, Michael had felt that it was just as easy to interpret Harper's apparent empathy as an interrogation tactic – a ruse allowing him to spin an ever more complex and absurd web of lies.

Having taken a shower, Michael went into the living room and decided to watch the previous night's recording from start to finish; hopefully, things would seem a little less equivocal the second time around. Maybe he was playing mind games with himself – maybe he should have taken Harper's comments much more on face value. Rewinding the video tape, he switched on the television and then went into the kitchen to make a cup of coffee and take a couple of paracetamol. Returning to the living room, he pulled apart the curtains but immediately realized he was going to have to watch the tape later. Before poring over the three hours of film, he had a clear duty to speak to the man now standing on the pavement outside, hesitantly checking the numbers of the houses on Balam Road against the crumpled piece of paper in his hand. Switching off the television and VCR, Michael went out of the living room and across to the front door.

'Hello, Naz. Come on in.'

'Oh, this is right house! I am very glad,' said Naz, grinning as he skipped up the last few steps to the front door.

'Come on through,' replied Michael, shaking Naz's hand.

'Thank you, thank you. Oh! Is nice place, Mick. Very nice.'

'Oh, thanks,' replied Michael a little guiltily – compared to the cramped conditions of the Turks' rented house, Balam Road no doubt appeared quite salubrious. 'Please, take a seat. D'you want a cup of coffee or something – the kettle's just boiled.'

'No, it's OK,' replied Naz, sitting down on the edge of the sofa.

'So, how's Mustafa and everyone …'

'Mick, I found him,' interrupted Naz excitedly. 'I found man you wanted.'

'Oh,' said Michael, slowly – this was going to be difficult. 'Right. Well …'

'Bad man. Very bad man and very … cunning. Cunning – I check word in dictionary.'

'Listen, Naz. Thanks for keeping an eye out for me and everything, but I was going to come and see you to tell you that …'

'No, is OK, no problem. This man should go prison many times. He make many people unhappy – so many, many people.'

'Yes, but, er …'

'But I must tell you now, not my people, your people.'

'Pardon?' asked Michael, quickly.

'I am sorry,' continued Naz, his expression becoming suddenly tinged with despondency. 'You tell me look for bad man in my world. But he is not in my world. He is in your world, so maybe he not right for you. I don't know.'

'So, he's not a trafficker bringing in immigrants into the country or a gangmaster or anything like that?'

'No, we work for him – me and Mustafa – but he pays us: he does not cheat us like Roger. No, he cheat English people. Good English people – like you.'

'What does he do exactly, this man?' asked Michael, with growing interest.

'Today you work?' asked Naz, his grin returning once more.

'Am I working today? No, no, I'm not.'

'Then you come with Nasruddin and you work for this man today. Then you see your own eyes, Mick, you see your own eyes …'

Thirty minutes later, Michael and Naz pulled up in front of a large three-bedroomed house in a quiet residential cul-de-sac. Walking up its broad driveway, Michael's first thought was that John Tysoe looked much more like a second hand car dealer than a builder. He wore a quilted black rally jacket with a logo of a red horse on the shoulder and the words 'Mobil Oil' stitched underneath. In his mouth was a half-smoked cigarette that somehow remained stubbornly fixed to his lower lip as he spoke to the man next to him, who, judging by his three piece suit was probably the owner of the house. The slight incline of his head and the way he held his palms outwards in reasoned entreaty similarly added to the impression that John Tysoe was very much the archetypal forecourt salesman. As Michael got nearer, however, he quickly revised this opinion. Tysoe had an extremely pronounced squint – his right eye being out of kilter with his left by at least twenty degrees – which, along with an unusually pale facial complexion and a livid shock of fiery red hair, served to make his appearance at one and the same time disturbingly eerie yet strangely intriguing.

'Well, I think that now we've got the major part of the extension done we should be able to complete the driveway in less than a week.'

'But that's what you said three weeks ago and absolutely nothing's happened since!'

'Oh, here are my chaps now!' replied Tysoe, cheerfully, turning towards Michael and Naz. 'I'm glad you two've finally decided to make an appearance, Mr Parker here has to be getting off to work!'

'Mornin',' said Michael, nodding at each of the two men in turn. Behind them he could make out the skeleton of a half-completed extension protruding from the back of the house.

'Hi,' replied the man, his forced smile barely concealing his irritation.

'So, you'll let me have the money for the paving slabs this evening then Mr. Parker ...?' asked Tysoe.

'Well, we'll just have to wait and see,' replied Parker, irritably. 'It depends on how much work gets done today – I mean, it really does. Now, I've got to get going. I'll see you when I get home at six o'clock tonight, like we said.'

'OK, Mr Parker, I'll be here, don't worry,' replied Tysoe, bidding the man farewell with a reassuring wave of the hand. Having watched the householder climb into his saloon car and drive away at pace, he then turned to face Naz and Michael.

'So, no Mustafa today, then?'

'No, no, he sick today,' replied Naz smoothly. 'This other friend of mine – Mick.'

'Hello, Mick – how d'you do?'

'Fine,' said Michael, extending his hand for Tysoe to shake.

'Good to meet you,' he replied, shaking his hand. The longer Tysoe looked at Michael, the more unsettled he felt – the deviant eye appearing somehow to be assessing him independently of the good eye. 'I suppose you've done this sort of work before, then?'

'Naz says it's repaving a driveway, right?'

'That's right.'

'Yeah. No problem.'

'Well, if you work half as hard as Naz does, I'm sure it won't be. Now, eighty pounds a day is what I pay – is that all right for you?'

'Fine,' replied Michael.

'Great. Well, I've laid the tools out for you already and Naz here knows what to do, so I'll leave you to it. I'll pop back again in the afternoon – I've got someone else I need to see now. OK, Naz?'

Naz nodded in response and then he and Michael watched Tysoe walk off down the opposite end of the crescent towards a small, unmarked blue transit van. Taking a step to his left, Michael tried to see if he could make out the number plate, but, although the vehicle was obviously quite new, the plate was illegible having been bent downwards underneath the bumper.

'Now, he goes to some other house,' said Naz beneath his breath. 'Find other people to cheat.'

'How many jobs does he usually have on the go at the same time, d'you know?'

'Ten, fifteen.'

'Really?' exclaimed Michael.

'Yes, is true, is true!' gasped Naz, excitedly. 'Mustafa and I meet two other men work for Tysoe before us. They say he crazy. Has many, many jobs on at once – but never finish even one. They work him two months, but then they leave – customers always angry they say. So, he ask me and Mustafa to work for him instead.'

As Tysoe's van pulled away, Michael and Naz turned and walked towards the pile of tools that were lying next to the porch. Looking at its neatly swept interior and the vase of ornamental pampas grass in the corner, Michael frowned thoughtfully. Clearly Tysoe's victims were pre-cisely the sort of middle-class householders to whom King and Tom were trying to appeal in *Criminal Britain*. The man himself was also strik-ingly photogenic – his weirdly sinister appearance being fascinating to observe. On the other hand, although Tysoe was obviously a serial con-man, undercover exposés of rogue tradesmen were nothing new, and having had his first idea about illegal immigrants so recently rejected, Michael wondered whether King and Tom might not find the idea of making cowboy builders the subject of the third documentary a little unoriginal. With a shrug, he leant over and took hold of the pick axe to begin breaking up the driveway; at this point, it just wasn't possible to tell. In any event, he had been planning to find some more casual labour for some time now, so he may as well work out the job until he had enough of footage of Tysoe ripping off Mr Parker to send to Tom. If Tom liked the idea, they could maybe take things further. If not, he would forget it and move on.

Turning to walk back across the driveway, Michael suddenly became aware that he was being watched. In the front window of the house stood a pretty, fair-haired woman of around thirty cradling a baby to her chest: Mr Parker must have told his wife to keep an eye on Tysoe's workmen whilst he was away, but it was clearly a task with which she felt uncomfortable. Letting the axe fall to his side, Michael nodded at her reassuringly and she smiled back in obvious relief and moved away from the window. At first he felt gratified by her response – she had been able to tell that he, at least, was a decent, hard-working man. But, as he once again raised the axe above his head to begin breaking up the paving stones, an image flashed hauntingly before his eyes of the small, white envelope that lay concealed along with the videotapes under the floorboards in Balam Road. Often, the spy had written, betrayal will appear to have left your side – but it will never be far away. His gesture had indeed reassured Mrs Parker, but it had been a lie – a calculated, deliberate lie. Criminals need victims and, for all his ultimately good intentions, Michael was about to play his part in ensuring that she and her husband became precisely that.

The work went well. Naz was as efficient and indefatigable as ever and the cool, late autumn weather proved ideal for their heavy manual labour. Finally laying down their tools just after five-thirty the two men reviewed their handiwork. The existing paving and the house's front wall had been completely demolished and broken up into hardcore to underlay the new driveway. As Naz lit up a cigarette, Michael put on his jacket, switched on his phone and made his way towards the house.

'Hello … hello …?' he called through the side door. Seconds later, Mrs Parker came sprinting down the hallway. Ever since she had seen the speed at which he and Naz were working she had been solicitously plying them with cups of tea and soft drinks every hour.

'Yes, yes, can I help you?'

'Er, have you got any turps? We've, er, finished for today and I just want to clean up a bit.'

'Turpentine, uhm, turpentine,' she said, hurriedly, 'let's see – there might be some under the sink. Come on in I'll have a look.'

'No, it's OK, I don't want to bring any dirt into your kitchen.'

'Oh, don't worry, don't worry. A bit of mess won't matter – I'm just so glad to have seen some work done today.'

As she bent down to open up the cupboard, Michael stood in the doorway and swivelled his shoulders gradually to get a panoramic shot of the Parker's neat, homely kitchen. Over the last few weeks he had been perfecting a series of similarly unobtrusive body movements to improve the dynamics of the footage.

'I'm ever so sorry I don't think we've got any.'

'Oh, it's OK, don't worry, Mrs Parker.'

'I am sorry – and you've worked so hard today, too.'

'Honestly, don't worry about it. I can clean up when I get home,' said Michael, politely, turning slowly to leave.

'Erm, excuse me …' she said, even before he had gone through the door.

'Yes?'

She bit her lip nervously before continuing. This was what he had hoped for. With luck he could get into her confidence and learn a little more about how she and her husband had come across Tysoe.

'Er, will you be coming back tomorrow?'

'I've no idea.'

'Oh. Doesn't Mr Tysoe tell you where you're going to be working each day, then?'

'No, no!' laughed Michael. 'I've never met the bloke before today, to be honest. I'm just a hired labourer, y'know? I work for all sorts of different people – I take whatever comes along.'

'Oh, I see,' she replied, her voice tinged with disappointment.

'He'll be here in a few minutes, though, why don't you ask him?'

'I will. Only the trouble is he doesn't always do what he says. In fact, he very rarely does.'

'That's builders for you.'

'That's exactly what I said to Maurice – my husband. He says we shouldn't pay him any more money until he finishes all the work, but we tried that before and he just disappeared for weeks. I mean I know we agreed stage payments and everything but the only time we get any work out of him is when we hand over more cash. It'll be winter soon as well. We've got to get it all finished now: it's not going to be possible to work in the rain and everything ...'

'Where did you find him?'

'In the local paper.'

Michael was just on the verge of asking whether she and her husband had tried to obtain any references, when he heard the sound of voices from the front of the house.

'Oh, there you are – that's him now.'

'Good,' she replied, taking off her apron and hastily wiping her hands on it. 'Tell him whatever he does not to leave, will you? I'll just call my husband in his car. He's always back at six on the dot, but I want to make absolutely sure ...'

She came out to the front of the house two minutes later just as her husband was pulling up in the street outside. As he got out of the car he was grim-faced, but the moment he saw the near complete transformation of the driveway his expression quickly changed.

'What did I tell you, Mr Parker?' exclaimed Tysoe, calmly. 'All we've got to do now is put down the screed and the paving stones and we're through. We'll be around again tomorrow and we'll only need two more days after that and we'll be finished.'

Mr Parker exchanged a cautiously optimistic look with his wife, but then frowned once more and walked over to confront Tysoe.

'Well, that's all well and good, but what about the extension? I mean you're asking me to part with almost all of the money and you've still got that left to complete.'

'It's the same situation with the extension,' said Tysoe, with a slightly mystified frown that seemed to imply that Mr Parker really was making an inordinate amount of fuss about nothing. 'There's only the glass left to go in and then all we've got to do is paint it up and we're finished.'

'Yeah, I know, you said that to us before, but then you never actually ...'

'D'you wanna come on inside and talk about it,' interrupted Tysoe, diplomatically raising his arm to usher Mr Parker into his house. 'I'm sure we can sort this out ...'

'Yes, yes OK ...' replied Mr Parker.

As Tysoe and the Parkers disappeared into the house, Michael sat down beside Naz on the one remaining side wall.

'What d'you reckon?' asked Michael, quietly.

'Driveway is no two days, I think. Is long job. Then one day for new wall, at least – bricklaying you cannot hurry. Paving, maybe ... hm ... four days – a week, perhaps.'

'As long as that?'

'Quicker to break things down than build them up, Micky.'

'What about that extension out there?'

'I no see exactly, but much to do, I think, much to do.'

A minute later, Tysoe re-emerged from the side door of the house.

'OK, thanks a lot Mr and Mrs Parker. See you again tomorrow. Goodbye now. Goodbye ...'

From the way that Tysoe was smiling as he made his way towards them, Michael guessed that Mr Parker had just parted with a further tranche of his hard earned cash.

'Well done today, lads – you've done a smashing job. Come on over to the van and we'll settle up.'

Just as Naz had described, Tysoe handed over their wages without argument. Watching Naz fold up the notes and put them in his top pocket, Michael began to understand why Tysoe was so keen to have Naz back to work for him again and again. Tysoe's modus operandi was clearly one of short, intensely productive spells of work sufficient to prise a payment out of his hapless victims, followed by a long period of inactivity during which their frustration and exasperation reached such a pitch that the only relief was the pitiful self-deception that the next payment would lead to Tysoe completing the job. Having counted his money, Michael decided to test out this hypothesis.

'D'you want us back here tomorrow, then?'

'Er, no, Mick, not tomorrow,' replied Tysoe, blithely contradicting what he had said to the Parkers just moments before. 'I've got another little job I need you both to do first, if that's all right.'

'Yeah, yeah, sure,' said Michael.

'Good,' exclaimed Tysoe, extracting a small piece of paper from the top pocket of his shirt. 'It's a kitchen job. Here's the address. See you about nine – OK?'

'Fine,' replied Michael.

'Great!' said Tysoe, walking around to the driver's door. 'Now, have yourselves a good evening, won't you, gents? Buy yourselves a pint or two, you deserve it.'

With a wink of his good eye, Tysoe got in and drove away. As his van went out of sight, Naz turned to Michael with a frown.

'He is bad man, I think.'

'Oh, yes, Nasruddin, I believe you're right,' answered Michael, quietly, 'I believe you're right.'

The second couple, Mr and Mrs Conrad, were even more well-to-do than the Parkers, occupying a large five-bedroomed house on the borders of Feltham and Witton. As soon as Michael pulled up into the broad driveway with Naz, he could tell by Mrs Conrad's pleasant wave of acknowledgement from the front window that this was the first day of the job and she had no idea whatsoever of the misery that lay in store for her and her family. Tysoe arrived five minutes later. Seeing his van pull up behind them, Michael switched on his mobile phone to begin filming and then followed Tysoe into the house. Although money was not discussed, Michael was nevertheless able to record a good fifteen minutes of Tysoe's fulsome reassurances to Mr Conrad that the extension and refurbishment of his kitchen would be completed to his absolute satisfaction in less than three weeks. When he left moments later, however, Tysoe once again quietly instructed Naz and Michael that they were to go to another house the following day. Responding that Mustafa was now fully recovered and that in any event he had another job arranged for the next couple of weeks, Michael asked if it would be all right if Tysoe paid him that evening for the day's work. Seeming to accept this explanation, Tysoe replied that he would and, giving Michael a brief, lop-sided smile, drove away.

The following morning, Michael put the video tape that he had taken of the Parkers into a sturdy jiffy-bag, and, leaving the mobile phone downloading footage of the Conrads, mailed it to Tom at the safe house. On the way back from the post office, he then stopped off at the all-day café on the Uxbridge Road for breakfast, returning to the flat just after eleven o'clock. The moment that he arrived at the steps to the front door, Harper was upon him.

'Where the fuck have you been?' he growled, his face livid with anger.

Michael's heart almost leapt up into his throat: he hadn't been expecting to see Harper again for at least another week, let alone find him waiting outside the flat.

'What's the matter? What's up?'

'I've been callin' you all mornin' – the inspectors are gonna be here any minute. Why haven't you got your mobile switched on?'

Michael was completely stumped for an answer: Harper had obviously been trying to call him over the last two hours whilst he had been away from the flat. Standing with his jaw gaping open, Michael felt the panic beginning to well up inside him. What was he to say? He simply had no excuse. Thankfully, before Harper had time to press for an answer to his question, Angela got out of the car in which the two of them had been waiting and sprinted across to the stairs to the flat.

'Get a move on you two,' she hissed. 'Quick!'

Hurrying up the steps behind them, Michael cursed his stupidity and lack of focus. He had taken his eye off the ball. Whilst researching cowboy builders – a subject that King and Tom would in all probability dismiss out of hand – he had compromised his investigation into the fraudsters.

'You said the inspection was gonna be in three weeks time!' he called out in the vain hope of defending his actions.

'I said about three weeks!' spat Harper over his shoulder.

'I told you we should have never have trusted this wanker!' snarled Angela at Harper as the three of them reached the landing in front of the door. Fumbling to get his keys into the lock, Michael turned and looked at her. She stared straight back at him − her eyes filled with naked antagonism. The moment they were inside, Harper slammed the door behind them, dashed across to the window and began anxiously looking up and down the street through a gap in the net curtains.

'What's the time?'

'Ten past eleven,' replied Angela, placing the small suitcase she had brought with her on top of the couch and hastily unzipping it. Taking out two framed photographs of herself, she turned and thrust one of them into Michael's hand. 'Put this in the bedroom.'

As Michael hurried towards the door, out of the corner of his eye he noticed the mobile phone still incriminatingly attached to the back of the video recorder. Pausing for a second, he thought about leaning down to unplug it, but Angela immediately detected that his step had faltered.

'Now!' she snapped.

Sprinting into the bedroom, Michael placed the photograph on the bedside table and then quickly returned to the living room.

'They're here!' hissed Harper, lurching sharply back from the window to ensure that he could not be seen from the road.

'Who is it, can you see?' asked Angela, not looking up from the task of positioning various items of female attire around the living room.

'Oh fuck!' gasped Harper.

'What?'

'It's Dill.'

'What!' cried Angela in horror, casting aside a blouse that she had just hung on a coat hanger and then rushing across towards the window. 'Oh, Jesus!'

'What's the matter?' asked Michael.

'I thought he'd been kicked off the inspection team!' exclaimed Angela, ignoring Michael's question.

'Well, he's obviously back on it now!' growled Harper. Over his shoulder, Michael could see two tall, well-built men making their way purposefully across the road towards the front of the flat.

'Come on, let's get out the back door,' said Angela, turning and hurrying towards the living room door. 'If Dill recognises either of us, we're finished. Mick'll have to do the interview on his own.'

'There isn't a back door,' interjected Michael.

'What!' exclaimed Harper and Angela in unison.

'There isn't a back way out – there aren't any stairs.'

'Oh, Christ alive!' raged Harper, furiously.

'It's too late to get out the front now,' cried Angela. 'They're almost here!'

'Have you got a back window?' asked Harper.

'Yeah.'

'Show us,' he replied, grabbing Angela's hand and dashing out into the hallway.

'You might be able to jump down on to the wall from here,' said Michael, opening up the kitchen window and pointing to the garden wall that separated the old lady's flat below from the street at the side.

'I'll never make it down there!' exclaimed Angela, staring aghast at the fifteen foot drop.

At the moment, the front door bell rang.

'Oh fuckin' hell,' cursed Harper. 'I'll kill Craig. He should've told us it was gonna be Dill!'

'Don't answer the door,' said Angela quickly, 'pretend we're not in.'

'That's no good!' blazed Harper. 'If Dill finds the place empty he'll arrange to have it put under surveillance. We'll never know what the bastard'll find out then.'

Sensing this was the moment to seize the initiative, Michael quickly cut in.

'He's seen both of you before, right? This guy, Dill.'

'Yeah,' replied Harper. 'It was over a year ago, but he's a sharp bastard.'

'OK. Ange, you wash your hair,' said Michael, pointing towards the bathroom door. 'Geoff, you go out through the window.'

'What?' gasped Angela.

'Wash your hair – in the bathroom. If you've got your head stuck inside the bath and your hair's wet you won't be so easy to recognise.'

Harper and Angela stared at each other indecisively, but when the front door bell rang a second time Harper delayed no further.

'Do it!' hissed Harper to Angela, turning and jumping up on to the window sill. As Michael left the kitchen, he had already taken the plunge down towards the wall.

'Take your clothes off as well,' said Michael, pushing Angela into the bathroom. 'Wrap a bath towel around you. If they see you half-dressed they won't stare too hard.'

As soon as Angela closed the bathroom door, Michael ran into the living room, unplugged the phone and, switching it back to record mode, slipped it into his top pocket. By the time he opened the front door the two inspectors were already half way back down the concrete stairs.

'Hello …' he called out after them. Stopping, they turned and looked back towards him.

'Mr Morgan?'

'Yeah.'

'My name's Dill. I'm from the Housing Benefits Office.'

'Oh, right, sorry – I was, er, out the back.'

'It's about your recent claim. D'you think we could have a word?'

'Sure, come on up,' said Michael, walking back into the flat. The moment he was out of their sight he rushed back into the living room, opened up the sideboard and frantically ran his eyes over the page of notes he had taken after Harper's visit.

Angela was Wendy.

They had met at a disco in Leeds.

'May we come in?' asked Dill respectfully, knocking gently on the living room door.

'Yeah, yeah,' replied Michael, stuffing the paper back in the drawer.

'Thank you, Mr Morgan.'

Michael watched Dill and his colleague walk across the living room and ease themselves down onto the low-slung, threadbare sofa. At first glance, Dill was by no means a remarkable figure, and, if he had passed him in the street, Michael would not have looked at him twice. As the inspector opened up his briefcase and extracted a pencil and notepad, Michael scrutinized his appearance more closely, trying to understand why it was that the fraudsters held him in such awe. He was about six feet tall and had a powerfully built frame, although his chin was under-sized and receded into his jaw slightly giving him a somewhat insecure, hunted look. His facial skin was extremely smooth and hairless – not naturally so, but as a result of having shaved with great care: here was a man, thought Michael, who simply did not leave the bathroom until every last hair had been painstakingly razored right back to its roots. His

174

clothes, on the other hand, were of generally low quality and had not been ironed. It was as Dill finally turned to look at Michael, however, that he at last began to appreciate why the inspector had been able to drive Harper and Angela into such a terrified panic. An ordinary person's gaze remains fixed on the object of its attention – but not Dill's. As he looked across the room, his grey-green eyes never once stopped moving, ceaselessly poring over Michael's face and body with all the patient intensity of a witch finder seeking out the devil's mark.

'Just a few questions first of all, if I may, Mr Morgan?' began Dill, his expression breaking into a smile that somehow made the soles of Michael's feet itch. 'When did you move in to this property?'

'Erm, July, sometime – end of July.'

'And where were you living before?'

'Up north.'

'Right, I see. What brought you down to London?'

'Looking for work.'

'Have you found any?'

'Just bits. Nothing permanent.'

'Are you claiming any other benefits?'

'No.'

'What about your wife?'

'What about her?'

'Is she working?'

'Yes.'

'As …'

'Waitressing, a couple of days a week. That's all.'

'Is she here at the moment?'

'Yeah, she's out the back, washing her hair.'

'Oh, right,' replied Dill, giving Michael another unctuous smile and then delving into his case for a few more papers. 'OK, Mr Morgan,' he continued, 'd'you think we could have a quick look around the property?'

'Sure,' replied Michael, standing and walking out into the hall.

'Who's your landlord, Mr Morgan?' asked Dill as he came through and joined Michael in the hall.

'Er, a bloke over in West Feltham.'

'What's his name?'

Suddenly, Michael froze, unable to remember the false name that

Harper had given him. Having stuffed the notes back into the drawer, it was going to look hugely suspicious if he had to go and check. Just at that instant, the sound of Angela turning on the shower became audible and, as Dill looked in the direction of the bathroom, the name suddenly came back to mind.

'Fry,' he blurted. 'Mr Fry.'

Dill turned and nodded at Michael and then began looking around the hallway. As he and his colleague were about to walk into the kitchen, Michael moved forward and knocked on the bathroom door. It was now or never.

'Wend! Wend!' he shouted through. 'There's a couple of guys here from the Housing. Are you decent? Wend?'

'What?' came Angela's muffled response.

'D'you need to have a look inside?' asked Michael, nodding at the bathroom door.

'No, it's …'

Before Dill had time fully to reply, Michael pushed open the door. Exactly as he had hoped, Angela was bent over the bath washing her hair, a towel draped around her half-naked body.

'Brian!' she screeched.

'Sorry, love,' said Michael closing the door quickly.

Dill and the other man exchanged a slightly embarrassed look and moved into the kitchen. Deciding it would be best to leave them to get on with the inspection, Michael went back into the living room. A minute later, Dill once again knocked respectfully on the door.

'OK, Mr Morgan, thank you very much. We're all finished now. We'll be on our way.'

'Oh, great, thanks,' said Michael, springing out of his seat and going into the hall where the two men were already on the verge of going through the front door. 'Was everything OK?'

'Yes, yes, fine,' replied Dill.

'Good,' said Michael, moving across the hallway to close the door with a huge feeling of relief. 'Thanks very much.'

'Oh, just one final thing I need to check,' said Dill, pausing on the threshold.

'Yes?'

'When did you say you moved in here again?'

'Erm, end of July,' replied Michael.

'Not the end of June?' asked Dill.

Looking into the inspector's face, Michael instantly realized his mistake. Michael Angel had indeed moved in at the end of July, but Brian Morgan had moved in at the end of June – or, at least, that was what he had written on his declaration.

'Oh, yeah, maybe you're right, perhaps it was the end of June,' he replied, realizing he had no option but to attempt to brush his mistake off as a lapse of memory. Dill exchanged a look with his colleague and then stared back at Michael. Once again his eyes narrowed as he scrutinized every detail of Michael's face. Finally, after what seemed like minutes but was in fact probably only a couple of seconds, he nodded and turned to walk back down the stairs.

'Good afternoon, Mr Morgan.'

As Michael closed the door, he tried to work out how suspicious his error must have seemed to Dill. Concluding that for the time being it was a much less pressing problem than having to explain to Harper why he had had his mobile phone switched off, he went back across the hallway to tell Angela that Dill had left.

'Ange. They've gone,' he called through the bathroom door. She didn't reply. Walking back into the living room he looked out of the front window just in time to see Dill and the other inspector driving away. The moment they were out of sight, Harper got out of his car and made his way gingerly back up the stairs.

'How'd it go?' asked Harper, walking through the door into the hallway.

'OK,' replied Michael. 'It was OK.'

'Where's Ange?'

'In the bathroom.'

At that moment, Angela emerged fully clothed but with her hair dripping wet. For a second the three of them stared at each other saying nothing. Once again Michael realized that he had to seize the initiative, and, placing his hands on his hips, let out a broad bellowing laugh.

'Fuckin' hell. That was close!'

As he continued laughing he could see Harper's face break into a smile. Angela, however, was scowling fiercely and shook her head in disgust as she walked into the living room to begin repacking her suitcase.

'You're right there,' conceded Harper.

'Pretty hairy. Wasn't it, eh, Ange?' said Michael, nodding in Angela's direction and then leaning forward and slapping Harper on the shoulder.

'Ha, fucking, ha,' called Angela humourlessly from the living room. 'Come on, Geoff. Let's get out of here.'

With a wink at Harper, who was now obviously seeing the funny side of things, Michael went into the bedroom, retrieved the photograph of Angela and gave it back to her. Snatching it out of his hand, she slipped it inside the suitcase, zipped it up and marched out of the flat.

Michael stood in the doorway, watching them walk down the stairs to their car. Half way down, Harper turned around and grinned at him. Nodding by way of reply, Michael closed the front door and then went back inside the flat. Leaning with his back up against the wall, he exhaled deeply and then closed his eyes for several seconds as the waves of relief and satisfaction swept over him. That grin meant everything. After such a desperately close shave with the inspectors, it would have been almost impossible for Harper to have faked such a spontaneous and natural expression: for all his earlier agonizing and despite the slip-up with his mobile phone, Michael was now certain that Harper didn't suspect him. As for Angela, although it was obvious that she both disliked and distrusted him, his idea of having her wash her hair had definitely saved her from apprehension by the authorities and without doubt she was in his debt for that. Moreover, it seemed to Michael that his own relative levity must come as a blessed relief to Harper compared to Angela's frigid cheerlessness. With a self-approving smile he rubbed his hand over his forehead. He had done it. He had achieved his first major objective of gaining the confidence of one of the gang members. Trust between strangers is only ever truly forged in adversity, and, as long as he made sure to do everything he could from now on to avoid coming directly between Harper and Angela, he should be able to use the day's experience as a means of insinuating his way still further into the gang. However, as he stepped forward to walk back down the hall, these reassuring thoughts were driven right from his mind. In the hallway, on the floor – lying flush against the skirting board and unnoticed in all the confusion – was a postcard; it must have arrived in the second delivery that morning. Kneeling down he picked it up and turned it over. It was amber.

Tom was calling him in.

178

Chapter 7

Two days later, Michael went to the safehouse, leaving Balam Road at
six a.m., just before first light. Silently closing the front door, he walked
down the concrete steps and surveyed the early morning scene before
him. The misty streets, ethereal in the diffuse amber glow of the streetlights, were totally deserted – even the normally busy Uxbridge Road
was empty of traffic. Walking around the corner to the small patch of
waste ground where he parked his car, he buttoned up his jacket against
the cold – winter was coming early this year. Unlocking the car door,
he looked across the road at the garages opposite and thought of Dill.
From what Harper had said, and from what he had seen of the inspector at first hand, it was all too easy to imagine him lurking in the
shadows behind the garages, a huge pair of binoculars around his neck
and a thermos flask bulging in the pocket of his faded Burberry. Turning
on the ignition, Michael struggled once more to try to determine
whether his having confused June with July had been enough to
provoke Dill's suspicions to the point of his actually deciding to mount
a surveillance of the flat. It seemed unlikely, but of the two errors that
Michael had made so far, it nagged him far more than the fact that he
had been downloading footage from the mobile when Harper had tried
to call him on it. Much as he had grown used to the phone, he could
always take Jim up on his offer to attempt to make a second, slimline
phone, or even ask him to rig up a completely different concealed
camera system altogether. On the other hand, even though he was
certain that Harper did not suspect him, both he and Angela were
clearly extremely wary of Dill, and, if the inspector were to take it into

his mind actively to start following Michael, they might well decide he was too much of a liability and stay as far away from him as possible in the future.

Half way to the safe house he stopped at a service station and bought some eggs and a loaf of bread for breakfast. When he arrived, however, he found the refrigerator already fully stocked. Walking over to the kitchen table, he picked up the copy of *The Mail* that was lying there – it was dated three days previously: Tom had mentioned that he sometimes stopped at the safe house overnight when he was going through a very heavy spell of work at the office and had obviously done so in the last few days. Having cooked breakfast and washed up, Michael waited until half past eight and then called through to the Tower. Tom replied that he would jump in a cab straightaway and, less than a half an hour later, came through the front door.

'You look well,' he said, unbuttoning his coat and then walking down the hallway to shake Michael's hand. His grip was firm and warm. It was good to see him again.

'You, too.'

'Thanks,' replied Tom, with a smile. 'Let's go on through, I'll give you the news.'

'I've just put some fresh coffee on,' replied Michael. 'It should be ready in a couple of minutes.'

'Good man, good man ...' said Tom walking through into the living room and sitting down at the brightly polished, mahogany table.

'This is new,' remarked Michael, taking the seat opposite him.

'Oh, yes, well, I thought I ought to get a few decent sticks of furniture in the place – you know, make it a bit more comfortable for you.'

'Thanks.'

'My pleasure. So,' continued Tom, his face rapidly becoming serious, 'I'm sorry about the postcard, it must have come as a bit of a shock. I hope your having suddenly to disappear like this didn't cause you any difficulties, but I couldn't really wait until you made contact next.'

'No – no problem.'

'Good. I'm glad to hear that,' he replied, slipping off his jacket and draping it over the arm of the sofa. 'All right, let me get straight to the point. Do you remember Windsor Finance, the venture capital division of King Media?'

'Yes – vaguely.'

'Just over a month ago they were approached by a television production company called Thomas Buckleys. Have you ever heard of them?'

'No. Never.'

'Me neither. They're small – a five-man band apparently – but they're all experienced broadcasters and from what I can gather a pretty competent crew. Anyway, the reason for Buckleys' approach was that they're looking for finance for a pilot episode of a new TV documentary they're hoping to produce – fifty per cent finance, in fact: they've got a pledge for the other half of the cash from Dutch state TV dependent on their finding a co-sponsor in the UK. Windsor liked the proposal and sent it off to the Tower where it went through several more sets of hands before eventually making its way on to Henry's desk for the final, royal seal of approval. Normally, he doesn't bother to examine these things in too much detail, but on this particular day he was a little less busy than most and he read their proposal all the way through.'

'And?'

Tom's eyes narrowed and he leant back in his chair before answering.

'We have competition, I'm afraid.'

'What?'

'Yes. As it stands, Buckleys' project isn't exactly the same as ours but it's pretty close.'

'In what way?'

'Drugs. It's a two-part documentary about drugs. Just like us, they're planning to have an investigator go out and film drug dealers using undercover cameras.'

'Is that really so similar?'

'If that was where the resemblance ended, no. The problem is that their editorial approach is more or less identical, I'm afraid.'

'How d'you mean?'

'In their proposal document Buckleys go into great detail about their intention to try and give the dealers a face. You know, not just film them selling the stuff, but go beyond that and acquaint the viewers with them as people; go to their homes, film their families, etcetera etcetera – it's Henry's original concept right down to a tee. What's more, they say if the pilot's successful they intend to produce a follow-up series along the same lines.'

'Shit.'

'That was his reaction. Mine, too.'

'When are they planning to start this?'

'Just as soon as they get the finance.'

'How did Henry reply, then?'

'Well, he's stalled them for the moment – asked for more details – but he can only hold things up for so long. Sooner or later they'll get fed up being given the run-around and go elsewhere for the money, and as they've already drummed up fifty per cent of the cash, it shouldn't be too difficult to find.'

'What are we going to do?'

'That's what I brought you here to discuss,' replied Tom, gravely. 'Now, just you sit tight for a few minutes – I'll go and get the coffee. One sugar, right?'

'Yeah, thanks.'

As Michael listened to Tom moving around in the kitchen, the full impact of his news began to sink in. Judging from what he had said, Buckleys would be up and running as soon as they had secured their second tranche of finance. With perhaps five or six months for filming and roughly the same amount of time for editing, post-production and scheduling they could be on the screen in under eighteen months – six months ahead of *Criminal Britain*. Up until this morning Michael's darkest fears had revolved around Dill and the mobile phone, but whereas both problems would be a blow to the first investigation, neither would force him to abandon the series altogether; Buckleys' documentary, however, appeared to have the potential to do precisely that. As Tom walked back in and put the mugs of coffee down on the table, his expression was disturbingly grim.

'So, does King think that we should throw in the towel, then?' asked Michael, apprehensively.

'Well,' said Tom, retaking his seat, 'I have to admit that when Henry and I first talked things through it was one of the options that we con- sidered: Buckleys' documentary is so similar that there's a very real risk of us coming across as a copy-cat programme. And, as I think I've said to you before, if there's one thing in the world Henry can't abide, it's coming second – that's not how he got where is today. You'll be glad to hear, though, that less than twenty-four hours later we'd completely ruled out the idea – we were absolutely determined to find some way of beating Buckleys to it.'

'Why? What happened?'

182

'John Tysoe happened.'

'Tysoe?'

'Yes, we played the tape you sent me,' replied Tom, shaking his head in admiration. 'Where on earth did you find him? His face! It's just so perfect, so … criminal – he's the absolute epitome of what we're looking for in the series.'

'You liked him, then?'

'I did. I did. And as for Henry – he just sat and gawped. I can't remember the last time I saw him so impressed. It would be an absolute tragedy if the British public never got to see Tysoe's face – those were his exact words. Tysoe's good enough for a whole documentary in his own right – easily.'

'You really think so?'

'Oh, yes, definitely.'

'You don't think cowboy builders as a topic is sort of a bit, well, unoriginal?'

'Not at all. The public can never get enough of people like that. Never!'

For a moment, Michael almost shook his head in disbelief – he would never have imagined such a response. When he had sent the video, he had walked away from the post office almost certain that King and Tom would dismiss his suggestion out of hand. Instead of being the cause of a second embarrassing rejection, however, it seemed that Tysoe might have rescued the entire series.

'So, what are we going to do about Buckleys then?' asked Michael.

'Well, we only have two choices, really. The first is to rethink the format in some way. Reading between the lines of their proposal, we're pretty sure they've got an undercover reporter just waiting to go: we think they've recruited him or her already.'

'Really?'

'Yes. So, as we have four documentaries to make and they have only one, it's almost inevitable that they're going to get there first.'

'So, what's the other option?'

Clasping both hands around his mug of coffee, Tom leant forward and stared straight into Michael's eyes.

'Run the first three investigations concurrently rather than sequentially.'

'What?'

'Do them in parallel, rather than one after another.'

Michael was about to reply, but instead drew in his breath and thought for several moments. Tom was still staring at him straight-faced – he was obviously deadly serious.

'That'd be impossible, though, surely,' he said eventually. 'I mean, it'd be confusing, dangerous ...'

'That's what we thought at first, but then we hit on the answer – why not make your Michael Angel personality appropriate not just to the first documentary, but to the first three?'

'What d'you mean?'

'Well,' said Tom, sitting forward on his seat, his eyes once again bright with enthusiasm, 'the essence of your success so far has been the credibility of your persona, has it not? You walk and talk and think like Michael Angel, don't you? The labourer from up north who's come down to London looking for a job.'

'Yes ...'

'So what happened when Michael Angel arrived in London? Talk me through his progress.'

'He met up with Harper and ...'

'No, before that – before Harper – when he first started looking for work.'

'Well, he ...'

'He got cheated by that man Roger, didn't he?' interrupted Tom, excitedly. 'But then he got smart: because you have to wise up in the big city – it's a jungle and you won't survive otherwise. He met Roger first and then got to know Harper afterwards, and when Harper said how about we do each other a favour – make a bit of money by a fraudulent housing benefit claim – he jumped at the chance. That was his first step on the ladder. The second was Tysoe. He took him up to eighty pounds a day and although Tysoe's screwing his customers, he's paying Michael Angel all right. So, what's his third step on the ladder, then? What does Michael Angel do next?'

'Tell me,' he replied, staring straight back into Tom's shrewd, calculating face.

'He gets even smarter. He's a big chap – well-built, tough – but presentable with it. So, he carries on with odd bits of casual building work here and there, but from now on, two or three nights a week ...'

Tom left the sentence trailing.

184

'What?'

'He gets a job as a doorman. A bouncer. In a night-club.'

'Why would he want to do that?'

'Good pay – better than he gets on the buildings. A bit of glamour, too. Smart suit, bow-tie.'

'And as regards the series?'

'Who controls the sale of drugs in night-clubs and discos?'

'Bouncers?'

'Exactly!' exclaimed Tom. ''Control the doors – control the floors' – that's what they say. Now, according to Buckleys' proposal, they're intending to concentrate on housing estates – suburbia in other words. But you can't just march in there willy-nilly and start filming criminals, as you know all too well from your experiences with Harper. You have to establish yourself first – it takes time. With the club scene, though, you can be right in the thick of it from day one: that gives us a big advantage over Buckleys straightaway. Also, we'll have at least two investigations going on in the suburbs already – Harper and Tysoe are both very much suburban animals – but night-clubs are a different environment altogether. We have to ring the changes in *Criminal Britain*, you know, make each episode that little bit different.'

'How do I get a job as a bouncer?'

'Through an agency. We've found you one already,' replied Tom, taking a sheaf of papers out of his briefcase and passing it across to Michael.

'The London-American Agency,' read Michael aloud.

'Your references are at the back there – from a club in the north of England where you worked for six months. False, of course, but I doubt they'll check.'

'How d'you know they'll employ me?'

'We don't, but they advertise all the time, so we guess there's got to be some sort of on-going demand for new people ...'

Standing up, Michael walked across the living room and looked thoughtfully out of the window. Henry and Tom's suggestion made a lot of sense. Ever since he had gone under cover, he had been acutely conscious of the fact that because he dare not rush things with Harper many of his days had been spent simply waiting around in the flat. It was a very poor use of time. As long as he didn't try and overdo things, it should be quite possible for him to work a few evenings a week in a club and still be able to track Harper and Tysoe during the day. And, as Tom had pointed out, rather than detracting from his Michael Angel persona, his temporary, night-time employment would lend it further credibility.

'What about the fourth documentary?' asked Michael, turning around to face Tom.

'Good point. Now, I don't want to underestimate Tysoe – he looks a pretty slippery customer to me – but I would have thought that compared to Harper, and probably the drugs investigation too, he's going to be relatively simple to wrap up. Do you agree?'

'Yes, I should think so; if you're satisfied for him to be the sole subject of the third documentary.'

'Oh, we are, we are.'

'Well, yes, then. He should be comparatively easy, I guess. The only problem might be establishing his precise motivation.'

'Well, I would've thought that's obvious – it's money, isn't it?'

'That's what I thought at first, but I'm not so sure now.'

'What d'you mean?' asked Tom.

'I mean there's some other dimension to his personality – something compulsive about the way he behaves. He's not just cheating one or two householders here and there, he's got literally a dozen on the go at any one time. It's not just the money, there's … I don't know … a strange pathology underlying what he does.'

'Do you think you'll be able to get close to him like you've done with Harper?'

'No, no chance. He never opens up. He's very secretive.'

'But you will be able to find out where he lives, won't you? Film his home and family and what have you?'

'Yes, I'm sure I will,' conceded Michael. 'It'll just be a question of tailing him for long enough. He's only one man, like you say, so sooner or later I should be able to find out what really makes him tick.'

'That's what we thought. So, our idea is to start the fourth investigation once you're happy you've more or less got him and a certain portion of the other two investigations in the bag. I mean, obviously, between then and now we've got to decide what the subject matter of the fourth documentary's going to be, but that's the basic idea. By this overlap approach we reckon we can halve the time to project completion.'

'Bringing the series to the screen when?'

'In a year's time – a good four of five months ahead of Buckleys: because, of course, whereas we know about them, they don't know about us. And, on top of that, we can also add to our lead by starting pre-production whilst you're still in the final stages of the investigations. That way, the moment you've finished, we'll be ready to go.'

'I see what you mean,' said Michael.

'Good. But listen, we don't want you to make the decision straight-away. As always, give it a bit of time – think it through. And, if you do go ahead like we suggest and things do start to get dangerous, you can pull out. Just like we've said all along. No regrets. No recriminations. Your safety in all of this is absolutely paramount.'

'OK – got you. I'll give it some thought and let you know later today. The idea sounds great, but there are going to be personal impli-cations – you know, as regards my family.'

'Absolutely, old chap. Take your time, take your time. '

'Thanks. Right. My turn now,' said Michael reaching into his jacket pocket and passing a video cassette across to Tom. 'Feast your eyes on this.'

'What is it?'

'The first half of the tape is a drinking session I had with Harper in the White Horse. Now, I'm not sure – see what you think – but it seems to me there might be a chance that the gang is politically motivated.'

'Really!'

'Yes.'

'Gosh! I said as much, didn't I?'

'You did.'

'Good lord!'

'It's only a possibility. I've played the tape several times and I'm still not sure myself.'

'OK.'

'The second half of the tape is the inspection by Housing Benefits – they came on Wednesday.'

'Already?'

'Yes. Ten days early. It caught me on the hop a bit.'

'Did it go off all right?'

'Yeah, eventually.'

'What d'you mean?' asked Tom, slotting the tape into the video recorder.

'Well, there were a few scenes of Harper and Angela before the inspectors arrived that I'd love to have recorded, but I couldn't get the camera out in time. I mean they were really panicking – you should've seen them.'

'Great!' exclaimed Tom, sitting down on the sofa and eagerly waiting for the video to begin. 'Things really are hotting up now, aren't they?'

'They are. Especially now that I've found out about Craig.'

'Who's Craig?'

Michael didn't reply: the tape had already started and he decided he may as well let Tom see for himself.

He returned to Balam Road at three o'clock that afternoon, having made two crucial decisions during the long drive back across London. Firstly, he was going to do as Tom and Henry had suggested: having already invested so much in *Criminal Britain*, he was unable to countenance the prospect of spending the rest of his life regretting that he had shied away from completing it when faced with a little competition. Secondly, in ten or eleven months' time, when it was all over, he would take a full year off work. By then, Jake would be sixteen years old – a young man: it would surely be time for them at last to get to know each other properly, not just as father and son, but as adults and as equals. Moreover, although running the first three investigations in parallel meant that Michael would be unable to take a few weeks away from his fictitious job in Geneva to visit Elizabeth and Jake, it advanced by a year the time that he would be able to reveal in full why he had disappeared in the first place. In that sense, perhaps Buckleys' documentary was a blessing in disguise: once the series was actually screened, Jake could scarcely fail to recognize and be impressed by what his father had achieved.

Taking the mobile phone out of the top pocket of his jacket, Michael stood in front of the living room mirror, positioning himself in such a way that the internal lens would catch his reflection as he spoke. He had tested the technique out a couple of times and had found that speaking directly into the mirror in this way created a really eye-catching visual effect. Also, the more narration he recorded now, the less he would need to add later.

'I'm calling the London Headquarters of the Trading Standards Authority,' he announced. 'There's a gentlemen there by the name of

Andrew Pollard whom I'm hoping will agree to talk to me about the problem of rogue traders. Let's see if I can reach him.'

'Good afternoon, Trading Standards Authority, may I help you?' replied the switchboard operator.

'Er, yes, please, could you put me through to Mr Pollard?'

'Just one moment …'

'Andrew Pollard.'

'Good afternoon, Mr Pollard. My name's Andy Byatt – I'm a freelance journalist. I'm doing a piece on cowboy builders and I was wondering if you'd be willing to give me the benefit of your advice on the subject.'

'Well, I'll help you if I can, Mr Byatt,' replied Pollard – his voice was affable yet authoritative. 'As far as I'm able, anyway …'

'Thank you. It's only a couple of quick questions, if I may.'

'Sure. Fire away.'

'Thanks. OK, first of all, are there any official figures – either from your office or from any other reliable source – on the number of building jobs each year in the UK in which householders claim to have been cheated by a cowboy operator? Is it one in twenty, or one in thirty or what? I'm just trying to get a feel for the overall numbers.'

'The Office of Fair Trading does publish statistics, but I'm afraid that isn't actually one of them. I can tell you, though, that last year we processed just over a hundred thousand complaints against building firms. It's our biggest category by far – has been for ages.'

'A hundred thousand?'

'Yes.'

'That's a very large number.'

'It is, but that's just the reported cases, of course. The vast majority of grievances simply never get pursued which is why I can't tell you exactly whether it's one in twenty or one in thirty. If you pressed me though, I'd say that for every one case we handle perhaps another nine or ten go unreported.'

'So, let me get this right,' said Michael, frowning gravely into the mirror. 'You're saying that around a million people a year in this country get fiddled by rogue builders?'

'Or claim to have been so, yes.'

'That's a huge number.'

'Yes, well, it's a big problem.'

'And how many of those complaints ever get satisfactorily resolved?'

'Of the grievances we handle, quite a lot; of the unreported ones very, very few. If you're a big company suing some other similarly large organization for breach of contract, this country's legal system is a fairly efficient means of seeking redress, but if you're an individual consumer, it's really not much use to you; cowboy builders are far too well versed in manipulating it, I'm afraid.'

'How do they do that?'

'Well, when they initially quote for a particular piece of building work they will always make sure they put as little as they can in writing – that takes out a whole swathe of claimants who, on having subsequently consulted a solicitor, find they don't have the evidence to substantiate their claims. However, even if a particular claimant does have a solid legal case, his solicitor will almost always advise him to drop it – you know, tell him not to throw good money after bad. That gets rid of most of those claimants who are left. On those rare occasions that a claimant does pursue the case all the way to court and does manage to get a ruling in his favour, he or she will almost always find that the damages they've been awarded simply aren't recoverable.'

'Why not?'

'Well, the builder will probably already have declared his company bankrupt. And because it won't have had any assets the ruling isn't really much use to the claimant – despite all the time, energy and money he or she will have expended in getting it. Sending in the bailiffs is similarly a waste of time. It might net the claimant five hundred pounds if he's lucky. To add insult to injury, a few weeks later the builder might well go and set up another company.'

'And then start ripping off people all over again.'

'Very often, yes.'

'Which brings me to my second question. If I've understood you correctly, very few cowboy builders ever get sent to prison. Am I right?'

'Yes. I mean for all the distress their activities cause, we're talking here essentially about civil, not criminal offences, so fines and community service are much more common sentences. If they repeatedly offend, though, judges sometimes do send them to prison.'

'Really?' asked Michael, moving closer towards the surface of the mirror.

'Yes, yes. It has been known to happen.'

190

'So, if a court were presented with convincing evidence of a given builder having systematically deceived, say, a dozen or so customers over a period of several months, d'you think the judge might award a custodial sentence?'

'Yes, that's quite possible, but the problem, of course, is compiling that evidence. One of the things cowboy builders rely on is the fact that their victims are almost always unaware of each other's existence and it's therefore all too easy for them to pretend when they are taken to court that the case in question was an isolated incident. I mean, a judge isn't going to send a builder to prison for five years for cheating someone out of a couple of thousand pounds, is he?'

'Thanks for your time, Mr Pollard, that's all I wanted to know,' said Michael, his face now only inches away from the surface of the glass.

'Oh, it's my pleasure. And do feel free to call me anytime by the way, we welcome all the publicity we can get.'

'Thank you, I will. Goodbye now.'

'Goodbye, Mr Byatt.'

Certain that his face would now be totally filling the screen, Michael paused for two seconds and then announced with quiet determination.

'Did you get that, John Tysoe? You're going to prison.'

His first job was at a night-club in Brighton called Fevah. Although Michael had prepared himself for the likelihood of having to travel some distance from Feltham, seventy miles was much further than he had anticipated. The people at London-American had said that they had been let down at the last minute by sickness, but he couldn't help thinking that probably all their other London-based temporaries had turned their noses up at the job. In either case, as a way of getting on good terms with the agency, he had decided to take it: it was only for five nights and the traffic would probably be quite light as he returned to Feltham in the small hours.

He arrived there earlier than he had intended, just before six o'clock in the evening. According to the directions that London-American had sent him there was an employee car park at the back of the building, but when he tried to pull into the road at the side he found a heavy, padlocked chain draped across it. Reversing back out, he made his way around the one-way system once again and then parked his car on the opposite side of the road to the club and waited for signs of life. Leaning back in his seat, he lit up a cigarette and surveyed the exterior of the building. Quite plainly the club had started life as a cinema – although the new owners had constructed a glitzy foyer and entrance area, the broad brick facia above left no doubt as to the building's original purpose. The street in which the club was located appeared to be right in the centre of Brighton's night-life district. Watching the groups of youths drifting in and out of the pubs, Michael found himself thinking of Jake. Within a few years this is precisely what he would be doing; perhaps he had even started to do so already. With a shake of his head, he opened the car door and stubbed his cigarette out on the kerb. Each successive investigation was becoming more and more personal to him. Harper might or might not be some sort of political extremist, but, in either case, a part of Michael couldn't help warming to him as an individual. Tysoe, on the other hand, had got right under his skin from the very word go and even though he hadn't communicated as much to Tom, he had decided to do everything in his power to make sure that he was sent to jail. And now, here he was entering the world of illegal drugs. Drugs that mercilessly slashed the bond between children and their parents – a bond, that in his own case, he was so anxious belatedly to try and forge. Winding up the driver's window, he got out of the car and locked it. He was sweating. He needed some air. All his professional life he had tried to remain dispassionate in his reporting, but now he could feel his own emotions being stirred up by the experiences he was undergoing. Having to abandon *Criminal Britain* because of Buckleys was one thing: having to do so because he had throttled a drug-dealer to death was another. From now on he knew he was going to have to keep a close eye on himself to make sure he didn't lose control.

Looking across the road, he noticed that a stocky, broad-shouldered man had just appeared out of the shadows and was unlocking the padlock and chain. Crossing the road, he went over to speak to him.

'Hi.'

'What d'you want?' replied the man, his cold blue eyes fixing Michael in an uncompromising, imperturbable stare.

'My name's Micky Angel. I'm from the London-American agency …'

'Oh, right,' replied the man, his tone of voice relaxing but his stony expression remaining unchanged. 'I'm Les. Come on in, I'll show you around.'

'Thanks,' said Michael, following him as he walked up the steps to the front entrance. 'So, er, you worked here long?' he continued, attempting a little light conversation.

'Too long,' replied Les, in a factual, rancourless voice. Selecting another key from the twenty or so on the heavy ring attached to his waist-band, he opened the door and stepped inside. The interior of the club was pitch black until Les disappeared into a cloak room and switched on the lights. Even allowing for the fact that the club was empty of customers and completely without atmosphere, Michael could tell that it had seen better days.

'You'll be on the front here with me,' said Les, relocking the front door and nodding in the direction of a gloomy passageway at the side of the cloak room. 'Come on, we get changed down 'ere.'

'OK,' answered Michael, trying not to appear too fascinated by Les's face, which for the first time he was now able to observe at close quarters and in proper light. The deeply pock-marked cheeks, the angular, tightly-shaven head and the penetrating blue eyes would doubtless be an asset to any hard-working bouncer. It was the bone structure, however, that Michael found really remarkable. His nose, jaw and cheek bones were prominent and well-defined, but yet at the same time indented with numerous subtle contours that seemed to indicate an inherent indestructibility.

'You can use that one if you want to,' said Les, pointing at a battered metal locker behind the door. 'What size are you? I'll get you a suit.'

'It's all right, I brought one with me,' replied Michael, lifting up the holdall he was carrying. According to Jim, it had taken the seamstress almost a whole day to micro-stitch the lens into the lining underneath the button hole on the lapel.

'As you like,' replied Les, opening up his own locker and beginning silently and methodically to get changed. Looking at his physique, Michael found it hard to guess how old he was: he could be anything between thirty-five and sixty. Whatever his age, Les was clearly an old hand and Michael decided not to insult his seniority by making further small talk or plying him with inane questions; if the older man had any words of wisdom to impart, he would be best left to do so in his own time.

'We open at seven, yeah?' said Michael, finally, after he had changed into his suit.

'Yeah,' replied Les, walking across the locker room to examine

Michael. 'Right, then. Let's have a look at you …' There was such authority in his voice, that without thinking Michael stood up and allowed himself to be frisked. The movements of Les's hands were so brisk and efficient that, even before Michael realized it, he had run his fingers underneath his lapels. Mentally, Michael smiled to himself in satisfaction. If the pinhole lens could escape this man's notice, it would escape anyone's.

'What's this?' said Les, at length, tugging lightly at Michael's black silk tie.

'What d'you mean?'

'You're here to watch my back, son: you'll have a hard job doing that if you're being strangled. Here you are – I've got a spare detachable you can borrow.'

Walking over to his locker, Les took out a clip-on tie and passed it across to Michael.

'Oh, thanks,' said Michael, unfastening the tie he had brought with him and putting it back in his holdall.

'Right, I've gotta go out and set up. You can stay 'ere and read the paper till seven if you like. The other staff'll be along in a bit.'

'No, I'll come around with you if that's OK,' replied Michael, cheerfully. 'Get to know where everything is.'

'Yeah, OK, if you like,' grunted Les.

Over the next twenty-five minutes, Michael accompanied Les though Fevah's various corridors and anterooms, checking toilets, fire doors and windows along the way. Les's systematic routine seemed somehow to relax him and he soon began to talk a little more freely about himself. He had been a bouncer for nearly thirty years – the last nine of them at Fevah – during which period the club had apparently changed both hands and names over half a dozen times. His title was head of security, but he effectively acted as caretaker and head barman, too. The club had a manager, but he only showed his face once every few months to check the books, leaving the club in the hands of its trusty, long-standing steward for the rest of the time. Fevah's current owners lived in the United States. Les had never met them.

Finally, at a quarter to seven, the round of preparations complete, Michael and Les arrived back at the downstairs bar.

'D'you want a drink before we open up, Mick?' asked Les, walking behind the counter.

194

'Yeah, all right. What are you having?' replied Michael, sitting down on one of the stools on the opposite side of the bar.

'Bitter lemon.'

'OK, me, too.'

'You been doin' this long?' asked Les, taking a couple of bottles out of one of the refrigerators and pouring them into two glasses.

'What doorkeepin'?'

'Yeah.'

'Not long,' lied Michael. 'I'm thinkin' I might stick at it, though. You know, make a career out of it.'

'Yeah?'

'Yeah, maybe. Don't know. What d'you reckon?'

'Wouldn't recommend it, son,' grunted Les, depositing the empty bottles in a plastic skip underneath the bar. 'Not if you've got any other options, anyway.'

'I haven't – only the buildings and I'm fed up with them. Besides, what's wrong with being a doorkeeper? You seem to have managed all right.' Instead of answering, Les just shook his head wearily and took a swig of his drink. Despite this phlegmatic response, Michael guessed that Les was flattered to receive such respectful recognition from a younger man. 'What'd your advice be if I did?'

'Did what?'

'Became a doorman, full time.'

Les considered the question for a few moments, pursed his lips and then replied.

'Stay fit. Stay sober … and always look into their eyes.'

'Whose eyes?'

'The punters' eyes – when a fight starts.'

'Yeah?'

'Yeah.'

'Why?'

'To see if they care or not.'

'What d'you mean?' answered Michael, quizzically. Les paused before replying – once again his face adopting the frightening, dead-pan expression he had worn when Michael had first met him outside.

'You'll see a fight every night in this job. Usually the trouble-makers are just pissed – got excited, lost control. They come at you, but when you look 'em in the eye, you can see they don't mean it. You clip 'em round the ear – they won't come back for more. But every now and then – I don't know, maybe once every two or three years – you'll meet him.'

'Who?'

'The one that doesn't care. The one that ain't gonna stay down unless he's unconscious – or dead.'

'What do I do then?'

'Get help. Get yourself some back-up as fast as you can.'

'And what do I do if I'm on my own?'

'Pray,' replied Les, gravely.

'I'll remember that,' said Michael, finally.

'You do that, son,' answered Les, picking up their two empty glasses and placing them in the automatic washer. 'Come on, time to go out front.'

As Les came out from behind the bar, Michael noticed a large metal cannister on the far wall with the words 'Amnesty Box' written on it. Sensing that his relationship with Les had progressed enough to risk a first, tentative enquiry, Michael pointed across the room at it.

'You get a lot of problems with drugs here?'

'Only the ones we sell ourselves,' replied Les, with a disparaging nod at the well-stocked bar behind him.

Tysoe's house was at the end of a quiet, dimly lit cul-de-sac in a small village a couple of miles south of Staines. Parking his car at the entrance to the street, Michael switched off his headlights and watched Tysoe get out of his van and make his way along the pathway of his large, modern, mock-Tudor home. Turning the key in the lock, Tysoe opened the front door and then looked back along the street – almost as though he suspected that someone might be watching him. Sinking back into the darkness of the car's interior, Michael recalled Tom's canny observation that Tysoe was a sharp operator and not to be underestimated.

'No ramshackle extensions, no half-completed driveways for John Tysoe,' observed Michael dryly into the mobile phone. He had begun recording an hour and a half ago, just before he and Naz had finished working for Tysoe on a house in East Feltham: thereafter he had followed him back to his home via two other houses at which he had stopped to make quotations for new jobs. Although Michael was confident that he understood Tysoe's modus operandi, it was still a mystery

196

to him why he went out of his way to cheat so very many people. Despite what Michael had learned from the Trading Standards Authority about how cowboy builders were rarely troubled by the law, his behaviour nevertheless seemed curiously reckless.

Checking his watch, he could see it was nearly half past seven. Although there was still almost an hour left before the end of the tape, he was worried that if he did walk down the cul-de-sac to try and get a closer shot of Tysoe's house he might well be spotted and so decided to call it a day and return to Feltham. Now that he knew the location of Tysoe's home he could come back a few days later and do some filming during daylight hours. Since he had started working for Tysoe again, he had learned nothing more about him so he didn't know whether he was married, but, judging by the house's fussily bourgeois appearance, Michael felt almost certain that he had a wife. At the rear of Tysoe's house he could just make out a double garage. He wondered what sort of car she drove.

Before returning to Balam Road, Michael decided to stop off at The White Horse for a drink, arriving there just before a quarter to eight. He hadn't seen Harper since Dill's inspection two weeks previously, even though he had popped into the pub for lunch a couple of times during his five-day stint at Fevah. In spite of the lack of contact Michael wasn't seriously concerned. The grin on Harper's face as he had walked away that morning had denoted comradeship not enmity, and, if Dill had subsequently raised any objection to the Morgans' fraudulent application, Michael would almost certainly have heard about it by now. Locking up his car, he made his way to the front entrance of the pub. Having bought himself a drink, he walked through into the main bar area. Harper and Angela were seated in an alcove, the air around them thick with the smoke of Harper's roll-ups. As usual, Angela was wearing her lurid dragon T-shirt and a sour, miserable expression on her face. Slipping his hand into his top pocket, Michael took out his cigarettes; there was still thirty minutes left of recording time on the tape.

'Well, long time no see,' said Michael, sitting down opposite them.

'All right, mate?' replied Harper, with a smile.

'Yeah, not so bad, you?'

'Where've you been the last two weeks?' interjected Angela, quickly.

'Around.'

'We went to your flat last night – and last week – you weren't there.'

'Yeah, well, I've been workin', haven't I?'

'Working!' said Angela, with a look of horror. It was a wonderfully unqualified response. Michael hoped it would come across as well on film.

'What, on the buildings?' asked Harper.

'A bit on the buildings, but in a club as well – I'm gettin' fed up with labourin'.'

'Well, anyway, your claim went through OK,' continued Harper. 'You'll be getting your first cheque tomorrow or maybe Wednesday.'

'Great,' replied Michael. 'I told you everything'd be fine, didn't I, Ange?'

In response Angela merely scowled and took a swig of her Breezer directly from the bottle.

'Come on round to my place once you've cashed it,' continued Harper. 'You can give me my cut then.'

'Yeah, all right,' responded Michael. 'Is Friday OK?'

'Yeah, whenever,' replied Harper.

'What about Dill?' said Angela, continuing to stare at Michael with narrowed eyes.

'What about him?'

'You haven't seen him snoopin' around, have you?'

'No.'

'You keep a look out, all right? Let us know if you see anything suspicious.'

'OK, I will, but listen, I've got an idea …'

So saying, Michael leant forward on his seat, lowered his voice and nodded at the two of them to move closer so that they could not be overheard. He and Tom had both given a good deal of thought as to what his next move should be once the Housing Benefit payments came through on Balam Road. After much discussion, they had decided to risk raising the stakes: it wasn't enough to skirt around the periphery of the gang any more – from now on he had to start getting right into their very midst.

'What sort of idea?' said Harper, cautiously.

'As Dill's not on our back, how about getting another property, eh? Doing the same thing all over again.'

'How do you mean?'

'Getting another property – you know. I'll find it and rent it out, then you get me another dead person's name and National Insurance number like before and then we'll sublet it and split the profit.'

To Michael's surprise, both Harper and Angela looked genuinely alarmed by this proposal.

'I dunno, Mick, it's risky,' replied Harper, uncertainly.

'It worked all right last time.'

'Yeah, I know, but we don't wanna go pushing things ...'

For a fraction of a second Michael thought about mentioning Craig – the gang member working inside Housing Benefits who had tipped them off about Dill's inspection. However, rather than stressing his knowledge of their activities, he began to sense that he should very quickly back right off: their frowning faces were clearly indicating that he had overplayed his hand.

'Well, suit yourselves,' he said, sitting back in his seat. 'It was just an idea. I mean, we don't have to if you don't want to ...'

'Give us some time to think about it, mate, all right?' said Harper, rubbing his hand thoughtfully over his stubbled chin.

'Yeah, OK, no problem,' replied Michael, brightly. Obviously, they still didn't fully trust him and, for all their high levels of organization, were clearly wary about taking on new properties. 'Shall I get the drinks in, then? Geoff?'

'Oh, yeah, thanks, Lager.'

'Ange.'

'No, I gotta get going.'

'Oh, go on, one for the road.'

'Vodka Breezer, then,' she grunted finally, with her customary lack of grace.

Taking his wallet out of his inside pocket, Michael slipped his jacket over the back of the chair as casually as he was able and then walked off to the bar. As he stood at the counter waiting for the barman to pour the drinks, he risked a look back at the table. Harper and Angela were deep in discussion and, as far as he could tell, the camera was just at the right proximity and elevation to pick up what they were saying. Once again he found himself blessing Jim's ingenuity – from their conversation he would hopefully be able to discover whether he had indeed overplayed his hand. A minute later the barman served the drinks and he returned to the table.

'There you are – a lager and a Breezer.'

'Thanks, Mick,' replied Harper. 'All right, we've had a word about your idea and we'll let you know OK? But if we do go ahead, we choose the property – not you.'

'Sure, no sweat – whatever you like,' replied Michael, picking up his glass with a feeling of relief. 'Cheers.'

'Cheers,' answered Harper.

He got back to the flat an hour later. Harper and Angela had stayed for one more drink and then left together – a slight, but distinct air of nervousness still hanging around them as they had climbed into Harper's car and driven away. Although tired after a full day's work and two and a half hours of having tracked Tysoe to his home, Michael decided to wait for the phone to get to the end of the tape so that he could download the conversation that Harper and Angela had had whilst he had been at the bar. The phone didn't finally switch itself off until a quarter to one, but the results were more than worth the wait. In the four months since he had gone under cover this was the most vital sixty seconds of filming he had yet made. Harper spoke first, once Michael was out of earshot.

'What d'you reckon?'

'I still don't trust him.'

'Why not?'

''Cos he's a fuckin' dope, that's why. If he screws up the inspection again like last time we're the ones who'll cop it – not him.'

'I'm more worried about Craig.'

'He won't let us down.'

'You say that, but Dill's back now. What if he fingers him, or the police?'

'It won't get that far. Craig's smart – you know that. The moment they get too close, he'll be out of there.'

'Exactly. Things can't go on forever: either Craig gets rumbled or he decides to cut and run. Either way we should get one last place in before he disappears – we need the money for Rick.'

'Rick's all right now. He's cool.'

'Oh, for Christ's sake, Ange, face facts.'

'What?'

'The guy's disturbed – psychotic.'

'He's been all right for the last month.'

'Of course, he has. But what happens if we can't find the money again – eh? Like last time.'

'Yeah, OK ...'

'He goes fuckin' ape-shit – that's what: he needs his gear. You might not be scared of what he'll do, but I am.'

'I said OK! OK!!'

'Here comes Mick. I'll tell him we'll think about it, all right?'

'All right. But we find the place, not him.'

'Yeah – good point.'

'There you are – a lager and a breezer.'

'Thanks, Mick ...

Sitting on the edge of the sofa, Michael was overcome with an intoxicating sense of excitement. Stopping the video, he replayed the vital section of film again. Everything about it was perfect: the tight, claustrophobic atmosphere of the alcove, the nervous, conspiratorial unease of the two fraudsters and, most of all, the crucial facts they had unwittingly revealed about their organization. Walking through into the hallway, Michael pulled up the carpet and slid the video tape in amongst the twelve others that he had so far collected. Pushing his hand right to the back of the underfloor compartment he pulled out the file that had been leaked to Henry King at *The Mail* and opened up the first page. There, just as he had remembered it, was the photograph of Richard Thompson, the man whom he and Tom had all long suspected of being the ringleader of the gang. Resting his back against the wall, Michael took a long hard look at the scratchy, black and white photograph and repeated to himself the words that Harper had spoken.

'You might not be scared of what he'll do, but I am ...'

The fraudsters weren't politically motivated – not in the least. They were just plain, old-fashioned common criminals; terrified of the law – but even more terrified of their leader.

October passed into November, and, just as King and Tom had suggested, Michael found the three investigations dovetailing together neatly during the more or less fixed weekly routine into which his life began to settle. Two or three days a week, he would work with Naz at one of the households that had been unlucky enough to have selected John Tysoe as their builder. Naz clearly found being involved in cheating people genuinely distressing and Michael was eventually forced to make up a story that he was a government inspector investigating tax evasion in the building industry, intending eventually to prosecute Tysoe once he had amassed sufficient evidence. Naz seemed happier after this, but although Michael was able to acquire a good deal more incriminating footage and even got as far as following Mrs Tysoe on a couple of frighteningly profligate shopping expeditions, he knew he was going to have to find a way of getting inside Tysoe's house and filming the spoils of his deceit before the investigation would be truly complete.

On Thursday nights he would go to The White Horse with Harper. Housing Benefits were now paying him on direct debit and although Harper always made sure he got his cut each month, he did not refer again to Michael's suggestion that they take out another property. For his part, Michael was content to let the matter ride for the time being. Another of the unforeseen advantages of running three investigations simultaneously was that he did not have to attempt to wrap the first of them up within six months as he and Tom had originally envisaged. Eventually, he knew that if Harper did not bring up the subject of a second property again, he would be forced either to do so himself or find some other means of infiltrating the gang in order that he could get to Craig and Thompson. In the end, he set himself a deadline of the end of the year. The patient approach had worked well for him from the start and the more relaxed he felt the more he would be able to gain Harper's confidence.

At weekends, Michael continued to temp for London-American. However, despite Tom and Henry's confident assertion that this would propel him into a vortex of narcotic dealing, in seven weeks he caught only a single, fleeting glimpse of anything that remotely resembled a drug transaction. By the beginning of December he began to worry that the approach was fundamentally misconceived: either the security personnel with whom he had so far worked did not control the supply of drugs, or, if they did, they kept their operations well out of sight of agency staff. So it was that three weeks before Christmas, Michael set off somewhat unenthusiastically to an interview that London-American had arranged for him at a top West-End night club that needed an extra guard on the door over the subsequent month to deal with the anticipated seasonal rise in custom. If the bouncers at Fevah and the other loosely-managed provincial clubs weren't running drugs to their dance-floors, what were the chances of the doormen so doing at an expensive, high profile, central London night-spot like Gog?

The club was huge – at least five times the size of any of those to which London-American had sent him so far. It was also considerably more up-market. Pulling open the heavy, frosted glass door of the entrance to the club's offices, Michael looked around the suavely decorated reception area. On the left hand side, below a giant expressionist canvas, stood a high-backed, six-seater leather sofa; on the right was a sweeping rosewood reception desk behind which sat a well-dressed young secretary. Waiting for her to come off the phone, Michael idly browsed through a copy of the club's brochure and then frowned to himself apprehensively. With an entrance fee of thirty pounds and cocktails at a tenner each, he imagined that the management at Gog would bend over backwards to crack down on any illegal activities that might compromise their lucrative catering and alcohol licences.

'Good morning – sorry to keep you waiting,' announced the receptionist, with a beaming, just-out-of-secretarial-college smile.

'That's all right. I've got an appointment to see, er, Mrs Honeywell.'

'Could I have your name, please?'

'Angel, Michael Angel.'

'Just take a seat, please, Mr Angel.'

Sitting down on the sofa, Michael unthinkingly slipped his hand inside his top pocket to switch on the phone, but then stopped midmovement and took the jacket off altogether, draping it over the armrest. The probability of his filming anything of interest on his interview was virtually nil, and, besides, the old-fashioned leather jacket looked more than a little déclassé in this chic environment. Gazing around the plush, air-conditioned reception he began to feel distinctly restless. This was a mistake – he should leave now – tell the agency he hadn't liked the look of Gog and get them to find him somewhere more downmarket. If he didn't make headway in the drugs investigation soon he faced the real prospect of being beaten to it by Buckleys.

'Mr Angel?' said a voice.

'Yes?' replied Michael, looking up to see a tall, slimly-built man in his late twenties standing waiting for him next to the reception desk. He had a goatee beard and wore a red velvet suit and an open-necked yellow shirt that ostentatiously revealed his pale, shaven chest. The contrast between his brightly coloured clothes and cold, sarcastic expression was extremely odd, putting Michael in mind of a rather sinister court jester.

'Would you like to come this way?'

'Thanks,' replied Michael, following him down the corridor

'Edwin. How d'you do?' said the man, idiosyncratically holding out his hand at shoulder height for Michael to shake.

'My name's Mick,' he answered, gripping it firmly.

'Charmed,' he replied, in a disdainful voice that suggested he was anything but.

'So what d'you do around here then, Ed?' replied Michael, deciding that one derisive response deserved another.

'Oh, this, that and the other,' replied Edwin, breezily, 'mostly the other. Do take a seat, Ma'am will be with you shortly.'

Taking hold of the door handle of the room at the end of the corridor, Edwin opened it just wide enough for Michael to have to squeeze past him in order to get through. Sitting down at the interview room's single wooden desk, Michael imagined that clubs like Gog probably exercised a powerful attractive force over the Edwins of this world: on a Saturday night there were doubtless dozens of queen bitches to be found mincing around the place.

In complete contrast, the Human Resources Manager was as straight as a die. Pretty, articulate and efficient, Mrs Honeywell appeared every inch a career professional. Having quickly run through Gog's history, ownership and employment policy in respect of temporary staff, she explained the shift system that they operated over the peak Christmas and New Year period during which Michael would be expected to make himself available up to three nights a week for a maximum of four weeks. When she got on to the subject of his references, he began to think that she was going to turn him down. No, she had never heard of the club in the North of England at which he had worked for six months. And, if it had indeed now closed down, could he get in touch with the previous owners and ask them to provide him with a contact address so she could check his references? His promising subsequently to try and do this seemed to placate her, but as he walked back down the corridor towards the entrance, he had already decided not to ask Tom to waste his time forging any documents to satisfy Mrs Honeywell. Gog was simply too up-market: he wouldn't take the job now even if they offered it to him. Just as he was about to go back out through the glass doors, however, an unmistakable voice came lilting across the reception area towards to him.

'Michael ...'

Turning around, he saw Edwin lounging against the far wall.

'Yeah?'

'Oh, no, no, no,' replied Edwin, shaking his forefinger back and forth like a school-master admonishing a naughty pupil for trying to bunk off home early. 'No finito. You've met Beauty – now it's time for the Beast ...'

Curious to discover what Edwin meant, Michael followed him across the reception and out through the main entrance. Edwin then took a sharp left and began to descend a narrow spiral staircase that Michael had not noticed on his way in. At the bottom was an unmarked wooden door which in turn gave way to a concrete staircase leading down to the basement. Following Edwin along the narrow echoing corridors, Michael allowed himself an ironic smile: even though he had decided not to take the job, it was interesting to note that for all Gog's marble floors and chromium plated walkways, below ground it was identical to all the other clubs at which he had so far worked. Pausing at an open doorway, Edwin knocked respectfully.

'What?' came a gruff, bellicose voice from deep inside.

Following Edwin through the door, Michael found himself in what at first appeared to be a small, dark cellar, empty save for half a dozen water pipes stretching from floor to ceiling on the far wall; the air in the room was cold and stale and somehow made him think of dungeons. On the left-hand side was a half-open door leading to another room from which purplish neon light was streaming. Raising his arm to indicate that from this point onwards Michael should proceed on his own, Edwin turned and made his way stiffly back out into the corridor. As he watched Edwin leave, Michael saw his right cheek twitch involuntarily.

'Fuckin' Christ!' snarled the voice, suddenly from the next room. 'Come on in, will you? I haven't got all day!'

Opening the door, Michael went on through to the small, window-less room beyond, at the far end of which was an ancient mahogany desk. The instant that Michael caught sight of the man seated behind it, he realized how frighteningly accurate Edwin had been in referring to him as a beast. With his rigid, muscular shoulders and pitiless feline eyes, he exuded more of an air of animal ferocity than anyone Michael had ever met. He wore a brilliant white doorman's dress-shirt, open at the neck, from the collars and cuffs of which protruded thick tufts of matted, flaxen-brown hair. Down the right hand side of his neck was a deep, ugly scar – long since healed, but still lividly coloured – that began just below his left ear and finished at the top of his chest, subtly distorting the symmetry of his face. His hands were large and powerful, with jagged, pointed nails that put Michael in mind of a leopard's claws. The jacket of his immaculate double-breasted suit was hung over the back of his chair at such an angle that Michael could see the label on the inside pocket; it was Savile Row, hand-made and one hundred per cent cashmere.

'You're Michael Angel, right?' growled the man.

'That's right.'

'Bit of a faggot name for a bouncer, innit?'

'If I want a punter to behave, I don't usually start by formally introducing myself.'

'Ha! Like it!' guffawed the man, with a rasping, brutal laugh. 'You prefer more direct means of persuasion, yeah?'

'When necessary.'

'My name's Kent,' grinned the man, revealing two rows of yellowed, sharp-edged teeth. 'They didn't tell you about me, did they?'

'No, they didn't.'

'Honeycunt upstairs does her job well enough, I won't take that away from her. You know, public face of the club and all that – PR's important in this business. Me? I'm much more low profile. I sort things out behind the scenes. Discreetly, you know? Without any fuss.'

'I see.'

'You will,' replied Kent, picking a copy of Michael's details up off the top of his desk. 'You're with London-American, right?'

'Yeah.'

'They said you're OK.'

'Did they?'

'Yeah. I phoned 'em to check – personally. She didn't think to do that – I did, though. Personal recommendations are important in this business. I set great store by 'em.'

'So you should.'

'We run a tight organization here. Tighter than anywhere you'll've ever worked. Everyone knows their place and everybody does what they're told to do … or allowed to do.'

Again the grin – this time openly threatening.

'Fine,' replied Michael.

In response Kent stared at Michael for several seconds, during which Michael felt the hairs on the back of his neck rise, as though his mind were being probed by a strange, animal sixth sense emanating from the creature in front of him.

'OK, that's it,' he said, finally, turning away and looking back at the papers on his desk. 'You can find your own way out, can't you?'

'I reckon so,' replied Michael, going back through the door.

Walking back down the corridor towards the exit, Michael decided that after all he would ask Tom to try and fix something up to satisfy Mrs Honeywell. For all the studied chic of Gog's public image, deep below the surface something very ugly was lurking.

The first couple of weekends were straightforward enough, but from the moment that Michael arrived for work on the Friday night of the third weekend, he was conscious of a strange atmosphere in the air. That evening, the entire top floor of Gog had been hired out by a private party of over two hundred and fifty people, and when he walked into the locker room at seven o'clock to get changed there was no one else around: the security staff were obviously going to be stretched very thin that night. Going through into the main part of the club, he met one of the barmen who told him that the party had been drinking steadily since three o'clock that afternoon and, during the last half hour, had begun to get a little unruly. Arriving at the front entrance at half past seven to start his shift, he found that only two of the normal team of five doormen were present.

'What's going on?' he asked Nigel, a burly West Indian ex-middle weight who was one of Gog's full-time staff. 'Where're the others?'

'Kent called 'em on the radio about ten minutes ago. They're up on the third floor with him now. I don't know what's goin' on – a couple of tables got knocked over or somethin'.'

Taking up his position on the opposite side of the entrance, Michael frowned to himself thoughtfully. Although the other members of Gog's security staff often contacted Kent on their walkie-talkies, he had not become personally involved in any of the minor security situations that Michael had so far observed. Tonight, however, he had clearly felt the need to leave his basement lair and sort things out on the third floor himself; even though Michael had only being working at Gog for just over two weeks, he sensed this was very much out of the ordinary.

Twenty minutes later, his three colleagues returned from the top floor and resumed their duties without comment, but, by ten o'clock, despite the gaiety of the steady stream of pre-Christmas merrymakers arriving at the front entrance, the atmosphere still seemed peculiarly tense. The first scuffle broke out ten minutes later.

Michael generally kept a sharp eye on the queue, but hadn't noticed the two tall men who had now reached the front of it until Nigel beckoned the first of them forward and began to check him.

'All right, all right, I'm clean,' said the first man, tetchily, pushing Nigel's hands away after just a few seconds and then making his way forwards towards the entrance.

'Hold it!' called out Nigel. 'Back, back …'

Ignoring the command, the man kept on walking, but within a flash Nigel sprang forward and caught hold of his arm.

'I said hold it!'

For a moment, it looked as though the man was going to comply and he spread his arms again to allow Nigel to check his pockets. No sooner had Nigel started to do so, though, than the second man rushed forward and shoulder-charged him, knocking him to the ground. Seeing Nigel fall forward and bang his forehead against the heavy, wooden entrance door, Michael span quickly around, grabbed the second man's arm, twisted it behind his back and then rammed him face first into the wall. Behind him he could sense rather than see that two of the other doormen had jumped forward and pinned the first man to the ground.

'OK, OK, cool it!' shouted Nigel, rubbing his temple gingerly as he got to his feet. 'Right, you two, out of here, now! And don't show your faces here again. Ever. Got it?'

Even before the queue had rearranged itself back into an orderly line the two men had disappeared out of sight. Within a few minutes the other doormen had settled down again and things seemed to get back to normal, but Michael found he couldn't put the incident out of his mind. At first, he thought he might be overreacting – the two men had probably been drinking and had no doubt been spoiling for a fight all night. The more he thought about it though, the more he began to wonder why the second man had said nothing when he had charged at Nigel. There had been no curse. No exclamation of anger. Nothing. If he hadn't lost his temper, then his actions could only have been pre-meditated.

Ten minutes later, the walkie-talkies went crazy. As the most senior member of staff, Nigel immediately started organizing the other doormen.

'Rod, Bill – you stay 'ere! You three, come with me now!'

Running quickly back through the club with Nigel and the two other security guards, Michael tried to make sense of the stream of messages pouring out of the walkie-talkies. It appeared that two fights had broken out simultaneously: one in the first floor bar and one on the third floor in the big private party. When they reached the lifts, Nigel told the other two bouncers to go up to the party and then dragged Michael with him towards the stairs to make their way up to the first floor bar on foot.

As they piled through the entrance doors into the bar, Michael could tell immediately that the fight taking place before him had not arisen spontaneously. Next to the counter, a man in a grey leather jacket was holding the barman with his arms pinned behind his back whilst another smashed him in the stomach with a baseball bat. As Nigel and Michael sprang forwards, the two men quickly turned on their heels and darted straight towards the emergency exit.

'You all right, George?' shouted Nigel at the barman.

'Yeah,' he hissed painfully.

'Come on,' called Nigel to Michael, not breaking his step as he ran towards the emergency exit to chase the two men. Michael followed, but had scarcely got through the doors than he was forced right back through them by the weight of Nigel's body. Although the two men had appeared to have fled down the stairs, they had in fact been waiting on the landing on the other side of the doors.

'Your turn now, shit-head,' jeered the man in the grey jacket, taking a step towards Michael and getting ready to swing the baseball bat at him. For a moment Michael hesitated, looking down at Nigel's prostrate form – he was clearly out cold and blood was seeping from a wound over his eye. Spurred on by Michael's reticence, the second man also took a step forward. It was two against one. Sensing that the element of surprise would be gone within an instant, Michael sprang forwards and threw a punch at the first man who, caught off-guard, dropped his baseball bat and fell down on to one knee. He recovered almost instantly, but, the moment he did so, a voice roared across the room from behind Michael.

'Mick!'

It was Kent. He had just come through the entrance to the bar and was running across it towards Michael. Seeing by Michael's reaction that reinforcements were on their way, the two men turned and ran down the stairs. Michael and Kent followed straight after, but, by the time they reached the ground floor, the emergency exit doors to the street outside were open and the two men were running off into the night.

'What happened, Mick?' asked Kent, breathlessly.

'They were tooled up – baseball bats,' replied Michael. 'I'm not sure, but I think they sneaked in a few minutes ago at the front when our backs were turned – a couple of their mates created a diversion.'

'Fucking bastards!' cursed Kent, angrily. 'How's Nigel?'

'Bad. They hit him hard. They might've fractured his skull.'

Pulling his walkie-talkie out of his inside pocket, Kent stabbed at the red call button and screamed into the receiver, 'Ambulance, first floor bar – quick. D'you read? Nigel's been hurt. D'you read?'

There was a blast of static and then a voice that Michael did not recognize hurriedly answered, 'It's on its way already. One of the guests on the third floor's been hurt. There's two more blokes up there causing trouble now.'

At this point Michael turned to go back up to help Nigel, but Kent suddenly grabbed him and dragged him down the stairs to the basement. As they ran through the corridors towards Kent's office, Michael tried to work out what was going on. The trouble had clearly been very carefully orchestrated and it appeared as though there were at least six men involved. Seconds later they were in Kent's room and he was tossing aside a filing cabinet to reveal a safe built into the wall behind it.

'Fuckin' lean on me? I'll fuckin' show 'em,' he growled, furiously. 'Take these! We'll go and sort out those other two cocksuckers on the third floor!'

From inside the safe Kent took out a couple of heavy leather coshes – Michael could feel the ball-bearings inside them as he pressed them into his hands. For a split second Michael got a glimpse inside the safe, which he could see was mostly filled with documents, but also contained a hand gun. Kent then slammed the safe to, turned on his heel and dashed back upstairs. As he ran down the corridor, Michael noticed that he had knuckle dusters on both of his fists.

By the time that they got to the third floor, the two men had already gone. The moment that Kent discovered this, he immediately hurtled back down the stairs, and, without waiting for the ambulance to appear, ran off to get his own car to take Nigel to hospital. Less than a minute later, he screeched to a halt outside the emergency exit and, with Michael's help, loaded Nigel carefully on to the back seat. Three minutes after that, they had pulled up outside a nearby hospital. Having helped Michael to carry Nigel into the entrance hall, Kent then rushed off to park his car.

The Casualty Department was in a state of total chaos. Speaking to a harassed, white-faced receptionist, Michael learned that an hour previously there had had been a pile-up in central London involving a car carrying four youths – all of whom were drunk – and a coach load of office workers on their way to a Christmas party. Coming out from behind her desk and helping Michael carry Nigel to a seat, the receptionist promised to do her best to get him seen to as soon as possible, although the doctors were rushed off their feet and he might well have to wait up to an hour. Moments later Kent reappeared. At Gog he had been a paragon of quick-thinking efficiency, but once in the waiting room amidst the crowds of sobbing and concussed revellers, he seemed to lose all self-control.

'An hour! We can't wait an hour!' he raged, turning around and grabbing a terrified Asian nurse by the arm, shaking her mercilessly. 'Get me a fuckin' doctor, now! Now!! My boy's been done bad.'

'It's OK, it's OK!' said Michael, stepping forward, and trying to break open Kent's vice-like grip. 'You stay here. I'll go and find a doctor. Leave her!'

Kent's bloodshot eyes were almost popping out of his head and he seemed utterly oblivious to Michael's protestations. At that moment, however, Nigel recovered consciousness and let out a long, painful moan.

'Let her go!' repeated Michael. 'I'll find a doctor!' Finally, Kent released the nurse and Michael scampered off down the corridor after her in search of the first person in a white coat he could find. He was in luck. At the far end of the corridor there was an examination area comprising two rows of four cubicles. Just as he arrived, the curtains were pulled back on one of these and a young male doctor emerged and began helping a patient to his feet.

'Doctor, look, I'm sorry,' gasped Michael, rushing over to him. 'I know you're buried, but I've got a mate of mine down there with a serious head injury. He's been attacked with a baseball bat. I think he might have a fractured skull.'

The doctor was just about to reply when all of a sudden a massive fight exploded in the waiting room behind them. A group of men who had been travelling on the coach had discovered the identity of the drunk driver who had caused the accident, and, seriously under the influence of alcohol themselves, had decided to mete out summary justice. For a second Michael and the doctor were separated as three Hospital Security Guards rushed down the corridor in between them to try and break up the mêlée. As the fight raged, Michael noticed the Asian nurse on his left hastily taking bandages out of a cupboard. Seeing Michael standing next to the doctor, she seemed to realize what he wanted and nodded hurriedly at the doctor as if to confirm that Nigel was indeed in a bad way.

'Can your friend walk?' asked the Doctor.

'I think so – just about.'

'OK, bring him down here,' he replied, moving quickly across to the sink to wash his hands.

Back in the waiting room, Kent and Michael supported Nigel on their shoulders and carried him down the corridor to the examination cubicle. Having checked Nigel's pulse and eye reactions, the doctor phoned through to the X-Ray department. Two minutes later, a porter appeared with a wheelchair, but no sooner had he helped Nigel into it, than he had to dash over to the cubicle opposite where a drunken youth in a soccer scarf had started to attack one of the casualty nurses. As the porter grabbed the hooligan, however, he himself was knocked to the ground, caught under the chin by one of the youth's flailing elbows. In that instant, all the frustration that had been building up inside Michael over the last two months exploded to the surface – the sight of the young woman desperately attempting to protect herself from the blows raining down on her head propelling him into an uncontrollable fury. The countless hours he had spent prowling around darkened night-clubs looking for drug dealing had been a total waste of time. Almost every single one of those nights he had either witnessed or had to break up a fight exacerbated by alcohol: compared to drink, other drugs were just nothing. What could King possibly expect him to discover that could be more socially destructive than this scene before him – a place of healing transformed into a chamber of hell? Forgetting *Criminal Britain*, forgetting Nigel and Kent, he rushed over to the opposite cubicle, grabbed the youth by his shirt collar, lifted him up into the air and slammed his body against the wall.

'You touch her again – you're dead,' he roared.

As the youth struggled to get free, his senseless, intoxicated eyes rolling wildly, Michael drew back his arm to punch him unconscious, but at that moment the porter got back to his feet, and, together with the doctor, leapt forward and dragged him away.

'Mick! Mick!!' shouted Kent, behind him. 'Come on! We've gotta get Nige' down to X-Ray.'

Turning his back on the infernal scenes in Casualty, Michael followed Kent as he pushed Nigel along the corridors towards the relative calm of the X-Ray department. As soon as they arrived, a fraught-looking technician told them they would have to wait ten minutes until the X-Ray machine was free and quickly ushered them into a small, empty side ward. As Nigel lay groaning on one of the beds, Kent paced restlessly backwards and forwards, furiously mumbling and cursing to himself, his voice echoing back eerily off the tiled walls. Having caught his breath and calmed down a little, Michael thought about asking Kent what had happened that night. Who were the group of men who had started the trouble at Gog and what was it that they wanted? Before Michael had time to put these questions into words, however, the door of the side ward in which they were waiting opened with a crash. There were three of them: the two men who had created the diversion earlier that night and the one that Michael had fought on the stairs – they were all carrying knives.

'You – back,' commanded the man in the grey jacket, pointing the long serrated blade of his combat knife at Michael. 'We don't want you.' Behind him, the third man – the one who had shoulder charged Nigel earlier that night – closed the door and stood looking back through the circular inspection panel, keeping careful watch on the corridor outside. On the bed, Nigel tried to raise himself upright, but straightaway fell dizzily backwards. Knives held aloft, the two men began to advance on Kent. Michael looked across the room at him. To his amazement, Kent was smiling

'You're dead already, you two,' he laughed. 'Fuckin' dead and buried.'

Instinctively, Michael took a step forwards to get around to the other side of the beds to where Kent was standing. To do so, however, he had to go past the man standing guard over the door who immediately turned and flashed his knife at him threateningly. Looking into his face, Michael felt his lungs suddenly empty of all oxygen. The man's eyes betrayed no emotion whatsoever – absolutely nothing. Swallowing hard, Michael fought to control his fear as Les's words ran terrifyingly through his mind. *Once – every two or three years maybe – you'll meet him: the one that doesn't care.*' Such was the man confronting him now.

'You had your chance,' sneered the man in the grey jacket, slowly closing in on Kent, who now stood with his back to the far wall. 'We offered to cut you in.'

For the first time in his life, Michael felt his courage begin to falter. It was an impossible situation. Even if he could survive a tussle with the man guarding the door, by the time he got past him the other two would already have slit Kent's throat. Again Nigel tried to get up, grasping hold of the curtain at the side of the bed which immediately snapped off the rail under his weight. As the curtain fell to the ground, it seemed as though time froze in the room: on the wall, above the bed, hitherto obscured by the curtain, was a chunky, red patient-alarm button. Straining with all his remaining strength, Nigel managed to lift himself up on to his left elbow and stretch his right arm towards the button.

'Get him!' hissed the man in the grey jacket to the man standing by the door. His boss's command was the man's undoing. In the fraction of a second before he stepped forward, his eyes flickered one last time towards the inspection panel and the corridor outside. It was all that Michael needed. In a single lightening movement he took one of the leather coshes out his pocket and hurled it at the man. It caught him full in the face. Leaping forward, Michael swung out his right foot and then kicked him as hard as he could in the groin. As he doubled up, Michael took out the other cosh out of his pocket and brought it crashing down on the back of his neck. The man fell forwards in a heap on the cold, stone floor. Taking a step sideways, Michael swung his right leg backwards again and, with all the strength he could muster, kicked the man full in the face. There was a sickening crack as his nose broke. *'He won't stay down,'* Les had warned, *'not unless he's unconscious – or dead'*.

Nigel hit the button. There was no sound, but in that instant everyone in the room knew that it was now only a matter of time before the hospital staff came running. The two men still left standing flinched undecidedly.

'I told you you was dead,' scoffed Kent.

Picking the first cosh up off the floor, Michael threw it across the room at Kent who caught it neatly in his left hand just as the man in the grey jacket lunged towards him. Jumping forward, Michael swung his cosh at the other man, but his timing was fractionally and disastrously wrong. The man dropped his weight on to his back foot, dodged the blow and, even before Michael could see him move, lashed upwards and outwards with his right hand, slashing Michael across the left cheek with his stiletto blade. At first there was very little pain, and Michael only knew that he had been cut when he put his hand to his face and felt the warm flow of blood running over his fingers. Taking a step backwards, he looked down at his hand and, as if triggered by the sight of the blood, a nauseating, stinging sensation shot up the side of his face. The blade had not simply just slashed his cheek, it had actually pierced it – the incision going right through into his mouth. Narrowing his eyes, the man facing him bent into a crouch, seemingly ready to pounce for the kill.

At that moment the door opened.

It was the X-ray technician. For a half-second his jaw dropped right open on witnessing the scene before him, but after that he didn't delay any further and within a flash disappeared back out again, the sound of his scampering feet echoing down the corridor. It ended the fight there and then. Turning to pick up their prostrate friend, whose face was now completely covered in blood, the two men carried him quickly out of the room and set off down the corridor in the opposite direction from the technician. Falling, rather than sitting down on the bed behind him, Michael put his hand to his face. By now the blood was not only pumping outwards down his cheek and neck but also inwards into his mouth. As he spat the gore out into a pool on the floor, Kent came into his line of sight holding a towel. Kneeling down in front of Michael, he lifted it up to his cheek. Bizarrely, he was still grinning.

'Press it down hard. And stick your tongue against the wound on the inside of your mouth. It'll stop the blood flow.'

The pain was excruciating, but Michael knew that what Kent had said was right and that he had to try and stem the bleeding. Gripping

Michael by the shoulders, Kent then leant forwards and, slowly positioning their heads side by side, whispered gently – almost tenderly – into his ear.

'You'll have a scar there all your life, Mick. But don't you ever be ashamed of it, you hear? Never. 'Cos it's my scar. My mark. It's what you got for helpin' me. I never forget my enemies. But I never forget my friends neither.'

To his left, Michael heard a loud gasp as Nigel got painfully to his feet. He hoped Nigel would be strong enough to help Kent carry him back to Casualty, because in a matter of moments he knew he was going to black out completely. As the darkness began to close in around him, Kent began speaking again, and, despite the nausea and pain sweeping through his mind, he felt himself smile at his words.

'Sorry you got dragged into all this, Mick. They were trying to sell drugs, you see; in Gog – in my fuckin' club. Can you believe it? No one gets away with that, mate. Not in my club. No one but me.'

Chapter 8

He was discharged from the private residential hospital in the third week of January. Christmas and New Year had been spent with his head shrouded in thick, chitin impregnated bandages specially designed for treating facial injuries. Having taken out the stitches, the surgeon had pronounced himself delighted with the way that the wound had healed, although on looking at his luridly discoloured flesh in the mirror Michael had been unable to share his optimism. Once the bruising had finally died down five days later, however, he realized why the physician had been so positive. Although there was no doubting the presence of the line across his cheek, the tissues either side of it were smooth and showed no signs of pinching: he had made a remarkable recovery. The ward nurses, who had at first been scrupulously sympathetic and solicitous – mindful of the psychological rather than the physical scars – very quickly became much more blasé and, in the final days before his discharge, almost began to lecture him about his injury: he should thank his lucky stars that within five minutes of having incurred it he had been able to receive treatment – the vast majority of victims who suffer serious facial scarring are not fortunate enough to be situated fifty yards away from an Accident and Emergency Unit at the time.

Kent had come to visit him twice, both times in the very early morning. Gog's private medical scheme covered all its employees, temporary as well as permanent, and he had therefore told him to take it easy at the hospital until he was fully recovered. Then, when he felt fit enough, there was a position waiting for him at Gog working weekends – Kent had already seen to it; he could have the job for as long as he wished. More significantly, Kent had also promised every now and then to find Michael what he termed a little 'extra work'. As to the drug turf war that had been the cause of the fight, he volunteered no further information, except at the end of the second visit to remark darkly that if the six men had children he hoped they were enjoying their recent Christmas presents because they were the last they would ever receive from their fathers.

The return journey to Feltham was a strange, surreal experience. Kent had offered to provide a chauffeur-driven car to take him from door to door but he decided to travel by train. It wasn't just that he didn't want to be seen arriving at Balam Road in anything as conspicuous as a limousine, but he also felt the need to be among ordinary people again to see how they reacted to his scar. In the event, not a single one of his fellow travellers gave him so much as a passing look, the hustle and bustle of journeying through the capital apparently depriving them of all curiosity. And so he sat on the train in a state of existential dislocation: expecting attention but receiving none; journeying back to a flat he seemed only ever to have inhabited in a dream and knowing that if he did return to those whom he thought of as his own they would avert their eyes from the alarming stranger with the worn leather jacket, cropped hair and scarred face.

The walk from the station to the flat was equally unsettling, the sights and sounds of Feltham seeming to belong to another world: an abandoned car on a patch of waste ground, its windows smashed and jagged, its seats strewn with litter; an old woman in an ancient worsted coat standing at a bus stop, trembling in the freezing wind; a council refuse worker, gingerly picking up the corpse of a dead fox and wrapping it in polythene sheeting. By the time he reached the Uxbridge Road he was almost convinced that the flat just wouldn't be there – that it simply didn't exist. Even when he arrived outside and began walking up the concrete staircase to the front door, he couldn't believe that the keys he held in his hand would fit the lock.

Sitting down on the sofa, he surveyed his drab, unfamiliar living room and tried to work out what he should do next. Making contact with Tom was the main priority, but he somehow felt unable to face him until he had had a couple of days to re-establish himself. Harper was next on the list, but he still hadn't worked out exactly what he was going to say to him about his five-week absence and his scar. Walking pensively through into the kitchen, Michael made himself a cup of coffee. It would have to be black because the milk in the fridge had long since curdled; he put in an extra spoon of sugar, but it still tasted bitter. In the end, he decided that first of all he would go and see Naz. He recalled that Tysoe had gone away on a winter break for Christmas and the New Year with his wife so his own absence shouldn't seem quite so pronounced. Finishing off his coffee, he took all the old food out of the fridge, put it in a bin liner and left to go Naz's house. Walking down the steps, he wondered whether the battery had gone flat in his car: he hoped not – if so, he would have to call someone out from a garage. Depositing the black sack in the dustbin at the bottom of the stairs, he pulled his jacket collar up against the cold and turned to walk off towards the waste ground at the rear. As he did so, he was just able to detect out of the corner of his eye the lace curtain in the downstairs flat flicker slightly.

Someone, at least, had noticed he was back.

Tom went white. Michael had tried to prepare him in advance on the phone, but he obviously hadn't fully taken things in. Sitting slowly down at the dining table, he swallowed hard and shook his head in a mixture of shock and self-recrimination.

'Oh, Christ. This is just what we didn't want to happen. Oh, I'm so sorry, my friend, I'm so sorry …'

'It's over now – it's done,' replied Michael, calmly. 'Don't blame yourself. I knew what the dangers were.'

'How did it happen? I should've realized something was up when you stayed out of contact for so long. I should've come to get you, like I promised I would – come around to your …'

'Tom,' interrupted Michael. 'It wasn't your fault, OK?'

'Who did this to you?'

'I got that job at Gog in the end – you know, the one you got me the extra references for. And, well, I'm still not exactly sure of the background, but the guy who runs their security – a bloke called Kent – was being leant on by some gang or other. They came in one night and caused major havoc: baseball bats, the works – I got in the way.'

'What did they want?'

'To muscle in on his operation.'

'What operation?'

'He's running drugs into the place.'

'Into Gog?' replied Tom, his eyes opening wide. 'Really?'

'I was surprised, too,' answered Michael, steadily, 'I mean it's such a high-class joint. Anyway, bouncers came up trumps in the end, Tom, just like you and King said they would. I must admit I'd almost given up hope, but eventually I found the drug connection we've been looking for.'

'Well, that's great news. I mean, well done, old boy, fantastically well done. Although at what a price … I really am sorry.'

'Thanks, but make that the last apology, all right?' replied Michael. 'I need you to think clearly for me. You can't do that if you let your judgement be clouded by misplaced feelings of guilt.'

'OK, I've got you. But you go careful from now on, do you hear? Very careful. For me.'

'I will, I will, don't you worry.'

'So,' said Tom, shaking his head sharply in an attempt to drive Michael's injury from his thoughts, 'how are you going follow it up?'

'It should be easy. Kent's got me a part-time job at Gog as a reward for my loyalty – working weekends.'

'Good.'

'I guess I just need to hang on in there until I can get some footage of gear being sold on to the kids. Kent's promised me some extra work as well, so I might be able to pick up some other good stuff, too. The guy's into all sorts of scams, I reckon.'

'When d'you start?'

'Whenever I like. I suppose I'll go in this Friday.'

'Right, well, fingers crossed, then. What about Harper? Anything new?'

'No, I'm afraid not,' replied Michael with a frown. 'Not since that tape I sent you of him and Angela in the pub.'

'When was the last time you saw him?'

'Over a month ago.'

'Not since your, er … this happened, then?'

'No. No.'

'Have you thought what you're going to do next?'

'Yes. I think the time's probably come to get a 'yes' or 'no' out of him on the second property.'

'I think you're right,' agreed Tom.

'If he doesn't cooperate, then I'll just have to go back to surveillance again. I've been really patient with him – we're good mates now and everything – but time's running out and if he's not going to play ball then my only option is the other gang members.'

'Who will you go after first?'

'Craig, definitely. I'm pretty sure he works in the same Housing Benefits office as Dill, so he shouldn't be too hard to find.'

'And then Thompson, yes?'

'Well, ideally, yes, but I'm not going to be able track him down without some sort of a lead. He's obviously left the address that was listed in the file so he could be anywhere.'

'What about Tysoe?'

'Almost done. I managed to get a lot of filming in before Christmas – including some of Mrs Tysoe. She appears to spend his money as fast as he earns it – if earn's the right word.'

'Are you back working for him now?'

'No, I just missed out because of still being in hospital. Naz is, though, with some other guy he's hired. They started work on a property belonging to some pensioners last week apparently, which was really annoying – some footage of him ripping them off would've been great. I reckon I can get back in in a couple of weeks, though.'

'How many more of Tysoe's jobs do you need to film?'

'None, really. It's more a question of staying with him until I can find a way of getting inside his house. As soon as I've done that I can pull out. I might go off and interview those pensioners as well if I get the chance, but then that'll be it.'

'So you're really very much on schedule, in fact.'

'Yeah, I'd say so. Gog was a big breakthrough and if Henry liked Tysoe's face, wait till he sees Kent's. The second house with Harper is a bit of a worry, but, yeah, basically, all three investigations are going well.'

Leaning back in his chair, Tom ran his hand over his chin for a few moments and then, for the first time since he had arrived, managed a smile.

'Have you given any more thought to the fourth documentary?'

'Not much, you?'

'Yes, we have, quite a bit.'

'And …?'

Before answering, Tom stood up and walked pensively over to the radiator by the window.

'Henry's very conscious of the fact that this is your series, and of the commitment we made to allow you to have your input on the third and fourth documentaries.'

As Michael looked across the room at his boss, he too began to smile. It was good to be with Tom again – good to observe all his familiar habits and mannerisms. Ever the diplomat, Tom clearly had something he wished to say but felt it judicious to skirt around the subject first.

'Yes. And ...'

'And we don't want to put you under any undue influence; you do understand that, don't you?'

'Come on, out with it, Tom,' said Michael, with a grin.

His circumlocution not yet having run its full intended course, Tom gave a mildly irritated frown.

'OK. It's like this. Henry thinks – and I'm in agreement with him – that the fourth documentary needs to be a little bit more, well ... racy than the other three.'

'Racy?'

'Yes, racy.'

'What d'you mean ... racy?'

'Well, we need to have an episode with a bit of spice in it, you know,' continued Tom, waving his hand back and forth expressively, 'at least one, anyway. We don't want it all to be too ... dry. I mean there are going to be trailers, aren't there, to attract viewers, yes? I mean, we're obviously going to be advertising both in advance and during the screening of the series ...'

Again Michael looked at Tom, staring into his eyes for several seconds before finally verbalizing what both of them knew to be true.

'You've already decided what the fourth documentary's going to be about, haven't you?'

Nodding his head almost imperceptibly, Tom walked forward, sat back down at the table again and slowly began to speak.

Although Michael didn't really have anything to discuss with Jim, on arriving at the camera shop the first thing he did was to glance in the direction of his workshop. The door was slightly open and it was dark inside so, on the assumption that Jim was out for the morning, Michael carried on walking into the main part of the store. The poster board was there just as he had remembered it, occupying the section of wall in the space between the new and second hand sections of the shop. Starting in the top left hand corner, Michael read systematically through each advertisement in turn. After a few minutes, the shop assistants stopped noticing him and, as a result, failed to observe his sleight of hand as he pulled two cards down off the wall in quick succession and then slipped them inside his jacket.

There was no answer at the first number. Calling it once again to make sure that he had dialled correctly, Michael listened to the ringing tone a few more times and then hung up. Taking the second card out of his pocket, he leant against the side of the phone booth and carefully examined it once more. The company's logo, which was in the middle of the card, was a free hand drawing and was all the more powerfully suggestive for it. It was the figure of the upper half of a young woman's naked body, picked out in gold ink on a black background. Her head was inclined slightly to the left and her eyes were half-closed in an expression of deep, rapturous sexual ecstasy. Between her breasts she held a large crucifix, the stem of which plunged downwards towards her groin disappearing beneath the words 'Heretic Films' in Gothic script which covered her hips and formed the base of the logo. Underneath, in poorly legible blue biro were a couple of lines of scrawled writing and a phone number. Picking up the receiver, Michael slowly dialled it. Trust Henry, Tom had said. Trust his instincts. He knows what the public wants and he's never wrong.

'Hello?' chirped a squeaky, high-pitched voice.

'Oh, er, hello. I'm ringing about the advert for a boom operator and sound recording engineer.'

'Oh, right,' answered the man.

'Have you found anyone yet or are you still lookin'?'

'Er, I'm not sure. Hang on a bit, I'll go and ask Len …'

For over a minute and a half there was complete silence. Just as Michael was about to hang up and try the first number again, the voice suddenly began speaking once more.

'Hello, you still there?'

'Yeah.'

'No, we haven't found anybody yet. What you doin' tomorrow?'

'Tomorrow?' asked Michael in surprise.

'Yeah, tomorrow?'

'Er, nothin'.

'Can you come round in the morning about ten?'

'Yeah, I should think so, what's your address?'

'Meet us outside Walthamstow tube – back entrance by the car park. There'll be two of us. Blue van.'

'Oh, yeah, all right, then. Do I need to bring any gear?'

'No, it's OK we'll have it all with us. What's your name?'

'Mick,' replied Michael, who had decided to continue using the same pseudonym for the fourth documentary, at least for the time being.

'OK, Mick, thanks for callin', see you tomorrow, mate.'

'Oh, right, great. So, er, how will I know what you look like then? Hello? Hello??'

There was no answer – the nameless respondent having already hung up. Thinking it would appear peculiar to call back, Michael frowned and walked slowly away from the phone booth, unsure exactly what to make of the conversation. His interview had lasted less than two minutes, over ninety seconds of which had been complete silence. Remembering that he had drawn a blank at all of the clubs at which he had worked before Gog, he shook his head in resignation and strode off towards Oxford Street and the train back to Feltham. He had to make a start on the fourth documentary somewhere and, for better or worse, it looked as though Heretic Films was going to be it.

He returned to Balam Road just before midday. Driving to The White Horse he looked around the bar for Harper, and, not finding him, went straight back out again and drove to his house: over a month had passed since they had last spoken and he couldn't afford to leave their next meeting to chance. Parking his car in the slip road, he turned off the engine but, instead of getting out, began to watch the house. On reflection, it would be better to try and meet Harper on his own, without Angela there to pour scorn and suspicion on what he had to say. If Harper left and went to the pub, he would follow him. If Angela herself left, he would wait until she was well out of sight and then go and knock on the door. Turning the engine back on to stave off the cold, Michael's thoughts turned to Elizabeth and Jake. Several times whilst he had been in hospital, he had thought of phoning or sending a card, but on each occasion had resisted the temptation: it wasn't just his own safety that was dependent on his cover story of working overseas, but theirs, too. As a result, it would be nearly the end of January before they received the New Year card that he had written at the safe house and given to Tom for posting from Geneva. Still, it was better late than never. Lighting up a cigarette, Michael wondered how Jake would feel in nine or ten months' time when *Criminal Britain* was actually screened. His initial thoughts on the subject had been that his son would probably be proud of him, but on consideration he began to worry that his fame might inspire jealousy amongst Jake's school friends. At sixteen years old, acceptance by one's peers was of paramount importance and it would be awful to think of his notoriety doing anything to damage his son's standing amongst them. No doubt Elizabeth would know how to handle the situation – she had always been expert at managing Jake; he would consult with her. As he was concluding that he could worry about it all in a year's time, he saw Angela leaving the house. Having waited until she was well out of sight, he got out of the car and made his way across the road.

'Well, look who it is,' said Harper, dryly. 'Micky Angel, man of mystery. Where the bloody hell have you … fuck me, what happened to your face?'

'Fight,' replied Michael, simply.

'Jesus. You'd better come on in,' said Harper, taking a step backwards and letting Michael walk into the hallway. 'Trouble back up north, was it?'

For a moment Michael was tempted to suggest that this was the case: to imply that his absence had been the result of having gone back to Yorkshire over the Christmas period and that he had got into a fight whilst he had been there would be quite credible. In the end, he decided to stick as close as possible to the truth.

'Nah, I got it workin' at a night club.'

'What, that joint down in Brighton?'

'No, I left them,' answered Michael, following Harper down the hallway into the kitchen. 'It was a place in central London – some wanker with a flick knife – it's my own fault, I should've been more careful.'

'Bad shit.'

'Yeah, I know. Listen, I'm sorry I haven't been in touch, I was in hospital for a bit. I've got your money here.'

Taking the envelope out of his inside pocket, he placed it on the kitchen table.

'D'you wanna cup of tea?' said Harper, ignoring the cash.

'Yeah, all right, thanks,' replied Michael, with relief: so far, Harper seemed to be taking his absence remarkably well.

'You just missed Ange, she's just gone out.'

'Oh, right. She OK?'

'Yeah, she's fine. So, how long were you in hospital for, then?'

'Oh, not long,' replied Michael, deciding it would best to play down his injury. As Harper turned his back and began making the tea, he looked surreptitiously around the kitchen. The last time he had visited the house they had gone into the living room which had been completely devoid of any clues that might be of help in his investigation. On the wall next to the fridge, he now spotted a framed photograph of Harper, Angela and two men sitting drinking in a pub garden. Later, if the chance presented itself, he would try and get a shot of it from the camera in his top pocket.

'They sewed you up well,' said Harper, turning around and looking at the scar once more.

'Yeah, yeah – they did a good job.'

'What about the police,' he continued, with a frown, 'were they involved?'

'Nah. Guy got away. I didn't even report it.'

'Just as well,' he grunted, pouring out the boiling water into two mugs. 'What did the club do?'

'They didn't give me any compensation or anything but they've offered me a job if I want it.'

'Yeah?'

'Yeah.'

'You gonna take it?'

'I suppose so. It's only workin' weekends, but I'm fed up with the soddin' buildings so I thought I might as well.'

'Oh, right.'

'I'm still like, er, a bit skint, though.'

'Yeah?'

'Yeah. I was wonderin' whether we could take out that second house we talked about. You know – before Christmas. I could do with the money.'

'Funny you should mention that,' replied Harper, casually, bringing the tea across and sitting down opposite Michael. 'I'd been thinkin' the same.'

'Yeah?'

'Yeah. I found a place while you were away 'n' all.'

'Did you? Great.'

Under the table, Michael clenched his fist in a mixture of triumph and relief. Once again the patience game had paid dividends.

'I even got a couple of identities sorted out for you and Ange as well.'

'Oh, yeah?'

'Yeah.'

'So, who am I this time?'

'Oh, I can't remember the name,' said Harper, picking up his tobacco tin. 'I've got all the stuff in the other room.'

At this point, Michael found himself in a quandary. Even though he knew about Craig, not to enquire how Harper was able to obtain these identities so easily might appear suspicious: it was the obvious question to ask. To do so, however, was to run the risk of appearing too inquisitive. In the end, Michael decided to chance it.

'So, where d'you get 'em from, then – these NI numbers and identities?'

In response, Harper merely frowned.

'Yeah, all right I was only askin',' said Michael, watching Harper bring his Rizla paper up to his lips and imagining that he would probably let the subject lapse at this point. Harper did reply, however, although once again only after a long pause.

'Friend of Angela's if you must know – from way back.'

'Oh, right. So, are we all set to go on this second place, then?'

'Not quite,' countered Harper, in an ominously soft voice.

'Why not?'

'Still one problem.'

'What's that?'

'Your mobile phone.'

Michael froze. In an instant, all Harper's affability had completely disappeared and he was now staring back at him from the opposite side of the table totally stone-faced.

'What about it?'

'Give it to me, Mick.'

Taking the phone from his top pocket, he passed it across the table to Harper who slowly weighed it up and down in his hand. As his expression became ever more dark and threatening, Michael struggled to maintain his calm.

'What the fuck's going on?' he growled, suddenly slamming the phone down on the surface of the table causing the plastic cover to shoot off at an angle. 'I rang you a dozen times on this bastard thing over Christmas – no answer.'

'Yeah, sorry about that …'

'Look, mate. I got a place lined up all right, but because I couldn't get in touch with you, somebody else rented it out first. The same thing happened that morning when Dill came round, didn't it? We could've been in seriously deep shit then 'cos of you. So, what's going on, eh? What d'you carry this thing around for all the time if you don't use it?'

Despite the fact that this was the one question that he had dreaded being asked for so long and that he now had no choice but to abandon the mobile phone altogether, Michael felt a thrill of satisfaction as one more piece of the fraud-ring jigsaw clicked into place. Harper had indeed grown to like him as a friend, but, at the end of the day, it counted for nothing. He and Harper each had their place in the criminal organization whose pyramidal structure Tom had astutely recognised. Michael had to defer to Harper, just as Harper had to defer to Thompson. Money went uphill, orders came down – it was an ancient law – and breaking it meant punishment and humiliation. All Michael could do now was to bow his head and take it.

'Yeah, you're right, sorry mate. I should've listened to you before. I'll get myself a new one.'

'Do that. A proper one with text and all that. And keep it turned on all the time, yeah?' said Harper, tossing the mobile on to the table in front of him.

'Yeah, yeah, I will. I'll get myself organized,' said Michael, sheepishly, scooping up the phone and cover and slipping them back into his pocket.

'Dead right you will. Now listen, I've found another place that's just as good and if I hurry I should be able to get it for us. But next time, when I call you, you fucking answer the phone – all right? And make sure you're there bang on the dot for the inspection, too. It won't be Dill again – we'll see to that – but you fuckin' be there, or we'll cut you adrift – forever. Got it?'

'I will. I promise.'

'Cool. Sermon over,' said Harper, his uncompromising severity disappearing just as quickly as it had appeared. Leaning forward and picking the envelope of money up off the table top, he took the notes out and stuffed them in his top pocket. 'Right, well, let's forget the tea and go down The White Horse, shall we? We got some catchin' up to do.'

'Excuse me. Are you Mick?'

'Yeah, yeah, I'm Mick.'

'Hello, I'm Len. Barry's out the back parkin' the van. Sorry we're a bit late; you been here long?'

'No, just a couple of minutes.'

'Oh, good. Come on. Down this way – follow me.'

Although Michael had never met a pornographer before, he was not without his preconceptions as to such a person's likely demeanour and appearance. Nothing about Len, however, remotely corresponded with any of them. Michael guessed that he was in his early fifties, but, with his shiny, brown shoulder-length hair and the spotlessly clean denims that hung loosely about his lanky, gangling frame, he looked more like a fifteen year old schoolboy allowed by his mother to attend his first rock concert on condition that she ironed all his clothes properly beforehand. Walking through the ticket barrier, Michael followed Len through the rear entrance of the station and out on to the forecourt beyond. He spotted the blue transit van straightaway, rudely positioned lengthways across two parking spaces. Leaning up against its dented off-side wing stood a chubby little man in a combat jacket incongruously clutching a bunch of carnations.

'Hello, you must be Mick. I'm Barry.'

His voice was even squeakier than on the telephone.

'Yeah, that's right. How d'you do, Barry?'

'Fine, thanks. Crikey, you should've told us you were such a big bloke – I don't know whether we'll have enough room for you in the back with all the gear.'

Michael was about to comment that Barry had hung up the phone long before they had had a chance to get around to discussing such matters, but he had already turned on his heel and was opening up the back of the van. Listening to the metallic clanks and bangs, which sounded more like he was demolishing their photographic equipment rather than rearranging it, Michael decided to take the opportunity to have a quick word with his partner.

'Er, Barry and I didn't actually talk money or anything on the phone. What's the score, exactly?'

'Oh, sorry Mick,' replied Len, apologetically, 'it's a hundred and twenty quid a day for the shoot plus your travel expenses. Is that all right?'

'Yeah, yeah that sounds fine. And, er, how often are you thinking of asking me to work for you?'

'Well, it depends on demand for our new titles really: once or twice a month maybe.'

'Oh, right.'

'Is that OK – I mean, if you haven't got too much work on at the moment.'

'No, no, I'm not too busy at the moment ...' replied Michael, recalling the summer afternoon at photographic college seventeen years ago when he had last handled a sound boom.

'Always on the assumption, of course,' added Len, solemnly, 'that we can establish a harmonious artistic and professional rapport.'

'Oh, of course, of course,' agreed Michael.

'OK, Mick,' shouted Barry, from the rear of the van. 'It'll be a bit of a squeeze but I think we can fit you in.'

There was absolutely no room to move in the back of the van and, jammed up against the window-less rear doors, Michael was unable to see exactly where they were going. At the end of the twenty minute drive, Barry finally brought the van to a halt and let Michael out. Standing on the dark, newly laid tarmac of the car park, he surveyed the scene before him. They were in the middle of a large, modern housing development situated, he guessed, on the extreme edge of London's north-eastern green belt. The three-storey flats had clearly been built down to a cost, but were nevertheless uniformly well-maintained. Michael imagined it was probably quite a nice place to live.

Levering himself out of the passenger seat, Len walked around to the back of the van to join Michael and Barry. Taking a small, peach-coloured envelope out of his top pocket, he opened it up and examined the letter inside; Michael could see that it was written on ornamental stationery, embellished around the margins by clutches of mauve blue bells.

'Sir Geoffrey Elton Towers. Number eleven,' he announced, cheerily, 'let's try over there, shall we?'

Despite its neat layout, the estate was very poorly signposted and the three men wandered around for almost fifteen minutes before they found the right flat. During this entire time, Michael did not see a single person and, as he stared up at the rows of net-curtained windows, could not help wondering to himself what might be going on behind them.

'Hello, is it Irene?'

'Yes.'

'I'm Len. This is Barry and Mick.'

'Hello. Oh, carnations! How lovely! Thank you. Come in, come in.'

The woman was in her late thirties, with dark auburn hair curled upwards at the ends in a style that reminded Michael of a famous black and white photograph of Jackie Kennedy. Her face was jolly rather than pretty, with a bubbly infectious grin that revealed a gap between her front teeth when she smiled. She was fairly short – only just over five feet tall – with a rounded figure that no doubt had once been voluptuous but was now well on the way to matronly. Len and Barry marched straight down the hallway after Irene, but as Michael followed on afterwards, he was rapidly overcome by a feeling of embarrassed disbelief. When she had first opened the door, he had naturally thought that she must be some sort of assistant, but, as they walked into the empty living room, it was startlingly obvious that she herself was to be the object of the afternoon's cinematic endeavours.

'Oh, I do like this,' commented Len appreciatively, looking around the flat's mock-Regency decorations. 'Tasteful. Very tasteful.'

'Oh, and Capo di Monte, too,' added Barry pleasantly. 'I've always liked Capo di Monte, me.'

'Oh, thank you,' grinned Irene, happily.

Turning to his left Michael looked at the large, verdigris cabinet that stretched along the entire back wall of the living room. He knew very little about antiques, but could nevertheless see that it housed an extraordinarily fine collection of the distinctive brightly-coloured figurines.

'Right. May I?' asked Len, pointing to the spotlessly clean chinoise sofa.

'Yes, yes, please sit down,' said Irene.

'Thank you,' replied Len. 'OK. Just a few forms to fill in before we get started …'

★

They arrived back at Walthamstow station just before four o'clock. Having parked the van in the station car park, Len pointed to the pub next door and suggested popping in for a quick drink, although Michael had in fact been thinking of nothing but a double whisky from the moment that they had left the flat. Leaving Len and Barry at the bar buying the drinks, he sat down at a quiet table at the back of the pub and, running the palms of his hands over his face, reviewed the events of the previous two hours. In terms of witnessing the most bizarre exhibitionist extremes of which the human species is capable, the experience had outranked any that he had had in his life so far by several orders of magnitude; in terms of Henry and Tom's idea for the fourth documentary, however, it had been a complete non-starter. Not only had Irene been twenty years too old, but she had also plainly been acting entirely under her own volition, having launched herself into her astonishing solo routine with the greatest of abandon and delight. As for the producers, it would be hard to imagine two individuals less threatening and exploitative than Len and Barry – or so it seemed on first impression, at least. Perhaps the best he could hope for from the afternoon would be to obtain some further background information from them and possibly one or two leads to other film-makers or agents.

'Oh, thanks, Len,' said Michael, taking hold of his drink. 'Cheers.'

'Yeah, cheers. Good afternoon's work,' replied Len.

'Yeah, cheers,' added Barry. 'Thanks for your help, Mick.'

'So, er, how did you discover Irene then?' asked Michael, tentatively.

'She found us.'

'Really?'

'Yeah, she wrote to us. We get letters from people all the time, telling us what they can do and what they've got. Women and men.'

'Oh, right,' said Michael, suddenly getting a flashback of Irene's enormous bush of pubic hair, the size of a dinner plate. 'And, er, is there much demand for, er, movies like hers?'

'Much more than you'd think,' replied Len.

'Yeah?'

'Oh, yeah. All these skinny nineteen year old cover models you see, they're not sex symbols – not really – they're just artificial creations made up to sell magazines. You ask your average bloke what sort of woman he'd like to spend a couple of hours in the sack with and it wouldn't be some scrawny supermodel, believe you me.'

'No?'

'Oh, Christ, no. They want a woman don't they? Not a broom handle. Somebody they can hold on to. You know, big, warm, cheerful.'

'Yeah, cheerful's important,' said Barry. 'Nice happy smiling face – not all moody and introspective.'

'She was good like that, wasn't she, Irene?' mused Len.

'Yeah, excellent,' agreed Barry.

'So, er, is this what you do all the time, then – this sort of video?' continued Michael.

'Oh, no,' responded Len. 'We do all sorts – you have to cater for every taste in our line of business.'

'Yeah?' asked Michael, thinking that perhaps the men from Heretic Films might yet prove to be of use to him after all.

'Oh, yes,' replied Len. 'We call ourselves the two witnesses – we've seen it all in our time, ain't we, Barry?'

'Sure have,' replied Barry. 'Anyway, did you enjoy it, Mick?'

'Er, yeah, yeah, it was great.'

'Good,' said Len, 'because me and Barry have, like, had a word and we think you're all right.'

'Yeah, we like your style,' said Barry. 'Discreet. Solid.'

'Oh, thanks,' said Michael, recalling the statuesque pose he had held throughout the afternoon – far more the product of his state of shock than a consciously adopted professional stance.

'So, if you feel you'd like to work with us again, we'd be very happy to have you.'

'Great.'

'We should be filming again in a couple of weeks, actually.'

'Yeah?'

'Yeah. We've been plannin' this one for absolutely ages.'

'It's gonna be a tricky one, mind you,' added Barry. 'We could end up in big trouble if certain people were to find out what we'd been up to – really big trouble – me in particular.'

'It won't half be good if we can swing it, though,' said Len enthusiastically.

'Oh, yeah, it'll be mega,' replied Barry, his eyes rolling gleefully.

'It's got a young blond in it 'n' all, Mick,' continued Len. 'I bet she'll be a lot more up your street than Irene.'

'Yeah. How old?'

'Nineteen. Gorgeous. Absolutely gorgeous.'

'Really?' replied Michael, trying not to show too much interest. Things were moving closer and closer to Henry and Tom's brief by the moment.

'Oh, yeah. So, what d'you reckon, then, you up for it?'

'OK. Why not?'

'It'll be at short notice and you're gonna need some portable sound recording gear. Have you got anything like that?'

'Er, no, but I know where I can get my hands on some fairly easily,' said Michael: there were several shops close to Jim's selling second-hand audio equipment – he could pop in late one afternoon before going on to work at Gog.

'Great!' exclaimed Len, lifting up his glass. 'So, here's to Heretic's next title, then.'

'Yeah,' added Barry, grinning lopsidedly. 'Here's to *Goosey, Goosey, Gander*. Our little pet project.'

'Ha! Like it, Barry!' laughed Len. 'Our pet project. A very apt description.'

'Thank you, Leonard,' replied Barry, politely acknowledging the compliment.

Raising his glass, Michael smiled, but, as he drank down the whisky, a cold chill ran the length of his spine at the thought of the type of film that the two men appeared to be planning.

Michael had been back at Gog less than two weeks before Kent honoured his promise of some 'extra work'. Towards the end of the Sunday night of his second weekend, one of the barmen came over to the front entrance to tell Michael to go down to the basement after he finished at two. Walking along the echoing concrete corridors and into the apparently functionless yet eerily disturbing anteroom, Michael was struck by the absence of all sense of time in Kent's underground realm: there simply weren't any temporal points of reference by which to orientate oneself – only the generators humming and the neon lights strobing night and day with the same unforgiving monotony. Kent, too, was unchanged – sitting at his antique desk and wearing the same expensively tailored clothes as the day of Michael's interview. Once again, he brought their meeting to a conclusion in less than a minute: no polite conversation, no wasted words, just a slip of paper on which was written the name and address of a warehouse in Lowestoft where they should meet on Monday morning. Walking back through the ante-room, Michael could see that Kent had scrawled "Eleven o'clock sharp" on the back of the note. That was in little more than eight hours time. He wondered if Kent ever slept.

Driving along the narrow Suffolk lanes, Michael pondered the question of whether Kent was bringing drugs directly into the country himself, or whether he was merely purchasing material that already had been smuggled in. All the signs suggested that it was the former. Having chatted to various staff at Gog, he had discovered that the club was part of the Ellis Group – an international and widely diversified entertainments conglomerate, a separate division of which imported and exported alcohol and drinks all over the world. This would surely provide an ideal cover for trafficking narcotics and it was difficult to imagine why Kent should have any interest in warehouses if he were not using them for that purpose. His operation was probably built upon a network of bribes paid to the warehouse staff and perhaps even to customs officials. Such a system, however, would doubtless regularly need maintaining and enforcing which, presumably, was why Kent had asked him along as hired muscle. Pulling into the car park in front of the large, well-secured warehouse, Michael went to switch the phone on in his top pocket, but then stopped mid-movement. For the moment he would hold fire – it might well be several hours before he discovered something of interest and didn't want the tape to have run out by then. Undoing his seat belt, he got out of the car and looked up at the sign at the entrance to the warehouse: on first glance at least, Carl and Ernst Logistics looked like a perfectly reputable establishment. On the other side of the car park, he could see Kent's Saab. Walking towards it, he felt his adrenalin begin to flow. After so many months of waiting, the drugs investigation was now moving forward at pace.

'All right, Mick?' asked Kent, getting out of his car. As usual, the three-piece suit that he was wearing was razor sharp.

'Yeah, fine.'

'This way,' he said, nodding in the direction of the reception.

'What are we here for then, exactly?' asked Michael, falling in to step with him.

'To scare the fuckin' life out of these cocksuckers,' replied Kent, curtly.

This brusque reply suggested to Michael that for the moment at least he should not quiz Kent further. Following him into the neat but sparsely decorated reception, Michael felt his palms go clammy. He would never be able to learn anything of Kent's operations unless he became a trusted assistant, but, in the very process of so doing, there was a strong possibility of his being called upon to employ strong-arm tactics. He could only pray that no one innocent would end up on the receiving end.

'My name's Kent. I've come to see Mr McDonald, the warehouse manager. Here's my card.'

'D'you have an appointment?' asked the receptionist.

'No, this is a spot check. Get him on the phone now, will you?'

'Oh, er, well, I don't actually know whether he's here and even if he is I'm not sure ...'

'He's here,' interrupted Kent. 'I checked. Get him on the phone now. Mr Kent. Ellis Group. I need to see him immediately.'

'Oh, OK, then, Mr Kent, would you like to take a seat?'

'No, I wouldn't,' he snapped, taking a step closer towards the receptionist's desk so that he was standing almost right over her. The woman swallowed and then looked across at Michael, panic plainly showing in her eyes. Letting his arms hang loosely by his side, as though ready for a fight, Michael glared aggressively back at her. Hastily, she picked up the telephone and made a call. The warehouse manager appeared almost straightaway.

'Good morning, can I help you?'

He was a short, stockily-built man in his early fifties, with a well-trimmed military moustache and a charcoal grey pin-striped suit. His expression was in the main indignant but also tinged with a certain air of bewilderment. Michael guessed that the spot check of which Kent had spoken was something very much out of the ordinary.

'Good morning, Mr McDonald,' growled Kent, barely moderating the belligerent tone he had adopted with the receptionist. 'My name's Kent from the Ellis Group. As I'm sure you know, we've been using your bonded warehouse for the last three months for transhipments to Europe and the Middle East.'

'Yes,' replied McDonald, cautiously. 'And what of it?'

'In the contract we signed with you, there's a clause allowing us to carry out two spot checks a year of your facilities.'

'Really? I wasn't aware of that.'

Sliding his hand into his inside pocket, Kent took out a buff envelope and handed it to McDonald.

'Page eight. Clause nineteen point four.'

Narrowing his eyes, McDonald looked first at Kent and then across at Michael, obviously trying to make sense of this unusual combination of contractual exactitude and bully boy hostility. After several seconds, he opened up the envelope and, having found the relevant clause, looked up at Kent again.

'It would appear you do, Mr ...'

'Kent. Can we get started? I estimate we'll need about two hours in all – if you've got your act together, that is.'

With a puzzled frown, McDonald put the contract back in the envelope and handed it back to Kent.

'By all means, but, er, may I ask why you felt the need to summon me in particular? I mean, you're surely not expecting me to accompany you on this inspection, are you?'

'It doesn't matter to me who takes me round ... and if you don't care about Ellis's business, it won't matter to you either.'

Once again McDonald's eyes narrowed and he stared at Kent, obviously fighting back the impulse to tell this belligerent boor and his skin head goon to leave the premises immediately. But, in the end, the long years of commercial conditioning asserted themselves and he turned and spoke quietly to the receptionist.

'Call Malcolm, will you, Elaine? Tell him to drop whatever he's doing and come over here now.'

'Yes, Mr McDonald.'

'Malcolm Grey is my deputy,' he continued through gritted teeth, turning to face Kent once more. 'He has overall responsibility for the running of the site, including the bonded facilities you are currently renting. He's been in the job for over twenty years and is the most appropriate person to show you around. I will, however, be asking him to write to me personally about every aspect of your inspection for my subsequent detailed review.'

'Good,' replied Kent, coldly. 'Let's hope he knows his stuff.'

It was half-past three before they left Carl and Ernst. Initially, the deputy warehouse manager Malcolm Grey had been confident and composed, but as the hours passed his self-assurance steadily began to disintegrate in the face of Kent's rigorous auditing skills and his seemingly encyclopaedic knowledge of warehouse practices. At first, it was minor procedural lapses: signatures that were not quite legible, missing duplicate copies. Then, it was poorly validated operating practices. When Grey sought to dispute Kent's appraisal in this regard, it only served to make him redouble his efforts until he found something seriously amiss. He succeeded in this just after half past one – right in the middle of the deputy warehouse manager's cancelled lunch hour. Carl and Ernst had only partially maintained their employee training records. There was no doubt that the training had taken place, but, without the records for it, how were they able to demonstrate that a given operator had received training for – and was therefore qualified to carry out – a given function?

As the day had progressed, Michael had become fascinated and confused in equal measures. The bonded warehouse system, whereby goods can be brought into the country without incurring import duty as long they are subsequently re-exported, obviously lent itself to abuse by drug traffickers. But, if that really was the reason for Kent's interest, why was he so fixated with ensuring that Carl and Ernst operated their systems correctly? Surely, this would be more likely to frustrate abuse, not facilitate it. Walking back across the car park with Kent, Michael could see McDonald and Grey standing in the reception looking thoroughly unsettled by the day's experience but yet, at the same time, plainly relieved that it had at last come to an end. He shared their sentiments entirely: time alone would tell exactly what Kent was up to – for the moment, all Michael could do was wait and see what happened next.

'You hungry?' grunted Kent, pressing the central locking release button on his key ring to open up his car.

'Yeah, I am.'

'Follow me. We'll stop off somewhere on the way.'

'On the way where?' asked Michael.

'On the way to see an old friend,' replied Kent, smiling for the first time since they had met that day.

After they left the motorway café, Michael followed Kent into London for a little over an hour, arriving in a suburb that he recognised as Brook Green just after six o'clock. The road in which they finally came to a halt was broad and quiet, with rows of large four storey

238

Edwardian houses on either side, all long since converted into individual flats. The street lighting was poor and an evening fog had just descended, but it was plain from Kent's gesticulation through the rear windscreen that he wanted Michael to stay in his own car for the moment whilst he made a call on his mobile phone. Switching off the engine, Michael drummed his fingers on the steering wheel and waited patiently to be summoned. A few moments later, his own mobile rang. It was the call that he had been dreading for almost three weeks. Heretic's porn movie was on for the next day at a house in Walthamstow – ten thirty sharp. Having hastily scribbled down the address, he read it back to Len and quickly finished the call. Trying to put the alarming prospect of what he was to face the next day from his mind, Michael slid back into his seat so that Kent could not observe him in his rear view mirror and then switched on the mobile to begin recording. Several times during the day he had thought about activating the phone but on each occasion had held on, waiting for concrete evidence of Kent's drug smuggling activities: he was glad now that he had been so patient. A minute later, Kent finished his own calls and, without turning around, waved his hand to indicate that Michael should join him in his car. Opening the passenger door of Kent's Saab and getting into the seat, he noticed that the internal lights did not come on. He guessed that it wasn't an electrical fault but that Kent had purposely removed the bulbs. The smell of the car's leather upholstery was unusually rich and strong.

'Flat four A,' said Kent. 'Basement. Can you see it over there?'

'Yeah, I can see it,' replied Michael, squinting through the darkness. The lights were off in the front room, but a dim glow coming from the glass panel above the front door suggested the presence of someone inside.

'It's owned by a bloke called Foss. Michael Foss, actually,' said Kent, with a grin. 'Michael – same name as you – funny that.'

'And …?'

'You met him a few weeks ago. Remember?'

'No.'

'No?' chuckled Kent, ironically. 'You should do. He left you with a nice little memento.' Swivelling around in his seat, he stretched out his hand and then turned Michael's chin so that he could see his scar. 'Remember now?'

Michael's heart began to race and, feeling a huge lump form in his

239

throat, he turned away from Kent and looked back across at the flat again. Staring through the gloom, he desperately strove to marshal his thoughts. How should he react? What should he say? If Kent had brought him here for the purposes of retaliation, how could he avoid getting involved in it whilst still maintaining his credibility?

'Yeah, I remember,' he replied, in a non-committal voice, turning back to look at Kent.

'He's on his own right now.'

'Yeah?'

'Yeah. A friend of his just rang him to check. And then he rang me. 'Cos he's not really a friend of Foss's anymore, you see. He used to be. But now he's, like, more a friend of mine, if you know what I mean. It's important in this world – knowing who your real friends are. I set great store by it.'

Still Kent was grinning and still Michael had no idea how to respond. Kent had obviously managed to turn one of Foss's gang members against him and had brought Michael here to help carry out a reprisal attack. Just as the silence reached the point at which he felt he absolutely had to say something, Kent reached into his inside pocket, took out a surgical glove and slowly put it over his right hand. Taking out the ignition keys, he then leant forwards and unlocked the glove compartment. For several seconds, Michael found himself unable to breathe. This was far worse than his worst fears – his very worst fears.

Kent had taken out a silencer and a gun.

'What about Juan Vucetich – you ever heard of him?' asked Kent, taking the cartridge out of the gun and checking the bullets.

Another name. You're out of your depth, screamed a voice in Michael's head. You're out of your depth! What was he to do?

'No,' he whispered, hoarsely.

'He was an Argentinean geezer. A copper – lived a hundred years ago,' mused Kent, screwing the silencer tightly on to the barrel of the gun, 'eighteen ninety – or somethin' like that. First law officer ever to convict a murderer on the basis of fingerprints. Some woman killed her son and then tried to frame her husband, but the stupid bitch left her prints all over the place so they nailed her: every villain's been shit-scared of fingerprints ever since. Not me, though. I think they're great.'

'Yeah? Why's that?' said Michael, forcing his vocal chords to work.

'Because you don't have to fight 'em – fingerprints, I mean,' replied

Kent, placing the gun in his lap and turning to face Michael once more. 'You can make 'em work for you. Know what I mean?'

'Yeah? How?' croaked Michael.

'Well, this is Foss's gun, isn't it? His own gun,' replied Kent, in a voice that seemed to imply Michael should already be aware of the fact. 'And there's only one way the police're gonna read it. Lonely man – no friends, drinks a lot – gets depressed one night 'cos his life's been a fuckin' waste of time and then blows his brains out. Suicide, innit? Gotta be. Case closed. Next please. What d'you say Mick, huh? Wouldn't take more than five minutes. If you want to, that is …'

Suddenly, Michael understood why Kent had brought him here. When they had first arrived, he had thought that it was part of the 'extra work' that Kent had promised him. But he had been wrong. Carl and Ernst had been work, but this was something altogether different. Kent wasn't asking Michael to assist him in killing Foss because he needed his help. He wasn't even asking him to do it as a test of his loyalty – his tone was far too relaxed for that, far too jocular. No, this wasn't a job. It was a demonstration of Kent's favour. He had already suggested to Michael that he had been planning to get his revenge on Foss and the other men, and, to his warped and violent psyche, offering Michael the chance to settle a score in the process amounted to an expression of goodwill.

'Nah, I never took it personal,' said Michael, trying to make the comment sound as off-hand as possible.

'He cut you up bad, Mick.'

'Yeah, I know, but it wasn't really my fight – it was yours. And besides, I draw the line at shooting people I don't know …'

'Suit yourself,' replied Kent, in a voice that carried a measure of disappointment but no apparent umbrage. 'I can always deal with him later …'

After returning to Balam Road, Michael fell into an exhausted sleep, but awoke in the small hours of the morning with the most terrifying dream he had ever had. He was a teenager again, back at boarding school. It was the summer holidays. All the other pupils had left, but he had stayed on, waiting for his father to collect him. Except that Kent was in the school, too, looking for his father – looking for him so that he could kill him. As Michael ran through the deserted cloakrooms and along the empty corridors, his horrified screams reverberated back off the battleship grey walls, filling his ears until his head shrieked with pain. Dad, you've got to hide. Dad, you've got to hide. The man wants to kill you. Through the refectory windows he could see his father's plum red Jaguar parked on the gravel driveway outside, but it was empty – he must have gone off to look for him in the school. But where? Where? And then he saw him on the first floor landing, smiling brightly and stretching out his arms in welcome. Hurtling up the broad stone staircase he rushed towards his father, but even before he had got half way, he saw Kent come up behind him and raise Foss's gun to the back of his head. Screaming, he called to his father to get out of the way, to run off as fast as he could. But, just as a look of alarm spread over his father's face and he turned to see who was behind him, the shot rang out.

It was 04:20. Staggering blindly out of the bedroom and through into the lounge he opened up the window and breathed in the early morning air. Outside the Uxbridge Road was completely quiet, but the silence did nothing to relieve the strange and terrifying feeling that now gripped his mind and overwhelmed his senses. It was a sense of having lost all control over events and his reactions to them; of being forced to undergo a terrifying, unendurable ordeal whose inexorable outcome would be his own destruction. The previous evening he had been asked to murder someone. He had done his best to make an astute response to this terrible request, and Kent had indeed postponed the planned killing, but such was the extreme nature of his character that he might just as easily have gone ahead and carried out the execution before Michael's very eyes. Within a few short hours, he was set to witness a spectacle of unimaginable degradation. For all Len and Barry's mild personal manners, the years of routinely recording the explicitly pornographic had clearly left them utterly desensitized to the abasement of human dignity. For an hour he lay on the couch smoking – unable to rid his mind of the sense of impending doom but too scared of what he might see if he closed his eyes and went back to sleep. As it began to grow light at five-thirty, he decided to make the journey to the opposite side of London before the traffic built up. When he got there he would find a quiet spot and grab a half hour's sleep in the back of the car. Perhaps the dreams would be gone by then.

To the casual passer-by, Maisie Road would doubtless have appeared quite charming that morning. The previous day's fog had vanished, burned off by a bright, luminous sun that would have graced the height of summer let alone the month of February. The rows of well-to-do three storey houses seemed to welcome the sunshine and one or two even sported hanging baskets filled with purple and yellow crocuses. Parking his car, Michael looked around to see if he could spot Len or Barry. On the opposite side of the road, he could just make out number forty-two – the house at which Len had said the film would be shot. With its brilliant stone frontage and sweeping bay windows, it was clearly one of the neatest and well-maintained properties in the street although to Michael, it appeared nothing less than a hideous, whited sepulchre. Fighting down a rising sense of disquiet, he opened the car window and flicked the ash off his cigarette. When he had left the flat, he had slipped a small bottle of whisky into his jacket pocket, but its presence was now more disturbing than reassuring. Never before had he felt that sort of need for alcohol. Was this how it was going to end, with his being driven to seek oblivion in drink? A minute later, Len pulled up in a large, white unmarked transit van. Locking his car, Michael walked over to him, his face grim with resignation.

'All right, Mick?' Len's voice was conspiratorial – excited. 'Have you brought your gear – the portable stuff?'

'Yeah. It's in the car.'

'Great. Get in. I'll tell you the plan.'

Walking around to the pavement, Michael opened up the passenger door and heaved himself up on to the front seat. Slamming the heavy door closed, he turned around to face Len, but was completely unprepared for the sight that greeted him as he did so.

'Michael Angel,' said Len. 'Sound engineer, right?'

Len was holding an old, battered paint brush, its bent bristles pointing squiffily upwards into Michael's face.

'Sorry?'

'Michael Angel,' repeated Len. 'Sound engineer, right?'

'Yeah …'

'Wrong,' replied Len, a beam of morning sunlight suddenly slanting through the windscreen and illuminating his freckled forehead. 'For the next ten minutes you are Michael Angel professional painter and decorator, come to put two coats of gloss on a set of kitchen windows.'

'What?'

With a grin, Len nodded towards the back of the van. Turning around, Michael could see that it was filled with interior decorating gear.

'It's all right, don't look so worried, mate – it'll be me that actually does the painting, not you.'

'I don't get it,' said Michael.

'The house we're gonna shoot the film in is owned by Barry's aunt Margaret. She's gonna be away until this evening, down at some Women's Institute's bash in Bournemouth, so we've got the place all to ourselves for the whole day. Oh, look, hang on, there's Barry now. Just remember what I said, you're a professional decorator, right? A professional – that's dead important.'

The three men arrived at the front door together. Taking a firm hold of the heavy brass knocker, Len banged it twice. Still not at all sure what was going on, Michael turned to look at Barry, who in complete contrast to his partner, appeared to be in a state of absolute terror.

'This is my aunt's house,' he squeaked, nervously. 'It's a brilliant place. It'll make a fantastic set. We've had our eye on it for years but she'll go mental if she finds out.'

'She's not gonna find out, though, is she?' snapped Len. 'Now, come on, Baz, pull yourself together, for Christ's sake. Don't bottle out now. Oh, good morning Mrs Fitzgerald, how are you today?'

Aunt Margaret was a tall, distinguished-looking woman in her early seventies, wearing an expensive, cream-coloured two-piece suit. In her right hand she was brandishing what Michael thought at first was some sort of surgical implement but was in fact a gigantic stainless steel hat-pin. When she spoke, her voice was shrill and high-pitched, but, unlike Barry's, carried an unmistakable edge of command.

'You're late. If the taxi wasn't late too I would have missed you altogether! Barry, what are you skulking around at the back there for? Come on through to the kitchen quickly. And, all of you, make sure you wipe your feet – this hall carpet shows the dirt terribly.'

The house was as magnificent as Aunt Margaret was formidable. Walking along the beautifully proportioned hallway with its tall, corniced ceiling and elegant wallpapered panels, Michael recalled the interior of Irene's flat. Despite her enviable collection of Capo di Monte, there was simply no comparison. This was the epitome of elegant, urban living. This was real class. Going through into the modern, designer kitchen, Michael looked across at the window frames which had already been sanded down and filled ready for repainting.

'Now, you must be the decorator, Mr Angel, am I correct?'

It sounded more like a scientific observation than a greeting. With the air of an entomologist striving to classify a small and annoyingly unusual insect, Aunt Margaret squinted myopically at Michael over the tops of her silver-framed spectacles.

'Er, yeah, yeah, that's right.'

'Good. Now, my nephew here tells me that you charge sixty-five pounds for an afternoon's work.'

'Sixty-five, er, yes, that's right.'

'My late husband Arthur decorated this house – and to an extremely high standard as I'm sure you can see. The windows here are the first thing that has needed doing since he passed away and I'm very much expecting you to maintain those same standards. D'you have any professional qualifications?'

'Er, yeah, yeah.'

'And they are what exactly?'

'Pardon?'

'What are they exactly – your qualifications?'

Again the obelisk stare. Michael wondered if that was what had finished off her husband Arthur.

'Well, er, I've got er …'

Out of the corner of his eye, Michael could see Len just about to come to his assistance but just at that precise moment the door bell rang.

'That'll be your taxi,' chipped in Barry, quickly. 'Have you got everything ready?'

'Er, yes, I have,' replied Aunt Margaret, irritably, 'but I really did want to talk to Mr Angel some more about the windows. It's most important the work gets done properly …'

'Don't worry, Mrs Fitzgerald,' continued Len, smoothly, 'when you come back the job'll be all done and the kitchen'll be absolutely spotless: and we'll make sure all the mess is vacuumed up afterwards, too.'

'Well, naturally,' she rasped, glaring at them fearsomely, before turning on her heel and marching briskly off down the hallway. Moving into the front room, the three men stood in the bay window and watched the taxi draw away; somehow, Michael even found himself waving. As the taxi did a right turn at the end of Maisie Road and disappeared out of sight, Len and Barry began to dance around the room.

'We've done it! We've done it!' they shouted, waving their arms in the air and then clasping each other in a delirious embrace. Michael, however, suddenly found himself beginning to feel desperately weary.

'Look, I've had enough of this,' he said, interrupting their celebrations. 'Tell me what's going on or I'm out of here.'

'Sorry, mate, sorry,' said Len, calming himself down, 'We've got the house for ten hours; two to do the painting, four to shoot the film, two to clear up afterwards and two spare just in case.'

'And what sort of movie is it? Come on, tell me.'

'Oh, it's got a great story-line,' said Len.

'Brilliant,' added Barry.

'I said what sort of movie is it – tell me,' insisted Michael.

'Posh housewife, right?' replied Len. 'Calls in the decorator one day, gets the hots for him and then they have it off in every single room in the house. There's twelve of 'em in all. That's why you need your portable gear – to go from room to room. It's gonna be awesome.'

'Completely awesome!' echoed Barry.

'Well, we hope it will be anyway,' continued Len. 'Heretic's only small – we never have the money for sets and things – so we have to make do how we can. Because we got this place for free, we had a bit more cash to spend on the actors and we've got a couple of semi-pro's in. Amanda should be here in about an hour and Barry's picking up Gert at Stansted at half eleven.'

'Actually, I'd better get a move on,' said Barry, suddenly. 'The traffic looked a bit heavy comin' down.'

'Yeah, OK, you get on your way and I'll see you back here about one. I'll start the paintin' straightaway. Actually, no, I'll get me and Mick a cup of tea first. Mick, how d'you take it? Mick, are you all right mate, you don't look too bright …'

Slumping wearily down on the sofa, Michael felt a huge wave of relief pour through him. Looking back up at the two men again – Len in his denims and heavy metal T-shirt and Barry with a tie on underneath his combat jacket, presumably for Aunt Margaret's benefit – Michael found himself smiling for the first time in how long? A month? Two months? How could he have ever thought these two men capable of even the smallest act of cruelty against man or beast?

'So, is going from room to room what gave you the idea for the title?' he asked, finally.

'What, *Goosey, Goosey, Gander?*'

'Yeah.'

'That's right!' exclaimed Len. '*Goosey, Goosey Gander*, where shall I wander …'

'Upstairs, downstairs and in my lady's chamber,' interrupted Michael, completing the quotation for him.

'Got it in one, mate,' grinned Len, spreading his arms grandly. 'In my lady's chamber … and in every other room in the house, too.'

'Including the attic and the cellar,' said Barry, turning to Len and adding as an afterthought, 'although we'll have to be a bit careful with the cellar: we don't want to drag any dirt up on to the hall carpet …'

She was a vision in black. After Barry had left, Michael had fallen into a deep sleep on the living room couch, but had awoken a little over an hour later on hearing a taxi pulling up on the gravelled driveway outside. Moving over to the bay window, he stood out of sight behind the heavy net curtains watching her as she got out of the cab and paid the driver. Shoes, jacket, shoulder-bag, hat – everything about her was black – the only exceptions being her long, blond hair and her blood red fingernails. As she walked up the steps and knocked the front door, Michael noticed that she even had a tattoo of a small black horse just below her navel, visible in the intriguingly sensual gap between the bottom of her blouse and the waistband of her low slung jeans. Hearing Len open the door and take her into the lounge, Michael made his way down the hall to meet Amanda May, the porn-star that Heretic had hired for the afternoon. Was she the girl that King and Tom had hoped he would find, enticed from an otherwise perfectly respectable middle-class background to work in the UK porn industry – the fastest growing in Europe? And if she was that girl, who had been the man who had lured her into it? Who was the faceless criminal behind her shame? When Tom had initially suggested this brief for the fourth documentary, Michael had had his reservations. Many women working in the porn industry did so as a matter of choice and it might well prove difficult to find one that exactly fitted the bill in the time he had available; and, even if he could, he would still have to track down her Svengali. As he opened the lounge door, however, Michael felt a thrill of anticipation. Despite the difficulty of the challenge that King had set him, there was something about Amanda May that had given him his first real sense of what he might achieve if he were able to succeed in it.

On entering the room, the first thing he noticed about her was her height: she was very small, probably only just over five feet tall. When she turned around to look at him, however, one feature – and one feature alone – captured his attention to the exclusion of all others: her complexion. As a student he had photographed his fair share of models, and thereafter as a professional photographer had gone on to take pictures of a number of world famous celebrities and beauties, but as regards facial complexion, none of them could match the perfection of the woman now standing six feet away from him. It wasn't simply the tone of her skin – with its wonderful peach-coloured luminosity – it was the uniformity of that tone, running all the way down from her smooth, even forehead to her taut, elegant neck.

'Oh, hello, mate,' said Len. 'Amanda, this is Mick our sound man.'

'Hello,' said Michael, 'how d'you do?'

'Fine, thanks,' she replied, 'you feelin' better now?'

'Sorry?'

'After your sleep,' she continued, with a grin, 'burning the candle at both ends, was you? Naughty boy.'

Her accent was pure East End and added enormously to her charm. Michael took to her instantly.

'Here, listen, Mick,' chipped in Len. 'I was gonna take Amanda around the house, but now you're up perhaps you'd do it. You haven't seen it all yet either and I've gotta do the last bit of painting. Don't wanna disappoint her ladyship, do we?'

Amanda giggled – she was obviously au fait with the Aunt Margaret situation.

'Yeah, yeah, sure,' said Michael.

'Barry just phoned, Gert's plane landed five minutes ago so they should be back about one. How long will you need to get ready, Amanda?'

'Oh, not long,' she replied, 'half an hour maybe.'

'OK,' said Len, checking his watch, 'have ten minutes to look around the house and then you can get started.'

'All right,' said Amanda.

'Use the first floor bedroom to do your make-up. It's got a nice big dressing table so you can spread out. We'll give you a shout when we're ready, all right?'

As they moved from room to room Michael was sorely tempted to switch on the camera in his top pocket and start quizzing Amanda about her background: Henry and Tom had suggested that he talk to as many female porn-stars as possible in his search for a respectable girl who had been enticed into the profession. In the end, though, he decided to use the time to gain her confidence: perhaps he could give her a lift back home afterwards or even suggest meeting up with her again for a drink one evening. Leaving her to get changed in Aunt Margaret's bedroom, which, he was surprised to note, contained a remarkable number of fluffy toys, Michael made his way back to the kitchen to help Len with the final preparations.

Gert arrived twenty minutes later; as his name suggested he was a Swede. Watching him get changed into the set of decorator's overalls that Len had brought, Michael asked Barry why Heretic hadn't chosen a British actor and was surprised to learn that it was generally accepted that the UK simply did not produce quality male porn stars. Apparently, this wasn't a question of physical appearance or even size – there were plenty of handsome, well-endowed men to be found – but rather one of stamina. You could get a decent hour or two out of a Brit, informed Barry, but if you wanted a man capable of performing all afternoon and well into the evening, you really had to go for a Scandinavian – or at a push a German. Michael was on the point of quizzing Barry more about this, when Len announced that filming was due to start in five minutes. Going into the front room, Michael strapped on the heavy, reel-to-reel portable tape recorder that he had purchased from the second-hand audio shop two doors down from Jim's and then brought it back into the kitchen for the final sound check. The moment he came through the door, Len, Barry and Gert dissolved into gales of laughter.

'Fuckin' hell, Mick,' said Len, resting his arms on the kitchen table to stop himself from falling over, 'where d'you get that thing, the British Museum?'

'It works OK,' replied Michael, quickly, 'don't worry – the sound's fine.'

'Jesus Christ, it's ancient,' giggled Barry. 'It must weigh a ton! Gert's the one that's supposed to be shagged out at the end of the film, not you.'

'Bloody hell and we thought we did things on the cheap!' continued Len. 'Is it solid state? We're not gonna have to send out for some spare valves half way through, are we?'

'I told you it works, OK,' contested Michael, looking down at the machine's solid wooden casing; on reflection, by wishing not to appear too well kitted-out, he may have gone back one technological era too many.

'Well, all right, it's your gear,' said Len, walking over to the hallway to call Amanda, 'but don't go suing us if you have a hernia, will you?'

'Hey!' shouted Barry to Len as he left the room. 'Ask Amanda if she's brought her nurse's uniform with her. Tell her we'll probably be needin' it later.'

After several more jokes at Michael's expense, Len returned and, at half past one precisely, the filming began. The opening scene was of Gert lazily painting the windows. Then, on hearing Amanda's approach in the hallway, Barry panned the camera around to get a shot of her as she stood poised at the kitchen threshold, pouting provocatively. She had changed out of her all black attire and was now wearing a pink silk dressing gown, the belt of which she had deliberately slung loose and low to reveal glimpses of her stockings and suspenders beneath. As she sidled seductively across the kitchen towards Gert, Michael couldn't help thinking that for all Len and Barry's assertions as to the film's dramatic excellence, the plot was in fact entirely formulaic and predictable. Even so, as Gert and Amanda began to kiss, Michael began concentrating intently to ensure that he positioned himself and his boom correctly whilst still being able to keep an eye on the actors and Len's directorial signals.

The first five scenes – kitchen, cellar, lounge, living room and downstairs hallway – all seemed to proceed according to the outline that Len had drawn up detailing the particular sexual activity that should take place in each of the rooms. When they got to the first floor, however, Amanda and Gert's liaison slowly began to take on a life of its own. The spare bedroom scene was supposed to see them in a doggy fashion pose on the bed, but as soon as they got through the door Gert grabbed Amanda by the hips and bent her over the dressing table. She willingly accepted this reorientation and although the ecstatic cries that she produced there were utterly authentic, it took Michael and Barry a good two minutes to find a position in the room that did not see them reflected back into the camera off one of the dressing table's three mirrors. The situation in the first floor office was even worse and Michael could see by the look in Len's eyes that he was starting to become a little annoyed. As Amanda began to fellate Gert underneath the desk, his excited exhortations suddenly switched into Swedish half way through and although reluctant to interrupt the dramatic flow, Len was forced to bring this to Gert's attention.

Things seemed to get back on track after this and the attic anal scene proceeded more or less to plan. As they went back down the attic stairs together, however, Amanda and Gert must have had some sort of verbal exchange because by the time Len, Barry and Michael caught up with them they were already acting out an entirely unscripted girl-on-top scene up against the first floor banister. When Len tried to shoo them on to the bathroom where the next scene was supposed to take place, he found that Amanda had tied Gert to the rails with her stockings. As Barry struggled to undo the tight nylon knots, Len lectured them on sticking to the director's instructions, but it was absolutely obvious to Michael that neither of them were listening to a word that he was saying. All the way through his sermon they simply stared fixedly into each other's eyes: somehow their intercourse had now gained a competitive edge and it had become a matter of pride to them not to orgasm before the other person did.

The moment that Gert was released they went absolutely wild. Abandoning all compliance to the script, the two actors writhed, grunted and humped their way through a series of increasingly athletic sexual positions against, behind and beneath whichever piece of first floor furniture next presented itself. Firstly Barry, and then Michael, looked across at Len questioningly, but on both occasions he shook his head sharply, having no doubt concluded that their spontaneity was superior to his own prearranged scenario. Following the sweat drenched couple for a second time into the spare bedroom, Michael looked at his watch. They had been going for fifty-one minutes. Amanda was now sitting on Gert's face. Standing up on to his toes so that he could hold the boom high enough above her head to ensure it was out of shot, Michael felt a stitch developing just under the right hand side of his rib cage. The tape recorder was now weighing so heavily on his arm that he was afraid he might drop it at any moment. The comments in the kitchen an hour previously about his ending up with a physical injury had just seemed liked empty jibes, but Gert and Amanda's sexual sparring was fast turning them into reality. Watching Gert's head thrash from side to side, Michael found himself wishing that Heretic had hired a Brit after all – the sooner the whole thing was over the better.

The orgasm, when it finally came, was absolutely thunderous, and, fittingly, took place in the master bedroom. By some ineluctable law of sexual chemistry, Gert and Amanda seemed simultaneously to abandon the struggle to outlast each other and threw themselves on the double bed together to thrash out the final few seconds of their encounter in a classic missionary position. Their joint vocal expression of ecstasy was so loud and prolonged that Michael was forced to turn the volume control down for fear of overloading the tape. Having slumped forward on to Gert's heaving chest, Amanda stretched out an arm, grabbed one of Aunt Margaret's fluffy toys and with her final last drop of energy playfully hit Gert over the head with it. Leaving the two exhausted actors giggling stupidly on the bed, Michael followed Len and Barry down the stairs to the kitchen. Having slipped off the heavy tape recorder, he sat down at the kitchen table opposite the two men and, as he did so, suddenly remembered the bottle of whisky in his jacket pocket.

'Fancy a shot?' he said, holding the bottle up in the air.

'Oh, good man,' exclaimed Len heartily, moving over to one of the kitchen cabinets to take out three sherry glasses.

'Don't use those!' called out Barry, quickly.

'What?' said Len.

'Don't touch 'em. She's got eyes like a hawk, that woman. If she sees the glasses're even an inch out of place, she'll know we've been drinkin'.'

'What shall we use, then?' asked Len.

'I know,' replied Barry, standing up and walking over to the draining board.

'Tea cups?' quizzed Len.

'Yeah. As long as we wash 'em back up afterwards she'll never notice.'

Having poured a shot of whisky into each of the porcelain Crown Derby cups, Michael handed one each to the two men.

'So, what d'you reckon to Amanda and Gert's performance, then?' he said. 'I thought they were great.'

'Well, it was a bit of a disappointment, I've gotta say,' grunted Len.

'Yeah, a tad unprofessional, I'm afraid,' added Barry, with a tone of lament in his voice.

'What!' cried Michael, unable to believe his ears, 'What d'you mean? I thought they were fantastic … weren't they?'

'Got a lot to learn, hasn't he, Barry?' said Len, with a sage shake of the head.

252

'He has, he has …' tutted Barry, wistfully.

'What did they do wrong, then?' queried Michael.

'You really don't know, do you?' replied Len.

'No, I don't – tell me.'

'Well, the end, obviously.'

'What about it?'

'Well, he didn't come in her mouth, did he?'

'Or even on her tits,' added Barry with disgust.

'We make porn, Mick – not sex education films,' explained Len, staring at Michael's still puzzled face. 'They're entertainers. They weren't supposed to be doin' all that for themselves, you know.'

'Well, they're young, I suppose,' conceded Barry, 'we shouldn't be too hard on 'em.'

'Nah, of course not,' replied Len, generously, 'I'm not gonna say anything. I mean, I wouldn't wanna hurt their feelings – they're good kids. Just give 'em ten minutes, shall we, and then we'll start all over again from the beginning again, eh? If that's all right by you, Mick?'

The shoot finished at four, but, instead of returning home as she had originally intended, Amanda hung around and helped the men tidy up the house. When they finally left an hour later, forty-two Maisie Road was, if anything, even more spotless than when they had arrived. Gert was booked on the last flight of the day to Gothenburg at eight-fifty and, as Amanda lived quite close to Stansted airport, she decided to come along with them to see him off. With two hours to go until boarding, they wandered over to the Fish and Chip shop in the airport complex and had a meal whilst waiting for the plane. As they sat eating the food, Gert began to entertain them. Not only was his English very good, but he turned out to be an incredibly talented mimic and in no time at all had everyone in fits of laughter taking off the accents of various travellers and passers-by. Michael's side was still aching from three hours of lugging the portable tape recorder around Aunt Margaret's house and, despite not wanting to see Gert go, it was a relief to be able to stop laughing when his plane was at last called. Having shaken hands with Len, Barry and Michael at least three times each, and having picked Amanda up off the ground in one final, enormous hug, Gert made his way through the departure gate and off towards the plane.

Michael arrived back at Balam Road just before ten o'clock. Through the open bedroom door, he could see his quilt – twisted and hanging half off the bed – just as he had left it at four o'clock that morning; except that the nightmare that had so tormented him now seemed to belong not only to another time, but to another person. Walking into the living room, he took the mobile phone out of his top pocket, and deliberately not attaching it to the VCR switched it to playback mode. Standing still for several seconds, he watched the footage that he had recorded at Maisie Road silently expire into nothingness. For a few short hours that day he had been a part of something – a member of a team, accepted for his skills and appreciated for his contribution. It was an experience that he had not expected, but which he would never forget, and he knew that he could not live at peace with himself if his actions were ever to cause the least harm or distress to those who had shared it with him. The media had the power to destroy good people just as easily as bad, and so, on the long motorway journey back to Feltham, he had made a solemn vow: he would include no footage of Len, Barry, Amanda or Gert in *Criminal Britain* and no reference to their names. Going into the bathroom, he switched on the shower and smiled to himself in the mirror. How ironic that the greatest pleasure he had yet derived in making the documentary series lay not in committing something that he had filmed to video tape, but in erasing it completely.

At first he didn't recognize the sound – he had only heard the ringing tone once when Jim had run through the prototype's various functions in his workshop. Leaping out of the shower, he dashed into the bedroom and, having wiped his hands dry on the bedspread, removed the tiny palm-held phone from its battery charger; Jim had told him to leave it permanently on charge when he was not actually carrying it, as he had had to crop the battery down to almost a third of its original size. Pressing the green receive button and putting the phone to his ear, he raised his eyes heavenwards in entreaty. Without telling Michael, Jim had been working on the prototype ever since he had first mentioned to him that he wanted a surveillance camera built into a much more modern-looking mobile; Jim had trialled it as thoroughly as he could in the workshop, but this was to be its first real test in the field.

'Hello?'

'Mick, it's Geoff.'

'Hello, mate, you all right?'

'Yeah, great. Got your new phone switched on, then?'

'Yeah, yeah, all the time. Reception's good, isn't it?' laughed Michael, praying that when he actually came to film Harper with the new phone its pictures would be equally sharp.

'Hm – not bad. But listen, the inspection on Milland Road is gonna be tomorrow – I just heard.'

'Great.'

'Half ten, all right?'

'OK.'

'Make sure you're there.'

'I will, no problem, I won't let you down.'

'You'd better not.'

'No worries, Geoff. I'll be there.'

'See you tomorrow, then.'

'Yeah, see you tomorrow, mate.'

Carefully clipping the second mobile back into its battery charger, Michael went back into the bathroom, switched off the shower, and, having draped a towel around his waist, lay down smiling on the bed. Yesterday his mental resolve had all but completely collapsed, but today, he was right back on top of things.

Harper: use the second property in Milland Road to worm his way deeper into the gang.

Tysoe: continue to work for him until he could film inside his house.

Kent: bide his time until the next piece of extra work.

Fourth documentary: get some contacts from Amanda.

He was back on top of things all right. Right back on top.

Chapter 9

'Is good see you again, Mick,' said Naz, sitting down in the passenger seat of Michael's car and reaching across to shake his hand; his grip was as firm and as powerful as ever.

'You, too, mate, how are you?'

'I am fine, I am fine,' replied Naz, although Michael could sense immediately that he was not in good spirits.

'Have you got the address of this place, then?'

'I have ... here,' said Naz, lifting himself up off the seat and pulling a crumpled piece of paper out of the back pocket of his jeans. 'Tysoe say we be there nine o'clock.'

'Pierrera Road, I know where it is. And you told him that you'd be bringing me this time, yeah?'

'I tell him, I tell him – he say, Micky, he's OK, he's good man.'

'Great.'

Strapping on his seat belt, Michael went to drive away from Naz's house, but stopped mid-movement and then turned to face him again. In the confined atmosphere of the car, the Turk's discomfort was almost palpable.

'You don't like doing this, do you? Working for Tysoe.'

'Oh, Mick, I so grateful you. You help me. You so good friend to me and my friends. You give me money – more money than I ever earn – but he is bad man. So bad man. I work for him three, four months now but I feel ... dirty.'

'It was those pensioners, wasn't it? Those old people.'

'Old people – he takes their money. He pays me with their money and I do not finish job for them … but if I stop to work for him then I let you down.'

Exhaling deeply, Naz raised his hands in the air in a gesture of help-lessness. Over his shoulder, Michael could see that one of the nearby houses had lost a window: the youths from the Abaddon estate must have been on the rampage again during the night. Naz had been the key link to Tysoe from day one, allowing Michael either to be involved in the builder's activities at first hand or simply to monitor to them at a distance as the work load of the other investigations permitted. Naz's position was thus absolutely critical to the successful completion of the documentary, and, despite the fact that the pressures of working for Tysoe were obviously taking their toll, Michael could not yet afford to let him relinquish it.

'Naz. If I tell you something, will you promise to keep it to yourself? I mean, this is serious – I could be in big trouble if you don't.'

'Yes …' replied Naz, cautiously. 'I promise you, Micky.'

Looking into his gentle, frowning face, Michael knew that the moment had come to tell him the truth. Having watched Naz's anxiety grow during the weeks since he had returned from hospital, he had increasingly come to feel that it would be the only way to secure his con-tinued cooperation: at this late stage in the documentary, he dare not risk any backsliding on the Turk's part. Putting his hand into his top pocket, he unclipped the mobile phone and held it in the palm of his hand.

'This isn't a phone, it's a camera. Those jobs we did before Christmas – the Parkers and the others – I filmed them all with this.'

Naz blinked twice in surprise and then took the phone from Michael's hand and examined it carefully.

'You no joke?'

'No. I'm not joking.'

'Where is lens? I know electronic camera – I train in Turkey.'

Putting his hand to his lapel, Michael lifted the top button up and pointed it towards Naz.

'It's in here. It's what called a charge coupled array. Wired up with ribbon cable through the lining of my jacket.'

'Is very clever, Mick, very clever,' said Naz, clearly impressed by the phone, 'tax inspector big job in England.'

'I'm not a tax investigator, Naz, I just told you that to put your mind at rest. I'm a reporter, actually – a journalist. I'm making a film about criminals in Britain: people like Tysoe who get away with it year in, year out – who lie and cheat and steal – but never get caught. When I've finished the film, I'm going to give it to the police so that they can prosecute Tysoe – put him in prison. But to be absolutely sure they've got enough evidence against him, I really need to follow him for one or two more jobs. If you can hang on that long, then that'll be it. I won't ask you to work for him anymore and you can go back to Turkey later this year, like you said, knowing you've done the people of this country a service.'

Naz paused for several seconds before answering, all the time staring intently into Michael's face.

'Is dangerous work you do, Michael Angel.'

'Yes, yes it is.'

'You are brave man.'

'Maybe,' conceded Michael, 'and maybe a bit stupid, too.'

'I don't think so,' replied Naz, his face at last breaking into a smile. 'OK, couple more jobs, then we finish. And after … we must have big, big party to celebrate – like with Roger, yes?'

'It's a deal,' grinned Michael, clipping the phone back into his pocket and then leaning forward to turn on the ignition. 'Come on, we'd better get a move on.'

'Michael, how are you?' exclaimed Tysoe. His squint seemed even more pronounced than Michael had remembered it: perhaps it was because he hadn't seen him for nearly two months.

'Fine thanks, you?'

'I'm OK. What happened to your face?'

'Fight. Somebody had a go at me.'

'Christ. No wonder you've been out of commission for so long. Still, you're ready for work, now, yes?'

'I am.'

'Great, great, well, good to have you back. OK, you two hang on here a tick and I'll just go and sort out Mr Spence …'

As was his habit, Tysoe marched up to the front door of the smart, three bed-roomed semi-detached leaving his two workmen waiting in the street outside. Carefully, Michael inched his way along the front wall to get within recording distance of the ensuing conversation with the householder. The most difficult thing about filming Tysoe was always the business discussions he had with his customers because wherever possible he attempted to ensure that these were undertaken without Michael or Naz being present. Michael doubted that this was because he specifically distrusted either of them, it was just one of his instinctive routines for precluding all forms of independent corroboration: as long as there were no witnesses and no paper work, it was always going to be the customer's word against his.

'Good morning, Mr Spence, and how are you today?'

'I'm fine thank you, Mr Tysoe, really fine ...'

To his left, Michael could see Naz's head drop in disappointment. It was another pensioner. Winking at Naz in an effort to cheer him up, Michael turned back around to face Tysoe and Mr Spence, but to his surprise the silver-haired old man suddenly stepped out of his house, closing the front door behind him.

'Come on around the side and I'll show you what I've done – I've got everything ready for you ...'

Not wanting to miss the ensuing discussion, Michael went through the front gate and followed Tysoe down the passageway at the side of the house and into the back garden. Turning around and seeing that Michael and Naz were there, Tysoe was just on the point of saying something but the old man began speaking first in his slow, deliberate voice.

'Right, Mr Tysoe, you said you needed a two and a half thousand pound deposit for materials, is that correct?'

'That's right, Mr Spence, mainly for the conservatory. I'll have my boys here knock down your old lean-to today, and I'll go off and buy the new one for you – the one you showed me in the catalogue.'

'Good, I thought that was what you said. Well, in that case, I can tell you I've got some excellent news for you.'

'And what's that, Mr Spence?'

'I've already bought it.'

'You've already bought what?'

'The conservatory,' announced the old man happily, as though telling a young grandson that he had anticipated his birthday wish and had the very present the child desired right there in his trouser pocket. 'You won't have to go and pick it up now; I've got it for you already.'

'I'm sorry, Mr Spence, I don't quite understand what you mean,' replied Tysoe, looking around the garden – there were indeed no signs of any building materials.

'It's up there in the shed at the top of the garden,' said Spence, cheerfully, 'in those special boxes – what d'you call 'em – flat packs.'

Tysoe's eyes narrowed and he flashed an angry look first at the shed and then at Michael. Although Michael knew that exactly the same thought was going through both of their heads, he kept his expression studiously neutral: if Spence had already bought the conservatory, that meant he didn't need to give Tysoe any money on deposit.

'Well, I'm sorry to say but that may have been something of a mistake on your part, Mr Spence,' said Tysoe, smoothly.

'Oh, really, and why's that, Mr Tysoe?' said the old man in a slow, deliberate voice. His baggy trousers and hand-knitted sweater exuded a folksy homeliness, but there was something about the tight line of his upper lip that suggested he was far shrewder than this avuncular appearance might imply.

'Well, builders like myself get pretty substantial discounts, because we buy in bulk, you see. If you've gone and paid too much for the materials, then I'm afraid I might not be able to maintain my original price.'

'You know, I thought about that,' said Mr Spence, raising his right forefinger sagely, 'so I asked my son-in-law – he works for the DIY store; he was the one that gave me their catalogue in the first place actually. I mean, he's only an accountant like, but he checked it out with his colleagues and they said he could get an employee's discount for me, 'cos I'm, like, family. Apparently, it's as big as anything they offer anyone in the trade; they do it to encourage their own people to take an interest in the firm's products.'

'Is that so, now?' asked Tysoe, dryly.

'Apparently. Anyway, what I'm suggesting – if it's all right by you, of course – is that I pay you and your men by the day from now on on a daily basis, based on the ten days you said it would take you to do the job. That way, you have a little bit of cash to keep you goin' and I get to keep an eye on the work. So there's no confusion, I've typed it all up for you. Here you are, have a few minutes to look over the details and I'll go and put the kettle on and make us all a nice cup of tea.'

As the old man turned his back on Tysoe, he smiled at Michael and then disappeared through his kitchen door. How had he known? Had he checked Tysoe out or had his son-in-law advised him? Whatever the means, Mr Spence had Tysoe completely over a barrel. If he pulled out now – having taken the time to make the original quotation and having hired two men for the first day – he would be the loser. If he did two or three days work and then subsequently failed to turn up, Mr Spence could simply switch to another builder, strong in the knowledge that Tysoe had none of his materials and none of his cash save that for which services had already been duly rendered. Averting his gaze so that he wouldn't make eye-contact with Tysoe and thus give any hint that he understood the true significance of what had happened, Michael went back down the alleyway to get the tools from the van. As Naz unlocked the rear doors he turned to Michael with a smile.

'Is smart old man, I think.'

'Yeah – dead smart.'

'But maybe is no good story for you, Mick, huh?'

'Oh, I wouldn't say that,' replied Michael. 'Actually, it's a bit of a bonus – a great example of how ordinary people can stand up to villains like Tysoe. I mean, did you see the look on his face?'

'Oh, yes. He was very angry.'

Taking a sledge hammer and a shovel out of the back of Tysoe's van, Michael was about to return to the house when suddenly he noticed the bunch of keys in the back door of the vehicle. Lowering his voice and making sure that he couldn't be seen by Tysoe who was standing at the end of the passageway reading Mr Spence's note, he turned to Naz.

'Naz. Are those Tysoe's keys?'

'Yes.'

'Does he let you have them often?'

'Sometimes. Why?'

'I'll tell you later.'

Picking up the tools, Michael walked back to the house with a spring in his step – if he could get his hands on the keys for long enough, it would be easy to get copies made.

But Michael was not alone in his contentment. Fifty yards away at the other end of Pierrera Road, a man in a beige-coloured Macintosh slipped back behind the tree he had been using for cover and, having pocketed his camera, turned and walked off towards his car with a smirk of satisfaction.

Mr May looked really quite infirm. When he finally appeared at the front door of his small council bungalow, Michael was certain that he would be unable to get out of his wheelchair and unlock the porch, but, lifting up a walking stick positioned next to the doorway, he leant slightly forward and then neatly jabbed at the catch with its rubberized tip. The porch door sprang open straightaway.

'Hello, is Amanda in?'

'You must be Mick.'

His voice was weak and very hoarse. Michael guessed that he had had part of his larynx removed – possibly because of cancer.

'Yes, that's right.'

'She told me you was comin'. She's down at Buyrite, down the road.'

'Sorry?'

'Buyrite – end of the street,' repeated Mr May, waving his walking stick to his left. 'The supermarket. She'll be off in ten minutes – at six. Go down and pick her up if you want, she'd like that.'

'Oh, er, OK, thanks,' replied Michael with a smile. Leaning forward, he went to put his arm inside the porch to shut the door, but Mr May obviously had the knack of closing it, too, and nodded at him to leave it. Smiling again, he walked back up the slanting pathway, which he now realized had been modified for wheelchair access, and walked back down the street in the direction that Mr May had indicated.

Buyrite was more of a large shop than a supermarket. Walking along the first of its two aisles, crammed to the ceiling with household items and foodstuffs, Michael imagined the long hours that its owners had to put in to ensure its continued survival: in a built-up area like this, one of the national supermarket chains was bound to have a store within half a mile or so. As he reached the end of the aisle, he turned to make his way back down to the exit and immediately caught sight of Amanda. She was sitting behind one of the shop's two check-out tills, chatting to an old woman as she weighed out her vegetables on a set of electronic scales. With a smile, Michael selected the best bunch he could find from a bucketful of slightly less than fresh flowers, and made his way down the aisle towards her. At a distance, with her hair tied back and in her shapeless blue and white cheque overalls, she could scarcely have looked more different from the stunning young woman he had seen emerging from the taxi two weeks previously. As he got closer, however, Michael found himself once more feeling thrilled – almost privileged – to be in her presence. There was no mistaking the magnificence of that complexion. One day, he would simply have to photograph it for himself.

'OK, Amanda, love,' said the customer at the check-out, sensing the arrival of Michael behind her, 'I'd better get going. You look after your-self now.'

'All right, Mrs Markham,' said Amanda, watching the portly woman heave her three plastic bags of shopping up off the counter and waddle away, 'mind how you go now.'

'I'll be all right, darlin', don't you worry,' called the woman over her shoulder.

'Yes,' said Amanda, turning to face Michael with a smile.

'Beautiful flowers for a beautiful lady,' replied Michael.

'Ah, hello, Mick!' she exclaimed, her smile broadening still further. 'Ha! I didn't see you come in. Did Dad send you round?'

'Yeah.'

'Sorry I wasn't back at the house to meet you.'

'That's all right – no problem.'

'You don't really want to buy those, d'you?'

'Yeah, of course I do – for you!'

'Oh, thanks,' she replied, taking the five pound note he was holding out and ringing it up through the till, 'that's really nice of you. Listen, you hang on a minute here, I'll just go out the back and get changed and then we can go.'

With a nod at the other till assistant, Amanda skipped down the aisle and disappeared through a door at the back of the shop. Within five minutes, the two of them were sitting in a small wine bar on the other side of the road from Buyrite. Going up to the counter, Michael ordered the drinks and then looked around the narrow, low-ceilinged room, empty save for a group of four office workers sitting at a table by the far wall. Apart from a couple of neon strip-lights behind the bar area, the wine-bar had no other illumination except for a single candle on each of the dozen or so tables. The atmosphere was nicely intimate – it was an ideal setting in which to talk to Amanda.

'So, how long have you worked at Buyrite, then?' asked Michael, putting the drinks down on the table.

'I don't work there full time, y'know.'

'No?'

'Oh, God, no. I just do the odd day there every now and then. I was a Saturday girl there for years and the owners are sort of like family friends now. Whenever they're a bit short-staffed they give me a call.'

'Oh, right. Anyway, listen, thanks for seeing me at such short notice.'

'No problem – my pleasure.'

'I got your number from Len, I hope you don't mind.'

'Nah, of course not. Has he sent you your copy of the film yet?'

'He has.'

'Great, innit? The house looks fantastic. I wonder what Barry's aunt'd say?'

'Have you ever met her?'

'No, what's she like?' asked Amanda, eagerly.

'Oh, scary like you wouldn't believe,' said Michael with a guffaw, leaning forward and taking a sip of his drink; although cheap, the house wine was surprisingly good.

'I got a card from Gert the other day,' she continued.

'Yeah?'

'Yeah, he's in the States. He's got a job over there for a month.'

'Really?'

'Yeah. I dunno how he swung it, the lucky sod. He's havin' a whale of a time apparently.'

'I wonder if he's taking off all the yanks' accents.'

'Ha, wouldn't surprise me! Mind you, they probably wouldn't even notice …'

'Yeah, you're probably right. So, what about you, then? Are you busy at the moment?'

'Nah. I take things easy, me. Why, you haven't gone and got me some more work, have you?'

Looking into Amanda's care-free, laughing face, Michael felt a lot more relaxed about revealing his true identity to her than he had been with Naz three days previously. Then, as now, his decision had been based on the conviction that without understanding his real motives the individual in question would not cooperate as he wished. The difference between the two was that in Naz's case, Michael desperately needed to keep him involved in the investigation, whereas with Amanda he had already vowed to exclude her from it. Similarly, whereas Naz could have used that information to wreck everything, neither Amanda nor the men from Heretic knew anything about him beyond his name and his mobile phone number and, if she reacted badly, he only needed to walk out of the door into the night and it would be next to impossible for any of them to trace him.

'No, I haven't got you some work, but there is something you could help me out with, though.'

264

'Oh, yeah, what's that, then?' replied Amanda.

'Information.'

'What sort of information?'

'Amanda, I'm not really a boom operator. I'm a journalist.'

'What?'

'I said I'm not a sound man, I'm a journalist. I work for one of the national news organizations. I'm doing a piece on the porn industry.'

'Are you havin' me on?'

'No, not at all.'

'Really?'

'Yes.'

'Does Len know?'

'No, he thinks I'm just a regular sound technician. And before you ask, I've no intention of selling you or Heretic out: there'll be no photographs or references to either of you in my piece and absolutely no names – not even pseudonyms.'

Amanda could tell that Michael was serious and she frowned for a moment, struggling to take in what she had heard. Across the other side of the bar, the four office workers broke into laughter as one of them finished telling a joke. Even if she didn't agree to talk him, he was really hoping they could part as friends.

'Well,' she said, cautiously, 'I suppose it depends on what you want to know.'

'Well, to start off with, how you got into the business in the first place.'

'I don't know whether I really am in the business. I mean, like I say, I take things pretty easy, me – I only do a couple of films a year and a bit of modelling every now and then …'

'Was that how you got started, then, through modelling?'

'No. A lot of girls do – it's an easy step from glamour to porn – but I just, like, went straight in at the deep end. I only started modelling afterwards – last year, actually.'

'So, how did you get into films, then?'

'A friend of mine called Bernie. I met her on holiday in Spain three years ago. She's been in the business for ages. She didn't tell me what she did at first, but we, like, met up when we got back – she doesn't live very far from here – and then one thing led to another and I ended up giving it a try.'

'Did she find you your first film?'

'Yeah, she did – and most of the ones I've done since. I mean, I only ever go on personal recommendation. I'm dead careful who I work with.'

'Because not everyone's as nice as Barry and Len?'

'Oh, God, yeah, not half – the stories! Bernie'd tell you. They treat you like a lump of meat most of them blokes. I don't need that.'

'Is that how most girls find work, then – through personal contacts?'

'Well, eventually, yeah, but in the beginning they usually go through an agent.'

'An agent?' asked Michael, quickly.

'Yeah, you know, like a theatrical agent; like real actors have, only for porn films. I mean these guys've got all the contacts – they'd keep you on your back seven days a week if you let 'em.'

'D'you know any agents like that? Unscrupulous ones, I mean.'

'Not personally. Bernie does, though. I can ask her for you if you like.'

'Would you? I'd appreciate that.'

'No problem. What d'you want – addresses?'

'Addresses, phone numbers – anything you can get.'

'Yeah, all right, I'll ask her.'

For a moment, Michael was tempted to ask for Bernie's phone number, but, mindful of his decision, decided not to press her any further. If she came back to him with the list – fine. If not, he would simply let the matter drop and go off in search of agents by himself. By the same token, he had agreed to do another film with Heretic at the end of the month, but was already planning the excuses he would give Len and Barry for making it his last. Afterwards, he would probably try and talk to the actress they were going to use – just as he was now doing with Amanda – but had no intention of contacting them again after that.

'Personal question, next …' he continued, with a smile.

'Go on, then.'

'Have you got a boyfriend? I mean a serious long-term one.'

'Yeah.'

'Who? Don't worry I'm not gonna mention his name, either. I'm just interested.'

'His name's Pete. He's in the army – royal engineers. I've got a picture of 'im if you wanna see it.'

266

'Have you? Yeah, I'd like to.'

Opening up her wallet, Amanda folded back several perspex flaps, inside the last of which was a snapshot of her and a young squaddie in his early twenties. Their heads were very close together – the picture had obviously been taken in a passport photo booth – and she had her hands on either side of his face as though keeping it steady for the camera. They were both grinning like schoolchildren.

'It was last summer – just before he went off to Cyprus.'

'He's a very lucky man, Amanda.'

'Hm, maybe,' said Amanda, gazing laconically at the photograph.

'Are you gonna marry him?'

'Dunno. He asked me. Maybe I should. He's a good bloke. We've known each other since we was ten. But I don't know whether I'm ready for all that yet. And besides, there's only me to look after my Dad. What about you, anyway?' she said, suddenly closing the wallet and turning to face Michael.

'Me?'

'Yeah, you. You married?'

'Separated.'

'I'm sorry.'

'Well, you know, these things happen,' replied Michael – Elizabeth's face all of a sudden flashing vividly to mind. What on earth would she say if she could see him now, sitting in a darkened wine-bar in East London with Amanda May, part-time check-out girl, part-time porn-star?

'D'you miss her?'

'Amanda,' replied Michael with an air of mock gravity, 'I'm supposed to be asking you the questions, not the other way round.'

'Oh, yeah, I forgot,' she replied with a laugh. 'But you can tell me about her – if you want to – I mean, if you'd like to that is …'

The bar was now almost entirely silent. On the other side of the room, the four office workers had gone quiet, each of them apparently lost for a few moments in their own thoughts. Amanda was smiling at him with all the friendliness and warmth that he had come to find so appealing during the short time that they had known each other. Michael blinked indecisively – uncharacteristically. For all her sympathetic charm, Amanda was still a complete stranger and he had never really confided in anyone about his separation, either at the time or in the six years since. On the other hand, he would probably never see her again after tonight and lately he had found himself thinking about Elizabeth more and more – maybe it would do him good to let those feelings out. And so, despite the voice in his mind cautioning him to return to asking Amanda about her life, he leant forward in his chair and began slowly to speak of his own.

The first person he saw when he got out of the taxi was Edwin, talking to a couple of caterers unloading trays of food from the back of a large refrigerated van. Walking around to the front of the cab, Michael paid the driver and then took a long, careful look at Mortlake Manor. It was the biggest country house he had ever seen, and the grandest, too – but for the enormous, modern swimming pool at the rear, it would easily have passed for an original eighteenth-century stately-home. Strolling along the gravel path towards the pedimented entrance portico, Michael slung his overnight bag over his shoulder and then slowly ascended the polished granite steps. Inside the bag was the white dinner jacket that Kent had insisted he wear for this, the next piece of extra work that he had arranged for him: in his ordinary black jacket he might well be mistaken for one of the guests rather than a member of the security staff.

'Oh, look who's here. Now I do feel safe …' scoffed Edwin sarcastically, brushing past Michael's shoulder and then scurrying off after the caterers down a side staircase that presumably led to the kitchens. Ignoring the jibe, Michael walked slowly through the huge, varnished oak double doors and into the central hallway, his footsteps echoing crisply on the black and white marble tiles.

'Mick! Up here, mate!' shouted a voice.

It was Nigel, leaning over the first-floor banister and smirking down at him good-naturedly. Making his way up the broad hardwood staircase, Michael felt a surge of excitement mixed with apprehension. The previous Saturday, when Kent had first told the two men that he had chosen them as doormen for the exclusive, all-night party a week later, he had given them the impression that it was a reward for defending him against Foss and his cronies at the hospital. As always with Kent, Michael had subsequently discovered that things were not as straightforward as they had originally seemed. The previous night, just before leaving Gog, he had received the customary two a.m. summons to Kent's basement office where he had given him a photograph of a man who would be at the party, telling him to keep a discreet eye on everything that he did. When Michael had asked who the man was, Kent had simply shaken his head and said he didn't need to know. Thinking that his instructions were complete, Michael had been about to leave, but it had been at that moment that his next big break had come. Getting up from his desk, Kent had walked across the room and, lowering his voice, had added, *'What we really wanna know, is how much coke he uses.'*

'We're over 'ere, man – it's great!' exclaimed Nigel, as Michael reached the top of the stairs. He then led Michael down another short flight of steps and into a wood-panelled corridor off which there were no less than eight separate bedrooms. 'That one's yours – I'm in 'ere.'

'What time's it all supposed to start, then?' asked Michael, glancing through the open door of his room – it had a four-poster bed and several pieces of what looked like genuine antique furniture.

'Eight,' replied Nigel, struggling to do up the top button of his dress shirt. 'Edwin wants us on the door from seven, though.'

'Does he now?' replied Michael. Since the day of his interview, he had seen Edwin less than a half dozen times at Gog but on every occasion had had to suffer a derisive put-down of the type just directed at him in the entrance hall. If Edwin insisted on continuing to snipe at him in this way, perhaps it was time to start returning fire.

'That's what the man said,' answered Nigel.

'Any of the bar staff here yet?' asked Michael.

'Yeah. Will and Steve are downstairs setting things up now.'

'OK, well, I'll see you down there in, say, twenty minutes, then?'

'Sure.'

With a nod at Nigel, he turned and walked into his room, quietly locking the door behind him. It had taken Jim's seamstress most of the morning to sew the lens into the top button of his recently purchased white dinner jacket and he hadn't had time to inspect it properly before he had left London. He was almost certain that she had maintained her same high standards, but just to be sure, he wanted a few quiet minutes alone to check it out.

The guests began to arrive from around ten past eight – the men mostly in black dinner jackets or dark suits, the women in evening gowns and long dresses. After an hour on the door and a couple of tours of inspection of the rooms given over to the party, it was quite apparent to Michael from the snippets of conversation that he overheard that despite the uniformity of their apparel they had a variety of different occupations. Quite a few appeared to be from the media – although plainly on the entertainments side, rather than journalism – but there was also a broad selection of business people, a smattering of politicians and even a couple of show-biz celebrities. Most guests arrived in taxis and, of those who came in their own cars, about a quarter brought overnight bags with them. By ten o'clock when the flow of guests had almost ceased, Michael estimated that perhaps a couple of dozen of them would be staying the night. Taking advantage of the lull in the arrivals, Michael left Nigel in charge of the door and wandered off towards the car park on the pretext of going for a cigarette. Having nosed around the ranks of Mercedes and Jaguars – discovering nothing of interest in the process – he turned to make his way back towards the front entrance and it was then that he heard a vehicle coming down the drive. As he made his way across the car park, the car went past him and pulled to a halt just ahead. When the driver got out and opened the boot, Michael was less than eight feet away from him.

It was the man in the photograph that Kent had given him.

'Shall I take your bag, sir?' he asked – blurting out the first thing that came into his head. Never having said anything remotely like that in his life before, he was conscious that his comment had somehow managed to sound at once both assertive and obsequious, and, when the man turned to look at him, he appeared quite taken aback.

'Er, yes, yes, thank you,' he replied, uncertainly. 'That's very kind of you …'

Taking hold of the man's rather old, but plainly top-quality Gladstone bag, Michael waited for him to lock up his car, and then swung his arm towards the front entrance to indicate the direction in which they should walk; having cast himself in the role of enthusiastic retainer, he had little alternative but to continue to maintain it.

'If you'll come this way, sir …?

The man walked behind him so Michael didn't get a chance further to study his face, but by the amber floodlights reflected back off the front of the house he was able to make out the initials B.S. stencilled in faded gold lettering on the side of his leather bag. Up ahead, he could see Nigel still standing by the entrance, thankfully looking in the opposite direction; he was going to have to manage the next few seconds very carefully.

'Sir is staying the night, I presume?' he said, falling in to step with the man.

'Yes, that's right.'

'And the name is …?'

'Sipkiss. Bernard Sipkiss.'

'If you'd care to follow me, I'll take you to the Porter – he'll show you to your room.'

'Oh, thanks.'

Dropping his shoulder slightly and giving the bag just the hint of a swing as though he were doing Sipkiss a favour by carrying it, Michael walked up the steps to the entrance just as Nigel turned around and spotted him returning.

'Is the Porter around?' he asked – he was now just far enough ahead of Sipkiss to be out of earshot.

'He's down the end there, I think,' replied Nigel.

'I'll just take this bloke's bag down for him. I'll be back in a tick.'

'OK, mate,' replied Nigel, seeming to accept this as a simple act of kindness on Michael's behalf.

The Porter was one was of the few staff working that night who was permanently based at Mortlake Manor and had his own room at the end of the entrance hall. Finding it empty, Michael quickly went over to the desk and searched for Sipkiss's name amongst the guest list.

'Ground floor annexe – room fifteen, sir,' said Michael, 'although I'm afraid the Porter's not here at the moment to take you over there …'

'Oh, that's all right,' said Sipkiss, calmly walking over to the rack of keys on the wall and taking down number fifteen. 'I'm sure I can find my own way.'

'Certainly, sir,' said Michael, handing him back his bag, 'down the corridor, turn left.'

'Thanks,' said Sipkiss turning on his heel with a smile.

As he watched him walk off down the corridor, Michael looked around to see if the Porter was about and then quickly slipped back inside his room. It was just as he had hoped: the rack contained both original and spare keys. Putting the spare number fifteen into his side pocket, Michael went back down the corridor to join Nigel at the front entrance. For the moment, he would bide his time, but later, if the opportunity presented itself, he would try and find five minutes to get inside Sipkiss's room.

★

The party was quite a formal affair and by twelve o'clock, when most of the guests had quietly made their way back to their cars or over to the huge line of taxis that had drawn up in front of the stables, Michael came to the conclusion that, with the possible exception of a trip to the dentists, none of them had ever been anywhere near cocaine in their lives. Over the next forty-five minutes, the occasion became still more subdued as the agency catering staff finished clearing away the buffet and tidied up the kitchens before themselves departing in the half dozen taxis that were left. At a quarter to one, Michael and Nigel finally closed the front entrance doors and went back into the now darkened bar area where the remaining twenty or so mainly male guests were drinking and talking quietly.

Sitting on a stool by the counter, Michael ordered a bitter lemon and then looked across at Sipkiss who was seated in one of the large leather sofas talking to a distinguished-looking but rather drunk elderly man. Several times during the evening, Michael had observed Sipkiss's behaviour, but on each occasion had been too far away to hear what he was saying and had thus been unable to determine much about him. His appearance gave away very little indeed, his sole distinguishing physical feature being a sharply receding hairline which made him look older than he perhaps really was. His general demeanour was also quite reserved – almost staid – and, in the absence of more specific information, Michael finally put him down as a civil servant or possibly a senior manager working in industry.

As Michael looked away for fear of being seen to stare, he caught sight of a young woman walking through a door at the back of the room. The moment he saw her, he understood why the two dozen men in the bar had hung around long after the other guests had departed: the swing of her hips and the extra layer of mascara she wore above her perfectly formed but perfectly cold eyes proclaimed one profession and one profession alone. Within a few moments, three more girls came in, followed finally by Edwin, who, having closed the door behind him, whispered something into the ear of the first girl and then stood watching with a peculiar air of approval mixed with distaste as they began to mingle amongst the guests. The arrival of the four call-girls brought about an immediate change in atmosphere and all at once everyone seemed to be drinking champagne. Seconds later the already revitalized party mood received a further shot in the arm when three young men came spilling in from the hallway, their arms around each others shoulders, laughing raucously. Grabbing several bottles of champagne off the bar, they went over to the back windows and within seconds had opened one up and stumbled out on to the patio in front of the swimming pool.

'Lights!' shouted the youngest of them, putting his head back through door and waving in the general direction of the bar. 'Where are the lights? We can't see a fucking thing out here! And turn the music up as well, will you?'

At the other end of the counter, Nigel nodded firstly at the barman, Will, to switch on the external floodlights and then at Michael in a manner that implied one of them had better go outside to ensure that the youths didn't drown themselves. In response, Michael got to his feet and, slipping quietly through the back window, looked for a position in the shadows where he could both watch the young men and continue to see what was going on in the bar. Having found a suitable spot behind an ornamental palm, he looked back through the tinted glass windows just in time to see Edwin bring in another three call-girls and Sipkiss slip his arm around one of them. On the far side of the bar, Nigel was now keeping a wary eye on the construction of an enormous but ultimately doomed champagne fountain and although the three youths were sprawled out on the pool-side furniture talking self-importantly about the stock market, within a few minutes they would no doubt be running riot again: this was the moment for which Michael had been waiting. Slipping a little further back behind the palm, Michael felt in his side pocket for the spare key and then took the mobile phone out of his top pocket and pressed 1-2-3. The annexe was only twenty yards to his left. If he hurried, he would be back before Nigel had even noticed that he had gone.

He returned to Balam Road at six o'clock on Sunday evening in a state of near mental and physical exhaustion. Sipkiss had been the penultimate guest to leave – not reappearing from his bedroom until after two p.m. – and Michael had had to spend the three hours prior to that avoiding the full-time Mortlake Manor staff as they went around the building clearing up the results of the previous night's mayhem. Seconds after he had recovered the camera from on top of the pelmet, the Porter had suddenly appeared at the door and asked him what he was doing. Showing him his mobile phone, Michael had explained that he had left it in the room by mistake the previous night after making a call on behalf of the guest who had been staying there. The Porter had accepted the explanation, but it had been a close call and Michael really hoped that the recording warranted the risks that he had taken in acquiring it. Knocking back a double whisky – the first drink he had had in three days – he immediately felt better and, having popped the tastiest-looking frozen meal he could find into the oven, walked through into the living room and connected the phone up to the VCR. Thankfully, the next day was a bank holiday Monday and so he had a full thirty-six hours to recover before starting a new job with Tysoe on Tuesday morning; he wasn't due back at Gog until the following Friday night.

The tape was dynamite. Even if Sipkiss wasn't married, the image of his handing over two fifty pound notes to the prostitute for the extras that she had so expertly provided would finish off all but the most robust career. Removing the tape, Michael wandered into the kitchen and thoughtfully ate his meal. Kent was obviously planning to get some sort of a hold over Sipkiss and, judging by the way that Sipkiss had indulged himself in the frenzied snorting session that had taken place in the bar at four a.m. that morning, cocaine was the means by which he intended to achieve that end. The tape, however, was a complete all-in-one blackmail package, although the circumstances in which Michael might choose to make it available to Kent – and thus whether it was actually worth anything to him – were as yet unclear. Concluding, finally, that it would be more than worth his while discovering who Sipkiss was and what he did, Michael took up the hall carpet and hid the tape amongst the others. Having taken a quick shower, he then went straight to bed.

He awoke with a start just before midnight. A throw-away comment by Kent had welled up from the depths of his memory and propelled him back to consciousness. Putting on his dressing gown, he went back to the store of video tapes, took out the relevant one and slipped it into the VCR. Shivering against the cold, he wrapped the dressing gown more tightly around his shoulders as he relived the terrifying two minutes in Kent's Saab when he had offered him the opportunity to kill Foss; the comment had been right at the very end of the conversation, he was certain he had remembered it correctly.

There!

Jamming his finger on the pause button of the remote controller, Michael rewound the tape and listened to the sentence again. *'Suit yourself. I can always deal with him later.'* Rewinding the tape, Michael returned it to the store under the hall carpet and, having switched off the lights, went back to bed. *'I can always deal with him later.'* Was Kent's usage of the personal pronoun just a random figure of speech? Because the previous Saturday in his basement office, when he had asked Michael to follow Sipkiss he had definitely said *'What we want to know is how much coke he uses.'* Was there any significance in the fact that he had used 'I' on the first occasion, and 'We' on the second? Could it be that Kent's vendetta with Foss and his friends was personal, but that in attempting to blackmail Sipkiss he was working with, or for someone else? Drifting slowly back off to sleep, Michael determined to discover two things as soon as he was able; firstly, who Sipkiss was, and secondly the identity of the owner – or owners – of Mortlake Manor.

Wednesday started well. Having had to complete Mr Spence's conservatory properly, Tysoe was cock-a-hoop that morning when he, Michael and Naz arrived at the home of a customer who, in Michael's eyes, appeared to be his most gullible victim yet. Mr Herbert, a quietly-spoken, good-natured man in his late forties, was a physics lecturer at one of the central London Universities and, without even asking for a receipt, handed over a two thousand pounds cash deposit to Tysoe for a loft conversion to his bungalow. Having spent the morning helping Michael and Naz to rip out half of his ceiling and a number of perfectly sound roof joists, Tysoe had then blithely announced to Mr Herbert that little more could be achieved that day and that he and his two men would be leaving after lunch. Once outside on the pavement, Tysoe had joked to Michael and Naz about reporting to a higher authority that afternoon and, having asked them to return the following morning at nine o'clock, had promptly disappeared. Taking advantage of the unexpected half-day holiday, Michael had dropped Naz off at his house – looking as troubled as ever – and then gone straight into London on the train to make enquiries at the Land Registry about Mortlake Manor.

That evening, as he walked back from the station to the flat, Michael passed the small park on Uxbridge Road that he had noticed on the first day that he had arrived in Feltham the previous July. Pausing for a moment, he leant on the railings and looked at a group of children playing on a small patch of AstroTurf. Parks had always held a special attraction for Michael. Some of his fondest memories of Jake's childhood had been the days on which he had returned after a week or two away on a story, gathered Jake up in one arm and the little yellow and red tricycle that he had bought for his second birthday in the other and headed off to the park a quarter of a mile away from their home. Recalling those profoundly fulfilling times together, Michael had an idea. When it was over – when the series had been filmed and brought to the screen – he would take Jake back to that very same park in North London to explain to him why he had disappeared for so long and what he hoped to do in the future to make up for it. His conversation with Amanda in the wine bar two weeks previously had stirred up memories of the years that he, Elizabeth and Jake had spent together as a family and not a day had gone by since without his wondering how and where he would tell his son about his life as an undercover reporter. With a nod of satisfaction, Michael moved away and continued his journey back to Balam Road. It was a great idea. The park would be a perfect location.

He was still in a cheerful mood as he approached the flat, but, as he began walking up the steps to the front door, his good humour evaporated in an instant. The old woman who lived downstairs had opened up a gap in the greying net curtains that hung in her front window and was staring at him with raw, undisguised malevolence. As soon as their eyes met, she immediately whisked them back into place and then disappeared out of sight. Unlocking the front door, Michael quickly went around the flat checking to see what might have happened to have occasioned such a display of hostility. Had the television switched itself on whilst he had been out and been blaring loudly through the floorboards? Had the taps flooded in the bathroom? Finding nothing, Michael began to make his dinner but found it very difficult to concentrate, the image of the reclusive old woman, scowling at him poisonously like a macabre medieval witch, having imprinted itself so deeply on his mind. Just as he had put the food on the table, the second mobile phone that he kept reserved for Harper began to ring.

'Hallo.'

'Mick?'

'Yeah.'

'It's Geoff. Where are you?'

His voice was nervous – angry.

'At home.'

'Get round here now.'

'What?'

'Just do it. Now, all right?'

The line went dead. Leaving his food on the table untouched, Michael grabbed his jacket and quickly left the flat. Struggling to keep calm as he drove to Harper's house he began feverishly re-examining the events of the last few weeks. Something had happened. Something was wrong – but he had no idea what. The inspection by Housing Benefits of the second property at Milland Road had proceeded without a hitch and the payments had started to come through exactly as planned. The second mobile phone was working perfectly – he hadn't missed a single call from Harper – and although he continued to carry the original mobile that Jim had made for him he had kept it well out of sight. The Thursday night drinking sessions had now resumed and seemed to be strengthening his relationship with Harper with each passing week. So what was it? Parking his car in the slip road of the industrial estate opposite Harper's house, Michael went to get out but then stopped and sat back in the seat. What if they had found him out and there was a reception party waiting for him at the house? Not just Harper, but Thompson and some of his men. The leaked file sent to King had indicated that the gang were pulling in two million pounds a year. What would the fraudsters be prepared to do to protect an income stream of that size? What would Thompson do if he flew into one of the rages to which Harper had referred? Quickly undoing his safety belt, Michael got out of the car and walked smartly over to the house. He couldn't afford to dwell on possibilities any further – he had to confront the reality of the situation.

'Come on through,' said Harper, gravely, 'Ange's out the back.'

She was standing looking out of the kitchen window, a cigarette in her right hand. Michael had never seen her smoke before; she was obviously in a state of extreme nervous agitation.

'What's up?' he said.

'You're up,' she replied, her voice seething with anger, 'you're fuckin' up.'

'I don't get you …' replied Michael, cautiously.

'Dill's on to you,' said Harper.

'What d'you mean he's on to me?'

'You're an open case again,' he continued. 'You have been for over two weeks now. He's actively investigating you right at this moment.'

'How d'you know?'

'Ange has got a mate inside Housing Benefits – he got a look inside your file this afternoon. It was on Dill's desk – Morgan, Balam Road.'

Closing his eyes for an instant, Michael struggled to maintain a grip on his objectivity – to force himself not to lose sight of the key facts: Dill was on to him, but Thompson wasn't here and by the looks of things there did not appear to be any direct threat of violence. He could not allow himself to panic. Whatever happened he had to keep calm.

'And what does it say?'

'It says you fucked up your dates on the inspection,' said Angela, bitterly. 'You couldn't bloody remember when you'd moved in, could you? You said July when it was supposed to have been June.'

'Why didn't you tell us you'd done that?' growled Harper. 'If we'd've known we could've done something – we could've been ready for this.'

Angela did not give Michael a chance to answer.

'Why didn't he tell us?' she scoffed, giving full vent to her rage. 'Why didn't he tell us? Same reason he nearly missed the inspection altogether. 'Cos he's a fuckin' moron, that's why! I told you we should never have dealt with him.'

'Why now?' said Michael.

'What?' spat Angela.

'Why now? Why's Dill suddenly got interested in me again now?'

'He put you down as a follow-up to check out later,' said Harper. 'Mixing up your dates wasn't enough for him to want to start investigating you at the time, so he left it three months. He went round again a couple of weeks ago and found the place empty.'

'Well, so what? I could've been out. That doesn't mean he's got anything on me, does it?'

'Jesus Christ,' exclaimed Angela in a mixture of disbelief and disgust. 'He's been followin' you ever since, you wanker! He's got a photo of you workin' on the buildings. You told him at the inspection you didn't have a job. You even made a point of tellin' him you'd got a bad back!'

'Why are you workin' on the buildings again, Mick?' said Harper. 'You told me you'd packed 'em in.'

''Cos I was helpin' out a mate. Do I need your permission for that?'

'Oh, fuckin' hell, what are we gonna do with this guy?' exhaled Angela, looking up at the ceiling as if to find some new reserves of strength amidst the grimy, faded paintwork. 'Look, dummy. The inspection is everything. It doesn't matter a shit what you do afterwards as long as you don't screw it up. The whole point in putting you on the list to be inspected in the first place is that the inspectors take you off it when they find out you're kosher. If you'd've got your facts right, we'd all be sittin' pretty now, but, as it is, Dill's on to you, which means he's on to us; we're next. We're your landlord, right? Here – at this address.'

Suddenly, Michael knew how he should play his hand. It was a complete departure from the plan he had been following for the last six months, but the revelation about Dill left him with no choice; he had to emerge from this debacle with his credibility intact. However, before he did so, he needed to check that he had understood correctly the vital piece of information that Angela had just given him – the final key fact that explained how the fraudsters' system operated.

'So is that how you work it, then? Your mate in Housing Benefits gets the inspectors to investigate the property you're renting, warns you when they're coming around and then, once they find there's nothing up, they close the case down?'

'Ten out of ten, Einstein. But it all relies on gettin' your facts right at the inspection. That's why we came round your house and talked you through it. If we'd've known you couldn't remember two or three simple names and dates we would'nt've touched you with a barge pole!'

'So, let's forget it, then,' retorted Michael, sharply.

'What?' said Harper.

'Let's fuckin' forget it, then!' he repeated, angrily, slamming his fist on the surface of the table. His newly conceived plan would more or less bring his relationship with Harper and Angela to an end, but, now that he understood the gang's system, they were not as important to him as they had been before. As he stared at their stunned faces, Tom's words pulsed through his mind. *'The answer lies in the Michael Angel persona you have developed.'* His guarantee of success lay not in simply acting out Michael Angel's life, but in actually living it. It was and always had to be his guiding principle.

'What d'you mean?' asked Harper, guardedly.

'I mean I'm workin' now – I've got a job up the West End – I don't need the money any more; not if all I'm gonna get out of you two is a load of shit. I mean whose idea was it for me to start fiddlin' Housing Benefits in the first place, anyway? I never came knocking at your door askin' you to help me out – you suggested it. So, sod it. I'll stop claiming tomorrow – knock both places on the head. If Dill's got nothin' on me then he's got nothin' on you then either, has he?'

Angela swallowed hard, her anger evaporating and giving way to a pitiful look of anxiety. Remembering the conversation that he had recorded in The White Horse

Michael knew that he had successfully played on the two fraudsters' principal weakness. *'We need the money for Rick,'* Harper had said. The two houses brought in over three hundred pounds a week. How would they find alternative revenue to continue paying Thompson? Still feigning resentment, Michael took his cigarettes from his top pocket, lit one up and threw the spent match on the surface of the table.

'Well,' he said, breaking the silence. 'That solves the problem, doesn't it?'

Harper and Angela seemed unable to speak, but simply continued to stare at one other. Finally, with a slight nod of the head, Harper turned to look at Michael.

'Drop Balam, keep Milland,' he said. 'Once it's off the list of open cases I'll get Craig to lose the Morgan file.'

'Yeah. Let's do that,' said Michael, caustically. 'You agree, Ange? I mean, let's make sure we all understand – let's not go getting our facts wrong, shall we? I don't want any more fuckin' grief out of you about this ...'

'OK,' she murmured, without looking at him.

'Right,' said Michael, taking out his wallet and slamming a sheaf of notes down on the table. 'Final month's rent on Balam Road. I'll ring up Housing Benefits first thing in the morning. See you around ...'

Walking back out into the night, Michael almost felt sorry for them. They were obviously way out of their depth – terrified of Thompson and what he would do to them if they stopped paying him his cut. Getting back into the car, he switched on the engine but then sat back in the seat for a moment as a thought suddenly occurred to him. As he had closed the front door, he had taken a final look down the hallway and had glimpsed Angela carefully counting out the money that he had left on the table. Could it be that just as he had regularly gone around to Harper's house to pay them, they regularly went around to

Thompson's house to pay him? Could it possibly be, indeed, that they were going off to pay him now? Angela's extreme state of anxiety may not have been the result of worrying about what Dill might do at some point in the future, but rather what Thompson would do the very next day if he didn't get paid. Switching off the engine, Michael sat and waited. It was entirely intuition, but it was worth a try nevertheless; he would give them an hour. In the event, they emerged less than five minutes later.

Despite the fact that it was now dark and he imagined that the fraudsters were far more concerned with what lay ahead of them, Michael stayed several car lengths behind: they had seen his car on a number of occasions and even at the risk of losing them completely he couldn't afford to be spotted on their tail. After driving down the Uxbridge Road for a half a mile, Harper did a left turn towards the old town, maintaining a careful thirty miles per hour all the way. Was it too much to imagine that Harper's sticking to the speed limit denoted a fearful reluctance to face Thompson? As Michael pulled up four car lengths behind them at a set of traffic lights, he began to plan what now appeared to be the final stages of the investigation into the gang of fraudsters. Once Harper had led him to Thompson's hideout, he could stake the place out until he could film him. After that, all that was left was to flush out the inside man, Craig. From what Harper had said it appeared as though he worked in the same department as Dill and should thus be fairly easy to find. Trying to control his excitement, Michael followed Harper down a narrow one-way street, all the time making sure that he kept his distance. What an irony that Dill – the man who had tirelessly tracked down so many fraudsters – had missed the most important of them all, right under his very nose.

At the end of the one-way street, Harper did a right turn and it was at that moment that Michael recognized exactly where they were: the second road down on his left was the one in which Naz lived. As he followed Harper over the railway bridge he began to feel uneasy – he had never actually been across it before but knew exactly what lay beyond. Coming down the other side of the bridge, Michael pulled up by the kerbside and watched Harper's car carry on for another twenty yards before disappearing down the next road on the right. Frowning, Michael lit up a cigarette and then turned his own car around and made his way back to Balam Road. Much as he had intended to follow

Harper all the way to Thompson's door, the sight of the enormous forbidding tower blocks that had come into view as he had driven over the bridge had left him in no doubt that his work for the night had to finish there and then. For Richard Thompson – arch-fraudster and extortionist – had his hideaway in a place with a reputation second to none; a place which only the most naïve would visit during the day and in which only the insane would wait around after dark.

Richard Thompson lived on the Abaddon estate.

Returning from Mr Herbert's on Thursday evening, Michael found an amber postcard waiting for him on the mat. As he knew he would be tied up at the weekend working three continuous nights at Gog, and as Tysoe still seemed to be in excellent spirits, he phoned him to ask if he could have the next day off. Leaving Balam Road at first light, Michael arrived at the safe house just after half past seven. Parking his car thirty yards away, he was about to get out when a woman came into view, opening up the driver's door of the car parked directly in front of him. Just as she was getting in, she turned her head momentarily to look at the car that had pulled up behind her. In the instant that their eyes met, Michael felt as though he had seen a ghost. In a sense, the woman was a ghost: a being from another life. It was Eva Osbourne – Tom's secretary. Thankfully, she was plainly in a hurry and showed no signs of having recognized him, driving away at speed the moment she started the engine.

As he arrived, Michael saw his deep frown reflected in the glass panel of the front door. The arrangement for an amber card was for him to go to the safe house first and then phone through to Tom to come and join him. Something must be pretty seriously up for Tom to have got his secretary to drop him off there beforehand so that he could meet Michael as soon as he arrived. Turning the key in the lock, a cold, fearful sensation suddenly spread through his stomach as he realized what the reason might be. Something had happened to Elizabeth and Jake. There had been an accident. Tom had fired off the amber card the previous afternoon and then come around to the safe house first thing to give Michael the news as quickly as he possibly could. Closing the door behind him, he sprinted quickly down the hallway and burst into the kitchen.

'What is it?'

'Oh, Jesus Christ!' exclaimed Tom – so startled that he let go of one side of the newspaper that he was reading.

282

'What is it – what's happened?'

'Oh, you surprised me! I wasn't expecting you yet.'

'It's nothing serious is it? I mean, it's not my family or anything …'

'No, no, don't worry,' responded Tom, recovering quickly. 'It's nothing like that. Gosh. You poor chap. You look scared to death. Come and sit down quick. I'll get you a cup of coffee.'

'It's just that I saw your secretary outside and I wondered what the hell was going on,' said Michael, slumping into the chair with relief.

'Oh, I see. Yes, sorry about that. I, er, got her to drop me off. She chauffeurs me around quite a lot nowadays, you know.'

'Oh, right.'

'She didn't see you, did she?'

'She did, but she didn't recognise me.'

'Good. Well, not good, really. Bad. Bit sloppy on my part, that. I should've come by cab really, shouldn't I?'

'Don't worry about it.'

'Sorry, old chap. But I, er, wanted to be here if you turned up first thing.'

'No problem,' said Michael. 'So, what has happened, then?'

'Well, it's not so good, I'm afraid,' replied Tom, gravely. 'It's Buckleys.'

'What about them?'

'Financed, filming and planning to be on the screen by the end of the year.'

'What!'

'I got it on the grapevine two days ago.'

'How? How did they manage it so quickly?'

'They're using more than one reporter.'

'What?'

'Three, in fact. And it seems things are going so well that they've decided to go ahead with the follow-up documentaries, too. It's getting more and more like our little show by the day.'

'Oh, Christ. So, where does that leave us?'

'Facing a very tough decision,' replied Tom, 'a very tough decision, indeed.'

'Meaning what, exactly?'

'Meaning at the absolute maximum you've got five months. Henry and I talked it through yesterday.'

'Five months!'

'Yes – to the end of September, to be precise.'

'You mean I have to finish everything by then?'

'Yes, if we decide to continue.'

'What d'you mean, if you decide to continue?'

'I mean we need to make a judgement now as to the realistic chances of your finishing all four investigations within the next five months. If you think you can, Henry'll pull every string there is: he'll guarantee you're on the screen before Buckleys. If not, then I'm afraid, well …'

Tom left the sentence unfinished. Letting his head rest on the back of the chair, Michael exhaled deeply and then closed his eyes in a mixture of fatigue and demoralized frustration. As it if wasn't enough having to contend with the likes of Thompson and Kent. Now he was faced with committing to a fixed deadline for completing all four investigations or seeing the entire series scrapped – all the dangers that he had risked, all the efforts that he had expended would have been for nothing.

'I don't believe this.'

'I'm sorry, old chap. But short of going around to Buckley's and filling their basement full of dynamite, there's not an awful lot we can do. It's just plain old-fashioned competition, I'm afraid – one of life's unfortunate realities.'

'Shit,' hissed Michael, leaning forward and rubbing the palms of his hands over his face.

'So, let's have a progress report. Come on, old boy. Nil desperandum. What's the news …?'

'Well, things are going well,' replied Michael, straightening up and turning to look at Tom once again. 'I mean up until two minutes ago, I would have said excellent but …'

As Michael looked at Tom full in the face, he found his voice trailing away to nothing. There was something about Tom's smile – it had a quality that he had never seen before and which he would never have imagined it possessing: a faint but unmistakable air of insincerity. Swallowing deeply, Michael struggled to comprehend what it could possibly mean. What was Tom really thinking? And then it hit him, in a sudden blinding flash of understanding that left his mind reeling in shock. Henry and Tom were losing interest in *Criminal Britain*. Tom Cranmer, the man who was always one step ahead, was asking for a progress report solely as a means of letting him down gently – as a prelude to declaring that he had no choice but reluctantly to bring the series to an end. There could be no other explanation. That was why he had got his secretary to drive him to the safe house. It hadn't been a lapse on his part – he was far too sharp for that: security only matters as long as there is something that must be kept secure.

'Are you OK, old chap?'

'Sorry?'

'Are you OK – you don't look good, at all.'

'No, no, it's just … sorry: all that worrying about Jake and Elizabeth – it, er, threw me a bit.'

'Forget the coffee,' said Tom, rising quickly from his seat, 'what you need is a shot of scotch.'

'Yeah, yeah, thanks, I will …'

'Me, too, I think …'

As Tom went across to the cabinet and took out a bottle of whisky, Michael forced his mind to concentrate – forced himself to focus on exactly what he should say next. Perhaps it was only natural that Henry and Tom weren't as enthusiastic as they had once been. He lived the documentary series twenty-four hours a day, but they only got glimpses of his progress following one of his infrequent visits to the safe house. For two months over the Christmas period he had disappeared completely; during that time he had given them absolutely nothing – nothing to maintain their interest. He had to revive it. He had to involve them once more. In the beginning – in the early days – King had been obsessed with the idea of *Criminal Britain*. He had to reinvigorate his zeal – send Tom back to him buzzing with enthusiasm. Picking up the glass, he threw the whisky back in one. The liquor tore at his throat and gullet, but mercifully seemed to bring his mind back into focus.

'OK. Right,' he began, trying to steady his voice and measure his words for maximum impact. 'From the top. Number one. I think I've done it – I think I've found Thompson.'

'Really?'

'Really. He lives on the Abaddon.'

'On the what?'

'The Abaddon. It's a sink housing estate on the outskirts of Feltham – derelict tenements, high rise flats – you know the sort of place. I followed Harper there two nights ago. It was dark, so I didn't actually venture on to the estate itself. I'm going back there next week during the day to stake Thompson out.'

'Good.'

'And I've cracked their system, too.'

'You have?'

'Yeah. Harper and Angela finally let on the other night. It's simple – wonderfully simple. The inside man Craig controls which properties the Housing Benefit Inspectors visit – that's the key to their system – that is their system, in fact. He sets up an inspection for each property, alerting the relevant gang member as to when it will take place. The Inspectors turn up, find that the people who are claiming benefit on the place actually do live there and then close the case down. End of story. After that, the gang can sublet the house or whatever, strong in the knowledge that the Inspectors won't come back again: those guys have got such a massive workload, they don't have the time to re-visit properties they've already checked out.'

'Clever. Very clever.'

'Isn't it just?'

'So, you're nearly there, then on the first investigation? Nearly finished.'

'Nearly. Thompson's not going to be easy to track down, but Craig should be a cinch.'

'Hm. So far so good,' said Tom, raising his eyebrows in unexpected approval. 'What about Tysoe?'

'I've found a way to get into his house. I got his front door keys off Naz and made some copies. I'm planning to stop working for him next week and then go in there as soon as I can after that.'

'Great.'

'Then all I've got to do is interview those two pensioners he cheated at the start of the year when I was in hospital. Then, I'm done. According to Naz, he ripped them off something awful; their house is still in a total state apparently. If I say I'm from the Trading Standards Authority they'll probably be only too pleased to show me around.'

'So, Tysoe's pretty much in the bag as well, too?'

'More or less.'

'Well, I'm sure Henry'll be pleased to hear that, but the sixty-four million dollar question, of course, is what about the drugs story? I mean we just have to be able to deliver on that one considering how advanced Buckleys are. How's it going?'

'Like a dream,' replied Michael, shaking his head admiringly. 'Henry's

286

idea of going under cover as bouncer? Perfect. I never thought it was going to be, considering the start I had, but now I realise it was absolutely inspired.'

'What's happened, then?'

'Kent is definitely dealing. Big time. Last weekend he sent me to a party at this posh country house called Mortlake Manor – cocaine all over the place.'

'Really?'

'Absolutely. The dispenser in chief was a guy called Edwin – he works at Gog too.'

'Hm, I see.'

'Yeah. But there's more – much more.'

'Go on.'

'Kent is trying to put the screws on someone – blackmail him. A guy called Sipkiss. That was why he sent me over to Mortlake Manor: he was a guest at the party.'

'What does he do, this fellow?'

'I don't know. I haven't found out yet. But what I did find out was that the Manor is owned by Alain Ellis – chairman of the Ellis Group, which also owns Gog, of course.'

'Sir Alain Ellis?'

'The very same.'

'A Knight of the Realm, eh? You don't really think he could be involved in all this, do you?'

'I don't know, but Kent flits from company to company within the Ellis Group pretty much at will. Last month I went to a bonded ware-house with him in Norfolk. He was there representing one of Gog's sister companies – he even produced a contract they'd signed. He wouldn't be able to do that without some seriously high-level support.'

'So, this could well go right to the top, then,' observed Tom.

'Possibly – who knows where it stops. But the higher it goes, of course, the bigger the story. And if I do find that the Ellis Group is rotten to the core – and I can prove it – just think of the publicity the series would get. I doubt Buckleys would be able to match it.'

'Hm, you're probably right.'

'Will you be in the office tomorrow?'

'Yes, I will.'

'Good. OK. When I get back, I'll send you a tape. It's footage of me and Kent in Brooke Green outside the house of a man called Foss. It's the scariest stuff I've filmed yet. When you get it, take it straight to Henry and show him: he's bound to be impressed – I looked at it myself again the other week and it gave me the creeps.'

'What's on the tape?'

'I won't say for now,' replied Michael, keeping his expression deliberately enigmatic – a little suspense would render the tape's dramatic effect all the stronger. 'Just take it to him and show him. You'll see what I mean.'

'OK,' answered Tom, slowly, 'I will. Which just leaves us with the fourth documentary. I don't suppose you've managed to make much progress there, have you?'

On arriving at the safe house that morning, Michael's intention had been to make absolutely no reference to Heretic, Amanda or Gert, having vowed to keep them out of the series. But that had been before he had known it might be scrapped and for a moment he was tempted to tell Tom all about them to demonstrate the progress he was making. No sooner had the thought entered his head, though, than he recalled the two hand-written pages of notes from the East European spy that Tom had given him in this very room just over seven months ago. Betrayal. Every line had spoken of the uniquely soul-destroying power of betrayal. No, he would keep his promise – he would not be able to live with himself afterwards if he didn't. However, just because he wasn't going to mention Heretic didn't mean that he couldn't be bullish about the fourth documentary as a whole. Leaning slightly forward, he grinned at Tom enthusiastically. The idea had, after all, originally come straight from King himself. If he talked things up a little, he should be able to maintain the great man's interest.

'No, actually, I've got off to a flying start.'

'Really?' asked Tom, his eyes opening wide: having only suggested the idea to Michael six weeks ago, his expectations had doubtless been very limited.

'Yes, I've managed to get myself on to the set of a porn movie next week.'

'Have you, now?'

'Yes, I have. I'll mail you the footage afterwards, if you like, you can show that to King, too,' said Michael, making a mental note to edit out anything that might incriminate Heretic.

'OK.'

'There are gonna be two girls in the film, apparently; I found out a few days ago. I'm gonna talk to them both afterwards, if I can – just like you and Henry suggested; take them out to dinner or something, find out how they got into the business and all that.'

'Good idea.'

'And, what's more, I've got someone in the know coming back to me with some names shortly; a list of the more unscrupulous agents in the business. I wouldn't be surprised if one of them turns out to be the guy we're looking for. Now that I've got Harper and Tysoe more or less behind me, I should have plenty of time to check them out …'

Sitting back in his chair, Michael watched Tom thoughtfully run his hand across his chin. It was the moment of truth. Michael had done everything that he could to convince him that completing the series within five months was possible. Watching him silently deliberate, Michael recalled the afternoon in his office when he had predicted that King would fire Cromwell, *The Mail*'s editor. Seven months later, that was exactly what had happened – whilst recovering in hospital at the start of the year Michael had read about it in one of the old newspapers in the patients' common room. It had been an extremely shrewd prediction on Tom's part, born of his unique understanding of King's mercurial character. Michael had become too isolated – had let himself get out of touch with the cut and thrust of events at the Tower. He needed Tom to fight for his interests now, just as much as he ever had done when he had worked for him at *The Mail*.

'I had a speech prepared, you know,' said Tom, finally. 'A sort of glory-in-defeat tribute: wonderful show, old chap; no-one on this earth could have achieved more than you have achieved, but time to call it a day, force majeure and all that. I think I would have found it a lot easier than what I actually am going to say …'

'Which is what?'

'The answer's yes – I will try and persuade Henry to let you keep going. But let's not kid ourselves, shall we? The time pressure you'll be under to meet the September deadline will mean that the temptation to cut corners is going to become almost overwhelming. And cutting corners means mistakes. With Tysoe and these pornographers you've just mentioned, that's maybe no problem. But with the fraudsters and Kent …' Tom shook his head grimly. 'It's a terribly selfish thing to say, but I don't want your coming to any further harm on my conscience. But the fact is you're close, aren't you? Very close. And what you have achieved so far is simply astounding – you really could emerge from this with something truly unique. So, yes, I will try and persuade Henry to let you carry on. But I must ask you to take care, my friend. Please, please, take care …'

Michael left the safe house an hour later, having asked Tom to call his contact in the Metropolitan Police – firstly to check out the Abaddon estate and secondly to discover as much as possible about Foss and Sipkiss; from here on in, he was going to need all the additional information that he could get. Unlocking the red BMW, he recalled the day seven months ago that he had got into it as one person and arrived in Feltham as another. He had driven off that morning intending to discover the truth about a gang of fraudsters, but what he had actually discovered had been the truth about himself. Pausing for a moment, he rested his forearms on the roof of the car and stared unseeing at the flats opposite. Not a night now passed without him lying awake and thinking of Jake – of regretting the years that he had spent pursuing his career at the expense of cultivating a relationship with his son. And, as for Elizabeth, his conversation with Amanda had led him to confront the deep feelings that he still had for her – she was and always had been the only woman that he had ever loved. Perhaps he was deluding himself that she could ever consider having him back – perhaps he had been doing so ever since their separation – but he knew for certain that the time had now come for him to ask.

With a shake of his head, he got into the car and began to strap on his seat belt. As he did so, he caught a glimpse of his face in the rear view mirror, whereupon, for several seconds, by some unfathomable psychological mechanism, he felt his two identities disentwine and begin to observe one another through the body that they both shared. From the rear view mirror, Michael Angel's scarred, hardened face glared sternly at him – his eyes filled with warning. I lost my family, his expression seemed to say, I lost them forever; don't make the same mistake. Nodding his head in acknowledgement, he stared unblinkingly back, until the strange mental fission receded and once again there was only a single person in the car.

Part Three
Betting High

Chapter 10

The dashboard's digital clock silently switched from twelve forty-six to twelve forty-seven. It was lunchtime. He should eat. Without taking his eyes off the house, Michael leant over and opened up the glove compartment, his fingers groping for the sandwich and the bottle of water inside: during six unbroken hours of surveillance not a single person had gone in or out of Harper's house – all the more reason for not letting his concentration drop now, even for a fraction of a second. Eating the food but not tasting it, Michael began to resign himself to the fact that the entire week might yield nothing new. Before his last meeting with Tom, he would have accepted this philosophically – long periods of waiting were an inevitable feature of investigative journalism – but now that he knew he had only five months to complete the series every unproductive second felt like an hour.

Things had been moving agonisingly slowly ever since the weekend. Kent had been away on Friday and Saturday, and when Michael had finally reported back to him about Sipkiss on Sunday night, his reaction had been surprisingly muted – despite Michael's assertion that Sipkiss had consumed easily as much cocaine as any other guest at the Mortlake Manor party. On Monday morning he had called Tysoe, pleading a slipped disk that would prevent him from working for the next couple of months. When Tysoe had accepted his story, he had been pleased to think that his weekdays would be free from then on, but three and a half fruitless days of staking out Harper's house had dampened his elation; either the fraudsters hadn't been back to the Abaddon estate or they had done so in the small hours of the morning. It was now Thursday noon.

If they didn't make their way there within the next twenty-four hours, it would be another five days at the earliest before he could resume surveillance – on Friday afternoon he had to go back to work at Gog and the following Monday was going to be taken up with shooting his second and final film for Heretic. Taking a sip of his water, Michael frowned, considering and then dismissing for the umpteenth time the idea of phoning Harper to suggest resuming their regular Thursday night drinking sessions. Just as Tom had said, he had to resist the temptation to cut corners – to force the investigation forward at a dangerously precipitous pace. He was Michael Angel and he had to act in character. His fierce Northern pride had been offended by the unfair allegations of incompetence that Harper and Angela had levelled at him and he had been fully justified in storming out as a result. It was now up to them to apologise to him, not the other way around. Moreover, by not paying Harper his regular weekly cut on the second house in Milland Road he was tightening the screws on the fraudster still further. Despite the growing feelings of impatience, Michael knew he had no choice but to sit and wait.

Just after ten to one his mobile rang. Putting the half-eaten sandwich down on the passenger seat, he took the phone from his top pocket and checked the number of the incoming call. It was Tom.

'Hello.'

'It's me. Can you talk?'

'Yeah, no problem.'

'Where are you?'

'Over the road from Harper's house. I've been staking it out all week.'

'Any joy?'

'No. Nothing.'

'They've not been back to the Abaddon estate yet, then?'

'No. They went out a couple of times yesterday, but just to the shops and things.'

'Good. I'm glad. You ought to know what you're up against before following them in there.'

'Has your mate from the Met been back in touch?'

'Yes. Just now.'

'And?'

'Most of it's lost apparently.'

'What d'you mean?'

'The estate – it's lost to the authorities: police, council, social services, just about everyone in fact.'

'What does 'lost' mean exactly?'

'It's a term the police use to describe an area they no longer control.'

'Don't they go in there at all, then?'

'Only in armed groups. Some of the tenement housing on the periphery of the estate is OK apparently, but it's anarchy in the tower blocks. No uniformed police officer has been in there in over two years.'

'What about crime? What happens when someone reports a break-in or something like that?'

'Most of the high-rise flats are either squats or crack-houses. There are a few residents left here and there, but only on the lower floors. If one of them rings up the police with a problem they put him or her straight on to the council. They get re-housed within a week – they go right to the top of the list.'

'So there's no rule of law in the place.'

'No – none at all. In a sense the estate isn't a part of the United Kingdom. I mean it's physically located here, but it's governed by, well, people like Thompson, I suppose.'

'Jesus,' exhaled Michael, recalling the devastation he had witnessed in the streets around the Abaddon: having wreaked their havoc, the youths from the estate obviously just returned there strong in the knowledge that the police dare not follow them.

'There are a dozen or so estates like it, apparently, up and down the country. Three or four in London, a couple in the Midlands, several more in Scotland and the North East. The authorities keep quiet about them – the Met especially – as you can imagine, they're not exactly keen to own up to the breakdown in order.'

'I see. What about Foss, did you get anything on him?' said Michael, putting to the back of his mind for the moment the question of exactly how he would approach the Abaddon estate.

'Yes. Known felon. Record of violent crime as long as your arm. GBH, robbery – you name it.'

'No surprises there, then.'

'No, none at all. And by the way, I showed Henry the tape of you and Kent outside his house.'

'And?'

'You were right. He was impressed. He said he was certain that

Buckleys would never come up with anything as visually powerful as that.'

'Good.'

'He did have his concerns, though.'

'About what?'

'About Ellis.'

'What about him?'

'He's a powerful man. Untouchable probably – or at least not with your resources and in the time you've got left. Henry says if you can pick up anything concrete on Ellis – fine – but first and foremost he wants you to concentrate on Gog. The focus must be on the young people at risk there from drug abuse.'

For a moment, Michael was tempted to argue this point, but instead bit his lip and let Tom's comment pass.

'OK. I'll try and spend as much time at the club as I can. Maybe I can find an excuse to go in there during the week as well.'

'Good idea. That was Henry's only reservation – apart from that he was very upbeat. He sees a definite continuity in the series now – a sort of thematic consistency, if you like – and it's very appealing to him. Play to it and he'll support you right down to the wire, I'm positive of that.'

'How do you mean?'

'I mean he's come to recognize *Criminal Britain* as a wonderful rogue's gallery of the villains who prey on middle England. That was probably his core concept all along, but you've done a fantastic job of realizing it. You've given Mr and Mrs Average a flesh and blood bogie-man for every single one of their very worst fears. Harper and Thompson take their taxes. Tysoe takes their savings. The pornographers lure their daughters into a life of vice ...'

'And Kent turns their sons into dope fiends.'

'Exactly!' exclaimed Tom.

'I'm glad he's pleased.'

'He is – he's behind you one hundred per cent, old chap. Take my word for it.'

'Thanks. That's good to hear. What about Sipkiss? Did you get me anything on him?'

'No, nothing – my friend at the Met drew a complete blank. I asked him to keep looking and he's going to try one or two other lines of enquiry. I'll let you know if he finds anything.'

'OK.'

'Listen. I've got to go now. But I'll call you soon, all right?'

'Fine.'

'Bye for now.'

'Bye, Tom.'

Clipping the phone back into the connector in his top pocket, Michael thought about eating the rest of the sandwich but then put it back in its wrapper and returned it to the glove compartment: he hadn't been hungry when he'd started it. Resting his hands on the steering wheel, he stared at the front door of Harper's house and went over in his mind once again the conversation with Tom. The news about the Abaddon estate couldn't really have been much worse. Anonymity was an absolute prerequisite of effective street surveillance. It was possible to find a kerbside in most areas of the country where you could sit in a car undisturbed for hours, but not in a place like the Abaddon – especially at night. How could he hope to concentrate on getting some proper footage of Thompson if he was looking over his shoulder all the time? He would have to think of a way around the problem – perhaps he could rent one of the lower floor flats to which Tom had referred and carry out his observation from there; it all depended where Thompson actually lived. At the same time, he couldn't afford to delay much longer in getting pictures of the inside man, Craig. He should be a much easier target because Michael knew where he worked, although the longer he left it the less time he would have to track him down if there were any unforeseen difficulties.

On the brighter side, the renewed vote of confidence from King was excellent news. Despite the painfully slow progress this week, he still had almost five months to finish his investigations; if he stuck to his modus operandi it should be enough. The only thing on which he disagreed with King was the question of Ellis. Without doubt, he had to trace the drug supply line from Kent to Gog and then on to its customers, but there was something far bigger going on inside the Ellis Group – he was certain of it. Furthermore, although Tom might proclaim King's unique empathy with the viewing public, he wasn't anywhere near as close to the story as Michael – he couldn't feel and smell the corruption inside Ellis – and, despite his earlier protestations of wanting to characterize Britain's faceless criminals, was obviously perfectly content simply to line them up as straightforward hate-figures. Leaning back in his seat,

Michael unscrewed the bottle of water and thoughtfully took a swig. King had given him his five months and he would therefore do everything that he could to meet the objectives that he had laid down. At the same time, he fully intended to follow his instincts and learn as much as he could about the Ellis Group's wider operations. Time would tell whether Sir Alain Ellis was really as untouchable as King supposed.

Babs had turned up dressed to kill. Taking her full-length leather coat and handing it to the waiter, Michael could see that not only did the skin-tight, purple dress that she was wearing stop right at the very top of her legs but it was also completely open at the back. Around her neck she wore a necklace of fine, white pearls that tapered into a point, accentuating her small but perfectly shaped bosom. Her hair was fastened tightly up above her head save for a single, wispy ringlet that coiled delicately downwards, coming to rest on her marble-white collar bone. She had rings on the fingers of both hands.

'Shall we have a drink at the bar first?'

'Sure,' she purred, turning and slipping her forearm inside Michael's; as they walked across the second floor restaurant together towards the bar, he could feel the swing of her hips against his thigh.

'What would you like? A cocktail, maybe?' asked Michael.

'Hm, good idea,' replied Babs, sitting down on the bar stool and crossing her long, elegant legs so that her foot rested up against his.

'The lady would like a cocktail,' said Michael to Will as he made his way along the counter towards them.

'OK, Mick,' replied Will, picking up one of the bar's enormous leather-bound cocktail lists and, in a single, deft movement, opening it up for Babs to read.

'A Scarlet Lady,' she answered, huskily. 'That sounds like me all over.'

'Mick?'

'Er, just mineral water for me, please – sparkling.'

With a friendly, courteous smile, Will turned around and began to fix the drinks. Resting her chin on her upturned palm and arching her right eyebrow, Babs gave Michael a sultry look of approval – she was clearly most satisfied with his choice of restaurant.

'So, how long have you worked at Gog, then?'

'A few months.'

'Classy place.'

'Yeah, not bad,' agreed Michael. He had in fact only ever been in the second floor restaurant at Gog once before, on his first day. Having had little more than a glimpse of its interior that afternoon, he couldn't remember much about it beyond a general impression of its expensive but somewhat aseptic aluminium décor. Looking at the subtle floor-lighting and the view of night-time Chelsea through the plate glass windows at the rear, Michael now realized what the interior designers had been aiming to achieve and could understand why Babs was so impressed.

'D'you bring all your girls here?' she asked, with a playful smile.

'Babs, I can honestly say you're the first,' replied Michael. Len had also given him the telephone number for Evelyn, the other girl in the second Heretic movie, but he had called Babs first because of her more outgoing personality.

'I'll take that as a compliment.'

'Please do. So, where are you from, then?' asked Michael, shifting his position slightly to ensure that her face was directly opposite the jacket pocket of his newly purchased double breasted suit. Jim's seamstress had sewn a lens into it two days ago: she had concealed one in every jacket he now owned – perhaps it was time he started asking for a discount.

'London. Lived here all my life,' replied Babs, breezily. 'You?'

'Up North, originally. I moved down here last year.'

'I thought your accent was a bit different.'

'Perhaps I'll lose it if I stay here long enough.'

'That'd be a shame.'

'Thanks. So, how long you been workin' in the movies, then?'

'A couple of years.'

'D'you like it?'

'It's a job – you know. Or, rather it's not a nine to five job. I tried that. It wasn't my scene at all.'

Looking into her smouldering, sardonic eyes, Michael recalled the five-hour filming session the previous week in the West London hotel room. Unlike Amanda, who simply projected her unqualified sexuality directly on to the screen, Babs delighted in playing the tease, which she achieved through a seemingly limitless array of facial gestures ranging from the sullenly pouting to the openly libidinous. Michael had no doubt that if she were to employ such facial expressions in an office environment it would drive the men wild and the women even wilder.

'But you've not worked for Heretic before?'

'Heretic?' replied Babs, quizzically.

'Heretic Films. You know Len and Barry ...?'

'Heretic! Is that what they call themselves?' she exclaimed.

'Yeah. Didn't you know?'

'Peculiar name.'

'A couple of characters, though, aren't they?'

'A couple of weirdoes, more like,' said Babs, adding as an after-thought, 'Sorry, they're not friends of yours, are they?'

'Sort of.'

'At least they knew what they were doing, I suppose. Which was more than could be said for – what was his name – Eliot. I could have strangled that little shit by the end ...'

On arriving at the hotel suite at lunch time, Len had cheerfully informed Michael that they would be shooting a Heretic speciality that day – an FFM: the porn industry acronym for a film featuring two women and one man. But the moment that the 'M' part of the equation had come through the door, Michael had sensed that irrespective of Heretic's experience of the genre, things were not going to proceed well. Eliot had turned out to be a mere five feet two and was apparently only comfortable working with women of a similar stature – the agency who had supplied him having failed to inform Heretic of this vital fact. Despite Len's solemn assurance that he had no intention of standing all three performers in a line, Eliot's insecurity had manifested itself on several critical occasions during filming. At first Babs and Evelyn had taken this in their stride, but by the time they had left at half-past six that evening, both looked as though they would have happily thrown him out of the hotel room's fifth-storey window.

'So, you think they're quite good at their job, then?'

'Who – Len and Barry?'

'Yeah.'

'Yeah – they're not bad.'

'Have you worked with many producers and film companies?'

'A few.'

'How d'you, like, protect yourself? I mean, there are some bad-ass guys out there, right – especially amongst the agents?'

'Oh, yeah, some of them are vile, but word gets around – you know.'

'Who was the worst you ever worked with, then?'

'The worst?' replied Babs, with a frown. 'I dunno whether I really want to remember that. A guy called Luxman, probably. D'you know him?'

'No,' said Michael, with a shake of the head, wondering if Amanda's friend Bernie knew Luxman. A full three weeks had passed since they had met at the wine bar without a sign of the list she had promised, although he had by no means given up hope of her keeping her word.

'Total arsehole,' spat Babs. 'Never again.'

'Well,' said Michael, seeing Will approach with the drinks and sensing that, for the moment, he should pursue the subject no further, 'here's to Luxman and Eliot – never to be worked with again.'

'I'll drink to that,' replied Babs with a smile.

Taking a sip of his water, Michael sensed the presence of someone else at the far end of the bar and, turning his eyes to the left, saw that it was Edwin.

'Would you excuse me for a moment?' he said.

'Sure,' replied Babs.

Walking along the bar towards where Edwin was standing quietly sipping a glass of Sebor, Michael strove to control a sudden rush of nervous self-doubt. Clenching his fist behind his back, he sternly told himself to keep calm. Approaching Edwin wasn't something that had just occurred to him – it wasn't a spontaneous act. He had been thinking about it for over a week and had no reason to rebuke himself for acting out of desperation or panic.

'Hi,' said Michael, in what he hoped was a convincingly casual voice.

'Well,' replied Edwin, ironically, 'like the place so much we're spending our weekdays here too, then?'

'Something like that.'

'Who's the flesh-pot?' continued Edwin, nodding at Babs who was talking to Will as she sipped her cocktail from a tall, gold-leafed glass.

'A friend,' replied Michael.

'Hm. Curves in all the right places, I suppose. Not that I'm any judge of such things.'

'Listen, I, er, wanted to ask you something,' said Michael, lowering his voice to a confidential tone.

'I'm all ears,' replied Edwin, with more than a hint of dismissive boredom.

'Coke. Can you get me some?'

'Sorry?'

'Cocaine. I want to buy some. I, er, noticed two weeks ago, at the Manor, you were, er …?'

'Giving it out,' replied Edwin, dryly.

'Yes. I mean, I'm not asking this as a favour, I'll pay for it, of course.'

'Why don't you ask your boss?'

'Well, like I say, I saw you the other night and besides, I don't want to end up too much in his debt.'

At first Edwin did not respond, but simply looked Michael up and down, seemingly scrutinizing every aspect of his appearance. Finally, sliding a silver cigarette case out of the inside pocket of his jacket, he looked him straight in the eye and spoke in a voice that, for once, held no trace of irony.

'You know, I think I may have underestimated you,' he said, removing one of the cigarettes, but not lighting it. 'Just dumb muscle, I thought. But you're learning quickly, aren't you?'

'I do my best.'

'You're right not to ask too many favours of Kent. He might decide to call them all in at once and that could be quite … painful for you – take my word for it.'

'I'll remember that.'

'Do. He had his favourites before you, you know – a whole string of protégés – and where are they all now, one might ask?'

'No idea.'

'Me neither,' replied Edwin, finally lighting up the cigarette and then fanning away the smoke with his slim, pale hand. 'The coke's no problem – although I will expect you to be discreet, of course.'

'Of course.'

'I'll drop by later with some. Pay me when you can.'

'That's great. Cheers.'

'You're welcome.'

'Right, well, I'll, er …' said Michael, nodding in the direction of Babs. In response, Edwin gave a fey wave of the hand that seemed to acknowledge that the conversation was over, but just as Michael turned his back he spoke again.

'There are other ways up the ladder, you know.'

'Sorry?' said Michael, turning around to face him again.

'In Ellis. If you ever get weary of all the strong arm stuff …'

Looking into Edwin's languorous, grey eyes, Michael could see that he clearly wanted him to understand that this was a proposition.

'I'll remember that, too,' he answered, with a respectful nod of his head.

'I hope you will,' replied Edwin, lifting the absinthe glass to his lips in a gesture of salutation.

A wave of excitement mixed with relief surged through Michael, and, as he made his way back along the bar towards Babs, he almost felt like shouting out in triumph. The conversation had lasted less than a minute, but he had probably advanced the investigation more in that time than in the previous two months. It wasn't simply that he now knew that Kent and Edwin were both players within a structured, integrated organization, but that another door into that organization through which he could gain further access to its secrets had now opened up. Picking up an olive from one of the dishes on the bar, he popped it in his mouth and smiled to himself, thinking of Tom. The fact that Edwin had said he would drop by later with some coke strongly suggested that there was a stash of it somewhere in the club.

'Good morning. Department of Social Security.'

'Can I speak to Craig?'

'Craig …?'

'I dunno his second name. He works in the same office as Mr Dill.'

'Who's calling?'

'I'd rather not say.'

'Oh, right, well, actually, there is a hot-line number you should ring, it's …'

'I only wanna talk to Craig,' interrupted Michael. 'I've got some important information for him.'

'Right, er, OK, hang on a moment, please. I'll see if he's available …'

For several seconds the line went quiet. Frowning, Michael looked through the window of the phone box towards the roof of the abandoned warehouse two hundred yards away from which he intended to film Craig. Judging by the telephonist's reaction and the fact that Craig was apparently able to influence which properties were inspected, he was probably a senior departmental or section manager, in which case, he might not even agree to speak to Michael, let alone meet him.

'Hello.'

'Is this Craig?'

'Yeah. Who's this?'

His voice was relaxed – unhurried.

'My name doesn't matter. I've got some information for you.'

'What about?'

'A bunch of fraudsters – in Feltham – on your patch.'

'Where did you get my name?'

'Friend of a friend.'

'Who?'

'I'd rather not say.'

'So, what d'you know about these … fraudsters then?'

Michael paused for a moment, smiling in admiration. Craig's lightly inquisitive, casual tone sounded totally natural, but he knew all too well what it felt like trying to keep your voice steady whilst your intestines churned at the thought that the day you had been dreading for so long might finally have arrived. If he was to capture Craig on film, he needed mercilessly to exploit that fear, not allowing him the time to think or consult with the other fraudsters.

'They're big – really big. They must be doin' you for – God, I don't know – hundreds of thousands a year. They've got loads of properties – they're dead well organized: they've got fake National Insurance numbers – everything.'

'What exactly have you got on these people – I mean what sort of information?' replied Craig, his voice still holding firm.

'Everything. Names, addresses, everything. It's all yours if you want it.'

'Why? Why d'you want to give me this?'

'Revenge. Someone I wanna pay back.'

'OK,' continued Craig, slowly, clearly not trying to sound too interested. 'Can you bring it here?'

'What, to Housing Benefits?'

'Yeah.'

'No fuckin' way,' exclaimed Michael. 'If I get seen in there with you I'm dead – they'd kill me if word got back to 'em. No, meet me. I'll bring the stuff with me.'

'Where?'

'Barretts on the High Street. Main entrance. Twenty minutes.'

'Twenty minutes? I can't. I can't just …'

'What d'you mean, you can't?' interrupted Michael, angrily. 'Listen.

I'm leavin' town in an hour. If you can't meet me now, I'll have to post the stuff in.'

'No, don't do that,' replied Craig, just a little too quickly. 'It's OK, I'll be there.'

Again Michael smiled to himself: Craig was clearly desperate not to risk letting Dill or any of his other colleagues get their hands on the information before him in case it related to the very fraud ring in which he was involved.

'What'll you be wearing?'

'Er, brown jacket – black trousers.'

'Wait by the main doors. I'll make contact once you arrive.'

Abruptly terminating the call, Michael made his way as quickly but as inconspicuously as he could towards the alleyway at the side of the warehouse and then padded silently up the fire escape's rusted metal stairs. Taking the portable video camera that he had bought at a high-street electrical shop the previous morning, he rested it on the moss-covered concrete ledge at the edge of the roof. When he had decided to call Craig at his office, claiming to have a file of information on a group of fraudsters, he had known that there was always a chance that it would panic him so much that he would just turn and run. Thankfully, though, Craig seemed to have taken his carefully crafted bait: if the anonymous caller's information related to the gang for which he was the inside man, he need only pick it up and then destroy it – if not, he would lose nothing by slipping out of the office for half an hour or so. Switching the video camera on, Michael focused its zoom lens on the front doors of the department store and patiently began to wait.

Craig came into view ten minutes later. At first, Michael didn't realize that it was him, despite the fact that he was the only person to have stood waiting outside the store during that time and was clearly wearing a brown jacket and black trousers. He was so young – so very, very young: if Michael hadn't known that he had been working for the Housing Benefit office for at least three years he would have put his age at little more than sixteen. Shaking his head gently so as not to unsteady the camera, he watched the slimly built young man lean up against one of the plate glass windows to the left hand side of the main doors and slowly light up a cigarette. Even at this distance, Craig was a remarkably inconspicuous figure, seeming to blend in completely with the lunch-time shoppers milling in and out of the store. With his quiff of brown hair and pale, fresh-faced complexion, he put Michael in mind of an altar boy or a court page, standing in the midst of some grand, choreographed state ceremony utterly unnoticed by everyone present; he hoped the long range images would faithfully capture this astonishing inconspicuousness.

After four or five minutes, Michael stopped filming but continued to observe Craig through his micro-binoculars. Several minutes later, Craig turned slowly on his heel and began to walk away, quickly disappearing from sight amongst the crowd of high-street shoppers. Packing up the camera, Michael wondered what Craig was thinking at this moment. Had he realized that the phone call had been a set-up to flush him out into the open? Would he now alert Thompson and the other fraudsters? Or, had he concluded that the anonymous caller had simply got cold feet at the last minute and he could do nothing now but wait and see what, if anything, might happen next? If Craig did alert Thompson, it wouldn't necessarily be a bad thing. Michael had at last been able to blow smoke into the serpent's nest – if it came out to confront the threat, he would be waiting there to catch it.

Parking his car at the end of the crescent, Michael sat and waited for Mrs Tysoe to leave her house for the Sports Club, just as she did every Monday, Wednesday and Thursday morning. Having tailed her there several times before Christmas, Michael had strongly suspected that she was still maintaining the same routine, but, just to make sure, had followed her to the Club twice during the last two weeks: unlike her husband, her schedule had proved to be reassuringly predictable. He looked at his watch. It was five to ten – she should be out at any moment. When he had left Balam Road that morning, his mood had been bordering on the exultant. Having visited the two pensioners the previous week in the guise of a Trading Standards Inspector and having filmed every detail of the unfinished work on their would-be kitchen-dining room, he had known that once he got inside Tysoe's house, the first documentary would effectively be over. However, now that he was only minutes away from it, he felt strangely deflated. Perhaps it was because he wouldn't really be satisfied until he had handed all the video evidence over to the police and they actually initiated legal proceedings. Angrily checking himself, he slammed the fist of one hand into the open palm of the other. He was letting his mind wander. For now, he had to focus all his faculties on the task of making absolutely sure he got in and out of the house unobserved. There could be nothing worse than operational negligence at this late stage: it would be one thing not to be able to complete the four investigations in time for the September deadline, it would be another to have to abandon the series altogether because of arrant carelessness.

At 10:02 precisely, Mrs Tysoe came hurrying out of the front door. Sitting bolt upright, Michael strained to make sure he caught sight of her sports holdall, but then slipped quickly back into his seat. He couldn't afford to make himself too conspicuous. Watching her open up the boot of her Audi convertible and swing the holdall inside, he swallowed hard and tried to relax. He had to calm down. She was right on schedule – everything was fine; she was even wearing her track-suit. Watching her reverse out of the driveway, Michael again considered whether he should follow her to the Sports Club to make absolutely sure that she hadn't changed her routine that morning: it was only twenty minutes there and back and he would still have well over an hour to look around the house before she returned. The problem with that strategy was Tysoe himself. According to Naz, they were starting work that day on a new property in Twickenham, but there was still a chance – albeit somewhat remote – that he would decide to wander off mid-morning and go back to his home. Naz had promised to phone Michael the moment he went off-site, but he had nevertheless set himself a target of being out of the house by eleven o'clock – a full hour before lunch. Turning around to pretend to look at something on the passenger seat, Michael heard the purr of the Audi's engine as it went gliding past. He would wait five minutes in case she had forgotten something – then he would go in.

'So, now at last we get to see inside the home of Mr John Tysoe,' said Michael, into the microphone of his mobile phone. 'I've got to make sure I look confident about this …'

Getting out of the car, he walked across to the pavement and then marched straight down the crescent, keeping his eyes firmly fixed on the front door: if anyone was watching it was important that they saw nothing diffident in his body language. Thankfully, Tysoe's house had a deep, brick-built porch and he knew that once he was inside he could only really be observed by someone standing in the front garden or directly facing him in the street. Having gone through the gate – and carefully closing it after him – he took the bunch of keys from his pocket and began sifting through them as he walked down the path: if someone did see him, he wanted them to get an impression of efficiency and deliberateness. To this end he had dressed in his new double-breasted suit and had brought a briefcase with him – if one of the neighbours were watching they would hopefully imagine he was a business associate of Tysoe's or perhaps someone like an estate agent. Once in the sanctuary of the porch, he allowed himself a surreptitious glance over his shoulder. There was no movement in the crescent. No sound. Nothing. Stage one complete.

'If Tysoe's got an alarm, then I'm in big trouble,' he whispered, more for dramatic effect than anything, but as he opened the second of the front door locks and walked on into the house, his heart almost stopped. Although there was no bell-box on the outside of the property, at the end of the hallway he caught sight of a flashing infra-red sensor: Tysoe had indeed installed an alarm system and must have purposefully hidden the bell-box out of sight. Standing half-in half-out of the door, he looked around for a control panel to see if he could find some way of neutralizing the alarm – they were almost always located next to the front door. Spotting it beside the hall telephone, he moved quickly forward and was just about to turn the key in the centre when he stopped mid-action and smiled. Mr Tysoe might well have been shrewd enough to have installed an intruder alarm system – and even concealed its external bell-box – but it was less than useless if his wife couldn't be bothered to turn it on.

'So, let's see what the standard of workmanship is like in Mr Tysoe's house, shall we?' said Michael, closing the front door and then walking down the richly carpeted hallway to the rear of the house. 'Perhaps we can start with the kitchen …'

He had been in the house for less than ten minutes when he started to sense that something was wrong. It began with a telephone call. Walking into the hall from the lounge where he had been photographing Tysoe's antique oak drinks cabinet, he looked at the telephone and waited for the answering machine to click in. It didn't – it wasn't switched on. The phone stopped after six or seven rings, but just as Michael went back into the lounge it started again – on this second occasion ringing only three times. Going back into the hall, Michael stood and stared uncertainly at the handset for several seconds. The second call meant that whoever it was that had phoned either hadn't been sure of the number or, expecting the person they were calling to be in, had thought that they must have misdialled. With a shake of the head, he turned on his heel and went back into the lounge: then again, it could just have been a wrong number.

Five minutes later, as he mounted the stairs to the first floor, he had almost forgotten the phone call, but the moment that he put his hand on the smooth, varnished banister, it came ominously back to mind. There was a window ledge next to the front door that he hadn't noticed when he had come in. On it was a black, leather purse. Opening it up, he could immediately tell that it was Mrs Tysoe's. Why had she left the house without her purse? And did she always leave the alarm off when she went out, or had she only done so today because she knew she would be back in a few minutes? She had taken her sports holdall with her — he had seen it with his own eyes — and the phone call could indeed have been a wrong number, but he couldn't rule out the possibility that, after all, she had changed her routine that morning and might be back at any second.

Sprinting into the living room, he opened up a small gap between the net curtains and stared down the crescent. It was as quiet as it had been all morning. Frowning, Michael unclipped the mobile phone from his top pocket and then checked the signal strength: it was at maximum — if Naz had been trying to call he would certainly have got through. Walking back out of the lounge he stood in the middle of the hall and then looked at his watch. Ten twenty-seven. Decision time. Although his rational mind was quietly counselling him that the purse and the alarm were consistent with the behaviour of a spoilt, lackadaisical woman and that the phone call had probably been an entirely coincidental event, deep inside his brain a powerful instinct was warning him to get out now while the going was still good. He considered the possible alternatives. Leaving immediately and returning the following Wednesday appeared the most attractive option, but, concluding that whereas Mrs Tysoe might follow a predictable routine that day, her husband probably wouldn't, Michael finally settled on a compromise. He would stay another fifteen minutes until a quarter to eleven, but check the window every sixty seconds.

Hurrying to complete the filming of the first floor he almost missed the walk-through wardrobe. Between the doors to the bathroom and the second bedroom was another door which he guessed led to a storage or airing cupboard. The moment that he opened it to confirm this, however, he knew that he had found the definitive image that he had been seeking. The door led into a purpose-built wardrobe that ran from floor to ceiling across the entire width of the house. On the left hand side was a cupboard filled with about thirty women's dresses and suits, each neatly wrapped in polythene: Mrs Tysoe obviously had everything that she wore dry-cleaned. It was the right-hand cupboard, however, that left him gasping in a mixture of awe and disgust. He had never seen so many pairs of shoes in his life – there were easily over a hundred – all of the very highest quality and all seemingly unworn. Right from the start of the investigation he had wondered why Tysoe went out of his way to cheat quite so many people, but had never for a moment thought that mere vanity could spawn such unhappiness.

'When you ask Mr John Tysoe to work for you,' he said, taking a pair of designer high-heels out of their heavy, gold-embossed box and holding them up for the camera, 'Your money won't end up in bricks and mortar. It'll end up here.'

It was the final, authoritative comment on the greed and callousness of the Tysoe's tawdry existence. Having filmed the walk-through wardrobe once again to be absolutely sure he had sufficient footage – this time standing inside and facing outwards on to the hall – Michael closed the door and paused for a moment. To his right, was a staircase leading to the second floor attic conversion. Tempting though it was to go up and make comparisons with the destruction of Mr Herbert's roof, he went through into the front bedroom instead, and, having checked that the coast was clear, decided to leave. It was still only twenty-one minutes to eleven, but the walk-through wardrobe had sealed it. He had seen everything that he needed to see. His six-month investigation of John Tysoe had now finished.

As Michael closed the front gate behind him and took one final look at the house, he thought of Naz. Whereas he couldn't hope to reproduce the wild spontaneity of the party that they had had after he had recovered the Turks' money from Roger, a celebration of sorts that night was definitely in order – he would go to the off-licence in the afternoon and pick up some drinks. Still more pleasing to Naz himself, though, would be the prospect of being able to tell Tysoe that he was no longer going to work for him. And six weeks after that, of course, he would be back in Turkey, reunited with his family. It made Michael smile to think

310

of their reunion. Before Naz left, he was planning to give him five thousand pounds of the money that Tom had deposited for him in the safe deposit box. It was the very least he deserved.

Michael was still smiling as he turned away from the house, but his face froze rigid as he looked back down the crescent: Mrs Tysoe's car had just turned into it and she was driving straight towards him. In the fraction of the second that they spotted each other, Michael swung his briefcase forwards to make it look as though he were in motion – as though he were walking past her house rather than having just emerged from it. Keeping his eyes fixed firmly on his own car he walked straight ahead, ignoring the look that Mrs Tysoe gave him when her car drove into his line of sight. The moment that she had driven past him, he crossed to the pavement on the other side of the crescent and continued towards his car. Unlocking the boot and placing the briefcase inside, he could see out of the corner of his eye that she had parked her own car in front of the house and was standing beside it staring back in his direction. Concluding that it would appear far too suspicious if he didn't look at her at all, he decided to give her a momentary glance after getting into his car and putting on his seat belt. He was glad that he did, for he looked up just in time to see her walking down the path towards her front door, her sports holdall in her right hand. She had obviously been suspicious – but not so suspicious as to try and get his registration number or even watch him as he drove away. He couldn't be a hundred percent certain, but he imagined that once she was inside the house and found nothing disturbed, she would forget about the stranger in the street outside. Sighing with relief, Michael did a three-point turn and, without looking behind him, drove out of the crescent. He would never know what had happened that morning – where Mrs Tysoe had been, who had telephoned her and whether the two events were in any way connected. But he didn't care. He had got away with it. And, more to the point, he now had everything he needed to ensure that, at the very least, John Tysoe's life was now going to become as uncomfortable as that of anyone he had ever cheated.

When he got back to Balam Road, there was a letter from Amanda waiting for him on the mat: Mr M Angel – PO Box 1110, Middlesex. Hastily opening it up, he walked into the kitchen to make himself a cup of coffee, but stopped on seeing the first name on the list and went into the lounge and poured himself a glass of whisky. Toasting Amanda's health, he threw the drink back in one and then let out a whoop of satisfaction. Things could simply not have gone better that day. The series was on a roll: Tysoe was in the bag and the first name on the list that Amanda had got from her friend was none other than Simon Luxman – the agent whom Babs had mentioned over dinner. Looking at the clock and seeing that it was nearly twelve, Michael decided to treat himself to lunch at a restaurant and then take the afternoon off. He desperately needed the rest. Tomorrow was Friday – the first day of his weekend shift at Gog – and the following week he had to start the prolonged night-time surveillance of Harper's house. This was just the right time to relax and recharge his batteries. In the evening, he would download the film of Tysoe's house and then go to Naz's for a celebration. Taking the whisky glass into the kitchen and swilling it under the tap, he turned to go back out of the flat again. At that moment, his mobile phone rang. It was Tom.

'It's me. Can you talk?'

'Yeah, I'm in the flat.'

'My contact in the Met just called me. I've, er, got some news.'

'Great. Is it Sipkiss?'

'No, it's Foss.'

'Foss? What about him?'

'My friend caught sight of his name on a report. He wouldn't've stopped to read it normally, but he remembered that I'd been asking about a man called Foss so he picked it up and read it through ...'

'And?'

'I, er, don't quite know how to tell you this ...'

'What's happened, Tom? Tell me.'

'He's dead.'

'What!'

'Foss is dead.'

'Oh, my God. When?'

'Three days ago. The police found him in his flat – back of his head blown off. Suicide they reckon. They're not treating it as suspicious ...'

Although the Turks – and Naz in particular – obviously had an excellent time that evening, Michael could not enjoy himself. Towards the end of the night he did find himself relaxing a little, but his spirits soon sank once more when he walked into the lounge and caught sight of one of the Abaddon estate's three tower blocks through the front window. He had finished off the investigation of his first criminal that day, but it somehow only made the remaining investigations appear all the more daunting: although Tysoe was a thoroughly repellent character, he didn't go around killing people; Foss's death had invested *Criminal Britain* with an altogether more serious dimension. Driving home just after midnight, Michael mulled over his reactions to the news once again. Four months ago, Foss had given him a scar that he would carry for the rest of his days and, if Nigel hadn't distracted him by activating the patient alarm, might well have gone on to kill him. Nevertheless, Michael felt no satisfaction at his murder and on the contrary wished that he was still alive. Since starting the documentary series he had never once felt the desire to take revenge on anyone for what they had done to him personally and although Foss's dispute with Kent predated Michael's appearance at Gog, he still felt in some way responsible for his death.

He awoke late on Friday morning, tired despite a long sleep and still feeling emotionally numbed by the previous day's news. In the hope of snapping out of it, he decided to download the footage of Tysoe's home that he had taken the previous day. Opening up the drawer beneath the VCR and discovering that he had run out of blank tapes, he went into the hallway and took up the carpet: the second undercover filming session at Mr Herbert's bungalow had lasted less than twenty-five minutes and the cassette on to which he had downloaded it was therefore empty from that point on – the forty-five minutes of footage would fit in easily. Carefully connecting the phone to the VCR, he inserted the tape and sat back to watch. The natural light in the house had been excellent and the images proved to be crystal clear – the best he had yet recorded. Despite this, Michael found himself strangely detached from the pictures of which only two days previously he had felt so proud. Leaving the tape half wound in case at some point in the future he might need the ninety minutes that was still unused, Michael returned it to the underfloor storage area. Having banged the tacks back into place with the heel of his shoe, he then sat down cross-legged on the grimy, threadbare carpet for several minutes, staring listlessly down the hallway. The fact was he wouldn't really be able to feel truly satisfied with any one of the investigations until he had completed them all. Tysoe was behind him now. If he wanted to recover his equanimity, he had no choice but to get back to work.

★

Friday night at Gog did indeed restore Michael's mental composure. It was an ordinary, uneventful shift most of which he spent in the first-floor bar chatting to Nigel. Furthermore, just before leaving at two a.m., he got a message from Kent, asking him to come and see him before starting work the following day. It was welcome news: the investigation was on the move again.

Walking along the underground corridors towards Kent's office at six o'clock the next afternoon, Michael's thoughts turned to his conversation with Edwin the previous week. What had happened to the so-called favourites who had come before him and why would it be painful for him if Kent were one day to call in all his favours at once? Arriving at the office, Michael went to knock on the heavy door of the ante-room but stopped mid-movement, having spotted something about it that he hadn't noticed before. It was sound-proofed. Not only that, but in complete contrast to the ancient, cracked plaster in the interior of the ante-room, the workmanship was obviously very recent. Somehow, he knew that Kent had had the door installed himself rather than it being an existing feature of the office that he had moved into. But why? With a shake of the head, Michael stepped forward and knocked twice. His only hope of solving the many unanswered questions about Kent would be to start following him outside Gog. Hearing the gruff, guttural summons from inside his office, Michael gritted his teeth and went in. If he did start trailing Kent, he would need to exercise extreme care to ensure that he wasn't spotted: not only did Kent possess extraordinary animal cunning, but he also seemingly lived and breathed his criminal activities twenty-four hours a day.

Putting the subject of surveillance to the back of his mind, Michael walked across the ante-room. Kent had no doubt summoned him here to discuss his next piece of 'extra work' and whether it was Sipkiss, an incoming shipment of cocaine or something completely new, he had to keep himself focused. The moment that he went through the second door into the office itself, however, he could tell straightaway that this assumption had been totally incorrect. As always, Kent was sitting at his desk, but this time his jaw was set rigid and his eyes seemed to bore straight into Michael's head.

'You wanted to see me,' said Michael.

For several seconds Kent did not speak. When finally he broke the silence, his voice was low and chillingly calm.

314

'I'm disappointed in you, Mick.'

'Yeah …?'

'Very disappointed. I thought I knew you better.'

'What d'you mean?' replied Michael, feeling his vocal chords beginning to tense. Kent hadn't brought him here to offer him some more work. Something was wrong – drastically wrong.

'I don't like secrets, me.'

'I don't know what you're talkin' about.'

'Dangerous things – secrets. People think they can keep 'em to themselves, but they always come out in the end.'

'Is that so?' said Michael, swallowing hard.

'It is,' answered Kent, nodding his head slowly. 'Take my word for it.' Standing up from behind the desk, he stood facing Michael, kneading his right fist into the palm of his left hand. 'I was a regular good Samaritan wasn't I, eh? Put you in hospital when your face was all slashed to fuck; gave you a job here, bits of extra work on the side 'n' all.'

'And I was very grateful,' replied Michael, quickly.

'Grateful? Grateful?' laughed Kent, ironically. 'Not the word I'd use. Cos you've been workin' for someone else all along, haven't you, eh? Divided loyalties – that's what they call it …'

'I don't know what you're talking about …'

'Oh, Micky, don't take the piss, that'll just make me even more upset,' said Kent, the smile spreading across his face only serving to make him look all the more menacing. 'Just come clean. It'll be better for you in the end.'

Michael's mind raced furiously as he struggled to comprehend what he had just heard. Up until this moment, Kent had never shown himself to be even the slightest bit suspicious of Michael and, indeed, had never had any reason to be so. How could he have suddenly leapt from that position to having discovered that Michael Angel was not the man he appeared to be? Instinctively, Michael looked to his left at the door through which he had just walked to see if someone was hiding in the shadows of the anteroom: if Kent could have a criminal rival like Foss executed then he would surely have no qualms about arranging a similar fate for a traitor like Michael. But the ante-room was empty and the door to the corridor was open. If Michael turned and ran now, he could get away. It didn't make sense.

'Maybe I'll just wait for you to tell me,' he replied, finally. Whatever happened, he shouldn't volunteer any information – he had to make Kent speak first so that he could discover what he knew or what he simply suspected.

'Films. You make films, don't you – eh? On the quiet. But I know all about 'em, now …'

So saying, Kent took another step across the room towards Michael, dropping his arms loosely to his side. Michael felt faint. The unthinkable had happened: he had been uncovered. A wild assortment of memories and images flashed before his eyes: Tom and King standing in front of the flickering log-fire in the penthouse above the Tower; the group of toddlers playing in the park in Feltham; Foss lying in a pool of a blood in the ground-floor flat in Brooke Green. At no point in the past ten months had he once thought about what he would do if he was totally unmasked, and now that it had happened he had no idea what to say – no lines prepared for this most awful of eventualities. Instead his mind had simply seized up – paralyzed by a terrified feeling of dread.

'Er, yeah, well …' he mumbled.

'You still can't believe I've found out, can you?' continued Kent, suddenly taking a step sideways and resting his arm on one of the filing cabinets. Michael's head began to swim crazily. Kent was toying with him.

'No.'

'I've got my sources, y'know. Nothing goes on around 'ere without me finding out …'

'I know …' replied Michael, his voice seeming to speak without the conscious control of his mind.

'D'you get a get a buzz when you're doin' it, eh?' continued Kent with a leer. 'Does it give you a hard-on?'

'No.'

'Some people'd say you was sick.'

'Maybe.'

'So, what am I gonna do with you, eh? What would be, as they say, an appropriate response to this?'

'I dunno.'

At that moment, Kent suddenly turned and pulled open one of the drawers of the filing cabinet. As he put his hand inside, Michael looked on in horror, realizing too late that the opportunity for escape had gone: Kent wouldn't need an accomplice to hold him down if he was going to shoot him. Falling, rather than stepping backwards, Michael felt his shoulders rest against the back wall of the office. As though in slow motion, Kent's hand was coming out of the cabinet. Michael's whole body felt like lead. He couldn't move. Why hadn't he taken his chance to turn and run?

'There is only one answer, I suppose,' continued Kent, turning to face Michael, 'more money. I obviously ain't payin' you enough, am I?'

Instead of the pistol that he had been expecting, Kent was holding a bottle of whisky and two glasses.

'Well, don't fuckin' walk off, you dozy cunt, come on over and have a drink. It's not every day you get a pay rise.'

As though in a dream, Michael walked forward and took the glass. The whisky was wonderfully harsh, burning his throat and neck, and, although he had no idea what was going on, the mental paralysis that had gripped him seemed to have receded, at least in part.

'Thanks,' he croaked.

'Naughty films, eh? You dirty fucker,' laughed Kent, punching Michael on the shoulder. 'I dunno. No wonder you never chase the pussy in the club. You're fuckin' surrounded by it as soon as you get out of the place, aren't you?'

In a flash, Michael realized what had happened. The previous Wednesday, in the second-floor restaurant, whilst he had been talking to Edwin, Babs had been chatting to Will, the barman – and Will, of course, was another of Kent's favourites, having been one of the two bar staff that Kent had sent to the Mortlake Manor party.

'Yeah, well, it's a bit of fun, you know.'

'Bit of fun? Is that what you call it?' replied Kent, coming so close to Michael that he could smell the whisky on his breath. 'Are they good, anyway, your films?' he whispered.

'Yeah, they're all right.'

'Couldn't – like – get me one, could you?'

'Yeah, sure. Why not?'

'Something hardcore, all right?'

'Yeah, yeah, sure.'

'It's not for me. It's for some friends of mine. They have a little appreciation society, y'know? They meet up every now and then. I thought I might take it along and show 'em.'

'All right, I'll, er, bring you something in tomorrow,' replied Michael, a lurid image springing to mind of a darkened room filled with smoke and a group of men clustered around a flickering video screen.

With a grin, Kent walked away, closed the filing cabinet and sat down on the edge of his desk. Taking in a huge gulp of air, Michael let himself give in to the enormous feeling of relief that was rushing through him. It had been a desperately close call. If Kent's bizarre sense of irony had led him to string Michael along for just a few seconds more, he would have bolted and everything that he had worked for would have been lost. Nevertheless, it had been a lesson well-learned. Blinded by the success that he had achieved in using Babs as a means of visiting Gog mid-week, he had failed to appreciate the possible implications of her having spoken to Will without his being present.

'I'll have a word with Honeycunt, all right?' said Kent. 'Get your wages bumped up a bit. We've got to hold on to our best staff, haven't we? I'm sure that's what it says in all her manuals, anyway …'

'Right, thanks,' replied Michael.

'Go on, then, sling your hook,' said Kent, nodding in the direction of the door.

'Oh, OK, cheers,' said Michael, turning to leave. Just as he reached the door, however, Kent spoke again. As always, there was a second agenda – a wheel within the wheel.

'Oh, and Mick, one more thing …'

'What?' said Michael, turning around to face him again.

'Watch your back for the next few days, all right? Be careful what you do – where you go.'

'Why's that?'

Walking across to Michael again, Kent reached up and touched his cheek, gently running his forefinger along the line of his scar.

''Cos some old scores are being settled right at this very moment. Foss is out of the way now, but his men are still on the warpath, so keep your head down, you hear? I wouldn't want you to get in the way. But don't worry, it'll all be over in a week or two and then I've got plans for you, Micky. Serious plans.'

He arrived back at Balam Road just after three a.m. Having paid the taxi driver, he sprinted quietly but quickly up the concrete steps and opened the front door. Although the discussion with Kent had almost terrified him out of his wits, thereafter the Saturday night shift hadn't

318

been too tiring and, long before he had left at two o'clock, he had decided that on returning to the flat he would go straight back out again and begin the first of the night-time surveillances of Harper's house. Clipping the mobile phone into the top pocket of his jacket, he checked his watch. Twelve minutes past three. He would stay outside Harper's house until around nine a.m., grab some sleep during the day and then recommence surveillance the following night after returning from Gog. Sooner or later Harper and Angela had to go back to the Abaddon estate. If they hadn't been going there during daylight hours, then they must have been doing so at night.

Walking away from the flat towards his car, he thought he sensed a slight movement to his left. Turning, he looked around – it had come from the curtains of the ground floor flat. With a shake of his head, he carried on walking to the car. It may just have been his imagination – he hadn't seen the wizened old lady once since the day three weeks ago that she had glared at him through the window. However, even if she was spying on him, there was absolutely nothing he could do about it and besides, a radical new plan had been forming in his mind over the last two or three days for the final phase of the series, which, were he to adopt, would put him well beyond the ken of her evil eye.

Despite trying to force himself to stay awake, he dropped asleep at about five-thirty but awoke with a start just before six. Harper and Angela were coming out of the house. Snatching the micro-binoculars up off the passenger seat, Michael managed to get their faces in focus as they walked down the steps and along the street towards Harper's car. Starting the engine, but not putting on his lights, he drove to the other end of the slip-road and waited for them to emerge from the street opposite. They came out thirty seconds later. Following them down the Uxbridge Road, Michael tried to rein in his excitement. It was perfectly possible that they were not going to the Abaddon estate at all. Although Angela clearly spent a lot of time at Harper's house, she didn't actually live there, which presumably meant that she had a place of her own somewhere else; perhaps the location of her house was all that he was going to discover. Within two or three minutes, however, Michael became so convinced that the estate was their eventual destination that he decided to take an alternative route there, speeding down parallel side streets to ensure that they didn't spot him following them and that he got there before they did.

He parked behind a cluster of dilapidated garages on the very edge of the estate. For over two weeks he had been considering what he should do when Harper and Angela eventually did lead him there and had concluded that he dare not park his car on the estate itself – even if it meant losing sight of them: if he sat inside the car he would be a sitting duck and if he left it and walked away, even for a few minutes, he might return to find it vandalized. Slipping the binoculars into his pocket, he got out of the car and waited in the shadows next to the garages for their car to appear. A minute later, they pulled into the main approach road and then made their way down the central avenue that ran through the middle of the estate. Running as quietly as he could to the end of the line of terraced houses on the other side of the garages, Michael put his binoculars to his eyes to see that Harper had come to a halt three hundred yards away and that Angela was just getting out. Without any apparent exchange of words or sign of farewell, she then walked briskly off whilst Harper turned the car around and began driving back down the central avenue – straight towards Michael. Looking hastily left and right to make sure that no one was watching, he jumped over the railings of the house on his left and hid in the front garden. As soon as Harper had driven past him, Michael ran back to his vantage point just in time to see Angela disappear through a set of double doors. With a frown, he set off at a noiseless run down the central avenue keeping as much as he could to the shadows. It was just as he had feared: Angela had gone into one of the Abaddon estate's three tower blocks.

Coming to a halt opposite the main entrance, Michael found himself confronted with the perilous decision that he had long known he would have to make if Harper or Angela did indeed go into one of the high-rise blocks: whether to wait around outside and see if he could spot them, or whether to go in after them. At that moment, he suddenly became aware of movement directly behind him. To his left was a line of boarded-up tenements at the rear of which, on a patch of land that had presumably once been back gardens, a group of five or six youths were gathering in the pre-dawn gloom. Moving out of sight up against a wall, Michael strained his eyes to try and make out what was happening, but the street lights in front of the houses had been smashed and it was impossible to see exactly what they were doing. Seconds later, though, there was a bright flash and the sudden, unmistakable whooshing sound of petrol being ignited. It was then that Michael knew that his decision had effectively been made for him. Within moments the bonfire that they had started would be fully ablaze and, in the light that it cast across the estate, he could easily be seen. The youths were all in their mid teens and the tallest of them was at least twelve inches smaller than him, but if they came at him in a pack he would be finished within seconds – especially if they had knives. Slipping away as quietly as he could towards the main entrance, Michael looked momentarily upwards at the tower block and, in that exact instant, caught sight of Angela about eighty feet above him. She was just about to close the curtains of what looked liked a bathroom window, but had paused mid-movement on seeing the flames on the waste ground opposite. A second later, she disappeared behind the drapes – but it had been more than long enough for Michael to work out her location. She was on the fifth floor in the rear flat.

The entrance foyer stank of urine and was pitch black except for a single light above one of the two lifts. Despite the fact that the lift looked as though it was still operational, Michael made his way gingerly across towards the staircase, making sure not to disturb any of the rubbish strewn across the concrete floor: it was important that no one saw or heard him coming. Pausing for a minute in the darkness of the second-floor landing, Michael stood and listened carefully, straining to interpret the subtle concoction of sounds reaching his ears – at this point, it was the only information he had about the strange and menacing environment into which he had ventured. To his left he could hear a baby crying: there were obviously still some families remaining in the block, just as Tom had said. From an external window on his right came a sudden loud curse followed by a snatch of excited laughter: the youths who had started the bonfire were taunting and bating each other. Underlying these and a number of other tantalizingly indeterminate sounds, he could hear the steady, muffled thud of a drum beat. Someone seemingly close by was playing rap music, although given the peculiar acoustics of tower blocks Michael imagined that they could just as easily be twenty floors above him as in the flat directly opposite. Resuming his upwards ascent, he made his way through the third and fourth floors, stopping only once on discovering a landing where the lights had not been smashed. He was desperate for a cigarette but knew that he couldn't possibly light one up. Frowning, he continued on his way. He had never been anywhere like this in his life before. Even the hand-rails were covered with graffiti.

On arriving at the fifth floor, he went straight past the landing and up the next set of stairs to check out what was on the sixth – he wouldn't feel secure without knowing what was directly above him. Although the lights were not working on the sixth floor, he could see straightaway that at least two of the four flats were unoccupied by virtue of the fact that their front doors were missing. The landing was also strewn with rubbish – sticks of splintered furniture and a tattered single mattress. From this floor upwards he guessed that the squats and crack-houses began in earnest. Walking stealthily back down to the intermediate landing, he stooped into a crouch and surveyed the fifth floor. The flat on the left was Thompson's. The light was too poor to tell much about it, but it was good enough for him to make out two crucial features. Firstly, the door was not the original one that had been supplied with the property, but a stout hardboard panel with a thick reinforced lintel, and secondly there was no letter-box or aperture of any nature whatsoever. Taking a deep breath, Michael moved three more steps down the staircase and looked at the broad window that was situated at the end of the fifth-floor landing. This was the key feature that he had to check out on this first foray – it was from this window that he would be able to determine the nearest point from which he might mount a long-distance surveillance. Pausing for several seconds more to make sure that no one was coming, Michael went down the final half dozen steps to the landing and across to the window.

It couldn't have been worse. Not only was the window at least forty feet above any of the houses on the Abaddon, but it also faced in the opposite direction to the other two tower blocks. Beyond the estate itself, the nearest high point was the railway bridge a third of a mile away – but even that was of an insufficient elevation. Sliding back into the shadows, Michael swore below his breath. Even with a telephoto lens, mounting a long-distance surveillance of the front door of Thompson's flat was plainly impossible. Looking around the landing, he tried to work out if there was a spot in which he could place a remote device, but this thought was immediately driven from his mind by the sound of voices from the staircase. Two, or possibly three men, were coming down the stairs from one of the upper landings.

He reacted instantly. Without waiting for the voices to come any closer, he sprang over to the staircase and began to hurry back down to the ground floor. This first reconnaissance might well have yielded more problems than solutions, but if he was caught hanging around outside Thompson's flat he might never get the chance to carry out a second one. As he walked briskly away from the front entrance, two of the youths by the bonfire looked peremptorily in his direction, but he immediately slipped into the shadows and long before he reached the safety of the garages he was certain that he was not being followed. Walking around the car, he checked to see if there were any signs of damage, but clearly no one had interfered with it. Switching on the head lights, he did a three-point turn, swung the car around and, in under a minute, was back on the main road. It was over: he had carried out his first reconnaissance of the Abaddon estate and had survived.

Driving back to Balam Road, he reviewed his night's work. On the positive side, he had at last located Thompson's flat. This was not only the final major step in the investigation of the fraudsters, but also completely freed up the next five nights that he had mentally reserved for the surveillance of Harper's house: now that he had to complete the series by the end of September, time was of the absolute essence. On the negative side, there was no proximate location from which he could observe the front entrance of Thompson's flat. This left him with only two options: either to position a remote camera on the landing or attempt to mount an observation of some other part of the flat. The latter was definitely the safer way of acquiring the footage of Thompson that he was seeking. Although he hadn't had the opportunity to go around to the far side of the building, he knew by the design of the other tower blocks that the flat had two windows at the rear – one for the living room and one for the bedroom. As long as he could find a suitable position, he should be able to see right inside it with a telephoto lens.

The unexpected development that night had been Harper dropping Angela off at Thompson's flat and then leaving her there by herself. Fighting back an involuntary shiver, Michael wondered what Thompson might possibly want of her beyond his regular cut from the properties that she and Harper were renting: the last time that he had seen her, she had seemed utterly terrified of what might happen if she couldn't pay up. Harper had said that Craig was an old friend of Angela's, and, as a fervent anarchist, he himself clearly had no scruples about ripping off the state. Beyond that, however, it wasn't at all clear how they had got mixed up with the gang or the nature of their relationship with it. Somewhere along the line perhaps they had wanted out, but had found that Thompson wouldn't let them. With a shrug, Michael put the whole issue to the back of his mind – he would probably never find out: once he had acquired some footage of Thompson, the second of his documentaries would effectively be over.

The flat was cold, but he didn't bother to put on the heating or even take a shower. He was physically and mentally exhausted – what he needed now was bed. Hanging his jacket on the hook by the front door, he suddenly remembered the porn video that he had promised Kent: he had better put it out now so he didn't forget later. He groaned wearily as he knelt down and took up the carpet – his thighs and calf muscles were stiff from hours of standing outside Gog and the lack of proper sleep. Squinting in the gloom beneath the floorboards, he ran his fingers over the tapes one by one looking for the half-wound cassette that contained the first cut of the FFM movie that Heretic had sent him. It hadn't been properly edited yet and he had only had time to watch the first half, so he had no idea what Kent or his seedy friends would make of it. However, apart from the tape of Amanda and Gert – which he had no intention of showing anyone, let alone Kent – it was the only porn movie he had so it would have to do. Checking his watch and seeing that it was nearly half past seven, he walked into the bedroom and set the alarm clock for three pm. It had been a long, long night, although with a bit of luck he should be able to get six hours sleep before having to return to Gog.

'Can I come in?' asked Michael, putting his head around the door of the workshop.

'Sure,' replied Jim, looking up from his bench and raising a welcoming hand towards the chair opposite, 'take a seat.'

'Thanks.'

'So, what have you got for me today, then,' asked Jim, flashing Michael his customary asymmetrical grin, 'another jacket?'

'Not clothes this time,' answered Michael, 'hardware.'

'Oh, right, well, fire away, then,' said Jim, with obvious interest, leaning forward and resting his slim, bony wrists on edge of his work bench. 'I'm always happy to help out a good customer.'

'I need a wireless surveillance camera; the smaller the better, no visible antenna and with a transmission range of about a thousand yards.'

'Colour?'

'No, but it does need to be infrared for night vision; it has to have its own power supply as well.'

'OK.'

'Also, I want it to be camouflaged.'

'As what?'

'I'm not sure. What have you got?'

'Well, all sorts of things. Where're you planning on puttin' it?'

'In a stairwell. It's fairly dark in there, but anything shiny or sleek is still going to stand out. I mean, it can't have a polished aluminium housing or anything like that …'

Rubbing his hand over his smooth, unstubbled chin, Jim thought for several moments. This was perhaps the seventh or eighth time that Michael had visited his workshop and on each occasion the diminutive engineer had been wearing the same monastic-grey polyester shirt. He wondered if he owned any other clothes.

'I think I know what you want,' said Jim, finally, standing up and squeezing his way around to the other side of the workbench. 'Hang on, I'll be back in a tick.'

He returned a minute later and placed a small pyramid of black plastic on the bench in front of Michael.

'This is neat,' he said, retaking his seat. 'The lens is in the sloping section at the front but you can't actually see it – it's one way tinted glass. You say you wanna record from a stairwell, yeah?'

'Yeah.'

'It should be just right, then. On staircases and in lifts and places like that, people generally face forwards, right? And, of course, as you wanna record their faces, it means that their eyes and your camera are gonna be looking directly into each other – so unless you can disguise the camera really well, they'll spot it. Not this one, though.'

'Why not?'

'It goes on the floor with the lens facing upwards at forty-five degrees. It's no good for close-ups, but if that's not what you're after, it's perfect. It's almost invisible in a dark corner or somewhere like that, and if you put it inside something – like an empty coke can or what have you – you're laughing. Nobody'll ever see it.'

'What's the transmission range?'

'Not a thousand yards, I'm afraid – I mean, that is a long way – it'll do maybe seven hundred at a push. Depends on how many walls you've got between it and the receiver and how thick they are.'

'It looks good. What about the receiver?'

'Oh, we got dozens of different types. Are you gonna be waiting in a building or a car or what?'

'A car.'

'You just need a standard unit, then. It's no problem – I can rig you one up to run off your cigarette lighter.'

'Great,' said Michael, feeling reassured, as always, by the engineer's breezy air of confidence, 'which brings me to your next technical challenge.'

'Go on.'

'I've got to tail someone's car.'

'Right ...'

'But whatever happens I can't let them see me. I'll need to track them at a distance of a mile or a mile and a half – something like that.'

'Can you get at their car?'

'What d'you mean?'

'Can you attach a transmitter to it?'

'I should think so.'

'Piece of piss, then,' said Jim, sitting back in his chair with an air of finality.

'How?'

'GPS.'

'Which is what'

'Global positioning satellites.'

'What, those dashboard navigator things?'

'The very same. When you have a GPS system installed in your own car, the transmitter's fitted inside it so that the satellites track you – telling you where you are. All we have to do is take the transmitter out and attach it to the other guy's car – that way, the satellites'll tell you where he is. It's dead simple'

'I haven't got a GPS system in my car, though.'

'Dosen't matter. I can fit one for you, or I can do you one up in a briefcase – you can power it from your cigarette lighter again, or off the mains if you want to operate it from home.'

'Can you fit it with a recording function?'

'What, sound?'

'No, no – I mean what I'd really like to know is where the car goes not just when I'm looking at the screen, but when I'm not there: if I'm asleep or doing something else.'

'Hm,' said Jim, with a frown, 'it should be possible. Is it all right if I wire the receiver up to a computer, rather than to a GPS monitor? It'll be a bit bulkier to carry around.'

'No problem.'

'OK, well, what I'll do, then, is give you a motion sensitive transmitter, so it only comes on when the target car's moving; you can use that as a software trigger to get the computer to record for you. You'll need a big hard disk, mind you, but nowadays that isn't a problem.'

'Great. When can you get it all done for me, then?'

'Oh, I dunno. Two weeks?'

'No, too late. I really need it tomorrow.'

'Tomorrow!'

Without replying, Michael opened up the sports holdall at his feet. Shifting to one side the camera and the two telephoto lenses he had just bought in the second-hand section of the shop, he took out the heavy buff envelope underneath and placed it emphatically on the bench top. If Henry King wanted the series finished by September, then he was going to have to pay for it.

Drawing in his breath, Jim looked at the wads of notes spilling out of the open envelope and then smiled in compliant surrender.

'Well, like I say, always happy to help out a good customer ...'

Having picked up the equipment from Jim last thing on Tuesday afternoon, Michael went straight to Gog for an early evening drink. The staff were all glad to see him and paid no attention when he left at eight-thirty through the employees' exit; the underground car-park was deserted and it took less than thirty seconds to install the transmitter between the bumper and number plate of Kent's Saab. He got back to Balam Road just before ten o'clock and immediately set about acquainting himself with the computer. Jim had not only typed up a page of instructions but had also thoughtfully provided him with some extra security software so that the lap-top could only be accessed by means of two eight digit codes. As the GPS screen sprang to life, Michael shook his head in admiration. The street map was absolutely precise and, at maximum zoom, even displayed house numbers: with this system, he could track Kent's car anywhere in the world. Fixing himself a cup of coffee, Michael decided to sit and wait for the small green dot on the screen to move. Knowing Kent's nocturnal habits, it might well be three or four o'clock in the morning before he left Gog, but Michael knew that it was pointless his going to bed – he was too excited.

In the end, he only had to wait just over an hour. At a quarter past eleven, he went in to the living room from the kitchen where he had been ironing shirts to see a green line slowly snaking its way across the map on the screen. Sitting down at the living room table, he stared on in fascination. It was an amazing surveillance tool. Not only did the GPS system indicate the car's current location, but the computer also kept an exact record of the route that it had taken to get there. A little over ten minutes later, the dot came to a halt. Kent had crossed the Thames and had stopped at a tiny back street in Belgravia called West Halkin Mews. Leaning back in his chair, Michael tried to recall the district. From memory, it was mostly extravagant boutiques and ludicrously over-priced pied-à-terres. Taking a pad from the bookcase, Michael wrote down the address: the computer seemed to be functioning perfectly well, but he ought to keep a hard copy of the information just in case it subsequently crashed. Two minutes later, the dot began to move again, slowly making its way back to Gog. Kent had been at the address for less than three minutes. Who could he have visited for such a short space of time? Smiling, he went back into the kitchen – he had left the iron on and it was starting to smell. Home. Kent had gone home to pick some-thing up: something he needed or had forgotten. Kent lived in West Halkin Mews. Michael was sure of it.

He left the GPS system running continuously for the next two days, finally closing it down on Thursday lunch time and then neatly packing it away in the brief case that Jim had provided. During the forty-two hour surveillance session, Kent had made a total of seven journeys: six short hops between Halkin Mews and Gog and one two-hour return trip to the Essex countryside. Packing his newly acquired camera and two telephoto lenses in his sports holdall, Michael went down to his car and set off for Fyl Lane, Essex – the road which the GPS system had told him had been Kent's eventual destination. From Feltham he esti-mated it would take about two and a half hours to get there: he would thus have all of the afternoon and evening to see what he could discover before returning to Balam Road for a final all-night surveillance session until the small hours of Friday morning.

Fyl Lane was very narrow with barely enough room for two cars to pass each other, although the houses either side of it were simply enormous. Having driven up and down the lane twice, he decided that he would be too conspicuous parking there and so began to look for a suitable place nearby from which he could carry out his surveillance; he was glad he had brought the two telephoto lenses with him. At the top of the lane was a track leading to a small copse next to which was a parking space large enough for two cars; he guessed it was a local beauty-spot. Positioning his car in the middle of the two spaces so as to deter any sightseers from parking next to him, he looked around to make sure he was completely alone and then surveyed Fyl Lane through the smaller of the two telephoto lenses. There were twelve properties in all, each of which was at least fifty yards apart from its neighbours: this was the very top end of the luxury stockbroker belt – he doubted that any of the houses cost less than five million pounds. Before leaving, he had expanded the GPS map to its very largest magnification, and, although it had not provided numbers for the houses in Fyl Lane, he was almost certain by the position in which the green dot had come to rest that Kent had visited the third house from the end. Getting out of the car, Michael took out the larger of the lenses and balancing it on the roof began examining every visible inch of the house.

The first thing he noticed about the large, red-brick house was its security. With a shake of his head, he recalled Thompson's flat on the Abaddon estate. Each of the two properties, in their own way, was a formidable fortress. With Thompson's flat, getting to the front door was the big challenge, whereas with Fyl Lane that was where the problems really began. The house had at least three separate security systems: electronically operated gates, a CCTV system and a panoply of infra-red security lights. Even more unusually, it had a special type of bullet-proof glass fitted into the office area at the side of the house. Michael had only ever seen that particular type of glazing once before, in the home of a former Secretary of State for Northern Ireland. Each individual pane was about six inches long by four inches wide, but was an inch and a half thick, diffracting the light from inside the room as though through a fish-eye lens. However, despite all the security, the house was clearly a home.

There was a large, brown teddy-bear pressed up against one of the first floor windows, and, in the back garden, Michael could make out a well-used aluminium climbing frame.

As if to confirm this impression, just after twenty to five, a large four-wheel-drive Range Rover drew up in front of the gates. Quickly priming the camera, Michael began to take a succession of shots. The mother was in her late thirties, blonde, well-dressed and with a distinctive finishing-school poise indicative of an extremely exclusive education. The younger of the two children, a boy, looked about nine years old and was plainly in a hurry to get to the toilet. Michael wondered how far the family travelled to school everyday. The second child was a girl of about thirteen and, despite her pigtails and boater, exuded an unmistakable air of aloofness and disdain. Michael disliked her instantly on sight. The fourth occupant of the car was a man in his early thirties, but was obviously not the woman's husband – rather, he was as much of a feature of the house's security as any of the electronic devices with which it had been equipped.

The next five hours were uneventful, and, after darkness had completely fallen, Michael began to think about returning to Feltham. Through various windows in the house he had observed the children relaxing, having their tea, doing their homework and then, at last, preparing for bed. In all he had taken about forty photographs but had still not quite been able to determine the family's exact social status. The level of security definitely suggested government, but the wealth could only really have come from private enterprise. At ten past nine, Michael finally decided to leave. He would eat in the twenty-four-hour café on the Uxbridge Road and then set up the GPS system and let it run by itself overnight. Just as he had put his cameras away and zipped up his holdall, however, he noticed a car coming to a halt outside the house. Taking the camera and telephoto lens back out, he tore off the lens cap and hastily screwed the two pieces of equipment back together. Cursing his lack of foresight at not having purchased a proper night-lens he waited patiently for the driver to walk underneath one of the security lights so that he could get him in focus. One thing, at least, he now knew for certain: the owner was not a government official – his car was a brand new, super-charged Bentley. As the man got to the front door, Michael got a clear view of his face and fired off three shots. The light wasn't ideal, but he reckoned the prints should be sharp enough to make out the man's face.

Driving back to Feltham, Michael pondered Kent's connection with the house in Fyl Lane. Never having seen Sir Alain Ellis, he couldn't be sure that he had been the driver of the car, but it seemed highly likely. What he couldn't understand, however, was why Ellis would permit a man like Kent to get anywhere near his family – if they had to meet, why didn't they do so in central London? Concluding that he really needed to see a picture of Ellis, he resolved to stop off at a photographic library the following afternoon before going on to Gog. Parking his car on the waste ground at the back of Balam Road, Michael checked his watch: ten-thirty five – it would be interesting to see when he got back inside the flat and switched on the GPS system whether Kent was now at the club. Reaching the top of the stairs, Michael put down the holdall and then took out his door key. As he went to put it in the lock, however, his heart missed a beat: the door was already open.

Leaving the holdall on the step, Michael went through the door. Switching on the lights, he rested his weight on his back foot, in case the intruder was still in there and was just about to charge at him. The hall, however, was deserted. Walking quietly forward, Michael went over to the far end of the hallway and then slowly inclined his head first left and then right: the kitchen and the bedroom were both empty – if the intruder was still here, he had to be in the living room. Balling his fists Michael ran through the door, ready for the fray, but the living room, too, was deserted. The intruder had gone. With a grimace, he went back to the front door, picked up his holdall and then checked the front door locks. They had both been jemmied. Locking the door with the bolt at the bottom, he began walking around the flat again, checking each room in turn, but nothing appeared to have been disturbed. Suddenly, the most awful thought occurred to him and, dashing back out into the hall he ripped up the carpet. The videos were still there – every single one of them. Going back in to the dining room, he looked around once more: as far as he could recall, everything was in exactly the same place as he had left it that morning. Frowning, he went back into the bedroom to check in there once again. And then, at last, he realized what was missing. The small black briefcase that he had left in the space between the bottom of the bed and the cupboard was no longer there.

The GPS system had been taken.

Chapter 11

There were plenty of suspects, but just as many arguments to discount each of them. Kent was probably top of the list, having been the object of the GPS surveillance. But even if he had found the transmitter behind his number plate, how had he been able to trace it back to Michael so quickly? And besides, from his point of view, the surveillance equipment was scarcely the issue: what possible benefit could he obtain by taking it but leaving Michael free? Foss's gang was next – or rather, those members that were still alive. Kent had gone out of his way to tell Michael to keep his head down, so the feud had obviously not yet fully been settled. But, once again, of what benefit would the GPS system have been to them? Having located his flat and broken into it, surely they would have been much more likely to have waited in the dark and then tried to attack him. A random act of burglary was another possibility. Undermining that theory, however, was the fact that in an area like Feltham, housebreakers were almost exclusively drug addicts looking for cash to feed their habits, yet no money had been taken and moreover, from the moment that Michael had entered the flat, he had had the distinct feeling that the intruder had been after something specific. Another possible suspect was the old lady downstairs. When this thought had first occurred to Michael he had dismissed it straightaway. Later, though, when he recalled the fact that he had sensed movement at her window the previous Saturday at three o'clock in the morning, he began seriously to consider the possibility that the old crone's voyeuristic compulsions could no longer be satisfied merely by observing him at a distance. Thinking back even further to the day that he had first rented out the flat, he remembered that the estate agent had skated over the subject of the old lady downstairs all too quickly.

Michael spent all of Friday morning and most of the afternoon arranging for the front door and lintel to be replaced. When the emergency repair workmen finally left at four-thirty, he went into the bedroom and packed his clothes for the night's work at Gog. He walked to the train station with a mounting sense of foreboding: facing Kent was going to be a nerve-racking experience. In actual fact, however, Michael saw no sign of him whatsoever that night and, as his shift neared its end and no summons was forthcoming, he began to wonder whether Kent was the number one suspect after all. To confirm this, as soon as the chance presented itself, he resolved to go back to the car park and check if the transmitter was still wedged behind the bumper of the Saab. Returning to Balam Road at three a.m., he walked cautiously up the stairs, mentally preparing himself for the sight of the door having been breached once more, but it was just as he had left it that afternoon. Whoever had carried out the burglary had obviously had no reason to come back – or at least, not yet.

Fixing himself a cup of coffee, Michael stood at the kitchen window and stared unseeing at the houses at the rear of the flat. He had come to two conclusions. Firstly, following the theft of the GPS system, he had decided to adopt the radical new plan that he had been formulating over the last few weeks for the final phase of the series. It was, however, such a departure from the way in which he had conducted the investigations so far that he really needed to talk it through with Tom; next week he would arrange a meeting at the safe house. Secondly, he was now certain that he would be unable to work out who had broken into his flat until either they made another move, or until he uncovered new information. Accordingly, given the time constraints under which he was operating, he couldn't afford to let the break-in hold him up any further. Walking into the bedroom, he opened up the wardrobe and took out his micro-binoculars and the remote surveillance equipment that he had purchased from Jim. It was time for his second night-time foray into the Abaddon estate.

He decided to park behind the garages again. In the intervening week someone had dumped a washing-machine there and, as he pulled in off the road, he had to swerve sharply to avoid it. Slipping the micro-binoculars into one pocket and the small, pyramidal transmitter into the other, he locked the car and, taking a deep breath, made his way on to the estate. As he cautiously slipped between the shadows of the central avenue, he was alarmed to discover that he felt even more uneasy than he had the previous Saturday: there had been no wind on that occasion, but tonight it was blowing strongly and he knew that his hearing would not pick up the sound of someone approaching until they were right on top of him. Reaching the wall opposite the entrance to the tower block in which Thompson lived, he waited for over a minute, trying to pick out signs of movement on the patch of waste ground where he had seen the youths lighting the bonfire, but there was clearly no one around. Continuing on towards the second tower block, he hid underneath an elevated walkway and, as the moon came out from behind a cloud, looked slowly around – he was now right in the very centre of the Abaddon estate. To his far left, on the extreme edge of the estate, was a railway embankment. Taking out his binoculars, he tried to see if there was a suitable position on it from which he might be able to film Thompson's flat, but the only spot that afforded a clear view of the tower block was not perpendicular to the building: unless Thompson stood right up against his window, he wouldn't be able to see him. Frowning, Michael carefully scanned the area once again. The situation was just as bad as he had feared: short of renting one of the tenements at the back of the estate – which would be both risky and time-consuming – filming the rear of Thompson's flat was no more possible than filming the front.

Which meant he had only one option left.

Again he went first of all to the sixth floor to check that there was no one above him. The mattress and bits of furniture appeared to have been unmoved – he supposed that the entire floor was indeed unin-habited. Returning once more to the fifth, he ducked quickly under-neath the staircase and looked back across the landing towards the front door of Thompson's flat. Not only was there a direct, uninterrupted view of the door, but the stairwell itself was so murky that it would be very difficult to spot the transmitter even if you knew it was there. As he stooped down on both knees, Michael ran his fingertips over the concrete floor – it was both flat and dry. He was in business. Taking the transmitter out of his pocket, he slipped off the back cover, pressed the activation switch and then positioned it squarely next to the brick stair-case. Although the signal would have to pass through at least two walls, the garages where he intended to wait with the receiver unit were only five hundred yards away: he should be well within range. Crouching stock still for a further thirty seconds, Michael strained his ears for the sound of anyone moving; hearing nothing, he then made his way back to the ground floor. Striding quickly across the foyer towards the front doors, he shook his right fist in triumph. He had done it. The battery life of the transmitter was at least fourteen days. Thompson was bound to come out during that time and, the moment he did so, his second *Criminal Britain* investigation would effectively be over.

Stepping out into the night, Michael turned to his left to make his way back to the garages and it was at that moment that three men suddenly came into view. They were walking shoulder to shoulder towards the entrance of the tower block, but the instant that they saw him they immediately fanned out. As he heard the sound of the door closing behind him, he knew that there was no escape – he had no choice but to confront the trio of heavily-built West Indians now blocking his path.

'What you doin' here, rufyaan?' growled the first man.

Michael let his hands fall loosely by his side so as not to appear to be adopting an overtly aggressive posture. For several seconds he stood in complete silence, staring apprehensively at the men and listening to the wind whistling across the estate. How was he to respond? What was he to say to these three dark angels of the night?

'You deaf, maan? Huh?' said the first man, taking a step forwards. Around his neck Michael could see that he was wearing a thick, solid-gold chain. Opening and closing his eyes, Michael racked his brains for a credible reply. It looked as though the very worst thing imaginable had happened: he had stumbled right into the path of three Yardies from one of the crack-houses on the upper floors of the tower block.

'He am foist, methinks,' said the second man, with apparent amusement – his shining white teeth flashing in the darkness.

'Maybe foist. Maybe Abram man,' said the third, suspiciously.

Swallowing hard, Michael forced himself to resist the temptation to take a step backwards. This was their turf, their language, their world – but he couldn't afford to show that he was intimidated, not even for a second.

'I'm looking for someone,' he said. His voice was firm and loud. Inside, his guts were churning, but at least he sounded confident.

'Your sistah?' volunteered the second man. 'She am still back there where we left her, maan – up against yon wall.'

The second and third men began to laugh out loud, but the first had clearly already lost patience. Reaching inside his leather jacket he pulled out a huge silver handgun, took two steps forward, and, with his free hand, grabbed the front of Michael's shirt and pushed him back against the doors. The man was incredibly strong – like a heavy-weight boxer. Michael felt his self-assurance begin rapidly to drain away.

'What you doin' here, rufyaan?' he barked.

The barrel was right between Michael's eyes and seemed entirely to block out his vision. Sensing, rather than seeing the other two men come up behind the first man, Michael heard one of them grudgingly remark.

'This am the danger zone, but he think we am cony.'

'My son,' said Michael, hearing the fear and desperation in his voice. 'I'm looking for my son.'

'Wherefore your saan be here?' asked the first man, narrowing his eyes.

'He ... he ... takes drugs. He hangs around these places.'

'You play me faalse,' said the first man, languidly lowering the barrel of the gun so that it rested on Michael's top lip. Below the man's left eye, Michael could make out a three-inch long scar and, in that instant, realized that it was essential to keep his own face turned to the side: if they saw his scar, his story as a concerned father would be instantly blown apart.

'It's the truth,' whispered Michael. 'Jake. His name's Jake ...'

'No,' replied the first man, shaking his head gently. 'No saan. No Jake. You flip the script. You am the cunning maan.'

'It's true. It's true.'

'You look for saan – three, four in the mornin'?' he continued, doubt-fully.

'Yes. Yes. I look for him at night especially ... it's, it's when he goes out to get them – his drugs ...'

Without removing the gun, the first man inclined his eyes to the man on his left who shrugged in response, seemingly already bored by the interrogation. Suddenly releasing Michael, the first man slipped the weapon back inside his leather jacket and took a step backwards.

'You come here again, rufyaan,' he said, languorously pointing a finger at Michael's chest, 'you come one more time to this ken – it am your termination.'

336

Lowering his head so as not to make eye contact, Michael slunk off to his left and moved quickly away into the night. By the time he plucked up the courage to look back, some thirty yards further on, the three men had disappeared inside the tower block. Taking out his cigarettes, he realized his hands were shaking: if they had seen his scar, or checked in his pocket and found the micro-binoculars, he might well have been dead by now. Back at the garages, he walked quickly towards his car, the stainless-steel drum of the abandoned washing machine observing him in the darkness like a giant, dismembered eye. Opening up the boot, he took out the receiver unit, put it on the front seat and then went over to the garages again to make sure no one was watching. Cautiously driving to the very edge of the slip road, he looked around once more and, with still shaking hands, plugged the receiver into the cigarette lighter socket. It was then that he realized the full extent of the catastrophe that had overtaken him that night.

The screen was blank – there was no signal from the transmitter.

Getting on the train to Gog the following afternoon, Michael closed his eyes, leant his head back against the head-rest and tried to navigate a path through the constellation of permutations that filled his mind to overflowing. Kent, Thompson, Foss's gang, the Yardies, the person who had stolen the GPS system – it seemed as though whatever he did next, he would be bound to antagonize one of them; the problem was that he was making too many enemies too fast. Showing his ticket to the guard, Michael ran his hand over his face and stared out of the train window at the abandoned factories and rows of disused warehouses on the outskirts of Feltham. He was deathly tired. He had hardly slept at all after returning to the flat, and, during one of the many periods of waking, had come to the conclusion that he could no longer afford to dismiss the notion of a worst case scenario in which he might be forced to cut and run. If things simply did get too hot, escape might one day be his only option. Similarly, if he did want to emerge from the series alive, he would also have to lower his expectations. In the case of the fraudsters, this might mean having to abandon altogether the idea of getting any footage of Thompson or even so much as a simple photograph. He had the video film of Craig as well as a tape recording of their phone conversation, and literally hours of footage of Harper and Angela; in reality, he had already achieved his principal objective of characterising the

337

gang and, much as he had long believed that filming Thompson would be the jewel in the crown of the investigation, if it meant getting his head blown off by the Yardies he had met the previous night, he might be forced to sacrifice it.

The Saturday night punters queuing up outside the front entrance were in particularly high spirits and he had great difficulty concentrating on his work. On a number of occasions, Nigel looked across at him to make sure that he had checked out a particular clubber jostling to get in, but each time Michael failed to respond until he actually called out to him. Finally unable to control his irritation, Nigel pointedly asked him if he was ill. In response, Michael shook his head and grunted that he was OK: in fact, he was wandering vainly through a succession of past mental reconstructions and imaginary future scenarios. One minute he was back on the fifth-floor landing, reliving each step in the activation procedure – what had he done wrong, why hadn't the transmitter worked? The next, he was picturing himself standing in front of Kent, watching him take the tiny GPS bug out of his top pocket and drop it on the cracked varnished surface of his old, battered desk.

A summons to Kent's underground lair did indeed come that night. By the time that he made his way along the underground corridors at five to two – overtired and drained of all energy – Michael had already prepared himself for the real possibility that he had been unmasked. Thinking it through, the security at Fyl Lane had probably been his downfall. During his surveillance of the property he had thought all along that it had been he who had been observing the inmates of the house – in fact, it must have been the other way around. He had remained up on the knoll for over five hours, but their own long-range cameras had probably picked him up within minutes. A succession of telephone calls must have quickly followed, the last of them being from Ellis himself to Kent. He could almost hear Kent's embittered, disbelieving response: 'Six foot tall; well-built; scar on his left cheek? Yeah, I know who that is. Leave me to deal with him.' Knocking on the door, Michael waited for Kent to call him through. Once again, just as on the occasion when he had confronted the Yardies outside the tower block, Jake's face sprang to mind. Not just for his own sake, but for that of his family, he had to make sure he got out of this final encounter alive.

'You wanted to see me?'

Kent was sitting at his desk and although he scowled at Michael as he

338

entered the room, it was clearly a look of irritation rather than one of furious betrayal; for the moment, at least, Michael's cover appeared still to be intact.

'Yeah,' he grunted. 'I need you on Tuesday at the warehouse.'

'That Carl and Ernst place?'

'That's right. I've got a very important shipment comin' in. I want you to watch my back.'

'What time?'

'Two. Can you be there?'

'Sure.'

'Don't fuck up, eh?' said Kent, his expression remaining broodingly hostile.

'I said I'll be there,' insisted Michael: his cover was indeed still intact, but Kent was obviously annoyed with him about something.

'I hope so. I want you to keep your mind on the job, Mick. I don't like part-timers and I don't like being made to look a wanker in front of people who are important to me.'

'What d'you mean?'

'This,' said Kent, opening up the drawer and taking out a video cassette. As he tossed it on to the surface of his desk, Michael recognized it as the FFM movie that he had given him the previous week.

'What about it?'

'I said my friends were into porn – not DIY.'

'I don't know what you mean,' replied Michael, blankly.

'It's a video of a couple of blokes fixing a roof for Christ's sake. I showed it to my friends on Saturday. They're important people, Mick. I kept on fast-forwarding the tape but the only cunt on display was me. So, from now on, you make sure you keep your mind on the job, all right? I fuckin' pay you well enough for it.'

Suddenly, Michael realized what had happened. He must have got the FFM movie and the video of Naz and Tysoe working on Mr Herbert's bungalow mixed up. Right from day one, he had scrupulously rewound all the surveillance tapes before returning them to storage. Consequently, as he had flicked through the cassettes in search of the FFM movie that he hadn't had time to watch all the way through, he had simply been looking for a half-wound tape. However, in those final, few exhausted moments before collapsing into bed, he had completely forgotten the other cassette he had purposefully left half-wound in case he needed to download any footage before he could buy some more blank tapes.

'I'm sorry about that,' he blurted, attempting to recover as quickly as he could. 'I must have got it mixed up with some of my home movie stuff. I used to work on the buildings back up north, you see, and ...'

'Just get out of here, Mick,' interrupted Kent, gruffly. 'I got work to do. And don't fuckin' screw up on Tuesday, all right?'

It had been Tysoe who had stolen the GPS system – Michael was ninety-nine per cent certain of it. Because he had already completed the Tysoe documentary, he hadn't thought to include the builder amongst the list of possible suspects, but, as he sat in the back of the mini-cab on the way home to Feltham and ran through the events of the previous month picturing them from Tysoe's point of view, he concluded that it had to have been him. Firstly, Michael had called to say that he was sick and wouldn't be available for work for at least a couple of months. Two weeks later, Naz had abruptly stopped working for him altogether. In the meantime, Mrs Tysoe must have told her husband about the shifty-looking man in the red BMW whom she had seen outside their house. By themselves, these events would probably only have provoked Tysoe's suspicions. If, however, he had returned to see the two pensioners on the pretence of coming back to finish the job but in fact to swindle them out of more money, and if they had mentioned the visit that they had had from the tall man with cropped hair from the Trading Standards Authority, he would have realized that Michael Angel was not the person he had seemed. The following day, he would call the pensioners to confirm, although the more he thought about it, the more it seemed to be the only conceivable explanation. The GPS receiver system was a personal computer. If Tysoe suspected Michael of being a reporter or an investigator of some sort, on breaking-in, he would have no doubt attempted to locate and remove the material that Michael had amassed on him and, as all the videos and photographic prints were under the floor boards and none of the cameras in his bedroom contained film, the only possible remaining storage medium was his lap-top.

As the taxi pulled up on the corner of Balam Road, Michael felt much of the pressure of the last few weeks fall from his shoulders. Having paid the driver, he walked leisurely towards the grass verge in front of his flat. The escapade with the videos may well have once again

340

brought him within a fraction of a second of discovery by Kent, but, nonetheless, in two days time, he would be meeting him outside Carl and Ernst to check the shipment that he was at such pains to bring in to the country. If it was drugs, it meant that both the second and third documentaries were now nearing completion. Smiling to himself at this astonishing reversal in his fortunes, he stopped beside one of the trees on the verge and lit a cigarette. When he got in, he would have a celebratory night-cap and then crash out – he felt as though he could sleep for a month. No sooner had this thought occurred to him, though, than once again he was right back on his guard. At the top of the concrete steps leading up to the flat, in the small alcove by the front door, someone was moving around. Hiding behind the tree he tried to figure out who it was. Checking his watch he could see that it was now three-fifteen. Would Tysoe be out this late? And, if he was, wouldn't he have just broken in again? Why would he hang around on the step outside? Deciding to risk another quick look, Michael peered once more towards the front door and then realized who it was: just like him, the person outside the flat was also smoking a cigarette.

'What the hell are you doin' here?' said Michael, leaning over and putting his key in the lock.

'What d'you think I'm doing?' replied Babs, mockingly. 'Waiting for you, of course.'

'It's three o'clock in the morning.'

'So?' she countered.

'How long have you been here?'

'Not long,' came the chirpy reply. 'About half an hour.'

'How did you find out where I live?' asked Michael, opening the door.

'I rang Will – the barman. He got your address for me,' she replied, casually flicking on the light switch and disappearing into the hall. 'Come on, I'll make us a cup of coffee.'

Too tired out to object, Michael closed the front door and walked down the hallway. In the kitchen, Babs had already located the cups and was putting the kettle on. Going into the lounge, Michael switched on the light and, with a weary smile, looked around the sparsely furnished room. Ironically, he almost felt sorry for Tysoe – after his own lack of success on the Abaddon estate he knew all too well the frustrations that came with an abortive break-in. Tysoe must have been livid when he had got the computer home and found it protected by two encrypted access codes.

'Sugar?' enquired Babs, as Michael entered the kitchen.

'No, thanks,' he replied, sitting wearily down opposite her at the table.

'So, how are you?' she asked, smiling and putting the mug of coffee to her lips.

'I'm fine. Actually, no I'm not – I'm exhausted. The last forty-eight hours have been just unbelievable.'

'Really? Ooh, tell me all about it.'

'Babs, look. I don't want to appear inhospitable or anything, but let me call you a cab to take you home, I can't …'

'Don't!' she interrupted, raising both hands in a sudden and vigorous gesture of rebuttal. 'Don't, please.'

'Babs …'

'Don't!' she cried. 'Just listen to me first. Please!'

'OK,' said Michael, hearing a real note of distress in her voice. For several seconds she sat in silence, her facial muscles seemingly poised for speech but yet somehow unable quite to proceed with it. Finally, brushing her long wavy hair back from the side of her face, she regained her composure and began to talk.

'Men ask me out a fair bit, I suppose. Most times, though, when they take me to dinner, they just ramble on about themselves all night and then it's straight back to their place. I guess that's mainly my fault for the sort of men I choose. But you – you were different. You …,' her brow furled as she struggled to find the right words, 'you wanted to know about me. You asked me all about myself and what I do. And then, when you took me home, you didn't try and come in or anything – even when I offered. You were polite – a gentleman. You didn't treat me like a whore. Not many men have behaved that way towards me and I was, well, really grateful to be shown that sort of respect – just for once, y'know?'

Staring at her pretty, vulnerable face – stripped of the masks of sarcasm and coquetry with which she habitually defended herself – Michael remembered the East European spy's dire warning about the uniquely soul-destroying power of betrayal. Three or four times since embarking upon *Criminal Britain*, he had had occasion to appreciate the profundity of those words and here again tonight, he knew he was facing one more manifestation of their dreadful truth. He had used Babs for his own ends. In so doing, he had touched upon a deeply felt sensitivity – a tragedy, perhaps – that lay at the very heart of her existence. How could he even think of turning her away now, when she had come to him for help?

'OK,' he conceded. 'You can stay, but I wasn't joking, y'know – I am absolutely exhausted. I don't think I'll be much use to you between the sheets.'

A playful smile reappearing about her lips, Babs leant slightly forward and, curling a lock of hair around her forefinger, purred in response.

'Oh, we'll see about that …'

The pensioners had been away for a long weekend and Michael wasn't able to confirm that Tysoe had indeed been back to see them until just before he left for Carl and Ernst on Tuesday morning. Getting into the car to begin the two-hour drive to the warehouse, he pondered the question of what the rogue builder might do next. On consideration, his attempting another break-in seemed fairly unlikely: with the element of surprise on his side, Tysoe might reasonably have been expected to discover all the incriminating material that Michael had on him the first time around, but not on a second occasion. A physical confrontation appeared equally improbable: Michael was a lot bigger and taller than him and anyway he worked by means of deceit, not violence. On the other hand, Michael doubted that Tysoe was simply going to disappear and forget all about it. On balance, he calculated that his next move would be to attempt to initiate some sort of dialogue – perhaps to try and buy Michael off or at least to discover more about his intentions. Arriving at Apex Corner and accelerating up the slip road on to the motorway, Michael reflected once more on the importance of Tom accepting his new plan; if it came off, the next time that Tysoe would see him would either be on television or in court.

He arrived at Carl and Ernst at twenty to two, positioning his car in a spot that would allow him to film Kent as he pulled into the car park: if a large consignment of drugs had indeed arrived at the warehouse, he wanted some footage of the Saab coming through the front gates. Just after ten to two, Michael spotted movement inside the reception. Mr McDonald, the warehouse manager, and his deputy, Malcolm Grey, were waiting for Kent to turn up; he had obviously given them such a rocket on the first inspection that they were anxious to ensure that nothing went wrong second time around. Five minutes later, Kent arrived. Waiting in front of his BMW, Michael filmed him getting out of the Saab and striding purposefully towards the reception. In his dark full-length overcoat and with a twisted curl of satisfaction about his lips, Kent had the air of a commissar marching off to supervise a firing squad. A verbal greeting felt inappropriate somehow, and so he simply nodded and fell into step with Kent as he strode unblinking towards the reception.

'Good afternoon Mr Kent, Mr Angel!' exclaimed McDonald, attempting warmth but conveying only anxiety.

'Mr McDonald,' replied Kent, curtly.

'Good to see you again and let me say first of all how much we appreciate your giving us advance notice of your visit.'

'No problem,' answered Kent.

'Excellent. So, if you'd like to come through to my office, perhaps we can go through the list of actions from the last inspection. You'll be pleased to hear that ...'

'No,' interrupted Kent, 'don't need to see those.' Slipping his hand inside his coat, he instead pulled out a dog-eared slip of pink-coloured paper. 'This is what we're interested in,' he continued. 'This shipment – we'd like to take a look at it.'

Blinking nervously, McDonald took the paper from Kent and passed it hesitantly to Grey: obviously Kent was not going to give them the luxury of reviewing the deficiencies he had identified last time, or even of carrying out the same type of inspection. From where Michael was standing he could see that the paper was a copy of an Air Way Bill. Having checked the number, Grey quickly moved across the reception to a computer terminal and typed it in.

'Yeah, we've got it,' said Grey. 'A single container. Came in two days ago. Warehouse D, area 3.'

'That's a secure bonded warehouse, right?' asked Kent.

'Yeah, that's right,' confirmed Grey, 'just like you requested.'

'Good, good,' said McDonald, clearly reassured by his deputy's response, 'so, no problem, then – we can go across there now if you like.'

'No,' retorted Kent.

McDonald visibly flinched: it was Kent's second straight negative within the space of ten seconds.

'Sorry?' he asked.

'This is an unaccompanied inspection – I think you'll find we're allowed to do them under the terms of contract. Just give us the keys to the storage area concerned and we'll go and have a look for ourselves.'

McDonald looked a little uncomfortable at the prospect of not being able to keep an eye on what Kent and Michael might discover, but Grey seemed genuinely perplexed by the request.

'There isn't much to see in D3,' he said, with a frown, 'it's just a container store, that's all.'

'So I guess we'll just have to make sure our inspection's all the more thorough, then, won't we?' replied Kent.

'Just get Mr Kent the keys, Malcolm,' said McDonald stiffly, glaring at Grey for having unnecessarily provoked Kent.

'OK …' murmured Grey, shrugging his shoulders and then leaning across to unhook a set of keys from a board on the wall.

Storage area D3 was indeed nothing more than four concrete walls and a corrugated iron roof punctuated by two small skylights. The moment that Kent had locked the door behind them, however, his face seemed to glow with excitement. Walking straight over to one of the grey, unmarked forty foot containers, he took a second set of keys from his inside pocket and began to undo the two giant padlocks.

'Keep your ears pinned back, Mick,' he hissed, straining to lever the first padlock out of its clasp, 'I don't want those two wankers creeping up on us.'

Not wanting directly to ask about the contents of the container and imagining that anyway he would find out soon enough, Michael stood with his back against the door: Kent was just over ten yards away – despite the relatively low level of light, the pictures should be fairly sharp. All he needed now was the dialogue to go with them.

'If this is a bonded warehouse,' he called out, 'aren't the containers supposed to stay sealed?'

'You're right, they should. And I don't make a habit of opening 'em 'cos it could get us into trouble – but this one's special. There's a little somethin' in 'ere for me.'

'So you wouldn't trust those two to get it out for you, then?' prompted Michael.

'What, McDonald and his side-kick?'

'Yeah.'

'Nah – they're not on the payroll, they're legit,' replied Kent. 'Mind you, that's exactly why we need 'em …'

Having removed the second padlock, Kent opened up the container, the doors emitting a metallic screech as he drew them apart. Inside, Michael could see there were several rows of wooden crates packed tightly together in a solid block; between the crates and the roof of the container was a gap of about five feet – just large enough for a person to walk around.

'Pass us a crowbar,' called Kent, taking a step backwards and then jumping panther-like up on to the crates. Taking a crow bar from a rack on the wall, Michael went over to join Kent who was now examining the Air Way Bill paperwork with a flashlight. The crates were all made of newly cut wood and the interior of the container smelled fragrantly of pine.

'Come on up and give us a hand, will you?' said Kent, turning the flashlight on to broad beam and suspending it from a hook on the ceiling. 'The packing cases are numbered. 666 is the one I want.'

Jumping up to join him, Michael stooped his head and began checking the numbers stencilled on each crate.

'This is it,' he called out, finding the case labelled 666 up against the right flank of the container.

'You hold the light,' said Kent, removing it from the ceiling and switching it back to narrow beam, 'I'll open it up.'

Shining the flashlight over Kent's shoulder, Michael watched as he quickly jemmied open the lid and pulled it back to reveal the layer of polystyrene packing beneath. Plunging his hand into the pink foam chippings, Kent then pulled out two pieces of black metal – each wrapped inside a polythene bag: obviously the drugs had been stashed inside a consignment of machine parts.

'There we go,' he commented, happily, putting the two pieces of metal to one side on top of the adjacent crate, 'all safe and sound.'

To Michael's surprise, Kent then proceeded to nail the lid of the crate back down, collect up the two metal parts and make his way back out of the container. Switching off the flash light, Michael followed afterwards. Within two minutes Kent had completely resealed the container such that it looked exactly the same as when they had arrived.

'Go and check the corridor,' ordered Kent, with a grin, 'I want to try out my new toy, but things might get a bit noisy.'

Walking over to the entrance door, Michael looked through the inspection panel to the corridor outside – it was completely empty.

Turning around, he could see that Kent had moved across to a work bench by the far wall and was starting to unpack the two metal parts. Frowning, he went over to join him: whatever the pieces of metal might be, they didn't appear remotely connected with drugs.

'What are those things, then?' he asked.

'Not things – thing,' replied Kent, carefully folding up the two polythene bags and slipping them inside his coat pocket, 'they fit together to make a stun baton.'

'A stun baton?'

'That's right. But not just any old stun baton – this one's special.'

'Yeah?'

'Yeah,' confirmed Kent, his voice a mixture of excitement and admiration. 'The first thing is the power. Most batons run off batteries, but this one's electromechanical. There's a ratchet built into the handle – here; you twist it a couple of times until it builds up a current. Like this. I'll show you ...'

Slotting the probe into the handle – which Michael now realized was in fact made of lacquered wood – Kent turned it until it gave a click. Once assembled the baton was quite small – only about seven inches in length – and looked totally inoffensive, resembling a set of curling tongs. Taking hold of the hand grip, Kent then twisted several times; the baton made very little noise and there was no apparent indication as to whether it was charged up or not.

'That's it,' explained Kent, 'simple as that.'

'What d'you use it ...'

Before Michael could finish the question, Kent suddenly flicked his wrist to the left and discharged the baton on to Michael's arm. Michael screamed in agony – the pain was excruciating: an intense feeling of burning at the point of contact and a jolt of energy that seemed to transmit itself through his entire nervous system.

'Fuckin' hell!' exclaimed Michael, placing his hand over his forearm and rubbing it furiously, 'what did you do that for?'

'It works, then?' chuckled Kent.

'Jesus, you're dead right it does!'

'Just wait a few seconds – just wait,' said Kent, 'you'll be surprised how quickly the pain goes away.'

Rubbing his arm several times more, Michael did indeed find that the pain soon died away. Seemingly oblivious to Michael's discomfort, Kent leant back against the work bench and continued to enthuse about the stun baton's technical features in a manner that somehow chillingly reminded Michael of Jim.

'And that, of course, is the other special feature of this design – low power. If I'd've done that to you with a commercially available stun baton – you know, those anti-mugging devices you get in the States, you'd've been out cold – hospitalized even. I mean, they deliver three-quarters of a million volts some of them. Way over the top ...'

'Oh, that makes me feel much better,' replied Michael, sourly.

'Don't be like that now, Micky,' laughed Kent, waggling the baton at Michael in a gesture of reproof, 'it was just my little joke.'

'Some joke,' grunted Michael, resentfully, but at the same time wanting to find out why Kent wanted this dreadful implement. 'So, what do you use it for, anyway?'

'Gettin' people to talk, of course. Like I say, the commercial ones are no fuckin' good: apply 'em more than twice and the bloke just blacks out. With this one, though, you can go on for hours – and what's more they don't leave a mark afterwards either. Amazin' innit?'

'So, you mean that thing's an instrument of torture?'

'Yeah, fuckin' brilliant, innit?' smirked Kent, holding the baton at waist height and then jerking it upwards in a brutal stabbing gesture. 'A specially designed rear-entry model. Imagine gettin' this shoved up your arsehole, eh? Fuckin' hell you wouldn't half squeal!'

A wave of nausea swept through Michael's stomach, and for a moment he felt like vomiting. Holding back the bile, he forced himself to conceal his disgust and concentrate on the task at hand. Kent was relaxed, voluble – he had to keep him talking: trading instruments of torture was an even more horrific crime than drug-smuggling. Was there no end to Kent's criminal activities?

'So, how many of those things are there in the container?'

'Fifty. They're made in South America. I asked the company to throw in an extra one for me – come in right handy, it will.'

'Who are they being shipped to, then?'

'Ooh, couldn't tell you that, Mick,' replied Kent, carefully unscrewing the handle from the probe. 'But if you think about it you can probably guess. They came from South America, they're banned in Europe, so that only leaves one place really ...'

'The middle east?'

'Got it in one.'

'Isn't it illegal, shipping this sort of stuff through the UK – even if it is a bonded warehouse.'

'What sort of stuff's that?' asked Kent, with a look of mock innocence.

'Stun batons.'

'They're not stun batons. They're just machine parts, aren't they? That's what it says on the shipping documentation anyway.'

'But what if the customs people came in and inspected the warehouse?'

'Well, they could find 'em I suppose and work out what they're used for, but I doubt it. My guess is if they did decide to inspect the warehouse they'd never even get as far as checking this container – they'd've turned round and gone home long before that.'

'How can you be so sure?'

''Cos Carl and Ernst's a top quality operation – they've got every certification under the sun: BS202, ISO9000, you name it. I mean, customs inspectors get to see some right ropey joints, but the moment they get in 'ere in they can tell it's kosher: every 't' crossed, every 'i' dotted. Why d'you think I spend so much time leanin' on those two arseholes back there? I want 'em to run a good ship here – it's the best protection you can get.'

'Oh, right, I see what you mean.'

'Not that we put much through this warehouse. Just the odd special shipment every now and then, you know, for our Arab friends or what 'ave you.'

'Are you making a lot of money on this, then?' asked Michael, deciding to risk another direct question.

'Nah. It's just a sweetener, this stuff. A bit of service to help smooth the path for the real business, y'know?'

'And what's that?'

'Now, that really would be telling ...' answered Kent, buttoning up his coat and turning towards the exit. 'Come on, let's go and have a poke around somewhere else before we go back. I can't leave without findin' something to put the shits up those two – they'll think I'm goin' soft otherwise.'

Just over a mile from Carl and Ernst, Michael stopped and pulled into a petrol station. Having watched Kent's Saab disappear off into the distance towards London, he waited another two minutes and then turned around and went back to the warehouse. Malcolm Grey was most obliging. Yes, he could make copies of all the paperwork relating to the container in D3, and if Mr Angel would care to take a seat for a few minutes he'd put them in an envelope for him. Two hours later, Michael was back in Feltham. Downloading the day's footage on to video tape, he played it back twice, made a copy for Tom and put it into a padded envelope. Sitting down at the dining table, he wrote him a brief note saying that they must meet at the safe house first thing on Friday morning and then addressed the envelope for his personal attention at the Tower; if he posted it first thing next day, Tom would get it on Thursday morning.

Lying awake in bed that night, Michael reviewed the significance of the day's events. The Ellis Group was clearly utterly corrupt, using their international trading network to traffic everything from drugs to instruments of torture. As a journalistic scoop, he had stumbled on one of the stories of the decade and undoubtedly the greatest of his career. As regards the series as a whole, however, it was going to mean a radical revision of his priorities. It was now the last week in April and he had only four months left to finish all the investigations. If the Ellis Group was to be the most important of these, and if he was therefore to give it the full attention it deserved, the other two investigations were necessarily going to have to suffer as a result. In the case of the fraudsters, he would make one last effort to get a picture of Thompson and then call it a day – the Abaddon estate was just too difficult to penetrate. As for Simon Luxman, the agent who was now his chosen target for the fourth documentary, he would just have to fit him in around the full-time investigation of the Ellis Group whenever and wherever he could.

He returned to Fyl Lane early the following afternoon. Parking his car once more on the knoll, he set about scrutinizing every visible aspect of the house's security systems. Since concluding that Tysoe had carried out the burglary of his flat, he had discounted as a panic reaction the idea that there were long-range, external cameras mounted on the house, but he nevertheless needed to examine every inch of its exterior for anything or anyone that might inadvertently detect his presence: twice before he had provoked Kent's suspicions – he was not going to get away with it a third time. Having satisfied himself that he could not be seen from the house, Michael settled down for a full day's observation; members of the family, staff, visitors – he would photograph them all.

Just after two his mobile phone rang. Looking at the LCD display, he stared suspiciously at the incoming number for several seconds. Suddenly realizing that the caller was in fact returning his own call from earlier that day, he leant on the roof of the BMW and, without taking his eyes off the house in the distance, pressed the receive button and put the phone to his ear.

'Hello, Andy Byatt.'

'Hello, this is Professor Richard Jerram from the University of London.'

'Oh, good afternoon, Professor Jerram, thanks for returning my call,' replied Michael. He had got the Professor's name from Lloyd Hall, the social sciences researcher who had produced the report on benefit fraud for Tom.

'My pleasure. I'm sorry I wasn't here to speak to you in person earlier.'

'Oh, no problem – thank you for getting back to me so quickly.'

'So, I understand from your message you're doing a piece on the international trade in instruments of torture,' boomed the Professor, heartily. Lloyd Hall had said that Jerram was not just a deeply knowledgable lawyer and criminologist, but also a gifted and charismatic lecturer. An image flashed through Michael's mind of a distinguished-looking septuagenarian in a grey suit and red polka dot tie standing at the front of an auditorium packed with undergraduates.

'Yes, that's right.'

'Lucky you: I'm sure you'll get to meet some thoroughly charming people.'

'Oh, I have done already.'

'Well, I must say at the outset, Mr Byatt, I'm by no means an expert on the subject, although I do have something of a passing knowledge, I suppose. What is it you want to know exactly?'

'Well, firstly, the degree to which the trafficking in instruments of torture is linked to the arms trade,' replied Michael, recalling Kent's talk of a sweetener: if the Ellis Group were trying to ingratiate themselves with an Arab state for the purposes of gaining a large contract, arms would seem to be the most likely candidate.

'Oh, they go pretty much hand in hand.'

'Really?'

'Oh, yes – not that the arms industry would ever admit it, of course.'

'No?'

'No. If you were to ask any of the major European or American armament manufacturers about their involvement in instruments of torture they'd throw up their hands in horror. And with seeming justification, too: they're sophisticated engineering companies producing multi-million dollar weapons systems – they don't make thumbscrews. It's only when you get to the other end of the supply chain, of course, that you can properly appreciate the connection.'

'Which is …?'

'Well, in those countries that practise torture, the government officials who buy the missiles for the army are usually the same chaps who buy all the nasties for the secret police; and, of course, the way to keep in with such people is to supply them with everything that they want. The British arms industry does its best to cater to their requirements accordingly – as do the bureaucrats and civil servants that regulate it.'

'Are you saying the British Government actively supports the trade in instruments of torture?'

'Oh, no, it's more a case of passive collusion. Britain is a waning power, Mr Byatt. In order to punch above its weight internationally, its political classes have long espoused the manufacture and brokerage of arms. Instruments of torture get dragged into the frame occasionally because that's what the customers want. And when they do, I'm sure the diplomats and the arms companies don't actually dirty their hands with them. No, they'll know people who know people. Discreet phone calls will be made to old friends. You know how these things work …'

Frowning grimly, Michael stared across the freshly sown fields at the magnificent red-brick mansion beyond. Sir Alain Ellis's public persona was that of the gentleman entrepreneur, the charismatic businessman whose acumen and panache had built up a world-beating entertainments corporation, but the Professor had put his finger exactly on the true character of Ellis's business and Michael knew that he could not rest until he had ripped to shreds the hypocritical façade behind which it hid.

'So, what about the regulations?'

'I beg your pardon?'

'The regulations. I mean there are laws, aren't there? Laws that specifically prohibit the manufacture or brokering of instruments of torture. Surely if it could be demonstrated that a given arms company had broken or flouted those regulations then they could be brought to justice, couldn't they?'

'I'm afraid it's not quite as simple as that,' replied the Professor, cautiously.

'What d'you mean?'

In response, the Professor inhaled deeply, as though preparing himself for a long, involved explanation.

'Well – to condense an entire year's sociology of crime lectures into a couple of minutes – there are many ways of categorizing criminals, Mr Byatt. The most instructive, I believe – and the one to which I find myself returning again and again – is their classification into three groups based on the strategies they adopt to avoid apprehension. The first group comprises what we might call the desperados: the bank robbers – the Bonnie and Clydes, if you like. These people are predators, essentially. They live on the fringes of society, come into it for a short time, break its laws and then dash off again and hole up somewhere out of town. Now, this type of criminal behaviour, although much loved in the popular imagination, is actually quite rare because it's not sustainable: the perpetrators being highly conspicuous and thus all too easy to apprehend. Are you with me so far?'

'Yes,' replied Michael.

'The second group is the largest of all and consists of what one might loosely term career criminals – everyone from burglars to embezzlers. As a rule these people would prefer to bend laws rather than break them. If they do break them, they attempt to do so in a way that minimizes the risk of apprehension. Unlike the first group, these criminals live very much inside society and their criminality is sustainable; in some cases, they can carry on their whole lives without detection.'

'I know the sort of person you mean,' said Michael, an image of Tysoe's squinting face quickly springing to mind.

'The third group is the most sophisticated of all: criminals who far from attacking society, work to integrate themselves into its very highest levels – to become, in effect, part of its establishment. Now, these people fear the law least of all because they can influence its procedures from the inside, and even – in some extreme cases – actually pass laws that legitimize their activities. The most notable example of this group in modern times, of course, would be the Nazis. In the Weimar republic, it was against the law to appropriate the wealth and possessions of an ethnic minority, so what did Hitler do? Took over the Government and then changed the law, thus legitimizing what hitherto had been utterly illegal.'

'So, are you saying that arms dealers know how to manipulate the law in their favour? That they're too savvy to be caught – too well connected?'

'That's part of what I'm saying, but it goes a lot deeper than that. You see society is not just governed by external laws – by written legislation – but by internal laws, too: by the laws that we carry around with us in our heads. It is these laws that really determine our moral perceptions of right and wrong – far more effectively than anything on the statute books – and it is these laws which our third category of criminals seeks to influence. For these individuals, reducing or removing legislative barriers to the particular criminal act they wish to perpetrate is, of course, highly desirable, but, ultimately, the safest means of all of avoiding apprehension is to ensure that society does not regard that act as criminal in the first place. Again, look at the Nazis. Hitler was all too conscious of the fact that it wasn't enough merely to change the law, he had to change the way people thought as well. That was why he put so much effort into his propaganda programmes. And they worked – and in an astonishingly short period of time, too. After the war, many German villagers claimed not to have known the purpose of concentration camps next to which they'd been living for years. Some of them were lying, no doubt, but most of them had simply just been very effectively conditioned. Human beings are social animals, Mr Byatt, and therefore highly suggestible. If properly cultivated, they can be persuaded over time to look at something as grotesque as a death camp and perceive it as just an ordinary civic building – a power station or something similarly mundane. They may look, but they will not see, or if they do see, they will not feel.'

'I'm still not sure I entirely get your point, Professor.'

'Mr Byatt, perhaps I shouldn't be asking you this, but do you have a particular individual or company in mind? So far you have been speaking in general terms, but I have the distinct feeling that you're actually investigating a given organization for involvement in torture and the arms trade. I don't want to know the details, of course, but am I on the right track?'

'Yes, you are.'

'Then you must understand this,' continued the Professor, gravely. 'British-made arms maim and kill; they tear the human body to pieces as effectively as any on the planet. For Britain to continue as an arms exporting nation, it must ensure that its citizens either fail to see, or fail to be moved by, that essential fact. Consequently, rather than turning to the legal system or the machinery of state for assistance in your investigation, you must expect them to be ranged against you. In short, you must recognise that you are not taking on the law breakers, but the law makers.'

'OK. I see what you mean.'

'Good luck, Mr Byatt – you'll need it: I fear that you have a mountain to climb and that it will be a long and lonely endeavour.'

'You may be right, Professor Jerram.'

'Call me again, if I can be of any help.'

'I will. Thank you.'

'Goodbye, Mr Byatt.'

Slipping the phone back into his top pocket, Michael rested the telescopic lens on the roof of the car and then thoughtfully lit up a cigarette. The Professor was right – the cards were stacked against him: the chances of bringing down a powerful establishment figure like Ellis were very slim. His only hope would be to insinuate his way still deeper into the organization to obtain irrefutable proof of Ellis either directing, or in some way being involved, in Kent's activities. Staring fixedly at the house, Michael wondered whether this was possible in a mere four months: circumstantial evidence would not be good enough – he was going to need chapter and verse. As he pondered the challenge, Michael spotted Ellis's Bentley pulling up at the front gates. Checking his watch, he was surprised to find that it was only two fifteen. He hadn't expected Ellis to be back for hours yet. What was he doing home so early? On refocusing the camera, he soon realized why, when Ellis straightaway walked back out of the house with his daughter and began packing a number of bags into the Bentley's capacious boot: they were obviously going out together somewhere for the afternoon. Quickly but carefully unscrewing the telephoto lens, Michael decided to follow them. He had intended to carry out a full day's observation of the house, but he somehow instinctively sensed that he should instead take this opportunity to trail Ellis and his daughter. Opening the door of the BMW, he placed the camera and lens on the back seat and then started off down the knoll. He would have to hurry – they would be out of the driveway and off down Fyl Lane in a matter of seconds.

He had been following the Bentley for just under half an hour when, driving past a large, well-preserved Gothic church, he realized that Ellis was going to Mortlake Manor: he had noticed the church's spire when he had passed through the village on the train six weeks previously. Knowing that the telephoto lens would not be effective at any more than two thousand yards, Michael tried to recall the geography of the area around the Manor. The surrounding fields were fairly flat, but he did remember seeing a line of hedgerows to the east of the property; he would park behind them if he could find a suitable lay-by.

In the event, he had to leave his car over a mile away: although providing excellent cover, the hedgerows he had remembered were so dense and unbroken that he was unable even to see the Manor, let alone photograph it. Pulling into a pub car park, he looked down the gently sloping valley towards the Manor house in the distance and then whistled softly to himself on spotting a small concrete bunker positioned less than five hundreds yards from it: as long as he took care to stay well out of sight, he would be close enough to use his video camera. The pub was closed and as there appeared to be no one around, he locked the car and, under cover of the trees, made his way guardedly along the perimeter of the intervening fields towards the bunker.

The door was locked with an ancient brass padlock. Looking through one of the murky, cobweb-covered windows, he was able to make out an assortment of agricultural tools inside, including a giant, six-foot scythe whose recently whetted blade glinted menacingly in the gloom. Crouching down on one knee, he began unpacking the handicam, but, as he did so, sensed movement to his left. Checking the position of the sun to ensure that it did not glint off the lens, Michael raised himself upright again and aimed the camera in that direction, but a nearby hedge was blocking his view. Going around to the back of the bunker, he found a foothold on a rusted, iron bracket and, taking care not to damage the handicam as he climbed, carefully hauled himself up onto its corrugated roof.

The Manor was now fully visible and such was the slant of the bunker's roof that he was certain that if he stretched out flat on his stomach he could not be seen from it. Lying face downwards, he pushed his foot up against a metal joist to ensure that he did not slide backwards and then took out the camera. The sight that greeted him when he got it into focus was so perfect that he simply lay still for several seconds shaking his head in disbelief – his gamble to follow the Bentley rather than remain at Fly Lane had paid off beyond his wildest dreams. Ellis and his daughter, each mounted on a superb thoroughbred horse, were slowly riding from the Mortlake Manor stables towards a nearby field containing a dozen or so dressage fences. In their immaculate equestrian apparel and with the stunning neo-classical building glowing in the afternoon sunlight behind them, the two riders moved straight-backed and imperious across the verdant spring landscape. Gently tightening the zoom, Michael focused in on Ellis's daughter as she positioned her mount ready for the first of the fences. Again he was struck by the extraordinary air of cruelty in the young girl's features which her black velvet helmet and brilliant white silk cravat seemed somehow to accentuate. When she began expertly steering her horse over the fences, he turned the camera on Ellis, seated resplendent on his stallion of palest beige as he looked on in silent approval. The scene was indeed perfect and Michael smiled ruefully as he recalled the nerve-racking thirty minutes he had spent inside Tysoe's home. It had taken him over six months to get into his house and photograph his walk-through wardrobe – six months to obtain the one, definitive image that summed up Tysoe's squalid existence. But yet today, on the very first occasion that he had followed Alain Ellis, he had managed the exact same feat. For here was Ellis's very quintessence – here was a man who traded in the agony and death of his fellow human beings so that he might ride out like a lord.

It took well over three hours to get back to Feltham. As he walked up the concrete steps to the flat, he wearily rubbed the small of his back with his fist. The journey from one side of London to the other was hard work at the best of times, but he had driven straight into the evening rush hour and it had been a long, uncomfortable ride. Depositing the telephoto lens in the bedroom, he went through to the living room and set the handicam up to download the footage he had taken at Mortlake Manor on to video tape. Having poured himself a glass of water, he cast his mind forward to the meeting with Tom at the safe house the following morning. The tape that he had sent him of the stun-batons at Carl and Ernst, along with the material he had obtained today would finally dispel any lingering doubts that he or King might still have about his investigation of the Ellis group. Moreover, with Tysoe already in the bag and the investigation into the fraudsters all but complete, Michael was virtually certain that Tom would agree to his new plan for the final stage of the series. Things were going well. Opening up the freezer, he thought about cooking himself a meal, but he hadn't had time to go shopping for a couple of weeks and it was virtually empty. Instead, he decided to take a shower and then turn in early – he would eat the following morning when he got to the safe house – what he needed now more than anything was sleep.

He arrived at half past seven. Thinking that Tom might already be waiting for him, he called out as he walked through the front door, but, even as his voice echoed down the hallway, he could sense that the house was empty. Moreover, it was cold and smelled faintly musty: after the scare that they had had last time with his secretary, Tom must even have given up staying there overnight when he had been working late at the office. Going on through into the kitchen, Michael switched on the central heating, and, without bothering to check the fridge, turned around and went straight back out to buy some provisions from the shop on the common.

Having cooked breakfast and read the papers, Michael decided to play the tapes that he had bought for Tom. The footage of the Yardies struck him as particularly impressive. Of everything that he had filmed so far, the pictures themselves were technically speaking of the poorest quality, but the impenetrable blacks and hazy greys only served to add to their impact; the Abaddon estate really was a terrifying place and he was glad that his next visit to it would be his last. Switching off the VCR, Michael looked at his watch and frowned – it was nearly ten o'clock. What was holding Tom up? Finally, after a further twenty minutes of pacing around the living room, he decided to call him. He had to start work at Gog at five-thirty and, to be on time, he would have to be washed and shaved and on his way out of Balam Road by four-thirty at the latest. Time was running short. Taking the mobile from his top pocket, he dialled Tom's private number at the Tower.

'Good morning, can I help you?'

358

Michael winced. Tom's secretary – again.

'Could I speak to Mr Cranmer, please, it's Mr Angel.'

'I'm sorry, Mr Angel, I'm afraid he's in a meeting at the moment.'

'Oh, I see. Could you get a message through to him, then?' replied Michael, clenching his fist in irritation: although he had sent the Carl & Ernst video by first class post, it had obviously not found its way through to Tom in time.

'I'm sorry, no,' answered the secretary, in her clipped, nasal tone. 'He asked not to be disturbed.'

Fighting down the impulse to shout back at her down the phone, Michael bit his lip and responded calmly, but forcefully.

'It's very urgent I speak to Mr Cranmer. D'you understand? Very urgent. I sent him something that has been delayed but which we must discuss today.'

'If you mean that video tape,' answered Tom's secretary, dismissively, 'it arrived yesterday.'

'What?' replied Michael, completely stunned by her response. 'How did you know about that? It was marked for his personal attention.'

'Because I'm his personal secretary, that's why,' came the curt reply. 'I open all his mail whatever it says on the outside. Anyway, as I've told you, it did arrive – I put it in his in-tray myself along with all the other post yesterday. Now, the meeting finishes at twelve, so Mr Cranmer may have time to speak to you then. If you would care to tell me your number, I'll let him know you called.'

Michael was flabbergasted. If Tom had got the tape the previous day, why hadn't he come to the safe house? What other meeting could possibly have been more important than this? And, if he couldn't get out of it, why hadn't he rung Michael to tell him? In any event, whatever the reasons, he couldn't go back to Feltham that day without having seen Tom and he certainly wasn't going to be given the brush-off by his secretary.

'Listen to me,' he said, pointedly. 'Listen to me carefully. This is a matter of the utmost urgency. No matter what Mr Cranmer may have said to you, go into the meeting now and tell him that Mr Angel is coming to see him in his office at twelve o'clock and that he should be there to meet me. D'you understand what I've said?'

'Yes, I do Mr Angel,' replied the secretary huffily, 'but as I already told you, he instructed me not to …'

'Just do it,' interrupted Michael, his voice trembling with anger, 'and do it now.'

The Tower was exactly as he remembered it, but, catching sight of his reflection in the mirror in the lift, he knew that he bore no resemblance to the person who had come here a year ago to see Henry King in his penthouse flat. Shortly afterwards, he and Tom had agreed never again to meet at the Tower in case he was spotted by someone working there who might inadvertently compromise his Michael Angel cover story. Staring at his shaved head and gaunt features, that precaution now seemed almost absurd: he could probably spend the whole day walking up and down the building and not be recognised once. Striding out of the lift and down the corridor, he prepared himself for a showdown with Tom's secretary, but, as he turned the corner he could see that Tom was already standing waiting for him.

'Come on in, old chap, come on in,' said Tom, ushering him into the room and closing the door behind him.

'Where were you?' asked Michael, his voice quivering with the pent-up frustration of five continuous hours of waiting. 'Why didn't you call?'

'Look, I'm sorry, I'm sorry,' replied Tom, avoiding Michael's eyes as he walked around to the other side of his desk. 'Things were just crazy yesterday. I can't explain everything now. It's all very complicated, but ...'

'What's so complicated about a thirty-second phone call?' interrupted Michael. 'If I'd've known you were tied up today, we could've met tomorrow or on Sunday. You've had a whole day to get in touch.'

'Listen, I said I'm sorry. I know you're out there risking your neck ...'

'Fucking right I am!' exploded Michael, stabbing his finger resentfully at Tom and then glaring around the interior of his plush, comfortable office. 'You told me you'd be there whenever I needed you. So where were you? I've been sitting around the safe house all morning – I've gotta be back in Gog at half past five.'

'Look,' said Tom, finally finding the courage to meet Michael's gaze. 'For the last time, I'm sorry. I know I said I'd be there for you twenty-four hours a day and I know I've let you down. But listen, *Criminal Britain* might be the only thing in your life, but it isn't the only thing in mine. That may sound harsh, I know, but I'll just have to ask you to accept it, OK? I had a very, very difficult situation to deal with yesterday. I didn't get the chance to read your note properly until an hour ago and by that time you were already on your way here. Try and think beyond your own circumstances for a few seconds – just for a few seconds. Something personal came up – something very personal to me and I had to deal with it.'

Walking over to the window, Michael looked out over the skyscrapers of the city of London. It was because Tom moved so successfully through the world of journalism that he had been able to offer him the chance to make the series in the first place. The stresses of working undercover were distorting his sensibilities – he was back in the real world now; he had to calm down and readjust.

'OK. OK,' he replied, turning and looking across at Tom. 'I'm sorry.'

'So am I. So, let's just put this whole thing behind us and get on, shall we? I really want to hear what's been happening, all the latest news – everything.'

'All right.'

'Good.'

'So,' said Michael, walking over to the seat opposite Tom, 'what did you think of the tape that I sent you, then?'

'I haven't had a chance to see it yet.'

'What!'

'I said things have been difficult for me these last couple of days. I haven't seen it yet. But you can tell me all about it now, OK?'

Slumping down into the seat, Michael exhaled heavily and rubbed his eye with the flat of his hand. Although he had gone to bed early the previous night, he hadn't slept well.

'Three days ago,' he began, striving to keep his tone of voice as measured as possible, 'I went to the warehouse again with Kent. There's a container of stun batons in there bound for the Middle East. Ellis is supplying them through one of his offshore companies. I managed to get my hands on the shipping paperwork and I'm having it checked out now, but I'm almost certain it's a sweetener for an arms deal he's trying to secure with the Arabs.'

'And that's what's on this tape, is it?' said Tom, taking it out of the padded envelope.

'Yeah.'

'Good. OK. So, what about the drugs?'

'What?'

'The drugs,' repeated Tom. 'I mean I'm sure this is all good stuff, but we agreed last time that you'd concentrate on drugs being sold to the kids in the club. What's the progress on that?'

Michael stared incredulously across the table at Tom. His expression was absolutely serious: the revelation about the torture equipment had gone completely over his head.

'Tom,' continued Michael, patiently. 'I don't think you get me. These stun batons are instruments of torture – specifically designed to be inserted into the victim's anus; thousand of volts directly into the intestines. The pain they inflict is agonizing – excruciating.'

For a couple of moments, Tom closed his eyes and there was silence in the room. Frowning wearily, he then ran his hand slowly and purposefully over his forehead.

'I'm sure they're ghastly things,' he said, finally. 'But look, we need to work together on this series. We need a concensus on your activities otherwise the whole thing is going to go horribly, horribly wrong. Now, I know you've been under a lot of strain, but I think you've forgotten what we agreed …'

'I'm not the one who's forgotten what we agreed,' interrupted Michael, feeling his temper spiral out of control once more, 'you are. The criminal without a face. That's what King said that first night – right here in this very building. The guy who gets away with it year after year after year – unknown, unrecognized, unpunished. Those were his exact words and Ellis is that criminal – par excellence. So, why are you bottling out now? Eh? Wrong sort of victims again, is it?'

'No, no …' said Tom, shaking his head despairingly.

'Has Henry warned you off Ellis? That's what it is, isn't it? Because he's a knight of the fuckin' realm, I suppose – not some scumbag off a housing estate.'

'No, nothing like that.'

'No?'

'No. To tell you the truth, I haven't spoken to Henry since the last time I saw you.'

'What!' exclaimed Michael, staring back at Tom in abject disbelief. Had it happened again? Had the series once more managed to slide right down the list of Tom and Henry's priorities, even though only a month had passed since the last meeting at the safe house?

'I know what this looks like,' replied Tom, quickly. 'I know you're thinking Henry and I aren't enthusiastic about the project anymore –

that we've stopped supporting you – but that really isn't true. The fact is he just hasn't been in the country since the beginning of April. He's been dashing off all over the place – the States, Australia – the man's a workaholic. He's due back in about ten days. I'll bring him up to speed, then.'

'I'd appreciate it if you would ...' replied Michael, pointedly.

'But he is going to ask about the drugs,' countered Tom, opening up a drawer and taking out a bottle of whisky and two glasses. 'He's bound to. What am I supposed to tell him?'

'Tell him exactly what you told him last time,' said Michael, fighting back the waves of exasperation once more. 'Tell him the truth. I'm getting further and further into Ellis's organization and, by the beginning of September, I'll have all the evidence of drug pushing that he needs – and a lot more on some far more important things, too. Show him this as well while you're there.'

'What is it?' queried Tom, passing Michael a glass of whisky and taking the tape back in return.

'Take a look,' he replied. 'It's some film I took of Ellis and his daughter yesterday.'

Walking across his office, Tom inserted the tape into his VCR and then stood back to watch. On the broad, high-resolution plasma screen, the pictures were much crisper and clearer than on the cheap twenty-two inch TV in Michael's flat and, within a matter of moments, he found himself once more transported back to the beautiful yet soul-chilling scene he had witnessed twenty-four hours previously.

'Yes, OK.' said Tom, as he pressed the pause button a couple of minutes later. 'It's good background material.'

'What?' exclaimed Michael.

'It's good background stuff,' repeated Tom, a little nervously. 'I mean, yes, yes – I'll certainly show it to Henry ...'

Looking at Tom's embarrassed yet slightly perplexed expression, Michael was utterly nonplussed for a reply. The scene at Mortlake Manor was one of the most perfect he had ever filmed – an idyllic pastoral episode that at one and the same time exuded death and decay – yet it appeared to have left Tom completely unmoved. Turning to look once more at the screen, Michael stared at the freeze-frame of Ellis's daughter, her fine but pitiless features furled in concentration as she steered her mount towards one of the fences. Had Tom gone blind? Why had his appreciation of the scene been so superficial? And then, suddenly, in a blinding flash of comprehension, the Professor's words came back to mind and Michael at last realized the full significance of what it was that he had been trying to tell him. *'They will look,'* he had said, *'but they will not see. Or, if they do see, they will not feel.'* Slumping slowly backwards into his chair, Michael felt all his resentment melt away to be replaced instead by a terrible, bleak sense of loneliness. He had gone to the safe house that morning in need of a boost to his morale – desperately looking forward to sharing his achievements and ideas with Tom. But the Professor had been right. He had a mountain to climb and could not expect help from anyone along the way. Staring once more at the blank, puzzled look on Tom's face, he knew there was no point in trying to explain the full significance of the Mortlake Manor footage: by themselves the pictures were simply not enough. The only way he would ever convince Tom would be to amass a complete and utterly incontrovertible case against Ellis. Chapter and verse – it was his only hope. Averting his eyes from Tom's, he leant forward and numbly took a sip of his whisky. He would wrap up the meeting and then go. There was nothing more for him here.

'There's something else I've got to you tell you,' he said, finally – his voice flat and dispassionate and somehow sounding as though it belonged to another person.

'What?'

'I'm pulling out of Feltham – in two weeks.'

'What? What d'you mean?'

'I'm leaving Balam Road.'

'Why? Where are you going?'

'I'm gonna rent a flat in the West End. Short term let – three months.'

'Why?'

'Acting in character, like you always said,' he answered, wearily. 'Michael Angel's moving up in the world. Balam Road was OK when he came down to London as a labourer, but he's working at Gog now – getting good money. I'm going to have to spend a lot more time at the club over the next three months, so I need a flat close by.'

'I see.'

'Besides, Feltham's getting too hot,' he added, taking the second video tape of the Yardies from his jacket pocket and passing it across the desk. 'Take a look at this. Show it to Henry, too.'

'What is it?'

'Trouble.'

'What sort of trouble?'

'The Smith and Wesson sort,' replied Michael, standing up turning to leave. 'I've gotta go now. I'll see you.'

'Hang on, old chap, you've only just got here!' said Tom, seemingly more disturbed by Michael's sudden listlessness than by his previous display of anger. 'I mean, what about the fourth documentary – the pornographers?'

'When I'm not working at Gog,' said Michael, continuing to walk towards the door. 'I'm going after a guy called Luxman. I'm almost certain he's the man Henry wanted me to find.'

As Michael looked back across the room and finally met Tom's gaze, his boss went to speak but at that precise moment his phone rang. Frowning, he stabbed at the button and leant forward to talk into the microphone.

'Yes. What is it?' he snapped.

'Your lunch appointment, Mr Cramner,' said his secretary. 'Mr Williams has just arrived in reception. Shall I ask them to send him up or …?'

'Tell him to hang on for a few moments,' replied Tom, irritably.

Not waiting for Tom to speak, Michael opened the door to leave.

'Wait a second!' called Tom.

Turning around, Michael looked across the office once more. Opening his mouth, Tom again went to say something, but, clearly sensing that a further apology would only make matters worse, instead took out his wallet.

'This,' he said, opening it up and pulling out a slip of paper. 'Take it.'

'What is it?' asked Michael.

'It's Sipkiss,' answered Tom, quietly. 'I've found him for you.'

Kent was in excellent spirits at the weekend and summoned Michael to see him on both the Saturday and Sunday nights – on the second occasion offering him the opportunity to work full-time at Gog. Having thanked him, Michael asked for a few days to consider the matter: although he had every intention of accepting the offer, he decided it would be better not to appear too keen. Returning to complete his shift, Michael felt genuinely elated as he left Kent's office – a full-time position at Gog was now exactly what he needed. However, as he walked back through the ante-room outside and caught sight of the water pipes on the far wall, the smile of satisfaction left his face. Recalling what Kent had said at Carl and Ernst about wanting his own stun-baton, he suddenly had a dreadful intuitive feeling as to the way in which it would be used: because the door leading to the corridor was soundproofed, the cries of anyone hand-cuffed to the pipes would be inaudible elsewhere in the building. Walking back up the staircase to the club, Michael wondered just how much Ellis knew about Kent's terrifying life of violence: the more he could prove in that regard, the greater his chances of getting Ellis put away for a very long time.

On Monday morning he went to see Jim and ordered another GPS system. Having spent the afternoon going around the estate agents looking for flats, he then went straight on to Gog to meet Evelyn, the second female star of the FFM movie. When he brought up the subject of Luxman, she replied that she had never worked for him but was all too well aware of his reputation. She then went on to relate a couple of unpleasant experiences of her own at the hands of similarly unscrupulous agents within the industry. It was the final confirmation he needed. Added to what he had learned from Babs and Amanda's friend, Bernie, Michael was now certain that he had found an ideal subject for the fourth documentary; as soon as he left Feltham, he would start to track him down.

He awoke on Tuesday morning in two minds as to what to do that day. Although he had intended to stake out Sipkiss's house with a view to discovering why it was that Kent wanted to bribe him, he had had an idea during the night as to how he should make his final attempt at capturing Thompson on film – a problem that had been plaguing him ever since planting the malfunctioning transmitter. After Harper and Angela had learned that Dill had put Michael Angel back on the list of active suspects, he had stopped claiming housing benefit on Balam Road. He was, however, still receiving benefit on the second property he had taken out in Milland Road and, although he had stormed out on Harper after their argument, he still owed him his cut of six week's rent. He only had a few days left in Feltham, but, if Harper and Angela went to the Abaddon estate during that time and he were able to follow them, he could knock on the door of Thompson's flat whilst they were actually in there on the pretence of wanting to speak to them. It would be a risky move, but he could claim that he was going back up north to Yorkshire in a hurry and wanted to pay off his debt on Milland Road before he left. As Thompson in turn took a cut of everything that Harper made, he would be unlikely to refuse. Concluding finally that he needed more time to think about the idea, Michael decided to stick to his original plan for the day and carry out an initial reconnaissance of Sipkiss's house.

He got there just after seven o'clock. Parking his car twenty yards away, Michael scanned the house in his rear view mirror. It was an expansive, three-storey South London property, well-maintained for the most part save for a number of small but tell-tale signs of disrepair: as far as he could see, it was the only building in the street with its original Edwardian roof. Looking at the other properties, Michael could easily imagine why Kent and Edwin had chosen Sipkiss as a target for coercion: keeping up with neighbours such as these and maintaining a coke habit at the same time would put strains on even the fattest salary. Deciding to drive around the block again and park in a position that would allow him to photograph the front of the house, Michael turned the ignition key, but, at that precise moment, caught sight of Sipkiss coming out of his front door. Switching off the engine, he watched the scene unfolding in his rear view mirror. Sipkiss, dressed in a three piece suit, was saying goodbye to his wife – a dark-haired woman in her early thirties. Just as it seemed as though the farewells were over and he began to move down the path, a toddler of about eighteen months suddenly appeared at the door, followed moments later by a girl in her late teens that Michael guessed was the child's nanny. A further round of goodbyes followed until a little over a minute later he got into his car and drove away.

Following Sipkiss's Jaguar through the south circular traffic, Michael took the note that Tom had given him out of his top pocket and cast his eyes over it again. Sipkiss worked for a company called Milton Dynamics. It was obviously a manufacturer of defence equipment, but the key question was its exact relationship with the Ellis Group. The day after visiting Carl and Ernst, he had sent the Air Way Bill and related paperwork to an investigation agency that specialized in ascertaining the real ownership of companies by unraveling the webs of offshore holding companies and cross share certificates employed by those who wish to conceal their investments. They had promised to give him a full breakdown by the end of the week, but he was already more or less certain that the trail that began with the South American producer of the stun batons would eventually connect with Milton Dynamics.

Just after eight o'clock, Sipkiss pulled into a small industrial estate comprising about thirty or so modern, red-brick buildings and parked his car in a personalized space. Having watched him take his briefcase out of the boot and disappear inside the building, Michael drove around the corner and parked in a lay-by. Opening up the glove compartment he then took out a large black and white photographic print of Sipkiss with the Mortlake Manor prostitute, put it into an A4 envelope, sealed it and marked it 'Mr Adrian Sipkiss – Highly Confidential'. He would drop it through the letter box around nine fifteen – there was no security camera on the front door and most of the employees should have arrived for work by then so it was unlikely that he would be seen.

He met Sipkiss two days later. Ideally, he would have liked to have given him a full week to fret over the photograph, but time was tight and, judging by what he had seen of Sipkiss's family situation, he imagined that he would already be desperate enough to get his hands on the originals. He chose Putney Bridge for the meeting place: it was less than half a mile from Milton Dynamics and Sipkiss could easily get there in his lunch time. Waiting beside the lamppost in the third alcove along, Michael watched Sipkiss stride angrily towards him.

'The porter,' he spat, with undisguised loathing. 'You were the porter that carried my bags, weren't you? I should've guessed it was you. What d'you want? Money, I suppose.'

Ignoring the question, Michael lit up a cigarette and, turning around, leant his elbows on the stone balustrade and looked out over the Thames towards London.

'Well, you just listen to me,' continued Sipkiss, coming up beside Michael and lowering his voice so that none of the passers-by on the bridge could hear, 'because you don't know who you're dealing with, mate. I've got friends that are way out of your league – they'll tear your bollocks off and ram then down your throat as soon as look at you, so you can stuff your fucking blackmail where the monkey puts its nut. Got it?'

'D'you mean Kent?' replied Michael, softly. Casually flicking the ash off his cigarette, he then turned around and looked at Sipkiss – the colour had completely drained from his face. 'Don't expect him to help you. He was the one that got you into all this in the first place.'

'How … how d'you know about him?'

'Never mind how I know,' replied Michael, taking an envelope from his inside pocket and then passing it to Sipkiss. 'Just shut up and look at these.'

Looking back out over the Thames, Michael did his best to keep his face completely expressionless. Despite what he had just said, the worst possible thing that could happen would be for Sipkiss to tell Kent that the tall, shaven-headed porter from the Mortlake Manor party was blackmailing him for information about Milton Dynamics. Instead, he had to convince Sipkiss that although he was even more unscrupulous than Kent, he would be prepared to hand over the photographs if he got what he wanted. It would be a very delicate balance to maintain.

'Enough?' asked Michael, turning to look at Sipkiss.

'Enough,' he mumbled, handing back the envelope.

'No, you keep 'em. I've got plenty more.'

'What is it you want?' asked Sipkiss, dejectedly slipping the envelope inside his coat pocket.

'This is the deal,' continued Michael, sternly, 'so keep quiet and listen. What I want is information, not money. What I'm offering is the complete set of negatives in exchange for it. If you don't give me that information, or if you lie, copies of the photographs go to your wife, your employer and to a number of other …'

'What information d'you want?' interrupted Sipkiss.

'I told you to keep quiet and listen,' replied Michael, 'I haven't finished talking yet. Whatever happens, this is the only time that you and I will ever meet. The decision that you make in the next sixty seconds is the one that you will have to live with for the rest of your life. Bullshit me now and there will be no second chance. And also, you should understand this. Although I can fuck up your life forevermore, all you can do is mildly inconvenience mine. That's because the information you've got is important to me, but it isn't absolutely essential. D'you understand what I've said?'

'Yes, yes,' replied Sipkiss, his eyes seeming to glaze over slightly.

'Right. There's an arms deal coming up soon. You know the one I mean. I want you to tell me everything you know about it – right from the very beginning – and exactly why it was that Kent and the others came to you.'

'How do I know you'll give me the photos back if I tell you?'

'You don't,' answered Michael, flatly, 'and I won't give them back to you straightaway, either. It may take weeks or even months before I find out whether you've told me the whole truth or not. But one thing's for certain: if you don't give me the information I want within the next minute, your wife'll have those photographs by the end of the week.'

Raising his eyes heavenwards, Sipkiss inhaled deeply and then hunched his shoulders – clearly weighing up the risks and uncertainties of the terrible situation in which he found himself. Resting his back against the alcove, Michael wondered whether Kent had just bribed him with cocaine or whether money had changed hands, too, but, almost as soon as the question had occurred to him, Sipkiss took a step forward and began to speak.

Chapter 12

The entrance to Miranda Close was barred by two tall, wrought-iron gates. Bringing his car to a halt in front of them, Michael looked across at the control panel to see if there was an intercom, but, at that moment, they began slowly and grandly to part of their own accord. Driving through and gazing at the imposing array of modern, three-storey executive homes beyond, he had no doubt that although the gates opened automatically during the day, a security access card would be required at night: wealth like this always protected itself after dark.

He spotted the house straightaway, being the only one of the twenty or so properties in the close undergoing any form of building work. Coming to a halt ten yards short of the driveway, Michael switched off the ignition, and, looking around, immediately caught sight of Naz perched on top of a wooden platform above the roof. With a laconic smile, he watched the Turk unbolt a section of scaffolding and then expertly punt it down a plastic chute at the side of the house. Naz's last building job was clearly almost complete; by the end of the week, he also would be leaving Feltham forever. Stretching over on to the back seat, Michael slipped the envelope out of the inside pocket of his leather jacket and got out of the car. Leaning up against the near-side wing, he sat watching Naz work with a mixture of admiration and regret. Much as his life had been enriched by having known this charming, conscientious man, and much as he would like to imagine that they would one day meet again, he knew in his heart that this was to be their final farewell.

'Naz!' he called out. 'Naz!'

'Micky!' shouted his friend in response, grinning and holding up his forefinger to indicate that he would be down in a minute.

Despite the fact that he had come to say goodbye to Naz, as he sat waiting by his car, Michael felt more cheerful than he had for months: over the past five days he had made two major breakthroughs and his spirits had brightened enormously as a result. The first of these had come about as a consequence of Sipkiss's revelations on Putney Bridge. Milton Dynamics had won a contract to upgrade and refit the Saudi Arabian fleet's torpedo system. As project director, Sipkiss had responsibility for choosing the subcontractor to supply the associated radar guidance equipment. From amongst the various companies who had bid for this, Kent was bribing him to select a Norwegian engineering group by the name of Fobors. The corporate diagram provided by the investigation agency to which Michael had sent the Air Way Bills from Carl and Ernst subsequently confirmed that Fobors was fifty-one percent owned by the same Ellis subsidiary that owned the South American manufacturer of the stun batons. Kent and Ellis's objectives were thus patently clear: by procuring cocaine and prostitutes for the decision maker at one end of the supply chain and instruments of torture for those at the other, they were making absolutely sure that the contract went to Fobors. The second major breakthrough had followed on just two days later. Having signed a three-month rental agreement on a furnished flat in Soho, Michael had phoned Simon Luxman and, posing as a film producer intending to produce a string of porn movies, had invited him there for a meeting the following week. Tempted by the prospect of supplying Michael with a series of girls for these, Luxman had readily agreed. It had been a critical breakthrough for the fourth and final documentary, and, although Michael knew that he dare not succumb to complacency, it was clear that the end of his work was now in sight.

'Micky, is good see you,' said Naz, striding towards Michael with his hand extended for him to shake.

'Good to see you, too, mate,' replied Michael, gripping his hand warmly, but feeling once again a pang of sadness: Naz had on the same faded cheesecloth shirt that he had been wearing the day that they had met just under a year ago.

'You phone last night, yes?'

'Yeah, that's right. Mustafa told me where you'd be. Good job?'

'Oh, yes, is good job,' grinned Naz, nodding in the direction of the four other men working on the sight, 'roof extension – good quality work, very good quality.'

'Not like Tysoe, then?'

'No, no,' laughed Naz, 'not like Roger, too.'

'So, you're off on Friday afternoon, then – is that right?'

'Yes, yes.'

'You must be looking forward to seeing your family again.'

'So much, Micky, so much. I think you know.'

'Yeah, I know,' replied Michael, thinking of the day in a little over three months time when he would at last be able to see Jake and Elizabeth again.

'And you. You go, too, yes?'

'Yeah, that's right. I'm leaving Balam Road tomorrow afternoon.'

'Your business – is finished?' enquired Naz, confidentially.

'More or less.'

'I very happy for you Micky. You good man.'

'So you always told me,' smiled Michael. 'But listen, I've got something for you before you go.'

'Yes?' replied Naz, his bright, innocent eyes sparkling happily.

'This,' said Michael, handing over the envelope.

'What is this?' asked Naz, his face suddenly crumpling in concern. Michael could not help smiling, knowing that whenever in the future he thought of Naz, he would always recall the extraordinary rapidity with which the Turk's expression could shift between emotional extremes.

'It's a present, Naz. A money order. It's for you and your family.'

'No, no, I not take, Micky, it is not …'

'Listen,' interrupted Michael, as sternly but as gently as he could, 'you've earned this money – every penny of it – and it will make me unhappy all my life if you don't take it. You helped me so much and many others too in a way that you'll never know. Please, take it, Naz. It means a lot to me.'

'OK, my friend,' said Naz finally, taking the envelope reluctantly from Michael's hand. 'I will share with Mustafa and the others.'

'That's great – do that,' replied Michael, happily. 'And when you get the chance, have a party and think of me, yeah?'

'Oh, yes, party!' exclaimed Naz, his face beaming once more. 'When we remember Mick, we remember big party. Mick is man for big party!'

As they stood smiling at each other, Michael spotted a man in a white helmet whom he guessed was the site foreman looking down at Naz from the platform on the roof. In a way he was glad that Naz had to get back to work – it was how he would like to remember him.

'Look, you'd better go, Naz, they're waiting for you.'

'OK, OK,' he replied, and then, with his face still smiling, held out his hand once more for Michael to shake. 'Thank you, Micky. I never forget you – I never forget what you did for me while I stay in England.'

'And I'll never forget you either, Nasruddin. Never.'

Watching Naz climbing up the scaffolding, Michael gave him a final wave and leisurely turned to go. As he walked back along the pavement, he noticed a woman in the neighbouring house standing waiting on the driveway by her car. Realizing that his own vehicle was partially blocking her exit, he gave her a quick, apologetic wave of the hand to indicate that he was now leaving. For a moment, their eyes met, but, in the very instant that she smiled at him in polite acknowledgement, Michael felt as though his whole world had come to a thunderous, cataclysmic halt. Seeing the look of consternation on the woman's face and watching her car keys slip from her hand on to surface of the driveway, he knew that for the first time since he had become Michael Angel, he had been recognized by someone from his former life. The house next to the one at which Naz was working was owned by Charlotte Gray – Elizabeth's best friend.

'My God,' she exclaimed. 'It's you, isn't it?'

'Yes, it's me, Charlotte,' replied Michael, walking slowly towards her.

'Are … are you back now?'

'You dropped your keys,' said Michael, leaning down to pick them up off the driveway and wondering how on earth he was going to explain his presence in the close in which she lived.

'Thanks,' she replied, taking the keys from him. 'Sorry. I mean, I was just so surprised to see you.'

'Ha! Me, too.'

'So, have you left Geneva now, then?' she continued, but even as her composure seemed to return, her eyes once more opened wide in astonishment. 'My God, what happened to your face?'

'Oh, that,' said Michael, trying his best to appear offhand. 'Well, it's a long story – a very long story. But look, I've got to ask you, how are Elizabeth and Jake?'

'What?'

'Elizabeth and Jake – how are they?'

For several moments Charlotte appeared completely unable to reply. Watching her normally composed, intelligent face go totally blank, Michael felt a rush of panic overtake him – perhaps there had been an accident. Before he was able to question Charlotte about this, however, she suddenly snapped right back to normal.

'They're fine, they're fine,' she replied. 'I saw them only two days ago, actually. Jake's just done his GCSE's.'

'How did he get on?'

'Well, I don't know,' she stuttered, tripping over her words, 'the, the results aren't out until August.'

'Yeah, I know that,' laughed Michael. 'But how did he think he got on? I mean, was he happy with how they went or what?'

'Yes, yes, very happy,' replied Charlotte, adding rather awkwardly, 'well, he's a bright boy – you know that.'

'Is something wrong, Charlotte?' asked Michael, suspiciously.

'No, no,' she replied hastily, 'but anyway who was that you were talking to? Was it one of the men working on next door's roof?'

'Yeah, yeah – I owed him some money,' replied Michael, casually.

'Oh. So, are you living around here now?'

'No, no, I'm in central London. I just got myself a flat there last week. I'm moving in tomorrow actually.'

'So your job on the continent is finished, then?'

'No, not entirely, but it should be within a couple of months. I'll be moving back here permanently then.'

'OK, I see. Oh, well, good!' exclaimed Charlotte, her expression suddenly brightening to a degree that seemed oddly disproportionate to what he had just said.

'Listen, er, I've got to go now,' said Michael, 'but tell Elizabeth and Jake that I'll be in touch soon, will you? I haven't been too good at writing over the last year, but could you tell them I'm planning to make it up to them – especially Jake, yeah?'

'Yes, yes, certainly,' answered Charlotte, once again with a seemingly unnatural degree of enthusiasm.

'And everything all right with you and your family?' asked Michael.

'Great. Great.'

'Good, well, I'll, er, be off then,' said Michael, smiling and turning to make his way back to the car. 'And, I'll, er, get out of your way, too.'

'Oh, thanks, thanks. Bye,' replied Charlotte, returning his smile and then uncharacteristically fumbling her keys as she tried to find the right one to open up her car.

Driving the three miles back to Feltham, Michael was anxious and puzzled in equal measures. She was obviously hiding something. Although he didn't like Charlotte Grey, he had always recognized her as a person of singular drive and intelligence. What could have happened to Elizabeth and Jake to have reduced her to such a state of nervous evasion? Of course, his sudden appearance on her driveway had been a shock, dressed as he had been in his casual clothes and with his ear ring and scar. But she appeared to have got over that surprise fairly quickly and had only really started to equivocate when he had mentioned Elizabeth and Jake. On the other hand, he somehow knew that she hadn't been lying when she had said that she had seen them two days ago and that they were both well. Parking the car on the waste ground behind his flat, Michael checked his watch. It was twelve twenty-five. Knowing that Tom would just be about to go to lunch and not wanting to discuss his family life over the phone, he decided instead to call him at the weekend and ask if they could meet at the safe house at the beginning of the following week. So far, he had only ever asked Tom to forward postcards to Elizabeth from the continent, but on this occasion he had already made up his mind to ask him actually to phone her. Considering Tom's failure to turn up at the safe house the previous week, it was the least he could do for him.

He parked his car on the slip road of the industrial estate twenty-five minutes later, a little after one o'clock. Switching off the engine, he felt a strange stab of nostalgia on seeing both Harper's house two hundred yards away and, through his rear view mirror, the spot where Roger had first picked him up. Although he would be leaving the following day, he knew that he had experienced so much during his time in Feltham that its sights and sounds would stay with him for the rest of his life. Taking the microbinoculars from his inside pocket, he focused firstly on the ground floor and then the two upper floors of the house to see if he could detect any signs of movement. As usual, though, Harper had the blinds down and so, putting the binoculars on the passenger seat, he lit up a cigarette and prepared himself for the long wait. He had decided to split the surveillance into two parts: the first period from lunch time through until ten o'clock that night; the second from five o'clock the following morning until the early afternoon. If Harper or Angela didn't emerge during that time or, if they did but didn't go to the Abaddon estate, he would call it a day – he would leave Feltham with no photograph of Thompson other than the one which he had brought with him in the file that had been leaked to Henry King at *The Mail*.

Just after two o'clock, Harper came out. Sitting bolt upright in his seat, Michael grabbed the binoculars and watched him slowly make his way down the road towards his car; executing a hasty three-point turn, he then quickly drove to the other end of the slip road. Following Harper down the Uxbridge Road, he began to feel decidedly nervous: he had so resigned himself to the likelihood of the fraudster not going back to the Abaddon estate during the relatively short time that he intended to keep him under surveillance, that he hadn't fully thought through what he would do and say if he did.

Parking his car behind the garages ten minutes later, Michael switched off the engine and sat deep in thought for almost five minutes, poring over everything that he had managed to learn about Richard Thompson during the past fourteen months. With no criminal convictions and only one long-distance photograph on record, he was clearly both an elusive and deeply mistrustful character. He was also violent and unpredictable – prone to savage mood swings that apparently could be exacerbated by his drug addiction. '*What happens if we can't find the money again?*' Harper had said. '*He goes fuckin' ape-shit – that's what. He needs his gear.*' How would this unstable, tyrannical character react to Michael's story? Thompson was at the apex of a pyramid of fraudsters that in all probability extended way beyond the seventeen people listed in the original file. But would his avarice overcome his suspicious nature? Taking a deep breath and checking his jacket once more to ensure that the three hundred pounds were still there, Michael switched on the mobile in his top pocket and got out of the car. If things got too dangerous he would cut and run, go to ground for twelve hours and then return to Balam Road in the middle of the night: he had very little to pack and could be on his way to his new Soho flat within fifteen minutes. Once he had gone, no one from Feltham would ever be able to trace him.

The entrance hall was just as dingy as when he had been there last in the small hours of the morning, the little sallow daylight that did pass through the discoloured panes seeming to be sucked straightaway into the murky, litter-strewn corners. Making his way up the stairs two steps at a time, Michael listened intently for any sounds that might indicate the presence of the Yardies; he was almost certain that they inhabited one of the very top floors but, if by chance he were to meet them on their way down, he would never make it to Thompson's flat. Reaching the fifth floor, he cast a brief, rueful glance in the direction of the stairwell where he had hidden the malfunctioning transmitter, then stepped forward and rapped his fist on the door. The noise echoed loudly around the landing. Taking a step backwards he strained his ears to detect any answering sounds from the floors above. Ominously, he heard a door open and, a moment later, what sounded like footsteps. Staring at the thick, unmoving timber panel in front of him, Michael felt an overwhelming urge to turn and run. The footsteps were now clearly audible on the staircase. The photograph of Thompson wasn't worth the risk – it never had been – it was time to go.

At that exact moment the door opened.

'Mick!'

It was Harper.

'Hello, Geoff.'

'What the fuck are you doin' here?'

'I've got somethin' for you.'

'What?'

'Money.'

Harper's dumbfounded expression quickly gave way to one of alarm, as, looking over Michael's shoulder, he, too, appeared to hear the sounds of the footsteps coming down the stairs.

'Get inside quick.'

The hallway was narrow and dark. As Harper closed the sturdy wooden door, Michael could see that it had three heavy-duty bolts on it. Sliding two of these into position, Harper turned and stared at him through the gloom.

'What's this about money? And how did you find me here, anyway?'

Striving to appear as casual as possible, Michael tried not to gabble his cover-story: it was tenuous and flimsy, but it was all that he had got.

'Remember the house in Milland Road?'

'Yeah.'

'I owe you your share of the rent – six weeks' worth. I'm leavin', you

378

see. Going back up north – tomorrow. I'm gonna try and patch things up with my family and I didn't want to go still owin' you the money, like.'

'How did you know I was here?'

'I went round your place just now. You were just drivin' off when I got there so I followed you. I'm off early tomorrow, you see, and I didn't know if you'd be back before I left …'

Cringing mentally at this explanation, Michael prepared himself for further questioning but, miraculously, Harper seemed to accept it, and, turning to walk down the corridor, led him into the flat. This was it. At last he was to come face to face with Richard Thompson.

'You'd better come on in, then …'

Walking through the door, Michael found himself in a surprisingly normal looking lounge-living room – there was wallpaper, potted plants and a pine dresser filled with crockery. In the corner of the room was a large television, in front of which, sprawled out on a dark blue couch, a distracted-looking youth in his late teens lay watching children's television.

'Ange,' called out Harper, 'Ange. It's Mick.'

A moment later Angela appeared at a door on the other side of the room which Michael guessed led through into the kitchen.

'What are you doin' here?' she asked, her eyes opening wide in alarm. 'What's up?'

Staring into her surprised, anxious face, Michael felt his throat suddenly go completely dry. Something was wrong – terribly, terribly wrong. This wasn't the hideout of a vicious megalomaniacal criminal. As usual, Angela had her dragon T-shirt on, but, over the top of it, she was wearing an apron.

'It's all right, don't worry,' said Harper, calmly, answering on Michael's behalf. 'Mick's brought us the money on Milland Road. Remember that house we helped him take out a couple of months back …'

'Oh, right …' replied Angela.

For a moment there was an uncomfortable silence, broken by both Harper and Angela realizing at once that the youth stretched out on the couch was now looking at Michael.

'Oh, er, Mick, this is Ange's son,' said Harper, awkwardly.

'Hi,' said Michael.

In response the young man did not answer, but merely continued to stare quizzically at Michael for several seconds before turning his glassy, vacant eyes back towards the television. The anxious silence reasserted itself straightaway and Michael could see that for some reason Angela was extremely uncomfortable with his being in her son's presence.

'Er, I tell you what, Mick,' said Harper, clearly also conscious of Angela's unease, 'you go and take a seat out on the balcony, I'll get us a couple of beers, all right?'

'Er, yeah, OK,' replied Michael walking over to a half-open set of French windows on the other side of the living room. Angela seemed in two minds as to whether to stay with her son or return to the kitchen, but once again Harper tactfully stepped in.

'It's only, Mick, Ange,' he said, gently. 'Don't worry. I'll get the beers. You get on with the cooking ...'

Sitting down on one of the two plastic garden chairs crammed into the narrow balcony, Michael looked out over the estate in bitter self-recrimination. Everything had seemed to indicate that Richard Thompson operated the fraud ring from this flat – but clearly he didn't live here. The young man lazing casually in front of the television; the furnishings; the very smell of the place – this was obviously Angela's home. How could Michael's assumptions have been so drastically wrong? Moreover, much worse than not having found Thompson at the flat, was the fact his absence completely undermined Michael's understanding of the gang. Turning and seeing Harper coming through the French windows with two bottles of beer, Michael desperately strove to marshal his thoughts. Having already told Harper that he was leaving to go back up north the next day, he could not credibly show his face in Feltham again. He either now had to discover from Harper his exact connection with Thompson or face up to the fact that the entire investigation was fundamentally flawed.

'Cheers,' said Harper, raising his bottle in the air in salutation.

'Cheers,' replied Michael.

'You know, I miss our Thursday nights down The White Horse,' continued Harper, taking out his tobacco tin and opening it up to roll a cigarette.

'Yeah?'

'Yeah.'

'Me, too.'

'Listen, Mick, er, I owe you an apology – we both do. We were dead hard on you last time we met. You were right – it wasn't your fault that Dill started following you. Ange feels real bad about what she said and everythin' – so do I.'

'That's all right.'

'Nah, it's not all right. You'd've never started claiming if it hadn't been for us. We talked you into it.'

'Forget it.'

'You caught us at a bad time, though, I'm afraid.'

'Yeah?'

'Yeah. Ange's lad in there, Rick. He's on the run, you see.'

'Yeah?' replied Michael, masking his extreme self-exasperation by taking a deep swig of the beer. How could he ever have been so stupid as to let himself assume that the Rick of whom Harper had spoken in The White Horse was necessarily Richard Thompson?

'Yeah. Well, he's had it tough all his life – poor bastard,' said Harper, lowering his voice slightly and casting a wary glance towards the kitchen to make sure that Angela was out of earshot. 'They used to think he was simple when he was a kid, but about five years ago he started having fits. The doctors were still trying to find out what was wrong with him when he got four months in a youth detention centre for aggravated burglary. The fits got worse inside and then, on top of it all, he got beaten up in there and lost his hearing in one ear. After he came out, Ange did everything she could to keep him away from his mates, but he slipped out one night and got nicked again. Bad company, eh? This was two years ago. He broke bail just afterwards, he's been hiding out here ever since.'

'So is this Angela's flat, then?' asked Michael.

'No, it's her mother's council flat actually – or it used to be – she got re-housed about five years ago. After Rick broke bail the police were lookin' for him, but everyone knows they're too scared to come on to the Abaddon, so we came back one night and opened the place up again. It was amazin' – it was exactly the same as Ange's mum had left it. The block's full of all sorts of fuckin' criminals and junkies, mind you, but it's safer than my place – or safer for Rick, anyway – he'll never survive another stretch inside. The dealers upstairs leave him alone; they know he's a bit touched. Ange can look after herself and I buy the odd bit of gear off 'em so we get on all right. The big problem is getting his drugs.'

'What d'you mean?'

'The fits take him in different ways. Sometimes he goes wild – you know, completely berserk – but at other times, he just falls into this sort of depressive collapse. The only medication we've found that works is this stuff called Topirimate – it's an anti-psychotic. We daren't risk trying to get it on prescription – if the doctors gave him up to the police he'd be straight back inside – so we have to buy it on the black market. Costs a bloody arm and a leg, though: it's stolen to order from pharmacies. Anyway, he's been all right the last few weeks – touch wood – he seems to have stabilized, but when we saw you last he was all over the fuckin' shop and the dealer we were using had just doubled his price. Ange had been up with him all night – he'd been crying for hours – that's why she was so strung out with you …'

Looking back through the window into the flat, Michael could see that Angela had now taken off her apron and was quietly ironing a shirt at the back of the room. Watching her slow patient movements, punctuated every few seconds by a maternal glance at her son, Michael at last understood the real meaning of the conversation that he had recorded in The White Horse.

'Is that why you started fiddling housing benefits, then?' asked Michael, turning to face Harper. 'To get the money for Rick's drugs?'

'More or less,' replied Harper, casually, relighting his roll-up and then flicking the spent match over the top of the balcony. 'We don't need the money when he's like this – when he's stable. But when he kicks off he can get through five hundred quid's worth of Topirimate in a week. Frightening it is. Christ knows what we're gonna do now that Craig's pulled out.'

'That's your mate on the inside, isn't it?'

'Not my mate,' replied Harper, disparagingly, 'Ange's – she went to school with his sister. He's done a bunk now. He called us up last week – reckoned he'd been rumbled. Probably just as well, really. Sooner or later we're gonna have to start finding the money somewhere else. If we ever get got caught we might end up inside and then Rick really would be in the shit.'

'Did Craig get you a lot of properties?' asked Michael, praying that Harper would carry on with his explanation.

'Nah, not really. Apart from the ones we did with you, the most we ever had on the go at any one time was two – and that was only when

Rick got really sick. No, we weren't into it in a big way, but Craig was – he got in with some real heavyweight gang. They were ripping off fuckin' millions apparently.'

'Yeah?'

'Yeah.'

'Bloke called Thompson was the ringleader. Bought himself a villa in Spain on it, so I heard. Anyway, listen, have you closed down Milland Road now – I mean, have you signed off?'

'Yeah, last week.'

'That's probably the best thing you could have done as it happens – now that Craig's gone we've no idea what's going on inside Housing Benefits and if Dill caught up with you again or somethin' we wouldn't get to hear about it. But look, keep the rent, right? I appreciate your bringing it round, but it sounds like you'll need it much more than we will. I'm glad you've patched things up with your family, mate. You always did miss 'em, didn't you …?'

Driving back from the Abaddon estate to Balam Road for the last time, Michael felt sick to his core. For months the phantom of betrayal had stalked him: probing, plotting, waiting for the day that it could step forward from the shadows and inject its poison into his soul. Now, finally, he knew what the East European spy had meant. There could be no *Criminal Britain* without telling the story of Harper and Angela, and no telling of their story without mentioning Rick. Watching, but not seeing the shoppers milling along Feltham High Street, Michael realized that he had misconstrued Harper's character and motivations right from the very beginning – that he had failed to notice the deep protective instinct that hid beneath his veneer of cynicism. He had thought that the fraudster had befriended him because he himself had been lonely. In fact, Harper had pitied the sad, solitary Northerner who had asked him for a game of pool one lunch-time, just as he had pitied his wayward nephew Jez and the simple, starry-eyed youth who watched children's cartoons during the day and wept uncontrollably into his mother's lap at night. Once the documentary was screened, Michael doubted that Harper or Angela would get a custodial sentence: the extent of their fraudulence was insignificant compared to that of Thompson and Craig. By betraying Harper's friendship, however, he had guaranteed them an infinitely crueller sentence: Rick's inevitable return to custody.

Arriving at the flat, Michael downloaded the conversation that he had had with Harper on the balcony and, in an effort to put it from his mind, straightaway hid the video cassette under the floorboards in the hall. In all, there were now over twenty cassettes in there – the complete record of his year's work. Despite the feelings of self-loathing at his calculated act of betrayal, Michael knew in his heart of hearts that the following afternoon, when he got to the flat in Soho, the first thing that he would do would be to find an equally secure storage area for the tapes: he would make his documentary about Harper, Angela and Rick, although how he was going to live with himself afterwards was another matter.

Walking back down the hall, he was just about to go into the lounge when he heard a noise outside the front door. Turning back around again, he went towards the net curtain to look through, when suddenly there was a sound of splintering wood and the door burst open with an enormous crash. Stepping instinctively on to his back foot, Michael was completely unable to defend himself when the two massive dark shapes came hurtling down the hallway towards him. Doubling up as the fists smashed into his groin, shoulders and head, Michael then found himself propelled into the lounge and pushed backwards into one of the dining chairs. Within a second his hands were behind his back and he heard two distinctive sharp clicks: he had been handcuffed to the chair.

'Rufyaan,' drawled a voice to his left. At that moment, the two men stood back and Michael saw the black, leather-jacketed Yardie who had held the gun to his face on the Abaddon saunter lazily into the room. 'Again you come my ken this day. Wherefore? Wherefore that be …?'

Without turning to look at Michael, the man continued walking slowly across the room, finally slumping down into the arm chair next to the window. Sinking low into the seat and spreading his legs broadly apart, he then languidly waved his right hand at the two other men who immediately set about ransacking the cupboards and shelves, dashing everything they found out on to the floor. When they had finished, one of them noticed the mobile phone still connected to the VCR. Unplugging it, he passed it to the man in the chair who scrutinized it carefully for several seconds before slipping it into his inside pocket. Looking at Michael, he then slowly raised his right eyebrow, inviting him once again to answer his question. Staring at his huge, powerful frame and remembering the manner in which last time his anger had flared so violently, Michael knew that he dare not risk repeating the same cover story. This was a man with little patience and no pity; only the truth would save him.

'I lied to you the other day,' said Michael. 'I wasn't looking for my son. I'm a reporter. I went to the estate looking for a man called Richard Thompson. I had a tip-off he was hiding out in that tower block – the one where you found me. I went back there again today to look for him, but he wasn't there. That's the truth. In the room next door to this – in the bedroom – you'll find some cameras and various telephoto lenses. Go and check if you want to.'

In response, the man simply laughed – a humourless, ursine rumble that seemed to emanate not from his mouth or throat but from somewhere deep in his chest. Raising himself out of the arm chair, he then stepped forward and, taking hold of Michael by the chin, turned his head slowly so that his scar was fully visible.

'Reporter? No reporter.'

'Cave boy am repaataa!' giggled the second man.

'It's true!' exclaimed Michael, but, no sooner had he spoken than the third man suddenly sprang forwards, pulling a reel of masking tape out of his pocket. Tearing off a strip he then stuck it over Michael's mouth. Although he knew that it was pointless to try and escape, Michael nevertheless began to shake himself violently around in the chair. In response, the leader nodded at his two henchmen who each grabbed one of Michael's shoulders, forcing their weight down on to him so that he was completely unable to move. His face still wearing the same amused smile, the leader then put his hand into the side pocket of his leather jacket and took out a small, red, barrel-shaped object about six inches in length. Looking on in horror, Michael watched as the man stuck his thumbnail into the Swiss army knife and pulled out a gleaming, hooked blade.

'This am my little scorpion,' he said, proudly, flourishing the curved blade as though it were a scorpion's tail. 'It help you talk, rufyaan.'

As the man stepped forward, Michael summoned up all his energy to overturn the chair, but again the two men were too strong for him. Grabbing the collar of Michael's T-shirt, the man then hooked the blade into it and dragged it downwards in a scything movement, revealing his bare chest. Resting the tip of the blade on Michael's right pectoral, he curled his lips into a huge, beaming grin and then, bringing his weight down to bear on the knife, dug the blade in and pulled.

With his mouth taped-up, Michael's scream turned in on itself, reverberating through his torso and limbs and forcing his body into a series of helpless spasms. After what felt like minutes, but was probably only seconds, Michael's eyes were able to focus once more and he looked up to see the leader staring back down at him and pointing to his chest in amusement.

'Scar to match your face, maan,' he laughed.

Lowering his head to look downwards, Michael was overcome with nausea at the sight of the blood pumping out of the deep gash in his chest. Fighting to stay conscious and maintain his concentration through the peels of sadistic laughter echoing in his ears, he racked his brains as to what he could say to convince the men that he was telling the truth: in a moment they would pull the tape from his mouth, but he would have only seconds to speak – he had to make sure that what he said was credible. As the leader wiped the bloody knife on his trouser leg, Michael suddenly thought of Tom. That was the answer. He would get them to call Tom. It was mid-afternoon. He should be in his office now. He could convince them. As the leader stood over him once more, Michael readied himself to tell him to call the switchboard first – that way, he would know for definite that Tom worked at *The Mail*. Instead of pulling off the masking tape, however, the leader suddenly swung his arm back and then punched him violently in the mouth. As his head whip-lashed backwards and then forwards again, Michael felt a wave of hopeless desperation overtake him. The beating was just going to go on and on. Thinking that he was an undercover police officer, or possibly a hired killer from another gang, the men no doubt believed that he would not reveal the truth until they had tortured and beaten him to within an inch of his life. Looking on in abject terror, Michael waited for the second excruciating stab of pain as the leader positioned the blade on the other side of his chest. But it never came. Instead, over his muffled, petrified cries of panic, a single quietly spoken word resounded throughout the room

'Back.'

The three men and Michael all looked to their left. A man was standing just inside the lounge doorway with a pistol held at waist height. It was Kent.

The men stood upright in surprise and took a step backwards, but, looking at their expressions and the way their eyes darted back and forth between each other, Michael could see that they were obviously thinking of jumping Kent: the room was narrow and it was three against one. Kent, however, had clearly already considered this probability and had no intention of surrendering the initiative.

'You, you,' he said pointing the gun at the leader and the man on Michael's left. 'In the middle of the room. Get down on your knees and raise your arms.'

Again the three men exchanged a glance, but as soon as they had done so, Kent fired the gun. In the confines of the narrow living room the noise was deafening. The shot was so close to the leader's head that he instinctively ducked down as the bullet went whizzing past his cheek.

'Next one takes your face off,' growled Kent, raising the gun. 'Now, on your knees!'

Within an instant the two men that he had pointed to had dropped to the floor. Taking several steps to his left to gain a wider firing angle, but not taking his eyes off the men, Kent called out to the third.

'You. What's your name?'

'Doc T,' responded the man.

'OK, Doc T, you get to do the honours. Take the tape off his mouth and then go back and kneel down next to your mates, real slow.'

Pulling the tape of Michael's mouth, the man went over to join the other two in the middle of the room.

'How you doin', Mick?' asked Kent, cheerily.

'I've been better,' gasped Michael. 'But, listen, I'm handcuffed into the chair. I can't move.'

'Who's got the keys?' asked Kent. The man called Doc T nodded his head. 'Undo the cuffs,' continued Kent, his voice low and threatening. 'Slow – got it?'

Getting back up again, Doc T walked around to the back of the chair and undid the left hand cuff. But then, having shifted position slightly as though moving around the chair to unlock Michael's right hand, he suddenly turned on his heel and sprang towards Kent.

Kent raised the gun as though to fire, but Doc T caught his right wrist in time and lifted his arm high into the air. For a fraction of a second, Michael was convinced that he had managed to surprise Kent, but, as Doc T brought up his right fist to smash it into Kent's face, Michael realized that it had in fact all been a clever feint on Kent's part.

He had something in his other hand, and, in a flash, had stabbed it into Doc T's throat before he had time to land his blow.

With a voltaic crackle, the Yardie soared through the air, crashing into the other two men in a tangle of limbs just as they had raised themselves to their feet to help him. Clutching his Adam's apple, he then let out a series of agonized, stentorian groans. Looking back at Kent, Michael could see that in his other hand he was holding the stun baton.

'Told you it'd come in handy one day, Mick, didn't I, eh?' grinned Kent, coolly, kneeling quickly down on one knee, picking up the keys to the handcuffs and then passing them to Michael.

Undoing the second cuff, Michael raised himself painfully to his feet. From his other pocket Kent then produced another pistol and, having passed it to Michael, turned and looked at the three Yardies.

'Now, listen to me you fuckin' thick, black bastards,' he spat, contemptuously. 'You're so far out of your fuckin' league I couldn't even begin to explain what you've got yourselves into. So, I'll keep it simple. Come back here again and you're dead. Fuck with me again and you're dead. That's all you need to know. Now, piss off.'

With the guns trained on them and with Doc T still retching in pain, the men gave up all hope of resistance and within seconds were out of the door and staggering down the front steps towards their car. Having made certain that they had driven off, Kent then quickly slipped out of the lounge, returning a few moments later with several folds of kitchen towel.

'Come on, sit down,' he said, levering Michael into a dining chair and then picking up the roll of masking tape off the floor.

'Thanks,' said Michael. 'I thought I'd had it then.'

'Ha! Now we're equal, eh, Mick?' laughed Kent, pulling Michael's shirt back and, getting right up close to his chest, positioning a thick fold of kitchen towel over the wound. 'Remember that night back in the hospital? I thought I'd fuckin' had it then, too. It was 'cos you jumped that geezer by the door that I'm still 'ere today.'

'What did you come round for, anyway?'

'That's why I came round,' replied Kent, simply.

'What? What d'you mean?'

'The men in the hospital – Foss and his mates – that's why I came round.'

'I don't get you ...' said Michael.

'They're all dead, Mick. That's what I came to tell you. I said I'd 'ave 'em all by Christmas, didn't I? Ha! They only just made it past Easter! I wanted to tell you that you don't have to keep you head down any longer. Took me fuckin' ages to find this place, mind you – which was just as well really: if I'd've got here any earlier your spades would've had us both. As I was pullin' up in the car I noticed them getting out of theirs. How d'you get involved with 'em anyway? Fuckin' Yardies! Are you off your head?'

'It's a long story,' replied Michael, wondering how he was going to explain the presence of the three drug dealers in his flat.

'Tell me on the way to hospital,' said Kent, pulling Michael's shirt back over the now completed make-shift bandage. 'You need stitches quick.'

The Saab's air-conditioning was crisp and soothing and, despite the pain in his chest, Michael found that his mind was thinking clearly again. He had driven back from the Abaddon estate absorbed in his betrayal of Harper's friendship and had not noticed the Yardies following him back to Balam Road. It had been nothing short of divine providence that Kent had arrived there just a few moments afterwards: he doubted that there was anyone else in the country capable of dealing with three such characters single-handedly.

'I hope you don't mind me saying this,' said Kent, accelerating away from Apex Corner towards the nearby A&E unit at Middlesex Hospital, 'but it's a right fuckin' dump this place. What're you livin' round here for?'

'Well, it was all I could afford when I got here from up north. I was skint. I've found another flat now, though. In Soho.'

'Thank Christ for that. So, are you gonna be takin' the job, then?'

'What job?'

'The job. Full time – at Gog. Remember.'

'Oh, yeah – yeah, I am,' replied Michael – having always intended to accept the job, it had slipped his mind that he had not actually confirmed as much to Kent. 'Sorry, I never got back to you. You weren't there last weekend otherwise I'd've told you.'

'Yeah, I was off freezin' my bollocks off in the fiords,' laughed Kent. 'Well that's good news anyway. I'm pleased.'

Although Michael smiled in response, inside his mind a voice cried out in frustration. Every time he had met Kent, right from the very first day he had started work at Gog, he had always made sure to record everything that he said, but because the Yardies had pocketed his mobile phone, he hadn't been wearing it when Kent had showed up. Worse still, he'd forgotten to get it back off them when Kent had sent them packing. As a result, he had just failed to capture this vital piece of supporting information: if Kent had spent the weekend in Norway, then he must surely have been visiting Fobors. Leaning his head back on the headrest, Michael closed his eyes for several moments, wondering what the Yardies would do with the phone. He had deliberately not stored any numbers in its address book and Jim had disabled the last number redial function, so they would probably give up on it fairly quickly; perhaps it had already been tossed into one of the piles of trash on the Abaddon estate. For the next few days he would have to use the second, palm-held mobile that he had acquired solely for the purposes of communicating with Harper; once he had moved into the Soho flat he would order another one from Jim.

'So, how d'you get involved with those guys, anyway, then?' asked Kent.

'Oh, I've been buyin' gear off 'em,' replied Michael, casually. 'We had a bit of a disagreement about the price.'

'You mean you were buyin' drugs – off them?' asked Kent, shaking his head in disbelief.

'Yeah.'

'Ah, you should've told me. I could've got 'em for you.'

'Yeah?'

'Yeah, of course,' replied Kent. 'I control all the gear goin' into the club. And a load of other places, too.'

'Yeah?' replied Michael.

'Yeah, of course I do. In fact, I was thinkin' I might make it part of your new responsibilities – now you're on board full-time, like.'

'Sounds great.'

'Looks like you've got more experience than I'd thought. Edwin's been doin' it for the last year or two but he's on his way soon – the boss has got other plans for him …'

For a moment, Michael was tempted to question Kent as to what Edwin would be doing for Ellis, but decided that it might be pushing his luck too far. Also, they were nearing the hospital and he wanted to

390

make sure that Kent didn't miss the turning: the make-shift bandage had worked well so far, but he could already feel a trickle of blood seeping out of the side of the kitchen towel and down into the waistband of his trousers. Pulling up on the double yellow lines outside the A&E unit, Kent switched off the ignition and, having checked that they were not being overlooked, quickly took the gun out of his pocket and slipped it into Michael's hand.

'Listen, I can't come in with you, I'm supposed to be somewhere else now, but take this just in case. I don't think your Caribbean mates'll be comin' back, but you never know.'

'Thanks.'

'Get yourself sewn up good and proper. I'll stop by tomorrow if I've got time.'

So saying, Kent placed his left hand on Michael's leg and squeezed hard. Surprised at this affectionate gesture but conscious of the spreading wet patch underneath his arm, Michael nodded briefly in response and then levered himself out of the car.

He got back to Balam Road just after seven o'clock in the evening. Keeping the gun in his jacket pocket, he walked warily over to the twenty-four hour café on Uxbridge Road to get himself a proper meal. Although the doctor in A&E had given him a pain-killing injection, he felt feeble and light-headed, not having eaten anything since the snack that he had had before going off to see Naz that morning. Sitting down by the window, he looked back across the road in the direction of his flat: Kent had been confident that the Yardies would not come back, but he was not so certain. At this point, he realized that he was sitting in the same seat he had occupied the first time that he had come to the café the day that he had arrived in Feltham. Lighting up a cigarette he sat pensively waiting for his food to arrive. Despite everything that he had achieved since, he could not afford the luxury of self-congratulation. He might well be slipping quietly away from Feltham the following afternoon, but he would never be really secure until the day in just over three months' time that Michael Angel disappeared off the face of the earth forever.

He slept badly. The pain-killing injection began to wear off just after midnight and the pills that the Doctor had given him didn't seem to have any effect. Several times during the night he heard noises, and, taking the gun from under his pillow, padded silently out into the hallway to make sure that there was no one there. As the morning drew near, however, he began to worry less about the Yardies than the way that Kent had got so close to him when dressing his wound and the peculiar squeeze on the leg that he had given him before driving away. A month ago, in the second floor restaurant, Edwin had given him a warning, the possible significance of which he now almost dared not contemplate. *'You're right not to ask too many favours of Kent. He might decide to call them all in at once and that could be quite painful for you – take my word for it.'* What if Kent was a homosexual? What if his brutal, violent nature extended into his sexual proclivities – into a hyper masculinity that could only be satisfied by being the dominant partner in a relationship with another male? *'He had his favourites before you, you know,'* Edwin had said. *'A whole string of protégés – and where are they all now, one might ask?'*

Hearing a noise at the front door, Michael awoke with a start and then leapt sideways straight out of bed. Grabbing the gun off the bedside table he trained it on the hallway. Chest heaving, he then lay back against the bedroom wall, closed his eyes and allowed himself a fleeting smile of relief. It had been the postman. Looking at the clock and seeing that it was half-past nine, he picked the bottle of pills up off the bedside table and examined the label with approval. Just before four a.m., he had taken a second dose, and, although he had not expected any result, they had obviously knocked him out for over five hours. Putting the safety catch back on the gun, he slowly got changed, being careful not to raise his right arm too high in case he opened up the stiches, and then went into the kitchen to make some coffee.

Having finished his second cup, he felt considerably better and began to plan his movements for the day. Although he was leaving the flat, he had decided to carry on renting it for the next four months. During that time it could act as a bolt hole or temporary stopover if things got too hot at Gog or in Soho. Accordingly, he had decided to leave the TV, the VCR and some other small household items. The tapes and most of his clothes, however, he would take with him, and, to that end, he had purchased two small suitcases the previous weekend. It would take about an hour to drive into central London and, as the estate agent had said he could pick up the keys any time after twelve o'clock, he decided he may as well start packing straightaway.

Walking out of the kitchen towards the hall cupboard where the suit-cases were stored, he opened the door but then stopped dead in his tracks. Lying squarely in the middle of the hall carpet was a postcard. He picked it up and then exhaled in intense irritation. It was red: the signal that he and Tom had agreed to indicate that he should cease operations immediately and go straight to the safe house. Slamming the cupboard door, he went into the living room to call Tom on the second mobile phone. Finding that the battery was not charged up, he shoved it into the top pocket of his jacket, went into his bedroom, and, cursing loudly, began to put on his shoes. He knew exactly what had happened. King had come back from his gallivanting overseas and, having discovered from Tom that Michael had still not yet got close to the drug pushing at Gog, had issued instructions for him to come in. Well, he had news for both King and Tom. He had done it — just as he had said he would. Slipping on his jacket and checking that he had enough change, he left the flat and made his way to the callbox on the corner of the Uxbridge Road.

'Hello, can I speak to Mr Cranmer, please?'

'Who's calling?'

'It's Mr Angel.'

'I'm sorry, Mr Angel, but I'm afraid he's in a ...'

'Then get him out of the fucking meeting!' roared Michael into the receiver. 'I need to speak to him now! This instant, right?'

For a moment the line went dead and Michael thought that Tom's secretary may have hung up. Rubbing his hand over the top of his head in annoyance, he fought back the urge to lash out a foot and kick the inside of the phone booth. He shouldn't have flown off the handle like that, but his patience was now almost completely exhausted. It was bad enough that Tom and King were prevaricating at this crucial stage, but to be held up by Tom's secretary each time he needed to speak to him was simply adding insult to injury.

'Hello?'

'Tom, it's me. I got your card. It's King, isn't it?'

'Yes, yes,' replied Tom, quietly.

'Listen. There's been a development. It's good news — it'll put his mind at rest. I'm in, Tom. I'm in. Last night Kent confirmed again that he controls drug distribution inside the club. But, more than that, he's asked me to handle it for him — put me in charge of it. I can get all the footage King needs and all the stuff I promised you besides.'

For a moment there was a strange, mournful silence. Michael was just about to ask Tom if he was still there when he exhaled heavily and began to speak.

'Oh, dear God. You haven't heard have you?'

'Heard what?'

'About Henry.'

'What about him?'

'I tried to call you yesterday afternoon but there was no answer on your mobile.'

'Yeah, somebody stole it, but what's happened to King anyway?'

'You haven't seen the news on the television or in the papers or any-thing ...'

'No, I haven't. What's happened Tom. Tell me!'

'He's dead,' replied Tom, flatly. 'Henry's dead.'

'What!'

'He died yesterday afternoon: collapsed at his home, first thing in the morning – a heart attack. They rushed him into hospital, but it was no good – they couldn't save him. He passed away just after two o'clock.'

'Oh, my God ...'

'I got there just after they'd admitted him but he was already in a coma – I didn't even get the chance to speak to him before he died. I called you a dozen times, but you didn't answer, so in the end I sent the card. I thought by the time you got it you'd have heard and you'd know what it meant. I'm sorry. This must be an enormous shock for you.'

'What are we going to do?' said Michael, looking out of the window of the call box in stunned bewilderment.

'I'm afraid there's nothing we can do,' said Tom, solemnly. *Criminal Britain* is over, old chum. It's finished. It has to be. It's time for you to come in.'

'But I'm so close!' gasped Michael. 'I'll, I'll be finished in just a few months – in a few weeks. We'll have everything we need ...'

'I understand how you feel and I know you're confident of complet-ing all the investigations, but without Henry I can't guarantee we can get the series screened. He was the one who could pull all the strings – who could make everything happen. You can't go on taking further risks without the assurance of knowing that it will actually make it on to the air. It'd be madness to do that – absolute madness.'

'No, no,' countered Michael, desperately, 'we'll find somebody else to screen it. The latest stuff I've got on Ellis and the others, it's dynamite. It'll make fantastic viewing …'

'I'm sure it would, old chap. But we're not the only fish in the pond. There's Buckleys, too, remember? Even while Henry was alive the September deadline was going to be close, but now he's dead we just won't be able to move fast enough.'

'But I've put so much into this, Tom. My whole life. I can't give up now.'

'But it's too dangerous,' insisted Tom. 'What if something happened to you? I just couldn't have that on my conscience. It was bad enough last time when you were knifed in the face.'

'Don't worry about that. It's my risk. It always has been, right from the beginning.'

'No, no – I can't.'

'Tom, listen to me. I'm begging you, please. If you'd only take a look at the latest stuff I've got …'

Suddenly, Michael became conscious of a peculiar hollowness on the line and, when Tom's secretary began to speak, he realized that she had cut in moments before and had been waiting for a lull in the conversation.

'Mr Cranmer, I'm terribly sorry to interrupt you, but I have Mr Scott on the other line. It's about Mr King.'

'OK, OK, tell him to hold – I'll be with him in a minute,' said Tom, the echoing sound disappearing and the line once more returning to normal. 'Sorry about that, old boy. It's complete pandemonium in the Tower – it's gone totally mad – I've been here since six trying to sort things out. But listen, you have to pull out now. Go straight to the safe house. It's the only thing to do. I'll call you there later. OK?'

'Tom, please.'

'I've got to go, old boy. I'll call you. I promise.'

Replacing the receiver, Michael pushed open the door of the phone box and, walking down the street as though in a dream, made his way back to Balam Road. Over the past year, dozens of potential calamitous scenarios had passed through his mind that might result in him having to abandon the series, but none with the devastating finality of that single, sixty-second phone-call. Going through the front door, he walked slowly around the flat – the place that had been his home for almost a year. During that time he had risked so much and had over-come every challenge that had confronted him – the prospect of now having to leave Feltham with nothing to show for it was unthinkable. How could he ever again look forwards to the future with optimism – surely the rest of his life was going to remain forever tainted by sour regret at having been cheated out of the-once-in-a-lifetime prize that should have been his? Sitting down at the kitchen table, he buried his head in his hands and forced himself to think. It was bad enough that he had worked so hard and had sacrificed so much, but if *Criminal Britain* was never screened, how would the world ever come to know the truth about Ellis? He simply had to find some way of completing the investigation.

Half an hour later, the answer came to him. Tom had said that he had been working since six o'clock that morning. The previous week when they had met in his office he had seemed abnormally tired and fraught, referring to something that had gone amiss in his personal life. Adding to this the sudden shock of King's death and the frenzied confusion it had evidently created in the Tower, it was hardly surprising that Tom had rec-ommended abandoning the series – even his naturally optimistic charac-ter must be wilting under such intense pressure. In the calm, intimate atmosphere of the safe house, however, he might well see things differ-ently. Perhaps it was not too late to find another media organization that could sponsor the series, who would share the enthusiasm and vision that King had demonstrated when first he had proposed the concept. That had been over a year ago, but now, of course, Michael had already com-pleted the first two investigations and was within a few weeks of com-pleting the other two. Irrespective of Buckleys' progress with similar subject matter, there had to be a chance, and if Michael did not try to take it, then he would truly spend the rest of his life burdened by self-recrimination. He would go to the safe house, get Tom to join him there that evening and do everything that he could to convince him.

Packing a light overnight bag, he left the flat and went down to his car. Deciding that the traffic would be too heavy at that time of the day in central London, he set off for the safe house around the south circu-lar. He had been travelling less than thirty minutes when he saw the first signpost for Barnes. Frowning, he recalled what Charlotte had said, or rather had left unsaid, the previous day. If there was one thing in the world more important to him than finishing *Criminal Britain*, it was

Elizabeth and Jake. Looking at his watch and seeing that it was only just after twelve o'clock, he decided to take a diversion and drive past their flat. Tom probably wouldn't be able to make it to the safe house until the evening, so he had plenty of time, and, more than anything at that moment, what he needed was reassurance – reassurance that those he considered his own would value and respect what he had achieved and the dangers that he had faced.

The moment that he pulled into the car park, he knew that something was wrong. He had wanted only to see some small sign of life, some indication that Jake and Elizabeth were still there – still going about their lives in the ordered respectability of their third-floor flat. Even at fifty yards away, however, he could tell that it was completely empty: there were no lights, no furniture and no curtains. Leaving the car door open, he walked across the grass verge towards the tall, red-brick building and looked up in utter disbelief. Where had they gone? What could have happened to them in the last year to have occasioned such a complete change in their circumstances? When last he had talked to Elizabeth, she had spoken only of stability – of her intention to stay in her job and to keep Jake at the school at which he was doing so well. Had they moved to another house? It would seem the obvious explanation, but it would not account for why Charlotte had been so evasive. Staring up at the deserted flat above him, Michael was filled with a terrible sense of foreboding. Elizabeth and Jake hadn't moved a few miles away to another apartment. They had gone. Gone forever.

He was back at Miranda Close half an hour later. Not waiting for the automatic gates lugubriously to part, he ran his car up on to the pavement, jumped on to the adjacent wall and, ignoring the pain in his chest, leapt over the iron railings. Running down the Close, he could see straightaway that Charlotte's car was there. She knew where they had gone. She must do. Rapping three times hard on the front door, he stood on the step clenching his fists and waiting for her to appear.

'Where are they? Where are they, Charlotte?'

Her look of surprise and alarm quickly gave way to one of steely antagonism, as, taking several step forwards, she moved to within a few inches of his face.

'I wouldn't tell you for the world,' she hissed.

'Charlotte, you've got no right. You can't keep that information from me.'

'If Elizabeth had wanted you to know, you'd be correct in that assertion: I would be morally bound to tell you. But she didn't. She told me that she didn't. And I've no intention of going against her wishes.'

'Why? Why didn't she want me to know where they've gone?'

'Why?' laughed Charlotte. 'Why? Why do you think? You ruined that woman's life. She could have anybody for a husband, with her looks and intelligence. But she had to go and choose a selfish, self-obsessed egomaniac like you!'

'Charlotte, I know you never liked me, but something happened this last year. It's too difficult to explain, but it's all over now and ...'

'Oh, it's all over, all right!' she scoffed. 'You're dead right it's all over. You're out of their lives forever and, my God, am I pleased to see it! Maybe at last Elizabeth'll get a shot at the happiness she deserves, now she's finally been able to put you behind her.'

'Charlotte, please,' begged Michael, feeling the tears of frustration beginning to well into his eyes. 'You don't understand, I've been waiting for this day for a whole year. Waiting for the time that I could get to see them and explain everything.'

'Keep your explanations,' snapped Charlotte. 'Keep them to yourself. They don't want to hear them and neither do I.'

Turning on her heel, Charlotte went to back inside her house. Taking a step forward, Michael clasped her forearm, but, twisting it violently, she shrugged off his grasp and went back into the hallway. Clutching his hands together in a last, desperate plea, Michael called out to her once more.

'Charlotte, I'm begging you.'

'I'd rather die than tell you where they're going,' she replied and, with a final look of implacable enmity mixed with disgust, closed the door.

Waiting for the gates to open, Michael looked at his car on the other side of the railings, crazily mounted at an angle on the pavement. It was no wonder that Charlotte had regarded him with such repugnance: with his cut lip, scarred face and filthy clothes, he must have appeared a truly pathetic figure. Opening up the driver's door, he slumped into the seat, resting his hands and forehead on the steering wheel. What next? What next for the man with two lives, both of which were rapidly spiralling into ruin? For a moment he thought of Tom, but he was totally caught up in dealing with the aftermath of Henry King's death and was anyway already urging him to abandon the series; he wouldn't have the time to find out where Elizabeth and Jake had gone. Sitting bolt upright again, Michael suddenly realized that, after all, there was a glimmer of hope. Charlotte might well be judgmental and self-righteous, but she was also unfalteringly grammatically pedantic. As she had been closing the door, she had said that she would rather die than tell him where they were going. Her use of the future tense could only mean that wherever their destination might be, they had not yet departed for it. Switching on the ignition, Michael turned the car through a hundred and eighty degrees and made his way back off the estate. Reaching the end of the road, he drew the car up sharply and then looked alternately left and right, trying to decide where best to go next. With a sudden surge of resentment, he abandoned the idea of going to Clapham – Tom might have got him into all this but he certainly wasn't going to get him out of it. That just left Balam Road or the new flat in Soho. With the first mobile phone stolen and the battery in the second completely dead, he turned left and began to make his way towards Central London. The estate agent had promised that the phone would be on from the moment that he moved in.

Tom had been calling the safe house regularly since lunch time. Putting down the receiver for the seventh or eighth time, he frowned and looked his watch. It was almost four o'clock. If Michael hadn't got there by now, he wasn't going to go at all. Opening up the bottom drawer of his desk, he went to take out the bottle of whisky, but then caught sight of the small, black deposit-box next to it. Unlocking it, he took out the two keys inside and held them in his hand. They were the keys to Balam Road – the first thing that he had received from Michael, eight days after he had gone undercover. Shaking his head, Tom poured himself a glass of whisky, but, instead of drinking it, stared guiltily at the amber coloured liquid. His parting words to Michael, before he had left the safe house and gone off to Feltham had been that if things ever got tough, he would immediately drop whatever he was doing and come and get him; twenty-four hours a day, seven days a week. When, if not now, should he honour that promise? When, if not now, should he repay the debt of trust which, in all honesty, he had been party to betraying? Leaving the whisky undrunk, he took his jacket off the coat stand and made his way grimly towards the door.

'I'm, er, just going out for a couple of hours ...'

'Where?' she asked, anxiously.

He didn't answer, although he guessed she probably knew.

True to his word, the estate agent had made sure that the phone was connected. As soon as Michael heard the reassuring burr of the dialling tone, he punched out 118 383 on the dial. Directory enquiries gave him the school's number straightaway.

'St Benedicts. Hello.'

'Hello, could I speak to Elizabeth Macheson, please?'

'Oh, I'm afraid not,' replied the voice, cheerily. 'The school's closed for Easter holidays now, but, anyway, she's left.'

'Really?' replied Michael, trying to instill his voice with just the right degree of surprise. 'This is Andy Byatt from the National Union of Teachers here, we've got a refund for her on her subscription. Where should I send it? Have you got a forwarding address?'

'Well, somebody in the office'll know, but there's nobody there this week — it's the caretaker you're talking to.'

'Oh, right,' replied Michael, shaking his fist in frustration. He should have remembered that the schools were out now.

'But anyway, I'm not so sure that pounds are gonna be much good to her where she's going.'

'No?' asked Michael, his tone of polite interest belying the shocked realization of what he had just heard.

'No. She's off to Australia, isn't she?'

'Australia?' gasped Michael.

'Yeah. Emigrating. Her and her son. We had a leaving do for her last week. A proper lady she was, Miss Macheson — we're all going to miss her.'

'D'you know where in Australia?' asked Michael, trying to maintain the genial tone in his voice.

'Oh, I can't remember exactly — some school over there. Ring back next week and there'll be somebody in the office, then. They'll tell you.'

'Oh, OK, just one final question. D'you know whether she's actually gone yet? I could always send the cheque to her home address if she's still in the country; I've got it here, it's in Barnes.'

'No, I'm afraid you've just missed the boat there, too,' said the care-taker, ''cos I know for a fact she's already moved out. She's off tomorrow in fact — she told me at the do — a week on Friday she said. That'd be tomorrow, wouldn't it? Yeah, that's right. Don't suppose she'll have the time to pay it in before she goes, will she? What with last-minute arrangements 'n' all.'

'Oh, right, thanks, you've been very helpful,' said Michael.

'My pleasure. Bye now.'

On seeing the damage around the door frame and lintel, Tom felt a shiver of fright pass along his spine: he had known all along that Michael had been living in constant peril, but the flecked paint and splinters of wood were far more suggestive of those dangers than all the video footage he had seen. Taking out the keys, he went to open the door, but then turned and looked back behind him; he hoped that whoever had done this wasn't still hanging around in the early evening shadows. At the end of the hallway, he paused and looked around the flat; it was even smaller and pokier than he had imagined. Going into the dining room, he put the keys down silently on the table and then took out his mobile to check the signal strength: if Michael phoned to say that he had gone to the safe house after all, he would immediately set off and join him – the quicker he got out of this awful place the better. Cautiously moving over to the sofa, he slowly ran his hand over the surface, worrying that it might dirty his raincoat if he sat down, but then immediately felt ashamed of the gesture. Michael had put up with these conditions for nearly a year – what right had he to be so fastidious? In the hope of staving off the rising sense of claustrophobia, he went over to the door to turn on the light but then changed his mind: the last thing he wanted to do was draw attention to his presence. Walking back across the room, he opened up the wall cupboard, and, with a smile, noticed the bottle of whisky on the bottom shelf. Having found a glass in the kitchen, he returned to the living room and poured himself a stiff double; nothing wrong with a shot of Dutch courage. Slumping down onto the sofa, which despite its obvious age proved to be surprisingly comfortable, he leant his head back and closed his eyes for a few seconds. He was dog tired – he'd been up since five. Watching the evening sun set through the living room windows, he all of a sudden began to feel strangely at peace. Maybe this wasn't such a bad way to end his day after all. Sitting in silence with a fine single malt, honouring a promise to a friend.

Michael wasn't sure how long he'd been walking. He had eaten, too, but couldn't remember where. Stopping in a doorway, he stared down the brightly-illuminated Soho street at the crowds of theatre goers and office workers bustling back and forth. When he had put the phone down on the caretaker, all conscious thought had simply drained away from his mind – caught in the hiatus between two lives, his identity had self-arrested, no longer aware of itself or anything around it. Reaching into his pocket for a cigarette and finding only his lighter, he gave a puzzled frown and then decided to set off back to his new flat – there was bound to be a tobacconist on the way. Except, he couldn't exactly remember where the flat was. It didn't matter. If he kept on walking he would eventually come across it. Passing by a shop window, he caught sight of his reflection in the plate glass – or rather the reflection of someone that he knew must be him. As he stared at the expressionless face, bruised and unshaven, deep inside his mind a thought flickered into life: a final, dying spark of self-motivation. There couldn't be that many flights to Australia. He had to find his way to the flat and he had to sleep. The following morning he would call the airports and then all the travel agents in the Barnes area. Elizabeth would have bought the tickets locally. She had always liked the personal touch.

Kent found that he was speeding. Gradually taking his foot off the accelerator, he slowed down until he slipped back under the speed limit. Neither his name, nor his car registration number, nor any other personal detail had ever found its way into a police officer's note book; if possible, he wanted to keep it that way. Smiling, he looked at the clock on the dashboard. Half-past seven. He hadn't been speeding because he was late – he had simply said that he would drop by Michael's flat the next day if he had the time – no, the fact was that he was excited. There was no other word for it – he knew that distinctive tickling feeling in his pelvis and spine. He had left it too long, of course. There had been the odd encounter, here and there, and a few passable interrogations in the anteroom next to his office, but there was no proper thrill without a proper chase. He had known from the very beginning that it would take time with Michael – and, of course, he had had to test his loyalty – but everything was now finally falling into place. Soon he would be moving to Soho – only a mile from his own flat. And then, once he was working permanently at Gog, it would only be a matter of time. He imagined it was going to be well worth the wait.

Pulling into the slip road in front of Michael's flat, Kent grimaced in disappointment. The lights weren't on. He wasn't in – probably off filming pussy somewhere. Turning off the engine he sat in the darkness and gazed slowly around. What a shithole. He'd never been to Feltham before and, if he had any choice in the matter, he never would again. Leaning back in his seat, he scratched his chin thoughtfully, trying to decide what to do. Maybe he'd take some time out for ten minutes, hang around a bit to see if Michael showed up. Suddenly, however, he was right back on his guard again – his eyes narrowed, the hair on the back of his neck stiff and alert. It was a car. The driver had come to a halt in front of Michael's flat and was looking up at it quizzically. Slipping his hand into his pocket, Kent took hold of his gun, but almost straightaway released it. The man had undoubtedly come to see Michael, but was an altogether different proposition from the three Yardies that he had so enjoyed humiliating the previous day. This man was nervous, hesitant – not at all self-confident. Staring through the Saab's one-way smoked glass windows, Kent wondered for a moment whether he had come to buy some gear off Michael, but then dismissed the idea. The man was anxious, certainly, but not in the way punters were anxious. He was too sly-looking for that. He was a villain – Kent knew it in an instant: he had a sixth sense for these things. Seeing the man get out of his car and walk hesitantly towards the flat, Kent slipped noiselessly out of the Saab and followed him along the pavement. As Michael wasn't in, maybe he'd have a word with his ginger-haired, boss-eyed friend instead, whose face – come to think of it – all of a sudden seemed strangely familiar. Where had he seen him before? Perhaps it had been at the club. No. It couldn't have been. Michael never brought his friends to Gog. So where? And then, as the man suddenly sensed someone behind him and looked nervously around, the memories came flooding back and Kent remembered everything: the darkened room; the sudden unexpected rush of embarrassment and, worst of all the laughter – the laughter from men whom he had been so much hoping to impress.

They made their approach through the alleyways that ran between the back gardens of the houses behind Balam Road. Jo'dan had had a girlfriend who'd lived just two streets away and he knew that by going down the gullies they could come out unseen on the waste ground behind the flat. Pausing in the darkness next to an ancient, moss-covered concrete garage they checked their weapons. They'd gone for Uzis in the end. Doc T had wanted to bring a sawn-off: his Adam's apple had taken the full force of the stun baton's discharge and he still couldn't talk properly. He wanted the big mother to suffer – blow half his face off with the shotgun and then leave him to bleed to death, but Zel, their leader, had counselled caution. The white guys were no fools and once the three of them got in there, they daren't give them a chance – they needed a massive explosion of firepower. Sawn-offs were OK for scaring bank-clerks, but Uzis did twenty rounds a second – three machine-pistols firing together at once could cut an ox in half. All the same, Jo'dan had insisted on taking his sawn-off as well and wouldn't back down even when a fight had started. In the end, the other two had given in as long as he agreed to go in first.

Seeing the neon glow from the streetlights on the main road up ahead, Zel stopped and rubbed some cocaine into his gums. He was even more amped up than Doc T: he hadn't been batonned, but as leader he'd been the one to suggest they follow the bald guy, Micky, to his flat in the first place and the one to decide that they had to go back for revenge. His plan was simple enough; from the waste ground to the side wall of the building, from the side wall to the stairs and then route one – straight through the front door. Nodding grimly to the other two that it was time to move in, Zel began walking the final few yards down the alleyway towards the waste ground. Letting Doc T go next, Jo'dan watched as he took the sawn off out of his inside pocket and was just about to follow after him when suddenly Zel stopped and raised his fist. It was a police siren. Waiting for it to pass, Zel stood quietly in the darkness, but within a few seconds it was obvious that the police vehicle had come to a halt nearby. Putting out his hand to gesture to the other two to wait, Zel peered around the wall at the end of the alley. Seeing him stand upright and then slowly shake his head in disappointment, Jo'dan and Doc T hurried forward to join him: it wasn't a police car – it was a fire engine. For nearly a minute, the three men stood side by side, watching the flames climb higher and higher into the sky. The bald guy's flat was an inferno – they had been cheated of their revenge. With a final disgusted shake of the head, Zel then turned and walked back down the alley into the darkness. Turning to follow, Jo'dan took several steps after him, but, seeing Doc T still staring resentfully at the blazing building, called out into the night.

'Forget it, maan. Babylon am already burnin'.'

★

They were leaving from Heathrow at three o'clock – flight QA21 to Sydney. Hastily locking the front door of the Soho flat, Michael ran down the stairs two steps at a time and out on to Dean Street. Thirty seconds later, he was in a cab and on his way to terminal three. Checking his watch, he then leant forward and offered the driver an extra hundred pounds to put his foot down. It might only knock five minutes off the journey, but as the plane was due to depart in just over three hours it could make all the difference.

Not waiting for the taxi to come to a halt, Michael tossed three fifty pound notes through the hatch towards the driver and dashed off in the direction of the nearest revolving door. Hurtling through into the forecourt beyond, he looked around for the Quantas check-in desks. In front of him, a young woman with a trolley piled high with luggage had just thrown herself into the arms of an approaching man: journey's end – lovers meeting. He was in arrivals: departures was on the floor below. He needed to get down the escalators quick.

Scanning the rows of passengers queuing at the half dozen Quantas check-in desks and seeing no sign of Elizabeth or Jake, Michael looked at his watch. Five to one. There were still two hours and five minutes to go before the plane was scheduled to take off, but he was almost certain that he had missed them. Elizabeth had always been scrupulously well organized and for a journey of such importance had no doubt arrived in plenty of time. Keeping half an eye on the check-in desks, Michael made his way hurriedly across to the Quantas information desk. He now had no alternative but to throw himself on the mercy of the airline.

'Hello,' said the woman behind the counter. 'Can I help you?'

She was in her early thirties, well presented and obviously very bright. Looking into her warm, intelligent eyes, Michael sensed that at least he would have a chance with this woman. Resting his forearms on the counter, he lowered his voice and spoke with as much candour and clarity as he was able.

'I want to ask a favour of you. A very great favour. My ex-wife and son are booked on QA21 to Sydney leaving in two hours time. I believe they may already have checked in and be on their way to the gate. I couldn't get to see them before they left. I was in a car accident, you see, two days ago. I only got out of hospital last night. Is it possible that you could get a message through to them saying that I'm here and would like to say goodbye to them before they go?'

'I'm terribly sorry, sir,' replied the woman, politely, 'but I'm afraid if they're already checked in – it's against security regulations for them to come back through departures.'

'I understand that and if they were returning to England in a few weeks I wouldn't be asking you. But they're not. They're emigrating. I won't be able to see them again, for, well, I don't know, a very long time. I was planning to go to their house the day before yesterday, but I couldn't and now they're leaving, thinking that I don't care – that I couldn't be bothered to make the effort to see them before they went …'

Making no attempt to conceal his cut lip and the bruising on his face, Michael stared straight into the woman's eyes. For nearly a year he had been acting – masking his true thoughts and emotions. Now, he only hoped that he could convey to her some small measure of his real feelings. Seeing her brow furl in sympathy, he immediately knew that she had sensed that his distress was genuine.

'Oh, dear, I see,' she replied. 'So, er, what shall we do?' Resting her hands on the computer keyboard, she then smiled at him helpfully. 'Well, let's have your wife's name, first of all, shall we? I'll look and see if she really has already checked in.'

'Macheson. Elizabeth Macheson.'

'Macheson … Macheson … yes, yes, I've got her. Right, er, could I just ask you to wait over there for a moment, sir? I need to make a quick couple of calls.'

Moving to the far end of the counter, Michael watched as the woman picked up a telephone and began to dial. If the airport authorities didn't allow Elizabeth and Jake to come back for a few minutes so that he could speak to them and explain, he would then be left with only one choice – to buy a ticket and actually follow them to Australia. Clutching the travel bag that he had brought with him from Balam Road, he blessed his foresight in having packed the fake Michael Angel passport that Tom had had made for him. In four hours time he was due to go to work at Gog. Three days later, he had a meeting scheduled with Simon Luxman. But now neither of those commitments seemed to matter. Nothing mattered any more, in fact, but the woman and the young man on the other side of the departures gate who in a few hours time might disappear from his life forever.

406

'Sir? Excuse me, sir?'

'The woman was calling him. Turning around, he moved quickly over to the counter.

'Yes?'

'I've got permission from airport security for your wife and son to pop back for a few minutes if they agree that they want to see you. They're calling them over the tannoy now, but I'm afraid you're not going to get very long with them. To save time, would you like to go straight over to door fifteen and wait for them? It's just the other side of the central departures gate down there on the left; it's locked on this side, but wait in front of it – if they do agree to see you, they should come out in a few minutes.'

'I can't thank you enough for this,' said Michael.

'My pleasure, honestly,' replied the woman, beaming broadly. 'Just go down there and wait and they should be out shortly.'

Sprinting through the crowds of passengers past the departure gate, Michael located door fifteen and stood impatiently waiting for it to open. Ten minutes passed. Thinking that perhaps Elizabeth and Jake had not heard the tannoy announcement, Michael looked nervously across the airport forecourt. The Quantas information desk was too far away to risk running all the way back again to check – they might come out just as he left. What was he to do? At that moment, though, the door suddenly opened and a security guard let Elizabeth come through. She had grown her hair long again, just as it had been when they had got married, and she was wearing a smart two-piece suit. Michael felt as though his heart would melt. She looked absolutely beautiful.

'Only a couple of minutes, Madam, please. Just knock when you want to come on back through,' said the guard, closing the door behind him.

'Hello, Elizabeth,' said Michael.

'What's happened?' she replied, anxiously, turning to face him. 'They said something about a car accident. Oh, my God, your face!'

'I haven't been in a car crash, Elizabeth,' he said, slowly, 'and I haven't been working in Geneva for the last year either.'

'What? What d'you mean?'

'After I spoke to you last, I didn't leave the country. I took a job as an undercover reporter. I changed my identity. For nearly twelve months I've been living under a fictitious name. I've been working on building sites, in night clubs – all sorts of different places. That's why I wasn't able to see you and Jake. I've met some pretty bad people along the way and I couldn't risk them trying to get at me through you.'

'And … did they do that to your face?'

'Yes, yes, they did.'

'Oh, I see,' she said, quietly.

'So, where are you going, then?'

'Australia. I've got a headmistresses's job there. Wonderful school. Great facilities. Jake and I went at Christmas. He fell in love with the place straightaway. His exams are over now and, well, after I got offered the job, we discussed it and just decided to go.'

'Oh,' he replied, numbly.

'How did you find us?'

'Charlotte. She tried to hide the fact that you were going, but I knew something was up. She said …' His voice began to falter – he could barely bring himself to repeat the words. 'She said that you'd told her that you didn't want me to know where you were going.'

'Yes, yes, that's right,' replied Elizabeth, averting her eyes.

'Oh, Liz, I know I haven't been in touch for ages, but it was because of this job. If you only knew how much I've been looking forward to …'

'It wasn't the job,' interrupted Elizabeth, sharply.

'What?'

'For you, this job – whatever it was – might have been different,' she continued, 'but for Jake and me it was exactly the same as all the others.'

'What d'you mean?'

'I mean you shouldn't think we didn't want you to know where we're going because you haven't been in touch for the last year. It's not that. It's because you've never been in touch. You've always been somewhere else. Always absent – away. As a husband, as a father …'

'That's not true. I mean, I know I wasn't around as much as most fathers, perhaps, but I always found time to see Jake; to spend a bit of quality time with him.'

Looking back up again, Elizabeth flared in anger.

'Quality time?' She gasped. 'Quality time? That's your problem all over – you believe your own bullshit! Being a parent isn't about being there for the good times. It isn't even about being there for the bad times. It's just about being there full stop. I had to raise Jake by myself! He had to grow up by himself – without a father. Sure, you wandered in every now and then between jobs, but then you just disappeared

408

again. It was no life for us. We were never a family or anything remotely approaching it. You know that. We went through all this before the separation.'

'And I regret it so much now.'

'Oh, it wasn't all your fault,' she conceded. 'It was me, too. I knew that you'd never had much of a family life yourself – with your mother dead and your father off in Kenya all year round. But I just pushed that to the back of my mind because I didn't want to face the facts: you were the first man that I fell in love with and I married you on a wing and a prayer, with no regard to who you really were – to who you really are. You're a fanatic – a zealot. You always have been and you always will be. That's why you've been so successful at your job. I gave up expecting you to change a long, long time ago. We're not going to Australia to get away from you. We're going because we already are away from you – we have been for years.'

'But Jake,' continued Michael, desperately. 'I've so much wanted to see him for the last year. Is he there now? Could you call him?'

'I don't think that would be a good idea,' responded Elizabeth, quickly.

'What?'

'I don't think it would be a good idea for you to see him.'

'Why not?'

'Because ...' She frowned – reluctant to say the words. 'Because, well, he resents you.'

'He resents me?' gasped Michael.

'Yes. If you must know. He resents you're not having being around for me. I suppose it's an adolescent thing. He's sixteen. He sort of sees himself as being responsible for looking after me. For protecting me.'

'I've got to see him. You've got to tell him that ...'

'No,' interrupted Elizabeth, once again averting her eyes. 'No, it's too late. Years too late. I'm sorry. Don't make this any more difficult for me than it already is, please. I've got to go now. I'll miss the plane.'

So saying, she turned and knocked on the door.

'Please, Elizabeth,' he begged, 'please let me explain what's happened. I'm so sorry for neglecting you both. And I want to tell you how I feel about you. I've had time to think, you see, I want to tell you that I still ...'

But even before he could finish the sentence, his words trailed off as the door opened and she quickly slipped through.

For twenty minutes, he walked aimlessly around, desolate and inconsolable. He knew in his heart that everything that Elizabeth had said had been correct. Both by upbringing and temperament he had been a poor husband and father – he had admitted as much when she had asked him for a separation. But over the last year he had changed. Finally, he knew that he was capable of what other men had always seemed able to achieve so naturally: to partition his time and energy fairly between himself and his family. To discover that the only woman he had ever loved had long given up on him and that the son he so much wished to know now despised him was simply unbearable. Standing by the window, he looked down at the taxi rank opposite. Was he now to get into one of those cabs and go back to the Soho flat? It seemed impossible. It was impossible. Everything that he loved and wanted was leaving on that plane. If he did not follow, there was no point in living any more.

Sprinting over to the departures board he checked the flights. QA21 was leaving in fifty-five minutes. It was too late to purchase a ticket and anyway it might alarm Elizabeth and Jake if they were to see him on the plane. That morning, though, when he had been ringing around the travel agents, he had discovered that there was another flight to Sydney an hour and a half later. Finding it on the departures board and seeing that it was Thai Air, he looked around for the ticket counter. He would hole up in Sydney for a couple of days, locate Elizabeth and Jake and then make contact.

Walking through hand baggage inspection twenty minutes later, he began to feel almost normal again. Handing over his travel bag and leather jacket to the security guard and watching him put them through the X-ray machine, he thought of Tom. He, too, had had a problem in his personal life recently. At the time he had mentioned it, Michael had been totally unforgiving – he hadn't even asked him what it was about. It was a reaction of which he now felt deeply ashamed. When he got to the gate he would call him and apologize. Then, when he got on to the plane, he would have a good meal and sleep. He had never been to Australia before. He was almost looking forward to it.

'Excuse me, sir.'

'Yes.'

'Would you just mind coming over here for a moment?'

Walking over to his left, Michael suddenly became conscious of the tension in the atmosphere. His jacket and bag had gone through the X-ray machine, but had then been put on a separate table whilst no less than three security officers crowded around a monitor scrutinizing images of them. As the operator of the machine leant forward and tapped a key on the console, Michael suddenly saw an enlarged X-ray image of the mobile phone in his top pocket appear on the monitor. Instantly, Jim's words came hauntingly back to mind. *'The tape mechanism's moulded into the casing. It's completely invisible – the only way to spot it would be an X-ray machine or something like that.'*

Quickly, Michael thought up an alibi. It was a new model. It had a tape function – for recording memos. But, at that exact moment, just as he was about to speak to the two approaching security guards, the woman to whom he had spoken at the Quantas information desk walked through the body scanner directly behind him. Why had she left her desk? What task had taken her away from information and led her to go to departures? Michael realized that he would never know but, as their eyes met, she instantly recognized his face. Seeing the cluster of security personnel examining his jacket and the two guards now standing at his shoulder, she stopped and then walked across and spoke to the operator of the X-Ray machine. In under a minute two police officers carrying machine guns had arrived and before Michael knew it, he found himself sitting in an unmarked room waiting to be questioned.

Checking his watch, he realized that there were less than three minutes to go before Elizabeth and Jake's plane departed. Looking at the armed police officers guarding the door, he knew that escape was impossible; the two most important people in his life were leaving for the other side of the world and he could not follow them. And, with that realization, it was as though the room in which he was sitting had simply ceased to exist and the entire earth had opened up beneath him. He was falling downwards – faster and faster into an enormous, bottomless pit. His eyes could no longer see and he tried to cry out but nothing was coming from his mouth. Then, over the sound of the air rushing past his ears, he began to hear voices up above him. Two, perhaps three people were speaking – it was difficult to tell exactly. For some strange reason they seemed to be talking about Tom – saying that he was dead and it was all to do with a canister of petrol they had found close to the flat in Balam Road. And then there were questions. Why was he going to Australia? Wasn't his passport fake? At first, Michael tried to answer, but the voices grew fainter and fainter and it had become so dark that it was impossible to tell where they were coming from.

Part Four

A Good Defence

Chapter 13

The first thing that Miles noticed about the courtroom was how cold it was. The cells in the basement of Kingston Crown Court had been hot and stuffy, but the moment that he was escorted through the narrow rear door into the dock of court five he immediately became conscious of the sharp drop in temperature. The dock itself was surprisingly large with enough room for at least half a dozen defendants. Walking slowly to the chairs at the front, he felt disoriented and slightly agoraphobic: after five months of cells and interview rooms, it was strange to find himself in so much open space once more. Having been steered into one of the chairs by the dock officer who then sat down directly behind him, Miles rested his forearms on the varnished beech wood ledge and looked down at the busy but noiseless preparations taking place in the courtroom below.

To Miles's left, his solicitor Brian Malde had just opened up a large, black brief case and was searching through the documents inside, finally extracting a transparent binder filled with several pages of his careful, hand-written notes. On the bench in front of him, Owen Drake QC, Miles's barrister, stood deep in thought, drinking water from a transparent plastic cup and staring unseeing at the far wall of the courtroom. He was a tall, well-built man in his early fifties whom Miles had met for the first time two days previously. As they had sat waiting for him to arrive in the interview room at the remand centre, Malde had been fulsome in his praise of Drake. A trenchant, war-horse circuit barrister of over thirty year's experience, Drake was the ideal defence advocate for a complex and challenging case like this. His solicitor's build-up had no doubt been intended to reassure Miles, but he had had no illusions: 'complex and challenging' was simply legalese for 'high probability of conviction', although when Drake had finally appeared, he had nevertheless been impressed by his personal charisma and striking air of shrewdness, which his gown and wig seemed now to emphasize still further. To Drake and Malde's right sat the team of barristers and lawyers for the Crown. Although Miles had never seen any of these half dozen people before, he immediately recognized the woman standing at the front of their group nearest to the judge's podium. Just over five feet tall, her heavy black gown hanging loosely from her slight shoulders, Neera Pahklava QC was easily the smallest and most physically inconspicuous person in the courtroom. Yet, as counsel for the prosecution, it was this diminutive, thirty-six year old Asian woman whom Drake and Malde had warned Miles that he had reason to fear more than anyone else at court. What neither they nor she realized, however, was the true sentence that would inevitably follow if she were to be successful in securing his conviction. For, if he were to be found guilty, Miles was more or less certain that he would be dead within a matter of months.

He had been in the remand centre less than a week before he had realized that Kent was trying to have him killed. At first the other prisoners had chatted to him, but, within a couple of days, as they had begun one by one to avert their eyes and turn their backs, he could sense that the word had got around that he was a marked man; Miles Coverdale had crossed the wrong people – he knew too much. The first attack had come on the Saturday night on the way back from the canteen. Two men, one white one black, had suddenly sprung into the corridor and tried to drag him into an empty cell. He had landed a blow in the first man's face and was struggling with the other when a prison warder had rushed forward and broken up the melee. The next morning he had started working out. It had been physically punishing at first, but his muscles had soon become accustomed to the non-stop round of press-ups, skipping and shadow boxing. More than strengthening his body, however, the work-outs had helped fortify his mind – numbing the anguish of knowing that Elizabeth and Jake were a world away and that Tom had died trying to pull him out of Feltham. Within two months, he had become a totally isolated figure in the remand centre, the other prisoners looking on in fear and suspicion at the shaven-headed man with the scarred face whose body came more and more each day to resemble that of a prize-fighter. When the second attack had finally come, he had known that he had to respond without mercy. He had borne his second assailant no malice. The tall, tattooed Geordie who had lunged at him in the courtyard was himself no doubt being threatened by Kent or was so desperate for gear that he would have attacked his own mother with the smuggled-in kitchen knife. But, as he had broken the man's arm and then his nose, smashing his face into the concrete of the courtyard wall, he had known that although his fellow prisoners wouldn't tell the guards about the incident, they would certainly tell each other. And, indeed, a third attack had never materialized. It would be different, however, if he were to be convicted of Tom's murder. In remand centres, even the most hardened criminals still clung on to hope – if they became lifers, they had nothing left to lose.

'All rise!'

Snapping out of his thoughts, Miles got to his feet and watched the various ushers and court officials do likewise as the judge entered the courtroom and took his seat. The right honourable Bain McKay was a tall man who stooped forwards slightly as he walked. His facial expression was somewhat ponderous, yet at the same time astute and thoughtful, betokening an unhurried, deliberative mind. Malde had said that McKay had a reputation for preferring not to interfere with the trial process unless advocates seriously slipped up – in which case he could be quite merciless. This, Malde had suggested, had to be good for them. Pahklava had a formidable intelligence, but was known to have an impulsive streak: if she were to get carried away and then be reprimanded by McKay, it could only count in Miles's favour.

'All manner of persons who have anything to do before my lord the Queen's justice, draw near and give your attendance,' announced the clerk of court. After everyone had retaken their seats, there was a short pause whilst the usher slipped through a door on Miles's left. Moments later a sharp knocking sound broke the silence.

'Jury in court!' announced the clerk of court, crisply.

As the group of fifteen or sixteen would-be jurors filed in, Miles turned and looked at them steadily. Although his scar was not on the cheek that faced them, there didn't seem much point in attempting to hide it by keeping his head turned to one side: they would be bound to spot it eventually. Moreover, Malde had told him at all times to try and look confident, making sure that his body language projected not the terrified dread of being found guilty but the certain knowledge of being innocent. To his left, Miles could see that Drake was reviewing his notes in a manner that seemed to imply that he was not going to object to any of the jurors. Watching the first of them pick up the Bible and begin reading the oath, Miles recalled his own experience as a juror in this same courthouse two years previously. For two hours in the jury room on the final day, the young woman called Jo had stood alone against the other eleven jurors. Never once losing her calm, she had argued that they should credit the mumbled, preposterous story of the mini-cab driver who had sworn, seemingly against all the evidence, that the vacuum cleaner he had given his wife for her birthday had not been stolen. Smiling ruefully, Miles wondered if one of the twelve people to be chosen would show such courage on his behalf, once his own incredible tale had been told.

As the swearing in and affirmations continued, Miles glanced at the public gallery adjacent to the dock, which was occupied by about a dozen or so men in dark clothing, all of whom he took to be journalists. Would Kent be there later? Certainly he was being called as a prosecution witness, but would he sit in the gallery from the first day? Looking up at the powerful strip lights suspended from the tall courtroom ceiling, Miles wondered for the thousandth time what had happened that fateful night. He was certain that it had been Kent who had taken the canister of petrol out of the cupboard next to the front door and poured the gasoline through the letter box. He was also more or less certain that Kent had not known that Tom had been in the flat: the arson attack had been an explosion of anger at having discovered that he had been betrayed by the man that he had known as Michael Angel and had been directed at him and no one else. What Miles did not know was what had occasioned that outburst and how much of his investigation into the Ellis Group Kent had subsequently been able to unravel. He guessed that his trying to have him murdered in the remand centre had been a desperate attempt to forestall awkward questions about the Group's activities coming up at the trial. Having been unsuccessful, Kent and Ellis had then no doubt changed tack – spending the last three months making sure that every aspect of their illegal activities was thoroughly covered up. In between the defence and prosecution teams was a third lawyer – Miles could see him sitting unobtrusively on the rear bench, pen and paper at the ready, waiting for the proceedings to begin.

This man, Malde had informed him, was a so-called watching brief: a legal representative appointed by Ellis to look after his interests during Miles's trial. Kent and Ellis's plan thus seemed clear: maintain the customary respectable public image of the Ellis Group during the trial, wait for the inevitable guilty verdict and then quietly have him silenced once, as a convicted murderer, he was safely behind bars.

As soon as the swearing in procedure had finished, the clerk of court stood up once more.

'Are you Miles Coverdale?' he asked.

'I am,' replied Miles.

'Miles Coverdale. You are charged on this indictment with the murder of Thomas Cranmer. How do you plead, guilty or not guilty?'

'Not guilty.'

With a respectful nod at the judge, the clerk of court retook his seat. Turning to face the jury, the judge began solemnly to speak.

'Ladies and gentlemen of the jury,' he said, 'as you have just heard, this is a murder trial. Now, as I'm sure you are aware, murder is a crime which the law treats with the utmost seriousness and for which the punishment is automatically a life sentence. I know several of you have sat on juries earlier this week and that what I'm going to say next will therefore already be known to you. Nevertheless I will repeat it, for it is all the more important in a trial of this magnitude. I would ask you all not to discuss this case with anyone outside the courtroom or even with each other until you retire to the jury room to consider your verdict. If anyone approaches you, either inside or outside of the court, in connection with this case, I would like you to tell one of the officials here at court.

'My role in this trial is to rule on the law – yours is to decide whether the defendant is guilty or not guilty as charged. If at any time during the trial you have any questions, or if you find you are unable to understand certain aspects of the case, please write your query down on a note and pass it to the usher over there. She will give it to me, and I will do my best to answer you.'

With a grave but reassuring nod at the jury, the judge turned his eyes towards the prosecution counsel. Having gathered together her notes, Neera Pahklava stood up and looked across the courtroom at the jury. Drawing in his breath, Miles sat slightly forward on his seat. This was it. His day of judgement was beginning.

★

'Ladies and gentlemen of the jury,' she began, 'it is my job to present to you the case for the prosecution. The first thing that I need to do is explain the indictment. The defendant, Miles Coverdale, is, as you have just heard, charged with the murder of Thomas Cranmer. Now, for the defendant to be found guilty of this charge, I must prove to you, beyond all reasonable doubt, not simply that he killed Thomas Cranmer, but that he did so intentionally – with full knowledge aforethought. That word 'intentional' is extremely important, ladies and gentlemen, and I want you to try and keep it in your minds at all times if you can. Because it is the intention to kill that renders the defendant guilty of this crime. If we, the prosecution, cannot prove that intention, then he is not guilty as charged and should walk free. I believe, however, that we can prove this to you and, to that end, will be bringing before you over the next few days both powerful forensic evidence and a number of witnesses who will leave no doubt in your mind as to the defendant's guilt.'

Miles looked quickly across at Malde as Pahklava drew breath: if she did have an impulsive streak there had been no sign of it so far in her cool, measured delivery.

'What I'm going to do next, ladies and gentlemen, is give you a basic outline of the events in this case as we, the prosecution, understand them. Directly afterwards, my colleague here, the counsel for the defence, will respond with his summary – his understanding – of those same events. Thereafter, I will summon the witnesses of whom I have just spoken and the defence, in turn, will call their own witnesses to support their case. It will then be up to you, the jury, to decide on the basis of the evidence with which you have been presented, whether you believe the defendant is guilty or not guilty.

'The defendant, Miles Coverdale, was a newspaper photographer by profession and worked for several years for *The Mail*, directly reporting to the deceased, Thomas Cranmer. Just under two years ago, Mr Coverdale was sacked by Mr Cranmer. His dismissal, which was extremely fraught and acrimonious, was witnessed by a number of colleagues on that newspaper, two of whom will be giving evidence later. In the argument between the two men, the defendant repeatedly threatened Mr Cranmer. He spoke openly of revenge – of getting his own back on the man who had ended his career at *The Mail*. And, indeed, the defendant's career did take a dramatic turn for the worse after his dismissal. Unemployed, and with no significant financial resources to fall back on, he was forced within a few short months to move out of the flat that he had occupied for many years and rent a far more modest property in Feltham, West London. You will hear from witnesses how he then began to gamble and drink; how his behaviour became ever more unruly and violent; how, in fact, his life began to fall apart.

'By September of that same year, the defendant was working as a casual, unskilled labourer on a succession of building sites and it was at this time, to supplement his meagre income, that he began fraudulently to claim housing benefit on his rented flat. In February of the follow-ing year, he went on fraudulently to claim housing benefit on a second property. On both occasions he used false identities and on both occa-sions filed a claim for a spouse that did not exist. Despite having slipped so low in the world, or possibly because he had slipped so low, the defendant did what we all might have done in similar circumstances – he began to dream. To dream of getting his old job back – of returning to journalism. To dream of transforming his shabby, unfulfilled life into something worthwhile. Thomas Cranmer and he had once been friends. And so it was that he contacted him again – despite the unpleasantness that had surrounded his departure from *The Mail* – suggesting that he make a documentary series about crime and the criminals that he was encountering in the circumstances in which he then found himself. Thomas Cranmer wanted no part of this. Later, ladies and gentlemen, you will hear from Thomas Cranmer's secretary about how he rejected this suggestion. You will also hear about how the defendant persisted with his proposal, pestering him to take up his brilliant idea. You will hear of the defendant's increasing desperation – about how he began to stalk Mr Cranmer, about how he stormed into his office, demanding that he support him in his would-be documentary. And, finally, members of the jury, you will hear how the defendant took the revenge that he had so terrifyingly predicted: luring Thomas Cranmer to his flat, hiding out of sight and leaving the door unlocked for him to enter and then pouring gasoline through the letter box to burn him to death.

'The defendant, Mr Coverdale, was arrested the following day trying to leave the country for Australia on a false passport. When questioned by the police, he had no alibi whatsoever for the night of Mr Cranmer's murder: no one had seen him since that afternoon and he could not account for his movements. Following his arrest, the police took his fingerprints and they were found to match those on the canister of petrol that had been left discarded a few yards from the crime scene.

'Ladies and gentlemen of the jury, this is in many ways a tragic case – the story of a man whose life disintegrated into failure, fantasy, vengeful obsession and eventually murder. It is a case nevertheless for which the evidence of guilt is overwhelming and for which, I believe, you will find the defendant guilty as charged.'

As Pahklava sat down and poured herself a glass of water, Miles scrutinized her pretty, impassive features. So far, she was playing her hand very much as Malde had anticipated, attempting to paint a picture of continuous and sustained decline rather than stressing any one particularly powerful aspect of her case, such as the petrol canister covered with his fingerprints. Seeing Drake get to his feet to reply with his opening statement, Miles was immediately struck by the difference between the two advocates. Drake was considerably larger than Pahklava physically and, being positioned on the left hand side of the court, seemed to tower over the jury as he turned to face them. Pahklava's voice was featureless and nasal and she had very much given the impression that she had been following a prepared script. Drake's powerful baritone, on the other hand, simply rippled with charm and spontaneity.

'Good afternoon, ladies and gentlemen. Having heard my learned friend here tell you that she is going to prove that the defendant killed Thomas Cranmer, you're probably expecting me to tell you that I am going to prove that he did not. You might be surprised to learn, then, that I cannot prove this to you and moreover have no intention of trying – none whatsoever.'

Pausing momentarily for dramatic effect, Drake unhurriedly slipped his right thumb inside his waistcoat pocket and grinned amiably at the jury. Looking at their bemused faces, Miles appreciated how adept Drake was at injecting his larger than life personality into his oratory. It remained to be seen, however, whether he was able to use that facility to significant effect.

'What I do share with my learned colleague, however, is that I, too, will be asking you to bear a particular word in mind during the course of this trial. But before I tell you what it is, I need to take you back to an event that predates the defendant's dismissal from *The Mail* by a little over three months – to March the fifteenth of that year, to be precise. On the day in question, a package was delivered to the offices of *The*

Mail. It was addressed to Mr Henry King – the paper's owner – and was marked for his personal attention. That package, sent anonymously, contained a file, and, in that file, were the photographs, names and addresses of a gang of social security fraudsters based in Feltham, West London. That gang, between them, had over the previous eighteen months defrauded the DSS out of somewhere in the region of two million pounds. A legal case had been prepared against this gang, but could not be put to the Crown Prosecution Service because the evidence had been compromised. The person who had compiled the file was so outraged at their having escaped justice that he or she leaked it to *The Mail* in the hope of exposing them.

'Henry King stared at the file every day solidly for nearly two weeks. It was a fantastic story, but he couldn't publish it – not without proof. But then, he had an idea. An idea he shared with Thomas Cranmer, his features editor. Why not send an undercover reporter to penetrate this gang? To follow them, film them, and then turn that film into the first of a documentary series about Britain's faceless criminals. Thomas Cranmer thought it was a brilliant suggestion: this country loses billions every year in social security fraud, so it was a major public interest story.

'A week later, Henry King and Thomas Cranmer summoned the defendant, Mr Coverdale, to a secret meeting at the offices of *The Mail* and asked him to be that reporter. They judged that he was uniquely qualified for the job: resourceful, intelligent, clear-headed and with over fifteen years experience as a photo-journalist. It would, of course, they told him, be a dangerous assignment: with that much money involved they had to assume that the gang were unscrupulous, probably violent men. It would be such a dangerous assignment, in fact, that Mr Coverdale would have to completely change his identity in order to penetrate the gang and, for security purposes, only the three of them could ever know who he really was and what he was really doing.

'Two days before the defendant was arrested, Henry King died of natural causes – a heart attack. The following day, Thomas Cranmer went to Feltham to bring back the undercover reporter whom he and King had sent to infiltrate the gang a year beforehand. He met his death that night through a tragic set of circumstances upon which I will elaborate later. But it wasn't Miles Coverdale who killed him. He and Thomas Cranmer were still the best of friends and had been all along. The acrimonious dismissal had been a fake, fabricated by them so that anyone who later tried to check would be unable to make a connection between the photographer who had once worked for *The Mail* and the hard-drinking, unskilled labourer whose identity he had assumed. And this, ladies and gentlemen of the jury, is why I cannot absolutely prove to you that the defendant did not kill Mr Cranmer. The only other two men who knew of the documentary that the defendant was making are both dead. Moreover, nothing was ever committed to print that I can now put before you to confirm that the defendant was working for them – no written employment contract, no letters, no faxes, nothing. So conscious were those three men of the risks that Mr Coverdale would face, that they were meticulously careful not to keep a record of what they were doing – and when two of them died, all independent substantiation died with them.

'A hopeless case, then?' announced Drake, suddenly, raising his voice lustily and flashing the jury an amused, ironic smile. 'I might as well pack up my bags and go home! Not at all, ladies and gentlemen, not at all.' Taking a couple of steps forward, he leant up against the edge of the jury box and stared at them good-humouredly. 'Did you ever do a really big jigsaw puzzle, when you were a child? You know, one of those enormous things with a thousand pieces. Or have you ever watched a child try and complete one? If you have, then you might have noticed that sometimes they force two pieces together that aren't supposed to fit with each other. And sometimes they can even actually work around the false joint such that if you look at the jigsaw from a distance you can make out the picture. But when you examine it closely ...' Raising his hand, Drake moved it backwards and forwards slowly, as though running it over an unseen surface and suddenly discovering a flaw. 'Aha! Something doesn't quite fit here.

'Which brings me to the word that I told you earlier I wanted to you to bear in mind throughout this trial. That word, ladies and gentlemen, is 'doubt'. The prosecution will indeed bring before you witnesses, arguments, evidence, which, just like the jigsaw I mentioned, will seem superficially sound. The picture will look fine – and for one very good reason.' Resting his hand on to the ledge at the front of the jury box, Drake rapped his knuckles down on the wooden surface, emphasizing each word in turn. 'Because those three men made absolutely damn sure that everything would appear to fit. But as we press and probe and examine, one by one we'll find those tell-tale flaws – and when we've found them, they will call into doubt the prosecution's entire version of events; the picture will just not look right. And that is my point. You see, in a court of law the defendant isn't required to prove his innocence. Rather it is the responsibility of the prosecution to prove that he is guilty and where there is significant doubt – and in this case, I assure you we are going to find plenty of that – only one verdict is possible: not guilty.'

'Could you state your name, please?'

'Thomas Cromwell.'

'And what is your profession, Mr Cromwell?'

'I recently took early retirement – before that I was a newspaper editor.'

'... your last position being editor of *The Mail* – is that correct?'

'Yes.'

'When was that – when did you retire from *The Mail*?'

'About eighteen months ago.'

'And how long had you been its editor?'

'Three and a half years.'

'Do you recognize the defendant, Mr Cromwell? The man over there in the dock.'

'I do.'

'Could you tell the court who he is?'

'His name is Miles Coverdale.'

In the two years since Miles had last seen Cromwell, his appearance had changed dramatically. He had always been of stout build, but had obviously gained a further three or four stones in the interim, endowing his already disdainful features with an air of bloated truculence. His clothes, which used to have a sprightly if somewhat self-consciously foppish quality, now appeared ill-fitting and scruffy, as though having been neither cleaned nor repaired for a very long time. Recalling the many occasions that he had seen Cromwell swaggering through the Tower, Miles wondered how he had felt that morning when Henry King had called him into his office and in a few short moments taken his entire empire from him.

'Thank you, Mr Cromwell,' responded Pahklava. 'Now, how exactly is the defendant known to you?'

'He used to work for *The Mail* – as a photographer.'

'For how long?'

'Six or seven years, I think. He joined before I did, but I'm pretty sure it was something like that.'

'So, he was one of the existing members of staff whom you inherited when you became editor?'

'That's right.'

'What was your opinion of Mr Coverdale?'

'My opinion?'

'Yes, your opinion. What did you think of him?

Cromwell shrugged derisively, as though having being asked to describe an insect that he had found in his salad.

'Not much, to be honest.'

'And why was that?'

'Well, he was never there for a start. I mean one expects photographers to be out and about, but I always got the impression he felt he could do whatever the hell he liked.'

'D'you think he was a bad photographer, then?'

'No, I wouldn't go so far as to say that.'

'But he was on a semi-permanent contract.'

'That's right.'

'Could you explain the significance of that to the court please, Mr Cromwell?'

'Well, it meant that he wasn't important enough to *The Mail* to be made a permanent member of staff, but we paid him as though he was to get first rights of refusal on his work.'

'Thank you, Mr Cromwell. Now, could you tell me, did you witness the defendant's dismissal from *The Mail* by Thomas Cranmer?'

'Oh, yes – I could have hardly failed to: practically the whole building saw it.'

'Could you describe what happened?'

'Yes, it was about ten in the morning. He'd asked to see Tom in his room for a chat, but when he got in there he started making all sorts of demands. More money, changes here, changes there. Tom told him where to get off, but he got abusive. The whole thing then spilled out of Tom's room into the office outside: we have – we had – a sort of open-plan arrangement at the Tower, you see. At one point Coverdale even threw this computer keyboard thing at him. That was it. Tommy fired him on the spot.'

426

'How did the defendant respond to that?'

'More abuse.'

'And did he threaten Mr Cranmer?'

'Oh, yes.'

'Do you remember what he said?'

'Well, I can't remember his exact words, but it was stuff like 'I'll get you back for this. Don't think you can get away with it. It's me that keeps you in your job.' That sort of thing.'

'And then he left.'

'Yes.'

'Did you ever see him again after that?'

'No.'

'What happened to the defendant after he was dismissed from *The Mail*, do you know?'

'Well, the rumour I heard was that he'd picked up a bit of work on the continent – which was hardly surprising, really: he wasn't going to be able to get a job on another British paper after that performance.'

'Thank you, Mr Cromwell. Just one final question. To the best of your knowledge, before Mr Coverdale's dismissal, how was he regarded by Thomas Cranmer and Henry King? Would you say that they had con-fidence in his abilities?'

'Tom? Maybe. Confidence of sorts, I suppose you could say; he tolerated him. Henry? No. I doubt he even knew he existed.'

'Thank you, Mr Cromwell.'

As Pahklava sat down, Drake got up and smiled broadly at Cromwell who looked back at him with a mixture of contempt and mistrust.

'Mr, er, Cromwell. In the dismissal incident to which you have just referred you described Mr Coverdale as abusive. Would you also describe his conduct as violent?'

'Yes, I would.'

'To your knowledge had he ever been violent or abusive before – whilst he was in the employ of *The Mail*?'

'No, not that I recall.'

'So, it was something of a surprise that he behaved in that way – something completely out of the ordinary, yes?'

'Yes, I suppose it was,' conceded Cromwell.

'Ladies and gentlemen,' said Drake, turning to face the jury. 'Please be aware that the defendant is a man of a good character and reputation, having neither been charged nor convicted of any crime in his entire life. His behaviour at the time of his dismissal was thus completely out of character – both personally and professionally.'

Having stared at the jury for several seconds to emphasize this point, Drake turned around again to face the witness box.

'Now, Mr Cromwell, you mention that the defendant was on a semi-permanent contract.'

'That's right.'

'Because, you say, he wasn't important enough to be made a permanent member of staff.'

'Yes.'

'Were semi-permanent contracts common at *The Mail*?'

'Far too common in my opinion – and not for just photographers either – there was a whole raft load of hangers-on there when I arrived.'

'How many other such photographers did the newspaper retain on semi-permanent contracts at the time of Mr Coverdale's dismissal, can you recall?'

'Oh, I'm not sure,' replied Cromwell, hesitantly. 'If I took a guess, I'd say maybe, er …'

'Four,' said Drake, 'to save you the trouble of having to estimate and so that the jury may know precisely. It was four.'

'If you say so.'

'Wasn't it actually the case,' continued Drake, 'that although there may well have been a surfeit of employees retained on semi-permanent contracts when you arrived at the paper, by the time of Mr Coverdale's dismissal, such contracts had in fact become a privilege – a benefit reserved solely for the most sought-after news photographers? Top industry professionals who could sell their work more or less wherever they wanted, and who could therefore command the salary of a permanent contract without the more tedious responsibilities customarily associated with them – such as having to attend the office regularly.'

'No, I wouldn't say that's correct.'

'Really?'

'No,' insisted Cromwell, acerbically, 'they're just the left-overs from the old days. Dross. Scroungers.'

At this point, Drake paused and took a deep breath, as though gathering himself to confront this assertion. Instead, he left it unchallenged and merely looked momentarily across the court towards the jury. For a split-second, Miles then saw a curl of satisfaction play about his lips: Cromwell's jaundiced resentment was becoming more apparent by the moment.

'Mr Cromwell, can you recall what the circulation of *The Mail* was on the twelfth of March of the year before last – in your final year as its editor?'

'Of course I can't!' exclaimed Cromwell.

'Would you be surprised to learn it was three point one million?'

'No. That sounds quite feasible.'

'What was *The Mail*'s average daily circulation for that year, d'you know?'

'I'm not sure.'

'Roughly.'

'Two and a half million?'

'Two point three million – according to the Press Association.'

'Well, they should know, I suppose.'

'That day – the one I just mentioned – it was special. Circulation was up by almost eight hundred thousand. Can you recall why?'

'No, I can't,' replied Cromwell, becoming visibly irritated. 'I can't recall any individual circulation figures from two years ago, let alone the reasons for them.'

'Then let me tell you. Circulation was up on that day because the front page featured a particular photograph: a photograph of a junior Minister for Overseas Development and his alleged mistress in a hotel room. It was an exclusive photograph and it was taken by the defendant. D'you remember it now?'

'Vaguely.'

'Mr Cromwell, I put it to you again that Miles Coverdale was on a semi-permanent contract because he was one of the most accomplished news photographers in the country. A man who could single-handedly boost a newspaper's circulation by over three quarters of a million – a man who had no need to be tied down to the responsibilities of a permanent contract because his work was in such demand.'

'You can put it to me as many times as you like,' retorted Cromwell, 'but that doesn't mean I have to agree with you. In my experience creating a successful newspaper isn't about individuals who may or may not contribute a particular piece of work, it's about quality, image, tradition and a whole lot of other things, too.'

'Thank you, Mr Cromwell,' replied Drake, looking down at his notes.

Interpreting this gesture as indicating that the questioning had finished, the editor was just about to turn and leave when Drake suddenly looked up again.

'Oh, er, just one final question, if you would, please, Mr Cromwell?'

'Yes?'

'At the time of your 'retirement' from *The Mail*, would you say that Thomas Cranmer and Henry King had confidence in your abilities?'

Instantly the atmosphere in the courtroom became tense and Miles could see that Pahklava was about to appeal to the judge that Drake was badgering the witness. Drake, however, was one step ahead of her and, before she could speak, directly addressed the judge himself.

'I ask, your honour, because I am seeking to establish the nature of this witness's relationship with Thomas Cranmer and Henry King and the likelihood of his being privy to their plans in respect of the defendant.'

In response, the judge did not speak but nodded slowly once.

'Well, Mr Cromwell. Did you have their confidence?'

'Yes, I would say that I did. My retirement was by entirely mutual agreement.'

'And how has *The Mail*'s circulation fared in the year since your departure?'

Again Pahklava stood up, but it was the judge who spoke first.

'Mr Drake,' he said quietly, 'could we make it the last question about circulation figures, please?'

'Of course, your honour,' replied Drake, glibly. 'You were about to respond, Mr Cromwell. *The Mail*'s average circulation since your departure? I have the figure here if you can't quite recall it.'

'I believe,' replied Cromwell, acidly, 'it is just below three million.'

'You are entirely correct, Mr Cromwell. Two point eight million, in fact. An improvement of approximately sixteen per cent. No more questions, your honour.'

As Cromwell lumbered out of the witness box, Miles could see several of the jurors exchanging glances in a manner that seemed to suggest that Drake's questioning had gone some way to achieving his stated aim of revealing flaws in the prosecution's case. It was at this point that they and everyone else in the courtroom suddenly turned their eyes towards the public gallery. Leaning slightly forwards and looking to his right, Miles quickly realized why everyone had become so distracted: making their way between the assembled ranks of journalists to the available seats at the front were two women who appeared to have slinked into the courtroom straight out of one of Kingston's night clubs. With their plunging necklines, shoulder pads and vividly colourful make-up, they stood out amongst the scruffy hacks like two white water-lilies in the middle of a huge stagnant pond. It was Babs and Evelyn. Imagining how the two women would appear to the obviously middle-class jury, Miles kept his gaze firmly fixed on the witness box where a fat, bearded man in his mid-fifties had just taken the oath.

'Could you state your name, please?'

'Leonard Britten.'

'And what is your profession, Mr Britten?'

'I'm a publican. I run The White Horse in East Feltham.'

'How long have you managed The White Horse, Mr Britten?' asked Pahklava.

'Ten years.'

'Thank you. Now, I'd like to ask you if you recognize the defendant – the man over there in the dock.'

'Yeah, yeah – I do. His name's Micky Angel.'

'Michael Angel, ladies and gentlemen,' announced Pahklava, turning momentarily to face the jury, 'was one of the names that the defendant assumed after he moved to Feltham. Indeed, it was the name under which he was travelling when he was arrested trying to leave the country. I beg your pardon, Mr Britten – sorry – to continue. Could you tell me how you became acquainted with the defendant – the man you knew as Micky Angel?'

'He started coming to the pub, about a year – eighteen months ago.'

'And what was the event that first really brought him to your attention?'

'How d'you mean?'

'Well,' replied Pahklava, lifting two sheets of paper up off the desk in front of her, 'in your statement to the police back in July – I'm sure you recall the one to which I refer – you mentioned a disagreement that took place in your pub one day.'

'Oh, yeah,' replied Britten, reluctantly, 'I know what you mean now. Yeah, he got into an argument with a bloke called Jez – he was a regular at the pub.'

'And what was their disagreement about, Mr Britten?'

'A game of pool.'

'And that was when you first started noticing the defendant?'

'Yeah, yeah.'

'How often did he come to your pub?'

'Three, four times a week.'

'And what did he do when he was there?'

'He used to sit in the corner, mostly, reading.'

'What did he read?'

'*The Racing Post.*'

'That's a paper about horse racing, yes?'

'Yes.'

'Did he gamble – did he bet on the horses?'

'Yeah. He used to, like, go back and forwards between the pub and the betting shop over the road.'

'And you picked up his newspapers a few times didn't you, when you were clearing up – you said so in your statement.'

'Yeah.'

'And the back pages were all covered with writing and pencilled calculations.'

'That's right.'

'Consistent with a man who bets regularly.'

'Yeah.'

'Was the defendant ever involved in any other trouble in your pub?'

'Yeah – he was.'

'When was that?'

'About, I don't know, six weeks after he started comin' in.'

'Could you tell the court what happened?'

'Yeah, it was, like, a Friday night. This bloke was drinkin' at the bar – I dunno who he was – and he owed Mick some money. Mick came in, and they had a bit of a punch-up, and then he left.'

'It was more than a bit of a punch-up, surely, Mr Britten,' urged Pahklava. 'There was a considerable amount of damage – smashed furniture, broken glasses, etcetera etcetera.'

'Yeah, it was a fair old ruck.'

'And did you hear the defendant threaten the man, just before he left?'

'Yeah, yeah, he did say somethin' to him.'

'And what was it exactly?'

'He said he'd 'ave him if he ever showed up in the pub again.'

'What were his exact words, d'you remember?'

'Erm, I'm not really sure,' replied the publican, uncomfortably.

'Weren't they 'If I ever see your face in here again, you cunt, I'll fucking kill you'? That's what you told the police he said.'

To his left, Miles could sense the jury collectively draw breath: Drake clearly did not have a monopoly on discomforting witnesses. Holding Britten's witness statement aloft, Pahklava was staring at him adamantly over the rim of her thin, gold-framed spectacles.

'Yeah, I think that's what he said,' mumbled Britten.

'A little bit louder, if you please, Mr Britten, so the jury may hear you.'

'Yes. Yes. That's what he said.'

'What did he do then?'

'Sorry?'

'The defendant – after the other man had left the pub?'

'Oh, er, he bought some drinks.'

'What – to drink in the pub?'

'No, no. To take away.'

'What did he buy, can you recall?'

'Some lager. A bottle of Bells.'

'Thank you, Mr Britten,' concluded Pahklava, with a cold smile.

'Just two questions, if I may,' announced Drake, as he took to his feet. 'The disagreement with the man called Jez. D'you know what it was about?'

'Yeah. Micky beat him at pool. They had, like, a bet on the side, but Jez wouldn't pay up.'

'Would an argument normally follow in a situation like that – in your experience as a publican?'

'Oh God, yeah. It's asking for trouble.'

'The other man, Jez. Did he do that sort of thing a lot?'

'What – wind people up?'

'Yes.'

'Yeah, all the time. A right nuisance he was. He's inside now.'

'And would you describe the defendant as a nuisance – as a problematic customer?'

'No, not at all, he was all right, Mick.'

'Because you didn't in fact ban him after the second incident of which you spoke, did you?'

'No, the other bloke owed him money – a week's wages – he had it comin' to him if you ask me.'

'Possibly so, Mr Britten,' observed Drake, wryly. 'Which brings me to my second question. After the defendant had threatened the man, he bought some drinks to take away, yes?'

'Yeah.'

'What else did he do?'

'How d'you mean?'

'Did he pay for the damage caused – even though it was he who had been wronged by the other man?'

'Yeah, he did – he gave me a hundred quid.'

'Thank you, Mr Britten.'

With a shrug and slightly despairing nod in Miles's direction, the publican left the witness box. Watching him walk towards the court-room exit, Miles felt a peculiar stab of regret. He had seen the portly figure of Britten many times behind the counter, but hadn't realized that the publican had known his name. He obviously had, though, and moreover was clearly troubled that he had left the jury with a less pos-itive impression of Michael Angel than the one that he himself had formed. Despite his predicament, as Miles watched Britten waddle out of the courtroom door, he was surprised to find himself overcome by a strange feeling of nostalgia for those long-lost afternoons he had spent reading *The Racing Post* in the warm, smoke-filled bar at The White Horse.

Dill was looking decidedly smug – like a star pupil summoned to stand up on stage with the teachers at end-of-term assembly. As Miles listened to him take the oath, he thought of Harper. During the intensive ques-tioning by the two detectives at the police station the day after he had been arrested on suspicion of Tom's murder, Miles had deliberately played down his involvement with Harper and Angela, inventing a fic-titious address for them to ensure that the authorities stayed off their scent. Even when he had eventually been charged, he still could not bring himself to tell the police anything more about Harper and Angela, despite the fact that he had spent months patiently insinuating himself into their lives and they, more than anyone, could lend credence to his story of having moved to Feltham in order to make a documentary series for King Media. The image of Rick plaintively waving him goodbye as he had left the flat was always before his eyes, and always in his ears were the words of the East European spy who had warned that he would be tormented by memories of betrayal long after time had dimmed all other recollections of his life under cover. It was only when the police had interviewed him again in the remand centre two months later, telling him that they had drawn a blank at the address he had given for Harper and Angela, that he had finally told them about their flat on the Abaddon estate. By that time, word of his arrest had long been out on the street and Harper and Angela had surely fled. A week later, a small team of armed police officers had gone to the fifth floor flat in the early hours of the morning. Two days after that, when he had discovered from Malde that they had found it deserted, Miles had felt a great sense of relief despite the fact that his only chance of ever seeing Elizabeth and Jake again lay in his being found not guilty.

'Could you state your name, please?' said Pahklava.

'Michael Dill.'

'And what do you do for a living, Mr Dill?'

'I'm a Housing Benefit fraud officer at the Department of Social Security in East Feltham.'

'Do you recognize the defendant, Mr Dill, and, if so, by what name was he known to you?'

'Yes, I do,' replied Dill. 'I knew him by the name of Brian Morgan.'

Out of the corner of his eye, Miles could see one of the jurors raise his eyebrows slightly: it was the third name in as many hours.

'Could you tell the court the circumstances in which you became acquainted with the defendant? Do please refer to your notes if you so wish.'

Taking a small notebook from his inside pocket and holding it ostentatiously at arm's length, Dill began to speak.

'On October the fourteenth last year, myself and a colleague went to try and establish the authenticity of a housing benefit claim submitted by a Mr Brian Morgan of 144 Balam Road, Feltham. He was claiming for himself and his wife – a Mrs Wendy Morgan; both of them were present when we visited the property. One of the first questions I asked Mr Morgan after I entered the flat was when he had moved in. He replied that he had been there since July, but I'd checked his claim forms just a few minutes beforehand and noted that he had been claiming housing benefit on the property since June.'

'So what did you do?'

Lowering the note-book, Dill turned and addressed the jury directly with an air of pompous self-importance.

'As a Housing Benefit fraud officer, I have been trained in certain interrogation techniques. Accordingly, rather than questioning Mr Morgan further on this point, I went on to check other aspects of his claim – making myself a mental note to return to this issue later.'

'Thank you, Mr Dill, please continue.'

With a respectful nod at Pahklava, Dill raised his note book once more.

'Subsequently discovering that all other aspects of the claim appeared genuine, my colleague and I left about fifteen minutes later. It was as we were walking down the steps at the front of the flat that I again asked Mr Morgan when he had moved in. On this second occasion, Mr Morgan corrected himself, saying after all that he had arrived in June – just as he had written on his claim form.'

'So, what did you decide to do then, Mr Dill?'

'I made a note to follow up again in three months.'

'Why was that?'

'Well, I wasn't sure whether the Morgans were legitimate or not. Mr Morgan's mistake could have been genuine. I reckoned that if I went back in three months and there were still signs of occupation I'd probably let the matter drop. We've got a lot of people attempting to defraud the Housing Benefits system, so at some point you've got to give up on those ones who look more or less authentic and move on.'

'Is that what you did, then – go back three months later?'

'Yes.'

'And what did you find?'

'The flat was completely deserted. I visited it once in late December, once in January and I also drove past it a few times after that but there were no signs of life.'

Involuntarily, Miles brushed his forefinger across his scar, remembering the month he had spent in the private hospital with his head swathed in bandages.

'What did you conclude, Mr Dill?'

'That the two people claiming to be Mr and Mrs Morgan probably didn't live there and had probably falsified their claim. That's the way these people usually work. Claim on one flat, stay there for a couple of weeks and then move on to another and start claming on that.'

'But you did eventually find the defendant, didn't you – the man claiming to be Mr Morgan?'

'Yes, I did.'

'Ladies and gentlemen,' declared Pahklava, addressing the jury but looking at the court usher, 'I want you now to take a look at exhibit one. This is a photograph taken by Mr Dill of the defendant working as a casual labourer on a residential property in Feltham.'

Giving a copy to the judge, the usher then walked around to the front of the jury box and handed out the remaining sheets to the jurors. Watching Pahklava holding her copy aloft as she waited for the jury to examine theirs, Miles was immediately struck by the remarkable similarity in page layout between the photograph of Brian Morgan and the format of the seventeen photographs that had been leaked to *The Mail*: both were printed on A4 paper and in both cases the photographs themselves occupied the same proportion of the top left hand corner of the page. Miles was still pondering this resemblance as Pahklava began speaking once more.

'Mr Dill, could you explain how you came to take this picture?'

'Yes. On February the twenty-second, I went to visit the flat in Balam Road one final time. I'd made up my mind that if there were still no sign of the Morgans I'd make arrangements to have their benefit cut. I arrived about seven thirty in the morning just as Mr Morgan was leaving. Knowing that he and Mrs Morgan's claim was based on their supposedly low income, I followed him to see if he was working. That was when I took the photograph.'

'And what did you do then?'

'I filed a report – asking my manager whether we should investigate Mr Morgan further, prosecute him there and then, or just stop his benefit altogether.'

'But that report was never actioned, was it?'

'No.'

'Why not?'

'Three days later, Mr Morgan made contact with the Housing Benefits office and signed off.'

'And as long as he wasn't claiming benefit, there was no point in pursuing him further?'

'That's correct.'

'Thank you, Mr Dill.'

Drake paused for several seconds before beginning his cross-examination. Miles did not know whether this was simply because he was marshalling his thoughts or whether he was consciously trying to unsettle Dill. In either case, his delay certainly produced that effect, for, as the seconds passed in silence, Dill shuffled nervously back and forth in the witness box.

'Mr Dill,' said Drake, finally, in an ominously low voice. 'The man known to you as Mr Morgan did indeed sign off as you have just described in February of last year, but that wasn't the last you heard of him, was it?'

'No.'

'Could you tell the court when next he came to your attention?'

'Yes, yes, I can,' replied Dill, speaking just a little bit too rapidly. 'It was about four months ago – in June, I think. I was contacted by some people from CID. They told me that they had arrested a man who'd supplied them with information about Housing Benefit fraud in Feltham.'

'And that man was Mr Coverdale, yes – the person whom you had previously known as Mr Morgan?'

'That's right.'

Looking across at Dill, Miles recalled the way the two detectives had stared on in astonishment as he had written down from memory the names and addresses of the seventeen fraudsters. Although he had been almost certain that they could no longer be found there – especially Harper for whom he had given a false address – he had remembered that before embarking on *Criminal Britain* Tom had had their names checked out and had found that several of them had criminal records. Sure enough, later that day, the detectives had returned to the subject and, although Miles could tell that they still didn't believe his alibi, it was obvious that they were interested in learning as much as they could about the gang of fraudsters. It was then that he had told them about how he had flushed out Craig and how he had learned that Richard Thompson had made so much money with Craig's assistance that he had eventually decamped to Spain. In the end, it hadn't prevented the detectives from charging him with Tom's murder, but if there was one weakness in the prosecution's case it was that although all the tapes and documents had been destroyed in the fire there was no denying that

Miles had supplied the police with vital criminal intelligence about the fraudsters.

'What was this information, could you tell the court, Mr Dill?'

'Yes, er, Mr – the defendant – had given the police the name of a man who had worked for several years at the Housing Benefits office in Feltham who'd been helping fraudsters to cheat the system.'

'What was the name of that man?'

'Craig Gleeson.'

'And where had he worked?'

'The Housing Benefit office in Feltham.'

'Yes, you have already stated that,' countered Drake, sharply. 'Which department exactly?'

Dill paused before answering, the right side of his face seeming to twitch slightly.

'My department.'

'Your department, Mr Dill?'

'Yes, that's right.'

Again Drake looked down at his notes and paused before continuing. Somehow, Drake had instinctively sensed that Dill was as ashamed of his failures as he was proud of his achievements – a situation which Miles had no doubt he was intending mercilessly to exploit.

'What was Mr Gleeson's modus operandi?'

'I beg your pardon?' responded Dill, with a puzzled look.

'His way of working,' replied Drake, carefully enunciating each word. 'How exactly did he perpetrate his fraud?'

'Well, he was in charge of arranging our inspections. In exchange for a share of the rent money, he'd make sure that we inspected a given property at a certain time so that the fraudsters he was in league with could prepare for our visit.'

'How many housing benefit fraudsters did Craig Gleeson work with, do you know, Mr Dill?'

'Er, we're not sure yet, exactly – we're still sort of checking through all the back records – but we reckon he pretty much sold himself to all comers, really.'

Drake smiled. Dill's evasion was only going to make his final admission all the more painful.

'Roughly, Mr Dill,' urged Drake. 'Roughly, how many?'

'Possibly as many as a hundred.'

'I'm sorry, I couldn't quite hear that, Mr Dill.'

'As many as a hundred,' repeated Dill.

'Thank you. And what was the resultant loss to the Department of Social Security arising from the redoubtable Mr Gleeson's activities? Has your department been able to calculate that yet?'

'No, not exactly,' said Dill, swallowing visibly.

'But, once again, you are able to give the court an estimate, aren't you?'

'It may run into the millions,' murmured Dill.

'Millions of pounds!' exclaimed Drake, loudly, turning to face the jury. 'I'd like you to take note of that, ladies and gentlemen. Earlier, you will recall the prosecution's comments about the defendant living in a fantasy world, but yet here we have a representative of the Housing Benefit office telling us that he was responsible for identifying the key individual in an enormous housing benefit fraud. Some fantasy!' Turning back to face Dill, Drake smiled at him with warm condescension. 'And where is Craig Gleeson now, d'you know?'

'The police haven't been able to trace him. He's on the run somewhere.'

'But he won't be getting another job in Housing Benefits, will he, because his name and photograph have been circulated throughout the country – am I correct?'

'Yes, yes, they have.'

'As has a description of how his system worked. No-one else is going to get away with that particular scam again, are they?'

'No, I believe not.'

'Right, Mr Dill,' said Drake, closing in for the kill. 'Let's sum up, shall we – so that we may be sure that we have all understood the facts? You uncovered a housing benefit fraud perpetrated by the defendant amounting to several hundred pounds; he uncovered a fraud running into millions. Craig Gleeson operated right under your nose for over five years without your having the slightest clue of what he was up to; the defendant tracked him down in less than twelve months. Would you say that's an accurate summing up of the situation?'

'Yes, but you can't blame me for that!' blurted out Dill, angrily. 'If they'd've listened to me we could've nailed the bastard two years ago!'

'Thank you, Mr Dill,' replied Drake coldly. 'I have no more questions.'

With Dill's exasperated outburst, Miles suddenly understood why the

440

photograph of him as Brian Morgan was identical in layout to those that had been leaked to *The Mail*: they had all been taken by Dill. It was the only explanation. Dill clearly lived and breathed his job, staying out night and day to photograph those claimants he suspected of fraud. Two years ago, he must somehow have managed to establish a common link between seventeen of the fraudsters which had led him to believe that they were an organized gang. Once his suspicions had been translated into a full-blown investigation, however, Craig must have stepped in and in some way managed to undermine it. In frustration and resentment at being forced to abandon the case, Dill had then leaked the file to *The Mail*. Shortly afterwards, Miles further surmised, Craig may also have tried to engineer Dill's dismissal, because at the Balam Road inspection, Harper had commented to Angela that he had thought that Dill had been kicked off the inspection team. Only this series of events would explain Dill's comment that Housing Benefits could've nailed Craig two years ago. Placing his hands firmly on the ledge of the dock for support, Miles felt his excitement mounting as he watched Dill leave the stand and the judge dismiss the jury for the afternoon. If he was right – and he was almost certain that he was – Dill could help substantiate his claim to have been working for Tom all along and thus prove his innocence. Standing up with the rest of the courtroom as the judge retired to chambers, Miles fixed his eyes on Malde. As soon as possible he had to tell his solicitor what he now understood.

Chapter 14

Having gathered up the newspapers and letters from the porch floor, Mary Lamb retreated quickly back into the hallway, closing the heavy front door firmly behind her. She had never thought of herself as being especially sensitive to the cold, but these last few years it seemed as though any slight draft or stray gust of wind had the power to confine her to her bed for a week. Clasping the collar of her house-coat more tightly about her neck, she went into the living room and turned on the gas fire; she would warm herself in front of it for a few minutes and then go to her kitchen at the back of the house and make some tea. Of the dozen or so letters that morning, only one was for her – from her friend Gabriel in Lisbon. Having separated the remaining mail into two piles for Angus and Madeleine respectively, she placed them both on the table along with the newspapers. As she was about to turn away and sit down by the fire to read her letter, the headline of one of the articles suddenly caught her eye. For a moment, she felt quite faint and put out her hand to steady herself. Taking several deep breaths to calm her beating heart, she picked up the newspaper and read the first paragraph of the article. With a sigh, she then slowly slumped down into the armchair. It was just as she had feared: that dreadful story had made its way back into the news once again.

Gazing around the living room, she cast her mind back over the events of the last two years. When the time for Angus to resign had come, he and Madeleine had both been wonderfully brave, facing up to the cameras and questions side by side with dignity and composure. Within a few weeks, just as Mary had expected, the story had been all but forgotten and Angus had been able to set about rebuilding his political career with his customary patience and resilience. Although he had had to resign his ministerial post, he had still retained his position as an MP and in time had been able to regain much of the respect of which he had been so unfairly deprived. Their own household, too, had gradually returned to normal and it had been months since any reference to that event had cast a shadow over their domestic happiness.

Frowning, she picked up the newspaper again and read the article all the way through. Checking the other two newspapers and finding no reference to the story, Mary suddenly had an idea. What if she were to throw the first newspaper away? Neither Angus nor Madeleine had the time to read the papers except when they got home in the evening and, as the trial would probably be finished in a couple of days and was anyway clearly not an absolutely top headline story, perhaps it would all be over and done with before it came to their attention. Dismissing the idea as unworthy of the honesty and respect that the members of her family accorded each other, she got up out of the armchair and positioned the newspaper squarely in the middle of the living room table. They had had nothing to fear from the truth then and they had nothing to fear from it now. Switching off the gas fire and turning to make her way back to the kitchen, Mary smiled to herself: she had warmed up nicely now and was really looking forward to her mid-morning cup of tea.

Malde had been excited at first, although his mood had quickly turned to one of caution: Dill was a witness for the prosecution and could thus not be approached directly by the defence. If Malde wanted to confront Dill with Miles's suspicions, he had only two options – both of which had their respective disadvantages. Firstly, he could recall him to the witness box. As a means of unearthing the full truth, however, this strategy had its limitations: Dill would be under oath, but if he claimed to have little or no knowledge of the original investigation and denied outright sending the file to King, Malde would eventually just have to let the matter drop. The other option was to inform the police and have them interrogate him in detail. In that case, though, Dill would have the right to a legal counsel who might well simply advise him not to say anything at all. That evening Malde had left the courtroom deep in thought, undecided which of the two options he should pursue. The following morning, however, he seemed to have regained some of his initial optimism, and, as Miles entered the dock, he turned and beamed at him − lifting up his right hand and curling the thumb and forefinger together in an 'OK' gesture. Miles guessed that he had already passed the matter over to the police and that they had indicated their willingness to follow it up.

Sitting once again at the front of the dock, Miles waited for the jury to arrive. As they filed noiselessly into the jury box, he examined them one by one. For the most part, they were dressed in casual clothes, so it was difficult to tell much about each individual's particular social class or profession. Moreover, they all seemed to wear the same, blank unemotional stare that revealed virtually nothing of their thoughts or attitudes. In the end, Miles only felt confident enough to speculate about four of the twelve people who were to decide his fate. The first was a man in his late fifties, neatly dressed in a crisp worsted jacket and wearing a sober dark red tie. Such was this man's air of intelligence and authority that Miles imagined it might well be he who would eventually be chosen as foreman of the jury. At the other end of the jury box sat two men in their early twenties dressed in jeans and sweat shirts. Whereas on the second day most of the jurors had taken different seats from those that they had occupied on the first, these two men had decided to sit − or more accurately slouch − next to each other in exactly the same position. Somehow, Miles sensed that they would be unsympathetic to his case. Finally, in front of them, on the lower tier on the far right-hand side sat a woman in her early thirties. In contrast to the two men behind, she had clearly been concentrating intently all the way through the first day's proceedings, sitting forward on her seat and vigilantly watching the advocates and witnesses as each had spoken in turn. With her high forehead and simple tied-back hair, she reminded Miles of Jo − the juror who on the final day of his own court service had held out so tenaciously against what she had believed would be a travesty of justice. As he stared at the woman's face, she turned and looked at him for a moment and their eyes met. He smiled. It seemed the most appropriate thing to do. For her part, however, the woman merely maintained her expressionless gaze: he doubted that even if she already had the feeling that he was innocent she would have reacted any differently. At that moment the judge entered and their exchange of looks was broken off. Standing up with the rest of the courtroom, Miles clasped his hands behind his back and waited for the second day of his trial to begin.

'Could you state your name and rank, please?'

'Detective Inspector Mark Fly, Richmond Road CID.'

'Detective Inspector, could you begin firstly by describing the events of the night of May the eleventh last year?'

'Just after nine o'clock at night, the station received a call from the fire service requesting we attend the scene of a blaze at 144 Balam Road, Feltham, from which the body of a man had just been recovered. I and my fellow CID officer, Detective Constable James May, arrived at the scene a little over fifteen minutes later at nine twenty. I immediately gave instructions for the area around the fire to be cordoned off in order that a search might be undertaken.'

'Could you describe the scene – the state of the property as you found it?'

'Yes. 144 Balam Road is the first floor flat in a block of six terraced flats on a residential street set back from the main Uxbridge Road. When I arrived at the scene the fire had already been extinguished, but it had obviously been a very serious blaze: all of the first floor windows had been blown out and there was also extensive damage to the ground floor flat.'

'Was the dead man the only person who had been affected by the fire?'

'No. The resident of the ground floor flat – a Mrs Alice McCray – had also been trapped in the blaze and was rescued by the fire fighters attending the scene. Mrs McCray was then taken to hospital where she was treated for minor burns.'

'Ladies and gentlemen,' said Pahklava, turning to face the jury, 'you will be later hearing from Mrs McCray, the seventy-five year old widow living in the ground floor flat who, but for the timely intervention of the fire service, might well have been seriously injured or even died in the blaze. Now, Detective Inspector, if you could kindly continue and tell the court the name of the victim of the fire and exactly how it was that he died.'

'Yes, the victim, Mr Thomas Cranmer, died of asphyxiation – a fact confirmed by an autopsy which was carried out the following morning by Dr Thomas Doherty at West Middlesex Hospital.'

'When was the identity of the victim confirmed?'

'In the small hours of the morning,' said Fly, checking his note book, 'at a quarter-past two, in fact. His body was identified by his partner and personal secretary, Miss Eva Osbourne. The previous evening, Miss Osbourne had become alarmed that Mr Cranmer had not returned home and had contacted her local police station to report him missing.'

Clenching his hands together, Miles sat back in his chair and exhaled deeply. Even now, five months later, he still found the affair that Tom had been having with his secretary both difficult to understand and distressing to recall. All too aware of the antipathy between Miles and Eva Osbourne, Tom had found it impossible in the context of *Criminal Britain* to apprise each of them of the exact relationship that he was having with the other. So it was that he had told Miles nothing about the affair that he was having with Eva and his decision to leave his wife for her. As for Eva, for the sake of maintaining Miles's cover, Tom had fallen back on the original story that he and Miles had concocted of the disagreement between them that had led to his being dismissed from *The Mail*.

'Wasn't it the case, Detective Inspector, that not only did Miss Osbourne report Mr Cranmer missing, but that she also specifically told the police that she believed that he had gone to Feltham to see the defendant, having been implored by him to visit him at his flat that very night?'

'Yes, that was so. And it was because she was convinced that Mr Cranmer had gone to Feltham that we were able to ascertain so quickly that it was indeed he who had died in the fire.'

'You mentioned an investigation of the scene of the blaze. What did that reveal?'

'In a neighbouring garden one of my officers recovered an empty petrol canister which had been used to start the fire.'

'If the usher would be so kind, I would like to show the witness exhibit two.'

Taking the petrol canister which was heavily bagged in polythene from the usher, the detective examined it peremptorily and returned it to her.

'Yes, that is the canister we recovered.'

'Ladies and gentleman, this article is a little large and perhaps somewhat difficult to pass between you so I will ask the usher to bring it over and you may look it at as she carries it in front of the jury box.'

Having watched the usher do so, Pahklava continued.

'Detective Inspector, were the defendant's fingerprints found on the canister?'

'Yes, they were – as well as a number of very clear palm prints.'

'Thank you. And could you now tell us about the circumstances surrounding the defendant's arrest?'

'Yes,' said the detective, examining his notebook once more. 'On the afternoon of May the twelfth, at ten past four, I received a call summoning me to terminal three at Heathrow airport where a man answering the defendant's description had been arrested in the hand baggage inspection area. I arrived there a little before five o'clock and found the defendant in the custody of the airport police. He had been apprehended attempting to leave the country using a false passport in the name of Michael Angel. Concealed inside his coat and mobile phone were a number of surveillance devices which had been detected by the hand baggage X-ray machine.'

'Did you question the defendant?'

'Yes I did. Myself and my colleague DC James May.'

'How did he seem?'

'Distracted in the extreme,' replied the detective, with a shake of the head. 'One could even say traumatized.'

'Really?'

'Yes. Neither myself nor my colleague were able to illicit any responses from him whatsoever. He seemed to be in a different world.'

'What did you do, then?'

'Well, as he was completely unable to account for his movements the previous night and as we had heard from Miss Osbourne that she had feared for Mr Cranmer's life when he had not returned from visiting the defendant, I arrested him on suspicion of his murder.'

'Did you interview the defendant the next day?'

'Yes, I did – the next two days in fact – at Richmond Road police station in the presence of my colleague DC May and the defendant's solicitor Mr Brian Malde.'

'How did he seem, then?'

'He was much clearer on both occasions – much more coherent.'

'This second time, when you questioned him, what did he say about his whereabouts on the night of Thomas Cranmer's murder and what reasons did he give for attempting to leave the country the next day?'

'The defendant stated that he had been walking around Soho on the night of the murder, had not been seen by anyone and could not recall exactly where he had been. He also stated that he had been completely unaware that Mr Cranmer had died in the flat that he had been renting and that he had been attempting to leave the country in pursuit of his ex-wife and son who, he had discovered, were emigrating to Australia.'

'What did he say about his relationship with Thomas Cranmer?'

'He stated that he had been working for Mr Cranmer for the previous twelve months as an undercover reporter, but that Mr Cranmer had been forced to terminate their arrangement because of the death of Mr Henry King who had originally commissioned him to make the documentary series. He suggested that the most likely reason for Mr Cranmer having gone to his flat had been to try and 'pull him out'.'

'So, what was his explanation for how Mr Cranmer died, then? If he, the defendant, had not poured the petrol into his flat did he know who had done it?'

'The defendant stated that he did not know how the fire had started, but speculated that it might have been a reprisal attack carried out by one of the criminals that he claimed to have been investigating.'

'Thank you, Detective Inspector Fly, I have no more questions for you.' Pahklava was looking very satisfied as she sat down: Detective Inspector May was a remarkably solid-looking police officer who simply oozed credibility and she was clearly pleased with the way that he had presented both himself and his evidence. As Drake stood up to cross-examine Fly, Miles got the feeling that he had wisely decided not to attempt to pit himself directly against the policeman's obvious integrity.

'Detective Inspector Fly,' said Drake, in a friendly, casual voice, 'just a few questions if I may? Firstly, when you interviewed the defendant on the second day, on May the twelfth, you showed him the petrol canister, did you not?'

'Yes, I did.'

'Did he make any attempt to deny it belonged to him?'

'No, he did not.'

'He stated readily that it was his and did not challenge your assertion that the petrol it had contained had been poured through the letter-box of his flat in Balam Road resulting in the death of Mr Cranmer.'

'That's correct.'

'Thank you, Detective Inspector. Now, the defendant's alibi was that he had been working for Thomas Cranmer and Henry King all along as an undercover reporter, correct?'

'Yes, that's correct.'

'And, in support of this alibi, he mentioned three investigations to you in which he had been engaged for the purposes of making the documentary series commissioned by Mr Cranmer and Mr King.'

'Yes.'

'Could you tell the court what they were?'

'Er, yes,' said the detective, referring to his notes, 'he stated that he had been on the trail of a group of social security fraudsters, of a cowboy building firm run by a Mr John Tysoe and a drug-running operation centred on a night club in central London.'

'The court has already heard about the first of those – the social security fraud – but just to be absolutely certain, could you confirm once again that the information which the defendant supplied was of substantial benefit to the authorities in identifying an individual by the name of Craig Gleeson who had been responsible for defrauding millions of pounds worth of housing benefit allowances?'

'Yes, that's correct.'

'Thank you. To return to the second of those investigations – the cowboy building firm run by a Mr John Tysoe – what did you do when you learned about his alleged activities from the defendant?'

'We went to interview Mr Tysoe.'

'And did you subsequently establish that he had indeed been involved in swindling a number of householders by means of poor quality and incomplete building work?'

'Yes, we did.'

'So, two out of three, then?'

'I beg your pardon?'

'You were able to verify relatively quickly that two out of three of the investigations which the defendant claimed he was undertaking could be substantiated by firm evidence of criminal activity.'

'Yes, we were able to uncover evidence of criminal activity in those two cases,' replied the detective.

'What about the third case – the alleged distribution of drugs inside the West end night club, Gog. Did you follow that up?'

'We did.'

'And did you find any evidence to substantiate the defendant's claims?'

'No, we did not.'

'And when you told the defendant that, what did he say?'

'He said it was because he had completed the first two investigations, but not the third and was therefore not yet in possession of all the evidence he needed to prove his case.'

'Thank you detective inspector,' said Drake, with a broad smile, 'you have been most helpful.'

As soon as Alice McCray entered the witness box, Miles could tell there was something not quite right about her. Looking around the courtroom he tried to determine whether anyone else had spotted it. However, neither the gallery – where once again Babs and Evelyn were seated in the middle of a group of journalists and members of the public – nor the legal teams, nor the jury seemed conscious of anything amiss. Checking himself, he turned his gaze towards the old woman once again to see if he had been mistaken: perhaps it was because the image of her strange, manic face at the downstairs window the first time that he had seen her had had such a powerful impact on him that he could never really think of her in any other way again. The more he looked at her, though, the more he got the impression of a woman whose mind was not completely in touch with reality. Firstly, although it was a cold November day, she seemed to have arrived at court without an overcoat. Secondly, although the plum red cardigan that she wore was spotlessly clean, she had done the buttons up incorrectly, giving the whole of her upper torso a distorted, asymmetrical appearance. Lastly, staring at her deep blue goitred eyes, Miles could see that they were rolling slowly and seemingly independently of the rest of her body's movements.

'Could you state your name, please?' asked Pahklava, her hitherto sharp, nasal tones being replaced by a warmer, more maternal tenor – she was obviously intending to give this elderly, fragile witness the full kid gloves treatment.

For several seconds the old woman did not reply, but then slowly her brow began to furl aggressively, as though Pahklava had levelled at her not a simple question, but a deeply confrontational and insulting statement.

'Alice McCray,' she retorted, her voice rising provocatively – almost challenging Pahklava to deny that this was not so.

Pahklava's face dropped: there was obviously nothing the least bit frail about this old lady.

'Er, yes, thank you … and where do you live, Mrs McCray?'

'One hundred and forty two Balam Road, Feltham,' answered the old woman distractedly, raising her left hand and smoothing down her frizzy, grey-ginger hair. Around her wrist, Miles could see that she was wearing a thin, black wristwatch, the strap of which was starting to come undone.

'How long have you lived there, Mrs McCray?'

'Oh, over forty years,' she replied, ebulliently. 'Since it was built, you know.'

Again Pahklava flinched – this sudden display of pride somehow being more disconcerting than if the old woman had maintained her original tone of hostility.

'Thank you, Mrs McCray,' continued Pahklava, tentatively. 'Now, er, I'd like to ask you about the man who moved into the flat above you eighteen months ago, can you …'

'No point in asking me,' interrupted the old lady. 'I don't know anything about him.'

At that moment, Miles sensed the courtroom at last become aware that something was wrong. To his right, in the public gallery, several people all seemed to shift position at once. In front of him, Drake looked sharply up from his notes, staring firstly at the witness box and then immediately at Pahklava to see how she was going to react, but before she could continue the old woman began to speak again.

'I rarely saw him, you see, or just on a handful of occasions: he used to keep very odd hours. I saw some of the people who came to visit him, mind you. There was the one who jumped out of the upstairs window into my back garden when the social security came round. I didn't like him, at all – he looked like a big, filthy rat. Then there was the foreign one with all the chest hair …'

'Er, yes, thank you, Mrs McCray,' interrupted Pahklava. 'What I was going to ask was are you able to recognize him now – in the courtroom, I mean?'

'Yes, of course, I can – he's over there!' snapped the old woman, with the air of someone intensely irritated at having been asked to state the obvious.

'Thank you, er, thank you,' replied Pahklava, reaching her left hand out on to the table in front of her and repositioning her notepad slightly. Miles guessed that she had now decided to abandon the other questions that she had prepared in advance and concentrate instead on eliciting from Alice McCray her single, most essential piece of testimony – the testimony which would prove that it must have been Miles who had torched the flat whilst Tom had been in there. 'Now, the night of the fire. I'm sure you remember – May the eleventh this year? You told the police that you heard activity beforehand. Could you tell the court what it was?'

'Footsteps – two sets of footsteps – about ten minutes apart.'

'And they were both men's footsteps, yes?' coaxed Pahklava. 'You told the police they were both men: because you can tell the difference in sound between men and women when they walk up the stairs in front of your house, can't you? Your hearing is excellent, I understand.'

'I don't live in a house. I live in a flat.'

'Yes, yes, exactly – in front of your flat, I mean. So, they were both men's footsteps. Yes?'

'Yes.'

'In the case of the first set of footsteps, did the man actually go through the front door?'

'Yes, he did.'

'And did you think it was the defendant – the man who lived upstairs?'

'Yes.'

'Why?'

'Because I could hear him moving around.'

'Did you hear the key turn in the lock when he went in?'

'No.'

'Were you normally able to hear that sound from the upstairs flat?'

'Usually, yes.'

'So, if it hadn't been the defendant, presumably the door had been left open, otherwise this man – whoever he was – would not have been able to get in?'

'I suppose so. I don't know.'

'What about the second set of footsteps – ten minutes later, just before the fire started?'

'They belonged to a man, too.'

Clasping his hands together, Miles shook his head slowly. This second

452

person had surely been Kent, although it was still a mystery to him how he had discovered Michael Angel's true identity and why he had arrived at the flat just a few minutes after Tom.

'Good. But the second man didn't go into the flat, did he? Because in his case, you didn't hear the front door open or close. Instead, he ran back down the stairs again a couple of minutes later.'

'Yes, yes,' replied the old woman, dreamily. 'He didn't ring the bell – I would have definitely heard it if he had. And then, when he went back down the stairs in such a hurry, I remember thinking how strange it was because Mr Angel was already in. I supposed he was going to come back again later that night …'

'Thank you, Mrs McCray,' said Pahklava, smoothly: it seemed as though this witness was going to be able to give her evidence properly after all. 'So, the second man didn't spend much time at the front door. If you had to estimate, how long would you say he was there exactly? Two minutes, one minute …?'

'Mr Angel had several late-night visitors, you know,' said the old woman, utterly ignoring Pahklava's question. 'That's why I thought the man might come back later.'

'Yes, er, right, but to return to the duration of the …'

'There was a woman, once. Late one night.'

'Yes, but …'

'I can see her now!' exclaimed Mrs McCray suddenly, pointing an accusing finger at the public gallery. 'There she is. That slut over there!'

For a fraction of a second the entire courtroom locked rigid in consternation. Then, all at once, every single face turned and looked at Babs, who blinked, shuffled in her seat and then began to turn bright red.

'Ms Pahklava,' rasped the judge – his dry Scot's brogue breaking the embarrassed silence. 'If your witness is incapable of responding to the questions that you direct at her, then she must leave the stand.'

'I'm sorry, your honour,' replied Pahklava.

'And I heard them as well, you know – afterwards,' continued the old woman – completely oblivious to the judge's words. 'Through the ceiling.' Narrowing her eyes knowingly, she then added in a confidential whisper. 'They were doing it for over an hour.'

Pahklava had now gone nearly as red as Babs. Out of the corner of his eye, Miles could see that in the jury box the two young sweat-shirted men were whispering to each other in barely-concealed mirth.

'Mrs McCray,' exclaimed Pahklava, sharply and with an unmistakable note of anger in her voice. 'You must answer my question or you may be held in contempt of court. How long did the second man spend at the front door of the upstairs flat just before the fire started?'

'Oh, maybe two minutes, I suppose – no more,' replied the old woman off-handedly, as though she had just been asked the question for the first time.

'Thank you, Mrs McCray, I have no more questions,' replied Pahklava with obvious relief, sitting quickly down and examining her notes. To her left, Drake shook his head soberly to indicate that he did not wish to cross-examine. Seconds later, when the judge dismissed the court for lunch, Miles noted that his face had broken into the broadest of smiles.

It was just after two o'clock when Kent took the stand. The last time Miles had seen him had been five months ago when he had dropped him off at the hospital to get the wound in his chest stitched up, and somehow he had expected him to look much the same as he had done that day. The Kent that stood in the witness box, however, was very different from the suavely dressed man who had arrogantly parked his turbo-charged Saab on the double yellow lines in front of Accident and Emergency. Instead of his Savile Row suit, he was wearing a cheap sports jacket and a roll-neck woollen sweater. As Miles watched him take the oath, he wondered why he had deliberately dressed down for the occasion. One reason, no doubt, was the ugly, livid scar on the right hand side of his neck which even a shirt with a high collar could not fully conceal. More significantly, though, Miles concluded that Kent was trying to create the impression of being an honest, hardworking man. He was not the chief fixer in a multimillion pound international crime network; he was just an ordinary, straightforward security manager at a night club. Knowing that the jury would in all probability have a fair proportion of middle-aged men and women with teenage children, he was seeking to portray himself as a reassuring authority figure – precisely the sort of person they would hope to be in charge of their offspring when they themselves were not around. Looking to his left and seeing the watching brief sitting poised and alert, Miles shook his head grimly. It was just as he had thought: Ellis's aim was to get through the trial with the minimum amount of public relations damage, whilst in the process ensuring that the court returned a verdict of guilty. Thereafter, Miles would be at his mercy.

'Could you state your name and occupation, please?'

'Arthur Kent. I'm the head of security at Gog – it's a nightclub in Chelsea.'

His voice was quiet but assured. Knowing his rigorous attention to detail, Miles imagined that he had had been perfecting his delivery for weeks.

'Could you tell the court if you recognize the defendant, Mr Kent?'

'I do.'

'By what name and how was he known to you?'

'I knew him as Micky Angel. He started working at the club about a year ago as a doorman – just before last Christmas. We were a bit short of staff at the time: we hired him as a temp through an agency.'

'Was he good at his job?'

'Yeah. Well, we thought so at first, anyway.'

'What do you mean, Mr Kent?'

'I mean he worked hard and everything and did what he was told, but he had a tendency to sort of, well, lose it sometimes. He had a bit of a short fuse.'

'When did you first discover this?'

'About a week before Christmas, there was some trouble at the club. Three blokes got a bit drunk. We, er, asked 'em to leave but they wouldn't go and things ended up gettin' a bit rough. In the process, one of our guys, Nigel, got hurt so we took him to hospital to get him patched up – me and Micky that is.'

'The person to whom you are referring – the employee of yours who was taken to hospital – was Mr Nigel Reed, is that correct?'

'That's right.'

'And what happened at the hospital?'

'Well, while I stayed in the waiting room, Micky went off with Nigel to this sort of consulting room place so that he could be seen by the doctors. On the way, they ran into the three blokes that had been thrown out of the club. Micky went bananas. Laid into 'em big time. I mean, they'd just got a bit drunk, but he took it all personal.'

'He attacked them?'

'Yeah.'

'Did you witness this yourself?'

'No, I didn't – I only heard about it afterwards.'

'Your honour, if I may …?' said Pahklava looking towards the judge.

'Ladies and gentlemen,' said the judge, turning to face the jury. 'The counsel for the prosecution will now read to you what is known as an admission. An admission is a statement made by a witness whose evidence is relevant to the trial, but who is unable to attend in person. Now, I want you all to be clear on this point: an admission is just as much evidence as if the witness concerned had come to court and given it to you themselves; please treat it as such. In this particular case I understand that Mr Nigel Reed is now working …'

'In Malaysia, your honour.'

'In Malaysia, exactly. So, please proceed, Ms Pahklava.'

The admission backed up Kent's version of the fight at the hospital in every detail. As Pahklava read through it, Miles recalled the many occasions that he and Nigel had spent together standing outside the front entrance to Gog in the cold night air. How had they turned Nigel against him? Had Kent threatened him? He doubted it – or, at least, he doubted that he had done so directly. It was much more likely to have been a combination of lies and inducements. It wasn't difficult to visualize the scene: Nigel summoned to the underground office in the small hours of the morning to find Kent sitting in the gloom behind his old mahogany desk. Mick betrayed us. He was going to shop everyone at Gog to the police – including you. We've got to defend ourselves. Sign this and then get yourself over to Ellis's Casino in Kuala Lumpur – there's a job waiting for you there; we'll look after the rest. What other choice would an ex-boxer on the wrong side of forty have, when confronted with such a proposal?

Having finished reading the admission, Pahklava turned to face the witness box again.

'So to recap, Mr Kent, you didn't actually witness the defendant attacking the three men from the night club, but you learned about it later from Mr Nigel Reed?'

'That's right.'

'When did he tell you about it?'

'Six, seven weeks later. Micky kept on losing his temper with the punters – the customers, I mean. In the end everyone got to notice it and that's when Nigel told me about what had happened at the hospital. I think he'd, like, sort of kept it under his hat up until then 'cos he didn't wanna get Micky into trouble.'

456

'And it was at this time that you started to think that the defendant might be something of a liability?'

'Yeah, yeah, that's right. I mean, he only used to work weekends, but all the same it was a bit of a worry.'

'When did you eventually dispense with the defendant's services?'

'Well, er ...' murmured Kent, seeming to search his memory for the exact date. 'We kept him on till about the end of March, I think. Something like that – beginning of April, maybe.'

'What was the defendant's reaction to being asked to leave?'

'Kicked up a right fuss. Shoutin', swearin'. I always got the impression he never had any money – or he used to spend it as soon as he got it – and I think he'd been bankin' on us offering him a full-time contract.'

'Had you ever intended to offer him a full-time contract?'

'No. No way.'

'Thank you, Mr Kent. Just one more question before I finish. Gog is a very big night club, is it not?'

'Pretty big – a capacity of just over two thousand.'

'Do you have a drugs policy there?'

'Yeah, we do – a very strict one.'

'The measures that you take – are they in keeping with local authority guidelines?'

'Oh, yeah, definitely.'

'And did Gog in fact receive an award for good practice two years ago, issued by the local authority in recognition of your procedures?'

'Yeah, yeah, we did. I was very proud of it, too.'

'Thank you, Mr Kent. I have no more questions, your honour.'

As Drake stood up, Miles could see the frustration etched into his face. Drake fully believed that Kent had been lying from start to finish, but, as no witnesses to the hospital incident had come forward and Gog's employees had closed ranks, Kent's version of Miles's time at the nightclub was going to have to stand more or less unchallenged. Moreover, in preparing Miles's defence, Drake and Malde had reluctantly concluded that his case could only suffer if they attempted to go into too much detail about the web of illegal activities in which the Ellis Group was involved. The essence of the prosecution's argument was that Miles had been living in a fantasy world, and to summon a string of witnesses, all of whom would flatly deny the allegations against them, would be to

457

risk reinforcing that impression: how could so many people be lying and Miles alone be telling the truth? Instead, Drake had decided to adopt a more subtle approach: if fortress Ellis was too formidable to be breached by a frontal assault, the only remaining strategy was stealth.

'Mr Kent. Who owns Gog?'

On the bench behind Drake, the watching brief flinched: Miles imagined that he hadn't expected him to go straight to the subject of Sir Alain Ellis with his very first question. Kent, however, seemed more than ready for the challenge.

'It's part of the Ellis Group of companies,' he replied, simply.

'The manager director of which is …?'

'Sir Alain Ellis.'

'Besides your responsibilities at Gog, do you undertake other tasks for any of the other companies in the Ellis group?'

'Yeah, occasionally.'

'What, for example?'

'Oh, y'know, little things – this and that.'

'Oh, 'little things – this and that'?' echoed Drake, with heavy irony. 'Well now, would arranging the export of instruments of torture to the Middle East for the Ellis Group come under the heading of one of the little 'this and that' things that you do?'

'No,' replied Kent.

'No?' queried Drake.

'No,' he insisted – his facial expression a perfectly balanced mix of surprise and indignation.

Undeterred, Drake continued to press on.

'Perhaps it's slipped your memory. Let me try and refresh it for you. I'm referring to electro-mechanical stun batons manufactured by Progo Engenharia of Porto Alegre, Brazil – an engineering company in which the Ellis Group owns a forty per cent stake.'

'I don't know what you're talkin' about,' said Kent.

'Oh, really,' exclaimed Drake, sardonically. 'Right, well, let's try another little 'this and that' task then, Mr Kent. How about Fobors, Sweden? An armament company in which the Ellis Group similarly owns a significant stake. Did you visit them on the second weekend of March this year with a view to helping them secure an arms contract in the Middle East?'

'No, I did not.'

'No?'

Before Kent had time to deny it once more, the judge interrupted.

'Mr Drake. Neither the witness nor the organization by which he is employed is on trial here. Unless this line of questioning directly relates to the defendant, I must ask you to desist.'

'I'm sorry, your honour,' replied Drake, with a respectful bow, 'I will get to the point. Mr Kent, you have just stated that the defendant worked weekends.'

'Yes.'

'But you also arranged other work for him as well, didn't you?'

'Yeah, a couple of small jobs here and there,' replied Kent, nonchalantly.

'One of which was accompanying you to a warehouse in Lowestoft by the name of Carl and Ernst.'

'Yeah, that's right.'

'How many times did you visit that warehouse with the defendant?'

'Once or twice.'

'Which?' countered Drake, sharply. 'Was it on one occasion or on two occasions, can you recall?'

'Twice, I think.'

'In what capacity did you visit that warehouse?'

'How d'you mean?'

'When you arrived there, you handed over a business card to a Mr McDonald, the warehouse Manager. How did it describe you?'

'Oh, right, I get you now,' replied Kent, pretending that he had only just realized what Drake had meant. 'It would have said procurement executive, Ellis International Export. That's an Ellis subsidiary company that supplies Gog with alcoholic drinks from overseas – wines, champagne, that sort of thing.'

'Ah, good. We're getting a little closer to your 'this and that' responsibilities now. So, in addition to being the head of security at Gog, you are also a procurement executive for another company within the Ellis Group?'

'Yeah. Well, on paper, I suppose.'

'What do you mean 'on paper'? Either you are, or you are not a procurement executive for Ellis International Export.'

'Yeah, I am, but only because there's, like, a security element in the shipment and storage of drinks to the club. I mean, they're high value items and as security manager it's part of my responsibility to ensure that they're properly handled. The procurement title's just a sort of convenience, really …'

'Are you saying, then, that it was in connection with the supply of alcoholic drinks to Gog in Chelsea that you went to the warehouse with the defendant?'

'Yeah.'

'Not to check up on a consignment of torture batons bound for the Middle East?'

'Mr Drake,' interrupted the judge, irritably. 'The witness has already stated that he knows nothing of the matter to which you refer. I will not warn you again. Whatever your point is, make it now or let the witness leave the stand.'

Drake's lips puckered, as though to imply that he knew that he had taken things as far as he was able. In the witness box, Miles could see a smile pass across Kent's face. Drake's questioning had been crude and ineffectual. By launching straight into an attack on Ellis, he had provoked the judge's anger and thus effectively prevented himself from being able to make any further allegations; Kent would be out of the witness box in seconds, with no mention of Foss, Sipkiss, the drugs he trafficked into Gog or any of the other criminal activities for which he had prepared careful explanations. The moment that Drake spoke again, however, the smile was immediately wiped from Kent's face.

'So, why did you visit the bonded warehouse at Carl and Ernst, then?'

'What?'

'Why did you visit the bonded warehouse at Carl and Ernst with the defendant, rather than one of their ordinary warehouses? Bonded warehouses are for products to be transhipped through the UK, not for ones delivered to it.'

For a second Kent froze – the question had caught him off-guard.

'Oh, er, right,' he muttered, 'er, there was a couple of other things I had to look at for a colleague. He asked me to, er, check 'em while I was there – at the warehouse, that is.'

If Kent's earlier responses had not been quite so smooth, this answer might well have sounded convincing. However, his momentary hesitation and sudden lapse in confidence were in marked contrast to the image of the honest, plain-speaking man that he had spent the previous ten minutes creating. It was exactly what Drake had been hoping for.

460

Staring at Kent in silence for several seconds with his most acid look of disdain, he shook his head slowly and then turned to face the judge.

'I have no more questions for this … gentleman, your honour.'

Two minutes later the judge dismissed the court for the day, and five minutes after that, Drake joined Miles and Malde in legal room 1.54 in the basement of the courthouse.

'What did you think?' asked Drake, as he came through the door – taking off his wig and smoothing back his hair.

'Not bad, I suppose,' replied Miles.

'I thought it was good,' insisted Malde.

'We were never going to get that much out of Kent,' continued Drake, sitting down on the opposite side of the narrow table to Miles. 'Like I said, we simply don't have the witnesses – but I think at the end there he was wrong-footed just long enough for the jury to spot that something was up.'

'Absolutely,' added Malde.

'And now it's the weekend!' beamed Drake, putting his hands behind his neck and leaning back in his chair. 'And that's the impression the jurors are going to go away with, isn't it? Something rotten in the house of Ellis. Too glib, our Mr Kent, too glib by half. Can we get some coffee organized in here – I'm parched.'

'The machine's broken – I already asked,' replied Malde. 'You'll have to go up to the first floor, I'm afraid.'

'Oh, God, not again!' groaned Drake, good-humouredly. Leaning forward, he then reached over the table and squeezed Miles on the forearm. 'So, Mr Coverdale, as I say, we've ended on a good note. It's the weekend now; you just try and keep your spirits up.'

'That's right, Miles,' echoed Malde, 'it's been a good day – not just Kent, but the old woman, too.'

'Oh, yes!' chuckled Drake, rolling his eyes in mirth. 'She was a real bonus.'

'D'you think her evidence'll work in our favour, then?' asked Miles.

'Oh, definitely! She'll have a big psychological effect on the jury.'

'Why's that?'

'Well, they may not actually sit down and consciously think it through, but subconsciously they'll be asking themselves if the old woman isn't essential to the prosecution's case, then why did they call her in the first place? And if she is essential to their case – but yet she's clearly off her rocker – then it can't be much good, can it?'

'D'you think so?'

'Yes, I really do. Summoning her was the biggest mistake the prosecution have made so far. They're trying too hard, that's their problem. When the courtroom becomes a place of mirth, it almost always undermines the jury's confidence in the Crown's case: no one takes a farce seriously.'

'What about Dill – any news?' asked Miles, turning to face Malde.

'Yes,' he replied. 'The police are interviewing him tomorrow afternoon.'

'So, will we know the result of that by Monday?'

'Yes, we will. There's still plenty of time to recall him to the stand or submit an affidavit from him.'

'That's good news, then, really good news,' said Drake, smiling at Miles again. 'So, listen, I guess that's it for now, but as I say, you look after yourself over the weekend. Try and stay relaxed. The way things are going you could well be on the stand on Monday afternoon. We're going to need you in top form for that!'

'Thanks,' said Miles. 'I appreciate everything you're doing for me.'

'You're welcome, Mr Coverdale. You really are most welcome.'

Giving the two men a wave of thanks through the window of the interview room as they made their way back upstairs, Miles tried to fight back a rising sense of despair. Despite Kent's revealing slip and Alice McCray's ranting, the evidence was still stacked heavily against him. On Monday, Tom's secretary would take the stand – the prosecution's chief witness. Malde had shown Miles part of the written statement that she had given to the police and, for all Malde's optimism, Miles knew that essentially his defence rested on the jury believing his word against hers and that of the overwhelming majority of the other witnesses. Lighting up a cigarette, he sat and smoked in silence until the dock officer came and knocked at the door. It was three-thirty now and he would have to spend the next two and a half hours in the courtroom cells before being returned with the other defendants being tried that day to the secure overnight unit at Kingston police station. Stubbing out the cigarette, he stood up and got ready to go, but, to his surprise, the dock officer had not come to take him to the cells.

'You've got a visitor,' he announced.

462

'What?'

'You've got a visitor. Someone to see you.'

Miles stared at the guard in astonishment. Drake and Malde had clearly already left for the weekend and, in the five months since he had been arrested, not a single person had been to see him. For a moment he thought it might be Babs, but then straightaway dismissed the idea: after lunch, neither she nor Evelyn had reappeared in the public gallery, the prospect of going to the pub all afternoon no doubt being preferable to having insults hurled at them by Alice McCray.

'Who is it?' asked Miles.

The dock officer didn't answer, but merely nodded to his left to indicate that the visitor was coming down the corridor. Retaking his seat, Miles frowned – racking his brains as to who it might be. For a split second, a wild, delirious hope suddenly gripped him. What if it was Elizabeth and Jake? Could they be back? Could they have found out about his trial? At that moment, though, the door swung slowly open, and the sudden, heady feeling of hope disappeared, to be replaced by an even more overpowering sense of shame.

'Good afternoon, Mr Coverdale. We've never actually met, but my name is …'

'Yes, yes. I know who you are,' said Miles.

'Can I sit down?' he replied – his voice was rich and gentle.

'If you wish.'

Removing the scarf from around his neck the man sat down, rested his forearms on the table and then turned his large grey-green eyes towards Miles. His look was strange and spell-binding, filled with sympathy and understanding, yet at the same time conveying a powerful impression of tremendous inner personal strength; Miles had never seen anything quite like it in his life before.

'I hope you don't mind my having come to your trial.'

'Why?' replied Miles. 'Why did you come?'

'I don't know,' he answered, with a frown. 'I'm not sure.'

'Curiosity?'

'In part, perhaps.'

'But not to gloat, I think.'

'No, not to gloat.'

'What do you want?'

Angus Lamb paused before replying, continuing to stare fixedly at

Miles across the table. Under his gaze Miles somehow felt bare and exposed, as if those tranquil, mesmeric eyes could see right down into his soul.

'You're innocent aren't you?' he said, at last.

'Yes, yes, I am.'

'That must be terrible for you,' he sighed, shaking his head sadly. 'Alone here. Away from your family.'

'Yes, yes. It is.'

'Will you tell me about it?'

'What?'

'Tell me all about what you did – about what happened to you.'

'Why? Why do you want to know?'

'Your barrister mentioned instruments of torture. You were on the trail of people selling those ... things, weren't you?'

'Yes. I was.'

'I've seen something of the results of torture at first hand when I worked for the Ministry of Overseas Development. I've seen the awful suffering that they bring.'

'I can tell you if you want,' said Miles. 'It's rather a long story, though.'

'I've got plenty of time,' replied Lamb, with a smile. 'Besides I may be able to help you. Being a Member of Parliament might not count for much in these days of our neutered parliamentary democracy, but it can still open a few doors here and there. It got me in here for a start ...'

Miles swallowed, almost unable to believe what he had just heard.

'You? Help me?'

'Yes. Why not?'

'But ...'

'But what?'

'But I crucified you.'

In reply Angus Lamb merely stared back at Miles, his face showing nothing but compassion and pity. Finally, talking off his raincoat and folding it carefully on top of the spare seat, he sat back ready to listen.

Miles talked for over two hours. At first the words came slowly, but, as Lamb prompted him with questions here and there, he found himself loosening up, explaining the last eighteen months of his life, and a good deal of it beforehand, with an honesty and eloquence that he did not know he possessed. Listening to himself speak, he realized that this was the first opportunity that he had had to tell his story in full to another human being who was not in some way involved in the criminal case against him. It was a wonderfully therapeutic experience and, by the time he had finished, the depression that had gripped him earlier that afternoon had utterly vanished, despite the fact that the case against him was just as strong as it had ever been. Lamb seemed particularly interested in Harper and Dill, both of whom were involved in the critical early stages of the series and both of whom could corroborate Miles's efforts to infiltrate what he had understood to be the gang of fraudsters. Having learned that Dill was for the time being out of bounds to the defence or anyone connected with them, Lamb suggested he might try to find Harper over the weekend. Miles, however, was not optimistic. Even if Harper was still hiding out in London somewhere, he was a diehard anarchist who actively looked forward to the collapse of the British state. Why should he come to the rescue of a man who had betrayed his friendship with a view to exposing him and those he cared for on national television? Lamb, however, seemed undeterred and said he would make some enquiries as to Harper's whereabouts as well as following up one or two other ideas that had occurred to him. As Lamb picked up his coat and turned to leave, Miles felt an awful emptiness clutch at his stomach: what right had he to accept the help of a man whose life he had almost ruined? When he broached the subject, Lamb simply smiled. His wife, he explained, had never believed the story of his infidelity for a moment and, although his mother had been heartbroken at the time, it had been she who had told him about Miles's trial and encouraged him to go along to the courthouse. Then, having shaken Miles's hand and promised again to help if he could, Lamb went out of the room and down the corridor, leaving Miles still unable to credit the extraordinary display of magnanimity that he had just witnessed.

Since the last time that Miles had seen Eva Osbourne in the Tower five months previously, she had had her hair cut very short. As she walked straight-backed and poised towards the witness box, the whole courtroom turned to watch her: for the first time in the trial, Thomas Cranmer seemed to come to life as a human being. Here was the woman he had loved – the person with whom he had intended to spend the rest of his life. As soon as she began to read the oath, Miles immediately noticed the change in her voice. There was still the same sharpness, still the same clarity of enunciation, but the self-conceit had gone – incinerated along with her hopes and dreams that cold May night in a one-bedroom flat in Feltham. Looking at her gaunt, thin face, Miles was overcome by a great sense of pity. Somewhere, a world away, Elizabeth and Jake were living and breathing. Although he was uncertain whether he would ever see them again, the knowledge that they were alive was still a source of comfort. Eva Osbourne, however, would never be reunited with Thomas Cranmer or, at least, not until she joined him in death. As she handed the bible back to the usher and turned to face Pahklava, the courtroom looked on in absolute silence.

'Could you state your name, please?'

'Eva Osbourne.'

'And what is your profession, Miss Osbourne?'

'I'm a PA – a personal assistant.'

'Where do you work?'

'At the offices of *The Mail* newspaper.'

'And how long have you worked there?'

'Twelve years.'

'For the last three of those years, you were PA to Thomas Cranmer, were you not – up until his death in May?'

'That's right.'

'Could you explain to the court your relationship with Mr Cranmer, both personal and professional, starting from when you first began to work for him? If at any time you feel the need to pause and collect your thoughts, please do so, there is no hurry.'

To his left, Miles could see the members of the jury sitting grave-faced and attentive. Standing erect in the witness box, her head held high, Eva Osbourne was the very epitome of dignity in grief.

'Before I worked for Tom, I was PA to his predecessor – a man called Roderick Marshall. When he left to take up a position in the US, Tom inherited me as his personal secretary. We hit it off right away – we had a very good working relationship. He trusted me to do almost everything for him. As a PA, that's really important: if you know that your boss will back you up in your decisions, then it makes life so much easier for both of you. We were a good team. He was very supportive, very dependable – not always quite up to speed with things, maybe, but that's why he needed me, I suppose.'

'But your relationship didn't remain purely professional, did it?'

'No, it didn't. Tom was married, although he and his wife no longer really had anything in common: they never spent any time together – it was, well, just dead between them. Then, in May last year – the bank holiday weekend, actually – we'd been working late one night and he asked me to dinner afterwards. I didn't think anything of it, really. He was always dining out and I went along because I knew he'd be good company. Well, anyway, after that things just seemed to take on a life of their own and over the next few weeks, we got closer and closer and eventually became lovers.'

'When did things become really serious? When did you decide to make your relationship permanent?'

Lifting her hand, Eva Osbourne curled a lock of hair still more tightly behind her right ear. On the lapel of her expensive two-piece suit, Miles could see that she was wearing a red and gold broach. Somehow, he knew that Tom had bought it for her.

'By the start of this year we were pretty much seeing each other every night. I ... understood the commitment he had to his wife and was content to keep things as they were. I was happy with him and that was enough for me. Also, he could be, well, weak. No, I don't mean that – weak's not the right word. He was considerate of other people's feelings. More considerate than me, anyway, and I was fairly certain that he didn't want to break things off with her. But then one night he told me he'd had enough. He said he couldn't face living the rest of his life as a lie and had decided to ask her for a divorce.'

'And did he do that?'

'Yes, he did.'

'What was his wife's reaction?'

'She was ... difficult at first, but accepted the idea fairly quickly. There was a period of about, oh, two or three weeks or so of frantic backwards and forwards between their respective lawyers, but in the end they came to an agreement. I mean, maybe that's actually quite quick for this sort of thing, I don't know: I'd no experience of it before.'

'When was this? When was it exactly that Mr Cranmer asked his wife for a divorce and their solicitors became involved?'

'It was at the beginning of May. Just before he died. We were planning to get married as soon as it had all gone through.'

'Thank you, Miss Osbourne,' said Pahklava, 'I know this must be distressing for you.' Pausing for a moment out of consideration for the witness, she carefully repositioned her gown over her shoulders before recommencing. 'Now, I would like to ask you about the defendant. Do you recognize the man in the dock, Miss Osbourne?'

'I do,' she replied, turning towards Miles and staring at him with her grey, unemotional eyes. 'His name is Miles Coverdale. He used to work as a photographer at *The Mail*.'

'Could you describe the relationship between Mr Cranmer and the defendant? I'd like if you could in your answer to make reference to actual dates. It will help the court greatly in understanding how their relationship evolved.'

Eva Osbourne did not answer straightaway but paused for a moment, her brow furling as though struggling to put a particularly difficult concept into words.

'I think Tom pitied him, actually,' she said finally. 'He once told me that Mr Coverdale didn't have any proper friends, which was exactly what Tom did have – he was the most sociable, popular person I've ever met – and that was why he felt sorry for him, I suppose. Certainly Tom was very patient with him: because he was patient with everybody, I guess, and because Mr Coverdale did produce the odd good photograph for *The Mail*, so that's how their relationship was at first. I'm sorry, you said you wanted dates. What I meant was up until Mr Coverdale left last year, that's what their relationship was like – as far I understood it, anyway.'

'I think the court has understood very well what you mean, Miss Osbourne. Thank you. Please continue.'

'But Mr Coverdale's dismissal was a very bitter affair and Tom never spoke about him in the office after that. I think he felt a bit betrayed because he'd stuck up for Mr Coverdale so often in the past and he'd just rewarded him by throwing it all back in his face.'

'When was the next time you saw the defendant, after he had left *The Mail*?'

'It was in March this year. Tom had a flat in Clapham. It was where we used to meet to spend the night together. Then, one day, as I was driving off to work I saw Mr Coverdale sitting in his car outside – it was parked twenty yards or so away from the flat. I didn't recognize him at first because his appearance had changed so much and because he deliberately looked away when I saw him. But, later that day, it clicked and I realized it was him. I was sure it couldn't have been a coincidence, so that night I mentioned it to Tom. He didn't want to talk about it at first, but not long afterwards he asked if we could start meeting at my flat instead.'

'What was his explanation for that?'

'He didn't give one but I sensed it was something to do with Mr Coverdale. Then, a few weeks later, I found out it was because he'd been stalking him.'

'Stalking him?'

'Yes. I was opening Tom's mail one morning – this was in early April, I think – and there was this package containing a video tape and a letter. I put them in Tom's in-tray and didn't think anything more of them, but then the next day a man by the name of Mr Angel called asking to speak to him. I told him he was in a meeting at which point he became very abusive and hung up. Two hours later he turned up at the office. It was Mr Coverdale – I recognized him straightaway because I'd seen him in the car outside the flat. He was only in there with Tom for a few minutes, but when he came out afterwards he looked quite angry– well, sort of angry and disappointed at the same time – it's hard to describe. Anyway, I was really quite scared, so that night I asked Tom again what was going on. He didn't want to tell me, but I knew he was hiding something so I kept on at him until he did. And that's when he told me that Mr Coverdale had been following him and pestering him to support him with a project that he was working on.'

'Did he indicate that he was interested in the project?'

'Oh, absolutely not. He said that Mr Coverdale had nothing to do with *The Mail* any more and that I should forget all about him.'

'When did you see the defendant again?'

'About a month later. The day before Tom died.'

'Could you tell the court what happened that day?' asked Pahklava.

'Yes,' she replied, pausing momentarily to collect her thoughts. 'He rang at about ten o'clock in the morning – that is to say he rang under the name of Mr Angel. I told him that Tom was in a meeting, but he went absolutely mad – started screaming at me down the phone.'

'What did he say exactly, can you recall?'

'He said, "Then get him out of the f'ing meeting". So I went to find Tom, told him what had happened and he came back and took the call in his office.'

'Now, Miss Osbourne,' said Pahklava, leaning forward and gripping the edges of the lectern in front of her. 'I want you to be very, very clear on this next point and tell the court exactly what happened during that call.'

'After they'd been speaking for a minute or so,' she continued, steadily, 'there was another incoming call for Tom – it was from one of the directors. Because I wanted to let Tom know about that second call, and because, well, I was worried about what was going on with Mr Angel, I interrupted their conversation. There's a facility on the phone that allows me to do that.'

'And, as you interrupted, you heard part of the conversation between Mr Angel and Mr Cranmer, did you not?'

'Yes, I did.'

'What was Mr Angel saying?'

'Well, I only caught a couple of sentences, but what I heard him say was "Tom, I'm begging you, please. If you'd only take a look at the latest stuff I've got".'

'Those were his exact words?'

'Yes.'

'Are you sure about that?'

'Absolutely.'

'What did you understand the defendant to mean by those comments?'

'That he was still trying to get Tom interested in his project.'

To emphasize this crucial point, Pahklava turned to her left for a moment and stared pointedly at the jury.

'What happened then?'

'Tom left – at about four o'clock that afternoon.'

'To go to the defendant's flat?'

'Yes.'

'Did he say that was where he was going?'

'No, but I was certain that he was going to see Mr Coverdale.'

'Why were you certain?'

'Because of what Mr Coverdale had said on the phone earlier – because he'd been imploring Tom to go and have a look at what he'd got.'

'How did Mr Cranmer appear when he left the office that afternoon?'

'He looked very grim, very … determined. Mr Coverdale had been harassing him for weeks and I think he'd decided he had to put a stop to it once and for all.'

'Have it out with Mr Coverdale face to face, you mean?'

'Yes, yes. He knew it was upsetting me and I think it had really got to him too in the end.'

'Miss Osbourne, you've been very brave. This has been difficult for you, I know, and I want to thank you for your evidence. My lord.'

With a nod at the judge, Pahklava sat down. Looking to his left towards the jury, Miles caught sight of the man in the worsted jacket whom he had earlier thought might well be elected as foreman. His expression was solemn and deeply thoughtful: just as Malde had predicted, Eva Osbourne had indeed been the prosecution's most potent witness.

'Mr Drake,' said the judge, quietly. 'Do you have any questions for Miss Osbourne?'

'Just two, your honour,' said Drake, looking at her with a restrained, respectful smile. 'Miss Osbourne, you have just told the court that the first time the defendant came to your attention again after his dismissal from *The Mail* was in March this year when you saw him outside the flat in Clapham.'

'That's right.'

'I'd like to ask you, if I may, to cast your mind back several months before that time to a morning in October last year – the second week of October, in fact. On the Tuesday of that week, do you recall receiving a phone call in the office for Thomas Cranmer from the man calling himself Mr Angel? Take some time to think, if you wish ...'

As Eva Osbourne blinked and then once more absentmindedly curled her hair down behind her ear, Miles recalled the morning in the deserted sports centre when he had rung Tom to tell him of his very first success with Harper.

'No, I don't remember it,' she replied, finally. For a second she seemed on the verge of qualifying this remark – perhaps to suggest that she received a lot of calls for Tom and might well have forgotten it – but instead she kept silent and simply stared blankly back at Drake. Sensing that pressing her on this point would only produce a further, more categorical denial, Drake moved on.

'Then I have only more question for you Miss Osbourne – although it is a very important one. As I'm sure you are aware, the defendant has pleaded not guilty to the charge of murdering Thomas Cranmer and moreover claims that he was working for him all along under conditions of extreme secrecy. I want to ask you, therefore, if you think it possible that Thomas Cranmer may have kept this fact from you for the sake of protecting the defendant.'

'No, I don't think so,' she replied.

'How can you be so sure?' asked Drake.

'Because Tom shared everything with me,' she said, with a flash of her old arrogance.

'With the greatest of respect, Miss Osbourne,' said Drake, his eyes narrowing, 'that assertion does contradict what you said earlier. When my learned friend asked you about having seen the defendant outside the flat in Clapham, you responded, and I quote your exact words, "he did not want to talk about it": 'he' – meaning Mr Cranmer. You then went on to say with reference to the video tape that arrived in the post – and once again, I quote – "he didn't want to tell me, I knew he was hiding something." I would like to ask you therefore once again to explain to the court how you can be so sure that Mr Cranmer was not in fact keeping Mr Coverdale's documentary a secret from you?'

For a moment, it appeared as though Drake had Eva Osbourne cornered. Without in any way challenging her dignity or affronting her grief, he had been be able to point out that her stated evidence implied quite clearly that Tom had indeed sought to keep her in the dark about *Criminal Britain*. Her response, however, was a blow more devastating to the defence's case than anything Drake could ever have imagined.

'Because King Media had a stake in the other documentary, of course.'

Miles felt as though his heart had stopped beating. To his left, Drake blinked twice – seemingly unable to assimilate what he had just heard. On the prosecution bench, Pahklava opened her eyes wide in surprise.

'Could you explain what you mean?' asked Drake, a concerned, fearful look beginning to spread across his face.

'King Media was involved in another documentary using undercover reporters to examine drug dealers and other criminals. It was screened recently – a month or so ago, I think; I didn't see it, but I remember Tom telling me that Henry King had taken a fifty percent stake in it and that the concept was very similar to that which Mr Coverdale had been suggesting.'

Drake swallowed hard. Miles had told him about Buckleys' documentary and the prosecution were aware of it, too, but none of them had known that King Media had actually invested in it. This was new evidence – completely new – and it was a bombshell blow to the defence's case. Seeing Pahklava sitting bolt upright, her look of astonishment having turned to one of excitement, Miles closed his eyes at the enormity of the news.

'Why didn't you tell the police about this when they interviewed you after Thomas Cranmer's death?' asked Drake.

Eva Osbourne paused for a moment before answering. Opening his eyes again, Miles was just in time to see her leaning forwards in the witness box and then answer in her iciest, most contemptuous voice.

'Because they didn't ask me.'

Slumping down into the cracked, plastic chair in the legal room, Miles stared at the wall opposite, but saw nothing of its faded painted surface. Instead, before his eyes, was the final handwritten sentence of the letter from the East European spy that Tom had given him the morning that he had moved to Feltham as Michael Angel. 'And, last of all, my friend,' it had said, 'a warning: just as you intend to betray others, you must consider that others, in turn, may seek to betray you.' Such had been the spy's dreadful prophecy and so had it come to pass. Henry King had backed both horses. Knowing that it would be impossible to predict which of the two documentaries would be finished first, he had made sure that he had had a stake in both enterprises. Now, at last, Miles understood exactly why Tom had come to pull him out of Feltham the night that he had died. For months he had regarded it as a noble act on the part of his boss, but now he could see it for what it really was – a guilt-ridden gesture: guilt at his weakness at having succumbed to the temptation of using the empty safe house to carry on his affair with Eva Osbourne; guilt at having led Miles to believe that *Criminal Britain* was anything other than just one more commercial venture for King Media.

Drake and Malde were in grim mood when they entered the legal room ten minutes later. As they had left the court after Eva Osbourne's evidence and begun to make their way to the basement to see Miles, a second bombshell had landed. In the corridor outside the courtroom Detective Inspector Fly had been waiting to speak to them. Dill had flatly denied all involvement in or knowledge of the file that had been leaked to *The Mail*. Given that the only copy of it had been destroyed in the blaze at Balam Road and with no other evidence to corroborate Miles's suspicions, the police had not pressed Dill any further; the interview with him had lasted less than five minutes. In spite of these setbacks, both men vowed to continue fighting on Miles's behalf and fervently contended that they could still win the case: they had never banked on discovering the source of the file and, although the revelation about King's involvement with Buckleys had been a blow, it had been by no means fatal. Eva Osbourne had been the prosecution's last throw of the dice – now it was their turn to bring forward their witnesses. Both Tysoe and Amanda's testimonies would powerfully support their case, and Miles himself, once he took the stand, would be sure to convince the jury of his innocence. But, when the two men left five minutes later, he could see in their eyes that they had begun to sense that the pendulum was now swinging inexorably away from them and could not be brought back, though they pulled at it with all their strength.

Chapter 15

Just over an hour later, Miles walked up the steps of the witness box. At lunchtime he had been unable to eat and instead had stayed by himself in the legal room, descending minute by minute into ever greater depths of despair as he pondered the significance of Eva Osbourne's evidence. All through his time in Feltham, he had regarded *Criminal Britain* as being the one thing that would make his life complete, but what it had in fact done had been to remove from his life the one thing that was of any real value, whilst demonstrating at the same time the utter worthlessness of everything that remained. Seeing the jury to his left, Miles fought back the urge to drop his head in shame. How could he hope to defend himself in their eyes when he felt so debased in his own? Taking the bible in his hand, he slowly read the oath; the truth, the whole truth and nothing but the truth. During the long weeks on remand he had hoped that it would be the truth that would secure his eventual release, yet the more it was revealed, the more he came to realize the sham emptiness of his life.

'Could you state your name, please?' asked Drake.

'Miles Coverdale.'

'And what is your profession, Mr Coverdale?'

'I'm a photographer.'

'And it was in that capacity that you joined *The Mail* on a semi-permanent contract a little over six years ago – is that correct?'

'Yes.'

'Were you good at your job?'

'I gave them what they wanted, I suppose,' replied Miles, wearily.

Hearing the unmistakable note of tiredness in Miles's voice, Drake frowned. If the jury misconstrued this as apathy, it would be absolutely disastrous to his case.

'Meaning a succession of powerful and original photographs, yes?' prompted Drake, 'Two or three each year with unwavering consistency – many of which went on to make the front pages.'

'Yes,' replied Miles, dully – recalling the visit from Angus Lamb and wondering how many of his other victims had had the strength of character to rebuild their lives as he had done.

'And it was because of your success and reputation as a leading photographic journalist,' continued Drake, his voice smooth, but his eyes glaring daggers, 'that Thomas Cranmer approached you in March of last year with an idea for a television documentary series. Could you tell the court about the circumstances surrounding his proposal?'

Miles blinked and ran his hand over the top of his head. He had to snap out of it – if not for himself, then at least for Drake and Malde.

'The, er, concept originally came from Henry King, the owner of King Media. At the beginning of March last year, he received an anonymous letter containing the names and addresses of seventeen social security fraudsters living in Feltham. It set him thinking. These were the faceless criminals who sponge off society, but who the public never actually get to see. His idea was to send an undercover reporter to infiltrate the gang – to find out how they operated and then expose them.'

'And having discussed this idea with Thomas Cranmer, the two of them then approached you?'

'That's right.'

'What was your reaction to their proposal?'

'I was excited, I suppose. I mean, I knew it'd be dangerous, but it looked like the ultimate career move for someone in my position. King promised to syndicate the series throughout his entire organization. I could have become very famous.'

'Because it was such a dangerous venture, what precautions did you take?'

'Well, at the time, we understood the seventeen fraudsters all to be members of a single gang – this was how the person who'd leaked their names to *The Mail* had described them. What we didn't realize was that it was all down to a single individual on the inside at Housing Benefits who was selling his services to all comers ...' Miles paused for a moment, thinking of Dill. How would he feel when he learned that Miles had been found guilty? How would he feel when he discovered that he had been murdered in prison? Again, he tried to force himself to concentrate: he had to stop his mind wandering and let himself be led by Drake's careful questioning. 'Anyway,' he continued, 'believing them to be a group of professional criminals who wouldn't take kindly to having their gang infiltrated by a reporter, we knew we had to adopt some pretty extreme security measures.'

'And what were they?'

'Well, it was no good just changing my appearance; I had to change my whole identity. If the gang ever found out who I was – traced me back to *The Mail* and King Media – then they might try and take reprisals against me or members of my family. I wasn't going to let that happen, so Tom and I faked my dismissal so that if anyone ever went back to check they'd find no trace of me at *The Mail*. We then jointly put the rumour around that I'd taken a job overseas. I lay low for about a month after that and we then set about creating my new personality.'

'The man by the name of Michael Angel?'

'That's right. He couldn't be a Londoner – it would be too easy to check up on his background. So we made him come from a small village in Yorkshire; Tom got hold of a car with the right plates and then we dreamt up a life story for him. He was a labourer who'd split up with his wife and had come down south looking for work. The idea was for him to get friendly with one of the gang members. We guessed that they were claiming benefit on multiple properties and would need new faces to help ensure a continuous supply of false claims.'

'What other security measures did you take?'

'Various different things: no phone calls except from public call boxes – or at least not in the early days; no letters; all monies in cash so that our bank accounts couldn't be traced. We didn't know how sophisticated the gang was, but we had to plan for the very worst. This is the computer age: if I'd've been traced, I might've ended up with a bullet in the back of my neck.'

'Mr Coverdale, could you tell the court about the flat in Clapham?'

'We had to have somewhere to meet and I needed a bolt hole in case things ever got really dangerous and I had to get out quick. So Tom started renting a flat in Clapham. We had an arrangement whereby if there was anything I needed to discuss with him, I'd call him a day or two beforehand and then he'd meet me there.'

'How many times did you actually do that?'

'Four times.'

'In a period of ...'

'Just under a year.'

'Did you know that Thomas Cranmer was also using the flat to carry on an affair with his secretary?'

'No, I didn't.'

'But you did see her outside the flat one day?'

'Yes, I did. And before that I'd noticed on a couple of occasions how it had seemed quite warm and felt very lived in; after that, though – after Miss Osbourne and I saw each other, that is – they stopped meeting there. I could tell the difference straightaway.'

'Why do you think Thomas Cranmer went ahead and conducted his affair with Miss Osbourne at the flat when he had intended it as a safe house for you? Wasn't that something of an irresponsible act on his part?'

'Possibly so,' conceded Miles. 'My guess is that he didn't deliberately set out to do it, but that it sort of crept up on him over time. In the early days, he'd occasionally sleep in the flat overnight – he used to work late and it was very handy for getting into central London the next morning – and if he didn't get on with his wife, I suppose it was preferable to going home. Then, when he found himself getting closer to Miss Osbourne, well, I guess it must have seemed like the perfect location – convenient, discreet ...'

'Thank you, Mr Coverdale. I'd like to turn now to what happened when you actually moved to Feltham. What did you do when you first got there?'

'Tom and I had agreed that I ought to take things slowly – very slowly. I didn't want to risk alarming the gang by rushing in too quickly: they'd've smelt a rat straightaway. So, the plan was get somewhere to live, pick up casual work where I could and then search for each of the fraudsters in turn until I found one that I could approach.'

'And did Henry King also suggest that whilst you were on the trail of these people, you should keep your eye out for other criminal activities that might be the subject of subsequent documentaries?'

'Yes, he did. His idea was to call the series *Criminal Britain*. It was to be made up of four documentaries, each of which would expose villains who are normally faceless – that was to be the common theme running throughout. For the second documentary, he wanted me to look at drug pushers, but the third and fourth were to be up to me – based on whatever I found of interest whilst researching the first two.'

'And it was in this connection that you had the fight in The White Horse public house: the fight described earlier by its landlord, Mr Leonard Britten?'

'Yes. I had an idea to investigate illegal immigrant labour. One of the first jobs I got was on a building site with a group of Turkish labourers. We were working for a man called Roger doing groundworks. At the end of the week, though, he disappeared without paying us. I ran into him in the pub by chance. The fight came about as a result.'

'And was that why you threatened to kill him – in the heat of an argument following you and your fellow workers having been cheated out of a week's wages?'

'Yes.'

'Did you mean it – literally?'

'No, I didn't. I was really furious though. The man cynically exploited immigrants. He was one of the worst people I've ever met in my life.'

'But, all the same, you didn't pursue the subject of illegal immigrants as one of the documentaries, did you?'

'No. I got a fair way into it, but I never actually completed it.'

'Why not?'

'Tom wasn't keen on the idea – nor was King. They didn't think it was right for the series.'

'And by then, you were already beginning to make progress with the gang of housing benefit fraudsters.'

'Yes.'

For a moment there was a pause and the courtroom went silent – Drake having intended his question as a prompt to Miles to begin talking about Harper.

'So, Mr Coverdale,' he continued, 'could you tell the court the form that progress took?'

For a second, Miles felt slightly light in the head: this had been the moment he had been dreading for months. Although he had eventually told the police about Harper and Angela, the time had now arrived for him to inform on them in public. Reaching out to steady himself on the edge of the witness box, he took a deep breath.

'I became friendly with a man called Harper – Geoffrey Harper. He was one of the seventeen named people in the original file. One night, in late September, he suggested that we jointly put together a fraudulent housing benefit claim on my flat. He had a girlfriend, a woman called Angela Jones. Together we would pretend to be a Mr and Mrs Morgan using fake marriage certificates and other documents that they had acquired.'

'And did you go along with this suggestion?'

'I did. About three weeks later the housing benefits inspectors came to the flat and it was at that time that I first learned of the existence of the man called Craig Gleeson. Over subsequent months I was able to piece together more and more information about him, discovering eventually that it was he who was really responsible for the fraudulent housing benefit claims. The supposed gang of seventeen fraudsters had never really existed as such – the set-up was much more loosely organized and also much bigger than we'd imagined.'

'Mr Coverdale,' said Drake, slipping his thumbs inside his waistcoat pockets and walking slowly away from his desk, 'what had you and Thomas Cranmer originally planned to do once the investigation into the fraudsters was complete?'

'The original idea had been for me to resume my real identity for a month or two. I would need a break after having been under cover for so long and would want to see my family again – my son in particular. Once I'd recharged my batteries, the plan had then been for me to assume another made-up identity and go on the trail of drug dealers.'

'What happened to change that?'

'In early November, Tom got wind of another documentary series being made by a company called Thomas Buckleys. They'd approached one of the divisions of King Media for finance and Tom was able to discover that their format was almost identical to ours. Originally we'd planned to film over two years, but, if we'd've stuck to that, Buckleys' documentary would've beaten us to the screen by a good six months and, more to the point, our series would've ended up just looking like a copy-cat version of theirs.'

'So what did you decide to do?'

'Well, by this time I'd already settled on the subject matter for the third documentary. I'd got a job working for a cowboy builder called John Tysoe. He used to cheat families, pensioners – all manner of people:

he'd overcharge them and wouldn't complete the work properly. I'd already got a lot of film of him, so, after some discussion we decided to change our original plan.'

'In what way?'

'I would use the same Michael Angel identity for the first three documentaries and attempt to get them finished within a year. We planned on going into pre-production early, so it seemed achievable. Also, Henry had had an idea for the fourth and final documentary, so we had all our targets lined up – we just had to do them within a tighter time frame than we'd originally planned.'

'And what was his idea for the fourth documentary?'

'Pornographers. He wanted me to track down the agents who work behind the scenes and look at how they lured women into the industry.'

'Were you able to complete the third and fourth documentaries?'

'The third, yes, but not the fourth.'

'Ladies and gentlemen,' proclaimed Drake, turning to face the jury from the position that he had now taken up at the very back of the court, 'we'll be hearing from witnesses involved in the third and fourth documentaries later, but for now, Mr Coverdale, could you tell the court about the drugs investigation which you began to undertake in November of last year? The second of your four documentaries.'

'Henry King had always been keen on investigating pushers right from day one, so his idea was that Michael Angel should get a job as a bouncer in a night club. Security staff are sometimes involved in selling drugs and he figured it would be in keeping with the Michael Angel persona that we'd developed if I were to sign on with an agency supplying temporary security personnel to the night clubs. That way, I could check out a large number of clubs in a relatively short space of time. Also, because I'd only be working two or three nights a week I'd have plenty of time to work on the other investigations.'

'And was that what you did?'

'Yes.'

'How long was it before you came across any drugs?'

'Two weeks before Christmas I got a job working at the Gog night club. What I discovered led me to believe that certain individuals there were heavily involved in drug trafficking as well as a number of other illegal activities.'

'Did you manage to compile conclusive evidence of such?'

'No, I didn't. I was getting very close towards the end but Henry King died before I had a chance to complete my investigations.'

It was at this point that Miles realized why Drake had left his seat and begun walking around the courtroom. He was now standing right behind the watching brief, in such a position that he could see over his shoulder at the notes that he was taking. As the lawyer shifted somewhat uncomfortably on his seat, attempting at the same time both to write his notes and keep them covered up, Drake flashed a wink at Miles and then turned to face the jury. Knowing his advocate's distaste of the Ellis Group and knowing that he was needling the watching brief to try and raise Miles's spirits, he smiled to himself. Drake was a fine man and even if the final verdict was 'guilty', he could have nothing but gratitude for the help that he had given him.

'Ladies and gentlemen, you will recall some of the activities in which the defendant alleges that the Ellis Group was involved from my cross-examination last week of Mr Kent – their security manager, procurement executive, etcetera etcetera. As the judge rightly pointed out at the time, however, it is not that organization which is on trial at this time but Mr Coverdale. Accordingly, I will make no further reference to those allegations, save to ask the defendant to confirm what happened to all the evidence of criminal activity that he amassed during his time working undercover as Michael Angel. Mr Coverdale?'

'I had a number of concealed cameras and recording devices,' responded Miles. 'When I'd finished filming a particular incident or meeting, I used to download the footage onto video tapes which I stored under the floor boards in the flat in Balam Road. They were all destroyed in the fire.'

'Thank you, Mr Coverdale. I would like to move on now to the period leading up to the death of Thomas Cranmer. Miss Osbourne has testified to your visiting his offices in early April and arguing with him. Could you explain to the court what happened?'

'I was angry with Tom because he hadn't come to a meeting that I'd asked for at the safe house. I'd just had a really close shave and was pretty stressed out. It seemed to me that if I was willing to risk my neck every day to make the documentary for King Media, it wasn't too much to ask him to find an hour to come and meet me in Clapham.'

'Why didn't he come to that meeting?'

'He told me it was for personal reasons. I later learned that it was because of what was happening with his wife and Miss Osbourne.'

'And so you went directly to his office to speak to him?'

'Yes.'

'How did he react on seeing you?'

'He was very apologetic and, well, frankly a little guilty, too. He told me that it wouldn't happen again and that he'd be there for me in the future if I needed him.'

'What d'you think he meant by that?'

'Early on we'd agreed that if I ever got into trouble – serious trouble – he'd come and pull me out.'

'And it was for this reason that he went to your flat on the night of his death?'

'Yes, I believe so.'

'Could you tell the court what happened in those last forty-eight hours before his death?'

'Henry King collapsed on the Tuesday morning and was rushed to hospital. He died there a couple of hours later. That afternoon, thinking that King's death meant that even if I finished the series on schedule we might not be able to get it televised, Tom sent me a red post card. It was the signal that we had agreed to indicate that I should cease operations. The next morning I phoned him at the office. That was the call that Miss Osbourne overheard.'

'And so what she heard,' said Drake, staring intently at the jury, 'was not in fact your pleading with Thomas Cranmer to adopt a documentary series you had conceived of yourself, but to complete the one on which you had already been jointly working for over a year?'

'Yes. Tom was adamant that without King to pull all the right strings for us we probably wouldn't be able to get it screened.'

'Did you share his opinion?'

'No, I didn't. I was convinced that we ought to finish making it first and then worry about marketing it afterwards.'

'Did you ask him to come to your flat in Feltham that night to discuss the matter at greater length?'

'No, I didn't. In fact, he asked me to meet him at the safe house later that day. There was never any suggestion on my part that he go to Feltham.'

'But he did, nevertheless.'

'Yes.'

'Out of concern for you and to honour the pledge that he had made to 'pull you out' if ever things ever went wrong or got tough.'

'Yes, I believe so.'

'Where were you that night – the night that he went to your flat in Feltham?'

'About a month beforehand I'd decided to leave Balam Road and get a flat in central London. The two Feltham-based investigations were already complete and I'd taken up a short-term rental on a flat in Soho because it was closer to Gog, and because it was an ideal address out of which to operate for the fourth documentary.'

'The fourth documentary being about pornographers?'

'Correct.'

'And that's where you were that night – in the Soho flat?'

'Yes. I slept there: the evening I'd spent just walking around.'

'But you can't exactly remember where, can you?'

'No.'

'Why not?'

Turning to his left, Miles looked at the jury. From the very beginning Drake had asserted that they would find his story convincing and, certainly, Drake's own careful, structured questioning appeared to have invested his testimony with a definite cohesion. Scanning their faces, Miles got the distinct impression that they had grasped everything that he had so far said. Perhaps all was not lost. Perhaps if he could just reach their hearts as well as their minds, supplementing their comprehension with a degree of sympathy, they would be able collectively to acknowledge his innocence.

'I'd learned that day that my ex-wife and son were intending to emigrate to Australia. Almost a year had passed since I'd spoken to them and it had mainly been the thought of seeing them again that had kept me going during the long months in Feltham. I was absolutely devastated by the news. Added to Henry King's death and Tom's insistence that we couldn't go on, I suppose, well, I just fell into some sort of depressive trance. It seemed to me that everything that I'd worked for in my life, everything I'd ever wanted, was falling apart right before my very eyes.'

'And what did you discover about your ex-wife and son the following morning?'

484

'I rang around the travel agents and found that they were leaving that afternoon on a flight to Sydney.'

'So what did you do?'

'I went to the airport to see if I could persuade them to stay. I was ... well, I was going out of my mind: I thought I might never see them again.'

'And were you able to persuade them to stay?' asked Drake, gently.

'No, I wasn't. And I wasn't able to discover exactly where they were going either.'

'And so you decided to buy a ticket and follow them – yes? Thinking that you might perhaps be able to track them down and persuade them later.'

'Yes. By that time *Criminal Britain* just didn't seem to matter any more. All I wanted was to see them again. I'd planned to ring Tom before I actually boarded the plane – to tell him that he was right and that we should call it a day, but I was arrested before I got there.'

'And it was when the police began to question you that you first discovered that Thomas Cranmer had died the previous night in the flat in Feltham?'

'Yes.'

'Thank you Mr Coverdale.'

All through Drake's questioning, Pahklava had not looked up once, remaining hunched over the pad of A4 paper that she kept on the desk in front of her, making note after careful note. As she stood up to cross-examine Miles, he swallowed deeply in nervous anticipation, remembering Drake and Malde's stern warning prior to the trial: more than Kent, more than Ellis, more than anyone – it was Pahklava whom he should fear.

'Mr Coverdale,' she began, 'on the day of your arrest, when interviewed by the police at Heathrow Airport you made no reply to any of the questions that you were asked. Detective Inspector Fly said in his evidence, 'neither myself nor my colleague were able to illicit any responses from him whatsoever.' Why was that?'

Miles frowned. He had just explained the reasons for this. Was this a trick to try and unnerve him?

'I was in something of a state of shock, because my ex-wife and son were emigrating and because Tom wanted to bring the series to an end.'

'But this was the day after you had learned that your ex-wife and son were leaving. If you had been coherent enough that morning to phone around a number of travel agencies to discover the flight on which they were due to depart, and if, as you claim, you were not yet aware of Mr Cranmer's death, why were you unable to utter so much as a single word in your defence when questioned by the police?'

'As I said,' replied Miles, cautiously. 'I was in a state of shock.'

'Surely it would have to have been a most extreme state of shock totally to deprive you of the power of speech?'

'Well, maybe it was, yes.'

'But yet not that extreme. Because the following day you were able to be perfectly articulate once again, weren't you – giving the police a comprehensive and detailed account of the previous eighteen months of your life? The transformation in your mental state from one day to the next is thus extremely pronounced indeed. How do you explain that?'

Miles paused before answering. With her first question she had exposed an apparent contradiction in his evidence that had not even occurred to him before: she was right – his behaviour did look strange. Despite this, he could not let her rush him. He had to make his answers as measured and as clear as possible.

'I don't think I can give you the sort of explanation you're looking for. I don't have the medical knowledge to explain exactly why my mind reacted as it did. All I can do is describe the pressures I was under at the time and my behaviour in reaction to them.'

'If you find it difficult to explain,' replied Pahklava, raising a cynical eyebrow, 'then perhaps I can help you. I put it to you, Mr Coverdale, that far from being in a state of shock when you arrived at Heathrow airport, you were in a confident mood. No one had seen you pour the petrol through the letter box of your flat the previous night and the police had not yet issued a description of anyone they wanted to interview in connection with Thomas Cranmer's death. It was therefore extremely unlikely that they were on the trail of Miles Coverdale yet and, even if they were, you were travelling under the name of Michael Angel and would be out of the country in a matter of hours. But then you found yourself unexpectedly under arrest. You needed time to think; time to create an alibi. And so, whilst they interrogated you, you kept quiet, picked up what facts you could from their questioning and then thought through overnight the elaborate story that you gave them the following morning. Wasn't that the explanation for your sudden, here-today gone-tomorrow traumatic state?'

'No, it wasn't,' replied Miles, simply.

As Pahklava smiled humourlessly at Miles and her dark, shining eyes bored into his face, he began to understand what Drake and Malde had meant: it was her job to prosecute him to the very best of her formidable abilities and that was exactly what she intended to do.

'Mr Coverdale, at the time of Thomas Cranmer's death how many years had you been separated from your wife?'

'Six.'

'And you had not seen her or your son during the previous twelve months?'

'No.'

'Had you spoken to them on the phone or written to them during that period?'

'No. Tom and I judged it would be too dangerous. I did, er, get them a Christmas card which Tom forwarded from Geneva – apart from that, we had no contact.'

Turning so that she half-faced the jury, Pahklava frowned with theatrical incredulity.

'Mr Coverdale,' she gasped, 'are you really asking the court to believe that you could be plunged into a catatonic state by the departure of a woman from whom you had been separated for six years and with whom your sole communication in the previous twelve months had been a single Christmas card?'

Again Miles paused before replying. She had him cornered. To attempt to elaborate upon his denial would make it sound all the more feeble: simply to repeat it would just make him appear stubbornly evasive.

'Yes, I am,' he said, trying to keep his voice steady. 'I am asking the court to believe that.'

Raising both eyebrows and shaking her head slowly as if to imply that confronted with such blatant dishonesty there was nothing she could do but move on, Pahklava looked down at the pad on the desk in front of her to check her next question. Without daring to glance to his left at the jury, Miles fought back a rising feeling of panic. He had to continue to speak the truth, no matter how incredible it sounded and no matter how incriminating it might be: it was, and always had been, his only hope.

'Mr Coverdale, you have, er, claimed in your evidence that all along you were making a documentary series for King Media.'

'That's correct.'

'Prior to your dismissal from *The Mail* did you have any experience of television documentaries?'

'No, I didn't.'

'What about Mr Cranmer, did he?'

'Yes, he'd worked in television for ten years before he moved into journalism.'

'And did he ever comment on the way your documentaries were proceeding – give you advice, perhaps?'

'Yes, all the time.'

'What about back-ups of the film footage that you took. Did he ever advise you to make copies for safety's sake?'

'No.'

'Wasn't that something of an oversight on his part?'

'In retrospect, yes.'

'Because all the original footage that you claim you took was destroyed in the fire.'

'That's right. He did have a couple of copies of video cassettes that I'd made him of one or two particular incidents …'

'But they were never found, were they?' interrupted Pahklava.

'No. I think he hid them.'

'As part of the extraordinarily tight security measures upon which you had agreed, no doubt,' she mused, nodding her head ironically.

'Yes.'

'What was Thomas Cranmer's opinion about the time scales you were operating under? Five documentaries in a year does seem somewhat ambitious, to say the least.'

'There weren't five documentaries, there were four.'

'No, no, I believe you embarked upon five – unless my calculations are incorrect. Earlier you stated in response to a question from my learned friend here on the subject of the documentary about illegal immigrants, and I quote, 'I got a fair way into it, but I never actually completed it.'

'Yes, well, like I said, I didn't finish it.'

'OK, so let's call it four and a half then, shall we?' conceded Pahklava, sarcastically. 'What did Thomas Cranmer think about the advisability of attempting to handle such a large volume of work within the space of a mere twelve months?'

'We didn't set out to do that. As I already explained the plan had been to film it over two years, but a rival series forced us to compress it into a shorter time frame.'

'Ah, yes, I'm glad you mentioned that,' purred Pahklava, 'the rival series. Yes. At the beginning of the trial, my learned friend here spoke at considerable length of the solemn pact between you, Thomas Cranmer and Henry King, but wasn't that supposedly trusting, intimate relationship very much at odds with what the court now knows to be the truth? Namely, that King Media were in fact co-sponsors of the very series against which you claim to have been competing.'

'I believe that was a commercial decision on their part.'

'Did they tell you about it?'

'No.'

'So, what you're saying is that they deceived you, yes? Let you put your life at risk for a documentary series that they might not even have finally screened?'

'To a certain extent.'

'To a certain extent?' echoed Pahklava, her brow furling gravely. 'I'm sorry, Mr Coverdale, I'm having a great deal of difficulty understanding just exactly what you claim your relationship was with Thomas Cranmer and Henry King. Previously you indicated that it was very close, but now you're suggesting that they manipulated you. Is that correct?'

'Yes, I suppose they did,' replied Miles.

'Did you ever get a hint of what was going on – did you ever suspect that King Media was backing this allegedly rival documentary?'

'No, I didn't.'

'Did Thomas Cranmer continue to provide feedback on your work? Continue to be closely involved in what you were doing right up until the very end?'

'Yes, he did.'

'Oh, he did, did he?' As soon as Pahklava had spoken, Miles knew that she was going to use his response against him. 'In that case why did he go to your flat on the night of his death?'

'To pull me out. He'd asked me to go to the safe house that morning, but once he'd discovered that I hadn't gone there, he must have decided to come and get me. I think he probably felt guilty about not having been completely honest with me and wanted to demonstrate that we were still friends and that he still cared.'

'But why did he go to Feltham? Why didn't he go to the flat in Soho?'

'Because he didn't know I was moving there that day.'

Pahklava winced painfully.

'Again I have to say your response calls into doubt the relationship that you claimed you had with Mr Cranmer. If he was closely involved with your work, then surely he would have been aware of a matter of such import – of your leaving the flat that you had occupied for the last year and moving to a totally different location.'

'Henry King had just died – the entire organization was in turmoil. Our telephone call that morning was very short and I didn't think to mention that I was actually planning on leaving that day.'

'You didn't think to mention it?' repeated Pahklava, her voice trailing off in astonished disbelief.

'No, I didn't.'

Taking a deep breath to emphasize the degree of her scepticism, Pahklava turned over the next page of her pad. Looking across at the courtroom clock, Miles tried to work out how long he had been on the stand, but his mind seemed unable to derive any meaning from the positions of the hands on the clock face.

'Mr Coverdale,' said Pahklava, looking up once more. 'In your evidence earlier today you stated that you were able to track down Craig Gleeson, the inside man in the housing benefits office, by means of becoming friendly with two people by the names of Geoffrey Harper and Angela Jones.'

'That's right.'

'On the day after your arrest – once your powers of speech had returned – did you give the police an address for them?'

'I did.'

All of a sudden, Miles's throat felt horribly dry. Would he now be forced not only to betray Harper once again, but also to admit that he had lied to the police in giving them a false address?

'They couldn't be found there, could they?'

'No.'

'Two months later – on July the fourteenth, in fact – in response to police questioning you gave another address for these two individuals.'

'That's right.'

'A flat in a high-rise block on the Abaddon estate in West London.'

'Yes.'

'When the police got there, they discovered that the inhabitants appeared to have fled in a hurry, leaving behind their furniture and much of their personal belongings.'

'So I understand, yes.'

For a moment, Pahklava paused, her eyes staring at Miles with a piercing intensity that made his stomach feel queasy. Of the masses of evidence in the case, how had she somehow managed to sense the particular importance of this one fact?

'And they have never been found since, have they – Geoffrey Harper and Angela Jones?'

'No. I understand not.'

Again Pahklava paused, glaring fixedly at Miles. As the silence persisted, Miles could see that Drake appeared to be on the point of standing up, but, before he could, the judge's voice rang out around the courtroom.

'Ms Pahklava. Do you have a question for the defendant in this regard?'

'My apologies, your honour, yes, I do have a question,' she replied, turning to face the jury, 'but I'd like to make a point first, if I may. Ladies and gentlemen of the jury, the prosecution does not dispute that the defendant fell into the company of a number of housing benefit fraudsters, some of whose names he passed to the authorities after his arrest. What we do dispute, however, is that he became associated with those individuals because he had been asked to make a documentary series for King Media. Rather, we contest that the idea of a documentary occurred to him many months after his dismissal – after he had already amassed a number of criminal connections – and constituted a vain and desperate attempt on his part to claw his way back into journalism.' Turning back around, she faced Miles again. 'Mr Coverdale, I put it to you that rather than having a close and intimate relationship with Thomas Cranmer and Henry King, you had a close and intimate relationship with Geoffrey Harper and Angela Jones – two of the very fraudsters whom you claim you were investigating. Wasn't that why you gave an address for them to the police that you knew to be false, in order

491

that they might have time to make themselves scarce? Wasn't that why you only revealed their actual address several months later when you believed that they had long since escaped?'

He knew he couldn't lie, even though to admit to one falsehood would be to incline the jury to believe that he may have uttered many more and even though it would sever the bond of trust that he had built up with Drake and Malde to whom he had never fully revealed his exact relationship with Geoff and Angela. The truth was all that remained in his life and if he betrayed it now, the little self-respect that he still retained would be extinguished forever.

'Yes. I was friends with Geoffrey Harper and Angela Jones and yes, I did make up a fictitious address for them in the hope that the police wouldn't find them.'

Pahklava's face lit up in triumph. To her right, Miles could see that although Drake's expression had remained completely impassive, on the bench behind him, Malde had wearily dropped his head.

'And what about Craig Gleeson?' continued Pahklava. 'Were you friendly with him, too?'

'No, not at all.'

'No?'

'No.'

'Because he was never caught either, was he? When you told the police his name, were you aware that he also had already fled?'

'Yes, I was, but ...'

'Ah,' interrupted Pahklava, 'so he was an accomplice of yours, too, then?'

'No, no – you've got it wrong,' exclaimed Miles. 'I'd heard he'd left the Housing Benefits office, but that was all. I mean, I never even met the man.'

'Oh no, I have not got it wrong, Mr Coverdale,' retorted Pahklava; her cheeks now flushed red with excitement. 'I have got it right – entirely right. What I am suggesting is completely consistent with the facts; which is more than can be said for the cock and bull story that you have told this court. The truth is that you fell into the company of a group of social security fraudsters after you lost your job at *The Mail* – individuals with whom by your admission you became friendly until you were forced to inform on them to try and save your own skin. As for *Criminal Britain*, it was nothing more than a fantasy; a sad fantasy that

492

you enacted without the slightest support or encouragement from your former employers who were already committed to a similar project; a fantasy that consumed you with bitterness and eventually led you to carry out a murderous act of revenge against Thomas Cranmer.'

'No. That's not true. Tom and Henry King sent me to Feltham to make a documentary series – they were in touch with me all along.'

'A documentary series!' cried Pahklava, scathingly. 'What documentary series? What exactly did you discover in this "documentary series" of yours, Mr Coverdale? A dishonest employee in the Housing Benefits Office whose name, by your own admission, was known to literally hundreds of people? A cowboy builder? Oh, congratulations! You can find one of those on any street corner! Somebody in Soho making seedy films? Wow! Headline news! That was your documentary series? Not much to show for a year's work, was it? I mean, unless I've missed something. In which case, tell me, please – tell us all. What awe-inspiring truths did you discover during your time as an undercover reporter? What great revelation did you behold? We'd like to know. We really would ...'

As the echo of Pahklava's voice died away, Miles stared around the room in bewilderment, utterly at a loss for a convincing reply. But, as his eyes came to rest on the large rosewood plaque of the royal coat of arms suspended on the wall behind the judge and he recalled the morning two years ago when he had stood gazing at the exact same symbol outside the court house, a wave of understanding suddenly swept over him and he knew in an instant how he should respond. The answer to everything he had witnessed since first setting foot on St John's Road that chill, spring morning lay in what he now recognized to be a betrayal of the pledge the coat of arms swore to uphold. Focusing his eyes once more, he looked around the court room again. All through his time in Feltham he had dreamed of the millions of viewers who would one day see for themselves the criminals he had encountered. Assembled before him were fewer than thirty people, most of whom believed that he was a murderer. Nevertheless, he would answer Pahklava's question, for the time to declare the truth that had been made known to him had now come and its inherent value could not be diminished no matter how small or incredulous the audience. Drawing in a deep breath, he turned to face the jury.

'I went in search of seventeen people hiding in a London suburb –

what I found was a hidden nation of slaves. I went looking for the dealers who press drugs into the hands of our teenagers – what I found was a young man intoxicated beyond all self-control punching a nurse in the face. I went looking for a legal means to bring a con-man to justice – what I found were the legal means by which gun-runners and torturers evade it. I went looking for the pornographers and vice-merchants who supposedly possess a unique power to corrupt our morals – what I found were four people who treated me like a brother and a collection of Capo di Monte to die for.' Looking at the stunned expressions of the jurors, he gave a short mirthless laugh. 'None of this makes any sense to you, does it? I can see it in your faces. I can't blame you for that – it didn't to me either up until now. So let me tell you what I discovered, ladies and gentlemen of the jury – it's simple enough. This country's laws don't create order – this country's order creates laws.'

At first, Pahklava seemed about to respond, but, having glanced at the still puzzled jury, instead simply shook her head once in thinly veiled contempt and then turned and addressed the judge.

'I have no more questions for the defendant, your honour.'

When Miles arrived at the courthouse the following morning, he was surprised to find that he had been allotted a new dock officer, even though this was to be the final day of his trial. As soon as he came down the corridor towards him, Miles immediately recognized the large, bushy handlebar moustache as belonging to the first person that he had seen when he had arrived at Kingston Court for his jury service two years previously. According to his security badge, the man's name was Paul Jones and, as he began to chat to Miles whilst they made their way through the reception area towards the male cells, he could tell that his personality was quite different from that of the dock officer he had had for the last four days, with whom he had exchanged no conversation beyond the simplest of formalities. As he closed the cell door, Paul Jones offered to get Miles a cup of tea and, true to his word, returned with it two minutes later. Sipping the hot, sweet liquid and staring at the graffiti on the cell wall, Miles let his mind go blank, enjoying the solitude. These were probably his last few minutes alone as a free man. By lunchtime the jury would have retired to make their verdict; by evening his fate would be decided.

Twenty-five minutes later, he was back in the dock of court five.

494

Looking down on the courtroom below, he could see various tell-tale signs indicating that the legal process was approaching its final stages. To his right, the half dozen members of the Crown's legal team were casually chatting to each other and they appeared to have brought with them fewer of the thick files and reference books that had covered their desks over the past four days. The ushers and other court officials too seemed more relaxed and were similarly bunched together in a group talking quietly by the main exit. Only Drake and Malde appeared unchanged, each diligently scrutinizing his notes in preparation for examining the two witnesses that they were to summon that morning. Seconds later, the informal atmosphere quickly evaporated as the usher announced the judge's imminent arrival and everyone returned to their places.

Amanda was looking absolutely beautiful. As she walked into the witness box, she brushed her long blond hair back from the side of her face and Miles was able to appreciate once more the perfect tones of her complexion. Taking the bible from the usher she looked up, and spotting Miles for the first time in the dock, winked playfully at him before taking the oath. He felt as if his heart would melt. How long had it been since he had seen someone he counted as a friend? How long would it be before he saw such a person again?

Standing up, Drake smiled warmly at Amanda who nodded gamely at him in return.

'Could you state your name, please?'

'Amanda May.'

Although she was easily the smallest witness yet to have given evidence, her voice was chirpy and confident and carried throughout the entire courtroom.

'And what d'you do for a living, Miss May?'

'Oh, this and that,' she grinned. 'I haven't got a full-time job really.'

'But you do modelling and acting occasionally, I understand.'

'Yes, that's right. Every now and then.'

'What sort of modelling and acting?'

'Glamour, mostly. Erotica, sometimes. It depends on what I get offered, really.'

Looking to his left Miles could see that the jury appeared quite unmoved by this statement. Amanda's manner was so natural and unassuming that she could have announced that she walked on water for a living and they probably would not have batted an eyelid.

'D'you recognize the defendant – the man over there in the dock?'

'Yeah.'

'Could you tell the court who he is and how you came to meet him?'

'I knew him as Micky Angel. I first met him earlier this year – in February it was. I got a job workin' for a little company called Heretic Films. It was a one-day shoot in this house in North London. He was the sound man: y'know, operated the boom and all that.'

'Was he competent at his job?'

'Yeah, seemed to be.'

'When did you next hear from him after that?'

'About two weeks later. He phoned me up. He said he was in the area and asked me if I wanted to go out for a drink with him.'

'And did you do that?'

'Yeah.'

'What did he tell you about himself that night?'

'He said he was a reporter – working under cover – makin' a documentary for one of the big news companies.'

'And what sort of documentary did he tell you he was making?'

'About pornography. He asked me how I'd got into it and things. I told 'im I hadn't really – not as such: I mean I only do one or two films a year and I'm very particular who I work with then. So then he asked me if I could put 'im in touch with other people in the industry. He was lookin' to try and track down agents – the unscrupulous sort. I've got this friend of mine who, like, does it full-time, so I said I'd call her up and get some names for 'im. That was it, really.'

'Did you think he was genuine?'

'What, you mean a proper reporter?'

'Yes.'

'Seemed so – as far as I could tell, anyway.'

'And did your friend do as you requested?'

'Yeah, she did. She gave me a list and I sent it on to 'im.'

'Did you hear from him again after that?'

'No, I didn't. Next thing I heard he was, well, here, y'know.'

'Just to run over that again for the benefit of the jury: when you met the defendant for a drink and he told you that he was working under-cover it was in February this year.'

'Yes.'

'You're certain of that.'

'Oh, yeah, absolutely.'

'Thank you, Miss May.'

'You're welcome.'

As Pahklava stood up to begin her cross-examination, Miles noticed that she didn't look directly at Amanda but kept her eyes firmly fixed on her notepad.

'Miss, er, May. In the conversation that you had with the defendant – the night that he invited you out for a drink – what did he ask you about?'

Miles recognized Pahklava's tactics straightaway: just as in his own case, she must be trying unnerve Amanda by asking her to repeat herself.

'Well, like I said,' replied Amanda, with a slightly perplexed tone to her voice, 'he told me he was making a documentary and wanted to know about how I'd got into films and everythin'.'

'Did he ask you anything else about yourself?'

'How d'you mean?'

At this point, Pahklava at last looked up – to Miles's surprise he could see that she was smiling at Amanda in a friendly and most inoffensive manner.

'You know, did he ask you anything else about yourself – small talk, that sort of thing.'

'Well, yeah, he asked me if I'd got a boyfriend.'

'And how did you reply?'

'I said I had, but I told him he's, like, in the army and so I don't see him so much 'cos he's away.'

'And what did the two of you talk about after that?'

Amanda's brow furled for a moment, having obviously expected the cross-examination to revolve entirely around the issue of Miles's under-cover investigation.

'Erm, he went on about his documentary thing ...'

'Yes. And ...'

'And then he told me about his wife.'

'Oh, really? What did he say about her, Miss May?'

'Well, he said that they'd split up a long time ago and that he missed her and he was, well, a bit lonely and everything and ...'

'Thank you,' replied Pahklava, politely 'Now, the movie that you had shot two weeks previously with the defendant – what sort of film was it?'

'Erotica.'

'You took your clothes off in it, then?'

'Wouldn't've been very erotic if I'd've kept 'em on.'

It was a sharp riposte, but Pahklava did not look in the least bit phased.

'And you engaged in sexual acts with another actor – a male actor?'

'Yeah.'

At this point, Pahklava turned so that she was half-facing the jury and then dropped her elbow on to her lectern in an uncharacteristically relaxed pose.

'Miss May. Did it occur to you that the defendant's motives in asking you out that night might not have been exactly as he described them?'

'What d'you mean?'

'Well,' she continued, raising her right eyebrow suggestively, 'A man buys you a drink. He checks to find out whether you have a boyfriend. He tells you he's a secret undercover reporter and then pulls at your heart strings by telling you he's lonely. Surely you must have recognized what was really on his mind?'

'No. It wasn't like that!' protested Amanda.

'Oh, come now, Miss May, don't be coy. The defendant could scarcely fail to have been attracted by your obvious good looks and having so recently witnessed your, er, performance on the film-set, no doubt had good reason to believe that you were sexually uninhibited ...'

'No!'

'... and being uninhibited, hoped perhaps that you might consider bestowing your favours upon him.'

'No! No!!'

Seeing Amanda's embarrassment and distress, Miles felt a terrible rage well up inside him. To have been the object of Pahklava's mockery himself the previous day had been bad enough, but to witness one of the most genuine people he had ever known cheapened and humiliated in this way was more than he could bear. Clenching his fists, he began to rise to his feet – he didn't care if Pahklava sent him to his doom, but he was not going to allow her to get away with this. At that moment, though, he felt two powerful hands grip him by the shoulders and pin him to his seat.

'Don't!' hissed Paul Jones into his ear. 'Don't let yourself get held up for contempt. She'll have gone through all that for nothing otherwise!'

Still the anger raged inside Miles. In the jury box, one of the two young sweat-shirted men was nudging the other in the ribs and, holding up his hand, was whispering something to him behind it.

'I have no more questions for this witness your honour,' announced Pahklava, standing straight-backed once more.

As Amanda turned and walked out of the witness box she managed a final brave smile at Miles. Feeling the dock officer's hands slip from his shoulders, he sat forward in his seat and mouthed the words 'Thank you' at her twice. With a nod of encouragement and a wave of her tiny hand, Amanda then made her way across the courtroom and in a few, brief seconds was gone.

Tysoe had not dressed up for the occasion and, as he mumbled his way through the oath, looked even more disreputable than Miles remembered. He appeared quite haggard, too, as though he had slept little the previous night. Following Miles's evidence to the police, Tysoe's business had probably begun to suffer quite badly; he wondered how far they had proceeded with a prosecution against him.

'Could you state your name, please?' asked Drake.

'Tysoe. Johnny Tysoe.'

'You'll have to speak up Mr Tysoe; the jury will be unable to hear you.'

As Tysoe nodded in response, Miles noticed that he seemed to be holding his right shoulder slightly forwards, as though he had strained it or it had been damaged in some way.

'And what is your profession, Mr Tysoe?'

'I'm a builder.'

'Do you recognize the defendant – the man over there in the dock?'

'Yes, I do.'

'Could you tell the court what his name is and how he became known to you?'

'I never knew his real name,' he muttered. 'I knew him as Mick – Micky Angel.'

Drake frowned. He, too, had noticed that Tysoe appeared both surprisingly shabby and strangely listless.

'And how did he become known to you, Mr Tysoe?' he repeated.

'Erm, it was towards the end of last year. I started hiring him as a labourer. Casual stuff. A few days a week.'

'Who introduced you to him?'

'One of the other blokes I used to hire. He brought him along one day in place of his mate who was sick.'

'This was the man known as Naz – an illegal Turkish immigrant whom you employed for several months at the end of last year and the first half of this?'

'Yeah.'

'When did you first begin to suspect that the man you knew as Michael Angel was not in fact an ordinary labourer?'

'I don't think I ever did really. He always seemed fairly normal to me. He was a good worker and everythin'.'

On hearing this, Miles sat bolt upright in his seat and looked quickly across the court. Drake's face had completely dropped, whilst Pahklava had now stopped what she was writing and was staring at Tysoe in surprise.

'Mr Tysoe,' said Drake, gravely. 'When interviewed by the police on May the nineteenth this year, you commented and I quote, 'I had always wondered about him,' – him meaning the defendant – 'he never did seem quite like a normal workman to me.' Are you now saying that that was not the case?'

'Er, yeah,' mumbled Tysoe, 'yeah, that's right.'

'Then why did you tell the police that it was?' he snapped.

'They, er, they were on at me. They said that he was a reporter and that he had evidence of me overcharging people and what have you. I sort of thought I ought to go along with what they said.'

'Mr Tysoe,' challenged Drake, his face reddening with anger, 'may I remind you that you are under oath. I ask you again. When did you begin to suspect that Mr Angel was not a bona fide workman?'

'I don't think I ever did. I mean, I was confused when the police said that, I thought they were gonna … you know, I thought I had to go along with 'em to save myself.'

As Drake took a deep breath, clearly fighting to control his anger, Tysoe looked up and across the court. Because of his squint it was always difficult to know exactly what he was looking at, but, by the incline of his head, Miles guessed he had just stolen a glimpse at the public gallery. Leaning forward, Miles turned his head to the right and immediately caught sight of Kent sitting on the back row, smiling sardonically; he must have slipped into the courtroom earlier when Miles had not been looking. Sitting back in his chair, Miles understood what must have happened. Somehow, Kent had tracked Tysoe down.

'If you are now maintaining,' continued Drake, stiffly, 'that the police put this suspicion into your mind, how do you explain the fact that later in that same interview with them you stated, 'Micky disappeared about the end of March. A few weeks later my wife saw someone just like him in our road on her way home one day. When she got inside the house, she was sure that he'd been in there. That's when I really began to suspect there was something up with him.'

'Like I say, I was worried because they were going on at me, so I sort of exaggerated what my wife had said. I thought if I went along with what they wanted to hear they wouldn't be so hard on me in the end.'

'That's ridiculous!' snapped Drake. 'They didn't coerce you into saying this or anything else. You had your solicitor present with you during the entire interview.'

'They said they were gonna take me to court,' mumbled Tysoe, staring vacantly into space. 'I was … I was scared like.'

Drake was just about to speak again, when the judge intervened. His voice had a sharpness to it that Miles had not heard before.

'Mr Tysoe, let me get this right. Are you saying that you never once suspected that the defendant was anything other than a normal workman and that the witness statement that you gave to the police on May the nineteenth and duly signed that day was completely inaccurate in that regard?'

'Yes. Yes, your honour.'

'Mr Tysoe, by your actions you misled the police, wasted their time and that of this court. It is therefore my recommendation that you be charged accordingly. Ms Pahklava, do you have any questions?'

'No, your honour,' she replied.

'Take the witness down. The court will resume in fifteen minutes.'

As the usher led Tysoe away, Miles could see the relief spread across his face. It was obvious why he had contradicted his original statement: no punishment that the state could mete out for wasting police time could possibly compare with that which Kent would serve up if he had continued to stand by it. Told to dress down like the commonest of criminals and act out the part of a weak and impressionable fool, Tysoe had effectively discredited himself as one of the only two witnesses that the defence had been able to bring forward. As Amanda had been the other, and Pahklava's insinuations had so cruelly diminished her in the jury's eyes, all independent corroboration of Miles's story had effectively been discounted.

It was now his word against virtually every witness and all the evidence.

As counsel for the prosecution, Pahklava gave her summary first. As she began speaking, Miles sat upright in his chair, mindful of Malde's advice never to convey an impression of guilt via his facial expressions or body language. But, as Pahklava systematically ran through the Crown's case, reiterating her arguments and validating each of them in turn by means of witness or material evidence, Miles felt his shoulders begin to slump. Here was a violent man: Cromwell, Kent, Nigel and the publican at The White Horse had all attested to the fact. Here was a deceitful man, who by his own admission had lied to the police to protect his former accomplices. Here was a desperate, embittered man who, according to the murder victim's partner — the person who had been closer to him than anyone else alive — had stalked and intimidated his former boss for months. Here was a man with a unique knowledge of and connections to the murder scene: the only person in the world, apart from Eva Osbourne, who had known that Thomas Cranmer would be in the flat that night, and the only person whose fingerprints appeared on the canister of petrol that had brought about his death. Here was the man who had tried to leave the country under an assumed name less than twenty-four hours later. And, finally, here was the man who, for the next twenty fours, had been unable to explain to the police exactly why he had done so and whose eventual alibi only served to emphasize the bizarre fantasy that had compelled him to commit the crime in the first place.

As Pahklava sat down at the end of her summary, Miles found himself in the grip of a strange mental ambivalence. Although he was not guilty in one sense, perhaps he was in another. His life had been a sham and had indeed fallen apart in a manner not too dissimilar to that which Pahklava was describing. Perhaps it was right that he had been brought to justice and the court was utterly correct to dispense it. Even when Drake got to his feet and delivered a blistering, impassioned response, Miles could still not suppress the voice at the back of his mind telling him that it had somehow been ordained that he should come to this court and be judged on what he had been and done in his life. Only when the judge began his own summing up was Miles at last able to snap out of his distracted state and concentrate fully on what was being said: these were the last moments of his trial – the last words that the jury would hear before retiring to consider their verdict.

'Ladies and gentlemen,' said the judge, 'let me begin by reiterating our respective responsibilities. As I said earlier, it is your job to decide whether the defendant is innocent or guilty and mine to rule on the law. In arriving at your decision you must consider all the evidence that has been brought before you and how it relates to the indictment on which the defendant is charged. Now, you will have heard many times in this case the word 'intent'. This is a murder indictment and for you to deliver a verdict of guilty you must be sure – beyond all reasonable doubt – that the defendant intended to murder the victim. If what you have heard and seen over the last five days does not convince you of that intention, you should find him innocent – however compelling the other evidence may be as to the likelihood of his having committed the crime. In this regard, you may find yourselves persuaded by the evidence of Eva Osbourne who was convinced that the defendant lured Thomas Cranmer to his flat on the night of his murder, and by that of Mrs McCray, the woman who occupied the flat below the defendant's, who heard a man's footsteps shortly after Thomas Cranmer had arrived. You may similarly be persuaded by the forensic evidence, although you must reflect on the fact that just because no other fingerprints were identified on the canister of petrol, it does not necessarily prove that it was the defendant who used it on the night in question.

'In arriving at your verdict you must consider the character of the defendant and the relationship that he had with Thomas Cranmer. Whereas a number of witnesses have made reference to violent acts perpetrated by the defendant subsequent to his dismissal from *The Mail*, he was up until that time both a man of good character and a well-respected professional. Similarly, no evidence has been put before you that his relationship with Thomas Cranmer prior to his dismissal was anything other than cordial, although that in itself does not preclude their having fallen out in the acrimonious incident that was witnessed by a number of employees at *The Mail*. Finally, you must consider the defendant's alibi both in respect of the undercover documentary series which he claims to have been making for his former employers and in respect of his attempted departure from this country – the timing and manner of which you may or may not find indicative of guilt. Finally, ladies and gentlemen of the jury, if you have not already done so, please choose one of your number to be foreman and to speak for you when you return your verdict which must be unanimous. Thank you very much.'

As the jury began to stand up and make their way out, Miles looked around the court. The judge's summary had implied that the verdict was still in the balance, but Malde and Drake had their heads lowered as they gathered together their papers, whilst the Crown's team were openly smiling at each other. In between them, the watching brief had already packed up his notes and, as he turned to walk out, Miles saw him purse his lips and make a short, confident nod in the direction of the public gallery where Kent was still seated, wearing the same mocking smile. Sensing the dock officer get to his feet behind him, Miles desperately cast his eyes once again in the direction of the jury. The woman who had so reminded him of Jo, whom he had instinctively sensed might champion his cause, was on her feet, but, although he stared at her fixedly, pleading that she return his gaze, she seemed deliberately to be looking downwards – deliberately trying to ensure that she did not catch his eye. Feeling Paul Jones's hand on his forearm, Miles got up and turned shakily to walk back through the dock towards the exit at the rear. Reaching the door, he did not open it, but instead raised his arms and placed the flats of his hands on its smooth, painted surface. Into his mind had sprung a vivid image of Elizabeth and Jake. Somehow, at the very core of his being, he knew that if he walked through that door, he would never see them again.

Gently levering his way past, Paul Jones reached forward to open the door, but at that moment Miles suddenly heard raised voices behind him. Turning, he looked back down into the courtroom just as the main doors burst open and a wild, dishevelled figure came hurtling through. It was Angus Lamb, quickly followed by a court usher and a security guard both of whom were clearly trying to catch him and restrain him. Rushing straight over to the clerk of court, Angus Lamb engaged him in urgent, whispered conversation, all the time pointing towards Miles in the dock. Instantly, the atmosphere in the courtroom which, moments before, had been totally subdued, became intense and electrified. The jurors, who had been making their way towards the back of the court in a straggled line, stopped and stared in fascination at the

504

scene taking place before them. The judge then reappeared, his wig slightly askew, and, leaning over the parapet, glared angrily at Angus Lamb whose arms the security guard had now pinned to his sides. In a flash, Drake sprang out from behind his desk and began speaking to Angus Lamb. As Miles made his way back to the front of the dock to try and hear what was going on, the judge caught sight of him and instantly issued an order for both him and the jury immediately to be removed from the court. The last thing he heard as he went through the exit and back towards the cells was Angus Lamb raising his voice. Walking down the corridor, Miles felt his fears about Elizabeth and Jake subside. There was a still a chance that he might yet be found not guilty. There was still a chance that he might see them again one day. For he had heard Angus Lamb's impassioned voice calling out '… and he's waiting in the car outside!'

He remained in his cell for two and three quarter hours. At first he thought it would only be a matter of minutes before he would be taken back out again, but lunchtime came and went without any sign of his being returned to the courtroom. Paul Jones came into the cell no less than three times, on each occasion saying that he had no news but would be certain to tell Miles the moment that he did. Obviously, Angus Lamb had somehow managed to track down Harper and persuaded him to become a witness for the defence. No doubt the delay was being caused by Pahklava and the prosecution team trying to convince the judge not to admit Harper's evidence at this late stage. The more he thought about it, the more he imagined that the judge would have to consider most carefully the relevant legal procedures and precedents in such circumstances. For the hundredth time he thanked his good fortune in having Drake and Malde as his defence team. Whatever objections Pahklava might have raised, he could be absolutely sure they were fighting them tooth and nail as much as if their own lives depended on it.

The call finally came just after half past two. As Miles walked down the narrow corridor towards the entrance to the dock, his heart was in his throat. Angus Lamb might well have succeeded in getting Harper into the witness box, but would he tell the truth when he got there if to do so would be to run the risk of exposing both himself and Angela to subsequent prosecution? And, even if he did, would his evidence be enough to persuade the jury, given the damage that Pahklava and Kent had already inflicted on his alibi? The moment that Miles walked into the dock, however, all these considerations were immediately swept from his mind.

The courtroom was virtually empty. All the barristers, solicitors and court officials had gone with the exception of Drake, Pahklava, the clerk of a court and a single stenographer. The watching brief was similarly nowhere to be seen and the public gallery had been cordoned off and the door leading to it covered by a metal shutter. More remarkably still, the judge was already seated, as was the jury who stared at Miles with a strange curiosity as he made his way to the front of the dock and sat down.

'Ladies and gentlemen of the jury,' announced the judge, his voice echoing eerily around the near-empty courtroom, 'as the clerk of court has explained to you, a witness has come forward at the last moment whose evidence may be relevant to this case. I do apologize for the delay this has caused and thank you for your patience. Now, I understand that you all consented to sign the Official Secrets Act and have duly been given copies of it to retain. The court is most grateful to you for your willingness in this regard. Please accept my thanks.'

So saying, the judge nodded towards the exit. Miles watched as the usher who had been guarding the door turned and went back through it. Utterly mystified, he waited for the witness to appear. Whoever Lamb had brought to court, it was obviously not Harper. So who on earth could it be and what information could this person possibly have that had required the judge to request that the jury sign the Official Secrets Act?

Several seconds later the door opened, only then straightaway to be locked by the usher who remained waiting in the corridor outside. Leaning forwards in his seat, Miles stared on in astonishment at the man whom the usher had let in, as he strode purposefully across the court-room towards the witness box. He was in his early sixties, tall, broad-shouldered and with a crown of brilliant white hair that shimmered and coruscated under the bright courtroom lights. He wore a narrowly lapelled cotton jacket of such a deep, dark red colour that it might have been dyed in blood. His shirt, which was of fine, bright linen, was open at the neck and out of it a thick tuft of hair protruded, curling up from his powerful, sun-tanned chest. Turning to his left, Miles looked at the jury and saw that they too were transfixed by the sight of this mysterious, charismatic figure. But it was as the man picked up the bible and began to read the oath that the court truly held its breath. For unlike every witness who had so far proclaimed those words, he seemed not to be reading them, but to be speaking them as though they were his own.

'Could you state you name, please?' asked Drake.

'Albert Ryder.'

'Is that your real name? The name with which you were christened?'

'No, it is not,' answered the man. 'That name is now known only to myself.'

'But Albert Ryder is the name that you use and by which you have been known for the last forty years.'

'That is correct.'

'What is your profession, Mr Ryder?'

'I'm a security consultant.'

'And what does that entail?'

'Mostly design work – electronic security systems for banks, public buildings, that sort of thing.'

'But you have not always been a security consultant, have you?'

'No.'

'Could you tell the court about what you did when you were a younger man?'

'In my early twenties,' he replied, 'I was recruited by British Intelligence because of a particular Slavic language in which I am fluent – my mother having been a native of that country.'

'And you became a spy for them.'

'Yes.'

Unable to stop himself, Miles sat bolt upright in his seat, clenching his fists in triumph. Lamb had found the East European spy! Using his connections as a Member of Parliament, he must have been able to tap into the security community and track the man down.

'What did they require you to do?'

'For three years, I lived under an assumed identity in that country. During that time, I obtained certain intelligence information which I passed back to my controllers in London.'

'What happened at the end of those three years?'

'When my work was finished, I returned to England and adopted a new identity – that of Albert Ryder.'

'The identity you still hold today.'

'That's correct.'

'How many people still alive know of what you actually did?'

'Not many – and none of them know my original identity.'

'But nevertheless it is widely known that in the past you had been associated with the intelligence services?'

'Not widely known. But yes, in certain circles I have a, er, reputation, one might say.'

'In which connection, Mr Ryder, would you kindly tell the court what happened in the summer of the year before last?'

'Yes,' he replied, turning to face the jury. 'One day towards the end of June, or maybe early July, I received a phone call. It was from a man who would not give his name but who had been recommended to me, he said, by a mutual friend. He told me that he was engaged in sending an operative under cover to penetrate what he believed to be a dangerous criminal gang and asked me if I would be prepared to offer him my advice.'

'What sort of advice was it that he wanted?'

'Psychological. He said that the individual in question was going to have to live under an assumed identity for a number of months and that he anticipated that this would lead to his suffering considerable mental strain. He wanted me to give him advice as to how best he might deal with it.'

'What was your response?'

'I agreed.'

'And what was the advice that you gave him?'

'I warned him about betrayal. I knew from my own experience the damage that it can do to someone in such a situation.'

'And how did you communicate this advice?' asked Drake.

'By letter.'

'To which address?'

'To a post office box in London.'

'Do you remember the number?'

'No.'

'Did you keep a record of it?'

'No, I did not.'

'Thank you, Mr Ryder.'

As Drake sat down, several members of the jury drew breath or shuffled nervously in their seats. Despite the courtroom being almost empty, the atmosphere was more highly charged than it had been at any time during the trial. Standing up, Pahklava gathered together her notes and then fixed her jet-black eyes on Albert Ryder. In response, however, he merely smiled back at her in a manner that was at one and the same time both respectful and utterly self-composed. For three years he had survived the terrors of living alone and under cover behind the iron curtain: compared to that experience, giving evidence to Neera Pahklava held no fear for him. As if sensing this she blinked, as though the energy of her intimidating glare had been deflected straight back in on herself, and when finally she did speak her voice was quiet and noticeably deferential.

'Mr Ryder. Just a few questions, if I may?'

'Please.'

'Were you paid for the advice that you gave and, if so, how?'

'Yes. I was. I received a money order – from a Swiss bank. It was delivered by hand to my London office two days later.'

'The funds were thus untraceable and could have come, presumably, from anyone?'

'Yes.'

'Had you ever been asked for similar advice before that time – or indeed since?'

'Yes, I had – twice: once about five years ago and then once again a long time before that – well over twenty years ago.'

'Finally, did the person to whom you spoke indicate exactly who it was who was going under cover – in terms of their profession, I mean? Did they say they were a reporter or a police officer or what have you?'

'No, they didn't.'

'So, the undercover operative could have been any one of those?'

'They could indeed.'

'Thank you, Mr Ryder,' said Pahklava, quietly sitting back down again.

'Mr Ryder,' said the judge, sombrely. 'The court has no more questions for you. I would therefore like to say how grateful we are to you for your evidence. I understand that you travelled a considerable distance to get here today, with no guarantee that what you had to say would be heard.'

In response, Albert Ryder merely bowed his great, handsome head and then turned and walked slowly out of the witness box. Reaching the exit he knocked once on the frosted glass, and, whilst the usher unlocked the door, looked back across the courtroom at Miles. As their eyes met, he slowly lowered and then raised his head – a gesture so slight as to be almost imperceptible, but which nevertheless acknowledged the unique bond between them.

As soon as the door had been closed again, the judge began to speak.

'Ladies and gentlemen, once again I would like to thank you for your patience and perseverance. Before you depart to consider your verdict, I wish to offer you some further guidance. As I said previously in my summary, it is my job to rule on the law and yours to deliver a verdict. Notwithstanding that observation, and always bearing in mind that it is for you to decide whether the defendant is guilty or innocent, I believe that the unusual circumstances in which the final witness was brought before you require me to comment on his and other evidence in this case.

'According to Mr Ryder, he was contacted in June of the year before last by an unknown person seeking help for what he termed an under-cover operative. That person may indeed have been Thomas Cranmer, hoping to obtain assistance for the defendant. We do not know. It may just as easily have been one of the programme makers of the recently screened documentary in which the court has heard that King Media was involved, or indeed the makers of some other programme alto-gether. On the other hand, it may have been nothing to do with the media at all – as counsel for the prosecution has pointed out, the person who contacted Mr Ryder merely spoke of an operative; a term that may just as easily be used to refer to a reporter, a policeman, a soldier or indeed a member of the security services. Finally, you must consider that it could even have been the defendant himself – his phone call to Mr Ryder marking the genesis of his descent into the self-deluding fantasy of which the prosecution has spoken. As I say, we do not know. Mr Ryder's evidence, by itself, is simply insufficient for you to judge – and this leads me on to the point that I wish to make.

'Because Mr Ryder's evidence only emerged at the very end of this trial, it was presented to you separately – after you had already been asked to retire to consider your verdict. I would like to ask you there-fore to guard against the natural tendency to regard it as having extraor-dinary significance simply by virtue of that fact. It does not. You must therefore make your best endeavours to consider what you have heard this afternoon in the context of the evidence of the last five days. In that regard, I refer you to the summary that I gave before you went off to consider your verdict four hours ago. You will recall that I spoke of intent and its paramount importance in a murder indictment. You will recall that I spoke of the evidence given by Eva Osbourne and Alice McCray about the events on the actual day of the crime. Finally, you will recall that I spoke about the relationship that the defendant had to Thomas Cranmer and his attempted departure from this country the day after his death. As you retire to make your verdict, I ask you to bear all of these points in mind. Thank you, ladies and gentlemen.'

As the jury rose to leave, Miles looked at their faces one by one to attempt to discern something of their thoughts. Albert Ryder's evidence had given him hope – a glimmer of hope that the twelve men and women before him would return a verdict of innocent and that he might thus one day see Elizabeth and Jake again. The fact was, however, that the evidence was still overwhelmingly stacked against him. Moreover, he was and always had been the only suspect in the investigation: in finding him innocent, the jury would have to countenance the notion that an unknown person, for an unknown reason, had, on that one particular night in May, sought to pour petrol through the letter box of his flat at the exact time that Thomas Cranmer had been in there. Imagining this argument being thrown in the face of the juror who sought to champion his cause, Miles looked at the young woman, sitting on the far right of the lower tier of the jury box. Again he stared at her. Again he put all his energy into his gaze, imploring her to look up and catch his eye. Again, she continued to look downwards. Still Miles stared on. Still he willed her with all his might to turn and face him. Finally, as the juror next to her stood up and began to make his way through the narrow seats and she at last had room to get up and leave, she lifted up her head and looked at him. Although he met her eyes for less than a second, he almost reeled backwards with the intensity of the emotion with which her expression was charged. It was anger. There was no doubt about it. Tossing her head sideways, she then made her way between the seats and within a few, short seconds disappeared from view. As Miles made his own way back through the dock to the door at the rear, his brow was furled in thought, but, try as he might, he knew he could not fathom what her look had signified.

Epilogue

The hour between nine and ten o'clock in the morning was Billy's favourite part of the day. The night shift at the precision plastic components factory at which he worked finished at eight and, although he valued his job and liked his employers, he always firmly turned down their offers of overtime and made sure that he was on his way out of the factory gates by a quarter past at the latest. The traffic was almost always light because he was going out of London when everyone else was commuting in and he could usually rely on being back home by eight forty-five. As he approached the front door of his third floor flat he would be smiling, thinking of the sight that would inevitably greet him on the other side. His wife Jeanette would be clearing up the breakfast things, carrying them through from the dining room to the kitchen, whilst their three year old daughter Annabel would be sitting on the carpet playing with her toys. Slipping off his coat, he would go down on his hands and knees and join his daughter for ten minutes, whilst Jeanette got ready for work and packed up her things for nursery. At nine o'clock, as he went out on to the balcony and watched them make their way across the estate, waving occasionally to Annabel when she turned and looked back, Billy would feel a real sense of contentment: his work was done, his family were safe and secure in their daily routine and now he could relax.

The first thing he would then do would be to make himself breakfast. Jeanette had offered to prepare it for him times beyond count, promising to have it ready on the table when he arrived home, but she had enough on her hands looking after Annabel. Besides, he derived a certain satisfaction from the simple, unsophisticated task of frying up the eggs and grilling the toast, and the aroma of the cooking always seemed to clear away the smells of the vinyls and resins from the factory. After he'd washed the dishes, he would then go back out onto the balcony, smoke a cigarette or two and look out over the estate – watching the people beginning their day just as his was finishing.

On this particular morning, he had just stubbed out his second cigarette and was thinking about going back inside the flat to read the paper when he noticed a black cab drive on to the estate. As it came to a halt and the passenger door opened, Billy looked on with interest. He had never before seen the tall, powerfully built man who had just got out and, as he watched him go around to talk to the driver, he found himself wishing that he never would again. His ancient black leather jacket and tightly cropped hair were intimidating enough in themselves, but there was something else, too: something that Billy could sense rather than see, even though the man was well over thirty yards away. It was something other-worldly – something ghostly. With a shiver, Billy picked up his coffee cup and ash tray and went back inside the flat. The man was probably a bailiff or a repo man. The estate had more than its fair share of folk who'd reneged on their debts and one of them was no doubt in for a very unpleasant early morning call as a result.

Sitting down on the sofa, he picked up the paper but then remembered there were a couple of bills he had to deal with. Frowning, he looked across at the letter rack. He slept from ten until four and usually had a couple of hours afterwards for that sort of thing before having tea with the family and then going off back to work. Today, however, he had promised to take Jeanette to the supermarket, so there probably wouldn't be time. Putting down the paper, he walked over to the letter rack; he might as well get them out of the way now. As he sat down at the dining table, there was a knock on the front door. Putting the bills to one side, he walked over to answer it. It had better not be a door-to-door salesman. He hated being disturbed during his hour of quiet.

As Billy opened the door, his jaw dropped in a mixture of consternation and outright fear. It was the man from the taxi. Seeing the scar that snaked across his cheek and his powerful, muscle-bound frame, Billy was seized with the urge to slam the door, but, realizing that such a man could probably smash it down with a single blow and noticing that he had deliberately taken a step backwards in a clear attempt to put him at

514

his ease, Billy instead swallowed hard and resolved to ask him what he wanted.

'Yes?' he said – conscious of the croak in his voice.

For a moment, the man stood absolutely still, seeming to take in every aspect of Billy's face and appearance, and then slowly and deliberately, he gave a respectful bow of the head. Who was this wraithlike stranger who at one and the same time appeared so terrifying and yet so scrupulously courteous?

'I'm sorry to disturb you, Mr Clarke.'

His voice was soft – ethereal.

'Who … who are you? What d'you want?'

In response, he did not reply, but instead reached inside his pocket and took out a photograph which he held up at arm's length for Billy to see.

'I've come to see you … about this man.'

For a moment, Billy felt faint. Sensing that his knees might suddenly give way, he put out his hand to steady himself on the lintel.

'Come,' he gasped.

It was all that he could manage to say.

Indicating the man to sit down, Billy watched him walk around to the other side of the living room table and pull out a chair. Even without the alarming-looking scar, his face really was very unusual. His forehead was high and broad, his nose large and bulbous and his eyebrows and mouth both seemed to turn down at the ends as though his mind were permanently in a state of concentration. His cheeks were a healthy burgundy red and, along with the grainy lines around his temples and jaw, conveyed the impression of his having spent much of his life out of doors. His eyes were light blue and so luminous and uniform in colour as to appear almost artificial – like a pair of precision, optical instruments that had been skilfully grafted into his head. Resting his elbows on the table, the man looked across at Billy and smiled gently. It was a strangely complex expression: a mixture of humour and humility, of experience and common understanding, and, with it, Billy's anxieties about his personal safety completely disappeared. This man had not come to collect a debt; he had come to repay one.

Slipping his hand inside his jacket, the man took out the photograph that he had shown Billy at the door and put it on the table top between them. Again, Billy stared at the picture. It could almost be a holiday snap. An elderly man in a Hawaiian T-shirt and shorts standing with his arm resting on the trunk of a palm tree – his grinning, sunburned face smiling cheerily back at the camera.

Yet this was the face that had haunted Billy's dreams for years.

'His name,' began the man, 'is Arthur Bonham. He's a chemical engineer. He lives in the Middle East – in Oman – and, before you ask, he still has his light brown suit, although he's put on a few pounds since you saw him last and he tells me he finds it a little bit tight around the waist nowadays.'

'Who are you?' whispered Billy.

'This is something of a shock for you, isn't it?' replied the man.

'It certainly is.'

'Would you like to hear his story – from the beginning?'

'Yes, I would. Very much.'

'Then let me tell it to you, as he told it to me, over tea on the lawn at his mansion in Masqat City. Arthur Bonham was born in England in nineteen thirty-seven. After graduating from University, he married a woman called Lucy Ballard and not long afterwards they moved into a small house in Seymour Road, Hampton where they lived for the next fifteen years. He had a natural flair for business and had started his own company before he was twenty-five. He kept it small and specialized and it did well. But then tragedy struck Arthur and Lucy Bonham. Although she was only thirty-one years of age, his wife became afflicted with severe arthritis and was shortly afterwards confined to a wheelchair. Arthur found it almost impossible to look after her, and when her unmarried sister Elaine volunteered to move in to the spare room and help, he accepted the offer gratefully. For the next seven years, the three of them lived there together: Elaine and Lucy keeping each other company and Arthur working to build up his increasingly successful business.

In nineteen seventy four, his wife Lucy died. By that time, Arthur's company was almost entirely centred on the Middle East and within six months he had moved there permanently and applied for citizenship of Oman. Although his sister-in-law Elaine offered to vacate the house in Hampton so that he could sell it, Arthur begged her to stay and three years later handed it over to her completely. At first, he went back to see her once or twice a year, but Seymour Road was filled with painful memories and he had married again with an Omani woman and was settled in his new life. As the years went by, Elaine continued to write, but Arthur's responses were short and ever more infrequent. He kept on promising himself that he'd go back to England for a long holiday and spoil her for a couple of weeks, but deep down he knew that he wouldn't. And deep down, he was guilty: guilty that he'd turned his back on the woman who'd nursed his first wife for so long; guilty that he was her only family and he could no longer find the time for her; guilty that he could let himself be so very selfish ...'

At this point the man paused, his eyes glazing over sadly as if the story that he was telling had resonances in his own life.

'Three years ago, Elaine Ballard also died. At first, Arthur thought everything would wrap itself up without him having to be involved. She had left the house to charity and, by the time the news of her death had reached him, she had already been cremated so there seemed little point in going back to England. But over the next few days he found her demise preying more and more on his mind. Her death had uncovered that part of his life that he had kept buried for so long. Finally, after a week of sleepless nights, he called his sister-in-law's solicitors and asked if there was still time to see the house once more, before it was finally sold; he knew he could never rest until he had done so. They told him that it was due to be cleared the following week, but, that if he wanted to, he could go there at the weekend. The next morning he took a flight to Heathrow. You were the first person to speak to him when he got off the plane.'

'Why did the old woman's solicitors tell the police she had no surviving relatives? If they'd've told them about this Bonham bloke, I would never have been convicted!'

'According to her will, she didn't have any surviving relatives.'

'But surely they must've made a note of him asking for permission to go the house!'

'Elaine Ballard's solicitors are a very large city firm with twenty-three partners and a whole army of probate staff, clerks and secretaries. If one of them did make a note of Arthur Bonham's request to go to Seymour Road, it never ended up in the file that they showed to the police.'

Taking a deep breath, Billy looked up at the ceiling in exasperation. He had been branded a criminal by virtue of a clerical error.

'He remembers you, you know,' continued the man. 'Very well.'

'Does he?'

'Oh, yes. When he arrived at Heathrow he was in a pretty bad way. He'd hardly slept for a week and his mind was tormented by guilt and regret. After his first wife's death he had never really grieved properly, you see: just thrown himself into his work as a means of escape. His sister-in-law's death had stirred up thoughts and feelings that he had kept suppressed for over thirty years. When you approached him and asked if he wanted a taxi he was in a total daze. And when you stopped off at the supermarket to buy him some tea and milk, he saw it as a real act of kindness.'

'What happened with the vacuum cleaner, then? Where did he get it from?'

'Elaine Ballard had a houseful of cats. She'd kept them for company. When he got into the house, he found it thick with pet hair, so the following morning the first thing he did was to go into Kingston and get himself a vacuum cleaner. He bought it on a market stall. He says he can't remember much about it now beyond having thought at the time what a good bargain it was.'

'Oh, my God!' exclaimed Billy. 'That bloke Smith downstairs must've sold some to the stall owner.'

'No doubt,' replied the man, with a smile. 'Anyway, Arthur spent the next two days going through Elaine and Lucy's things. There were letters, photographs and numerous other mementoes of those fifteen years of his life that he had lost. On the Sunday morning, he retraced the steps of the walk that the three of them used to take to church: the young woman tragically struck down by illness, her husband pushing her wheelchair and her sister walking dutifully beside. That was the turning point, he said. At last he was able to put his marriage to Lucy into the broader context of his life as a whole, and, at last, he could properly grieve for the first woman that he had loved. The following afternoon, he booked his return flight and then, having searched for the piece of paper that you had given him, called you to ask you to take him back to the airport. As he sat waiting for you to arrive, he remembered how kind you'd been to him when you'd first picked him up at Heathrow. No longer having any need for the vacuum cleaner, he decided to ask if you wanted it.'

Leaning back in his chair, Billy shook his head. Now, finally, he understood the reasons for the injustice that he had suffered. What he still did not know, however, was the identity of the man who had explained it to him.

'But you,' he asked. 'Who are you?' The man had avoided the question first time around.

'I am ... an executor,' he replied, slowly. 'The executor of a man who died last year. Many people believe that once they die they will be judged on what they did whilst they were alive. But this man was judged before his death. He was not a bad man, I suppose, but he was not a good man, either. And, as he waited in fear and trembling for judgment to be pronounced, he made a number of promises about what he would do if damnation was not to be his fate. You were the first of those promises.'

Opening up his jacket, the man took a fat, manila envelope out of the inside pocket and laid it on the table next to the photograph.

'In here is an affidavit from Arthur Bonham detailing everything that I have just described to you, signed by him and duly witnessed by a registered Omani attorney in law. Also in the envelope you will find a letter of recommendation to a London solicitor by the name of Brian Malde. Trust him. He's a good man. I know. Take the letter and affidavit to him and he will arrange everything. It'll cost you nothing, Mr Clarke – all the expenses will be taken care of – and within three, maybe four months, your criminal conviction will be repealed.'

'Thank you,' replied Billy, staring at the envelope in amazement, 'but ... I still don't understand. I mean, why?'

In response, the man turned his head slightly and nodded in the direction of the gold-framed photograph of Jeanette and Annabel that Billy kept on top of the sideboard.

'They're your wife and daughter, aren't they?'

'Yes, yes, they are.'

'Look after them,' replied the man, softly. 'Look after them well.'

So saying, he stood up, and even before Billy had had time to thank him again, went through the front door and made his way soundlessly down the stairs.

Emerging from the ground floor stairwell, Miles paused for a moment and breathed in the fresh, summer air. It had taken him four months to track down Arthur Bonham, and, as he strolled slowly across the estate towards the waiting taxi, he cast his mind back to the moment that he had solemnly sworn to find him when, at ten past seven in the evening of the final day of his trial, the tall man in the worsted jacket and red tie had stood up to deliver the jury's verdict. Twice during the afternoon, the judge had informed them that they could adjourn until the following day, and twice they had rejected his offer – electing instead to stay in the jury room for five continuous hours until they had thrashed out their verdict. As the man had spoken those two simple words and Miles had felt the waves of relief flood through him, he had turned his eyes towards the young woman whom he had believed had been so instrumental in securing his release and gazed at her in abject gratitude. Whether his intuition had been correct or not, he would never know. For, in response, she had simply stared back straight-faced until, having thanked the jury, the judge dismissed them and they left the courtroom.

Twenty minutes later, he had walked out of the front entrance of Kingston Crown Court a free man. But, as he had stood on the deserted, wind-swept steps of the courthouse, staring at the late evening traffic moving anonymously around the ring-road, he had never felt more alone or empty in his life. He had no job, nowhere to live and the only family that he had were on the other side of the world. Where was he to go and what was he to do? But then, out of nowhere, he had heard what had sounded like a faint voice calling his name on the wind. At first, he had thought he must be dreaming: looking left and right, he could see there was no one around but himself – he was all alone, surely, all alone in the world. And then, all at once, on the pavement in front of him, Angus Lamb had appeared – his face calm and filled with sympathy, his arms outstretched beckoning him towards him. It was late. Miles must be hungry and tired. Would he come with him and share supper at his house?

As they had driven along in the car, Miles had been unable to speak – overcome by the nervous exhaustion of his trial and Angus Lamb's unimaginable kindness. However, when they had arrived at his Hampstead home and Lamb's wife Madeleine had opened the front door to greet them, he had lowered his head and begun to babble incoherently. He had no right to be there. No right to accept the hospitality of a house that he had once all but destroyed. But even as the words had tripped off his lips, he had felt her hand cradling his cheek, gently closing his mouth and lifting his face upwards until it was within a few inches of her own. 'We have all sinned,' she had said. 'We have all sinned.'

Having taken Miles's jacket and the polythene bag in which he kept his overnight things, Lamb had then slowly led him down the long hallway towards the annex at the back of the house. Their meal would be ready in about half an hour. Would Miles like to spend a few minutes talking to his mother whilst it was being prepared? Over the last few days he had told her all about Miles's ordeal and she had really been looking forward to meeting him. Twice Miles had knocked on the tall, heavily panelled, Victorian door. Hearing no response, he had finally let himself into the warm, dimly lit kitchen to see Mary Lamb seated beside the coal fire reading a letter. Catching sight of him at the door, she had beckoned him to come and sit opposite, but, even as he had rested his hand on the back of the ancient leather chair on the other side of the hearth, his legs had given way and his body had crumpled to the floor at her feet. For Mary Lamb had radiated an aura of pity and compassion beyond anything he had ever experienced in his life before, and, with every step that he had taken towards her, he had seen the anguish in her face as she had opened up her heart to share his pain. And then his head had been in her lap and he had begun to weep uncontrollably – great, salty globules of water that had poured from his eyes, drenching his face and chest; tears of gratitude and of regret, of relief and of shame.

Arriving back at the taxi, Miles tapped on the window and the driver sat up with a start: he had obviously dropped off to sleep for a few minutes. Opening the passenger door, Miles shifted his suitcase to one side and then sat down on the bench seat, fastening his safety belt as the driver restarted the engine.

'It was terminal three, wasn't it?' he called cheerily, over his shoulder.

'That's right,' replied Miles.

'Goin' anywhere nice?'

'Australia.'

'Oh, yeah? Which part?'

'I don't know yet.'

Looking in the rear view mirror, Miles could see the puzzled expression on the driver's good-natured face as he struggled with this response. For a moment, the man looked as though he was going to ask Miles to explain what he had meant but, in the end, he simply slipped the taxi into gear and began to drive away. Smiling, Miles returned to his thoughts. Today was the day to which he had been looking forward for almost six months: the day that he would at last be free to go in search of Elizabeth and Jake.

He had stayed at Angus Lamb's Hampstead home for nearly a month – spending his days wandering the chilly, wide-open heath and his evenings ensconced in the intimate warmth of Mary Lamb's kitchen. After two weeks, he had called Amanda and they had gone out to dinner together. It had been a nervous affair at first, with Miles desperately wanting to demonstrate his gratitude at every conceivable turn, but sensing that Amanda was becoming increasingly embarrassed by it. Half way through the meal, a thought had occurred to him as to how he might properly show his gratitude. Having learned from Amanda that she had never had a professionally produced portfolio to showcase her talents as a photographic model, he had offered to produce one for her and, a week later, the two of them had spent an afternoon together in a London studio. Having developed the prints the following day, Miles had then compiled them into the album that would be the last piece of professional photographic work he would ever undertake. Since showing the footage of Alain Ellis and his daughter at Mortlake Manor to Tom in the Tower, he had known that although he would remain a journalist for the rest of his life, he could never trust the camera again: something had died inside him that day. However, as he had dropped the completed portfolio off at the post office to send to Amanda, he had felt no sadness, only a thrilling sense of elation. It wasn't simply that she would be delighted with the results – although that in itself was heart-warming enough – rather, it was that although his art had been taken from him, something infinitely more important had taken its place. In the beginning, he had not even recognized that it had been there at all, and even now he was not sure of the precise moment that it had first been born inside him. Perhaps it had been in the witness box, when Pahklava had asked him what he had discovered in Feltham. Or perhaps it had been even earlier still, when Angus Lamb had visited him in the legal room and listened so patiently to his story. But, although he was uncertain when it had come to him, he had no doubts as to what it was – and no doubts, either, that it was growing stronger and ever more magnificent with each passing day.

'But you must have, like, a destination, though, surely?' announced the taxi driver, suddenly. 'I mean, on your ticket. You can't just be flying to Australia, can you?'

Even though the man had not spoken for almost a minute, he had obviously still been wrestling with Miles's enigmatic response. Seeing his mystified, well-meaning look, Miles took pity on him and explained.

'Yes, you're right, of course. I'm flying to Sydney. But then I have to go looking for someone – well, two people actually. I don't know where they are exactly, so that's why I'm not precisely sure where I'm going.'

'You're lookin' for two people in Australia and you don't know where they are?'

'Yes.'

'That won't be easy,' observed the driver, pessimistically. 'It's a big place.'

'Oh, I'll find them, all right,' answered Miles. 'Don't you worry.'

Looking into his rear-view mirror and seeing the absolute certainty in Miles's face, the driver shrugged, deciding to let the matter drop. For Miles was utterly convinced that he would find Elizabeth and Jake: Arthur Bonham had emigrated over thirty years ago and when he had begun to search for him he had not even known his name; his wife and son had been gone for less than twelve months. Jake would be nearly seventeen now and would not have seen his father for over two years and, although Miles suspected that his resentment towards him had not waned, he somehow knew that Jake would be willing to speak with him – not least because what he had to say would take only a matter of seconds. During his time in Feltham he had dreamt of walking in the park with his son for hours on end, regaling him with tales of his exploits and the terrible dangers that he had faced. But now he recognized the vanity of using *Criminal Britain* as a justification for his life-long inadequacies as a father and a husband. Now all he wanted was a few quiet moments with Elizabeth and Jake to beg for their forgiveness; to show them that he was strong enough to face the truth about himself and ask of them thereafter only what they felt able to give.

And it was because he had the strength to face that truth that he was now so certain that he could at last faithfully impart the truth to others. Not the truth that he had once cravenly purveyed – not the shallow, seductive images that polluted his age – but the word. For it was the word that had been born inside him. The spoken word. The written word. The word that lights the path to wisdom – the one and only means by which the human mind may properly interpret what the human eye has perceived. And just as he was certain that he would find his family, he was certain that afterwards, when he returned to these shores, he would be able to proclaim the truth to its people in a way that no one had ever done before. To speak the truth in a voice of such calm simplicity that little children would sit and happily listen. To speak the truth in a voice of such thunderous power that it would wrest the very heavens free of their foundations and bring them crashing down to earth for his fellow beings. He could build a New Jerusalem in this green and pleasant land – he knew it. He knew it in his heart, in his mind and in every fibre and sinew of his being. He knew it because he had the word. It was with him. Around him. In him.

'You're not cold in the back there?' asked the driver from the front of the taxi.

Looking up, Miles could see that he had just wound down the window.

'No, no, I'm fine,' he called out, feeling a pleasantly cool breeze begin to circulate around him.

In response the driver nodded contentedly. Looking at his watch, Miles estimated that they would be at the airport in about twenty minutes and so sat back in his seat to enjoy the ride. As the taxi then finally pulled out of the estate, turning on to a broad dual carriageway, the smell of newly mown grass wafted through the window into the back of the cab. Summer had been on the verge of breaking through for weeks, but now, at last, it was here. And, as the wonderfully fresh aroma filled his nostrils, Miles Coverdale smiled to himself. It was a good omen. A good omen for a man whose former life had come to an end that morning. A good omen for the man that he was about to become.

Reborn.

"Please read this book and be ashamed that you have sat back and let this happen."

DAVID BELLAMY

– botanist, broadcaster and environmentalist

"Hilarious in parts, but with a deeply serious message ..."

BUILDING FOR A FUTURE magazine

"I screamed with laughter."

SIR ROY STRONG – art historian and writer

"A shocking reminder of how ... fast our environment is being despoiled. Read it, then join an environmental pressure group."

TONY JUNIPER – Executive Director, Friends of the Earth

"Inventive writing ... it could make you weep."

EARTH MATTERS

Volume One:
ISBN 0 9536850 2 0
Price: £6.99

Volume Two:
ISBN 0 9536850 4 7
Price: £6.99

Also Available from Hilltop Publishing by PJ Goddard

Libidan

PJ Goddard's first novel tells the story of a pharmaceutical researcher who discovers a Viagra drug for women.

Part black comedy, part thriller, part allegorical tale, *Libidan* examines the heights to which humanity may ascend – or the depths into which we may fall – when our genome gives up its secrets.

Since its publication in 2001, *Libidan* has received widespread critical acclaim throughout Britain's literary and scientific communities.

Broadcasters: *'Highly entertaining.'*
JOHN HUMPHRYS – The *Today* Programme

Politicians: *'Imaginative, well-written and, in places, side-splittingly funny. Deserves all the success it gets.'*
JOHN BERCOW – MP

Literary reviewers: *'Head-shakingly funny. Goddard's dialogue is spot on and his motley cast of characters an absolute delight.'*
SHARON ELZING-SCHULZ
– Curled-up-with-a-good-book.com

Ethicists: *'A real achievement.'*
PROFESSOR RICHARD ASHCROFT –
Centre for Bioethics in Medicine, Imperial College, London

Environmentalists: *'A bawdy and hilarious tale of how a run-of-the-mill scientist stumbles across a discovery that promises great power and wealth, but ultimately delivers only corruption and ruin ... and a serious examination of the commercialization of scientific insight.'*
DR BRIAN JOHNSON
– Biotechnology Advisory Unit, English Nature

Scientific Journals: *'Here philosophy meets quantum physics, genetic engineering and the future of all mankind. Read it – you will never think or perceive the same way again.'*
JOHN MORRISON – Human Nature

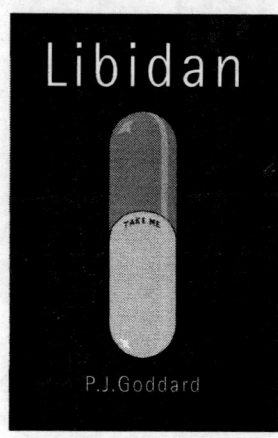